THE CERTIFIED SIX SIGMA
BLACK BELT HANDBOOK

SECOND EDITION

Also available from ASQ Quality Press:

The Certified Six Sigma Green Belt Handbook
Roderick A. Munro, Matthew J. Maio, Mohamed B. Nawaz, Govindarajan Ramu, and Daniel J. Zrymiak

Six Sigma for the New Millennium: A CSSBB Guidebook, Second Edition
Kim H. Pries

5S for Service Organizations and Offices: A Lean Look at Improvements
Debashis Sarkar

The Executive Guide to Understanding and Implementing Lean Six Sigma: The Financial Impact
Robert M. Meisel, Steven J. Babb, Steven F. Marsh, and James P. Schlichting

Applied Statistics for the Six Sigma Green Belt
Bhisham C. Gupta and H. Fred Walker

Statistical Quality Control for the Six Sigma Green Belt
Bhisham C. Gupta and H. Fred Walker

Six Sigma for the Office: A Pocket Guide
Roderick A. Munro

Lean-Six Sigma for Healthcare: A Senior Leader Guide to Improving Cost and Throughput, Second Edition
Chip Caldwell , Greg Butler, and Nancy Poston.

Defining and Analyzing a Business Process: A Six Sigma Pocket Guide
Jeffrey N. Lowenthal

Six Sigma for the Shop Floor: A Pocket Guide
Roderick A. Munro

Six Sigma Project Management: A Pocket Guide
Jeffrey N. Lowenthal

Transactional Six Sigma for Green Belts: Maximizing Service and Manufacturing Processes
Samuel E. Windsor

Lean Kaizen: A Simplified Approach to Process Improvements
George Alukal and Anthony Manos

A Lean Guide to Transforming Healthcare: How to Implement Lean Principles in Hospitals, Medical Offices, Clinics, and Other Healthcare Organizations
Thomas G. Zidel

To request a complimentary catalog of ASQ Quality Press publications, call 800-248-1946, or visit our Web site at http://www.asq.org/quality-press.

THE CERTIFIED SIX SIGMA BLACK BELT HANDBOOK

SECOND EDITION

T. M. Kubiak
Donald W. Benbow

ASQ Quality Press
Milwaukee, Wisconsin

American Society for Quality, Quality Press, Milwaukee 53203
© 2009 by American Society for Quality
All rights reserved. Published 2009
Printed in the United States of America
14 13 12 11 10 09   5 4 3 2

Library of Congress Cataloging-in-Publication Data

Kubiak, T.M.
    The certified six sigma black belt handbook / T.M. Kubiak and Donald W. Benbow.—2nd ed.
        p. cm.
        ISBN 978-0-87389-732-7 (alk. paper)
    1. Quality control—Statistical methods—Handbooks, manuals, etc.   I. Benbow, Donald W.,
1936–   II. Title.

    TS156.B4653 2008
    658.4'013--dc22

                                                                                    2008042611

Publisher: William A. Tony
Acquisitions Editor: Matt Meinholz
Project Editor: Paul O'Mara
Production Administrator: Randall Benson

ASQ Mission: The American Society for Quality advances individual, organizational, and
community excellence worldwide through learning, quality improvement, and knowledge
exchange.

Attention Bookstores, Wholesalers, Schools, and Corporations: ASQ Quality Press books,
videotapes, audiotapes, and software are available at quantity discounts with bulk purchases for
business, educational, or instructional use. For information, please contact ASQ Quality Press at
800-248-1946, or write to ASQ Quality Press, P.O. Box 3005, Milwaukee, WI 53201-3005.

To place orders or to request a free copy of the ASQ Quality Press Publications Catalog,
including ASQ membership information, call 800-248-1946. Visit our Web site at
www.asq.org or www.asq.org/quality-press.

Portions of the input and output contained in this publication/book are printed with permission
of Minitab Inc. All material remains the exclusive property and copyright of Minitab Inc. All
rights reserved.

∞ Printed on acid-free paper

Quality Press
600 N. Plankinton Avenue
Milwaukee, Wisconsin 53203
Call toll free 800-248-1946
Fax 414-272-1734
www.asq.org
http://www.asq.org/quality-press
http://standardsgroup.asq.org
E-mail: authors@asq.org

For Jaycob, my grandson:
This world is changing with each passing day—sometimes for the better, sometimes not. I will strive to carry your burdens until you are able to do so for yourself. May you always be blessed with the best that life has to offer and always strive to improve not just your life but the lives of others. On life's journey you will confront challenges that may seem impossible, but always know my strength and support will forever be with you. There will be many twists and turns, but always be faithful to your own values and convictions. Know that if you live life fully, you will surely achieve your dreams. I will always be there to help you find your way, but only you have the strength to spread your wings, soar high, and find your yellow brick road. When you follow your own path, there will be no limits to what you can accomplish.
—T. M. Kubiak

For my grandchildren Sarah, Emily, Dana, Josiah, Regan, Alec, Marah, and Liam.
—Donald W. Benbow

Table of Contents

CD-ROM Contents

Sample Examination Questions for Parts I–IX

Certified Six Sigma Black Belt—Simulated Exam

List of Figures and Tables

Part VI

Part IX

Preface to the Second Edition

In the spirit of customer-supplier relationships, we are pleased to provide our readers with the second edition of *The Certified Six Sigma Black Belt Handbook*. The handbook has been updated to reflect the most recent Six Sigma Black Belt Body of Knowledge, released in 2007.

As with all ASQ certification–based handbooks, the primary audience for this work is the individual who plans to prepare to sit for the Six Sigma Black Belt certification examination. Therefore, the book assumes the individual has the necessary background and experience in quality and Six Sigma. Concepts are dealt with briefly but facilitated with practical examples. We have intentionally avoided theoretical discussion unless such a discussion was necessary to communicate a concept. As always, readers are encouraged to use additional sources when seeking much deeper levels of discussion. Most of the citations provided in the references will be helpful in this regard.

A secondary audience for the handbook is the quality and Six Sigma professional who would like a relevant Six Sigma reference book. With this audience in mind, we have greatly expanded the appendices section:

- Although the Body of Knowledge was updated in 2007, we have elected to keep the 2001 Body of Knowledge so that readers can compare changes and perhaps offer recommendations for future Bodies of Knowledge.

- All tables were developed using a combination of Microsoft Excel and Minitab 15. Thus, the reader may find some differences between our tables and those published in other sources. Appendices 29–33 are examples of where such differences might occur. Note that years ago many statistical tables were produced either by hand or by using rudimentary calculators. These tables have been handed down from author to author and have remained largely unchanged. Our approach was to revert to the formulas and algorithms that produced the tables and then redevelop them using statistical software.

- The table for control constants has been expanded to now include virtually all control constants. To the best of our knowledge, this handbook is probably the only reference source that includes this information.

- Tables for both cumulative and noncumulative forms of the most useful distributions are now present—for example, binomial, Poisson, and normal.

- Additional alpha values in tables have been included. For example, large alpha values for the left side of the F distribution now exist. Thus, it will no longer be necessary to use the well-known conversion property of the distribution to obtain critical F values associated with higher alpha values. Though the conversion formula is straightforward, everyone seems to get it wrong. We expect our readers will appreciate this.

- The glossary has grown significantly. Most notable is the inclusion of more terms relating to Lean.

- A second glossary has been added as well. This short glossary is limited to the most common Japanese terms used by quality and Six Sigma professionals.

We are confident that readers will find the above additions useful.

As you might expect, chapter and section numbering follows the same method used in the Six Sigma Black Belt Body of Knowledge. This has made for some awkward placement of discussions (for example, the normal distribution is referred to several times before it is defined), and in some cases, redundancy of discussion exists. However, where possible, we have tried to reference the main content in the handbook and refer the reader there for the primary discussion.

After the first edition was published, we received several comments from readers who stated that their answers did not completely agree with those given in the examples. In many instances, we found that discrepancies could be attributed to the following: use of computers with different bits, the number of significant digits accounted for by the software used, the sequence in which the arithmetic was performed, and the propagation of errors due to rounding or truncation. Therefore, we urge the reader to carefully consider the above points as the examples are worked. However, we do recognize that errors occasionally occur and thus have established a SharePoint site that will permit readers to recommend suggestions, additions, corrections, or deletions, as well as to seek out any corrections that may have been found and published. The SharePoint site address is http://asqgroups.asq.org/cssbbhandbook/.

Finally, the enclosed CD contains supplementary problems covering each chapter and a simulated exam that has problems distributed among chapters according to the scheme published in the Body of Knowledge. It is suggested that the reader study a particular chapter, repeating any calculations independently, and then do the supplementary problems for that chapter. After attaining success with all chapters, the reader may complete the simulated exam to confirm mastery of the entire Six Sigma Black Belt Body of Knowledge.

—The Authors

Preface to the First Edition

We decided to number chapters and sections by the same method used in the Body of Knowledge (BOK) specified for the Certified Six Sigma Black Belt examination. This made for some awkward placement (the normal distribution is referred to several times before it is defined), and in some cases, redundancy. We thought the ease of access for readers, who might be struggling with some particular point in the BOK, would more than balance these disadvantages.

The enclosed CD contains supplementary problems covering each chapter and a simulated exam that has problems distributed among chapters according to the scheme published in the Body of Knowledge. It is suggested that the reader study a particular chapter, repeating any calculations independently, and then do the supplementary problems for that chapter. After attaining success with all chapters, the reader may complete the simulated exam to confirm mastery of the entire Six Sigma Black Belt Body of Knowledge.

—The Authors

Acknowledgments

We would like to express our deepest appreciation to Minitab Inc., for providing us with the use of Minitab 15 and Quality Companion 2 software and for permission to use several examples from Minitab 15 and forms from Quality Companion 2. This software was instrumental in creating and verifying examples used throughout the book.

In addition we would like to thank the ASQ management and Quality Press staffs for their outstanding support and exceptional patience while we prepared this second edition.

Finally, we would like to thank the staff of Kinetic Publishing Services, LLC, for applying their finely tuned project management, copyediting, and typesetting skills to this project. Their support has allowed us to produce a final product suitable for the ASQ Quality Press family of publications.

—The Authors

Part I
Enterprise-Wide Deployment

Part I

Chapter 1
Enterprise-Wide View

HISTORY OF CONTINUOUS IMPROVEMENT

> Describe the origins of continuous improvement
> and its impact on other improvement models.
> (Remember)
>
> **Body of Knowledge I.A.1**

Most of the techniques found in the Six Sigma toolbox have been available for some time, thanks to the groundbreaking work of many professionals in the quality sciences.

Walter A. Shewhart worked at the Hawthorne plant of Western Electric, where he developed and used control charts. He is sometimes referred to as the father of statistical quality control (SQC) because he brought together the disciplines of statistics, engineering, and economics. He describes the basic principles of SQC in his book *Economic Control of Quality of Manufactured Product* (1931). He was the first honorary member of the American Society for Quality (ASQ).

W. Edwards Deming developed a list of 14 points in which he emphasized the need for change in management structure and attitudes. As stated in his book *Out of the Crisis* (1986), these 14 points are as follows:

1. Create constancy of purpose for improvement of product and service.

2. Adopt a new philosophy.

3. Cease dependence on inspection to achieve quality.

4. End the practice of awarding business on the basis of price tag alone. Instead, minimize total cost by working with a single supplier.

5. Improve constantly and forever every process for planning, production, and service.

6. Institute training on the job.

7. Adopt and institute leadership.

8. Drive out fear.

9. Break down barriers between staff areas.

10. Eliminate slogans, exhortations, and targets for the workforce.

11. Eliminate numerical quotas for the workforce and numerical goals for management.

12. Remove barriers that rob people of pride of workmanship. Eliminate the annual rating or merit system.

13. Institute a vigorous program of education and self-improvement for everyone.

14. Put everybody in the company to work to accomplish the transformation.

Joseph M. Juran pursued a varied career in management beginning in 1924 as an engineer, executive, government administrator, university professor, labor arbitrator, corporate director, and consultant. He developed the Juran trilogy, three managerial processes—quality planning, quality control, and quality improvement—for use in managing for quality. Juran wrote hundreds of papers and 12 books, including *Juran's Quality Control Handbook* (1999), *Juran's Quality Planning & Analysis for Enterprise Quality* (with F. M. Gryna; 2007), and *Juran on Leadership for Quality* (2003). His approach to quality improvement includes the following points:

- Create awareness of the need and opportunity for improvement

- Mandate quality improvement; make it a part of every job description

- Create the infrastructure: Establish a quality council; select projects for improvement; appoint teams; provide facilitators

- Provide training in how to improve quality

- Review progress regularly

- Give recognition to the winning teams

- Propagandize the results

- Revise the reward system to enforce the rate of improvement

- Maintain momentum by enlarging the business plan to include goals for quality improvement

Deming and Juran worked in both the United States and Japan to help businesses understand the importance of continuous process improvement.

Philip B. Crosby, who originated the zero defects concept, was an ASQ honorary member and past president. He wrote many books, including *Quality Is Free* (1979), *Quality without Tears* (1984), *Let's Talk Quality* (1990), and *Leading: The Art of Becoming an Executive* (1990). Crosby's 14 steps to quality improvement are as follows:

1. Make it clear that management is committed to quality

2. Form quality improvement teams with representatives from each department

3. Determine how to measure where current and potential quality problems lie

4. Evaluate the cost of quality and explain its use as a management tool

5. Raise the quality awareness and personal concern of all employees

6. Take formal actions to correct problems identified through previous steps

7. Establish a committee for the zero defects program

8. Train all employees to actively carry out their part of the quality improvement program

9. Hold a "zero defects day" to let all employees realize that there has been a change

10. Encourage individuals to establish improvement goals for themselves and their groups

11. Encourage employees to communicate to management the obstacles they face in attaining their improvement goals

12. Recognize and appreciate those who participate

13. Establish quality councils to communicate on a regular basis

14. Do it all over again to emphasize that the quality improvement program never ends

Armand V. Feigenbaum originated the concept of total quality control in his book *Total Quality Control* (1991), first published in 1951. The book has been translated into many languages, including Japanese, Chinese, French, and Spanish. Feigenbaum is an ASQ honorary member and served as ASQ president for two consecutive terms. He lists three steps to quality:

1. Quality leadership

2. Modern quality technology

3. Organizational commitment

Kaoru Ishikawa (1985) developed the cause-and-effect diagram. He worked with Deming through the Union of Japanese Scientists and Engineers (JUSE). The following points summarize Ishikawa's philosophy:

- Quality first—not short-term profit first.

- Consumer orientation—not producer orientation. Think from the standpoint of the other party.

- The next process is your customer—breaking down the barrier of sectionalism.

- Using facts and data to make presentations—utilization of statistical methods.

- Respect for humanity as a management philosophy—full participatory management.

- Cross-function management.

Genichi Taguchi taught that any departure from the nominal or target value for a characteristic represents a loss to society. He also popularized the use of fractional factorial experiments and stressed the concept of robustness.

In addition to these noted individuals, Toyota Motor Company has been recognized as the leader in developing the concept of lean manufacturing systems.

Various approaches to quality have been in vogue over the years, as shown in Table 1.1.

Table 1.1   Some approaches to quality over the years.

Quality approach	Approximate time frame	Short description
Quality circles	1979–1981	Quality improvement or self-improvement study groups composed of a small number of employees (10 or fewer) and their supervisor. Quality circles originated in Japan, where they are called quality control circles.
Statistical process control (SPC)	Mid-1980s	The application of statistical techniques to control a process. Also called "statistical quality control."
ISO 9000	1987–present	A set of international standards on quality management and quality assurance developed to help companies effectively document the quality system elements to be implemented to maintain an efficient quality system. The standards, initially published in 1987, are not specific to any particular industry, product, or service. The standards were developed by the International Organization for Standardization (ISO), a specialized international agency for standardization composed of the national standards bodies of 91 countries. The standards underwent major revision in 2000 and now include ISO 9000:2005 (definitions), ISO 9001:2008 (requirements), and ISO 9004:2000 (continuous improvement).
Reengineering	1996–1997	A breakthrough approach involving the restructuring of an entire organization and its processes.
Benchmarking	1988–1996	An improvement process in which a company measures its performance against that of best-in-class companies, determines how those companies achieved their performance levels, and uses the information to improve its own performance. The subjects that can be benchmarked include strategies, operations, processes, and procedures.
Balanced Scorecard	1990s–present	A management concept that helps managers at all levels monitor their results in their key areas.

Continued

Table 1.1   Some approaches to quality over the years. *Continued*

Quality approach	Approximate time frame	Short description
Baldrige Award Criteria	1987–present	An award established by the U.S. Congress in 1987 to raise awareness of quality management and recognize U.S. companies that have implemented successful quality management systems. Two awards may be given annually in each of six categories: manufacturing company, service company, small business, education, health care, and nonprofit. The award is named after the late secretary of commerce Malcolm Baldrige, a proponent of quality management. The U.S. Commerce Department's National Institute of Standards and Technology manages the award, and ASQ administers it.
Six Sigma	1995–present	As described in Chapter 1.
Lean manufacturing	2000–present	As described in Chapter 1.
Lean-Six Sigma	2002–present	This approach combines the individual concepts of Lean and Six Sigma and recognizes that both are necessary to effectively drive sustained improvement.

VALUE AND FOUNDATIONS OF SIX SIGMA

> Describe the value of Six Sigma, its philosophy, history, and goals. (Understand)
>
> **Body of Knowledge I.A.2**

A wide range of companies have found that when the Six Sigma philosophy is fully embraced, the enterprise thrives. What is this Six Sigma philosophy? Several definitions have been proposed, with the following common threads:

- Use of teams that are assigned well-defined projects that have direct impact on the organization's bottom line.

- Training in statistical thinking at all levels and providing key people with extensive training in advanced statistics and project management. These key people are designated "Black Belts."

- Emphasis on the DMAIC approach to problem solving: define, measure, analyze, improve, and control.

- A management environment that supports these initiatives as a business strategy.

The literature is replete with examples of projects that have returned high dollar amounts to the organizations involved. Black Belts are often required to manage four projects per year for a total of $500,000–$5,000,000 in contributions to the company's bottom line.

Opinions on the definition of Six Sigma differ:

- Philosophy—The philosophical perspective views all work as processes that can be defined, measured, analyzed, improved, and controlled (DMAIC). Processes require inputs and produce outputs. If you control the inputs, you will control the outputs. This is generally expressed as the $y = f(x)$ concept.

- Set of tools—Six Sigma as a set of tools includes all the qualitative and quantitative techniques used by the Six Sigma expert to drive process improvement. A few such tools include statistical process control (SPC), control charts, failure mode and effects analysis, and process mapping. Six Sigma professionals do not totally agree as to exactly which tools constitute the set.

- Methodology—The methodological view of Six Sigma recognizes the underlying and rigorous approach known as DMAIC. DMAIC defines the steps a Six Sigma practitioner is expected to follow, starting with identifying the problem and ending with implementing long-lasting solutions. While DMAIC is not the only Six Sigma methodology in use, it is certainly the most widely adopted and recognized.

- Metrics—In simple terms, Six Sigma quality performance means 3.4 defects per million opportunities (accounting for a 1.5-sigma shift in the mean).

In the first edition of this book, we used the following to define Six Sigma:

Six Sigma is a fact-based, data-driven philosophy of improvement that values defect prevention over defect detection. It drives customer satisfaction and bottom-line results by reducing variation and waste, thereby promoting a competitive advantage. It applies anywhere variation and waste exist, and every employee should be involved.

However, going forward, we combined the definitions of Lean and Six Sigma and proffer a definition for Lean-Six Sigma. This is discussed in detail in Section I.A.4.

VALUE AND FOUNDATIONS OF LEAN

> Describe the value of Lean, its philosophy,
> history, and goals. (Understand)
>
> **Body of Knowledge I.A.3**

The term "lean thinking" refers to the use of ideas originally employed in lean manufacturing to improve functions in all departments of an enterprise.

The National Institute of Standards and Technology (NIST), through its Manufacturing Extension Partnership, defines Lean as follows:

A systematic approach to identifying and eliminating waste (non-value-added activities) through continuous improvement by flowing the product at the pull of the customer in pursuit of perfection.

ASQ defines the phrase "non-value-added" as follows:

A term that describes a process step or function that is not required for the direct achievement of process output. This step or function is identified and examined for potential elimination.

This represents a shift in focus for manufacturing engineering, which has traditionally studied ways to improve value-added functions and activities (for example, how can this process run faster and more precisely). Lean thinking doesn't ignore the valued-added activities, but it does shine the spotlight on waste. A discussion of various categories of wastes is provided in the waste analysis section of Chapter 27.

Lean manufacturing seeks to eliminate or reduce these wastes by use of the following:

- *Teamwork* with well-informed cross-trained employees who participate in the decisions that impact their function

- *Clean*, organized, and well-marked work spaces

- *Flow systems* instead of batch and queue (that is, reduce batch size toward its ultimate ideal, one)

- *Pull systems* instead of push systems (that is, replenish what the customer has consumed)

- *Reduced lead times* through more efficient processing, setups, and scheduling

The history of lean thinking may be traced to Eli Whitney, who is credited with spreading the concept of part interchangeability. Henry Ford, who went to great lengths to reduce cycle times, furthered the idea of lean thinking, and later, the Toyota Production System (TPS) packaged most of the tools and concepts now known as lean manufacturing.

INTEGRATION OF LEAN AND SIX SIGMA

> Describe the relationship between Lean and Six Sigma. (Understand)
>
> **Body of Knowledge I.A.4**

After reading the description in the last few paragraphs of Section I.A.2, Six Sigma purists will be quick to say, "You're not just talking about Six Sigma; you're talking about Lean too." The demarcation between Six Sigma and Lean has blurred. We are hearing about terms such as "Lean-Six Sigma" with greater frequency because process improvement requires aspects of both approaches to attain positive results.

Six Sigma focuses on reducing process variation and enhancing process control, whereas Lean—also known as lean manufacturing—drives out waste (non-value-added) and promotes work standardization and flow. Six Sigma practitioners should be well versed in both. More details of what is sometimes referred to as lean thinking are given in Chapters 29–33.

Lean and Six Sigma have the same general purpose of providing the customer with the best possible quality, cost, delivery, and a newer attribute, nimbleness. There is a great deal of overlap, and disciples of both disagree as to which techniques belong where. Six Sigma Black Belts need to know a lot about Lean (witness the appearance of lean topics in the Body of Knowledge for Black Belt certification).

The two initiatives approach their common purpose from slightly different angles:

- Lean focuses on waste reduction, whereas Six Sigma emphasizes variation reduction

- Lean achieves its goals by using less technical tools such as kaizen, workplace organization, and visual controls, whereas Six Sigma tends to use statistical data analysis, design of experiments, and hypothesis tests

The most successful users of implementations have begun with the lean approach, making the workplace as efficient and effective as possible, reducing the (now) eight wastes, and using value stream maps to improve understanding and throughput. When process problems remain, the more technical Six Sigma statistical tools may be applied. One thing they have in common is that both require strong management support to make them the standard way of doing business.

Some organizations have responded to this dichotomy of approaches by forming a Lean-Six Sigma problem-solving team with specialists in the various aspects of each discipline but with each member cognizant of others' fields. Task forces from this team are formed and reshaped depending on the problem at hand.

Given the earlier discussion, we believe a combined definition is required and proffer the following:

Lean-Six Sigma is a fact-based, data-driven philosophy of improvement that values defect prevention over defect detection. It drives customer satisfaction and bottom-line results by reducing variation, waste, and cycle time, while promoting the use of work standardization and flow, thereby creating a competitive advantage. It applies anywhere variation and waste exist, and every employee should be involved.

BUSINESS PROCESSES AND SYSTEMS

Describe the relationship among various business processes (design, production, purchasing, accounting, sales, etc.) and the impact these relationships can have on business systems. (Understand)

Body of Knowledge I.A.5

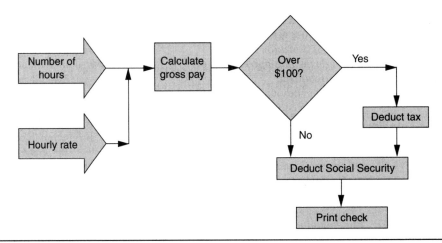

Figure 1.1   Example of a process flowchart.

Processes

A process is a series of steps designed to produce products and/or services. A process is often diagrammed with a flowchart depicting inputs, the path that material or information follows, and outputs. An example of a process flowchart is shown in Figure 1.1. Understanding and improving processes is a key part of every Six Sigma project.

The basic strategy of Six Sigma is contained in DMAIC. These steps constitute the cycle Six Sigma practitioners use to manage problem-solving projects. The individual parts of the DMAIC cycle are explained in Chapters 15–38.

Business Systems

A business system is designed to implement a process or, more commonly, a set of processes. Business systems make certain that process inputs are in the right place at the right time so that each step of the process has the resources it needs. Perhaps most importantly, a business system must have as its goal the continual improvement of its processes, products, and services. To this end, the business system is responsible for collecting and analyzing data from the process and other sources that will help in the continual incremental improvement of process outputs. Figure 1.2 illustrates relationships among systems, processes, subprocesses, and steps. Note that each part of a system can be broken into a series of processes, each of which may have subprocesses. The subprocesses may be further broken into steps.

SIX SIGMA AND LEAN APPLICATIONS

Describe how these tools are applied to processes in all types of enterprises: manufacturing, service, transactional, product and process design, innovation, etc. (Understand)

Body of Knowledge I.A.6

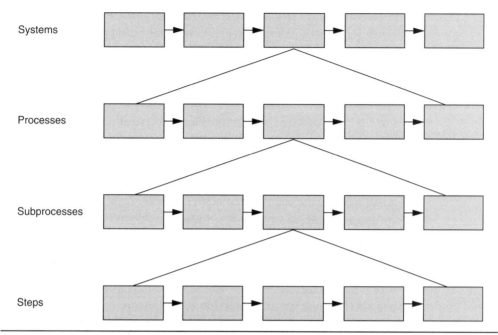

Figure 1.2   Relationship among systems, processes, subprocesses, and steps.

The most successful implementations of Lean and Six Sigma have an oversight group with top management representation and support. This group defines and prioritizes problems and establishes teams to solve them. The oversight group is responsible for maintaining a systemic approach. It also provides the training, support, recognition, and rewards for teams.

The following are examples of problems that would be assigned to teams:

- A number of customers of an accounting firm have complained about the amount of time the firm takes to perform an audit. The oversight group forms a team consisting of three auditors (one of them a lead auditor), two cost accountants, and two representatives from the firm's top customers. The oversight group asks the team to determine if the lead time is indeed inordinate and to propose measures that will reduce it. The team begins by benchmarking (see Chapter 5) a customer's internal audit process. After allowing for differences between internal and external audits, the team concludes that the lead time should be shortened. The team next uses the material discussed in Chapter 18 to construct a value stream map, which displays work in progress, cycle times, and communication channels. A careful study of the map data shows several areas where lead time can be decreased.

- A team has been formed to reduce cycle times on an appliance assembly line. The team consists of the 12 workers on the line (six from each of the two shifts) as well as the 2 shift coaches and the line supervisor. Although this makes a large team, it helps ensure that everyone's creative energy is tapped. The team decides to start a job rotation process in which each assembler will work one station for a month and then move on to the next station. After three months the workers universally dislike this procedure, but they agree to continue through at least one complete rotation. At the end of nine months, or one and a half rotations, the team acknowledges that the rotation system has helped improve standard work (see Chapter 29) because each person better understands what the next person needs. They are also better equipped to accommodate absences and the training of new people. The resulting reduction in cycle times surprises everyone.

- A team has been charged with improving the operation of a shuttle brazer. Automotive radiators are loaded on this machine and shuttled through a series of gas-fired torches to braze the connections. The operator can adjust the shuttle speed, wait time, gas pressure, torch angle, and torch height. There is a tendency to adjust one or more of these settings to produce leak-free joints, but no one seems to know the best settings. The team decides to conduct a full factorial 2^5 designed experiment with four replications (see Chapter 28) during a planned plant shutdown.

- A company is plagued with failure to meet deadlines for software projects. A team is formed to study and improve the design/code/test process. The team splits into three subteams, one for each phase. The design subteam discovers that this crucial phase endures excess variation in the form of customer needs. This occurs because customers change the requirements and because sometimes the software package is designed to serve multiple customers whose needs aren't known until late in the design phase. The subteam helps the designers develop a generic Gantt chart (see Chapter 17) for the design phase itself. It also establishes a better process for determining potential customer needs (see Chapter 15). The design group decides to develop configurable software packages that permit the user to specify the functions needed.

The coding subteam finds that those responsible for writing the actual code are often involved with multiple projects, leading to tension between project managers. This results in spurts of activity and concentration being spent on several projects with the resulting inefficiencies. The subteam collaborates with the project manager to establish a format for prioritization matrices (see Chapter 13), which provide better guidance for coders.

The testing subteam determines that there is poor communication between designers and testers regarding critical functions, especially those that appeared late in the design phase. After discussions with those involved, it is decided that for each project a representative of the testing group should be an ex officio member of the design group.

References

Crosby, P. B. 1979. *Quality Is Free*. New York: McGraw-Hill.

———. 1984. *Quality without Tears: The Art of Hassle-Free Management*. New York: New American Library.

———. 1990. *Leading: The Art of Becoming an Executive*. New York: McGraw-Hill.

Deming, W. Edwards. 1986. *Out of the Crisis.* Cambridge, MA: MIT Press.

Feigenbaum, A. V. 1991. *Total Quality Control.* 3rd ed. New York: McGraw-Hill.

Gryna, Frank M., Richard C. H. Chua, and Joseph A. DeFeo. 2007. *Juran's Quality Planning & Analysis for Enterprise Quality.* 5th ed. New York: McGraw-Hill.

Ishikawa, K. 1985. *What Is Total Quality Control?* Englewood Cliffs, NJ: Prentice Hall.

Juran, Joseph M., and A. Blanton Godfrey. 1999. *Juran's Quality Control Handbook.* 5th ed. New York: McGraw-Hill.

Chapter 2
Leadership

ENTERPRISE LEADERSHIP RESPONSIBILITIES

> Describe the responsibilities of executive leaders and how they affect the deployment of Six Sigma in terms of providing resources, managing change, communicating ideas, etc. (Understand)
>
> **Body of Knowledge I.B.1**

The definition and role of leadership have undergone major shifts in recent years. The leadership model that is most effective in the deployment of Six Sigma envisions the leader as a problem solver. The leader's job is to implement systems that identify and solve problems that impede the effectiveness of the processes. This requires two steps:

- Allocate resources to support team-based problem identification and solution

- Allocate resources to install corrections and ensure that the problems do not recur

This concept of leadership implies a good understanding of team dynamics and Six Sigma problem-solving techniques. Deployment of a culture-changing initiative such as the adoption of Six Sigma rarely succeeds without engaged, visible, and active senior-level management involvement. Initiatives starting in the rank and file seldom gain the critical mass necessary to sustain and fuel their own existence.

ORGANIZATIONAL ROADBLOCKS

> Describe the impact an organization's culture and inherent structure can have on the success of Six Sigma, and how deployment failure can result from the lack of resources, management support, etc.; identify and apply various techniques to overcome these barriers. (Apply)
>
> **Body of Knowledge I.B.2**

Many organizations have a structure and culture that were formed when an important goal was for the organization to continue running the way it always has. A highly centralized organizational structure tends to have more of this inertia than a decentralized one. Such a structure and culture tend to resist any change. An unintended consequence is that fundamental improvements are difficult to achieve. Some symptoms of such a system are listed here, with possible remedies:

- Symptom: A system that requires many signatures for expenditures discourages or delays improvements, particularly when signatories are busy or travel frequently.

    Remedies:

    – A multiple-signature e-mail procedure can be instituted.

    – Teams can be empowered with budgets.

- Symptom: Adherence to an "if it ain't broke, don't fix it" philosophy serves as a barrier to change.

    Remedies:

    – One company encourages employees to stop the assembly line when they see a problem or an opportunity for improvement. A wall clock reflects the number of minutes the line was stopped during the shift. They try to have 30–40 minutes of downtime per shift, because only when the line is down are they solving problems and making improvements.

    – Everyone must understand that an important part of his or her job is to make improvements. Incentives for these improvements must be provided.

- Symptom: Managers are not properly trained as change agents.

    Remedy: All personnel with management responsibilities need to understand the basics of change management (see Section I.B.3).

Project Champions are often the ones best able to break roadblocks. In many situations, the motto "No Champion, no project" is valid. Typically, the Champion is at an executive level of the organization. Sometimes the Champion is the process owner.

CHANGE MANAGEMENT

> Describe and use various techniques for facilitating and managing organizational change. (Apply)
>
> **Body of Knowledge I.B.3**

There was a time when a manager's job was to keep things running the way they always have, that is, to prevent change. Today it is understood that change is critical to an enterprise, and the management of changing processes has become a science of its own. Following are some common errors that managers need to avoid:

- Inadequate communication about coming changes. Management may assume that a single memo or meeting is appropriate, but people need to have time and an opportunity to digest and react to changes.

- Change-management function assigned to people without the preparation or resources to execute it.

- Improper or inadequate explanation of the change. Employees tend to fear and resist change that they do not understand.

For best results, a team with executive leadership should be charged with leading the change and advising top management of necessary actions. Effective communication is essential to success. The following steps are typical in the management of change:

1. Communicate the need for change. Use data regarding market share, competition, and prospects for expansion. Benchmarking (see Chapter 5) is a useful tool.

2. Communicate a view of a future state with a successful change.

3. Establish and communicate near-term, intermediate-term, and long-term goals and metrics.

4. Identify and use forces for change; identify and reduce barriers to change.

5. Communicate early successes and recognize those responsible.

6. Lock in improvements.

7. Establish the need for being a nimble, changing organization.

SIX SIGMA PROJECTS AND KAIZEN EVENTS

> Describe how projects and kaizen events are selected, when to use Six Sigma instead of other problem-solving approaches, and the importance of aligning their objectives with organizational goals. (Apply)
>
> **Body of Knowledge I.B.4**

Organizational goals must be consistent with the long-term strategies of the enterprise. One technique for developing such strategies is called hoshin planning. In this process, a company develops up to four vision statements that indicate where the company should be in the next five years. Company goals, projects, and relevant work plans are developed on the basis of these vision statements. Periodic audits are then conducted to monitor progress.

Once Six Sigma projects have had some success, there will usually be more project ideas than it is possible to undertake at one time. Some sort of project proposal format may be needed, along with an associated process for project selection. It is common to require that project proposals include precise statements of the problem definition and some preliminary measures of the seriousness of the problem, including its impact on the goals of the enterprise.

A project selection group, including Master Black Belts, Black Belts, organizational Champions, and key executive supporters, establishes a set of criteria for project selection and team assignments. In some companies the project selection group assigns some projects to Six Sigma teams and other projects to teams using other methodologies. For example, problems involving extensive data analysis and improvements using designed experiments would likely be assigned to a Six Sigma team, whereas a process improvement not involving these techniques might be assigned to a lean manufacturing team employing kaizen tools. Details on kaizen new product design should follow the Design for Six Sigma (DFSS) guidelines as detailed in Chapters 39 and 40.

The project selection criteria always have as key elements the furthering of organizational goals. One key to gauging both the performance and the health of an organization and its processes lies with its selection and use of metrics. These are usually converted to financial terms such as return on investment, cost reduction, increases in sales, and/or profit. Other things being approximately equal, projects with the greatest contributions to the bottom line receive the highest priority. More details on project metrics are covered in Chapter 16.

SIX SIGMA ROLES AND RESPONSIBILITIES

> Describe the roles and responsibilities of Six Sigma participants: Black Belt, Master Black Belt, Green Belt, Champion, process owners, and project sponsors. (Understand)
>
> **Body of Knowledge I.B.5**

Enterprises with successful Six Sigma programs have found it useful to delineate roles and responsibilities for people involved in project activity. Although titles vary somewhat from company to company, the following list represents the general thinking regarding each role. The definitions provided can be found in Appendix 34.

Black Belts

Black Belts work full time on Six Sigma projects. These projects are usually prioritized on the basis of their potential financial impact on the enterprise. Individuals designated as Black Belts must be thoroughly trained in statistical methods and be proficient at working with teams to implement project success. Breyfogle (2003) suggests that the number of Black Belts equal about 1% of the number of employees in the organization.

> *Black Belt (BB)—A Six Sigma role associated with an individual typically assigned full time to train and mentor Green Belts as well as lead improvement projects using specified methodologies such as DMAIC; define, measure, analyze, design, and verify (DMADV); and DFSS.*

Master Black Belts

Master Black Belts have advanced knowledge in statistics and other fields and provide technical support to the Black Belts.

> *Master Black Belt (MBB)—A Six Sigma role associated with an individual typically assigned full time to train and mentor Black Belts as well as lead the strategy to ensure improvement projects chartered are the right strategic projects for the organization. Master Black Belts are usually the authorizing body to certify Green Belts and Black Belts.*

Green Belts

A Green Belt works under the direction of a Black Belt, assisting with all phases of project operation. Green Belts typically are less adept at statistics and other problem-solving techniques.

> *Green Belt (GB)—A Six Sigma role associated with an individual who retains his or her regular position within the firm but is trained in the tools, methods, and skills necessary to conduct Six Sigma improvement projects either individually or as part of larger teams.*

Champion

A Champion is typically a top-level manager who is familiar with the benefits of Six Sigma strategies and provides support for the program.

> *Champion—A Six Sigma role associated with a senior manager who ensures his or her projects are aligned with the organization's strategic goals and priorities, provides the Six Sigma team with resources, removes organizational barriers for the team, participates in project tollgate reviews, and essentially serves as the team's backer. A Champion is also known as a sponsor.*

Executive

Successful implementations of Six Sigma have unwavering support from the company-level executives. Executives demonstrate their support for Six Sigma through their communications and actions.

Process Owner

Process owners should be sufficiently high in the organization to make decisions regarding process changes. It is only natural that managers responsible for a particular process frequently have a vested interest in keeping things as they are. They should be involved with any discussion of change. In most cases, they are willing to support changes but need to see evidence that recommended improvements are for the long-term good of the enterprise. A team member with a "show me" attitude can make a very positive contribution to the team. Process owners should be provided with opportunities for training at least to the Green Belt level.

> ***Process owner**—A Six Sigma role associated with an individual who coordinates the various functions and work activities at all levels of a process, has the authority or ability to make changes in the process as required, and manages the entire process cycle so as to ensure performance effectiveness.*

Reference

Breyfogle III, Forrest W. 2003. *Implementing Six Sigma: Smarter Solutions Using Statistical Methods*. 2nd ed. Hoboken, NJ: John Wiley.

Part II

Organizational Process Management and Measures

Part II

Chapter 3
Impact on Stakeholders

IMPACT ON STAKEHOLDERS

> Describe the impact Six Sigma projects can have on customers, suppliers, and other stakeholders. (Understand)
>
> **Body of Knowledge II.A**

Stakeholders are those who have a vested interest in the process and/or its outcomes. General stakeholders in an organization include customers, suppliers, employees, investors, and communities. Typically, process stakeholders include the following:

- Process operators and managers from all shifts

- Process customers, internal and external

- Process suppliers, internal and external

- Process design personnel

- Product design personnel

- Maintenance and logistics personnel

External suppliers to a process are those outside the enterprise that provide process inputs, including sources of materials, purchased parts, contracted services, electrical power, and so on. *Internal suppliers* to a process are departments or processes inside the enterprise that provide process inputs. Similarly, *external customers* to a process are those outside the enterprise who receive process outputs, while *internal customers* are those inside the enterprise who receive process outputs.

Suppliers of either type are responsible for meeting the requirements of their customers. Customers of either type are responsible for communicating their requirements to their suppliers.

The level of interest by individuals or groups may change over time, depending on economic, contractual, and other influences.

The most effective Six Sigma projects involve teams representing process owners and all stakeholders. There are several reasons for this:

- Stakeholders have the best knowledge base about the process
- Stakeholders tend to have the best ideas for process improvement
- Stakeholders are often the most aware of unintended consequences of process changes
- Stakeholders' buy-in is usually necessary to implement real process improvement

A Six Sigma project may impact stakeholders in the following ways:

- Process inputs may be altered, which changes the requirements to suppliers
- Process procedures may be changes that impact operators and managers
- Process outputs may be altered, which impacts customers
- Changes to tooling, preventive maintenance schedules, and so forth, impact the suppliers of those materials and services

Chapter 4
Critical to x (CTx) Requirements

CRITICAL TO x (CTx) REQUIREMENTS

> Define and describe various CTx requirements (critical to quality (CTQ), cost (CTC), process (CTP), safety (CTS), delivery (CTD), etc.) and the importance of aligning projects with those requirements. (Apply)
>
> **Body of Knowledge II.B**

The concept behind Critical to x (CTx), where x is a variable, is simply that x is an area or areas of impact on the customer. Critical customer requirements are usually expressed as expectations or needs, but not necessarily in quantifiable terms. Process CTxs represent measurable product or process performance characteristics and act to quantify the critical customer requirements. Let's look at some of the more familiar "x's":

- **Critical-to-Quality (CTQ)**—CTQs may include the physical dimensions of height, width, depth, and weight. They may even include the electrical characteristics of a product, such as impedance. They describe the requirements of quality in general terms but lack the specificity to be measurable. However, CTQs can be translated into measurable terms or critical requirements through the inclusion of customer-defined specifications. For example, the customer may specify that the weight of the product be between 15 and 20 pounds. Products outside these specifications will not meet the customer's critical requirements.

- **Critical-to-Cost (CTC)**—CTCs are similar to CTQs but deal exclusively with the impact of cost on the customer. However, CTCs and CTQs may be similar, yet stated by the customer for different reasons. For example, the weight of the product may also serve as a CTC. Again, the customer might require the weight to be between 15 and 20 pounds. However, the specification is necessary to achieve an impact on cost. Products heavier than 20 pounds may require more power consumption, thus increasing the cost.

- **Critical-to-Process (CTP)**—CTPs are typically key process input variables. In terms of the process, we might think of CTPs as the critical x's in the $y = f(x)$ equation. We may know and understand what the x's are (for example, temperature, pressure, humidity), but not necessarily their specific setting or level. Once the settings are determined or specified, they can be set to achieve a consistent y.

- **Critical-to-Safety (CTS)**—CTSs are stated customer needs regarding the safety of the product or process. Once more, consider the previous example of product weight. Product weight is the CTS variable. Though identical to the CTQ and the CTC, it is identified by the customer because any product heavier than 20 pounds has been shown to introduce a high rate of back injuries. Product weights less than 15 pounds have been shown to introduce a high rate of back injuries as well since the lower weight induces the operator to pick up and transport multiple products. So far, we have seen that CTxs may be identical across categories, but for different reasons.

- **Critical-to-Delivery (CTD)**—CTDs represent those customers with stated needs regarding delivery. Typically, one thinks of late deliveries. However, delivering too early may be a problem for some customers, as it represents excess inventory requiring payment before the need for such inventory arises. CTDs are translated into critical customer requirements through the quantification of these impact areas. For example, the customer may specify that products be received no earlier than two days prior to the delivery date and no later than one day after the delivery date.

Projects aligned with CTxs, and subsequently critical customer requirements, have the biggest impact on the customer and often on the business directly. A useful tool for ensuring this alignment or translation from critical customer requirement to CTx is the tree diagram—an example of which is shown in Figure 4.1.

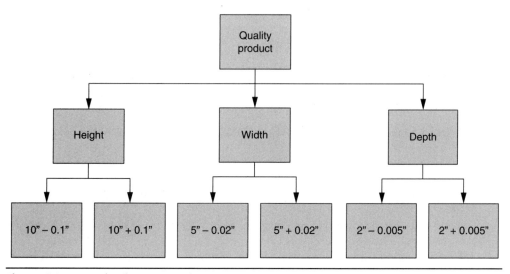

Figure 4.1   Example of a CTQ tree diagram.

Chapter 5
Benchmarking

BENCHMARKING

> Define and distinguish between various types
> of benchmarking, including best practices,
> competitive, collaborative, etc. (Apply)
>
> **Body of Knowledge II.C**

Improving processes and products is often aided by comparing the current state with outstanding processes or products. In some cases, the comparison will be with other divisions of the same company. In other cases, external comparisons are more appropriate. The use of these comparisons is called *benchmarking*. Benchmarking often assists a Six Sigma team in setting targets and finding new ways to achieve them. It is an especially helpful technique when a quality improvement team has run out of new ideas. Consider the following benchmarking example.

Example 5.1

A payroll department team charged with making improvements in the quality and efficiency of the department's work seeks out a company known for the quality of its payroll work. With that company's agreement, the team studies the payroll function, looking for ideas it can use in its home department.

The information for benchmarking may come from various sources, including publications, professional meetings, university research, customer feedback, site visits, and analysis of competitors' products. A downside of benchmarking within a particular industry is that it tends to put one in second place at best.

Benchmarking helps teams strive toward excellence while reducing the tendency to feel that locally generated ideas are the only ones worth considering. Moreover, it is important because it provides an organization with the opportunity to see what level of process performance is possible. Seeing a gap in process performance between what is and what could be helps an organization determine its desired rate of improvement and provides the ability to set meaningful intermediate stretch goals or targets. Benchmarking is useful for driving breakthrough improvement over continuous improvement.

There are four steps in benchmarking:

- Analyze the operation

- Know the competition and the industry leaders

- Incorporate the best of the best

- Gain superiority

Several types of benchmarking exist, and each has advantages and disadvantages:

- Internal benchmarking—provides easy access to other departments within the same company. However, the search for exceptional performance is often limited by the company's culture, norms, and history.

- Competitive benchmarking—forces an organization to take an external perspective. However, focusing on industry practices may limit opportunities to achieve high levels of performance, particularly if a given industry is not know for its quality.

- Functional benchmarking—compares similar functions typically outside the organization's industry and provides ample opportunities to seek out benchmarking partners.

- Collaborative benchmarking—refers to the cooperation between various functions or organizations to achieve benchmarking results. Collaborative benchmarking may permit access to specific benchmarking partners that may not exist with the other types of benchmarking.

Chapter 6

Business Performance Measures

BUSINESS PERFORMANCE MEASURES

> Define and describe various business performance measures, including balanced scorecard, key performance indicators (KPIs), the financial impact of customer loyalty, etc. (Understand)
>
> **Body of Knowledge II.D**

Many of the Six Sigma tools deal with analyzing numerical values. The metrics the organization chooses reflect its business philosophy and, to a large extent, determine its success. Unfortunately, many organizations use too many metrics, often lagging in nature, which may drown them in data and cause them to be unable to change with customer needs. This chapter lists some tools that will help in the selection and use of business performance measures.

Balanced Scorecard

The *balanced scorecard*, a term coined by Robert S. Kaplan and David P. Norton in the early 1990s, separates organizational metrics into four perspectives:

- **Financial perspective**—provides the organization with insight into how well its goals, objectives, and strategies are contributing to shareholder value and the bottom line. It provides shareholders with a direct line of sight into the health and well-being of the organization. Common metrics used for this perspective are given in the next section.

- **Customer perspective**—defines an organization's value proposition and measures how effective the organization is in creating value for its customers through its goals, objectives, strategies, and processes. The customer perspective is not easily obtained. Multiple approaches and listening posts are frequently required, which must be compared and reconciled to ensure a correct understanding of the customer's stated and unstated needs, expectations from the organization's products and services, and the strength of its customer relationships.

- **Internal business processes perspective**—includes all organizational processes designed to create and deliver the customer's value proposition. Organizations that perform these processes well generally have high levels of customer satisfaction and strong customer relationships since efficient and effective processes falling into this perspective can be considered to be predictors of the metrics included in the customer perspective.

- **Learning and growth perspective**—generally includes the capabilities and skills of an organization and how it is focused and channeled to support the internal processes used to create customer value. The development and effective use of human resources and information systems as well as the organizational culture are key aspects of this perspective.

Key Performance Indicators

Key performance indicators (KPIs) are both financial and nonfinancial metrics that reflect an organization's key business drivers (KBDs; also known as critical success factors [CSFs]). Organizations will benefit from the use of KPIs that are defined with the following criteria in mind:

- Quantitative and measurable

- Goal based

- Process based

- Strategy based

- Time bounded

Another way of defining KPIs is in terms of the SMART acronym:

- **S**pecific—KPIs should be laser focused and process based.

- **M**easurable—KPIs must be quantitative and easily determined.

- **A**chievable—KPIs may be set with regard to benchmark levels, yet remain obtainable. KPIs set at higher levels adversely impact employee morale and subsequently organizational performance.

- **R**elevant or results based—KPIs should be linked to the organization's strategies, goals, and objectives.

- **T**ime bounded—KPI levels should reflect a specific period of time; they should never be open-ended. Time-bounded KPIs can be measured. When an appropriate time frame is chosen, KPIs can create a sense of urgency and employee focus.

Some progressive organizations have developed and embedded their KPIs within the framework of the balanced scorecard. Common examples include the following:

- Financial
  - Return on investment
  - Return on capital
  - Return on equity
  - Economic value added
- Customer
  - Customer satisfaction levels
  - Retention rates
  - Referral rates
  - Quality
  - On-time delivery rates
- Internal business processes
  - Defect rates
  - Cycle time
  - Throughput rates
  - Quality
  - On-time delivery rates
- Learning and growth
  - Employee satisfaction
  - Employee turnover rate
  - Absentee rate
  - Percentage of internal promotions

These examples should be considered a starter set and subjected to the criteria identified earlier to ensure their appropriateness. Also, note that the metrics in these perspectives are not necessarily mutually exclusive and may very well overlap. For example, quality and on-time delivery rates appear in both the customer and internal business process perspectives. Customers judge an organization by these metrics and make determinations regarding the continuance of a business relationship with a supplier. On the other hand, these same metrics may be used by a supplier as a predictor of the customer satisfaction levels that might be achieved as a result of its internal business processes.

Organizational metrics do not end with KPIs. Lower-level metrics down to the individual process level may be required to support KPIs and to provide deep, meaningful, and actionable insight for organizations to effectively conduct and run their businesses.

Customer Loyalty

"Customer loyalty" is a term used to describe the behavior of customers—in particular, customers who exhibit a high level of satisfaction, conduct repeat business, or provide referrals and testimonials. It is the result of an organization's processes, practices, and efforts designed to deliver its services or products in ways that drive such behavior.

Many organizations recognize that it is far easier and less costly to retain customers than attract new ones. Hence, customer loyalty drives customer retention, and by extension, has a financial impact. However, customer loyalty can be a double-edged sword. Some organizations strive blindly to retain all their customers, including those that are unprofitable. In Chapter 15 we discuss the concept of customer segmentation. Customers may be classified as profitable or unprofitable. Conceptually, the idea of unprofitable customers is difficult to understand. Moreover, severing ties with this customer segment may be even more difficult, as it may be seen as highly unusual or simply "not done." Enlightened organizations understand this distinction well and act accordingly. Such organizations have gained insight into the cost of maintaining customer relationships through extensive data collection and analysis. This insight has given rise to such terms as "relationship costs" and "relationship revenue."

Organizations must be careful not to confuse loyal customers with tolerant customers. Customers have a zone of tolerance whereby a single bad experience or even a series of bad experiences spread over a sufficiently long time frame may strain the customer-supplier relationship yet keep it intact. However, the cumulative effects of such experiences may push a customer beyond his or her zone of tolerance, resulting in customer defection. At this point, a customer may deem that it is no longer worth maintaining the business relationship.

Organizations, especially those in a niche market or those that may be a single/sole source provider, should have a deep understanding of what drives their customer satisfaction levels and relationships. Limited competition or the cost of changing suppliers or service providers may be all that is keeping customers loyal. Given the right opportunity, these "loyal" customers may readily defect.

Part II.D

Chapter 7

Financial Measures

FINANCIAL MEASURES

> Define and use financial measures, including revenue growth, market share, margin, cost of quality (COQ), net present value (NPV), return on investment (ROI), cost-benefit analysis, etc. (Apply)
>
> **Body of Knowledge II.E**

When preparing a project report, it is common to state the project benefits in financial terms. Benefits that can't be stated financially, such as improved morale and improved team-building skills, are important and should be listed in the report, but the financial aspects usually dominate the benefit section of the report.

Common Financial Measures

Revenue growth is the projected increase in income that will result from the project. This is calculated as the increase in gross income minus the cost. Revenue growth may be stated in dollars per year or as a percentage per year.

An organization's *market share* of a particular product or service is that percentage of the dollar value that is sold relative to the total dollar value sold by all organizations in a given market. A project's goal may be to increase this percentage. During a market slowdown, market share is often watched closely because an increase in market share, even with a drop in sales, can produce an increase in sales when the slowdown ends.

Margin refers to the difference between income and cost.

Return on Investment

One of the most easily understood financial numbers is the return on investment (ROI):

$$\text{ROI} = \frac{\text{Income}}{\text{Cost}} \times 100\%$$

where *income* includes money that will be made as a result of the project, dollars saved, and costs avoided, and *cost* is the amount of money required to implement the project.

In basic terms, the ROI metric measures the effectiveness of an organization's ability to use its resources to generate income.

Another approach is to calculate the amortization time, that is, the number of months required for the enterprise to recover the costs of the project. This is known simply as the *payback period*.

Net Present Value

The net present value (NPV) of an amount to be received in the future is given by the formula

$$P = A(1 + i)^{-n}$$

where

P = net present value

A = amount to be received n years from now

i = annual interest rate expressed as a decimal

This formula assumes the money is compounded annually.

Example 7.1

In four years, $2500 will be available. What is the NPV of that money, assuming an annual interest rate of 8%?

$$P = 2500(1 + 0.08)^{-4}$$

$$P = 1837.57$$

Therefore, $1837.57 invested at 8% compounded annually will be worth $2500 after four years.

Suppose a project requires an investment of $1837.57 and will return $3000 in four years. Using the NPV approach, the gain is $500, assuming a compound annual interest rate of 8% per year. The interest rate is usually set by company policy on the basis of the cost of money.

Example 7.2

Suppose a project requiring an initial investment of $4000 pays $1000 every six months for two years beginning one year from the date of the investment. What is the NPV and the gain?

Net present value of the first payment = NPV_1 = $1000(1 + 0.08)^{-1}$ = 925.93

Net present value of the second payment = NPV_2 = $1000(1 + 0.08)^{-1.5}$ = 820.97

Example 7.2 *(continued)*

Net present value of the third payment $= NPV_3 = 1000(1 + 0.08)^{-2} = 857.34$

Net present value of the fourth payment $= NPV_4 = 1000(1 + 0.08)^{-2.5} = 824.97$

Net present value of the fifth payment $= NPV_5 = 1000(1 + 0.08)^{-3} = 793.83$

Total net present value of the income $= 4293.04$

Since the initial investment is $4000, the gain is about $293.04. **Note: This calculation assumes a lump sum payback at the end of four years.**

Cost of Quality

The standard categories of quality costs are as follows:

- **Appraisal costs:** Expenses involved in the inspection process
- **Prevention costs:** Costs of all activities whose purpose is to prevent failures
- **Internal failure costs:** Costs incurred when a failure occurs in-house
- **External failure costs:** Costs incurred when a failure occurs when the customer owns the product

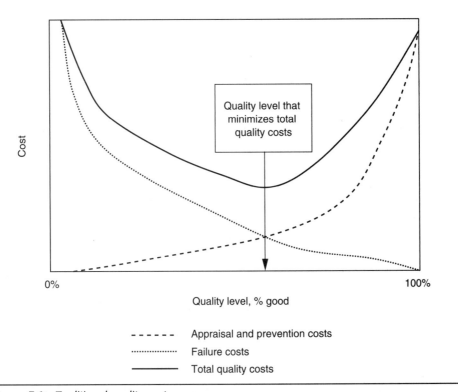

Figure 7.1   Traditional quality cost curves.

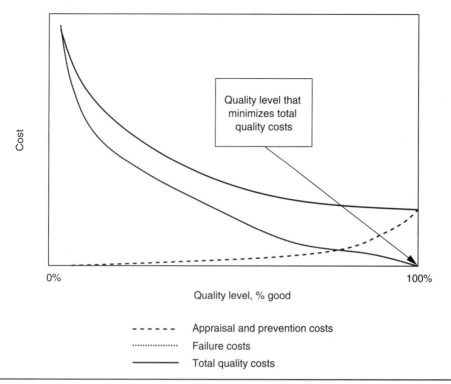

Figure 7.2   Modern quality cost curves. Adapted from Joseph M. Juran and A. Blanton Godfrey, *Juran's Quality Control Handbook*, 5th ed. (New York: McGraw Hill, 1999).

The total cost of quality is the sum of these four amounts. Cost-of-quality calculations have been successfully used to justify proposed improvements. However, it is essential that representatives from the accounting function be involved to ensure that appropriate conventions are used in such proposals.

It is the bias of most quality professionals that if businesses spent more on prevention, they could reduce the total cost of quality because failure costs and, in many cases, appraisal costs could be reduced.

The traditional way to sketch the relationship between quality costs and the quality level is illustrated in Figure 7.1. It indicates that as the quality level approaches 100%, appraisal and prevention costs approach infinity. The optimum total quality cost level is where the total quality cost curve is minimized. This optimum point is located directly above the intersection of the appraisal-prevention and failure curves.

Figure 7.2 demonstrates a different path of thought with regard to quality costs. It illustrates that if it was possible to achieve perfect quality (that is, 100% quality level), the total quality cost curve would be minimized with finite appraisal-prevention and failure costs.

Part II.E

Part III

Team Management

Part III

Chapter 8
Team Formation

TEAM TYPES AND CONSTRAINTS

The two general types of teams are *informal* and *formal*. *Formal teams* have a specific goal or goals linked to the organization's plans. The goal is referred to as the mission or statement of purpose of the team. The formal team may also have a charter that includes its mission statement, a listing of team members, and a statement of support from management. *Informal teams* usually have none of these documents and may have a more fluid membership depending on their needs.

Virtual teams are made up of people in different locations who may never meet in person. Instead, the team may meet using conferencing facilities, or they may conduct all communication through written words via e-mail. These teams are used when expertise is separated geographically or temporally.

Process improvement teams are formed to find and propose changes in specific processes. These teams are usually cross-functional, involving representation from various groups likely to be impacted by the changes.

Self-directed teams and *work group teams* usually have a broader and more ongoing mission involving day-to-day operations. They typically are in a position to make decisions about safety, quality, maintenance, scheduling, personnel, and so forth.

TEAM ROLES

> Define and describe various team roles and responsibilities, including leader, facilitator, coach, individual member, etc. (Understand)
>
> **Body of Knowledge III.A.2**

Teams seem to work best when various members have assigned jobs and others understand the team rules and dynamics. Following are standard team roles and typical duties.

Team Leader

1. Chairs team meetings and maintains team focus on the goal.

2. Monitors progress toward the goal and communicates this to the organization.

3. Manages administrative/record-keeping details.

4. Establishes and follows up on action assignments for individual team members.

Sponsor/Authorizing Entity

1. Selects objective and scope.

2. Organizes team.

3. Monitors progress via communication from the team leader.

4. Arranges for resources needed by the team.

Facilitator

1. Makes certain that all members have an opportunity for input and that a full discussion of issues occurs. In some cases, the facilitator chairs the meeting.

2. Helps the team leader keep the team on track.

3. Summarizes progress using visual aids as appropriate.

4. Provides methods for reaching decisions.

5. Mitigates nonproductive behavior.

6. Helps resolve conflicts.

Scribe/Recorder (May Be a Temporary or Rotating Position)

1. Maintains and publishes meeting minutes. May communicate action assignment reminders to individuals.

2. May use visual aids to record discussion points so all can see and react.

Coach

1. Works with the team leader and facilitator to move the team toward its objective.

2. Helps provide resources for completion of team member action assignments.

Team Member

1. Participates in team meetings.

2. Communicates ideas and expertise.

3. Listens openly to all ideas.

4. Completes action assignments as scheduled.

TEAM MEMBER SELECTION

> Define and describe various factors that influence the selection of team members, including required skills sets, subject matter expertise, availability, etc. (Apply)
>
> **Body of Knowledge III.A.3**

Every project must have representatives of the various project stakeholders (see Chapter 3). In addition, teams need members with technical knowledge and access to outside technical resources as needed. In addition, it is critical that all team members have basic teamwork training.

In some situations, team composition will change over the life cycle of the project. For example, design engineers may be involved in the concept phase and production personnel would be brought in for the pre-production/launch phase. Some team members may be in one, some, or all phases, depending on the nature of the project. Of course, care must be exercised to ensure that team members are brought in at the appropriate times. Waiting too long to involve production personnel may result in an elegant, yet nonbuildable product.

A team must be provided with the resources needed to complete team activities and assignments. This includes ensuring that team member participation is viewed as part of a team member's job and that adequate time is allotted to completing team assignments.

LAUNCHING TEAMS

> Identify and describe the elements required for launching a team, including having management support; establishing clear goals, ground rules, and timelines; and how these elements can affect the team's success. (Apply)
>
> **Body of Knowledge III.A.4**

Using teams to accomplish Six Sigma projects has become commonplace. Team members and team dynamics bring resources to bear on a project that people working individually would not be able to produce. The best teams with the best intentions will perform suboptimally, however, without careful preparation. There seems to be no standard list of preparation steps, but at a minimum, the following items should be performed:

- Set clear purposes and goals that are directly related to the project charter. Teams should not be asked to define their own purpose, although intermediate goals and timetables can be generated. Teams often flounder when purposes are too vague.

- Team members need some basic team-building training. Without an understanding of how a team works and the individual behavior that advances team progress, the team will often get caught in personality concerns and turf wars.

- A schedule of team meetings should be published early, and team members should be asked to commit to attending all meetings. Additional subgroup meetings may be scheduled, but full team meetings should be held as originally scheduled.

- Teams can succeed only if management wants them to. If clear management support is not in place, the wisdom of initiating the team is in question. Team members must know that they have the authority to gather data, ask difficult questions, and, in general, think outside the box.

- Team meetings should close with a review of activities individual team members will complete before the next meeting. Minutes highlighting these activities should follow each meeting.

- All teams should have a sponsor who has a vested interest in the project. The sponsor reviews the team's progress, provides resources, and removes organizational roadblocks.

There is an increase in the use of virtual teams—teams that hold meetings via the Internet or other electronic means. These teams require somewhat more attention to communication and documentation activities.

Part III.A.4

Chapter 9

Team Facilitation

TEAM MOTIVATION

> Describe and apply techniques that motivate team members and support and sustain their participation and commitment. (Apply)
>
> **Body of Knowledge III.B.1**

In many enterprises, people feel like anonymous cogs in a giant machine. They become unwilling to invest much of themselves in a project. An important part of team leadership is generating and maintaining a high level of motivation toward project completion. The following techniques have proved successful.

Recognition

Individuals like to be recognized for their unique contributions. Some forms of recognition include the following:

- Letters of appreciation sent to individuals and placed in personnel files

- Public expressions of appreciation via meetings, newsletters, and so forth

- Tokens of appreciation such as trophies, gifts, or apparel

Rewards

Monetary rewards are effective, especially when considerable personal time or sacrifice is involved. However, particular care must be taken with this type of reward. Frequently, the individual giving the reward delivers the same dollar amount to each team member without considering the amount of personal time, sacrifice, or results achieved by each team member. This is the easy route for the giver, but it may generate hard feelings within the team because all the members know the degree to which each team member participated. One way around this issue is to provide a set monetary limit for the entire team and allow the members to determine how the money is spent or divided.

Relationships within the Team

During team meetings, facilitators and other team members can enhance motivation by setting an example of civility and informality, relaxing outside roles, and exhibiting a willingness to learn from one another. Teamwork may be enhanced by celebrating the achievement of a project milestone. Some authorities suggest that participation and motivation are improved by referring to team sessions as workshops rather than meetings.

TEAM STAGES

> Facilitate the team through the classic stages of development: forming, storming, norming, performing, and adjourning. (Apply)
>
> **Body of Knowledge III.B.2**

Teams are said to go through several growth stages:

- **Forming**: Members struggle to understand the goal and its meaning for them individually

- **Storming**: Members express their own opinions and ideas, often disagreeing with others

- **Norming**: Members begin to understand the need to operate as a team rather than as a group of individuals

- **Performing**: Team members work together to reach their common goal

These four stages are considered traditional. Recently, however, two additional stages have been proposed:

- **Adjourning**: A final team meeting is held, during which management decisions regarding the project are discussed and other loose ends are tied up

- **Recognition**: The team's contribution is acknowledged

In Figure 9.1, the horizontal arrows indicate the standard stages of team development. The dashed arrows show alternate paths taken by teams in some circumstances. Without good leadership a team can backslide from norming or performing into a previous stage. If a team leader or facilitator observes signs of backsliding, he or she should remind the group of the goals and agenda and the need to press forward. Team members accustomed to working with one another on similar projects may be able to skip the storming stage and possibly the norming stage. There have also been examples of teams that go through the other stages and omit the performing stage.

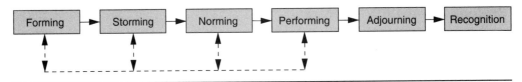

Figure 9.1 Team stages.

TEAM COMMUNICATION

> Identify and use appropriate communication
> methods (both within the team and from the
> team to various stakeholders) to report progress,
> conduct milestone reviews, and support the
> overall success of the project. (Apply)
>
> **Body of Knowledge III.B.3**

Lack of adequate communication is one of the most frequently noted causes of team failure. Serious effort toward improving communication should be made at each stage of team development. In some situations, such as large projects or those with geographical barriers, it is necessary to develop a formal communication plan.

Initiating the Team

A clear statement of goals and objectives is critical. If team members have been selected to represent groups or supply technical knowledge, these roles should be announced at the initial or kick-off meeting. The team's initiation should be in the form of a written document from an individual at the executive level of the organization. A separate document from each member's immediate supervisor is also helpful in recognizing that the team member's participation is important for the success of the team.

Team norms are often established at the first team meeting. They provide clear guidelines regarding what the team will and will not tolerate, and often define the consequences of violating the norms. Examples of team norms include the following:

- Being on time. A consequence of being late may be to put a dollar in a kitty that will be used at the team's discretion at a later date.

- Holding one conversation.

- Demonstrating civility and courtesy to all members.

- Accomplishing assigned tasks on time.

- Providing advance notice of being absent for a meeting.

- Participating in each meeting.

- Following a prepared agenda.
- Putting the team back on track when it strays from the agenda topic.

During the Life of the Team

Announcements of team meetings—including time, location, agenda, and such—must be made as early as possible. Minutes or a summary of the meeting should be provided immediately after the session.

Following Project Completion

Final reports and follow-up memos regarding disposition of team proposals should be provided to each team member.

Chapter 10
Team Dynamics

TEAM DYNAMICS

> Identify and use various techniques (e.g.,
> coaching, mentoring, intervention, etc.) to
> overcome various group dynamic challenges,
> including overbearing/dominant or reluctant
> participants, feuding and other forms of
> unproductive disagreement, unquestioned
> acceptance of opinions as facts, groupthink,
> floundering, rushing to accomplish or finish,
> digressions, tangents, etc. (Evaluate)
>
> **Body of Knowledge III.C**

Once teams have been formed, they must be built, because a true team is more than a collection of individuals. A team begins to take on a life of its own that is greater than the sum of its parts. The building of a team begins with well-trained members who understand roles and responsibilities of team members and how they may differ from roles outside the team. For example, a first-line supervisor might find himself deferring to members of his group in a team session more than he would outside team meetings. Teams are built with understanding and trust in fellow members; therefore, an early step in the building of a team should be informal introductions of each member, such as, "Tell us your name, a non-job-related interest, and what you hope the team accomplishes." This last request sometimes uncovers so-called hidden agendas. These are goals individuals have in addition to the team's stated goals and purposes. Whether or not such agendas are verbalized, their existence and importance must be recognized by team members. The most successful teams are able to suppress the hidden agendas in favor of team progress with the stated ones.

The best model for team leadership is the coach who strives to motivate all members to contribute their best. Productive teams occur when team coaches facilitate progress while recognizing and dealing with obstacles. The coaching function may be performed by team leaders or team facilitators or both. Figure 10.1 contains common team obstacles and associated solutions.

Obstacle	Solution
A person or group dominates the discussion	• Go around the team, asking each person for one comment or reaction. • Ask dominating people to summarize their positions or proposals and e-mail them to all team members. • If the dominating people react negatively to the suggestions of others, ask them for their ideas first or adopt the "no judgments allowed" rule from the brainstorming technique. • Speak to the dominating people between team meetings and request that they cooperate in making sure all voices are heard.
A person or group is reluctant to participate	• Be sure to welcome and express appreciation for every comment or contribution. • Form small subgroups that report to the full team. • Make action assignments for each person, with brief reports at the beginning of the next team meeting. • Speak to the reluctant people between team meetings and request that they cooperate in making sure all voices are heard.
A tendency exists to accept opinions without data	• Emphasize the importance of basing decisions on facts from the first meeting onward. • Raise the following questions: – Are there data that can support that? – How do we know that? – How could we verify that? – Who could collect some data on that?
Emphasis on consensus building has influenced a team to seek consensus too early (i.e., opposing views haven't had a fair hearing)	• Provide full opportunity for the expression of all views. • Support voices of dissent. • Ask individuals to play devil's advocate by opposing early consensus. • Be sure a preliminary written conclusion includes dissenting views.
Team members begin to air old disputes	• Make sure ground rules state the need for a fresh start, keeping history in the past. • Have a printed agenda, possibly with scheduled times for agenda items. A facilitator may say, "It's 3:10; let's move on to item number two." • Assign team members the job of collecting data regarding the issue in dispute.
The team is floundering because it has lost sight of its goals and objectives	• Make sure goals and objectives are clear and well understood at the first team meeting. • Start team meetings by revisiting goals and objectives and reminding the team where it is in its journey and which objective is next. • Use graphics based on PERT and Gantt charts (see Chapter 17) to help keep teams focused. • Bring in an outside voice, which often generates new ideas and approaches.

Figure 10.1   Team obstacles and solutions.

Continued

Part III.C

Obstacle	Solution

The team is rushing to meet its milestones or designated accomplishments without the benefit of a thorough study or analysis
 	
Note: When this occurs, the team risks the following:
• Suboptimizing
  – Unintended consequences (i.e., solving one problem but creating others)
  – Missing root causes
	• Encourage the team to study a far-ranging list of approaches and solutions. Use divergent thinking tools such as brainstorming and cause-and-effect diagrams to broaden the perspective.
	• When a change is studied, be sure it is clearly communicated to all who might be impacted. Actively seek input regarding possible unintended consequences.
	• If a root cause is "turned off," the problem should go away. Try toggling the root cause and observe whether the problem also toggles.

The team becomes troubled over the issue of attribution (i.e., who should get credit for an accomplishment)	• If an idea comes from outside the team, that should be acknowledged. • If an idea was advanced before the team was formed, that should be acknowledged. • Often, the source of ideas and concepts developed during team sessions is not known, but if one person or group is responsible, that should be acknowledged.
The team digresses too far from its goals and objectives	• Assign an individual or group to follow through on a side topic. • Set a deadline beyond which no effort will be spent on the topic.

Figure 10.1 Team obstacles and solutions. *Continued*

Chapter 11

Time Management for Teams

TIME MANAGEMENT FOR TEAMS

> Select and use various time management
> techniques including publishing agendas with
> time limits on each entry, adhering to the agenda,
> requiring pre-work by attendees, ensuring that
> the right people and resources are available, etc.
> (Apply)
>
> **Body of Knowledge III.D**

Time is perhaps the most critical resource for any team. Team meeting time must be treated as the rare and valuable commodity that it is. It is up to the team leader and the facilitator to make every minute count, although every team member has this responsibility as well. Some practices that have proved useful follow:

- Form an *agenda committee* that will generate the meeting agenda well in advance of the scheduled meeting. This group can be responsible for getting the resources called for by each agenda item. For smaller teams, the agenda is often prepared by the team leader.

- Use a *Gantt chart* (see Chapter 17) time line displaying milestones and dates, updating as needed.

- Publish *meeting agendas with time limits* on each item. Assign a timekeeper and stick to the schedule as closely as possible. Leave 5–10 minutes as a buffer at the end of the session.

- Publish *reminders of members' action assignments*. In some cases, the team leader will want to review progress on these assignments between meetings.

Chapter 12

Team Decision-Making Tools

TEAM DECISION-MAKING TOOLS

> Define, select, and use tools such as brainstorming, nominal group technique, multi-voting, etc. (Apply)
>
> **Body of Knowledge III.E**

Several useful tools are available for helping teams make decisions.

Nominal group technique (NGT) is used to prioritize a list of items. Each team member writes on a slip of paper the letters designating a list of items. For example, if there are four items, each team member writes the letters A, B, C, and D and then ranks each of the items, using a higher number for a higher ranking. The highest-ranking item would be marked "4," the next highest would be marked "3," and so on. The totals are compiled for each item and represent the team's consensus. Items with the highest totals are the priority items to be worked on by the team.

In *force field analysis*, illustrated in Figure 12.1, a goal or objective is first listed as the future or desired state. The lists in the two columns are produced from brainstorming or a similar technique. The first column, "Driving force," lists the things that help make the future state occur, and the items in the second column, "Restraining force," are those that prevent the future state from occurring. The team then ranks the two lists, using NGT or a similar tool. The team consensus

Future state: Number of errors is less than 3 per 100 documents	
Driving force	**Restraining force**
Pressure from customer A	Ambient noise level
Group incentive system	Weak spell-checker
Operator enthusiasm	Lack of training
Use of control charts	Inertia
Supportive management	Poor input data

Figure 12.1 Example of a force field analysis.

provides guidance on how to proceed. Depending on the organizational environment in which this technique is used, it may be more effective to focus on reducing or eliminating the restraining forces than to focus on sustaining or increasing the driving forces.

Multivoting is a variation of NGT in which each team member has 100 points to allocate to the items on the list as he or she feels appropriate, assigning the largest number of points to the highest-ranking item. Points assigned to each item are totaled and ranked accordingly. Items with the most points are worked on first.

Conversion/diversion refers to the two types of thinking that go into each of the team tools. Diversion refers to those team activities that produce a broad or diverse set of options. When a team needs a number of fresh ideas, diversion techniques are used. A brainstorming session or a session listing possibilities on a cause-and-effect diagram are examples of diversion. Once many options have been listed, conversion activities are used to narrow the list and prioritize items for action. Examples of conversion activities are NGT and multivoting.

Part III.E

Chapter 13
Management and Planning Tools

MANAGEMENT AND PLANNING TOOLS

Define, select, and apply the following tools: affinity diagrams, tree diagrams, process decision program charts (PDPC), matrix diagrams, interrelationship digraphs, prioritization matrices, and activity network diagrams. (Apply)

Body of Knowledge III.F

Affinity diagrams are used to produce numerous possible answers to an open question such as, What are some of the ways to reduce cycle time for process A? The first step is to brainstorm to obtain two dozen to three dozen responses. Each response is clearly written on a sticky note. The next step is to move the notes into 5–10 natural groups. Some authors suggest doing this in silence, with all team members participating as they prefer. If a note is moved between two groups several times, a duplicate may be made so that one can be placed in each group. The next step is to name each group. This may take several iterations before team consensus is reached. The last step is to draw lines enclosing all notes in a group with the group name. An example of an affinity diagram is shown in Figure 13.1.

Interrelationship digraphs are used to identify cause-and-effect relationships. A typical application begins with listing a half dozen to a dozen concerns on individual sticky notes and then arranging them in no particular order around the perimeter of a sheet of easel paper or a whiteboard. Start with the note at the 12 o'clock position and, moving clockwise, compare it with the next note. For each pair of concerns, determine which concern is more influential on the other and draw an arrow to indicate this. Do not draw an arrow if there is no influential relationship. Then compare the 12 o'clock note with the next note, again moving clockwise. After the 12 o'clock note has been compared with all the other notes, begin with the note clockwise from the 12 o'clock note and compare it with all the other notes that it has not been compared with. Repeat this process until all pairs of notes have been compared. In each case, ask, "Does A influence B more than B influences A?" Revise this diagram as necessary, using additional information or data if needed. An example of an interrelationship digraph at this stage is shown in Figure 13.2.

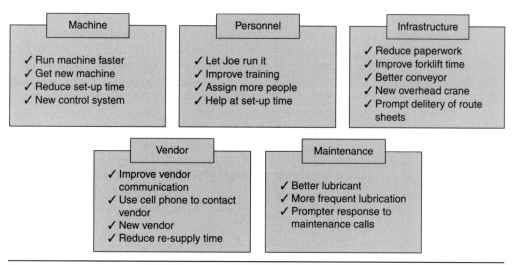

Figure 13.1   Example of an affinity diagram.

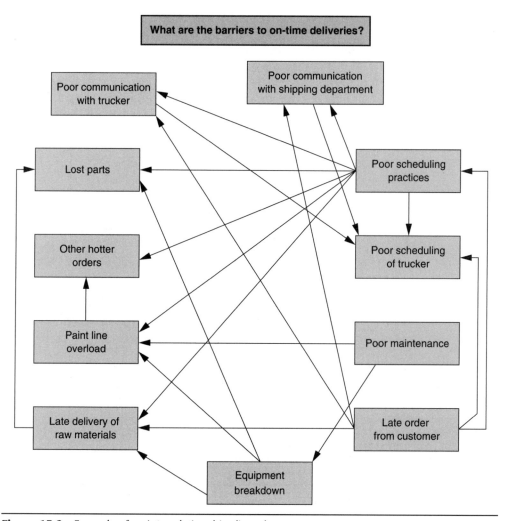

Figure 13.2   Example of an interrelationship digraph.

The next step is to find the note that has the most outgoing arrows. This note is called the driver. In the example, the driver is poor scheduling practices. The driver (or drivers if there is a tie or near tie) is often a key cause of the problem. The note with the greatest number of incoming arrows—poor scheduling of trucker—is called the outcome and is often used as a source of a metric for determining project success.

Tree diagrams help break a general topic into a number of activities that contribute to it. This is accomplished by a series of steps, each one digging deeper into detail than the previous one. A sticky note listing the general topic is posted at the top of the easel or whiteboard. Have the team suggest two to five slightly more specific topics that contribute to the general topic. Write each on a sticky note and post them in a horizontal row beneath the original general topic. For each of these new topics, have the team suggest two to five even more specific topics and post these on the next level down. Continue each branch of the tree as far as seems practical. Draw appropriate connecting lines. Review the tree by making sure that each item actually contributes to the item above it. The resulting diagram should provide specific activities that, when they occur, contribute to the general topic. An example is shown in Figure 13.3.

When a tree diagram is used to study defects, it is sometimes called a fault tree.

A *prioritization matrix* aids in deciding among several options. In the examples shown in Figures 13.4 and 13.5, the options are four software packages: A, B, C, and D. The team determines by consensus the criteria against which the options will be measured and the relative importance (that is, weighting) of each criterion.

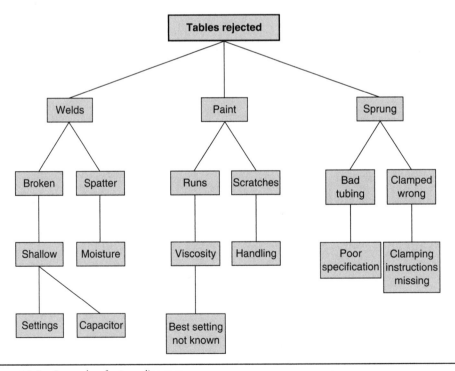

Figure 13.3 Example of a tree diagram.

Multivoting (discussed in Chapter 12) may be helpful. In the example, the criteria and their relative importance are as follows:

Compatibility: 0.25
Cost: 0.30
Ease of use: 0.40
Training time: 0.05
Total: 1.00

Each option is ranked for each criterion, with 1 being the lowest and 4 being the highest. A tie is handled by assigning each option the average values of the ranks. For example, if two options are tied for third place, the two ranks are third and fourth. These have values of 2 and 1, respectively, so each option receives a rank value of 1.5. In the example in Figure 13.4, packages A and C are tied for third place for cost. Thus, the two ranks are third and fourth, but with rank values of 2

Determine the most suitable software package					
		Criteria			
Relative importance	0.25	0.30	0.40	0.05	1.00
Option	Compatibility	Cost	Ease of use	Training time	Total
Package A	4	1.5	3	3	N/A
Package B	1	4	2	2	N/A
Package C	3	1.5	4	4	N/A
Package D	2	3	1	1	N/A

Figure 13.4   Example of a prioritization matrix—first step.

Determine the most suitable software package					
		Criteria			
Relative importance	0.25	0.30	0.40	0.05	
Option	Compatibility	Cost	Ease of use	Training time	Total
Package A	1.00	0.45	1.20	0.15	2.80
Package B	0.25	1.20	0.80	0.10	2.35
Package C	0.75	0.45	1.60	0.20	3.00
Package D	0.50	0.90	0.40	0.05	1.85

Figure 13.5   Example of a prioritization matrix—second step.

and 1, respectively. Therefore, each option receives a value of 1.5. Package B has the lowest cost (that is, highest rank), so it is assigned a value of 4. Package D has the next lowest cost, so it is assigned a value of 3. Packages A and C have the same cost, so each is assigned a value of 1.5.

The next step (as shown in Figure 13.5) is to multiply each of the option values by the relative importance (that is, criteria weights) and calculate the row totals. The option with the highest total represents the team's consensus and therefore its software package selection. From Figure 13.5, we can see that the team will select software package C.

A *matrix diagram* is typically used to discover and illustrate relationships between two groups of items. In Figure 13.6, the two groups are the units of a training course and the objectives of the course. The items in the unit group are listed across the top of the chart, and the items in the objectives group are listed down one side. The team examines each square in the matrix and enters one of three symbols or leaves the square blank, depending on the relationship between the items in the row and the items in the column. The most conventional symbols are shown in the example, although letters and numbers are sometimes used. The team then examines the completed matrix and discusses possible conclusions.

The *process decision program chart* (PDPC) is a tree diagram used to illustrate anticipated problems and list possible solutions. It may be treated as a dynamic

			Unit								
			1	2	3	4	5	6	7	8	9
	Review basics		⊙		⊙	O			Δ		
	Math skills		O	Δ	⊙			⊙	O		
	Communication skills							O			
	Attitude/motivation									Δ	
Objective	Sketching				⊙			O			
	Ohm's law					⊙	O	Δ			
	Kirkoff's law						⊙	O			
	Thevinev's law							Δ	O		
	Heisenberg's uncertainty principle										

⊙ = strong relationship
O = moderate relationship
Δ = weak relationship
blank = no relationship

Conclusions:
    Thevinev's law and communication skills covered only weakly
    Attitude/motivation barely covered
    Heisenberg's uncertainty principle not covered
    Unit 2 contributes very little toward objectives
    Unit 9 contributes nothing toward objectives

Figure 13.6 Example of a matrix diagram.

document to be updated as the project proceeds. An example is shown in Figure 13.7.

The *activity network diagram* (AND), also known as an arrow diagram, is similar to the PERT chart (discussed in Chapter 17). An example is shown in Figure 13.8.

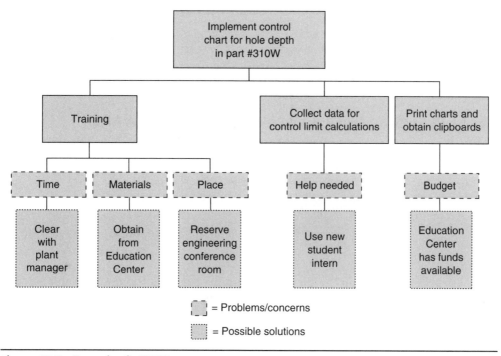

= Problems/concerns

= Possible solutions

Figure 13.7   Example of a PDPC.

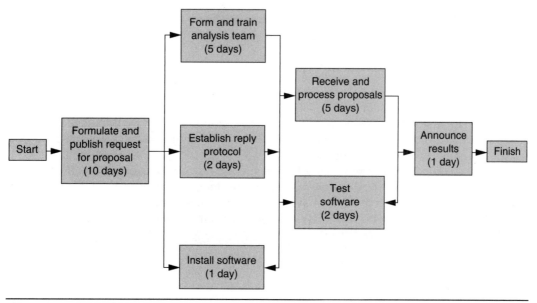

Figure 13.8   Example of an AND.

Part III.F

Chapter 14

Team Performance Evaluation and Reward

TEAM PERFORMANCE EVALUATION AND REWARD

> Measure team progress in relation to goals, objectives, and other metrics that support team success, and reward and recognize the team for its accomplishments. (Analyze)
>
> **Body of Knowledge III.G**

At specified points in the life of the team, its progress should be evaluated. The measurement system and criteria should be agreed upon in advance. Performance measures are usually numerical rather than narrative.

The criteria against which the team is evaluated must relate to progress toward goals and objectives. It is common practice to compare team progress against the time line established in a Gantt chart (see Chapter 17) or similar document. The following are typical criteria:

- **T**ime oriented ("Are we on schedule?")
- **O**bjective oriented ("Are we meeting our goals?")
- **M**onetary ("Are we on budget?")

A good mnemonic device for remembering the criteria is that the first letter of each criterion spells "TOM."

In addition to these criteria, teams have found self-evaluation at the end of each meeting to be useful. This process permits midcourse corrections and ensures meetings become more effective.

Recognition and rewards for team success help encourage future efforts (see Chapter 9). Team leaders can recognize the team's efforts as the team reaches various milestones. More formal reward ceremonies at the conclusion of a team's project might involve a higher level of management. Here are just a few of the possibilities:

- Evaluations that show personal strength and growth as a team member
- Tokens such as pins, small gifts, apparel, or meals
- Recognition through professional organizations
- Support for publication of results in professional journals
- Recognition in company newsletters
- Financial rewards based on cost savings resulting from the project

Part IV
Define

Part IV

Chapter 15
Voice of the Customer

CUSTOMER IDENTIFICATION

> Segment customers for each project and show how the project will impact both internal and external customers. (Apply)
>
> **Body of Knowledge IV.A.1**

An early step in any project is to seek the voice of the customer (VOC). The internal and external customers of a project include all those who are impacted by the project. For most projects the customers can be grouped into segments. This segmentation is driven by customer requirements and often includes the following categories:

- Internal and external
- Demographics
  - Age groups, especially for consumer goods
  - Geographical location, including climate, language and ethnic issues, and shipping considerations
- Industry types (for example, the project might impact customers in construction, agriculture, and stationary equipment industries)

When possible, a list of customers within a segment should be constructed. When a project team proposes changes of any type, all customers, internal and external, must be consulted, or at a minimum, the customers' concerns must be represented.

It is easy to underestimate the value of understanding and providing for customers' needs. For without customers, we have nothing!

CUSTOMER FEEDBACK

> Identify and select the appropriate data collection method (surveys, focus groups, interviews, observation, etc.) to gather customer feedback to better understand customer needs, expectations, and requirements. Ensure that the instruments used are reviewed for validity and reliability to avoid introducing bias or ambiguity in the responses. (Apply)
>
> **Body of Knowledge IV.A.2**

Statistically speaking, the most valid procedure for collecting customer data is to randomly select a reasonably large representative group of customers and obtain complete and accurate data on each one. But since this procedure is not possible in most situations, various other methods are employed. Each of the following methods compromises a statistical approach in some way:

- Written surveys can be sent to a randomly selected group of customers or potential customers, but it's seldom possible to get responses from all those selected. In addition, the accuracy of the responses is questionable. A carefully worded and analyzed survey can, however, shed significant light on customer reactions.

- Focus groups are an attempt to improve the depth and accuracy of the responses. Focus groups generally provide more accurate answers and the ability to probe deeper into issues or concerns on a real-time basis. However, the sample is often nonrandom and too small. As statisticians say, "The plural of anecdote is not data."

- Phone or in-person interviews permit a higher response rate than written surveys; however, as with written surveys, the respondents tend to be self-selecting and therefore nonrandom because many people decline to participate. A skillful interviewer can record customer feelings that written surveys wouldn't detect.

The data collected should be objective and designed to shed light on customer requirements. It is important to use several independent resources to obtain this information. Results from each resource should be compared to determine patterns of reinforcement or contradiction of conclusions.

Part IV.A.2

CUSTOMER REQUIREMENTS

> Define, select, and use appropriate tools to
> determine customer requirements, such as CTQ
> flow-down, quality function deployment (QFD),
> and the Kano model. (Apply)
>
> **Body of Knowledge IV.A.3**

The best customer data collection and analysis is useless unless there is a system to use the data to effect changes. This system should study each item of customer feedback to determine which processes, product, and/or services will be impacted. The volume and/or urgency of customer concerns will help determine the requirements that customers deem critical. Some type of criticality rating system should be applied to the feedback data (for example, a phone call from a customer is rated higher than a response to a questionnaire). Suppose, for example, that analysis of customer data identifies six areas where product quality is compromised. With the help of the criticality rating scale, perhaps two of the six would be deemed important enough to motivate immediate improvement projects. A number of other tools developed to aid in determining and meeting customer needs are listed in the remainder of this chapter.

Critical-to-Quality Flow-Down

Customer satisfaction generally falls into three dimensions:

- Quality
- Delivery
- Cost

Cost and delivery are easy to quantify. Customers are willing to pay x per item and expect its delivery y days after they place the order. Quantifying quality characteristics presents more of a challenge. One of the tools devised to help is called the critical-to-quality (CTQ) flow-down. Its purpose is to start with the high-level strategic goal of customer satisfaction and determine how this goal "flows down" into measurable goals. The nomenclature for the various levels is illustrated in Figure 15.1.

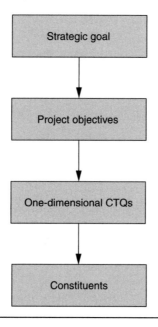

Figure 15.1   CTQ flow–down.

Example 15.1

High on Mid America Landscaping's list of strategic goals is customer satisfaction. A survey of past customers raised the need to establish a project team to ensure that customers understand the nature of the plants and trees they are purchasing. The team identifies a number of constituent parts to the problem. These constituents will guide the team. The CTQ flow-down diagram is shown in Figure 15.2.

Example 15.1 *(continued)*

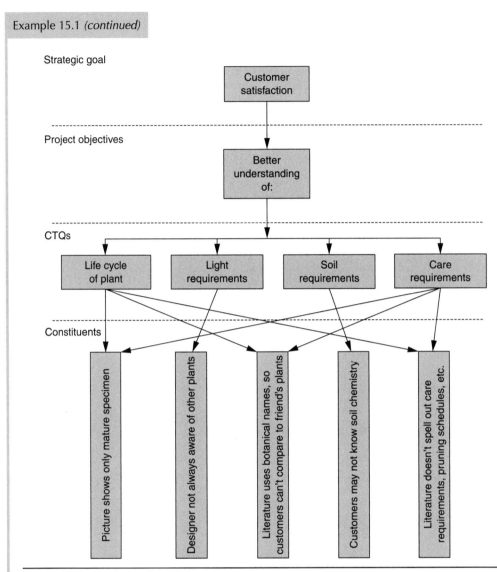

Figure 15.2   Example of a CTQ flow-down.

Quality Function Deployment

Quality function deployment (QFD) provides a process for planning new or redesigned products and services. The input to the process is the VOC. The QFD process requires that a team discover the needs and desires of its customer and study the organization's response to these needs and desires. The QFD matrix helps illustrate the linkage between the VOC and the resulting technical requirements.

A QFD matrix consists of several parts. There is no standard format matrix or key for the symbols, but the example shown in Figure 15.3 is typical. A map of the various parts of Figure 15.3 is shown in Figure 15.4.

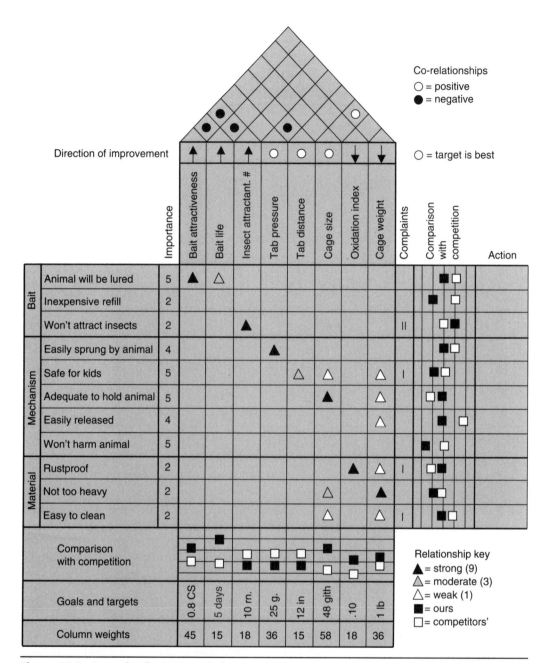

Figure 15.3   Example of a QFD matrix for an animal trap.

The matrix is formed by first filling in the customer requirements (area 1), which are developed from analysis of the VOC. This section often includes a scale reflecting the importance of the individual entries. The technical requirements are established in response to the customer requirements and placed in area 2. The

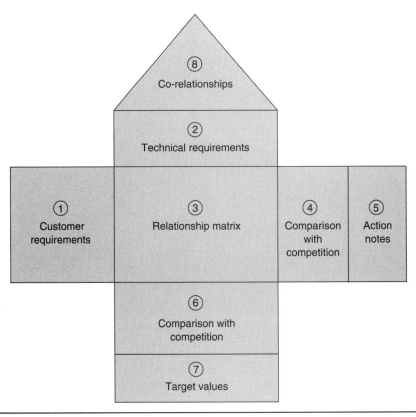

Figure 15.4   Map of the entries for the QFD matrix illustrated in Figure 15.3.

symbols on the top line in this section indicate whether lower (↓) or higher (↑) is better. A circle indicates that target is best.

The relationship area (3) displays the connection between the technical requirements and the customer requirements. Various symbols can be used here. The most common are shown in Figure 15.3.

Area 4, which plots the comparison with the competition for the customer requirements, is not always shown on QFD matrices. Area 5 provides an index to documentation concerning improvement activities.

Area 6, like area 4, is not always shown on QFD matrices. It plots the comparison with the competition for the technical requirements. Area 7 lists the target values for the technical requirements. Area 8 shows the co-relationships between the technical requirements. A positive co-relationship indicates that both technical requirements can be improved at the same time. A negative co-relationship indicates that improving one of the technical requirements will worsen the other.

The column weights shown at the bottom of Figure 15.3 are optional. They indicate the importance of the technical requirements in meeting customer requirements. The value in the "Column weights" row is obtained by multiplying the value in the "Importance" column in the customer requirements section by values assigned to the symbols in the relationship matrix. These assigned values are arbitrary; in the example, a strong relationship was assigned a 9, moderate 3, and weak 1.

The completed matrix can provide a database for product development, serve as a basis for planning product or process improvements, and suggest opportunities for new or revised product or process introductions.

The customer requirements section is sometimes called the "What," while the technical requirements section is referred to as the "How." This "What versus How" concept can be applied through a series of matrices intended to decompose the technical requirements to lower levels that can eventually be assigned as tasks. In addition, the basic QFD product-planning matrix can be followed with similar matrices for planning the parts that make up the product and for planning the processes that will produce the parts.

If a matrix has more than 25 customer voice lines, it tends to become unmanageable. In such a situation, a convergent tool such as the affinity diagram (see Chapter 13) may be used to condense the list.

Kano Model

Kano's model of customer satisfaction identifies several types of requirements that impact customer satisfaction. They are illustrated in Figure 15.5 and described in the next few paragraphs.

The Kano model separates customer requirements into several categories. They are shown as various curves on the graph in Figure 15.5, which has a horizontal

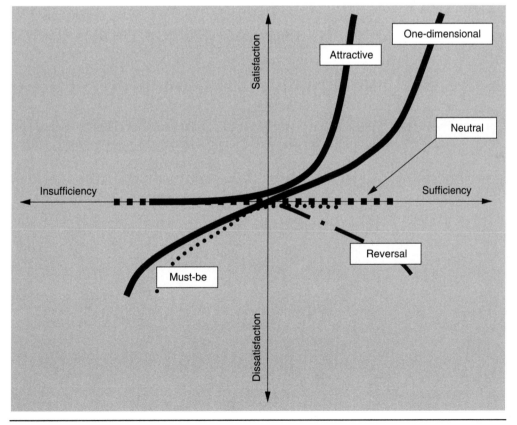

Figure 15.5   Kano model for customer satisfaction.

Part IV.A.3

axis going from insufficiency to sufficiency for the amount of the requirement that is met. The vertical axis goes from dissatisfaction to satisfaction.

Must-be requirements, or basic requirements, are those the customer assumes will be there, and, although they aren't in any specifications, the customer will be very dissatisfied if they are not there. The line labeled "Must-be" in Figure 15.5 is on the dissatisfied side when the specification is missing. When it is on the sufficiency side, it doesn't move very high into the satisfaction region. An example might be a shirt with a button hole that is sewed shut.

One-dimensional requirements are those in which the customer expects a certain level of sufficiency, and anything exceeding that level increases satisfaction. A computer connection may be advertised as having a certain data transfer rate. If the rate in use is less than the advertised rate, the customer is dissatisfied. However, transfer rates above the advertised rate will increase the level of satisfaction. The curve labeled "One-dimensional" crosses the origin of the axis system at the expected value.

Attractive requirements are the way to get to the heart of the customer. When present, they increase satisfaction, but their absence does not cause dissatisfaction, because the customer does not expect them. An example would be a set of kitchen cupboards that arrives with an extra corbel because the designer thought it would add a nice touch.

In addition to these three requirement types identified by Kano, two additional types of characteristics are sometimes used:

- *Neutral characteristics* don't bring satisfaction if present, nor do they cause dissatisfaction if absent. This could refer to features the customer didn't expect or features the customer rarely uses.

- *Reversal characteristics* refer to features the customer doesn't want and whose presence causes dissatisfaction. An example might be the beeping feature on a microwave.

An awareness of these features of customer satisfaction (and dissatisfaction) provides insight and guidance for the organization's goal of ever-improving customer satisfaction.

Chapter 16
Project Charter

A *project charter* is a document stating the purposes of the project. It serves as an informal contract that helps the team stay on track with the goals of the enterprise. Each charter should contain the following points:

- **Purpose**: Establishes goals and objectives

- **Benefits**: States how the enterprise will fare better when the project reaches its goals

- **Scope**: Provides project limitations in terms of budget, time, and other resources

- **Results**: Defines the criteria and metrics for project success

PROBLEM STATEMENT

> Develop and evaluate the problem statement in relation to the project's baseline performance and improvement goals. (Create)
>
> **Body of Knowledge IV.B.1**

The problem statement should be a concise explanation of a current state that adversely impacts the enterprise. In many ways, the problem definition phase is the most important phase of the DMAIC cycle. If this phase is not done thoroughly, teams may move on to subsequent phases only to stall and cycle back through "define." This phase should be emphasized, and teams should not move forward until the sponsor/process owner signs off on it.

The following are examples of well-defined problem statements:

- The reject rate for product X is so high that competitors are taking some of our market share

- The cycle time of product B must be reduced in order for the organization to remain competitive

PROJECT SCOPE

> Develop and review project boundaries to
> ensure that the project has value to the customer.
> (Analyze)
>
> **Body of Knowledge IV.B.2**

Six Sigma projects sometimes suffer from disagreement among the project team members regarding project boundaries. The process of defining scope, of course, can result in problems of the extremes:

- Project definitions with scopes that are too broad may lead a team into a morass of connecting issues and associated problems beyond the team's resources. Example: "Improve customer satisfaction" with a complex product or service.

- Project boundaries that are set too narrow could restrict teams from finding root causes. For example, "Improve customer satisfaction by reducing variation in plating thickness" restricts looking at machining processes that may be the root cause of customer problems.

- The tendency is to err on the side of making the scope too broad rather than too narrow. Individuals who have experience with projects and project management should be used in the definition and charter phases to help improve the probability of appropriate boundaries.

- Several tools are available to assist in setting a project scope:

  - Pareto charts to help in the prioritizing process and sometimes in support of project justification

  - Cause-and-effect diagrams to broaden the thinking within set categories

  - Affinity diagrams to show linkages between the project and other projects or processes

  - Process maps to provide visualization and perhaps illuminate obvious project boundaries and relationships

Collectively, these tools help the Black Belt zero in on the scope, and sometimes, even more importantly, what is out of scope. In fact, it is often necessary to state explicitly what is out of scope. Scope may be defined or limited by the following:

- Geography
- Demographics
- Organization structure

- Process boundaries

- Relationships (for example, suppliers, customers, contract personnel)

- Those using system A

In addition to defining what is in scope, teams will find it necessary to explicitly state what is out of scope as well. Though one would initially think that this should be obvious by simply stating what is in scope, many sponsors, team members, and other stakeholders often fail to make this important connection. For example, process B is in scope, whereas processes A and C are out of scope.

GOALS AND OBJECTIVES

> Develop the goals and objectives for the project on the basis of the problem statement and scope. (Apply)
>
> **Body of Knowledge IV.B.3**

The next step in forming the project charter is to establish the goals. Goal statements should be SMART:

- **S**pecific: This is not the place to be generic or philosophic. Nail down the goal.

- **M**easurable: Unless the team has measurable goals, it won't know whether it is making progress or whether it has succeeded.

- **A**chievable, yet aggressive: This is a judgment call; experience with project planning and execution will help in meeting this requirement.

- **R**elevant: The goal must be specifically linked to the strategic goals of the enterprise.

- **T**imely: The goal must make sense in the time frame in which the team must work.

Example 16.1 shows a SMART goal linked to the organization's strategic goals of customer satisfaction and quality.

Example 16.1

Improve the production yield for part A on process B from its current baseline of 60% to 90% within six months.

Part IV.B.3

PROJECT PERFORMANCE MEASURES

> Identify and evaluate performance measurements
> (e.g., cost, revenue, schedule, etc.) that connect
> critical elements of the process to key outputs.
> (Analyze)
>
> **Body of Knowledge IV.B.4**

Although one may argue with the statement, "If it can't be measured, it isn't worth doing," measurement of progress toward a goal is a critical part of a project definition. Since it is important that projects have a measurable impact on the enterprise, the common denominator of most metrics tends to be financial. However, an intermediate goal such as prompt response to customer orders would have associated measurements such as cycle-time reduction, document throughput, and shipping efficiency. Therefore, a performance measurement in this area should include specific goals for these measurements.

Similarly, the general project goal of increased profitability for a particular product line might have as a secondary metric the amount of cost reduction, which, in turn, could have a tertiary metric involving inventory reduction.

The improper choice of metrics may lead the project team in the wrong direction. The classic example is machine utilization. If an objective is to increase the percentage of the day that each machine produces parts, excess inventory will often be built. Similarly, if the bottom line of an accounting balance sheet is used as a metric, excess inventory may not be drawn down to a less wasteful level, because most accounting systems assume that inventory is an asset. Having a goal of increasing the ratio of direct to indirect labor sometimes leads a manufacturing team in the wrong direction, because moving people off the line into support positions may be the best path to process improvement.

All processes can be measured in terms of quality (that is, defects) and cycle time. Process cost flows from these two metrics. Reducing cost without focusing on reducing defects and cycle time is a recipe for disaster.

Chapter 17
Project Tracking

PROJECT TRACKING

> Identify, develop, and use project management
> tools, such as schedules, Gantt charts, toll-gate
> reviews, etc., to track project progress. (Create)
>
> **Body of Knowledge IV.C**

At specified points in the life of the team, its progress should be evaluated. The measurement system and criteria are agreed upon in advance. The criteria against which the team is evaluated must relate to progress toward goals and objectives. It is common practice to compare team progress against the time line established in a Gantt chart or similar document. Typical criteria (see Chapter 14) are:

- Time oriented ("Are we on schedule?")
- Objective oriented ("Are we meeting our goals?")
- Monetary ("Are we on budget?")

Example 17.1 illustrates use of the project planning and tracking tools.

Example 17.1

A team uses a mailed survey to obtain information on customer preferences. The team identifies the following activities necessary for project completion:

A. Construct survey questionnaire

B. Decide whether to buy or build software to analyze the data

C. Print and mail questionnaire

D. Buy or build software

E. Test software

F. Enter data into database

G. Use software to analyze results

H. Interpret results and write final report

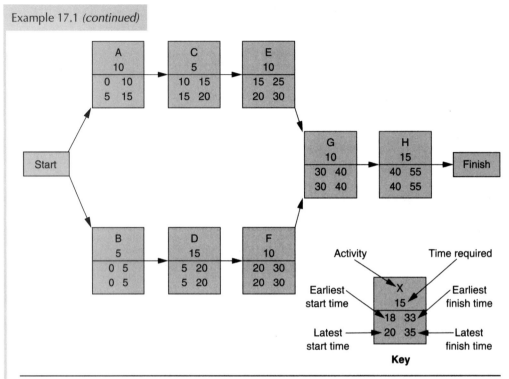

Example 17.1 *(continued)*

Figure 17.1 Project network diagram.

The team constructs the project network diagram shown in Figure 17.1 to show predecessor and successor relationships. The number directly below each activity letter indicates the number of days required.

As the key in Figure 17.1 indicates, the numbers below the line in each activity box provide data regarding start and finish times. *Slack time* for an activity is defined as:

$$\text{Slack time} = \text{Latest start time} - \text{Earliest start time}$$

Project Evaluation and Review Technique (PERT) and Critical Path Method (CPM) have essentially merged in current software packages. The *critical path* is the path from start to finish that requires the most time. In Figure 17.1, there are just two paths:

- Path ACEGH requires 10 + 5 + 10 + 10 + 15 = 50 days

- Path BDFGH requires 5 + 15 + 10 + 10 + 15 = 55 days

Therefore, BDFGH is the critical path. Software packages are available to identify and calculate the critical path for projects with multiple paths. If activities on the critical path are delayed, the entire project will be delayed. *Critical path time* is the time required to complete the project. The only way to complete the project in less time is to decrease the time for at least one of the activities. This is usually

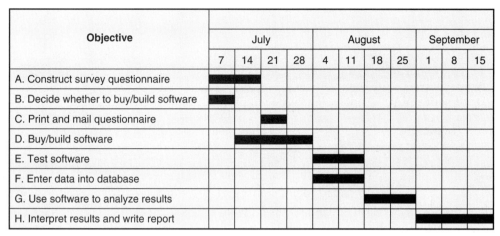

Objective	July				August				September		
	7	14	21	28	4	11	18	25	1	8	15
A. Construct survey questionnaire	███	██									
B. Decide whether to buy/build software	██										
C. Print and mail questionnaire			██								
D. Buy/build software		██	███	██							
E. Test software					███	██					
F. Enter data into database					███						
G. Use software to analyze results								███			
H. Interpret results and write report									███	██	

Figure 17.2   Example of a Gantt chart.

accomplished by putting more resources into one or more activities on the critical path. This is sometimes referred to as "crashing" the project. The information from the PERT/CPM analysis can be used to construct a Gantt chart, as shown in Figure 17.2.

The charts shown in Figures 17.1 and 17.2 have the advantage of being easy to understand while conveying essential data, and therefore they are often used for presentations to executive groups as well as tracking devices. Additional charts and diagrams can be produced for each of the activities listed. These graphical tools are also useful for tracking and evaluating the project at various phases and at final management reviews. Storyboards are sometimes used to convey project information involving changes that are easier to draw or photograph than to explain in words. A common application of storyboards is for before-and-after pictures, often called current state and future state, for a proposed project. This approach is appropriate for facility or product redesign projects. Storyboards for Six Sigma projects are often formatted into five sections labeled define, measure, analyze, improve, and control (DMAIC), with charts, figures, and documents illustrating the activity in each area.

Part V
Measure

Part V

Chapter 18

Process Characteristics

INPUT AND OUTPUT VARIABLES

> Identify these process variables and evaluate
> their relationships using SIPOC and other tools.
> (Evaluate)
>
> **Body of Knowledge V.A.1**

A process is a step or sequence of steps that uses inputs and produces a product or service as an output. Every process has inputs that are traditionally categorized as material, man, machine, methods, Mother Nature, and management. Some authorities include the measurement system as an input since it has an impact on the perceived output (see Figure 18.1).

Processes are often made up of smaller subprocesses. For example, a part may be produced using a process that has a machining step. This machining step may be thought of as a process whose steps might include clamping, turning, plunging, and facing. In addition, the plunging step is a process in itself. In a similar manner, a payroll process has subprocesses that include gathering time-clock information, making deductions, and so forth. The deduction process itself could be thought of as having subprocesses for tax deductions and insurance, among others.

When defining a process, it is important to identify its start and end points. If, for example, a team is charged with improving a process, it needs to know these process boundaries. Cross-functional processes may incur subprocess boundaries defined by the organizational structure, geography, and so on.

A thorough understanding of process inputs and outputs and their relationships is a key step in process improvement. Figure 18.1 lists process inputs and outputs.

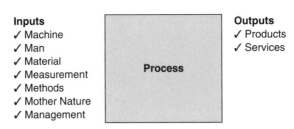

Inputs
✓ Machine
✓ Man
✓ Material
✓ Measurement
✓ Methods
✓ Mother Nature
✓ Management

Process

Outputs
✓ Products
✓ Services

Figure 18.1   Process diagram.

Suppliers	Inputs		Process	Outputs		Customers
	Description	Requirements		Description	Requirements	

Figure 18.2 Example of a SIPOC form. Courtesy of Minitab.

The *SIPOC* is another useful tool in the study of processes. The acronym stands for the key elements of a process:

- Suppliers—The internal and external providers of resources, materials, knowledge, and services that the process requires

- Inputs—The elements outside the process boundaries that feed the process so that it can function and produce outputs

- Process—The step or sequence of steps that is being improved

- Outputs—The measurable or assessable end products or services produced by the process

- Customers—People who receive the final products and the outputs of each process step

Developing a SIPOC constitutes completing the form shown in Figure 18.2. One key value of completing a SIPOC is the ability to create a connection from supplier to input to process to output to customer. When such linkages can't be clearly demonstrated, opportunities for improvement exist.

PROCESS FLOW METRICS

> Evaluate process flow and utilization to identify waste and constraints by analyzing work in progress (WIP), work in queue (WIQ), touch time, takt time, cycle time, throughput, etc. (Evaluate)
>
> **Body of Knowledge V.A.2**

Process flow improvement is a significant Six Sigma goal. As such, it implies the need for process flow metrics. Consider a generic process consisting of four steps (Figure 18.3).

This could be a business process such as generating an invoice, a government process such as serving a subpoena, a manufacturing process, or a design process. The following metrics may be used to evaluate flow in the process:

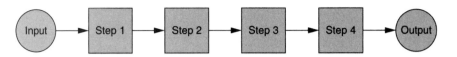

Figure 18.3 Generic process flowchart.

- *Work in progress* (WIP) is the material that has been input to the process but that has not reached the output stage. This includes the material being processed by the various steps and the material waiting to be processed by one or more steps. This may occur as inventory stored before a particular step or stored elsewhere. In the case of invoice processing, WIP would be the number of invoices that have started the process but that have not yet finished it. In general, the larger the WIP, the longer the time required to complete the process. WIP, although considered an asset by some accounting systems, is in many ways a liability because it requires space, environmental control, labeling, record keeping, and other upkeep expenses.

- *Work in queue* (WIQ) is the material waiting to be processed by some step in the process and is one component of WIP. It is important to segment the WIQ by step to help identify process bottlenecks or constraints. Also, it is desirable to maintain WIQ in "first in first out" (FIFO) order depending on the shelf life of the inventory.

- *Touch time* is the time that material is actually being processed by one of the steps. Again, it may be useful to segment the total touch time by step so that processes with large touch times may be readily identified for improvement purposes.

- *Takt time* is computed as follows:

$$\text{Takt time} = \frac{\text{Time available}}{\text{Number of units to be processed}}$$

The takt time is the rate at which the process must output completed items. Takt is similar to the word "drumbeat" in German, referring to the constant rate of output.

Example 18.1

Forty-eight subpoenas are to be served in 480 minutes. The takt time would be

$$\text{Takt time} = \frac{480 \text{ minutes}}{48 \text{ subpoenas}} = 10 \text{ minutes per subpoena}$$

- *Cycle time* is the average time for a particular step to complete one item. If the generation of working drawings in a design process requires an average of 32 hours, that is the cycle time for that step. If the cycle time is greater than the takt time, the required number of items will not be output. In situations where several people can be performing the step, we can compute the number of people required as follows:

$$\text{Number of people} = \frac{\text{Cycle time}}{\text{Takt time}}$$

Example 18.2

The takt time is 13 minutes, and the cycle time for a particular step is 38 minutes, therefore:

$$\text{Number of people} = \frac{38 \text{ minutes}}{13 \text{ minutes}} = 2.9 \text{ or 3 people}$$

Notice the number of people is rounded up.

- *Throughput* is the number of items or amount of material output from the process in a given period of time. For example, a takt time of 10 minutes per subpoena is equivalent to a throughput rate of 6 subpoenas per hour.

- *Value-added time* is the amount of time used for activities for which a customer is willing to pay. All other time is non-value-added and should be scrutinized for possible reduction, simplification, or elimination. Note that touch time may not be the same as value-added time.

- *Setup time,* also referred to as *change-over time*, is the time required to convert from producing one product to producing a different one on, say, a particular machine, process step, and so forth. This should be studied for each step with an eye toward making the process more flexible for mixed model operation.

In most cases, the ultimate goal of studying process flow is to implement a one-piece flow instead of a batch-and-queue operation.

PROCESS ANALYSIS TOOLS

Analyze processes by developing and using value stream maps, process maps, flowcharts, procedures, work instructions, spaghetti diagrams, circle diagrams, etc. (Analyze)

Body of Knowledge V.A.3

Process Maps and Flowcharts

A key step in understanding processes is the development of process maps and flowcharts. The format of these documents will vary with the situation, but in general, flowcharts show each step in a process, decision points, inputs, and outputs. Process maps usually contain additional information about the steps, including inputs and outputs, costs, setup time, cycle time, inventory, types of defects that can occur, probability of defects, and other appropriate information. Examples are shown in Figure 18.4.

Process maps and flowcharts enable a broader perspective of potential problems and opportunities for process improvement. Teams using these tools get a better understanding of individual and group goals.

Written Procedures

Almost every process can be improved by reducing variation. To do so, it is necessary to always do things the same way. One plant issues T-shirts that read: "The

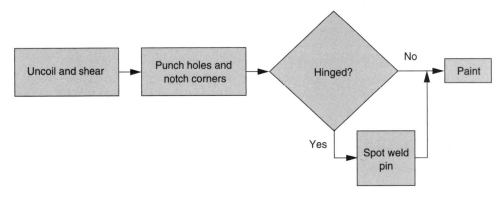

a) Flowchart for primary operations on sheet metal blower door

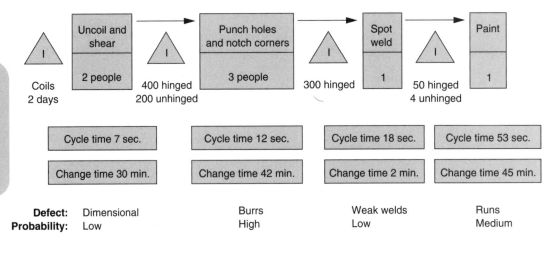

b) Process map for primary operations on sheet metal blower door

Figure 18.4   Process flowchart and process map example.

Right Way/The Safe Way/The Same Way." The best way to ensure that things are done the same way is to have written procedures and work instructions. The procedures tend to be more generic, often covering several processes and products and usually in text format. Work instructions are usually product specific and often include graphics showing discrete steps including defects to avoid, safety hazards, tooling required, and any information that ensures the job will be performed in a standard way. When generating work instructions and procedures, the people closest to the process must be involved. If more than one shift or workstation is affected, the appropriate people should participate. The most difficult aspect of documenting instructions and procedures is maintaining up-to-date versions. As workers find improvements or engineers change designs, the documentation must be updated to avoid problems, issues, defects, or obsolescence. Examples of written procedures and work instructions are illustrated in Figures 18.5 and 18.6, respectively.

Another useful tool for analyzing processes is known as the *value stream map*. Value stream mapping is a technique for following the production path for a product or service from beginning to end while drawing a visual representation of every process in the material and information flows.

The following steps illustrate how to develop and analyze a value stream map:

1. Produce a value stream map. Figure 18.7 shows some symbols that are used on value stream maps.

2. Analyze all inventory notes with an eye toward reduction or elimination. Inventory tends to increase costs for the following reasons:

   - Storage space may be expensive (rubber awaiting use in a tire factory is stored at 120°F; wood inventory may need to have humidity control).

   - Quality may deteriorate (think rust, spoilage, and so forth).

   - Design changes may be delayed.

   - Money invested in inventory could be used more productively elsewhere.

   - Quality problems that are not detected until a later stage in the process will be more expensive to correct if an inventory of wrong products has accumulated.

3. Analyze the entire value stream for unneeded steps. An example of a completed value stream map is given in Figure 18.8. Notice that

> 1. Place circuit board on fixture.
> 2. Connect tester and initiate test cycle.
> 3. Attach printout to board.
> 4. Remove board from fixture and place it on conveyor.

Figure 18.5   Example of written procedures.

Work instructions for Brazing A8106 to A8311

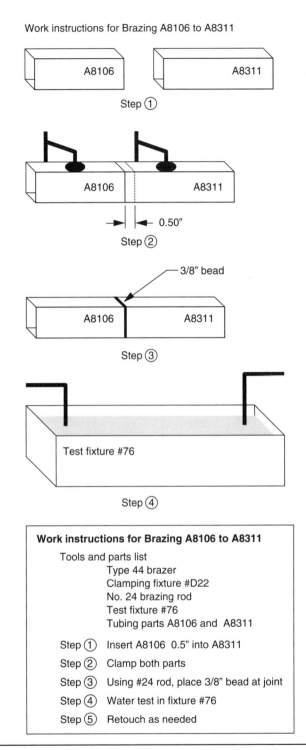

Work instructions for Brazing A8106 to A8311

Tools and parts list
        Type 44 brazer
        Clamping fixture #D22
        No. 24 brazing rod
        Test fixture #76
        Tubing parts A8106 and A8311

Step ①   Insert A8106 0.5" into A8311

Step ②   Clamp both parts

Step ③   Using #24 rod, place 3/8" bead at joint

Step ④   Water test in fixture #76

Step ⑤   Retouch as needed

Figure 18.6   Example of work instructions.

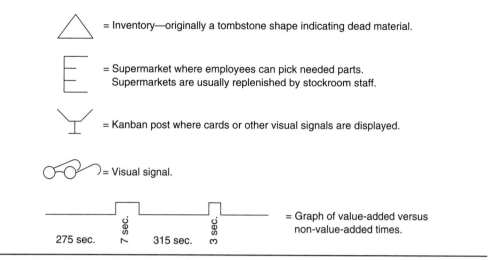

Figure 18.7   Example of the symbology used to develop a value stream map.

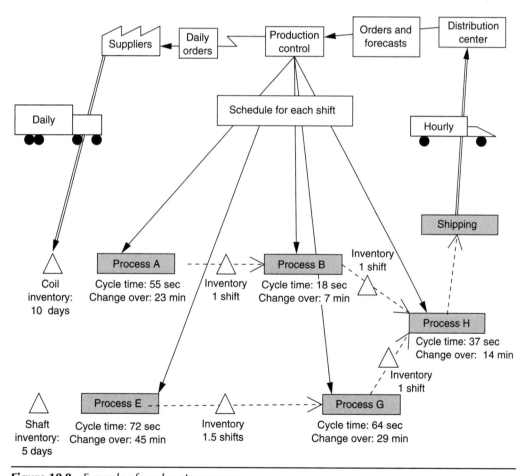

Figure 18.8   Example of a value stream map.

Part V.A.3

information about timing and inventory is provided near each shaded process box.

4. Determine how the flow is driven. Strive to move toward value streams in which the production decisions are based on the pull of customer demand. In a process where pull-based flow has reached perfection, a customer order for an item will trigger the production of all the component parts for that item. These components will arrive, be assembled, and delivered in a time interval that will satisfy the customer. In most organizations, this ideal has not been reached and the customer order will be filled from finished goods inventory. The order will, however, trigger activities back through the value chain that produce a replacement part in finished goods inventory before it is needed by the next customer to place an order.

5. Extend the value stream map upstream into suppliers' plants. New challenges occur regarding compatibility of communication systems. The flow of information, material, knowledge, and money are all potential targets for lean improvements.

Spaghetti diagrams refer to product flow paths in an organization. One example is shown in Figure 18.9. These diagrams are helpful in reducing waste and stream-lining process product flow.

A *circle diagram*, also known as a hand-off map, is used to show linkages between various items. Mark Blazey, in his book *Insights to Performance Excellence 2008*, uses these diagrams to show how the Baldrige Award criteria relate.

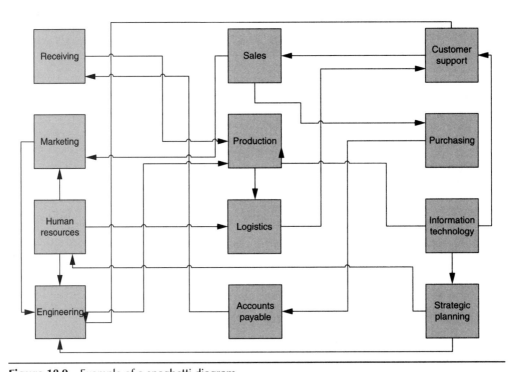

Figure 18.9   Example of a spaghetti diagram.

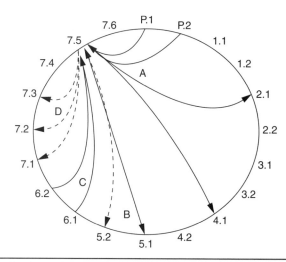

Figure 18.10   Example of a circle diagram. Used by permission from Mark L. Blazey, *Insights to Performance Excellence 2008: An Inside Look at the 2008 Baldrige Award Criteria* (Milwaukee, WI: ASQ Quality Press, 2008), 222.

Figure 18.10 shows linkages for the criterion entitled "Process Effectiveness Outcomes" (Item 7.5). Although Figure 18.10 depicts item numbers, other relevant descriptors, such as departments, processes, and individuals, may be used. The direction of the arrows indicates the flow of products, services, information, and the like. Circle diagrams are highly useful in that they readily depict predecessor and successor relationships as well as potential bottlenecks. Too many inputs or outputs from any given descriptor around the circumference of the circle may indicate a limiting function. Examination of these specific descriptors might prove highly insightful.

Part V.A.3

Chapter 19
Data Collection

TYPES OF DATA

> Define, classify, and evaluate qualitative and quantitative data, continuous (variables) and discrete (attributes) data, and convert attributes data to variables measures when appropriate. (Evaluate)
>
> **Body of Knowledge V.B.1**

Quantitative data are grouped into two types:

- Continuous (also called variable data)
- Discrete (also called attribute data)

Continuous data result from measurement on a continuous scale such as length, weight, or temperature. These scales are called continuous because between any two values are an infinite number of other values. For example, between 1.537 inches and 1.538 inches, there are 1.5372, 1.5373, 1.53724, and so forth.

Discrete data result from counting the occurrence of events. Examples might include counting the number of paint runs per batch of painted parts, counting the number of valves that leaked, or counting the number of bubbles in a square foot of floated glass.

Effort should always be made to move from discrete to continuous measurements. There are several reasons for doing this:

- Control charts based on continuous data are more sensitive to process changes than those based on discrete data.

- When designed experiments are used for process improvement, changes in continuous data may be observed even though the discrete measurement hasn't changed.

- Continuous or variable data contain more information than discrete or attribute data. Note that variable data can be transformed into attribute data, but the reverse is not true. For example, a part with a measured value of 7 inches exceeds the tolerance of 5 inches. Thus, the part would be considered a defective. However, because we measured the part, we know that it is not only defective, but by how much.

In these examples, perhaps the size of the paint runs or the amount of leakage or the size of the bubbles could be measured. Then, when process improvements are attempted, it may be possible to determine techniques that reduce bubble size, for instance, even though the number of bubbles may not change.

MEASUREMENT SCALES

> Define and apply nominal, ordinal, interval, and ratio measurement scales. (Apply)
>
> **Body of Knowledge V.B.2**

To avoid analysis errors, it is important to recognize the type of measurement scale used to collect data. There are four types of measurement scales:

- Nominal

- Ordinal

- Interval

- Ratio

Nominal scales classify data into categories with no order implied—for example, a list of equipment such as presses, drills, and lathes.

Ordinal scales refer to positions in a series, where order is important but precise differences between values aren't defined. Examples would be first, second, and third places in a marathon or letter grades in a course.

Interval scales have meaningful differences but no absolute zero, so ratios aren't useful. An example is temperature measured in °F, because 20°F isn't twice as warm as 10°F.

Ratio scales have meaningful differences, and an absolute zero exists. One example of a ratio scale is length in inches, because zero length is defined as having no length and 20 inches is twice as long as 10 inches. Other examples include weight and age.

SAMPLING METHODS

> Define and apply the concepts related to
> sampling (e.g., representative selection,
> homogeneity, bias, etc.). Select and use
> appropriate sampling methods (e.g., random
> sampling, stratified sampling, systematic
> sampling, etc.) that ensure the integrity of data.
> (Evaluate)
>
> **Body of Knowledge V.B.3**

The best data collection and analysis techniques can be defeated if the data have errors. Common causes of errors include:

- Units of measure not defined (for example, yards or meters?)
- Similarity of handwritten characters (for example, 2 or Z?)
- Inadequate measurement system
- Improper rounding or data truncation
- Batching input versus real-time input
- Inadequate use of validation techniques
- Multiple points of data entry
- Ambiguous terminology (for example, calendar or fiscal year?)

Example 19.1

The NASA team working with the Mars rovers uses the term "sol" to designate a Martian day, which is longer than an earth day. ("Yestersol" refers to the previous Martian day, apparently.)

To minimize error:

- Have a carefully constructed data collection plan
- Maintain a calibration schedule for data collection equipment
- Conduct repeatability and reproducibility (R&R) studies on data collection equipment
- Record appropriate auxiliary information regarding units, time of collection, conditions, equipment used, name of data recorder, and other characteristics that might be appropriate or useful in the future
- Use appropriate statistical tests to address outliers

- If data are transmitted or stored digitally, use a redundant error correction system

- Provide clear and complete instruction and training

If data are obtained through sampling, the sampling procedure must be properly designed to ensure statistical validity. Some of the available techniques are listed in the following paragraphs.

Simple *random sampling* is a procedure by which each item has an equal probability of being selected as part of the sample. One way to do this is to assign each item a number and arrange a set of numbered tags so that each tag number corresponds to exactly one item. The tags are thoroughly mixed in a container and one is chosen. The number on the tag identifies the item selected as part of the sample. If the population size is quite large, making up the tags can be time consuming. In this situation, random numbers generated by calculators or computer software can be used to select the elements of the sample.

If the population of parts to be sampled is naturally divided into groups, it might be desirable to use *stratified sampling*. For example, suppose 300 parts came from Cleveland, 600 came from Chicago, and 100 came from Green Mountain. A stratified sample of size 50 could be formed by randomly selecting 15 items from the Cleveland batch, 30 from the Chicago batch, and 5 from the Green Mountain batch. In other words, each group gets a proportional part of the stratified sample.

Sample homogeneity refers to the need to select a sample so that it represents just one population. This is desirable regardless of the type of sampling. In the case of the stratified sampling procedure, the population consists of the original 1000 parts, and stratification is used to help ensure that the sample represents the various strata. When selecting the data collection scheme for time-related data, the entire sample should be collected at the same time in the process so that it comes from the population being produced at, say, 9:00 a.m. and not some from 9:15 a.m., which may be a different population. In fact, the purpose of a control chart is to use sampling to determine whether the population at one time is different from the other populations sampled.

COLLECTING DATA

> Develop data collection plans, including consideration of how the data will be collected (e.g., check sheets, data coding techniques, automated data collection, etc.) and how it will be used. (Apply)
>
> **Body of Knowledge V.B.4**

Part V.B.4

Most organizations collect large volumes of data, sometimes far more than they are able to analyze effectively. Check sheets are often used to record the presence or absence of particular features. Some data are collected manually by having people record counts or readings on check sheets or forms. In some cases it is helpful to code data to simplify the recording process. For example, suppose several measurements of shaft diameters are to be recorded. The tolerance limits for shaft diameters is set at 1.5353 to 1.5358. The person doing the recording might read three values as 1.5355, 1.5354, and 1.5356 but record the last two digits only as 55, 54, and 56 for simplicity. Sometimes it is useful to code data by using an algebraic transformation. Suppose a set of data has mean μ and standard deviation σ. A new set of data may be formed by using the formula $y = ax + b$. That is, each element of the new set is formed by multiplying an element of the original set by a and then adding b. The mean μ_y and standard deviation σ_y of the new set are given by

$$\mu_y = a\mu + b$$

$$\sigma_y = |a|\sigma$$

Increasingly, data are automatically transmitted from a measuring device to a database. A contoured part may be clamped into a fixture and have dozens of readings made and recorded instantaneously. Potential advantages of this automatic gauging approach include improved precision as well as reduction of labor, cycle time, error rates, and costs. When considering automated inspection, attention must be paid to the possibility of high initial costs, including the possibility of part redesign to adapt it to the constraints of the measurement system. If the measured values are fed directly into the database, care must be taken to make certain that the communication link is reliable and free of noise. It is also useful to have a graphic output so operators can quickly spot erroneous data visually.

Chapter 20

Measurement Systems

MEASUREMENT METHODS

Define and describe measurement methods for both continuous and discrete data. (Understand)

Body of Knowledge V.C.1

Chapter 19 stated that there are two types of data. Similarly, quality characteristics are of two types: attributes and variables. Discrete or attribute data result from characteristics that are counted; for example, a pane of glass might have four bubbles, or a batch of resistors might include seven that don't conduct current. Tests such as these are called attribute screens because they may be used to screen out items that don't meet requirements, such as glass panes with more than six bubbles or resistors that don't conduct current.

Continuous or variables data result from characteristics that are measured rather than merely counted, such as length, diameter, and hardness. Many tools and methods have been devised for obtaining measurements. A few are listed in the following paragraphs.

Gage blocks are made of very hard materials and provide basic references for setting and calibrating gages. In use, a set of blocks is assembled with the total thickness equal to the desired dimension.

A typical 83-block set has the following blocks (dimensions in inches):

0.1001, 0.1002, . . . , 0.1009	(9 blocks)
0.1010, 0.1020, . . . , 0.1490	(49 blocks)
0.0500, 0.1000, 0.1500, . . . , 0.9500	(19 blocks)
1.0000, 2.0000, 3.0000, 4.0000	(4 blocks)
0.0500 wear blocks	(2 blocks)

With this set, a stack of blocks can be assembled to equal any dimension from 0.2000 to 12.000 to the nearest 0.0001. For example, 8.1234 can be produced by using the following blocks:

$$0.1004 + 0.1230 + 0.9000 + 3.0000 + 4.0000 = 8.1234$$

A set of gage blocks can be used to set precision measuring tools such as height gages.

Measurement tools can be grouped into five categories:

- Mechanical: Mechanical systems are used to amplify small movements

- Pneumatic: Air pressure or velocity is used to detect dimensional variation

- Electronic: Changes in characteristics such as resistance, capacitance, or inductance are converted to dimensional changes

- Light technologies: Wave interference is used to provide standards

- Electron systems: An electron beam microscope is used to make measurements

The following are descriptions of various measurement tools in common use:

- Caliper—whether equipped with a vernier scale, a dial, or a digital readout, it is essentially a very accurate steel ruler.

- Micrometer—uses precision screws to move a spindle relative to a fixed anvil to determine the distance between them.

- Transfer device (including spring calipers, spring dividers, and telescoping gages)—used to compare dimensions. They may also be used with a set of precision gage blocks to obtain measurements.

- Height gage—used with a flat surface plate, measures lengths and various geometric characteristics such as flatness.

- Sine bar—used to measure angles.

- Precision protractor—used to measure angles.

- Dividing head—used for measuring angle spacing on a circle.

- Optical comparator—projects an enlarged shadow of a part onto a screen along with a transparency showing tolerance limits. The user can visually determine if the part contours meet specifications.

- Ring gage—used to determine whether shaft diameters meet tolerance. They typically come in go/no-go pairs. A shaft that is in tolerance will fit into the go gage but not into the no-go gage. The standard ring gage may not detect out-of-round or taper defects on the shaft.

- Thread snap gage—used to determine whether external threads meet maximum and minimum material conditions.

- Functional gage—used to determine whether a part will fit with a mating part.

- Air gage—uses the velocity of airflow between the gage and the part to determine the dimension.

- Coordinate measuring machine (CMM)—uses electronic probes to provide very accurate measurements. A CMM is usually interfaced with a computer to collect, analyze, and store measurement data. Some models can be programmed to proceed through a series of steps measuring lengths, location, diameters, and so on.

Many fields have special tools to meet their unique measurement requirements. For instance, hardness of metals is often determined by using either the Brinnell or the Rockwell method. Tensile strength and other forces are often measured by using dynamometers. Titration is used to determine the amount of a given chemical constituent by measuring the volume of a reagent needed to cause a certain reaction.

When selecting a gage for use in an inspection process, the rule of ten is often used: The smallest increment of measurement for the device should be less than or equal to $\frac{1}{10}$ of the tolerance.

MEASUREMENT SYSTEMS ANALYSIS

> Use various analytical methods (e.g., repeatability and reproducibility (R&R), correlation, bias, linearity, precision to tolerance, percent agreement, etc.) to analyze and interpret measurement system capability for variables and attributes measurement systems. (Evaluate)
>
> **Body of Knowledge V.C.2**

In order to analyze a measurement system, it is important to understand several key concepts and how they relate:

- *Accuracy* is the closeness of agreement between a measurement result and the true or accepted reference value. The components of accuracy include:

  - *Bias*—This is a systematic difference between the mean of the test result or measurement result and a true value. For example, if one measures the length of 10 pieces of rope that range from 1 foot to 10 feet and always concludes that the length of each piece is 2 inches shorter than the true length, then the individual exhibits a bias of 2 inches.

  - *Linearity*—This is the difference in bias through the range of measurements. A measurement system that has good linearity will have a constant bias no matter the magnitude of measurement. In the previous example, the range of measurement was from 1 foot to 10 feet with a constant linear bias of 2 inches.

  - *Stability (of a measurement system)*—This represents the change in bias of a measurement system over time and usage when that system is used to measure a master part or standard. Thus, a stable measurement system is one in which the variation is in statistical control, which is typically demonstrated through the use of control charts.

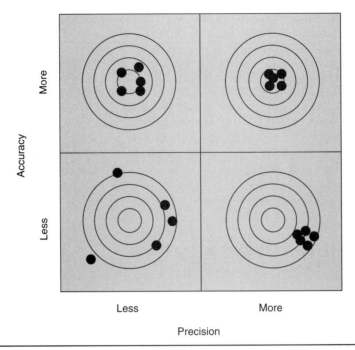

Figure 20.1   Accuracy versus precision.

- *Precision* is the closeness of agreement between randomly selected individual measurements or test results. It is this aspect of measurement that addresses repeatability or consistency when an identical item is measured several times. Figure 20.1 illustrates the relationship between accuracy and precision.

The components of precision include:

- *Repeatability*—This is the precision under conditions where independent measurement results are obtained with the same method on identical measurement items by the same appraiser (that is, operator) using the same equipment within a short period of time. Although misleading, repeatability is often referred to as equipment variation (EV). It is also referred to as within-system variation when the conditions of measurement are fixed and defined (that is, equipment, appraiser, method, and environment).

- *Reproducibility*—This is the precision under conditions where independent measurement results are obtained with the same method on identical measurement items with different operators using different equipment. Although misleading, reproducibility is often referred to as appraiser variation (AV). The term "appraiser variation" is used because it is common practice to have different operators with identical measuring systems. Reproducibility, however, can refer to any changes in the measurement system. For example, assume the same appraiser uses the same material, equipment, and environment but uses two different measurement methods. The reproducibility calculation will show the variation due to a change in the method. It is also known as the average variation between systems, or between-conditions variation of measurement.

- *Discrimination*—This represents the measurement system's capability to detect and indicate small changes in the characteristic measured. Discrimination is also known as resolution. For example, a tape measure with 1-inch gradations would be unable to distinguish between object lengths that fall in between the inch marks. Hence, we would say that the measurement system cannot properly discriminate among the objects. If an object to be measured was 2.5 inches, the measurement system (that is, tape measure) would produce a value of 2 or 3 inches depending on how the individual decides to round. Therefore, to measure an object that is 2.5 inches, a tape measure with finer gradations would be required.

- *Precision-to-tolerance ratio (PTR)*—This is a measure of the capability of the measurement system. It can be calculated by

$$PTR = \frac{5.15\hat{\sigma}_{ms}}{USL - LSL}$$

where $\hat{\sigma}_{ms}$ is the estimated standard deviation of the total measurement system variability. In general, reducing the PTR will yield an improved measurement system.

- *Gage repeatability and reproducibility (GR&R) study*—This is one type of measurement system analysis done to evaluate the performance of a test method or measurement system. Such a study quantifies the capabilities and limitations of a measurement instrument, often estimating its repeatability and reproducibility. It typically involves multiple appraisers measuring a series of items multiple times.

- *Percent agreement*—This refers to the percent of time in an attribute GR&R study that appraisers agree with (1) themselves (that is, repeatability), (2) other appraisers (that is, reproducibility), or (3) a known standard (that is, bias) when classifying or rating items using nominal or ordinal scales, respectively.

Every measurement system consists of the following key components:

- Measurement instrument

- Appraiser(s) (also known as operators)

- Methods or procedures for conducting the measurement

- Environment

Measurement system analysis can be categorized into two types:

- Variables

- Attributes

Variables

Three common methods fall into this category:

- AIAG method
- ANOVA method
- Control chart method

Each will be addressed separately in the following sections.

AIAG Method

Example 20.1

Figure 20.2 is an example of how to conduct a GR&R study. It uses the data collection sheet published by the Automotive Industry Action Group (AIAG) in *Measurement System Analysis* (1995). These steps provide a widely accepted procedure for analyzing measurement systems:

1. Label 10 parts with tags numbered 1–10 in such a way that the numbers on the tags aren't visible to the appraiser. Randomly place the parts on a work surface.

2. The first appraiser (we'll call him Al) chooses a part, measures the designated dimension, announces the reading, and hands it to the recorder. The recorder looks at the number on the tag and records the reading announced by Al in the appropriate column of row 1 (row labels are shown along the left margin).

3. Al measures the remaining nine parts and announces the reading for each. The recorder enters the values in the columns of row 1 according to tag number.

4. The 10 parts are again randomly placed on the work surface with the tag numbers not visible. Bill, the second appraiser, measures each one. The recorder enters Bill's readings in row 6 of the form, which is the row for trial #1 for appraiser B.

5. Cher, the third appraiser, repeats the procedure, and the recorder enters these values in row 11.

6. Now it's Al's turn to measure the 10 parts for trial #2. These readings are entered in row 2. Bill and Cher follow with their second set of readings, which are recorded in rows 7 and 12, respectively. (The appraiser order can be randomized if desired rather than A, then B, and then C as indicated here.)

7. Each appraiser completes the third trial of measurements, and these are recorded in rows 3, 8, and 13. This completes the data entry portion of the study. Figure 20.3 shows an example of the collected data.

Example 20.1 *(continued)*

		\multicolumn{10}{c}{Part}		
Row	Appraiser/ Trial	1	2	3	4	5	6	7	8	9	10	Average/ Range	Appraiser/ Trial

Gage Repeatability and Reproducibility Data Collection Sheet

Row	Appraiser/Trial	1	2	3	4	5	6	7	8	9	10	Average/Range	Appraiser/Trial
1	A1												A1
2	A2												A2
3	A3												A3
4	**Average A**												$\bar{X}_A$
5	**Range A**												$\bar{R}_A$
6	B1												B1
7	B2												B2
8	B3												B3
9	**Average B**												$\bar{X}_B$
10	**Range B**												$\bar{R}_B$
11	C1												C1
12	C2												C2
13	C3												C3
14	**Average C**												$\bar{X}_C$
15	**Range C**												$\bar{R}_C$
16	**Part Average**												$\bar{\bar{X}}_{Part}$
17	Maximum part average − Minimum part average =												R_{Part}
18	$(\bar{R}_A + \bar{R}_B + \bar{R}_C)$ / Number of appraisers =												$\bar{\bar{R}}$
19	$\bar{X}_{DIFF} = Max\,(\bar{X}_A, \bar{X}_B, \bar{X}_C) - Min\,(\bar{X}_A, \bar{X}_B, \bar{X}_C) =$												$\bar{X}_{DIFF}$
20	* $UCL_R = D_4\bar{\bar{R}} = (2.574)\bar{\bar{R}} =$												
21	* $LCL_R = D_3\bar{\bar{R}} = (0)\bar{\bar{R}} = 0$												
22	* $D_3 = 0;\ D_4 = 2.574$ for 3 trials												

Figure 20.2   Blank GR&R data collection sheet. Used with permission of AIAG. Adapted from AIAG.

8. Calculate the average and the range for each appraiser for each part tag number. The values go in rows 4 and 5, respectively, for Al; 9 and 10, respectively, for Bill; and 14 and 15, respectively, for Cher.

9. Calculate the values for row 16 by averaging the values in rows 4, 9, and 14.

10. Calculate the values for the "Average/Range" column for rows 4, 5, 9, 10, 14, and 15 by averaging the 10 values in their respective rows.

Example 20.1 *(continued)*

11. Calculate the value for the "Average/Range" column of row 16 by averaging the 10 values in that row.

12. Calculate the value for the "Average/Range" column of row 17 by using the formula given in that row.

13. Calculate the value for the "Average/Range" column of row 18 by using the formula given in that row.

14. Calculate the value for the "Average/Range" column of row 19 by using the formula given in that row.

15. Calculate the UCL_R by using the formula shown in line 20 along with the proper control chart constant values from row 22.

16. Compare each of the 10 R-values in row 5 to the UCL_R value calculated in row 20. Any R-value that exceeds the UCL_R should be circled. Repeat this for the R-values in rows 10 and 15. The circled R-values are significantly different from the others, and the cause of this difference should be identified and corrected. Once this has been done, the appropriate parts can be remeasured using the same appraiser, equipment, and so on as for the original measurements. Recompute all appropriate values on the data collection sheet as necessary.

Recall that repeatability is the variation in measurements that occurs when the same measuring system—including equipment, material, and appraiser—is used. Repeatability, then, is reflected in the R-values as recorded in rows 5, 10, and 15 and summarized in row 17. Repeatability is often referred to as equipment variation, but the individual R averages may indicate differences among appraisers. In the example in Figure 20.3, R_A is smaller than R_B or R_C. This indicates that Al has done a better job of getting the same answer upon repeated measurements of the same part than either Bill or Cher. Perhaps Al has a better technique, more skill, or sharper eyesight than the others. Investigation of this issue may provide an opportunity for variation reduction.

Reproducibility is the variation that occurs between the overall average measurements for the three appraisers. It is reflected by the X-values in rows 4, 9, and 14 and summarized in the value of $\bar{X}_{DIFF}$ in row 19. For example, had $\bar{X}_A$ and $\bar{X}_B$ been closer in value and $\bar{X}_C$ significantly different, then Cher's measurements would exhibit a bias. Again, further investigation would be necessary.

The next step in the study is to complete the GR&R report shown in Figure 20.4. A completed report based on the data from Figure 20.3 is shown in Figure 20.5. Each of the quantities in the "Measurement Unit Analysis" column will now be described:

- *Equipment variation (EV)* is an estimate of the standard deviation of the variation due to repeatability and is sometimes denoted σ_E or σ_{rpt}

- *Appraiser variation (AV)* is an estimate of the standard deviation of the variation due to reproducibility and is sometimes denoted σ_A or σ_{rpd}

Gage Repeatability and Reproducibility Data Collection Sheet

Row	Appraiser/ Trial		Part										Average/ Range	Appraiser/ Trial
		1	2	3	4	5	6	7	8	9	10		
1	A1	0.29	−0.56	1.34	0.47	−0.80	0.02	0.59	−0.31	2.26	−1.36	0.19	A1
2	A2	0.41	−0.68	1.17	0.50	−0.92	−0.11	0.75	−0.20	1.99	−1.25	0.17	A2
3	A3	0.64	−0.58	1.27	0.64	−0.84	−0.21	0.66	−0.17	2.01	−1.31	0.21	A3
4	Average A	0.45	−0.61	1.26	0.54	−0.85	−0.10	0.67	−0.23	2.09	−1.31	0.19	$\bar{X}_A$
5	Range A	0.35	0.12	0.17	0.17	0.12	0.23	0.16	0.14	0.27	0.11	0.18	$\bar{R}_A$
6	B1	0.08	−0.47	1.19	0.01	−0.56	−0.20	0.47	−0.63	1.80	−1.68	0.00	B1
7	B2	0.25	−1.22	0.94	1.03	−1.20	0.22	0.55	0.08	2.12	−1.62	0.12	B2
8	B3	0.07	−0.68	1.34	0.20	−1.28	0.06	0.83	−0.34	2.19	−1.50	0.09	B3
9	Average B	0.13	−0.79	1.16	0.41	−1.01	0.03	0.62	−0.30	2.04	−1.60	0.07	$\bar{X}_B$
10	Range B	0.18	0.75	0.40	1.02	0.72	0.42	0.36	0.71	0.39	0.18	0.51	$\bar{R}_B$
11	C1	0.04	−1.38	0.88	0.14	−1.46	−0.29	0.02	−0.46	1.77	−1.49	−0.22	C1
12	C2	−0.11	−1.13	1.09	0.20	−1.07	−0.67	0.01	−0.56	1.45	−1.77	−0.26	C2
13	C3	−0.15	−0.96	0.67	0.11	−1.45	−0.49	0.21	−0.49	1.87	−2.16	−0.28	C3

Continued

Figure 20.3 GR&R data collection sheet with data entered and calculations completed. Used with permission of AIAG. Adapted from AIAG.

Gage Repeatability and Reproducibility Data Collection Sheet

Row	Appraiser/Trial					Part						Average/Range	Appraiser/Trial
		1	2	3	4	5	6	7	8	9	10		
14	Average C	-0.07	-1.16	0.88	0.15	-1.33	-0.48	0.08	-0.50	1.70	-1.81	-0.25	$\bar{X}_C$
15	Range C	0.19	0.42	0.42	0.09	0.39	0.38	0.20	0.10	0.42	0.67	0.33	$\bar{R}_C$
16	Part Average	0.17	-0.85	1.10	0.37	-1.06	-0.19	0.45	-0.34	1.94	-1.57	0.00	$\bar{\bar{X}}_{Part}$
17	Maximum part average – Minimum part average =											3.51	R_{Part}
18	$(\bar{R}_A + \bar{R}_B + \bar{R}_C)$ / Number of appraisers = (0.18 + 0.51 + 0.33) / 3 =											0.3417	$\bar{\bar{R}}$
19	$\bar{X}_{DIFF} = Max(\bar{X}_A, \bar{X}_B, \bar{X}_C) - Min(\bar{X}_A, \bar{X}_B, \bar{X}_C) = 0.19 - (-0.25) =$											0.4447	$\bar{X}_{DIFF}$
20	* $UCL_R = D_4\bar{\bar{R}} = (2.574)(0.3417) = 0.8795$												
21	* $LCL_R = D_3\bar{\bar{R}} = (0)(0.3417) = 0$												
22	* $D_3 = 0; D_4 = 2.574$ for 3 trials												

Figure 20.3 GR&R data collection sheet with data entered and calculations completed. Used with permission of AIAG. Adapted from AIAG. *Continued*

Gage Repeatability and Reproducibility Report				
Part No. and Name:	Gage Name:		Date:	
Characteristics:	Gage No.:		Performed by:	
Specifications:	Gage Type:			

From data sheet:	$\bar{\bar{R}} =$		$\bar{X}_{DIFF}$		R_P

Measurement Unit Analysis			Percent Total Variation	
Repeatability – Equipment Variation (EV) $EV = \bar{\bar{R}} \times K_1$ $= \_\_\_\_ \times \_\_\_\_$ $= \_\_\_\_$	Trials	K_1	$\%EV = 100(EV/TV)$ $= 100(\_\_\_/\_\_\_)$ $= \_\_\_\%$	
	2	0.8862		
	3	0.5908		
Reproducibility – Appraiser Variation (AV) $AV = \sqrt{(\bar{X}_{DIFF} \times K_2)^2 - (EV^2/(nr))}$ $= \sqrt{(\_\_\times\_\_)^2 - (\_\_^2/(\_\_\times\_\_))}$ $= \_\_\_\_$	Appraisers	K_2	$\%AV = 100(AV/TV)$ $= 100(\_\_\_/\_\_\_)$ $= \_\_\_\%$ n = number of parts r = number of trials	
	2	0.7071		
	3	0.5231		
Gage Repeatability & Reproducibility (GRR) $GRR = \sqrt{EV^2 + AV^2}$ $= \sqrt{\_\_^2 + \_\_^2}$ $= \_\_\_\_$	Parts	K_3	$\%GRR = 100(GRR/TV)$ $= 100(\_\_\_/\_\_\_)$ $= \_\_\_\%$	
	2	0.7071		
	3	0.5231		
Part Variation (PV) $PV = R_{Part} \times K_3$ $= \_\_\_\_ \times \_\_\_\_$ $= \_\_\_\_$	4	0.4467	$\%PV = 100(PV/TV)$ $= 100(\_\_\_/\_\_\_)$ $= \_\_\_\%$	
	5	0.4030		
	6	0.3742		
	7	0.3534		
Total Variation (TV) $TV = \sqrt{GRR^2 + PV^2}$ $= \sqrt{\_\_^2 + \_\_^2}$ $= \_\_\_\_$	8	0.3375	$ndc = 1.41(PV/GRR)$ $= 1.41(\_\_\_/\_\_\_)$ $= \_\_\_$ ndc = number of distinct categories	
	9	0.3249		
	10	0.3146		

Figure 20.4 Blank GR&R report. Used with permission of AIAG. Adapted from AIAG.

- *Gage Repeatability and Reproducibility (GRR)* is an estimate of the standard deviation of the variation due to measurement system and is sometimes denoted σ_M

- *Part-to-part variation (PV)* is an estimate of the standard deviation of the variation due to the part differences and is sometimes denoted σ_p

- *Total variation (TV)* is an estimate of the standard deviation of the total variation in the study and is sometimes denoted σ_T

Gage Repeatability and Reproducibility Report						
Part No. and Name:		Gage Name:			Date:	
Characteristics:		Gage No.:			Performed by:	
Specifications:		Gage Type:				

From data sheet:	$\bar{\bar{R}} =$	0.3417	$\bar{X}_{DIFF}$	0.4447	R_{Part}	3.51

Measurement Unit Analysis				**Percent Total Variation**
Repeatability – Equipment Variation (EV) $EV = \bar{\bar{R}} \times K_1$ $\quad = (0.3417)(0.5908)$ $\quad = 0.2019$	Trials	K_1		%$EV = 100(EV/TV)$ $\quad = 100(0.2019/1.1458)$ $\quad = 17.62\%$
	2	0.8862		
	3	0.5908		
Reproducibility – Appraiser Variation (AV) $AV = \sqrt{(\bar{X}_{DIFF} \times K_2)^2 - (EV^2/(nr))}$ $\quad = \sqrt{((0.4447)(0.5231))^2 - ((0.2019)^2/(10)(3))}$ $\quad = 0.2296$	Appraisers	K_2		%$AV = 100(AV/TV)$ $\quad = 100(0.2296/1.1458)$ $\quad = 20.04\%$ n = number of parts r = number of trials
	2	0.7071		
	3	0.5231		
Gage Repeatability & Reproducibility (GRR) $GRR = \sqrt{EV^2 + AV^2}$ $\quad = \sqrt{(0.2019)^2 + (0.2296)^2}$ $\quad = 0.3058$	Parts	K_3		%$GRR = 100(GRR/TV)$ $\quad = 100(0.3058/1.1458)$ $\quad = 26.69\%$
	2	0.7071		
	3	0.5231		
Part Variation (PV) $PV = R_{Part} \times K_3$ $\quad = (3.51)(0.3146)$ $\quad = 1.1042$	4	0.4467		%$PV = 100(PV/TV)$ $\quad = 100(1.1042/1.1458)$ $\quad = 96.37\%$
	5	0.4030		
	6	0.3742		
	7	0.3534		
Total Variation (TV) $TV = \sqrt{GRR^2 + PV^2}$ $\quad = \sqrt{(0.3058)^2 + (1.1042)^2}$ $\quad = 1.1458$	8	0.3375		$ndc = 1.41(PV/GRR)$ $\quad = 1.41(1.1042/0.3058)$ $\quad = 5.09 \Rightarrow 5$ ndc = number of distinct categories
	9	0.3249		
	10	0.3146		

Figure 20.5 GR&R report with calculations. Used with permission of AIAG. Adapted from AIAG.

The "Percent Total Variation" column in Figure 20.4 shows for each type of variation the percent of total variation it consumes. Sometimes the right-hand column is based on the tolerance for the dimension. In this case, the value of TV is replaced by the tolerance.

In general, if the $\%GRR$ is:

- Less than 10%, the measurement system is considered acceptable

- Between 10% and 30%, inclusive, the measurement system is considered marginal

- Greater than 30%, the measurement system is considered inadequate

These criteria should be considered guidelines and dependent upon the situation at hand.

ANOVA Method

The data depicted in Figure 20.3 can also be analyzed using the analysis of variance (ANOVA) methods (addressed in Chapter 25).

Example 20.2

Figure 20.6 represents the results of an ANOVA using Minitab. The top source table illustrates that the interaction term (that is, parts by operators) is not significant. Thus, the term is removed, resulting in the second source table.

The third source table provides the variances for each component. Notice that the GR&R variation is relatively small with respect to the part-to-part variance. This is what we look for in a measurement systems analysis.

The last source table in Figure 20.6 depicts how much each component contributes to the total variation. The "SD" column provides the standard deviation for each component. Compare this column with the "Measurement Unit Analysis" column in Figure 20.5. The numbers are similar though not exact. This is due to the difference in the methods used. The "%Study Var" column shows the percentage contribution of each component. Compare these numbers with the "Percent Total Variation" column in Figure 20.5. Again, the numbers are similar but not exact.

Figure 20.7 is obtained from the "%Study Var" column from the last source table in Figure 20.6 and is frequently used to depict what is called the "components of variation."

Example 20.2 *(continued)*

```
Gage R&R Study - ANOVA Method

Two-Way ANOVA Table With Interaction

Source             DF        SS        MS         F        P
Parts               9    88.3619   9.81799   492.291    0.000
Operators           2     3.1673   1.58363    79.406    0.000
Parts * Operators  18     0.3590   0.01994     0.434    0.974
Repeatability      60     2.7589   0.04598
Total              89    94.6471


Alpha to remove interaction term = 0.25


Two-Way ANOVA Table Without Interaction

Source             DF        SS        MS         F        P
Parts               9    88.3619   9.81799   245.614    0.000
Operators           2     3.1673   1.58363    39.617    0.000
Repeatability      78     3.1179   0.03997
Total              89    94.6471


Gage R&R

Source              VarComp
Total Gage R&R        0.09
  Repeatability       0.04
  Reproducibility     0.05
    Operators         0.05
Part-To-Part          1.09
Total Variation       1.18


                                   Study Var   %Study Var
Source              StdDev (SD)    (6 * SD)      (%SV)
Total Gage R&R        0.30237      1.81423       27.86
  Repeatability       0.19993      1.19960       18.42
  Reproducibility     0.22684      1.36103       20.90
    Operators         0.22684      1.36103       20.90
Part-To-Part          1.04233      6.25396       96.04
Total Variation       1.08530      6.51180      100.00
```

Figure 20.6   Gage R&R Study—ANOVA method: source tables.

Example 20.2 *(continued)*

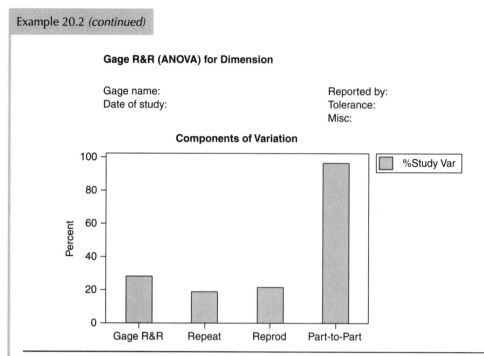

Gage R&R (ANOVA) for Dimension

Gage name: Reported by:
Date of study: Tolerance:
                                    Misc:

Figure 20.7   Gage R&R study—ANOVA method: components of variation.

With the ready availability of statistical analysis software, the ANOVA method represents a quick and easy way to analyze data obtained from a GR&R study.

Control Chart Method

Another method for analyzing GR&R data is through the use of $\bar{X} - R$ control charts.

Example 20.3

Figure 20.8 provides the source tables for this method. Notice the similarities and differences between these two tables and the last two tables in Figure 20.6 as well as the "Percent Total Variation" column from Figure 20.5. The answers are, indeed, similar.

Figure 20.9 is particularly interesting. Let's disregard the one out-of-control point on the range chart for operator B for the moment. Notice that each $\bar{X}$ chart is out of control. This is actually desirable since the R chart is based on repeatability error. If the $\bar{X}$ chart was in control, this would mean that part-to-part variation would be less than the repeatability variation. In other words, the part-to-part variation would be lost within the repeatability variation.

Part V.C.2

Example 20.3 *(continued)*

```
Gage R&R Study - XBar/R Method

Source                VarComp
Total Gage R&R          0.09
  Repeatability         0.04
  Reproducibility       0.05
Part-To-Part            1.22
Total Variation         1.31


                                   Study Var    %Study Var
Source                StdDev (SD)   (6 * SD)      (%SV)
Total Gage R&R          0.30589     1.83536       26.70
  Repeatability         0.20181     1.21087       17.61
  Reproducibility       0.22988     1.37925       20.06
Part-To-Part            1.10412     6.62474       96.37
Total Variation         1.14571     6.87428      100.00
```

Figure 20.8 Minitab session window output of the R&R study—$\bar{X}/R$ method: source tables for Example 20.3.

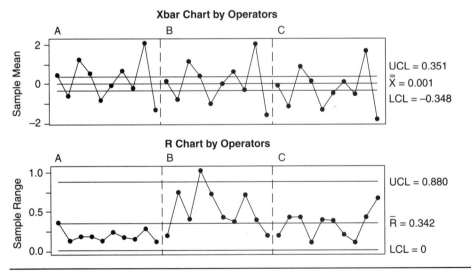

Figure 20.9 Graphical results of the GR&R study—$\bar{X}/R$ method: $\bar{X}$ and R control charts by operators (appraisers) for Example 20.3.

Part V.C.2

For a more detailed discussion on the use of the control chart method, see *The Six Sigma Handbook, Revised and Expanded* (2003), by Thomas Pyzdek.

Attributes

This section discusses two attribute methods using Minitab as the basis for the examples.

Attribute Agreement Analysis

Example 20.4

The data in Table 20.1 show the results of five new appraisers grading the written portion of a 12th-grade essay test. The appraisers graded on the 5-point scale: –2, –1, 0, 1, 2. In addition, each appraiser grade for a given test will be compared with a known standard grade for that test. Each appraiser graded each of the 15 tests. $\alpha = 0.05$ will be used.

Table 20.1 Attribute agreement analysis—data for Example 20.4.

Appraiser	Sample	Rating	Attribute	Appraiser	Sample	Rating	Attribute
Simpson	1	2	2	Duncan	8	0	0
Montgomery	1	2	2	Hayes	8	0	0
Holmes	1	2	2	Simpson	9	–1	–1
Duncan	1	1	2	Montgomery	9	–1	–1
Hayes	1	2	2	Holmes	9	–1	–1
Simpson	2	–1	–1	Duncan	9	–2	–1
Montgomery	2	–1	–1	Hayes	9	–1	–1
Holmes	2	–1	–1	Simpson	10	1	1
Duncan	2	–2	–1	Montgomery	10	1	1
Hayes	2	–1	–1	Holmes	10	1	1
Simpson	3	1	0	Duncan	10	0	1
Montgomery	3	0	0	Hayes	10	2	1
Holmes	3	0	0	Simpson	11	–2	–2
Duncan	3	0	0	Montgomery	11	–2	–2
Hayes	3	0	0	Holmes	11	–2	–2
Simpson	4	–2	–2	Duncan	11	–2	–2
Montgomery	4	–2	–2	Hayes	11	–1	–2
Holmes	4	–2	–2	Simpson	12	0	0

Continued

Example 20.4 *(continued)*

Table 20.1   Attribute agreement analysis—data for Example 20.4. *Continued*

Appraiser	Sample	Rating	Attribute	Appraiser	Sample	Rating	Attribute
Duncan	4	–2	–2	Montgomery	12	0	0
Hayes	4	–2	–2	Holmes	12	0	0
Simpson	5	0	0	Duncan	12	–1	0
Montgomery	5	0	0	Hayes	12	0	0
Holmes	5	0	0	Simpson	13	2	2
Duncan	5	–1	0	Montgomery	13	2	2
Hayes	5	0	0	Holmes	13	2	2
Simpson	6	1	1	Duncan	13	2	2
Montgomery	6	1	1	Hayes	13	2	2
Holmes	6	1	1	Simpson	14	–1	–1
Duncan	6	1	1	Montgomery	14	–1	–1
Hayes	6	1	1	Holmes	14	–1	–1
Simpson	7	2	2	Duncan	14	–1	–1
Montgomery	7	2	2	Hayes	14	–1	–1
Holmes	7	2	2	Simpson	15	1	1
Duncan	7	1	2	Montgomery	15	1	1
Hayes	7	2	2	Holmes	15	1	1
Simpson	8	0	0	Duncan	15	1	1
Montgomery	8	0	0	Hayes	15	1	1
Holmes	8	0	0				

Figure 20.10 illustrates the Minitab session window for this example. The output is typically divided into four parts:

- Each appraiser versus standard—The percent agreement table shows that both Holmes and Montgomery agreed with the standard on 15 out of 15 assessments, followed by Simpson with 14 out of 15, then Hayes with 13 out of 15, and Duncan trailing with 8 out of 15. With the exception of Duncan, all appraisers did well against the known standard. These results are confirmed with Fleiss' kappa statistics and Kendall's correlation coefficients. Notice Duncan's overall kappa was only 0.41176 while his correlation coefficient was the lowest at 0.87506. Figure 20.11 depicts in graphical form these same results using confidence intervals. It is obvious

Example 20.4 *(continued)*

```
Attribute Agreement Analysis for Rating

Each Appraiser vs Standard

Assessment Agreement

Appraiser     # Inspected   # Matched    Percent          95 % CI
Duncan                 15           8      53.33    (26.59,   78.73)
Hayes                  15          13      86.67    (59.54,   98.34)
Holmes                 15          15     100.00    (81.90,  100.00)
Montgomery             15          15     100.00    (81.90,  100.00)
Simpson                15          14      93.33    (68.05,   99.83)

# Matched: Appraiser's assessment across trials agrees with the known standard.


Fleiss' Kappa Statistics

Appraiser     Response      Kappa   SE Kappa          Z   P(vs > 0)
Duncan        -2          0.58333   0.258199    2.25924      0.0119
              -1          0.16667   0.258199    0.64550      0.2593
               0          0.44099   0.258199    1.70796      0.0438
               1          0.44099   0.258199    1.70796      0.0438
               2          0.42308   0.258199    1.63857      0.0507
              Overall     0.41176   0.130924    3.14508      0.0008
Hayes         -2          0.62963   0.258199    2.43855      0.0074
              -1          0.81366   0.258199    3.15131      0.0008
               0          1.00000   0.258199    3.87298      0.0001
               1          0.76000   0.258199    2.94347      0.0016
               2          0.81366   0.258199    3.15131      0.0008
              Overall     0.82955   0.134164    6.18307      0.0000
Holmes        -2          1.00000   0.258199    3.87298      0.0001
              -1          1.00000   0.258199    3.87298      0.0001
               0          1.00000   0.258199    3.87298      0.0001
               1          1.00000   0.258199    3.87298      0.0001
               2          1.00000   0.258199    3.87298      0.0001
              Overall     1.00000   0.131305    7.61584      0.0000
Montgomery    -2          1.00000   0.258199    3.87298      0.0001
              -1          1.00000   0.258199    3.87298      0.0001
               0          1.00000   0.258199    3.87298      0.0001
               1          1.00000   0.258199    3.87298      0.0001
               2          1.00000   0.258199    3.87298      0.0001
              Overall     1.00000   0.131305    7.61584      0.0000
Simpson       -2          1.00000   0.258199    3.87298      0.0001
              -1          1.00000   0.258199    3.87298      0.0001
               0          0.81366   0.258199    3.15131      0.0008
               1          0.81366   0.258199    3.15131      0.0008
               2          1.00000   0.258199    3.87298      0.0001
              Overall     0.91597   0.130924    6.99619      0.0000
```

Figure 20.10   Minitab session window output for Example 20.4.

Continued

Example 20.4 *(continued)*

```
Kendall's Correlation Coefficient

Appraiser      Coef    SE Coef         Z         P
Duncan      0.87506   0.192450   4.49744   0.0000
Hayes       0.94871   0.192450   4.88016   0.0000
Holmes      1.00000   0.192450   5.14667   0.0000
Montgomery  1.00000   0.192450   5.14667   0.0000
Simpson     0.96629   0.192450   4.97151   0.0000


Between Appraisers

Assessment Agreement

# Inspected   # Matched   Percent        95 % CI
         15           6     40.00   (16.34, 67.71)

# Matched: All appraisers' assessments agree with each other.


Fleiss' Kappa Statistics

Response      Kappa    SE Kappa         Z   P(vs > 0)
-2         0.680398   0.0816497    8.3331      0.0000
-1         0.602754   0.0816497    7.3822      0.0000
0          0.707602   0.0816497    8.6663      0.0000
1          0.642479   0.0816497    7.8687      0.0000
2          0.736534   0.0816497    9.0207      0.0000
Overall    0.672965   0.0412331   16.3210      0.0000


Kendall's Coefficient of Concordance

     Coef   Chi - Sq   DF        P
0.966317    67.6422    14   0.0000


All Appraisers vs Standard

Assessment Agreement

# Inspected   # Matched   Percent        95 % CI
         15           6     40.00   (16.34, 67.71)

# Matched: All appraisers' assessments agree with the known standard.
```

Figure 20.10 Minitab session window output for Example 20.4. *Continued*

Example 20.4 *(continued)*

```
Fleiss' Kappa Statistics

Response      Kappa    SE Kappa         Z    P(vs > 0)
-2         0.842593    0.115470    7.2971       0.0000
-1         0.796066    0.115470    6.8941       0.0000
0          0.850932    0.115470    7.3693       0.0000
1          0.802932    0.115470    6.9536       0.0000
2          0.847348    0.115470    7.3383       0.0000
Overall    0.831455    0.058911   14.1136       0.0000


Kendall's Correlation Coefficient

    Coef     SE Coef          Z         P
0.958012    0.0860663   11.1090    0.0000


* NOTE * Single trial within each appraiser. No percentage of assessment
         agreement within appraiser is plotted.

Attribute Agreement Analysis
```

Figure 20.10   Minitab session window output for Example 20.4. *Continued*

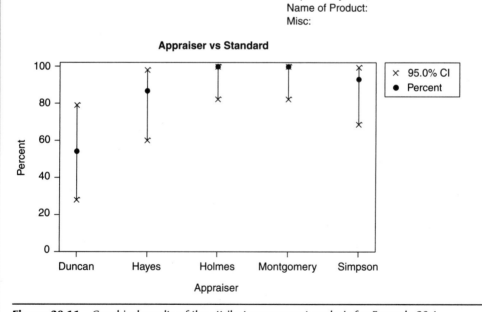

Figure 20.11   Graphical results of the attribute agreement analysis for Example 20.4.

Example 20.4 *(continued)*

that Duncan requires additional training on how to grade essay tests, and both Hayes and Simpson could stand a little brushing up as well.

- Between appraisers—Fleiss' kappa statistic assumes the level of disagreement among scores is the same (that is, the difference between a score of –2 and –1 is the same as the difference between a score of –2 and 2). Therefore, Fleiss' overall kappa statistic reflects value that indicates an unacceptable measurement system (that is, 0.672965). However, since Kendall's coefficient of concordance considers the difference between scores when the order of the scale is maintained, a high value is obtained (that is, 0.966317). This value is driven primarily by the fact that four of the five appraisers agreed on a minimum of 13 out of 15 trials.

- All appraisers versus standard—For reasons similar to "Between appraisers," Fleiss' overall kappa statistics is given as 0.831455, while Kendall's coefficient of concordance was 0.958012.

- Within appraiser—This table was not generated, because each appraiser assessed each test only once.

Attribute Gage Study—Analytic Method

An attribute gage study is used to determine the amount of bias and repeatability of a measurement system when the response is an attribute variable (that is, accept or reject). In such studies, reference values are known for each part and are selected at equal intervals across the entire range of the gage. Depending on the particular attribute gage study method chosen (for example, regression method or AIAG method), additional requirements may be placed on the characteristics of the parts, the number of parts per trial, and the number of parts used in the study. Therefore, for additional information when constructing an attribute gage study, the reader is referred to the tutorial or help files of the specific software. Also, the reader will find the second edition of the AIAG *Measurement Systems Analysis Reference Manual* useful in understanding the underlying theory.

Example 20.5

Table 20.2 shows the summarized data of 20 trials for each of eight parts. For each part, a reference value has been provided and the number of acceptances has been captured. The AIAG method will be used.

Figure 20.12 depicts the results of the attribute gage study analysis. The (adjusted) repeatability was determined to be 0.0458060, while the bias in the measurement system was 0.0097955. The t test indicates that the bias is significantly different from zero.

Example 20.5 *(continued)*

Table 20.2 Attribute gage study—data for Example 20.5.

Part number	Reference	Acceptances
1	–0.050	0
2	–0.045	1
3	–0.040	2
4	–0.035	5
5	–0.030	8
6	–0.025	12
7	–0.020	17
8	–0.015	20
9	–0.010	20
10	–0.005	20

Attribute Gage Study (Analytic Method) for Acceptances

Gage name: Reported by:
Date of study: Tolerance:
                                    Misc:

Bias: 0.0097955
Pre-adjusted Repeatability: 0.0494705
Repeatability: 0.0458060

Fitted Line: 3.10279 + 104.136 * Reference
R - sq for Fitted Line: 0.969376

AIAG Test of Bias = 0 vs not = 0
  T   DF   P-Value
6.70123 19   0.0000021

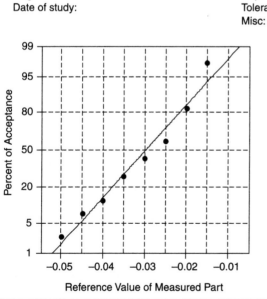
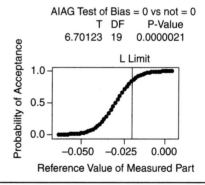

Figure 20.12 Graphical results of the attribute gage analysis for Example 20.5.

It should now be clear that whenever a process improvement project is undertaken, the measurement system should be one of the first things analyzed, for the following reasons:

- All data from the process are, in effect, filtered through the measurement system

- Measurement system variation often represents the most cost-effective way to reduce the total observed variation

MEASUREMENT SYSTEMS IN THE ENTERPRISE

Identify how measurement systems can be applied in marketing, sales, engineering, research and development (R&D), supply chain management, customer satisfaction, and other functional areas. (Understand)

Body of Knowledge V.C.3

Measurement systems are widely found throughout most functions of an enterprise. Let's consider the following examples:

- Human resources—Though they are not often thought of as measurement systems in the context of Six Sigma, performance appraisal/evaluation systems are widely used throughout most organizations. More often than not, these systems are wrought with bias and lack repeatability. Managers, or appraisers as we call them, frequently must use ill-defined criteria to assess an employee's performance, usually on an annual basis. Such measurement systems can have a profound and deep impact on an individual and his or her career. In some instances, a single (annual) data point is used to determine whether to terminate an employee. In some organizational structures, employees may have multiple managers/appraisers who provide input that might be highly polarized. This discussion of a performance appraisal/evaluation system quickly raises questions regarding assessor agreement within managers, between managers repeatability, each manager to standard, and all managers to standard. These terms should be familiar, as they form the basis for the attribute agreement analysis discussed previously.

- Marketing and sales—These functional organizations traditionally have used employee surveys to gauge levels of customer satisfaction, dissatisfaction, and loyalty as well as customer needs, wants, and other behaviors. Survey results are often fed to research and development functions to support and justify changes to product features and capabilities. Therefore, it is desirable that such surveys be highly reliable and well defined. More than once, unreliable surveys have wreaked havoc on organizations. Consider the American automobile industry in the early 1970s. These companies continued to build large, gas-guzzling automobiles, missing the changing trend in consumer taste for smaller, more fuel-efficient vehicles.

- Quality engineering—This function is often responsible for conducting various GR&R studies similar to those discussed previously. In addition, departments within this function usually are accountable for equipment calibration.

- Supply chain management—Probably the most common measurement system found in a supply chain management function is that of evaluating supplier performance and/or issuing supplier report cards. Supplier performance may be assessed inaccurately for a variety of reasons, such as inability to determine a defect, misclassification of defects, inaccurate data entry, or even poor definitions of what constitutes a defect or late delivery. Some organizations include subjective components of measurement for determining levels of service or the ease of doing business with the supplier. Measuring supplier performance is critical in many organizations, as such performance provides the foundation for determining rework and repair cost allocations and reimbursements and occasionally percent of profit sharing.

These are just a few examples of where measurement systems are routinely found in organizations. Their widespread use makes it imperative that they be adequate and sound to support their intended purpose. Without adequate measurement systems, organizational decision making may result in completely erroneous decisions that send an organization down a treacherous path. Alternatively, the basis for decision making deteriorates and decision makers must rely on gut feel or guesswork. Either way, the outcomes are undesirable.

METROLOGY

Define and describe elements of metrology, including calibration systems, traceability to reference standards, the control and integrity of standards and measurement devices, etc. (Understand)

Body of Knowledge V.C.4

The purpose of a gage traceability document is to show the relationship between a given measurement system and the standards maintained by the national government at the National Institute of Standards and Technology (NIST). The traceability document quantifies the uncertainty involved in the various measurement transfers, from NIST calibration down to a measurement made on a part. Measurement error is a source of variation. As such, it should be analyzed whenever a reduction in process variation is sought. It often happens that what was perceived as excess process variation was really excess variation in the measurement system. When reducing the total observed process variation, improving the measurement system is often the most cost-effective strategy.

The causes of measurement error can be placed in the usual cause-and-effect categories:

- Machine (equipment)
  - Lack of accuracy
  - Lack of precision
  - Gage instability over time
- Methods (procedures)
  - Wrong tool specified
  - Improper procedure specified
  - Failure to use specified tool or procedure
- Man or woman (appraiser)
  - Lack of training
  - Lack of physical ability
  - Lack of motivation
- Mother Nature (environment)
  - Temperature, humidity, atmospheric pressure
  - Lighting, noise conditions
  - Vibration
  - Electronic emission
- Materials (parts)
  - Instability over time
  - Lack of homogeneity
- Management
  - Inconsistent goals and objectives
  - Reward system inconsistent with stated goals and objectives
  - Atmosphere of mistrust and fear

Throughout this book we refer to the 7Ms. However, notice that this list contains only six "Ms." The missing "M" is measurement, which we have framed in terms of the root cause categories based on the remaining six "Ms."

Whenever measuring equipment is used, a calibration system should be in place to help ensure that the measurement system does its job. The main thrust of a calibration system consists of a schedule that requires each piece of measuring equipment to be calibrated on a regular basis. The time intervals between calibrations are based on the type of equipment and its uses. Calibration systems usually start with a relatively short interval for new equipment, with provisions for changing interval length depending on experience. If, for instance, an instrument has been in for several successive calibrations with no adjustment needed, the calibration interval may be extended. On the other hand, instruments frequently requiring adjustment may need shorter intervals. Some organizations set calibration quality goals of 95%, meaning that 95% of the instruments scheduled for calibration need no adjustment. Each instrument must have a label that plainly displays its due date. Some organizations install a procedure to notify users of pending calibration. In addition, a record system is required to document calibration activity. A system must also be in place for maintaining the calibration standards and equipment. This system should include a schedule for verifying that the standards are usable by checking them against recognized master standards.

Chapter 21
Basic Statistics

BASIC TERMS

> Define and distinguish between population parameters and sample statistics (e.g., proportion, mean, standard deviation, etc.) (Apply)
>
> **Body of Knowledge V.D.1**

In a statistical study, the word "population" refers to the entire set of items under discussion. For example, the population might be the set of parts shipped to customer B last Friday. It is typically not feasible to measure a characteristic on each item in a population; therefore, a statistical study will randomly select a sample from the population, measure each item in the sample, and analyze the resulting data. The analysis of the sample data produces *statistics*. Examples of sample statistics include sample mean, sample median, sample standard deviation, and so on. These sample statistics are used to estimate the corresponding population *parameters*.

It is traditional to denote sample statistics by using Latin letters, and population parameters by using Greek letters. An exception is made for the size that doesn't follow these criteria. Table 21.1 shows commonly used symbols.

The Greek letter μ is pronounced "mew." The Greek letter σ is a lowercase sigma. The capital sigma, Σ, is used to designate summation in formulas.

Table 21.1 Commonly used symbols.

	Population	Sample
Sample size	N	n
Mean	μ	$\bar{X}$
Standard deviation	σ	s

CENTRAL LIMIT THEOREM

> Describe and use this theorem and apply the sampling distribution of the mean to inferential statistics for confidence intervals, control charts, etc. (Apply)
>
> **Body of Knowledge V.D.2**

Suppose a population consists of the numbers 2, 3, and 4. The dot plot for this population would look like Figure 21.1.

Now randomly draw a sample of size $n = 2$, replacing the first before drawing the second. There are nine possible samples. These nine samples are shown in Table 21.2 along with the means of each sample.

The dot plot for the sample means is shown in Figure 21.2.

Note that this dot plot looks much different from the population dot plot in Figure 21.1. In Figure 21.2, the mean of the sample means is 3, the same as the mean of the population from Figure 21.1 However, the standard deviation of the distribution of the sample means is 0.577, while the standard deviation of the population

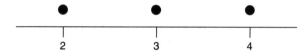

Figure 21.1   Dot plot for a simple population of three numbers.

Table 21.2   Sampling distribution of the mean.

Sample	Sample mean
2, 2	2.0
2, 3	2.5
2, 4	3.0
3, 2	2.5
3, 3	3.0
3, 4	3.5
4, 2	3.0
4, 3	3.5
4, 4	4.0
Total	**27.0**
Mean	**3.0**
Standard deviation of sample means	**0.816**

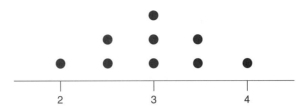

Figure 21.2 Dot plot of the sample means from Table 21.2.

shown in Figure 21.2 is 0.816. This procedure could be completed for other populations, but that exercise will be omitted here and a more general case will be considered.

Suppose the histogram for a large population looks like Figure 21.3 and a sample of size $n = 10$ is randomly selected from that population. Denote the mean of this sample $\bar{x}_1$. Now randomly select another sample of size $n = 10$ and denote its mean $\bar{x}_2$. Repeat this exercise 50 times, obtaining 50 sample means. Plot these sample means on a histogram. This distribution is called the sampling distribution of the mean. The standard deviation of this distribution is called the standard error of the mean and is denoted by $\sigma_{\bar{x}}$ and also by s_e. This sampling scheme gives rise to the following definition of the central limit theorem:

> *The central limit theorem (CLT) states that, regardless of the shape of the population, the sampling distribution of the mean is approximately normal if the sample size is sufficiently large. The approximation improves as the sample size gets larger.*

Of course, a nearly normal population will have a nearly normal sampling distribution of the mean for small sample sizes. Non-normal populations will require larger sample sizes for the sampling distribution of the mean to be nearly normal. Statisticians usually consider a sample size of 30 or more to be sufficiently large (see Figure 21.4). Chapter 22 provides more detail about the normal distribution. The following is a key fact that is useful in calculating confidence intervals and limits for control charts:

> *Given a random variable x with mean μ and standard deviation σ, if the variable x is normally distributed or the sample size n ≥ 30, the distribution of sample means is approximately normal with mean $\mu_{\bar{x}} = \mu$ and standard deviation $\sigma_{\bar{x}} = \dfrac{\sigma}{\sqrt{n}}$.*

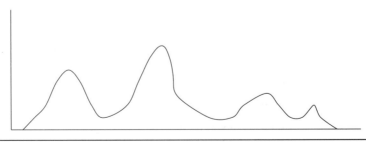

Figure 21.3 Example of a histogram from a large non-normal looking population.

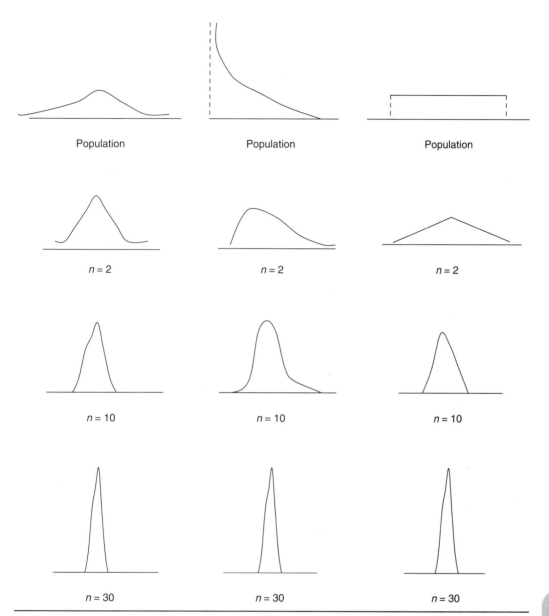

Figure 21.4   Examples of the impact of the CLT when sampling from various populations.

The CLT is the basis for calculating confidence intervals (discussed in Chapter 25) as well as for various hypothesis tests. Control charts, such as the $\bar{X}$ and R chart (discussed in Chapter 35), depend on the CLT since each point plotted on the $\bar{X}$ chart represents a sample mean.

DESCRIPTIVE STATISTICS

> Calculate and interpret measures of dispersion and central tendency, and construct and interpret frequency distributions and cumulative frequency distributions. (Evaluate)
>
> **Body of Knowledge V.D.3**

The purpose of descriptive statistics is to present data in a way that will facilitate understanding. The following data set represents a sample of diameters from a drilling operation:

> 0.127, 0.125, 0.123, 0.123, 0.120, 0,124, 0.126, 0.122, 0.123, 0,125, 0.121, 0.123, 0.122, 0.125, 0.124, 0.122, 0.123, 0.123, 0.126, 0.121, 0.124, 0.121, 0.124, 0.122, 0.126, 0.125, 0.123

What conclusions can be reached by looking at the data set? As presented, raw data provide little insight into underlying patterns and limit our ability to make meaningful conclusions. A frequency distribution, a dot plot, and a histogram of these data have been constructed in Figure 21.5.

x	Tally	Frequency
.120	I	1
.121	III	3
.122	IIII	4
.123	IIIIIII	7
.124	IIII	4
.125	IIII	4
.126	III	3
.127	I	1

Frequency distribution

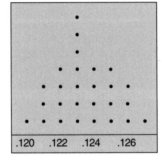

Dot plot

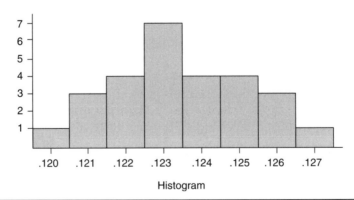

Histogram

Figure 21.5   Example of a data set as illustrated by a frequency distribution, a dot plot, and a histogram.

These diagrams reveal information about the sample data that was not obvious from the data list, such as the following:

- The spread of the sample

- The shape of the sample

- The approximate center of the sample

These three attributes (that is, spread, shape, and center) are important to understanding the data and the process that generated them.

The spread of the sample is also referred to as dispersion or variation and is usually quantified with either the sample *range* (defined as the highest value minus the lowest value) or the sample *standard deviation*. The sample standard deviation is defined computationally as

$$s = \sqrt{\frac{\sum_{i=1}^{n}(x_i - \bar{x})^2}{n-1}}$$

where

$\bar{x}$ = sample mean

n = sample size

If data for the entire population are used (rare in practical applications), the population standard deviation is defined computationally as

$$\sigma = \sqrt{\frac{\sum_{i=1}^{N}(x_i - \mu)^2}{N}}$$

where

μ = population mean

N = population size

The shape of a distribution is usually defined in terms of its kurtosis and skewness. *Kurtosis* refers to the overall peakedness or flatness of the distribution, while *skewness* measures the general symmetry of the distribution.

The center of the sample may be quantified in three ways:

- The *mean* is the arithmetic average of a data set.

- The *median* is the middle value of an ordered data set. If the data are composed of an odd number of data points, the median is the middle value of the ordered data set. If the data are composed of an even number of data points, the median is the average of the two middle values of the ordered data set.

- The *mode* is the most frequently found value in a data set. Note: There may be more than one mode present.

These three terms are known collectively as *measures of central tendency*. From the previous example, we have the following:

- mean $= \dfrac{3.333}{27} = 0.123$
- median $= 0.123$
- mode $= 0.123$

Of these three measures, the mean is the most useful in many quality engineering applications.

Table 21.3 summarizes the various descriptive measures.

If a column showing totals of the frequencies is added to the frequency distribution, the result is called a *cumulative frequency distribution*, as shown in Figure 21.6.

Table 21.3 Summary of descriptive measures.

Statistic	Symbol	Formula/Description
Measures of central tendency		
Mean	$\bar{x}$	$\dfrac{\sum\limits_{i=1}^{n} x_i}{n}$
Median	$\tilde{x}$	• Middle number of an ordered data set if there is an odd number of data elements • Average of the middle two numbers of an ordered data set if there is an even number of data elements
Mode	No symbol	Most frequent number of an ordered data set
Measures of dispersion		
Range	R	Highest value – lowest value
Sample standard deviation	s	$\sqrt{\dfrac{\sum\limits_{i=1}^{n}\left(x_i - \bar{x}\right)^2}{n-1}}$

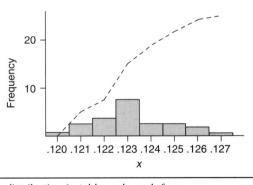

x	Frequency	Cumulative frequency
.120	1	1
.121	3	4
.122	4	8
.123	7	15
.124	4	19
.125	4	23
.126	3	26
.127	1	27

Figure 21.6 Example of a cumulative frequency distribution in table and graph form.

GRAPHICAL METHODS

> Construct and interpret diagrams and charts,
> including box-and-whisker plots, run charts,
> scatter diagrams, histograms, normal probability
> plots, etc. (Evaluate)
>
> **Body of Knowledge V.D.4**

Table 21.4 provides an overview of the graphical methods discussed in this section. The following paragraphs provide more information about those methods not already discussed.

Table 21.4   A comparison of various graphical methods.

Name	Purpose	Application	Interpretation
Tally	Provides a quick, informal histogram-like diagram.	Used to make a preliminary judgment on skewness, for example.	Grouping of tally marks near the center with few at the ends suggests a normal distribution. More tally marks at one end suggests skewness. Isolated marks at extreme ends suggests outliers. Evenly distributed marks suggests a uniform distribution.
Frequency distribution	Summarizes data from a tally column.	Especially useful if tally column cells have a large number of marks.	Grouping of values near the center with few at the ends suggests a normal distribution. More values at one end suggests skewness. Isolated values at extreme ends suggests outliers. A horizontal line across the tops of all bars suggests a uniform distribution.
Stem-and-leaf diagram	Provides information about the contents of the cells in a frequency distribution.	Useful when the behavior of the data within cells is needed.	If data values within cells are not fairly evenly distributed, measurement errors or other anomalous conditions may be present.
Box-and-whisker chart	Illustrates range, median, and location of middle 50% of data.	Used to provide more information than tallies or frequency distributions.	If the location of the center line of the box is not halfway between the low value and the high value, the distribution may be skewed. If the location of the center line of the box is not halfway between sides of the box, the distribution may be skewed. Long lines outside the box to high or low points may indicate outliers.

Continued

Table 21.4 A comparison of various graphical methods. *Continued*

Name	Purpose	Application	Interpretation
Scatter diagram	Detects possible correlation or association between two variables.	Used to help determine whether the equation for a linear regression line should be calculated.	If the plotted points tend to fall in a band that appears to be centered around a straight line, it would be appropriate to calculate the linear correlation coefficient and the parameters for a straight line.
Run chart	Provides a visual of a set of data over time.	Used when real-time feedback of process information is needed.	Trends and runs above or below the center line can be detected. Process adjustment based on the run chart may result in overadjustment. This can be remedied by using a control chart. See Chapter 35 for more information on control charts.

Data: .18 .24 .21 .17 .36 .34 .19 .25 .18 .22 .37 .24 .42 .33 .48 .56
.47 .55 .26 .38 .54 .19 .24 .42 .44 .11 .39

Measurement	Tally	Stem-and-leaf		Ordered stem-and-leaf	
.10–.19	‖‖‖	.1	8 7 9 8 9 1	.1	1 7 8 8 9 9
.20–.29	‖‖‖‖	.2	4 1 5 2 4 6 4	.2	1 2 4 4 4 5 6
.30–.39	‖‖‖	.3	6 4 7 3 8 9	.3	3 4 6 7 8 9
.40–.49	‖‖	.4	2 8 7 2 4	.4	2 2 4 7 8
.50–.59	‖	.5	6 5 4	.5	4 5 6

Figure 21.7 Stem–and–leaf diagrams.

A *stem-and-leaf diagram* is constructed much like the tally column except that the last digit of the data value is recorded instead of the tally mark. This diagram is often used when the data are grouped. Consider the example shown in Figure 21.7. The stem-and-leaf diagram conveys more information than the tally column or the associated histogram. Note that the ordered stem-and-leaf sorts the data and permits easy determination of the median.

The *quartiles* of a set of data divide the sorted data values into four approximately equal subsets. The quartiles are denoted Q1, Q2, Q3, and Q4. Q2 is the median. Q1 is the median of the set of values at or below Q2. Q3 is the median of the set of values at or above Q2.

The *box plot* (also called a *box-and-whisker diagram*), developed by Professor John Tukey of Princeton University, uses the high and low values of the data as well as the quartiles. This is illustrated in Figure 21.8. Once the data from Figure 21.8 are sorted, we have

$$63, 65, 67, 69, 71, 71, 75, 76, 76, 76, 81, 85$$

Minimum	= 63
Maximum	= 85
First quartile (Q_1)	= 68.5
Second quartile (Q_2)	= 73
Third quartile (Q_3)	= 76
Fourth quartile (Q_4)	= 85

Notice that quartiles need not be values in the data set itself. Also, the fourth quartile is equivalent to the maximum value.

Figure 21.9 shows how the shape of the dot plot is reflected in the box plot.

Box plots can be used to mine information from a database. In this hypothetical example, a stainless steel casting has a tight tolerance on the machined inside diameter (ID), which has been causing problems. The quality team has heard a number of proposed fixes. Some people believe the problem is caused by a slightly out-of-round condition on a cross section of the casting. Others feel there is a taper, and still others insist the problem is too much part-to-part variation. The question is, which type of variation is giving the most trouble? The team decides to measure the ID at three angles (12 o'clock, 2 o'clock, and 4 o'clock) at three locations along the bore (top, middle, and bottom) on five pieces. The resultant data and box plots are shown in Figure 21.10.

Figure 21.10 shows that the largest source of variation is part-to-part. The Pareto principle says that the part-to-part variation should be attacked first.

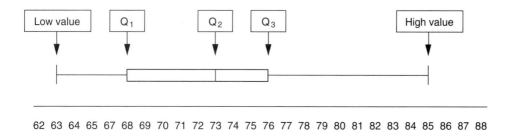

Figure 21.8 Box plot with key points labeled.

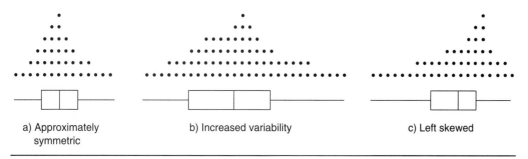

a) Approximately symmetric

b) Increased variability

c) Left skewed

Figure 21.9 Examples of box plots.

	Part #1			Part #2			Part #3			Part #4			Part #5		
	Top	Middle	Bottom	Top	Middle	Bottom	Top	Middle	Bottom	Top	Middle	Bottom	Top	Middle	Bottom
12	.998	.992	.996	.984	.982	.981	.998	.998	.997	.986	.987	.986	.975	.980	.976
2	.994	.996	.994	.982	.980	.982	.999	.998	.997	.985	.986	.986	.975	.976	.974
4	.996	.994	.995	.984	.983	.980	.996	.996	.996	.984	.985	.984	.978	.980	.974

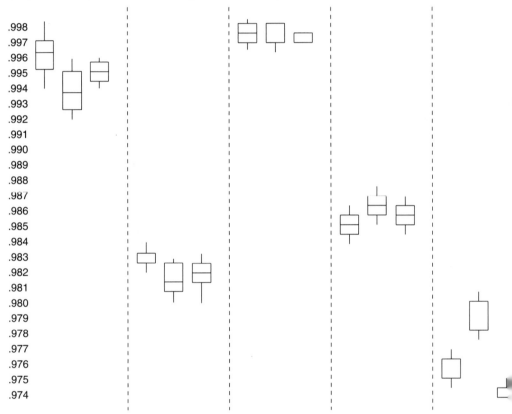

Which of the three variations is most prevalent? A box plot of these data:

Figure 21.10   Example of a multiple box plot.

Moreover, any improvements in out-of-round or taper may be masked by the large part-to-part variation.

Run Charts

If a specific measurement is collected on a regular basis, say every 15 minutes, and plotted on a time scale, the resulting diagram is called a run chart. A *run chart* is simply a basic plot of a specific process/product value on fixed time intervals. An example of a run chart is shown in Figure 21.11.

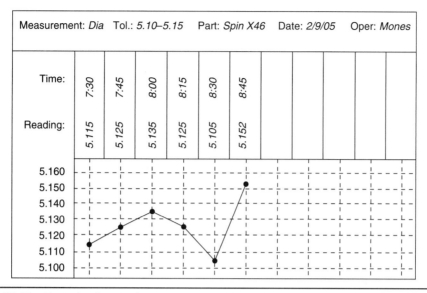

Measurement: *Dia*   Tol.: *5.10–5.15*   Part: *Spin X46*   Date: *2/9/05*   Oper: *Mones*

Figure 21.11   Example of a run chart.

Note: The natural variation in the process and in the measurement system tends to cause the graph to go up and down even when no significant change is occurring.

Scatter Diagrams

When several causes for a quality problem have been proposed, it may be necessary to collect some data to help determine the root cause. One way to analyze such data is with a *scatter diagram*. In this technique, measurements are taken for various levels of the variables suspected as being the cause. Each variable is then plotted against the quality characteristic to get a rough idea of correlation or association. For example, suppose an injection molding machine is producing parts with pitted surfaces. The following potential causes have been suggested:

- Mold pressure
- Coolant temperature
- Mold cooldown time
- Mold squeeze time

Values of each of these variables as well as the quality of the surface finish were collected on 10 batches. These data are shown in Table 21.5.

Four graphs have been plotted in Figure 21.12. In each graph, "Surface finish" is the vertical axis. The first graph plots mold pressure against surface finish. Batch #1 has a mold pressure of 220 and a surface finish of 37. Therefore, one dot is plotted at 220 in the horizontal direction and at 37 in the vertical direction. On each graph, one point is plotted for each batch. If the points tend to fall along a straight line, this indicates linear correlation or association between the two variables. If the points tend to closely follow a curve rather than a straight line,

Table 21.5 Data for scatter diagrams shown in Figure 21.12.

Batch number	Mold pressure	Coolant temperature	Cooldown time	Squeeze time	Surface finish
1	220	102.5	14.5	0.72	37
2	200	100.8	16.0	0.91	30
3	410	102.6	15.0	0.90	40
4	350	101.5	16.2	0.68	32
5	490	100.8	16.8	0.85	27
6	360	101.4	14.8	0.76	35
7	370	102.5	14.3	0.94	43
8	330	99.8	16.5	0.71	23
9	280	100.8	15.0	0.65	32
10	400	101.2	16.6	0.96	30

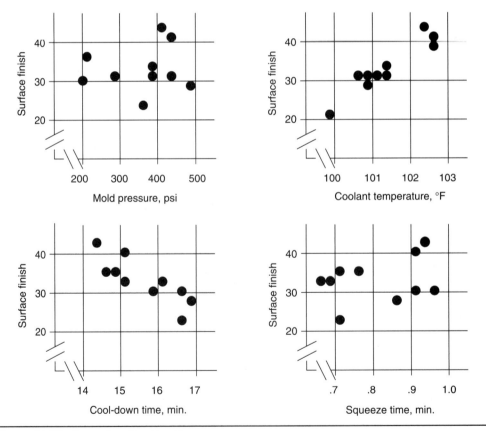

Figure 21.12 Examples of scatter diagrams.

there may be a nonlinear correlation. Note that high correlation does not imply a cause-and-effect relationship. A low correlation, however, is evidence that there is no such relationship.

The closer the points are to forming a straight line, the greater the linear correlation coefficient, denoted by the letter r. A positive correlation means that the line moves from the bottom left to the upper right. A negative correlation means that the line moves from the top left to the bottom right. If all the points fall exactly on a straight line that tips up on the right end, $r = +1$. If all the points fall on a straight line that tips down on the right end, $r = -1$. The value of r is always between -1 and $+1$, inclusive. This may be stated as $-1 \le r \le +1$. Most authorities suggest that the first step in analyzing a set of data for correlation is to construct a scatter diagram. If the points on this diagram tend to form a straight line, it makes sense to calculate the value of r.

Normal Probability Plots

Normal probability graph paper is designed so that a random sample from a normally distributed population will form an approximately straight line. This is illustrated in Figure 21.13. The procedure for using this paper follows:

1. Construct a cumulative frequency distribution.

2. For each row in the cumulative frequency table, calculate

$$\frac{\text{cumulative frequency}}{n+1}$$

   where n = sample size.

3. Multiply this result by 100 to convert it to a percentage. This value is known as the mean rank probability estimate.

4. Plot the first column of the table on the vertical axis and the last column on the horizontal axis.

The light dashed line in Figure 21.13 indicates that the points approximate a straight line.

The line is extended to provide an estimate of capability for the process. Assuming that the specification (or tolerance) for the dimension is 0.119 to 0.127, as indicated by the heavy dashed lines, the extended dashed line shows that about 4% of the parts will be below the lower specification limit and about 5% will be above the upper specification limit. If probability paper is not available, the approach demonstrated in Figure 21.14 may be used.

x	Frequency	Cumulative frequency	(Cumulative frequency) + (n + 1)	Mean rank, %
0.120	1	1	1/28	4
0.121	3	4	4/28	14
0.122	4	8	8/28	29
0.123	7	15	15/28	54
0.124	4	19	19/28	68
0.125	4	23	23/28	82
0.126	3	26	26/28	93
0.127	1	27	27/28	96
	$n = 27$			

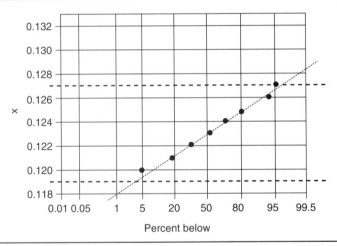

Figure 21.13   Example of the use of normal probability graph paper.

Sorted data	7.8	9.7	10.6	12.7	12.8	18.1	21.2	33.0	43.5	51.1	81.4	93.1
Normal scores	−1.59	−1.10	−0.78	−0.53	−0.31	−0.10	0.10	0.31	0.53	0.78	1.10	1.59

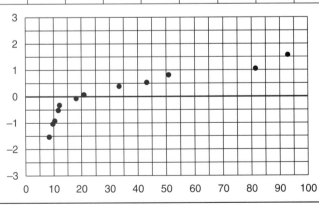

Figure 21.14   Example of a normal probability plot.

Example 21.1

Consider the following for developing a normal probability plot:

7.9, 9.7, 10.6, 12.7, 12.8, 18.1, 21.2, 33.0, 43.5, 51.1, 81.4, 93.1

- Step 1: Order the data from smallest to largest.

- Step 2: Select from the normal scores table the column corresponding to the sample size (see Appendix 25). Note: The normal scores were rounded to two decimals from those given in Appendix 25.

- Step 3: Plot the points and assess linearity.

Because the points do not form an approximately straight line, the sample probably did not come from a normal population.

VALID STATISTICAL CONCLUSIONS

> Define and distinguish between enumerative (descriptive) and analytic (inferential) statistical studies, and evaluate their results to draw valid conclusions. (Evaluate)
>
> **Body of Knowledge V.D.5**

One of the results from current technology is that we're drowning in data and thirsting for information. Statistical studies provide tools for squeezing information out of the data. The two principal types of statistical studies are usually called *descriptive (enumerative)* and *inferential (analytical)*.

Descriptive studies use techniques such as those in the previous two sections to present data in an understandable format. A long column of numbers is rendered more meaningful when the mean, the median, the mode, and standard deviation are known. A histogram or scatter plot squeezes additional information from the data.

Inferential studies analyze data from a sample to infer properties of the population from which the sample was drawn. This is especially important in those situations in which population data are unavailable or infeasible to obtain. Suppose, for instance, that one needs to know the mean diameter produced by a particular tooling setup on a lathe. The population would consist of all the parts that could be produced by that setup, which could take weeks or possibly years. Instead, a sample is selected, its properties studied, and a reasonable inference about the population mean diameter is obtained. In this case the mean of the sample would provide an approximation for the population mean. The amount of variation in the sample would provide information about how close that approximation is to the actual population mean. Inferential studies are covered in detail in Chapter 25, and this particular problem is addressed in the section on point and interval estimates. Inferential studies produce statements involving probabilities, confidence levels, and so forth; thus, the next chapter attacks this topic.

Part V.D.5

Chapter 22
Probability

BASIC CONCEPTS

> Describe and apply probability concepts such as independence, mutually exclusive events, multiplication rules, complementary probability, joint occurrence of events, etc. (Apply)
>
> **Body of Knowledge V.E.1**

Probability is defined in two ways:

- Classic definition—If an event, say *A*, can occur in *m* ways out of a possible *n* equally likely ways, then

$$P(A) = \frac{m}{n}$$

- Relative-frequency definition—The proportion that an event, say *A*, occurs in a series of repeated experiments as the number of those experiments approaches infinity. According to this definition, probability is a limiting value that may or may not be possible to quantify.

Almost all statistical activities are based on the rules of probability. This section lists and illustrates those rules, providing groundwork for the study of probability distributions, confidence intervals, and hypothesis testing.

The probability that a particular event occurs is a number between 0 and 1, inclusive. For example, if a lot consisting of 100 parts has four defectives, we would say the probability of randomly drawing a defective is 0.04, or 4%. Symbolically, this is written $P(\text{defective}) = 0.04$. The word "random" implies that each part has an equal chance of being drawn. If the lot had no defectives, the probability would be 0, or 0%. If the lot had 100 defectives, the probability would be 1, or 100%. The probability that event *A* will occur can be illustrated with a *Venn diagram*, as shown in Figure 22.1. The area in the rectangle is called the universe and has a probability of 1. The shaded area inside the circle represents the probability that event *A* will occur.

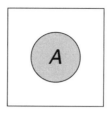

Figure 22.1   Venn diagram illustrating the probability of event *A*.

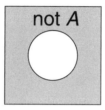

Figure 22.2   Venn diagram illustrating the complementary rule of probability.

Complementary Rule of Probability

The complementary rule of probability states that the probability that event *A* will occur is 1 – *P*(event *A* does not occur). Stated symbolically, $P(A) = 1 - P(\text{not } A)$. Some texts use other symbols for "not *A*," including –*A*, ~*A*, *A'*, and $\bar{A}$. The Venn diagram illustrating the complementary rule is shown in Figure 22.2, where the probability that *A* will occur is shown as the area inside the circle and *P*(not *A*) is the shaded area.

Addition Rule of Probability

Suppose a card is randomly selected from a standard 52-card deck.

Example 22.1

What is the probability that the card is a club?
There are 13 clubs; therefore, we have $P(\clubsuit) = 13/52 = 0.25$.

Example 22.2

What is the probability that the card is either a club or a spade?
There are 26 cards that are either clubs or spades; therefore, we have $P(\clubsuit \text{ or } \spadesuit)$ = 26/52 = 0.5.

We can see that $P(\clubsuit \text{ or } \spadesuit) = P(\clubsuit) + P(\spadesuit)$. Mathematically, we have

$$P(A \text{ or } B) = P(A) + P(B)$$

Part V.E.1

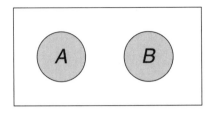

Figure 22.3   Venn diagram illustrating the addition rule of probability with independent events *A* and *B*.

Or, using the proper symbology, we obtain

$$P(A \cup B) = P(A) + P(B)$$

where $\cup$ is the symbol for "union" or "addition."

Note that this formula applies only when *A* and *B* are independent of one another.

The Venn diagram for the addition rule of probability is shown in Figure 22.3. Note that events *A* and *B* cannot occur simultaneously. Two events that can't occur simultaneously are called mutually exclusive or disjoint. This is demonstrated by the fact that the two circles do not intersect.

Example 22.3

Now let's consider the probability of selecting either a king or a club. Using the addition rule, we have

$$P(K \text{ or } \clubsuit) = P(K) + P(\clubsuit)$$
$$= 4/52 + 13/52$$
$$= 17/52$$

However, this is incorrect because there are only 16 cards that are either kings or clubs (that is, 13 clubs plus the $K\diamondsuit$, the $K\heartsuit$, and the $K\spadesuit$). The reason the addition rule doesn't work here is that the two events (that is, drawing a king and drawing a club) can occur simultaneously. Hence, they are not independent. We'll denote the probability that *A* and *B* both occur as $P(A \cap B)$. This leads to a generalized version of the addition rule:

$$P(A \cup B) = P(A) + P(B) - P(A \cap B)$$

where $\cap$ is the symbol for "intersection."

This generalized rule is always valid. For the previous example, we have

$$P(K \cap \clubsuit) = 1/52$$

since there is only one card that is both a *K* and a $\clubsuit$.

Example 22.3 Continued

$$P(K \cup \clubsuit) = P(K) = P(\clubsuit) - P(K \cap \clubsuit)$$

$$= 4/52 + 13/52 - 1/52$$

$$= 16/52$$

$$= 4/13$$

The Venn diagram illustrating the general version of the *addition rule* is shown in Figure 22.4. The circles in the figure are not disjoint since they clearly overlap. When circle A and circle B are added together, the intersection of the two circles will be counted twice. Therefore, we must subtract the intersection (that is, $P(A \cap B)$) to get the actual area of both circles.

Contingency Tables

Contingency tables provide an effective way of arranging attribute data while allowing us to readily determine relevant probabilities. This statement is best illustrated by the following scenario: Suppose each part in a lot is one of four colors (red, yellow, green, or blue) and one of three sizes (small, medium, or large). A tool that displays these attributes is the contingency table shown in Table 22.1.

Each part belongs in exactly one column, and each part belongs in exactly one row, so each part belongs in exactly one of the 12 cells. When the columns and rows are totaled, the table becomes the one shown in Table 22.2.

Using the data in Table 22.2, we'll illustrate how to use a contingency table through the following examples.

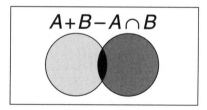

Figure 22.4   Venn diagram illustrating the general version of the addition rule of probability.

Table 22.1   Example of a contingency table.

Size	Red	Yellow	Green	Blue
Small	16	21	14	19
Medium	12	11	19	15
Large	18	12	21	14

Table 22.2 Contingency table for Examples 22.4–22.11.

Size	Red	Yellow	Green	Blue	Totals
Small	16	21	14	19	70
Medium	12	11	19	15	57
Large	18	12	21	14	65
Totals	**46**	**44**	**54**	**48**	**192**

Example 22.4

Find the probability that a part selected at random is red:

$$P(\text{red}) = \frac{46}{192} = 0.24$$

Example 22.5

Find the probability that a part selected at random is small:

$$P(\text{small}) = \frac{70}{192} = 0.365$$

Example 22.6

Find the probability that a part selected at random is both red *and* small:

$$P(\text{red and small}) = P(\text{red} \cap \text{small}) = \frac{16}{192} = 0.083$$

Example 22.7

Find the probability that a part selected at random is red *or* small:

$$P(\text{red or small}) = P(\text{red}) + P(\text{small}) - P(\text{red and small})$$

$$= \frac{46}{192} + \frac{70}{192} - \frac{16}{192}$$

$$= \frac{100}{192} = 0.521$$

Example 22.7 *(continued)*

Note that Example 22.7 uses the generalized addition rule to account for the overlap because parts can be both red and small simultaneously.

Example 22.8

Find the probability that a part selected at random is red *or* yellow:

$$P(\text{red or yellow}) = P(\text{red}) + P(\text{yellow})$$

$$= \frac{46}{192} + \frac{44}{192}$$

$$= \frac{90}{192} = 0.469$$

Note that in Example 22.8 parts cannot be both red and yellow simultaneously, so $P(\text{red and yellow}) = P(\text{red} \cap \text{yellow}) = 0$.

Conditional Probability

In the case of two events, A and B, conditional probability asks the question, What is the probability of B occurring given A occurred? This situation is formalized mathematically with the following definition of conditional probability:

$$P(B|A) = \frac{P(A \cap B)}{P(A)}$$

Let's continue with the data from the previous example. Now suppose that a part selected at random is known to be green.

Example 22.9

Find the probability that the selected part is large.
Using the previous formula, we are looking for

$$P(\text{large} \,|\, \text{green})$$

Also, we know

$$P(\text{green}) = \frac{54}{192} = 0.281$$

$$P(\text{green and large}) = P(\text{green} \cap \text{large}) = \frac{21}{192} = 0.109$$

Example 22.9 *(continued)*

Therefore, we can readily calculate

$$P(\text{large}|\text{green}) = \frac{0.109}{0.281} = 0.389$$

Alternately, we could have determined the probability directly from the table by noting that of the 54 green parts, 21 of them are large. Thus we would have computed the following directly:

$$P(\text{large}|\text{green}) = \frac{21}{54} = 0.389$$

Example 22.10

Find the probabilities directly from Table 22.2:

$$P(\text{small}|\text{red}) = \frac{16}{46} = 0.348$$

$$P(\text{red}|\text{small}) = \frac{16}{70} = 0.229$$

$$P(\text{red}|\text{green}) = \frac{0}{54} = 0$$

Now let's use the formal definition of conditional probability to compute Example 22.10:

$$P(\text{small}|\text{red}) = \frac{P(\text{small} \cap \text{red})}{P(\text{red})} = \frac{16/192}{46/192} = \frac{16}{192} = 0.348$$

$$P(\text{red}|\text{small}) = \frac{P(\text{red} \cap \text{small})}{P(\text{red})} = \frac{16/192}{70/192} = \frac{16}{70} = 0.229$$

$$P(\text{red}|\text{green}) = \frac{P(\text{red} \cap \text{green})}{P(\text{green})} = \frac{0/192}{54/192} = \frac{0}{54} = 0$$

Independent and Dependent Events

Two events, A and B, are said to be independent if and only if the occurrence of B has no effect on the occurrence of A (or vice versa). This can be stated mathematically as

$$P(A|B) = P(A)$$
$$P(B|A) = P(B)$$

Similarly, events A and B are dependent if and only if this formula does not hold. In this case, we have

$$P(A|B) \neq P(A)$$

$$P(B|A) \neq P(B)$$

Let's consider an example using Table 22.2 along with some of the problems we solved previously.

Example 22.11

Recall that

$$P(\text{small}|\text{red}) = \frac{P(\text{small} \cap \text{red})}{P(\text{red})} = \frac{16/192}{46/192} = \frac{16}{192} = 0.348$$

$$P(\text{small}) = \frac{70}{192} = 0.365$$

since

$$P(\text{small}|\text{red}) \neq P(\text{small})$$

Therefore, we can conclude that $P(\text{small})$ and $P(\text{red})$ are dependent events.

This brief introduction provides a solid foundation for discussing the multiplication rule of probabilities, which follows shortly.

Mutually Exclusive Events

Two events, A and B, are said to be mutually exclusive if both events cannot occur at the same time. Remember our previous example for which we sought $P(\text{red} \cap \text{green})$ only to recognize that according to our contingency in Table 22.2, a part cannot be both red and green at the same time. Hence, event A (that a part is red) and event B (that a part is green) are mutually exclusive.

Multiplication Rule of Probabilities

Recall the previous formula for conditional probability. If we rearrange this formula, we will obtain the multiplication rule of probabilities:

$$P(A \cap B) = P(A) \times P(B|A)$$

$$P(A \cap B) = P(B) \times P(A|B)$$

Let's consider a scenario whereby a box holds 129 parts, of which six are defective. We'll use this situation and study several examples to understand how multiplication rules work.

Example 22.12

A part is randomly drawn from the box and placed in a fixture. A second part is then drawn from the box. What is the probability that the second part is defective?

The probability can't be determined directly unless the outcome of the first draw is known. In other words, probabilities associated with successive draws depend on the outcome of previous draws.

Let

D_1 denote the event that the first part is defective

D_2 denote the event that the second part is defective

G_1 denote the event that the first part is not defective (that is, good)

G_2 denote the event that the second part is not defective (that is, good)

There are two mutually exclusive events that can result in a defective part for the second draw: good on first draw and defective on second *or* defective on first and defective on second.

Using the notation we just defined, we can write these two events as $(G_1 \cap D_2)$ and $(D_1 \cap D_2)$. Note that we are looking for the probability that both of these events occur (that is, $P(G_1 \cap D_2) + P(D_1 \cap D_2)$). Now we can readily write the probability equations that will help us solve the problem:

$$P(G_1 \cap D_2) = P(G_1) \times P(D_2 | G_1)$$
$$P(D_1 \cap D_2) = P(D_1) \times P(D_2 | D_1)$$
$$P(D_2) = P(G_1 \cap D_2) + P(D_1 \cap D_2)$$

Filling in the numbers, we have

$$\frac{123}{129} \times \frac{6}{128} = 0.045$$

$$\frac{6}{129} \times \frac{5}{128} = 0.002$$

$$= 0.0045 + 0.002 = 0.047$$

Example 22.13

Given the same scenario, what is the probability of selecting only one defective?

There are two mutually exclusive events that can result in drawing only one defective part: good on first draw and defective on second *or* defective on first and defective on second.

Using our notation, we can write these two events as

$$P(G_1 \cap D_2) = P(G_1) \times P(D_2 | G_1)$$
$$P(D_1 \cap G_2) = P(D_1) \times P(G_2 | D_1)$$
$$= P(G_1 \cap D_2) + P(D_1 \cap G_2)$$

Example 22.13 *(continued)*

Filling in the numbers, we have

$$\frac{123}{129} \times \frac{6}{128} = 0.045$$

$$\frac{6}{129} \times \frac{123}{128} = 0.045$$

$$= 0.090$$

Therefore, the probability of selecting only one defective is 0.090.

Table 22.3 summarizes the key probability equations and concepts described in this section.

Table 22.3   Summary of the rules of probability.

Axioms of probability

$0 \le P(\text{Event}) \le 1$

$\sum_{i=1}^{n} P(E_i) = 1$

Complementary rule

$P(A) = 1 - P(A')$

For two events A and B

Conditional probability

$P(A|B) = \dfrac{P(A \cap B)}{P(B)}$ for $P(B) > 0$

$P(B|A) = \dfrac{P(A \cap B)}{P(A)}$ for $P(A) > 0$

	Independent	Dependent
Events	$P(A|B) = P(A)$	$P(A|B) \ne P(A)$
	$P(B|A) = P(B)$	$P(B|A) \ne P(B)$
Addition rule	$P(A \cup B) = P(A) + P(B)$	$P(A \cup B) = P(A) + P(B) - P(A \cap B)$
Multiplication rule	$P(A \cap B) = P(A) \times P(B)$	$P(A \cap B) = P(A) \times P(B|A)$
		$= P(B) \times P(A|B)$
	Mutually exclusive	**Not mutually exclusive**
	$P(A \cap B) = 0$	$P(A \cap B) \ne 0$

COMMONLY USED DISTRIBUTIONS

> Describe, apply, and interpret the following
> distributions: normal, Poisson, binomial, chi
> square, Student's *t*, and *F* distributions. (Evaluate)
>
> **Body of Knowledge V.E.2**

This section and the following one provide information about several distributions. Information about several of the commonly used distributions is summarized in Table 22.4.

Normal Distribution

If X is a normal random variable with expected value μ (that is, $E(X) = \mu$) and finite variance σ^2, then the random variable Z is defined as

$$Z = \frac{X - \mu}{\sigma}$$

However, when $E(Z) = 0$ and the $Var(Z) = 1$, then Z is distributed as a standard normal variable. We will use the concept of the standard normal distribution extensively in later sections.

It is important to remember that the area between any two points under the standard normal curve can be determined from statistical tables such as those in the appendixes. This can best be understood with a few examples.

Table 22.4 Summary of formulas, means, and variances of commonly used distributions.

Distribution	Formula	Mean	Variance
Normal	$f(x) = \dfrac{1}{\sigma\sqrt{2\pi}} e^{-\frac{(x-\mu)^2}{2\sigma^2}}$ for $-\infty < x < \infty$	μ	σ^2
Poisson	$f(x) = \dfrac{e^{-\lambda}\lambda^x}{x!}$ for $x = 0,1,2,\dots$	λ	λ
Binomial	$f(x) = \binom{n}{x} p^x (1-p)^{n-x}$ for $x = 0,1,\dots,n$	np	$np(1-p)$
Chi square	$f(x) = \dfrac{e^{-x/2} x^{(v/2)-1}}{2^{v/2}\,\Gamma\left(\frac{v}{2}\right)}$ for $x \geq 0$, $v =$ degrees of freedom	v	$2v$
t	$f(x) = \dfrac{1}{\sqrt{\pi v}}\dfrac{\Gamma\left(\frac{v+1}{2}\right)}{\Gamma\left(\frac{v}{2}\right)}\left(1 + \dfrac{x^2}{v}\right)^{-(v+1)/2}$ for $-\infty < x < \infty$	0 for $v \geq 2$	$\dfrac{v}{v-2}$ for $v \geq 3$
F	$f(x) = \dfrac{\Gamma\left(\frac{v_1+v_2}{2}\right) v_1^{v_1/2} v_2^{v_2/2} x^{(v_1/2)-1}}{\Gamma\left(\frac{v_1}{2}\right)\Gamma\left(\frac{v_2}{2}\right)\left[\left(\frac{v_1}{v_2}\right)x + 1\right]^{\frac{v_1+v_2}{2}}}$ for $0 < x < \infty, v_1 > 0, v_2 > 0$	$\dfrac{v_2}{v_2-2}$ for $v_2 \geq 3$	$\dfrac{2v_2^2\left(v_1+v_2-2\right)}{v_1\left(v_2-2\right)^2\left(v_2-4\right)}$ for $v_2 \geq 5$

Example 22.14

Find the area under the standard normal curve between +1.22 standard deviations and +2.06 standard deviations, as illustrated in Figure 22.5.

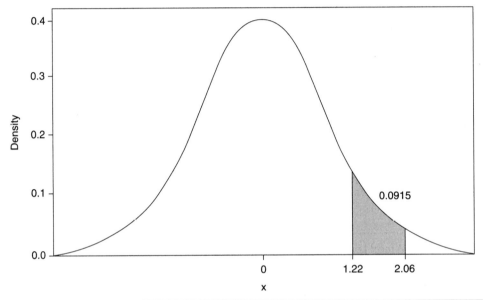

Normal Distribution Plot
Normal, Mean = 0, StDev = 1

Figure 22.5 Standard normal distribution for Example 22.14.

To find our area, we determine the area to the right of 1.22 and subtract the area to the right of 2.06.

Using the standard normal tables from the appendixes, we get the following:

$$\text{area to the right of } 1.22 = 0.1112$$

$$\text{area to the right of } 2.06 = 0.0197$$

$$\text{area between } 1.22 \text{ and } 2.06 = 0.0915$$

Therefore, the area under the curve between the two values is 0.0915.

For any data set that is normally distributed and for which the mean and the standard deviation are known or can be estimated, this technique can be used to determine the probability of falling between any two specified standard normal values or z-scores using

$$z = \frac{x - \mu}{\sigma}$$

Example 22.15

A product fill operation produces net weights that are normally distributed. A random sample has mean 8.06 ounces and standard deviation 0.37 ounces, as illustrated in Figure 22.6. Estimate the percentage of the containers that have a net weight between 7.9 and 8.1 ounces.

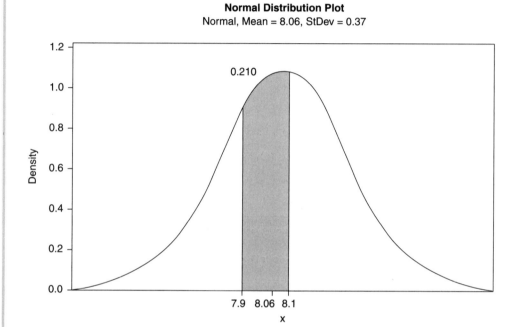

Figure 22.6   Standard normal distribution for Example 22.15.

To determine the number of containers, we must first calculate the z-scores for 7.9 and 8.1. Filling in the numbers, we have

$$z(7.9) = \frac{7.9 - 8.06}{0.37} = -0.432$$

$$z(8.1) = \frac{8.1 - 8.06}{0.37} = 0.108$$

Using the standard normal tables from the appendixes, we get the following:

area to the right of –0.43 = 0.6664

area to the right of 0.108 = 0.4570

area between –0.43 and 0.108 = 0.2094 = 0.210

Therefore, 20.94% of the containers have a net weight between 7.9 and 8.1 ounces. Put another way, the probability that a randomly selected container will have a net weight between 7.9 and 8.1 is approximately 0.2094.

Part V.E.2

Poisson Distribution

The Poisson is important to the Black Belt because it is used to model the number of defects per unit of time (or distance) and is the basis for the control limit formulas for the c and u control charts. The Poisson has also been used to analyze such diverse phenomena as the number of phone calls received per day and the number of alpha particles emitted per minute. The formula is

$$P(X = x) = \frac{e^{-\lambda}\lambda^x}{x!} \text{ for } \lambda > 0 \text{ and } x = 0, 1, 2, \ldots$$

The mean and variance of the Poisson distribution are both λ.

Example 22.16

The number of defects per shift has a Poisson distribution with $\lambda = 4.2$. A plot of this distribution is shown in Figure 22.7. Find the probability that the second shift produces fewer than two defects. Therefore, we will seek

$$P(x < 2) = P(x = 0) + P(x = 1)$$

Filling in the numbers, we have

$$P(X = 0) = \frac{e^{-4.2}4.2^0}{0!} = 0.015$$

$$P(X = 1) = \frac{e^{-4.2}4.2^1}{1!} = 0.063$$

$$P(X < 2) = 0.078$$

Example 22.16 *(continued)*

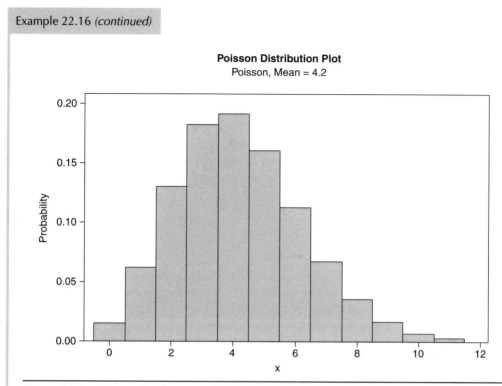

Figure 22.7   Poisson distribution with mean $\lambda = 4.2$ for Example 22.16.

Binomial Distribution

The binomial distribution represents a sequence of n Bernoulli trials.

If X is a random variable that equals the number of trials that result in a success, then X is binomially distributed with parameters p and n. The symbology relevant to the binomial distribution follows:

$$n = \text{sample size or number of trials}$$

$$x = \text{number of successes in the sample}$$

$$p = \text{probability of a success for each trial}$$

Key assumptions regarding the binomial include the following:

- Each trial is independent
- Each trial can result in only one outcome: success or failure
- $0 < p < 1$ and where p is constant for each trial

The term "success" can be defined in whatever way we deem appropriate. For example, a "success" might mean that a part sampled is nonconforming (that is, we have succeeded in finding a defect).

The binomial formula is as follows:

$$P(X = x) = \frac{n!}{x!(n-x)!} p^x (1-p)^{n-x}$$

Note: $x!$, pronounced "x factorial," is defined as $(x)(x-1)(x-2) \ldots (2)(1)$. Also, $0! = 1$ by definition.

Let's look at the formula for a moment. The term $p^x(1-p)^{n-x}$ from the binomial formula represents the probability of obtaining x successes in n trials while the term $\frac{n!}{x!(n-x)!}$ represents the number of ways in which the x successes in n trials can occur. With this brief background, we'll now look at an example of how the binomial distribution can be used.

Example 22.17

A sample of size six is randomly selected from a batch with 14.28% nonconforming. A plot of this distribution is shown in Figure 22.8. Find the probability that the sample has exactly two nonconforming units.

From the problem statement, we know that

$$n = 6$$

$$x = 2$$

$$p = 0.1428$$

Filling in the numbers, we have

$$
\begin{aligned}
P(X = 2) \quad &= \frac{6!}{2!(6-2)!} 0.1428^2 (0.8572)^{6-2} \\[2mm]
&= \frac{720}{(2)(24)}(0.0204)(0.5399) \\[2mm]
&= (15)(0.0204)(0.5399) \\[2mm]
&= 0.1651
\end{aligned}
$$

Thus, the probability that the sample contains exactly two nonconforming units is 0.1651.

Example 22.17 *(continued)*

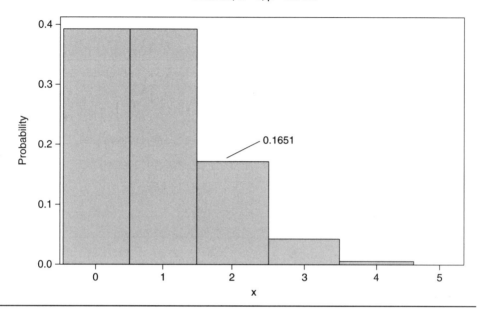

Figure 22.8 Binomial distribution with $n = 6$ and $p = 0.1428$ for Example 22.17.

Chi-Square (χ^2) Distribution

If we obtain a random sample $X_1, X_2, \ldots, X_n$ of size n from a population that is normally distributed with mean μ and finite variance σ^2, the random variable

$$\chi^2 = \frac{(n-1)s^2}{\sigma^2}$$

is distributed as a chi-square distribution with $n - 1$ degrees of freedom where s^2 is the sample variance.

The formula for the χ^2 will be useful later when we discuss hypothesis testing and confidence intervals.

Figure 22.9 illustrates the effects of various degrees of freedom on the chi-square distribution.

Part V.E.2

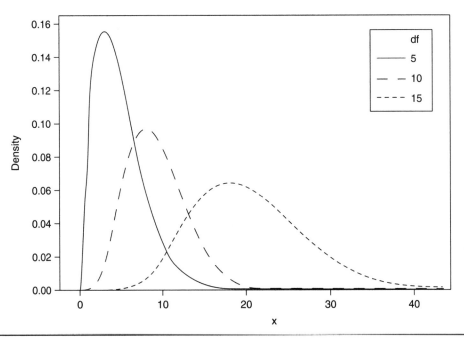

Figure 22.9 Example of a chi-square distribution with various degrees of freedom.

t Distribution (Also Known as Student's *t* Distribution)

If we obtain a random sample $X_1, X_2, \ldots, X_n$ of size n from a population that is normally distributed with unknown mean μ and finite variance σ^2, then T is distributed as a t distribution with $n-1$ degrees of freedom:

$$T = \frac{\bar{x} - \mu}{\frac{s}{\sqrt{n}}}$$

Recall that when we reviewed the normal distribution previously, we assumed that σ was a known value. In general, this is unlikely since σ is a parameter of a population. Of course, when it is unknown, we must resort to estimating it. This is where the t distribution becomes useful. In practical applications of this formula, μ is often assumed to be a known value, say μ_0, and σ is estimated by s, determined from the sample.

Typically, the t distribution is used when $n < 30$, but more importantly when σ is unknown. The t distribution is flatter than the normal distribution and has longer tails. As the degrees of freedom increase, the t distribution approaches the normal distribution. Figure 22.10 illustrates the effects of various degrees of freedom on the t distribution.

t Distribution Plot

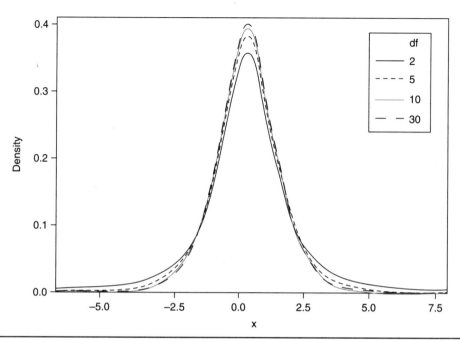

Figure 22.10 Example of a *t* distribution with various degrees of freedom.

F Distribution

If X and Y are two random variables distributed as χ^2 with ν_1 and ν_2 degrees of freedom, respectively, then the random variable

$$F = \frac{X/\nu_1}{Y/\nu_2}$$

is distributed as an *F* distribution with degrees of freedom ν_1 as the numerator and degrees of freedom ν_2 as the denominator.

This formula for the *F* distribution will be useful later when we discuss hypothesis testing and confidence intervals. Figure 22.11 illustrates the effects of varying the degrees of freedom in both the numerator and the denominator.

A beneficial key property of the *F* distribution follows:

$$F_{1-\alpha,\nu_1,\nu_2} = \frac{1}{F_{\alpha,\nu_2,\nu_1}}$$

If an α value table (that is, upper percentage points) is available, this reciprocal relationship is useful for determining the $(1 - \alpha)$ values (that is, lower percentage points). Of course, the reverse is true as well.

F Distribution Plot

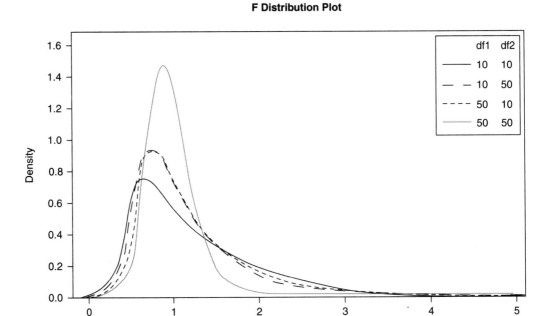

Figure 22.11 Example of an *F* distribution with various degrees of freedom.

OTHER DISTRIBUTIONS

Describe when and how to use the following
distributions: hypergeometric, bivariate,
exponential, lognormal, and Weibull. (Apply)

Body of Knowledge V.E.3

This section provides information about several other types of distributions useful in the practice of Six Sigma. Information about several of these distributions is summarized in Table 22.5.

Hypergeometric Distribution

The hypergeometric distribution is useful when sampling from a finite population without replacement (that is, a sample is drawn from a population, inspected, and set aside, and another sample is drawn from the remaining population). Whereas in binomial sampling the probability of incurring a success (for example, defect) remains constant from sample to sample, the probability of incurring a success in hypergeometric sampling changes from sample to sample (that is, sampling without replacement).

Table 22.5 Summary of formulas, means, and variances of other distributions.

Poisson	$f(x) = \dfrac{e^{-\lambda}\lambda^x}{x!}$ for $x = 0,1,2,\ldots$	λ	λ
Hypergeometric	$f(x) = \dfrac{\binom{K}{x}\binom{N-K}{n-x}}{\binom{N}{n}}$ for $x = \max\{0, n+K-N\}$ to $\min\{K,n\}$	np	$np(1-p)\left(\dfrac{N-n}{N-1}\right)$
Bivariate	The joint probability mass function of two discrete random variables: $$f_{XY}(x,y) \geq 0$$ $$\sum_x \sum_y f_{XY}(x,y) = 1$$ $$P(X=x, Y=y) = f_{XY}(x,y)$$	Depends on the joint probability mass function	Depends on the joint probability mass function
Bivariate normal	$f_{XY}(x,y; \mu_X, \mu_Y, \sigma_X, \sigma_Y, \rho) = \dfrac{1}{2\pi\sigma_X\sigma_Y\sqrt{1-\rho^2}} e^{\left\{\frac{-1}{2(1-\rho^2)}\left[\frac{(x-\mu_X)^2}{\sigma_X^2} - \frac{2\rho(x-\mu_X)(y-\mu_Y)}{\sigma_X\sigma_Y} + \frac{(y-\mu_Y)^2}{\sigma_Y^2}\right]\right\}}$ for $\begin{cases} -\infty < x < \infty \\ -\infty < y < \infty \\ -\infty < \mu_X < \infty \\ -\infty < \mu_Y < \infty \\ \sigma_X > 0 \\ \sigma_Y > 0 \\ -1 \leq \rho \leq 1 \end{cases}$	Conditional: $$\mu_{x|y=y_0} = \mu_x + \rho\sigma_x \dfrac{(y-\mu_y)}{\sigma_y}$$ $$\mu_{y|x=x_0} = \mu_y + \rho\sigma_y \dfrac{(x-\mu_x)}{\sigma_x}$$	Conditional: $$\sigma_{x|y=y_0} = \sigma_x\sqrt{1-\rho^2}$$ $$\sigma_{y|x=x_0} = \sigma_y\sqrt{1-\rho^2}$$

Continued

Table 22.5 Summary of formulas, means, and variances of other distributions. *Continued*

Exponential	$f(x) = \lambda e^{-\lambda x}$ for $0 \le x < \infty$	$\dfrac{1}{\lambda}$	$\dfrac{1}{\lambda^2}$
Lognormal	$f(x) = \dfrac{1}{x\sigma\sqrt{2\pi}} e^{\left[\frac{-1}{2\sigma^2}(\ln x - \mu)^2\right]}$ for $0 < x < \infty$	$e^{\mu + \sigma^2/2}$	$e^{2\mu + \sigma^2}\left(e^{\sigma^2} - 1\right)$
Weibull	$f(x) = \dfrac{\beta}{\alpha}\left(\dfrac{x-\gamma}{\alpha}\right)^{\beta-1} e^{-\left(\frac{x-\gamma}{\alpha}\right)^{\beta}}$ for $x \ge \gamma, \alpha > 0, \beta > 0$	$\gamma + \alpha\Gamma\left(1 + \tfrac{1}{\beta}\right)$	$\alpha^2\left[\Gamma\left(1 + \tfrac{2}{\beta}\right) - \left[\Gamma\left(1 + \tfrac{1}{\beta}\right)\right]^2\right]$

If X represents the number of successes in a sample, then X is distributed as a hypergeometric random variable with

$$f(x) = \frac{\binom{S}{x}\binom{N-S}{n-x}}{\binom{N}{n}} \text{ for } x = \max\{0, n+S-N\} \text{ to } \min\{S, n\}$$

The elements in this formula are defined as follows:

N = the finite population size

S = the number of objects in the total population classified as successes

$N - S$ = the number of objects in the total population classified as failures

n = the sample size

x = the number of objects in the sample classified as successes

$n - x$ = the number of objects in the sample classified as failures

Example 22.18

A batch of 100 parts, of which 25 are defective, has been received for inspection. Assuming sampling without replacement, what is the probability of obtaining three defects in a sample of size 10? Figure 22.12 illustrates the distribution of this example.

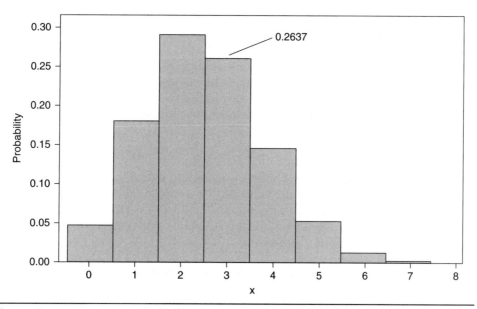

Hypergeometric Distribution Plot
Hypergeometric, N = 100, M = 25, n = 10

Figure 22.12   Hypergeometric distribution for Example 22.18.

Example 22.18 *(continued)*

Before we go too far, let's first define a "success" as the finding of a defect. Then from the problem statement, we can readily see that

$N = 100$

$S = 25$

$N - S = 75$

$n = 10$

$x = 3$

$n - x = 7$

Filling in the numbers, we have

$$P(X = 3) = \frac{\binom{25}{3}\binom{75}{7}}{\binom{100}{10}}$$

$$= \frac{(2300)(1.98 \times 10^9)}{1.73 \times 10^{13}}$$

$$= 0.2637$$

Bivariate Normal Distribution

If there are two random variables of interest that are dependent or vary jointly (for example, length and weight), each of which is normally distributed, the joint probability density function of the variables is distributed as a bivariate normal distribution. The bivariate normal distribution, along with the mean and the variance, is given in Table 22.5. An example of where the bivariate normal distribution might apply is when we are interested in determining the probability of meeting the specifications for both length and weight simultaneously.

Exponential Distribution

Recall that the Poisson distribution was used to model the number of defects per unit of time (or distance). By contrast, the exponential distribution allows us to model the time between defects and is a key distribution in the study of reliability engineering. Also, note that while the Poisson is a discrete distribution, the exponential is a continuous distribution.

If X is a random variable that equals the distance (or time) between successive defects from a Poisson process with mean $\lambda > 0$, then X is exponentially distributed as

$$f(x) = \lambda e^{-\lambda x} \text{ for } 0 \leq x < \infty$$

The cumulative exponential distribution is given as

$$P(X < x) = F(x) = \int_0^t \lambda e^{-\lambda x} dx$$

$$= 1 - e^{-\lambda t}$$

Example 22.19

Customers arrive at the self-checkout counter at the supermarket at a rate of five per hour. What is the probability that a customer arrives in less than 15 minutes? Figure 22.13 illustrates the distribution of this example, and it also includes an additional curve to demonstrate how the value of λ affects the shape of the distribution.

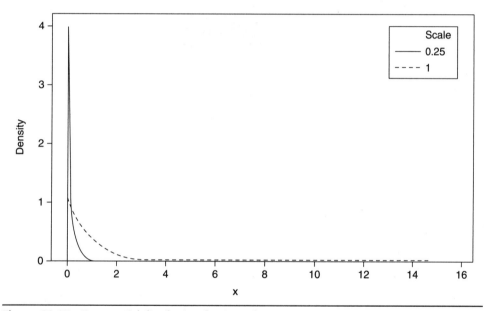

Figure 22.13   Exponential distribution for Example 22.19.

Before we can begin to solve this problem, we need to ensure that all time units are made consistent. Thus we need to convert the 15-minute time interval to 0.25 hours.

From the cumulative exponential distribution formula, we can determine

$$P(X < 0.25) = 1 - e^{-(5)(0.25)}$$

$$= 1 - e^{-1.25}$$

$$= 1 - 0.2865$$

$$= 0.7135$$

Lognormal Distribution

If a variable Y has a normal distribution with mean μ and finite variance σ^2, then the variable $X = e^Y$ has a lognormal distribution. This distribution has applications in modeling life spans for products that degrade over time. The probability density function for the lognormal distribution is defined as

$$f(x) = \frac{1}{x\sigma\sqrt{2\pi}} e^{\left[\frac{-1}{2\sigma^2}(\ln x - \mu)^2\right]} \text{ for } 0 < x < \infty$$

Example 22.20

Suppose the lifetime of a plasma television is distributed as lognormal with mean $\mu = 10$ hours and standard deviation $\sigma = 2$ hours. What is the probability that the lifetime of the plasma television exceeds 1,000 hours? Figure 22.14 illustrates the distribution for this example.

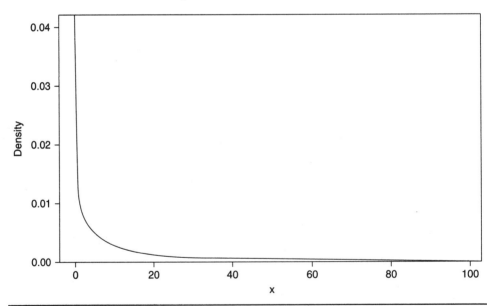

Lognormal Distribution Plot
Lognormal, Loc = 0, Scale = 10, Thresh = 0

Figure 22.14 Lognormal distribution for Example 22.20.

Example 22.20 *(continued)*

$$P(X > 1000) = 1 - P(X \leq 1000)$$

$$= 1 - P(e^Y \leq 1000)$$

$$= 1 - P(Y \leq \ln(1000))$$

$$= \Phi\left(\frac{\ln(1000) - 10}{2}\right)$$

$$= \Phi\left(\frac{6.9078 - 10}{2}\right)$$

$$= \Phi(-1.55)$$

$$= 1 - 0.9394$$

$$= 0.0606$$

Weibull Distribution

The Weibull distribution has the general form

$$P(x) = \alpha\beta(x - \gamma)^{\beta-1} e^{-\alpha(x-\gamma)^\beta}$$

where

α = scale parameter

β = shape parameter

γ = location parameter

The elegance of the Weibull function is that it takes on many shapes depending on the value of β, as shown in Figure 22.15. For example, when:

- $0 < \beta < 1$, the Weibull has a decreasing failure rate and can be used to model "infant mortality"

- $\beta = 1$, the Weibull is reduced to the exponential distribution with a constant failure rate

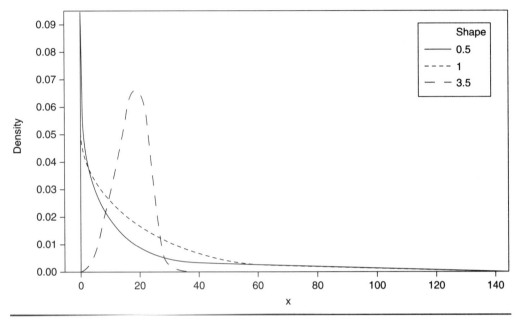

Figure 22.15 Example of a Weibull function for various values of the shape parameter β.

- $\beta > 1$, the Weibull has an increasing failure rate and can be used to model "wear out"

- $\beta = 3.5$, the Weibull is approximately the normal distribution, has an increasing failure rate, and can be used to model "wear out"

As a result, the Weibull distribution is one of the fundamental distributions in the study of reliability engineering.

Chapter 23
Process Capability

PROCESS CAPABILITY INDICES

> Define, select, and calculate C_p and C_{pk} to assess process capability. (Evaluate)
>
> **Body of Knowledge V.F.1**

Process capability is defined as the inherent variability of a characteristic of a product. It represents the performance of the process over a period of stable operations. Process capability is expressed as $6\hat{\sigma}$, where $\hat{\sigma}$ is the sample standard deviation of the process under a state of statistical control. Note: $\hat{\sigma}$ is often shown as σ in most process capability formulas. A process is said to be capable when the output always conforms to the process specifications.

The *process capability index* is a dimensionless number that is used to represent the ability to meet customer specification limits. This index compares the variability of a characteristic to the specification limits. Three basic process capability indices commonly used are C_p, C_{pk}, and C_{pm}.

The C_p index describes process capability in relation to the specified tolerance of a characteristic divided by the natural process variation for a process in a *state of statistical control*. The formula is given by

$$C_p = \frac{USL - LSL}{6\sigma}$$

where

 USL is upper specification limit

 LSL is lower specification limit

 6σ is the natural process variation

In simpler terms,

$$C_p = \frac{\text{Voice of the customer}}{\text{Voice of the process}} = \frac{VOC}{VOP} = \frac{\text{Tolerance}}{\text{Natural process variaton}} = \frac{USL - LSL}{6\sigma}$$

Occasionally, natural process variation is referred to as normal process variation, natural process limits, or natural tolerance.

C_p values greater than or equal to 1 indicate the process is technically capable. A C_p value equal to 2 is said to represent 6σ performance.

However, the C_p index is limited in its use since it does not address the centering of a process relative to the specification limits. For that reason, the C_{pk} was developed. It is defined as

$$C_{pk} = \text{Min}(C_{pk_U}, C_{pk_L})$$

where

C_{pk_U} is the upper process capability index and given by $C_{pk_U} = \dfrac{USL - \bar{x}}{3\sigma}$

C_{pk_L} is the lower process capability index and given by $C_{pk_L} = \dfrac{\bar{x} - LSL}{3\sigma}$

and

$\bar{x}$ = process average

σ = process standard deviation

USL = upper specification limit

LSL = lower specification limit

3σ = half of the process capability

Notice that the C_{pk} determines the proximity of the process average to the nearest specification limit. Also note that at least one specification limit must be stated in order to compute a C_{pk} value.

C_{pk} values of 1.33 or 1.67 are commonly set as goals since they provide some room for the process to drift left or right of the process nominal setting.

The C_{pk} can be easily converted to a sigma level using

$$\text{Sigma level} = 3C_{pk}$$

Note: When the process average is obtained from a control chart, $\bar{x}$ is replaced by $\bar{\bar{x}}$.

Example 23.1

A batch process produces high fructose corn syrup with a specification on the dextrose equivalent (DE) of 6.00 to 6.15. The DEs are normally distributed, and a control chart shows the process is stable. The standard deviation of the process is 0.035. The DEs from a random sample of 30 batches have a sample mean of 6.05. Determine C_p and C_{pk}.

$$C_p = \frac{\text{Tolerance}}{6\sigma} = \frac{6.15 - 6.00}{6(0.035)} = 0.71$$

Since the value of C_p is less than 1, the process is deemed "not capable."

$$C_{pk_U} = \frac{USL - \bar{x}}{3\sigma} = \frac{6.15 - 6.05}{3(0.035)} = 0.95$$

$$C_{pk_L} = \frac{\bar{x} - LSL}{3\sigma} = \frac{6.05 - 6.00}{3(0.035)} = 0.45$$

$$C_{pk} = \text{Min}(C_{pk_U}, C_{pk_L}) = \text{Min}(0.95, 0.48) = 0.48$$

A C_{pk} of 0.48 indicates that the process is even less capable relative to the lower specification limit.

Example 23.2

The data given in Table 23.1 were obtained from a control chart used to monitor the diameter of a cable. Determine C_p and C_{pk}.

Using Minitab to compute the process capability indices from the 20 subgroups in Table 23.1, we obtain the process capability analysis displayed in Figure 23.1.

Notice that the various process capability indices are all below 1, indicating the process that produces the cable is not capable of meeting the diameter specification limits. Some portion of the cable produced will be either too large or too narrow.

Example 23.2 *(continued)*

Table 23.1 Cable diameter data.

									Subgroup										
1	**2**	**3**	**4**	**5**	**6**	**7**	**8**	**9**	**10**	**11**	**12**	**13**	**14**	**15**	**16**	**17**	**18**	**19**	**20**
0.529	0.543	0.493	0.559	0.545	0.607	0.577	0.546	0.527	0.557	0.538	0.544	0.558	0.560	0.541	0.572	0.543	0.521	0.550	0.536
0.550	0.557	0.534	0.519	0.588	0.532	0.526	0.560	0.545	0.559	0.557	0.550	0.548	0.533	0.534	0.556	0.544	0.532	0.544	0.554
0.555	0.559	0.527	0.562	0.544	0.562	0.546	0.530	0.513	0.529	0.517	0.562	0.532	0.538	0.544	0.560	0.541	0.524	0.545	0.569
0.541	0.581	0.511	0.551	0.561	0.542	0.557	0.564	0.557	0.539	0.521	0.540	0.570	0.567	0.537	0.520	0.526	0.544	0.571	0.531
0.559	0.551	0.565	0.530	0.573	0.549	0.548	0.514	0.525	0.591	0.568	0.537	0.567	0.557	0.574	0.578	0.518	0.523	0.527	0.534

Example 23.2 *(continued)*

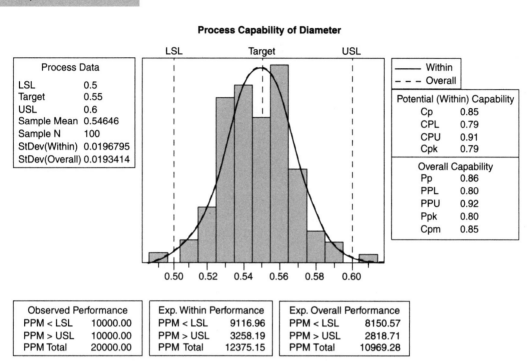

Figure 23.1   Example of a process capability analysis using the data given in Table 23.1.

PROCESS PERFORMANCE INDICES

> Define, select, and calculate P_p, P_{pk}, and C_{pm} to assess process performance. (Evaluate)
>
> **Body of Knowledge V.F.2**

Process performance is defined as a statistical measure of the outcome of a characteristic from a process that *may not have been demonstrated to be in a state of statistical control.* Use this measure cautiously since it may contain a component of variability from special causes of unpredictable value. It differs from process capability because a *state of statistical control is not required.*

The *process performance index* is a dimensionless number that is used to represent the ability to meet specification limits on a characteristic of interest. The index compares the variability of the characteristic to the specification limits. Three basic process performance indices are P_p, P_{pk}, and P_{pm}.

The P_p is computed as

$$P_p = \frac{USL - LSL}{6s}$$

where

USL is upper specification limit

LSL is lower specification limit

6s is the natural process variation

Similar to the C_{pk}, the P_{pk} is computed as

$$P_{pk} = \text{Min}(P_{pk_U}, P_{pk_L})$$

where

P_{pk_U} is the upper process capability index and given by $P_{pk_U} = \dfrac{USL - \bar{x}}{3s}$

P_{pk_L} is the lower process capability index and given by $P_{pk_L} = \dfrac{\bar{x} - LSL}{3s}$

and

$\bar{x}$ = process average

s = sample standard deviation

USL = upper specification limit

LSL = lower specification limit

3s = half of the process capability

Notice that the P_{pk} determines the proximity of the process average to the nearest specification limit. Also note that at least one specification limit must be stated in order to compute a P_{pk} value.

The P_{pk} is known as the potential process capability and is used in the validation stage of a new product launch. A state of statistical control is not required.

Process performance indices tend to be a bit larger than their corresponding process capability indices since they are often based on smaller sample sizes.

The C_{pm}, also known as the *process capability index of the mean*, is an index that accounts for the location of the process average relative to a target value and is defined as

$$C_{pm} = \frac{(USL - LSL)/2}{3\sqrt{\sigma^2 + (\mu - T)^2}} = \frac{USL - LSL}{6\sqrt{\sum\limits_{i=1}^{n} \dfrac{(x_i - T)^2}{n-1}}}$$

where

μ = process average

σ = process standard deviation

USL = upper specification limit

LSL = lower specification limit

T = target value (typically the center of the tolerance)

x_i = sample reading

n = number of sample readings

When the process average and the target value are equal, the C_{pm} equals the C_{pk}. When the process average drifts from the target value, the C_{pm} is less than the C_{pk}. The P_{pm} index is analogous to the C_{pm}.

Example 23.3

Recall the data given in Table 23.1. Determine the C_{pm}.
   Figure 23.1 depicts a C_{pm} = 0.85 against a target value of T = 0.55, indicating the process is not capable.

SHORT-TERM AND LONG-TERM CAPABILITY

Describe and use appropriate assumptions and conventions when only short-term data or attributes data are available and when long-term data are available. Interpret the relationship between long-term and short-term capability. (Evaluate)

Body of Knowledge V.F.3

The Difference Between Short-Term and Long-Term Capability

Significant confusion abounds, and contradictory statements pepper the literature with regard to meaning and determination of short-term and long-term capability and variability. The following provides a synopsis of a few key interpretations found in the literature:

- Breyfogle (2003) suggests that capability indices (C_p and C_{pk}) and performance indices (P_p and P_{pk}) be considered long term or short term on the basis of the method used to calculate $\hat{\sigma}$, an estimate of the process standard deviation. Table 23.2 summarizes the methods of computing $\hat{\sigma}$ as suggested by Breyfogle.

- C_p and C_{pk} represent long-term capability, while P_p and P_{pk} represent short-term capability. The AIAG suggests using P_{pk} for less than a 30-day production run (that is, short term) and C_{pk} for everything thereafter (that is, long term).

- Long-term variability = Short-term variability +1.5σ shift. This interpretation is based on the underlying assumption of Six Sigma, which is that a process will drift or shift ±1.5σ in the long term. When this drift is taken into account, 6σ process performance equates to 3.4 ppm; otherwise, 4.5σ process performance equates to 3.4 ppm.

Table 23.2 Methods of determining the standard deviation for use in process capability indices.

Method	Short term/Long term
$\hat{\sigma} = \sqrt{\dfrac{\sum\limits_{i=1}^{n}(x_i - \bar{x})^2}{n-1}}$	Long
$\hat{\sigma} = \dfrac{\bar{R}}{d_2}$	Short
$\hat{\sigma} = \dfrac{\bar{s}}{c_4}$	Short
$\hat{\sigma} = 1.047$ (moving median, $\tilde{R}$)	Short
$\hat{\sigma} = \dfrac{\overline{MR}}{d_2}$	Short
$\hat{\sigma} = s_{\text{pooled}} = \sqrt{\dfrac{\sum\limits_{i=1}^{m}\sum\limits_{j=1}^{n}(x_{ij} - \bar{x}_i)^2}{n_i - 1}}$	Short

Capability-Related Assumptions

The following three bullets identify the key assumptions related to capability indices:

- The data obtained from the process are stable. This assumption applies to the C_p and C_{pk} indices. The P_p and P_{pk} indices do not require this assumption.

- The individual process data elements are distributed approximately normally. When the data are not normally distributed, normality can be restored statistically using different data transformations. In addition, Minitab is able to analyze non-normal capability data.

- The specification limits are based on customer requirements—ideally, all specifications are based on customer requirements.

PROCESS CAPABILITY FOR NON-NORMAL DATA

Identify non-normal data and determine when it is appropriate to use Box-Cox or other transformation techniques. (Apply)

Body of Knowledge V.F.4

If the histogram of individual data elements indicates that the data are not normally distributed, the procedure described previously for determining the process capability indices will not yield correct values for the percentage of process output exceeding specifications. If precise values for the percentage values are required, the following approaches—all of which involve fairly complex calculations and are usually performed with the aid of statistical software packages—may be taken:

- Find another known distribution that fits the data—exponential, chi-square, Weibull, and F distributions are among the possibilities. A statistics software package is helpful in choosing the function and parameters that will provide the best fit for the data.

- Use nonlinear regression to fit a curve to the data and apply numerical integration to find the areas of the "tails" beyond the specification limits.

- Transform the data to produce a second variable that is normally distributed; various normalizing transformations are available. Among the most used are the Box-Cox transformation and the Johnson transformation. These transformations introduce a new variable that will have a "more normal" distribution.

  – The Box-Cox transforms the input data, denoted by Y, using $W = Y^\lambda$, where λ is any number typically between –5 and 5. The trick, of course, is to choose λ that produces a curve that is as close to normal as possible. Statistics software packages will use sample data to recommend a range for λ, often with a confidence interval. The user may choose a value in the range and observe the resulting curve, eventually choosing the value that best fits the situation. The package typically also generates values for the capability indices. Unfortunately, the Box-Cox transformation is limited to positive data values and often does not provide a suitable transformation. It also assumes that data are in subgroups.

  – The Johnson transformation is chosen from three different functions within the Johnson system. As a result, this approach usually finds an appropriate transformation. It does not assume data are in subgroups.

PROCESS CAPABILITY FOR ATTRIBUTES DATA

> Calculate the process capability and process sigma level for attributes data. (Apply)
>
> **Body of Knowledge V.F.5**

Part V.F.5

The customary method of defining process capability for attributes data is to use the mean rate of nonconformity. For p and np charts, it is $\bar{p}$. For c and u charts, they are $\bar{c}$ and $\bar{u}$, respectively.

Example 23.4

An electronics manufacturing process produces lots of size 64 and has a customer specification of no more than two nonconforming units per lot. The stable process has $\bar{p} = 0.025$. On a long-term basis, we would like the process to produce an average of two or fewer nonconforming units per batch. What percentage of the batches will meet this requirement?

Table 23.3 was developed using the binomial distribution. From this table, we can quickly determine that 78.47% of the batches produce fewer than three nonconforming units per batch. Thus, 21.53% produces more than two nonconforming units per batch.

Table 23.3 Binomial probabilities for Example 23.4.

Nonconforming units	Probability of occurrence
0	0.1978
1	0.3246
2	0.2622
Total	**0.7847**

A similar procedure will work for c and u charts using the Poisson distribution.

PROCESS CAPABILITY STUDIES

> Describe and apply elements of designing and conducting process capability studies, including identifying characteristics and specifications, developing sampling plans, and verifying stability and normality. (Evaluate)
>
> **Body of Knowledge V.F.6**

Example 23.5

Suppose a customer requires that a certain process output be 20 to 30. Examples of the 20 to 30 requirement might include:

• The arrival time for a delivery vehicle must be between 20 minutes and 30 minutes after the hour

• Manufactured pumps must produce between 20 psi and 30 psi

• The plating thickness must be from 20 mm to 30 mm

The 20 to 30 requirement in Example 23.5 is called the specification or tolerance.

One method of measuring process performance is to calculate the percentage of the process outputs that comply with the specification. This can be accomplished by measuring each output and dividing the number that meets the specification by the total number measured.

Conducting a Process Capability Study

The purpose of a capability study is to determine whether a process is capable of meeting customer specifications and to devise a course of action if it cannot.

Although authors differ on the specific steps of a process capability study, the general elements of any study include the following:

- Select a quality characteristic on a specific process for study. Ideally, a capability study should be performed for every quality characteristic. In practice, people familiar with the process are usually able to identify the few characteristics that merit a full capability study. These are the characteristics that past experience has shown to be difficult to hold to specification.

- Confirm the measurement system used to acquire the process data. Large measurement system variation can obscure the "true" process variation and will produce an unreliable estimate of process capability.

- Gather the data. Ideally, the data are readily available and are being tracked on a control chart. If not, collect data from the process—preferably randomly and with consideration given to rational subgrouping. Although the literature differs greatly on the appropriate number of subgroups, approximately 25–30 uniformly sized subgroups is usually sufficient. Subgroup sizes typically range from three to five.

- Verify process stability and ensure the process is in control. This can easily be accomplished using control charts. If the process is out of control, identify and eliminate special cause variation.

- Verify the individual data are normally distributed. Plot the data in a histogram and test for normality, which can be verified using a variety of statistics tests such as Anderson-Darling, Ryan-Joiner, Shapiro-Wilk, or Kolmogorov-Smirnov.

- Determine process capability. Apply the previously described methods. If the process is not capable, work to improve it.

- Update the process control plan. Once the process has achieved a desired level of capability, update your control plan to ensure the gains are maintained. If no control plan is present, create one.

Part V.F.6

PROCESS PERFORMANCE VS. SPECIFICATION

> Distinguish between natural process limits
> and specification limits, and calculate process
> performance metrics such as percent defective,
> parts per million (PPM), defects per million
> opportunities (DPMO), defects per unit (DPU),
> process sigma, rolled throughput yield (RTY), etc.
> (Evaluate)
>
> **Body of Knowledge V.F.7**

Natural Process Limits

As mentioned previously, natural process limits are known by several names in the literature: natural process variation, normal process variation, and natural tolerance. In all cases, these terms refer to the $\pm 3\sigma$ limits (that is, 6σ spread) around a process average. Such limits include 99.73% of the process variation and are said to be the "voice of the process." Walter Shewhart originally proposed the $\pm 3\sigma$ limits as an economic trade-off between looking for special causes for points outside the control limits when no special causes existed and not looking for special causes when they did exist.

Specification Limits

In contrast to natural process limits, specification limits are customer determined and are used to define acceptable levels of process performance (see Example 23.5). Said to be the "voice of the customer," specification limits may be one sided (that is, upper or lower) or two sided. The difference between the upper and lower specification limits is known as the tolerance.

The C_p index discussed previously brings together the concepts of "voice of the process" and "voice of the customer." Recall that the C_p is defined as

$$C_p = \frac{\text{Voice of the customer}}{\text{Voice of the process}} = \frac{VOC}{VOP} = \frac{\text{Tolerance}}{\text{Natural process variaton}} = \frac{USL - LSL}{6\sigma}$$

Example 23.6

A dimension has an upper specification limit (USL) of 2.130 and a lower specification limit (LSL) of 2.120. Data from the process indicate that the distribution is normal, and an $\bar{X} - R$ control chart indicates the process is stable and in control. The control chart was developed using subgroups of size five. The process average and the average range taken from the control chart are 2.1261 and 0.0055, respectively. Estimate the percentage of production that exceeds the specification limits.

Example 23.6 *(continued)*

From the problem statement, we know the process average is $\bar{\bar{X}}$ = 2.1261. The point estimate for process standard deviation is determined by

$$\hat{\sigma} = \frac{\bar{R}}{d_2} = \frac{0.0055}{2.326} = 0.00236$$

(The values for d_2 are given in Appendix 6.)

Computing the upper and lower Z statistics, we have

$$Z_U = \frac{USL - \bar{\bar{X}}}{\hat{\sigma}} = \frac{2.130 - 2.1261}{0.00236} = \frac{0.0039}{0.00236} = 1.65$$

$$Z_L = \frac{\bar{\bar{X}} - LSL}{\hat{\sigma}} = \frac{2.1261 - 2.120}{0.00236} = \frac{0.0061}{0.00236} = 2.58$$

The area beyond these Z values can be found by using the table in Appendix 12:

$P(Z_U > 1.65) = 0.0495$, or 4.95%, exceeds the upper specification

$P(Z_L > 2.58) = 0.0049$, or 0.49%, exceeds the lower specification

$= 0.0544$, or 5.44%, exceeds both specifications

Process Performance Metrics

There are numerous process performance metrics (not to be confused with process performance indices) used in Six Sigma projects, including:

- Defects per unit (DPU)
- Defections per million opportunities (DPMO)
- Throughput yield
- Parts per million (PPM)
- Rolled throughput yield (RTY)

Example 23.7

A process produces 40,000 pencils. Three types of defects can occur. The number of occurrences of each defect type are:

- Blurred printing: 36
- Wrong dimensions: 118
- Rolled ends: 11
- Total number of defects: 165

Defects per Unit

$$\text{Defects per unit (DPU)} = \frac{\text{Number of defects}}{\text{Number of units}} = \frac{165}{40,000} = 0.004125$$

Defects per Million Opportunities

To calculate the number of opportunities, it is necessary to find the number of ways each defect can occur on each item. For this product, blurred printing occurs in only one way (the pencil slips in the fixture), so there are 40,000 opportunities for this defect to occur. There are three independent places where dimensions are checked, so there are (3)(40,000) = 120,000 opportunities for dimensional defects. Rolled ends can occur at the top and/or the bottom of the pencil, so there are (2)(40,000) = 80,000 opportunities for this defect to occur. Thus the total number of opportunities for defects is

$$40,000 + 120,000 + 80,000 = 240,000$$

Therefore, defects per million opportunities (DPMO) is calculated as

$$\text{DPMO} = \frac{(\text{Number of defects})(1,000,000)}{\text{Total number of opportunities}} = \frac{165,000,000}{240,000}$$

$$\text{DPMO} = 687.5$$

Throughput Yield, Also Called Yield

$$\text{Throughput yield} = e^{-DPU}$$

In Example 23.7, the computation for the throughput yield is

$$e^{-0.004125} = 0.996$$

Parts per Million

Parts per million (PPM) is defined simply as

$$\text{PPM} = \text{DPU} \times 1,000,000$$

In Example 23.7, the computation for the PPM is

$$\text{PPM} = (0.004125)(1,000,000)$$

$$\text{PPM} = 4125$$

PPM is also used to refer to contaminants, as seen in the following example.

Example 23.8

Suppose 0.23 grams of insect parts is found in 25 kilograms of product:

$$\text{PPM} = \left(\frac{0.23}{25,000}\right) \times 1,000,000$$

$$\text{PPM} = 9.2$$

Rolled Throughput Yield

Example 23.9

Rolled throughput yield (RTY) applies to the yield from a series of processes and is found by multiplying the individual process yields. If a product goes through four processes whose yields are 0.994, 0.987, 0.951, and 0.990, then

$$\text{RTY} = (0.994)(0.987)(0.951)(0.990) = 0.924$$

Reference

Breyfogle, Forrest W. III. 2003. *Implementing Six Sigma: Smarter Solutions Using Statistical Methods.* 2nd ed. Hoboken, NJ: John Wiley.

Part V.F.7

Part VI
Analyze

Part VI

Chapter 24

Measuring and Modeling Relationships between Variables

CORRELATION COEFFICIENT

> Calculate and interpret the correlation coefficient and its confidence interval, and describe the difference between correlation and causation. (Analyze)
>
> NOTE: Serial correlation will not be tested.
>
> **Body of Knowledge VI.A.1**

The *sample correlation coefficient* r is a statistic that measures the degree of linear relationship between two sets of numbers and is computed as

$$r = \frac{S_{xy}}{\sqrt{S_{xx}S_{yy}}} = \frac{\sum_{i=1}^{n}(x_i - \bar{x})^2(y_i - \bar{y})^2}{\sqrt{\sum_{i=1}^{n}(x_i - \bar{x})^2 \sum_{i=n}^{n}(y_i - \bar{y})^2}} = \frac{\sum_{i=1}^{n}x_i y_i - \frac{\left(\sum_{i=1}^{n}x_i\right)\left(\sum_{i=1}^{n}y_i\right)}{n}}{\sqrt{\left(\sum_{i=1}^{n}x_i^2 - \frac{\left(\sum_{i=1}^{n}x_i\right)^2}{n}\right)\left(\sum_{i=1}^{n}y_i^2 - \frac{\left(\sum_{i=1}^{n}y_i\right)^2}{n}\right)}}$$

where $-1 \leq r \leq 1$.

Also, r is used to estimate the population correlation coefficient ρ. Correlation values of -1 and $+1$ represent perfect linear agreement between two independent and dependent variables. When r is 0, there is no linear relationship. If r is positive, the relationship between the variables is said to be positive; hence, when x increases, y increases. If r is negative, the relationship is said to be negative; hence, when x increases, y decreases. Figure 24.1 provides examples of different types of correlations.

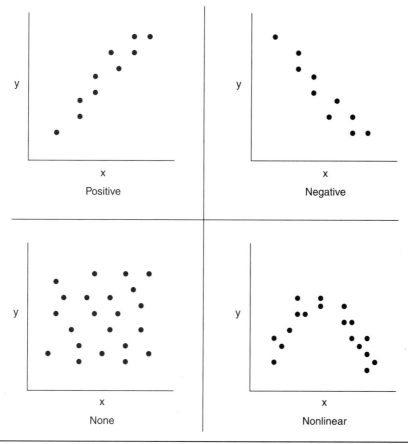

Figure 24.1   Examples of different types of correlations.

Example 24.1

Compute the correlations coefficient from the data given in the first two columns of Table 24.1.

Table 24.1   Data for Example 24.1.

	x	y	x^2	xy	y^2
	10	2	100	20	4
	15	3	225	45	9
	20	5	400	100	25
	15	4	225	60	16
Total	**60**	**14**	**950**	**225**	**54**

For convenience in computing the correlations coefficient, additional columns and totals have been added. From Table 24.1, we find that

Example 24.1 *(continued)*

$$\sum_{i=1}^{n} x_i = 60$$

$$\sum_{i=1}^{n} y_i = 14$$

$$\sum_{i=1}^{n} x_i^2 = 950$$

$$\sum_{i=1}^{n} x_i y_i = 225$$

$$\sum_{i=1}^{n} y_i^2 = 54$$

$$n = 4$$

Filling in the formula from earlier, we have

$$r = \frac{225 - \dfrac{(60)(14)}{4}}{\sqrt{\left(950 - \dfrac{60^2}{4}\right)\left(54 - \dfrac{14^2}{4}\right)}} = \frac{15}{\sqrt{(50)(5)}} = 0.9489$$

Another related value is the coefficient of determination, denoted r^2 where $r^2 \leq 1$. The *coefficient of determination* is the square of the correlations coefficient and represents the amount of the variation in y that is explained by the fitted simple linear equation. Similarly, the *adjusted coefficient of determination* (r_{adj}^2) is used with multiple regression because, unlike the R^2 statistic, the adjusted coefficient will increase when variables are added to the model that act to decrease the mean square error. r_{adj}^2 is given by

$$r_{adj}^2 = 1 - \frac{SS_E/(n-p)}{SS_T/(n-1)} = 1 - \frac{\sum_{i=1}^{n}(y_i - \hat{y}_i)^2 \Big/ (n-p)}{\sum_{i=1}^{n}(y_i - \bar{y})^2 \Big/ (n-1)}$$

where p is the number of coefficients fitted in the regression equation.

Correlations versus Causality

Correlation differs from causality. It is necessary to understand this important distinction in order to use regression analysis effectively. Causality implies correlations, but correlation does not imply causality.

Example 24.2

Empirical data demonstrate a strong correlation between height and weight in males. However, gaining weight does not cause one to grow taller. Hence, there is no causal relationship.

Hypothesis Test for the Correlation Coefficient

Recall that r is a sample statistic used to estimate ρ, the population correlation coefficient. As such, it will be useful to test the hypotheses

$$H_0 : \rho = 0$$

$$H_a : \rho \neq 0$$

As you might expect, such a test has been nicely defined. The test statistic for the hypotheses is given by

$$T = \frac{r\sqrt{n-2}}{\sqrt{1-r^2}}$$

where T has the t distribution with $n - 2$ degrees of freedom.

Example 24.3

Test the hypotheses that

$$H_0 : \rho = 0$$

$$H_a : \rho \neq 0$$

Use the data and result from Example 24.1. Assume $\alpha = 0.10$.
   Computing the T we have

$$T = \frac{0.9489\sqrt{4-2}}{\sqrt{1-(0.9489)^2}} = 4.2519$$

From Appendix 14, we find that $t_{\alpha/2,n-2} = t_{0.05,2} = 2.920$. Therefore, we reject the null hypothesis that $\rho = 0$.

Confidence Interval for the Correlation Coefficient

An approximation for the $100(1 - \alpha)\%$ confidence interval for ρ is given by

$$\tanh(\operatorname{arctanh}(r) - \frac{z_{\alpha/2}}{\sqrt{n-3}}) \leq \rho \leq \tanh(\operatorname{arctanh}(r) + \frac{z_{\alpha/2}}{\sqrt{n-3}})$$

where

$$\tanh(u) = \frac{e^u - e^{-u}}{e^u + e^{-u}}$$

Example 24.4

Construct a $100(1 - \alpha)\%$ confidence interval for ρ. Assume $\alpha = 0.10$, $r = 0.95$, and $n = 28$.

Using Appendix 12, we find that $z_{\alpha/2} = z_{0.05} = 1.645$. Filling in the formula from earlier, we have

$$\tanh(\text{arctanh}(0.95) - \frac{1.645}{\sqrt{28-3}}) \leq \rho \leq \tanh(\text{arctanh}(0.95) + \frac{1.645}{\sqrt{28-3}})$$

$$\tanh(1.8318 - \frac{1.645}{5}) \leq \rho \leq \tanh(1.8318 + \frac{1.645}{5})$$

$$\tanh(1.5028) \leq \rho \leq \tanh(2.1608)$$

Applying the identity for the $\tanh(u)$, we obtain

$$\frac{e^{1.5028} - e^{-1.5028}}{e^{1.5028} + e^{-1.5028}} \leq \rho \leq \frac{e^{2.1608} - e^{-2.1608}}{e^{2.1608} + e^{-2.1608}}$$

$$0.9057 \leq \rho \leq 0.9738$$

REGRESSION

Calculate and interpret regression analysis, and apply and interpret hypothesis tests for regression statistics. Use the regression model for estimation and prediction, analyze the uncertainty in the estimate, and perform a residuals analysis to validate the model. (Evaluate)

NOTE: Models that have non-linear parameters will not be tested.

Body of Knowledge VI.A.2

Regression analysis is a technique that typically uses continuous predictor variable(s) (that is, regressor variables) to predict the variation in a continuous response variable. Regression analysis uses the method of least squares to determine the values of the linear regression coefficients and the corresponding model.

The *method of least squares* is a technique for estimating a parameter that minimizes the sum of the squared differences between the observed and the predicted values derived from the model. These differences are known as residuals or experimental errors. Experimental errors associated with individual observations are assumed to be independent and normally distributed. It should be noted that analysis of variance, regression analysis, and analysis of covariance are all based on the method of least squares.

The *linear regression equation* is a mathematical function or model that indicates the linear relationship between a set of predictor variables and a response variable. *Linear regression coefficients* are numbers associated with each predictor variable in a linear regression equation that tell how the response variable changes with each unit increase in the predictor variable. The model also gives some sense of the degree of linearity present in the data.

Simple Linear Regression

When only one predictor variable is used, regression analysis is often referred to as simple linear regression. A simple linear regression model commonly uses a linear regression equation expressed as

$$E[Y|x] = \beta_0 + \beta_1 x + \varepsilon$$

where

> Y is the response for a given x value
>
> x is the value of the predictor variable
>
> β_0 and β_1 are the linear regression coefficients
>
> ε is the random error term
>
> $V[Y|x] = \sigma^2$
>
> $\varepsilon_i \sim N(0,\sigma^2)$

β_0 is often called the intercept and β_1 the slope.

Applying the method of least squares provides us with a line fitted to the data so that the sum of the squared residuals, $\sum_{i=1}^{n} \varepsilon_i$, is minimized. That fitted line takes the form of

$$\hat{y} = \hat{\beta}_0 + \hat{\beta}_1 x$$

where

> $\hat{y}$ is the response for a given x value
>
> x is the value of the predictor variable
>
> $\hat{\beta}_0$ and $\hat{\beta}_1$ are the linear regression coefficients

and

$$\hat{\beta}_0 = \bar{y} - \hat{\beta}_1 x$$

$$\hat{\beta}_1 = \frac{S_{XY}}{S_{XX}}$$

and

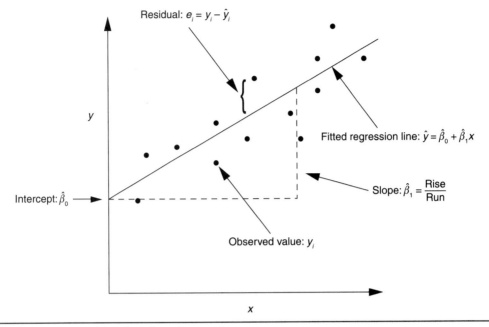

Figure 24.2 Graphical depiction of regression concepts.

$$S_{XY} = \sum_{i=1}^{n} x_i y_i - \frac{\sum_{i=1}^{n} x_i \sum_{i=1}^{n} y_i}{n}; S_{XX} = \sum_{i=1}^{n} x_i^2 - \frac{\left(\sum_{i=1}^{n} x_i\right)^2}{n}$$

Special note: Statistical notation varies greatly among authors. b_0 and b_1 are often used for $\hat{\beta}_0$ and $\hat{\beta}_1$, respectively.

Figure 24.2 illustrates the relationships that exist among all the concepts just discussed.

Example 24.5

Suppose a relationship is suspected between the ambient temperature T of a paint booth and paint viscosity V. If the relationship holds, then it may be possible to control temperature (predictor variable) in order to control viscosity (response variable).

Recall the data given in the first two columns of Table 24.1. The first step is to plot the data on a scatter diagram to determine if it is reasonable to approximate them with a straight line. Although a straight line can't be drawn through these four points, the trend looks linear, as shown in Figure 24.3.

The next step is to find the linear equation that best fits the data. We might guess at the following two equations:

1. $V = 1 + 0.2T$

2. $V = -3 + 0.5T$

Example 24.5 *(continued)*

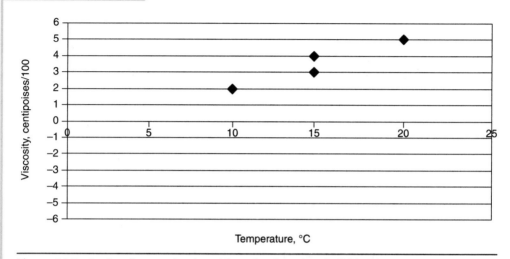

Figure 24.3 Scatter diagram developed from the data given in Table 24.1.

These lines, along with the data from Table 24.1, are plotted in Figure 24.4.

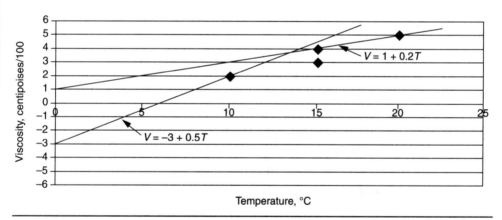

Figure 24.4 Scatter diagram from Figure 24.3 with two proposed lines.

Which of the lines fits the data better? To answer this question, we first construct a table for each equation comparing the actual value of V with the value V' predicted by the equation for each value of T. Doing so yields the values shown in Table 24.2.

After inspecting these tables closely, it would appear that the first equation fits the data better because the values predicted by the equation seem to come closer to the actual data values. But is there another equation that fits them even better? To properly address this question, it is necessary to have a basis for judging goodness of fit. A method frequently employed is called "least squares." For each line in Table 24.2, the value of residual $e = V - V'$ is computed and squared. These values are shown in Table 24.3.

Example 24.5 *(continued)*

Table 24.2 Computed values for the proposed lines in Figure 24.4.

$V' = 1 + 0.2T$			$V' = -3 + 0.5T$		
T	V	V'	T	V	V'
10	2	3	10	2	2
15	3	4	15	3	4.5
20	5	5	20	5	7
15	4	4	15	4	4.5

Table 24.3 Computed values for the proposed lines given in Figure 24.4 with residual values added.

$V' = 1 + 0.2T$					$V' = -3 + 0.5T$				
T	V	V'	e	e^2	T	V	V'	e	e^2
10	2	3	−1	1	10	2	2	0	0
15	3	4	−1	1	15	3	4.5	−1.5	2.25
20	5	5	0	0	20	5	7	−2	4
15	4	4	0	0	15	4	4.5	−0.5	0.25
			$\sum e_i^2$	2				$\sum e_i^2$	6.5

Thus, the equation with the least value of $\sum_{i=1}^{n} e_i^2$ is the better-fitting equation. The tables confirm the supposition that the first equation fits the data better.

Of course, guessing is not the most desirable way to determine the most appropriate straight line fit of the data. A more appropriate technique is the method of least squares.

Method of Least Squares

A straight line has the form $y = b_0 + b_1 x$. Formulas for finding b_0 and b_1 for the best-fitting line are given by

$$b_1 = \frac{S_{xy}}{S_{xx}}$$

$$b_0 = \bar{y} - b_1 \bar{x}$$

The supporting formulas from section VI.A.1 are repeated here for convenience:

$$S_{xx} = \sum_{i=1}^{n} x_i^2 - \frac{\left(\sum_{i=1}^{n} x_i\right)^2}{n}$$

$$S_{xy} = \sum_{i=1}^{n} x_i y_i - \frac{\sum_{i=1}^{n} x_i \sum_{i=1}^{n} y_i}{n}$$

$$S_{yy} = \sum_{i=1}^{n} y_i^2 - \frac{\left(\sum_{i=1}^{n} y_i\right)^2}{n}$$

where n is the number of data points.

Example 24.6

Recalling the data given in Table 24.1 and replacing x for T and y for V, we have

$$S_{xx} = \sum_{i=1}^{n} x_i^2 - \frac{\left(\sum_{i=1}^{n} x_i\right)^2}{n} = 950 - \frac{60^2}{4} = 50$$

$$S_{xy} = \sum_{i=1}^{n} x_i y_i - \frac{\sum_{i=1}^{n} x_i \sum_{i=1}^{n} y_i}{n} = 225 - \frac{(60)(14)}{4} = 15$$

$$S_{yy} = \sum_{i=1}^{n} y_i^2 - \frac{\left(\sum_{i=1}^{n} y_i\right)^2}{n} = 54 - \frac{14^2}{4} = 5$$

Solving for the coefficients, we obtain

$$b_1 = \frac{S_{xy}}{S_{xx}} = \frac{15}{50} = 0.3$$

$$b_0 = \bar{y} - b_1 \bar{x} = 3.5 - (0.3)(15) = -1$$

Thus, the best-fitting regression equation is given by

$$V = -1 + 0.3T \text{ or } y = -1 + 0.3x$$

and where $\sum_{i=1}^{n} e_i^2 = 0.5$ is minimized, as shown in Table 24.4.

Example 24.6 *(continued)*

Table 24.4 Residual values for the least squares regression line from Example 24.6.

$V' = -1 + 0.5T$				
T	*V*	*V'*	*e*	*e²*
10	2	2	0	0
15	3	3.5	−0.5	0.25
20	5	5	0	0
15	4	3.5	0.5	0.25
			$\sum e_i^2$	0.5

Confidence Interval for the Regression Line

As you might expect, confidence intervals can be calculated about the mean response at a given value of $x = x_0$. The $100(1 - \alpha)\%$ confidence interval is given by

$$\hat{y}_0 - t_{\alpha/2, n-2} S_\varepsilon \sqrt{\frac{1}{n} + \frac{(x_o - \bar{x})^2}{S_{XX}}} \le E\left[Y\middle|x = x_0\right] \le \hat{y}_0 + t_{\alpha/2, n-2} S_\varepsilon \sqrt{\frac{1}{n} + \frac{(x_o - \bar{x})^2}{S_{XX}}}$$

where

$$S_\varepsilon = \sqrt{\frac{\sum_{i=1}^{n} y_i^2 - n\bar{y}^2 - b_1 S_{XY}}{n - 2}}$$

is known as the standard error of the estimate.

Example 24.7

Compute the 95% confidence interval for the mean response using the data from Example 24.6 about $x_0 = 18$.

Using the results of Example 24.6 in conjunction with Table 24.1, we can compute

$$S_\varepsilon = \sqrt{\frac{54 - (4)(3.5)^2 - (0.2)(15)}{2}} = 0.5$$

$$\hat{y} = -1 + 0.3x = -1 + (0.3)(18) = 4.4$$

Example 24.7 *(continued)*

$$\bar{x} = 15$$

$$\bar{y} = 3.5$$

$$t_{\alpha/2,n-2} = t_{0.025,2} = 4.303$$

$$n = 4$$

Filling in the numbers for the confidence interval formula given earlier, we have

$$4.4 - (4.303)(0.5)\sqrt{\frac{1}{4} + \frac{(18-15)^2}{50}} \le E[Y|x = x_0] \le 4.4 + (4.303)(0.5)\sqrt{\frac{1}{4} + \frac{(18-15)^2}{50}}$$

$$2.9893 \le E[Y|x = x_0] \le 5.8107$$

It is important to note that this confidence interval applies only to the interval obtained at $x = x_0$, not the entire range of x values.

Prediction Interval for a Future Observation

In addition to confidence intervals, we can calculate a prediction interval about a future observation, y_0, at $x = x_0$. The $100(1 - \alpha)\%$ prediction interval is given by

$$\hat{y}_0 - t_{\alpha/2,n-2}s_\varepsilon\sqrt{1 + \frac{1}{n} + \frac{(x_o - \bar{x})^2}{S_{XX}}} \le y_0 \le \hat{y}_0 + t_{\alpha/2,n-2}s_\varepsilon\sqrt{1 + \frac{1}{n} + \frac{(x_o - \bar{x})^2}{S_{XX}}}$$

Example 24.8

Compute the 95% prediction interval for the next observation using the data from Example 24.7 about $x_0 = 18$.

Filling in the numbers obtained from Example 24.7, we have

$$4.4 - (4.303)(0.5)\sqrt{1 + \frac{1}{4} + \frac{(18-15)^2}{50}} \le y_0 \le 4.4 + (4.303)(0.5)\sqrt{1 + \frac{1}{4} + \frac{(18-15)^2}{50}}$$

$$1.8272 \le y_0 \le 6.9728$$

Notice that the width of the prediction interval is much wider than the corresponding confidence interval at $x = x_0$.

Hypothesis Test for Regression Coefficient b_1

Recall that b_1 represents the slope of the regression equation. Although we can test the slope of the line against any value, we typically test to determine whether the slope is zero. In this case, the following hypothesis test is appropriate:

$$H_0 : \beta_1 = 0$$

$$H_a : \beta_1 \neq 0$$

This hypothesis tests whether x can be considered a meaningful predictor of y. In other words, does a relationship exist between the two variables? The corresponding hypothesis test statistic is

$$t = \frac{b_1 - \beta_1}{s_{b_1}}$$

where

$$s_{b_1} = \sqrt{\frac{s_\varepsilon^2}{S_{xx}}} = \frac{s_\varepsilon}{\sqrt{S_{xx}}}$$

For a two-side hypothesis test, the test statistic is compared to $t_{\alpha/2, n-2}$ and rejected if

$$t > t_{\alpha/2, n-2} \text{ or } t < -t_{\alpha/2, n-2}$$

Example 24.9

Using the results obtained from the previous examples, test the following hypotheses at $\alpha = 0.05$:

$$H_0 : \beta_1 = 0$$

$$H_a : \beta_1 \neq 0$$

Filling in the numbers from the test statistics, we obtain

$$t = \frac{b_1 - \beta_1}{s_{b_1}} = \frac{0.3 - 0}{\frac{0.5}{\sqrt{50}}} = 4.24$$

The critical values of $t_{\alpha/2, n-2}$ are −4.303 and 4.303. Since the test statistics values are within these values, we do not reject H_0.

Multiple Linear Regression

When multiple predictor variables are used, regression is referred to as multiple linear regression. For example, a multiple linear regression model with k predictor variables uses a linear regression equation expressed as

$$Y = \beta_0 + \beta_1 x_1 + \beta_2 x_2 + \ldots + \beta_k x_k + \varepsilon$$

where

Y is the response

$x_1, x_2, \ldots, x_k$ are the values of the predictor variables

$\beta_0, \beta_1, \beta_2, \ldots, \beta_k$ are the linear regression coefficients

ε is the random error term

The random error terms in regression analysis are assumed to be normally distributed with a constant variance. These assumptions can be readily checked through residual analysis or residual plots. See hypothesis tests for regression coefficients discussed earlier. Note: Other regression techniques are available when the input and/or output variables are not continuous.

Multicollinearity occurs when two or more predictor variables in a multiple regression model are correlated. Multicollinearity may cause the coefficient estimates and significance tests for each predictor variable to be underestimated. Note: The presence of multicollinearity does not reduce the predictive capability of the model—only calculations regarding individual predictor variables. However, including correlated variables does add to the overall model complexity and will likely increase the cost of data collection, perhaps needlessly.

Due to the tediousness of the calculations involved in computing the coefficients in multiple regression, software programs are often employed.

MULTIVARIATE TOOLS

> Use and interpret multivariate tools such as principal components, factor analysis, discriminant analysis, multiple analysis of variance (MANOVA), etc., to investigate sources of variation. (Analyze)
>
> **Body of Knowledge VI.A.3**

Multivariate analysis comprises a variety of tools used to understand and reduce the data dimensions by analyzing the data covariance structure. The following common tools are used to support multivariate analysis:

- *Principal components* are used "to form a smaller number of uncorrelated variables from a large set of data. The goal of principal components analysis is to explain the maximum amount of variance with the fewest number of principal components." See Minitab 15. Principal components have wide applicability in the social sciences and market research.

- *Factor analysis* is used "to determine the underlying factors responsible for correlations in the data." See Minitab 15.

- *Discriminant analysis* is used "to classify observations into two or more groups if you have a sample with known groups. Discriminant analysis can also be used to investigate how variables contribute to group separation." See Minitab 15.

- *Multiple Analysis of Variance (MANOVA)* can be used to analyze both balanced and unbalanced experimental designs. MANOVA is used to "perform multivariate analysis of variance for balanced designed when you have more than one dependent variable. You can take advantage of the data covariance structure to simultaneously test the equality of means from different responses." See Minitab 15. The advantage of MANOVA over multiple one-way ANOVAs is that MANOVA controls the family error rate. By contrast, multiple one-way ANOVAs work to increase the alpha error rate.

Each of these tools will be explored through the use of examples.

Example 24.10

Using the census data collected in Table 24.5, perform a principal components analysis using Minitab. Determine which factors contribute the greatest to the variability.

Table 24.5 Census data for Examples 24.10 and 24.11. Obtained from Minitab.

Population	School	Employ	Health	Home
5.935	14.2	2.265	2.27	2.91
1.523	13.1	0.597	0.75	2.62
2.599	12.7	1.237	1.11	1.72
4.009	15.2	1.649	0.81	3.02
4.687	14.7	2.312	2.50	2.22
8.044	15.6	3.641	4.51	2.36
2.766	13.3	1.244	1.03	1.97
6.538	17.0	2.618	2.39	1.85
6.451	12.9	3.147	5.52	2.01
3.314	12.2	1.606	2.18	1.82
3.777	13.0	2.119	2.83	1.80
1.530	13.8	0.798	0.84	4.25
2.768	13.6	1.336	1.75	2.64
6.585	14.9	2.763	1.91	3.17

Example 24.10 *(continued)*

Setup:

Choose *Stat > Multivariate > Principal Components*. Select all five data fields for *Variables*. Select "correlations" for type of matrix. Select "Scree plot" in the *Graphics* dialog box. The resulting analysis is depicted in Figures 24.5 and 24.6.

```
Principal Component Analysis: Pop, School, Employ, Health, Home

Eigenanalysis of the Correlation Matrix

Eigenvalue   3.0289    1.2911    0.5725    0.0954    0.0121
Proportion    0.606     0.258     0.114     0.019     0.002
Cumulative    0.606     0.864     0.978     0.998     1.000


Variable        PC1       PC2       PC3       PC4       PC5
Pop           0.558     0.131    -0.008    -0.551     0.606
School        0.313     0.629     0.549     0.453    -0.007
Employ        0.568     0.004    -0.117    -0.268    -0.769
Health        0.487    -0.310    -0.455     0.648     0.201
Home         -0.174     0.701    -0.691    -0.015    -0.014
```

Figure 24.5   Example of a principal components analysis using the data given in Table 24.5.

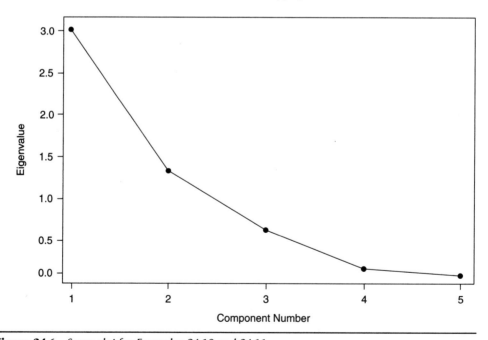

Scree Plot of Pop, ..., Home

Figure 24.6   Scree plot for Examples 24.10 and 24.11.

Example 24.10 *(continued)*

Analysis:

The eigenvalue row in the top table of Figure 24.5 provides the variance of each component. For instance, population has a variance of 3.0289. Notice the second and third row. Population, school, and employment contribute 60.6%, 25.8%, and 11.4%, respectively, to variability. Taken together, the first two factors account for 86.4% of the variability, while the first three account for 97.8%. The scree plot shown in Figure 24.6 is simply a graphic depiction of eigenvalues. Conceptually, this plot is similar to a Pareto chart of variances. The principal component score for factor 1 (that is, population) is given by

$$\text{PC1 Score} = 0.558Population + 0.313School + 0.568Employment \\ + 0.487Health - 0.174Home$$

Scores for the other factors can be determined in the same manner from the bottom table in Figure 24.5.

Example 24.11

Using the census data collected in Table 24.5, perform a factor analysis using Minitab.

Factor Analysis: Pop, School, Employ, Health, Home

Principal Component Factor Analysis of the Correlation Matrix

Unrotated Factor Loadings and Communalities

Variable	Factor1	Factor2	Factor3	Factor4	Factor5	Communality
Pop	0.972	0.149	-0.006	-0.170	0.067	1.000
School	0.545	0.715	0.415	0.140	-0.001	1.000
Employ	0.989	0.005	-0.089	-0.083	-0.085	1.000
Health	0.847	-0.352	-0.344	0.200	0.022	1.000
Home	-0.303	0.797	-0.523	-0.005	-0.002	1.000
Variance	3.0289	1.2911	0.5725	0.0954	0.0121	5.0000
% Var	0.606	0.258	0.114	0.019	0.002	1.000

Factor Score Coefficients

Variable	Factor1	Factor2	Factor3	Factor4	Factor5
Pop	0.321	0.116	-0.011	-1.782	5.511
School	0.180	0.553	0.726	1.466	-0.060
Employ	0.327	0.004	-0.155	-0.868	-6.988
Health	0.280	-0.272	-0.601	2.098	1.829
Home	-0.100	0.617	-0.914	-0.049	-0.129

Figure 24.7 Example of a factor analysis using the data given in Table 24.5.

Example 24.11 *(continued)*

Setup:
Choose *Stat > Multivariate > Factor Analysis*. Select all five data fields for *Variables*. Select "Scree plot" in the *Graphics* dialog box. The resulting analysis is depicted in Figures 24.6 and 24.7.
Analysis:
Although the five factors fit the data perfectly, we can see from the top table in Figure 24.7 that the last two factors (health and home) add little to the total variance. As a next step, we might consider performing two separate factor analyses—one for the first two components and one for the first three components.

Example 24.12

Using the salmon data collected in Table 24.6, perform a discriminant analysis using Minitab to be able to classify a newly caught salmon as being from Alaska or Canada.

Table 24.6 Salmon data for Example 24.12. Obtained from Minitab.

Salmon origin	Freshwater	Marine	Salmon origin	Freshwater	Marine
Alaska	108	368	Canada	129	420
Alaska	131	355	Canada	148	371
Alaska	105	469	Canada	179	407
Alaska	86	506	Canada	152	381
Alaska	99	402	Canada	166	377
Alaska	87	423	Canada	124	389
Alaska	94	440	Canada	156	419
Alaska	117	489	Canada	131	345
Alaska	79	432	Canada	140	362
Alaska	99	403	Canada	144	345
Alaska	114	428	Canada	149	393
Alaska	123	372	Canada	108	330
Alaska	123	372	Canada	135	355
Alaska	109	420	Canada	170	386
Alaska	112	394	Canada	152	301
Alaska	104	407	Canada	153	397
Alaska	111	422	Canada	152	301
Alaska	126	423	Canada	136	438
Alaska	105	434	Canada	122	306

Continued

Example 24.12 *(continued)*

Table 24.6 Salmon data for Example 24.12. Obtained from Minitab. *Continued*

Salmon origin	Freshwater	Marine	Salmon origin	Freshwater	Marine
Alaska	119	474	Canada	148	383
Alaska	114	396	Canada	90	385
Alaska	100	470	Canada	145	337
Alaska	84	399	Canada	123	364
Alaska	102	429	Canada	145	376
Alaska	101	469	Canada	115	354
Alaska	85	444	Canada	134	383
Alaska	109	397	Canada	117	355
Alaska	106	442	Canada	126	345
Alaska	82	431	Canada	118	379
Alaska	118	381	Canada	120	369
Alaska	105	388	Canada	153	403
Alaska	121	403	Canada	150	354
Alaska	85	451	Canada	154	390
Alaska	83	453	Canada	155	349
Alaska	53	427	Canada	109	325
Alaska	95	411	Canada	117	344
Alaska	76	442	Canada	128	400
Alaska	95	426	Canada	144	403
Alaska	87	402	Canada	163	370
Alaska	70	397	Canada	145	355
Alaska	84	511	Canada	133	375
Alaska	91	469	Canada	128	383
Alaska	74	451	Canada	123	349
Alaska	101	474	Canada	144	373
Alaska	80	398	Canada	140	388
Alaska	95	433	Canada	150	339
Alaska	92	404	Canada	124	341
Alaska	99	481	Canada	125	346
Alaska	94	491	Canada	153	352
Alaska	87	480	Canada	108	339

Example 24.12 *(continued)*

Setup:

Choose *Stat > Multivariate > Discriminant Analysis.* Select "Salmon Origin" for *Groups*. Select "Freshwater Marine" for *Predictors*. The resulting analysis is depicted in Figure 24.8.

```
Discriminant Analysis: SalmonOrigin versus Freshwater, Marine

Linear Method for Response: SalmonOrigin


Predictors: Freshwater, Marine


Group       Alaska      Canada
Count          50          50


Summary of classification

                     True Group
Put into Group    Alaska    Canada
Alaska               44         1
Canada                6        49
Total N              50        50
N correct            44        49
Proportion        0.880     0.980


N = 100            N Correct = 93          Proportion Correct = 0.930


Squared Distance Between Groups

           Alaska      Canada
Alaska    0.00000     8.29187
Canada    8.29187     0.00000


Linear Discriminant Function for Groups

              Alaska    Canada
Constant     -100.68    -95.14
Freshwater      0.37      0.50
Marine          0.38      0.33
```

Figure 24.8   Example of a discriminant analysis using the data given in Table 24.6.

Continued

Example 24.12 *(continued)*

```
Summary of Misclassified Observations

                                            Squared
Observation    True Group   Pred Group   Group   Distance   Probability
        1**      Alaska       Canada      Alaska    3.544       0.428
                                          Canada    2.960       0.572
        2**      Alaska       Canada      Alaska    8.1131      0.019
                                          Canada    0.2729      0.981
       12**      Alaska       Canada      Alaska    4.7470      0.118
                                          Canada    0.7270      0.882
       13**      Alaska       Canada      Alaska    4.7470      0.118
                                          Canada    0.7270      0.882
       30**      Alaska       Canada      Alaska    3.230       0.289
                                          Canada    1.429       0.711
       32**      Alaska       Canada      Alaska    2.271       0.464
                                          Canada    1.985       0.536
       71**      Canada       Alaska      Alaska    2.045       0.948
                                          Canada    7.849       0.052
```

Figure 24.8   Example of a discriminant analysis using the data given in Table 24.6. *Continued*

Analysis:

The probability of correctly classifying an Alaskan salmon is 88%, while the corresponding probability for a Canadian salmon is 98%. A newly caught fish can be identified by using the linear discriminant functions provided in Figure 24.8. The function providing the highest discriminant value would be used. The two functions are

$$Alaska = -100.68 + 0.37 Freshwater + 0.38 Marine$$

$$Canadian = -95.14 + 0.50 Freshwater + 0.33 Marine$$

Example 24.13

Using the plastic film data collected in Table 24.7, perform a MANOVA using Minitab to determine the optimum levels for extruding plastic film.

Setup:

Choose *Stat > ANOVA > Balanced MANOVA*. Select "Tear," "Gloss," and "Opacity" for *Responses*. Select "Extrusion" and "Additive" for *Model*. Select "Matrices (hypothesis, error, partial correlations)" and "Eigen analysis" in the *Results* dialog box. The resulting analysis is depicted in Figure 24.9.

Analysis:

The p values from the four statistical tests indicate that "Extrusion" and "Additive" are significant at $\alpha = 0.05$, while the interaction term "Extrusion * Additive" is not significant. The partial correlations matrix indicates that the three partial correlations (tear-opacity, gloss-tear, and opacity-gloss) are small. Therefore, a univariate ANOVA for the three responses may be acceptable. The eigenvalue analysis provides

Example 24.13 *(continued)*

Table 24.7 Plastic film data for Example 24.13. Obtained from Minitab.

Tear	Gloss	Opacity	Extrusion	Additive
6.5	9.5	4.4	1	1
6.2	9.9	6.4	1	1
5.8	9.6	3.0	1	1
6.5	9.6	4.1	1	1
6.5	9.2	0.8	1	1
6.9	9.1	5.7	1	2
7.2	10.0	2.0	1	2
6.9	9.9	3.9	1	2
6.1	9.5	1.9	1	2
6.3	9.4	5.7	1	2
6.7	9.1	2.8	2	1
6.6	9.3	4.1	2	1
7.2	8.3	3.8	2	1
7.1	8.4	1.6	2	1
6.8	8.5	3.4	2	1
7.1	9.2	8.4	2	2
7.0	8.8	5.2	2	2
7.2	9.7	6.9	2	2
7.5	10.1	2.7	2	2
7.6	9.2	1.9	2	2

```
ANOVA: Tear, Gloss, Opacity versus Extrusion, Additive

MANOVA for Extrusion
s = 1    m = 0.5    n = 6.0

                    Test                 DF
Criterion         Statistic     F   Num  Denom      P
Wilks'             0.38186   7.554    3     14   0.003
Lawley-Hotelling   1.61877   7.554    3     14   0.003
Pillai's           0.61814   7.554    3     14   0.003
Roy's              1.61877
```

Figure 24.9   Example of MANOVA using the data given in Table 24.7.

Continued

Example 24.13 *(continued)*

```
SSCP Matrix for Extrusion

                Tear      Gloss     Opacity
Tear           1.740     -1.504      0.8555
Gloss         -1.504      1.301     -0.7395
Opacity        0.855     -0.739      0.4205


SSCP Matrix for Error

                Tear      Gloss     Opacity
Tear           1.764      0.0200    -3.070
Gloss          0.020      2.6280    -0.552
Opacity       -3.070     -0.5520    64.924


Partial Correlations for the Error SSCP Matrix

                Tear        Gloss      Opacity
Tear           1.00000     0.00929    -0.28687
Gloss          0.00929     1.00000    -0.04226
Opacity       -0.28687    -0.04226     1.00000


EIGEN Analysis for Extrusion


Eigenvalue     1.619      0.00000    0.00000
Proportion     1.000      0.00000    0.00000
Cumulative     1.000      1.00000    1.00000


Eigenvector          1          2          3
Tear            0.6541     0.4315     0.0604
Gloss          -0.3385     0.5163     0.0012
Opacity         0.0359     0.0302    -0.1209


MANOVA for Additive
s = 1    m = 0.5    n = 6.0

                      Test                  DF
Criterion        Statistic      F    Num   Denom     P
Wilks'             0.52303    4.256    3      14   0.025
Lawley-Hotelling   0.91192    4.256    3      14   0.025
Pillai's           0.47697    4.256    3      14   0.025
Roy's              0.91192
```

Figure 24.9 Example of MANOVA using the data given in Table 24.7. *Continued*

Example 24.13 *(continued)*

```
SSCP Matrix for Additive

           Tear    Gloss    Opacity
Tear     0.7605   0.6825     1.931
Gloss    0.6825   0.6125     1.732
Opacity  1.9305   1.7325     4.901


EIGEN Analysis for Additive


Eigenvalue   0.9119    0.00000    0.00000
Proportion   1.0000    0.00000    0.00000
Cumulative   1.0000    1.00000    1.00000


Eigenvector        1          2          3
Tear          -0.6330     0.4480    -0.1276
Gloss         -0.3214    -0.4992    -0.1694
Opacity       -0.0684     0.0000     0.1102


MANOVA for Extrusion*Additive
s = 1    m = 0.5    n = 6.0

                          Test                  DF
Criterion              Statistic      F    Num  Denom      P
Wilks'                  0.77711    1.339    3    14    0.302
Lawley-Hotelling       0.28683    1.339    3    14    0.302
Pillai's               0.22289    1.339    3    14    0.302
Roy's                  0.28683


SSCP Matrix for Extrusion*Additive

            Tear      Gloss     Opacity
Tear      0.000500   0.01650    0.04450
Gloss     0.016500   0.54450    1.46850
Opacity   0.044500   1.46850    3.96050


EIGEN Analysis for Extrusion*Additive


Eigenvalue   0.2868    0.00000    0.00000
Proportion   1.0000    0.00000    0.00000
Cumulative   1.0000    1.00000    1.00000


Eigenvector        1          2          3
Tear          -0.1364     0.1806     0.7527
Gloss         -0.5376    -0.3028    -0.0228
Opacity       -0.0683     0.1102    -0.0000
```

Figure 24.9   Example of MANOVA using the data given in Table 24.7. *Continued*

Example 24.13 *(continued)*

insight into how the mean responses differ among the levels of the model terms. Only the first eigenvalues for both "Extrusion" and "Additive" are non-zero and therefore have any meaning. The highest absolute value of each eigenvalue for each of the first eigenvectors indicates that "Tear" has the greatest difference in means between the two levels. The second highest is for "Gloss," followed by "Opacity."

Multivariate tools are more complicated than many of the other quantitative tools in the Six Sigma professional's arsenal. Although they are powerful and easily implemented with statistical software, the interpretation of the results is more subjective and caution is required.

MULTI-VARI STUDIES

> Use and interpret charts of these studies and determine the difference between positional, cyclical, and temporal variation. (Analyze)
>
> **Body of Knowledge VI.A.4**

Multi-vari analysis is a powerful graphical technique for viewing multiple sources of process variation. Sources of variation are categorized into families of related causes and quantified to reveal the largest causes.

Typical categories are positional, cyclical, and temporal. *Positional variation* is often called within-part variation and refers to variation of a characteristic on the same product. *Cyclical variation* covers part-to-part variation. *Temporal variation* occurs as change over time. For example, a study of the variation in hardness of a metal part might involve collection of hardness data at different locations on the part for positional variation. The study might find average hardness on consecutive parts to detect patterns of cyclical variation. It might also involve the average hardness of parts selected from production on several days, providing information on the temporal variation.

Six Sigma professionals find multi-vari studies useful in their constant battle to reduce variation. This is because once the predominant type of variation has been identified, the list of possible causes is greatly reduced.

Example 24.14 *(Mini Case Study)*

A cast stainless steel part has a tight tolerance on its machined inner diameter because a piston that moves inside must make a good seal. The part is a closed-end cylinder with a cast "ear" on one side and is illustrated in Figure 24.10. The problem is that the pistons are leaking. Machinists consider this a nightmare design because the

Example 24.14 *(continued)*

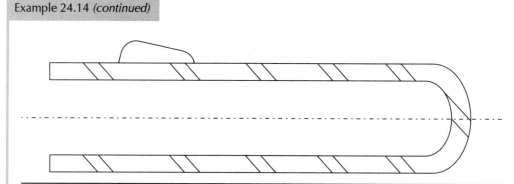

Figure 24.10   Stainless steel casting with critical ID.

walls are too thin, the depth is too great, and the dead end adds to the problems. A team has been assigned to work on the problem. One team member thinks the lathe chucks are clamping too tightly and squeezing the part out of round. Another member wants to change the tooling. Many of the ideas have been tried in the past with little improvement.

To initiate a multi-vari study, a data collection scheme that will capture types of variation must be designed. The data can be displayed on graphs that will aid in identifying the largest type of variation. To cover the within-part variation, the inside diameters (IDs) were measured at the top, middle, and bottom, as indicated by the section lines T, M, and B in Figure 24.11. Additional within-part variation was measured by checking for out-of-round conditions. To detect this out-of-round variation, the ID was measured at three different angles: 12 o'clock, 2 o'clock, and 4 o'clock, with 12 o'clock at the ear shown on the top.

To capture the variation over time, five pieces were selected at approximately equal time intervals during a shift. All measurements were obtained with a dial bore gage and recorded on the data sheet shown in Figure 24.11. The measurement results from five parts from one shift are shown in Table 24.8. What can be learned by looking at these numbers? Very little. Plotting the numbers on a graph, as shown in Figure 24.12, does point out an interesting pattern, however.

A visual review of Figure 24.12 may help answer the question, Which type of variation is most dominant: out-of-round, top-to-bottom, or part-to-part? Some help may come from drawing a different type of line for each type of variation, as shown in Figure 24.13. In this figure it is fairly clear that the most significant variation is caused by part-to-part differences; therefore, the team brainstormed possible causes for part-to-part variation. People with ideas on how to reduce other variation, such as out-of-round, were asked to hold those ideas until later. It was finally hypothesized that the part-to-part variation was caused by the casting process, and a new foundry that could do precision casting instead of investment casting was located. The new batch of precision cast parts arrived, and again five parts were selected from a shift. The machined parts were measured, and the results are shown in Table 24.9. Notice that a more discriminating measurement system was introduced for these castings. A graph of the data appears in Figure 24.14.

Example 24.14 *(continued)*

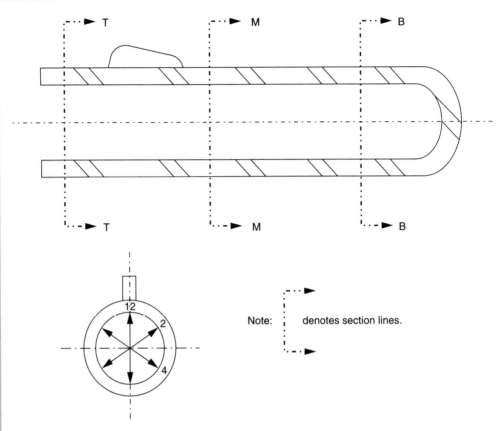

The 12 o'clock measurement is the diameter from 12 o'clock to 6 o'clock.
The 2 o'clock measurement is the diameter from 2 o'clock to 8 o'clock.
The 4 o'clock measurement is the diameter from 4 o'clock to 10 o'clock.

Angle	Section T-T	Section M-M	Section B-B
12 o'clock			
2 o'clock			
4 o'clock			

Figure 24.11 Data collection sheet.

Example 24.14 *(continued)*

Table 24.8 Casting data for Example 24.14.

Angle	Part #1			Part #2			Part #3			Part #4			Part #5		
	T	M	B	T	M	B	T	M	B	T	M	B	T	M	B
12	0.998	0.992	0.996	0.984	0.982	0.981	0.998	0.998	0.997	0.986	0.987	0.986	0.975	0.980	0.976
2	0.994	0.996	0.994	0.982	0.980	0.982	0.999	0.998	0.997	0.985	0.986	0.986	0.976	0.976	0.974
4	0.996	0.994	0.995	0.984	0.983	0.980	0.996	0.996	0.996	0.984	0.985	0.984	0.978	0.980	0.974

Example 24.14 *(continued)*

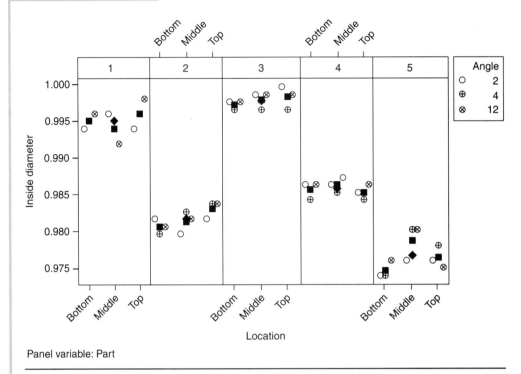

Figure 24.12 Multi-vari chart of data from Table 24.8.

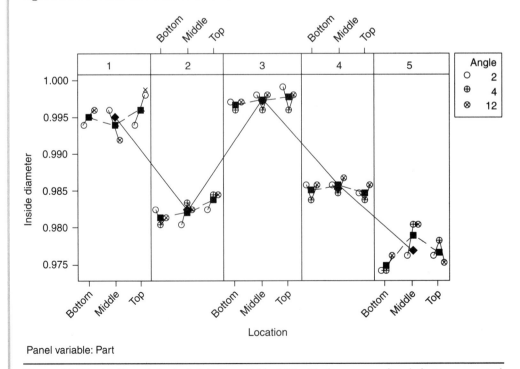

Figure 24.13 Multi-vari chart of data from Table 24.8 with the means of each factor connected by lines.

Example 24.14 *(continued)*

Table 24.9 Casting data for Example 24.14 with precision parts.

Angle	Part #1			Part #2			Part #3			Part #4			Part #5		
	T	M	B	T	M	B	T	M	B	T	M	B	T	M	B
12	0.9835	0.9845	0.9805	0.9815	0.9850	0.9830	0.9825	0.9820	0.9825	0.9845	0.9840	0.9830	0.9815	0.9810	0.9840
2	0.9820	0.9810	0.9825	0.9850	0.9825	0.9810	0.9850	0.9845	0.9845	0.9810	0.9825	0.9820	0.9845	0.9825	0.9815
4	0.9850	0.9830	0.9835	0.9830	0.9815	0.9845	0.9820	0.9830	0.9825	0.9825	0.9815	0.9810	0.9835	0.9835	0.9820

Example 24.14 *(continued)*

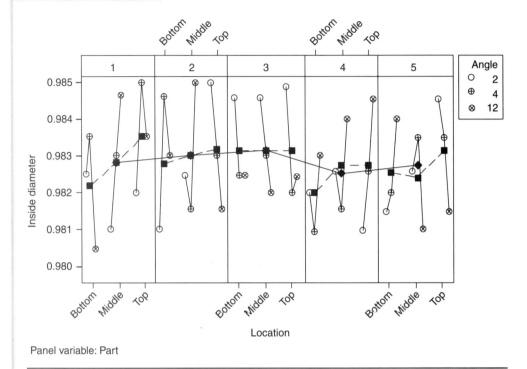

Panel variable: Part

Figure 24.14 Multi-vari chart of data from Table 24.9 with the means of each factor connected by lines.

Does it appear that the part-to-part variation has been reduced? Assuming that the part-to-part variation remains relatively small, which type of variation is now the most dominant? Figure 24.14 suggests that the out-of-round variation is now dominant.

The team then began to discuss possible causes for out-of-round variation. At this point some team members returned to the theory that chuck pressure was causing the part to be squeezed into an out-of-round contour. A round hole was then machined, and when the chuck pressure was released, the part snapped back to a round contour that left an out-of-round hole. They suggested a better pressure regulator for the air line feeding the pneumatic chuck. One observant person who focused on the top of the hole, where the out-of-round should be most prominent, noticed that sometimes the 12 o'clock dimension is the longest (as in part #4) and sometimes another dimension is longer (see the numbers in Table 24.9). Since the parts are always chucked with the same orientation, the chuck pressure could not be the cause. The team members wondered if there might be a pattern relating the various orientations and the diameters, so they placed orientation numbers by each dot, as shown in Figure 24.15, and tried to find a pattern. Unfortunately, no pattern was discovered and the relationship seemed to be random.

Example 24.14 *(continued)*

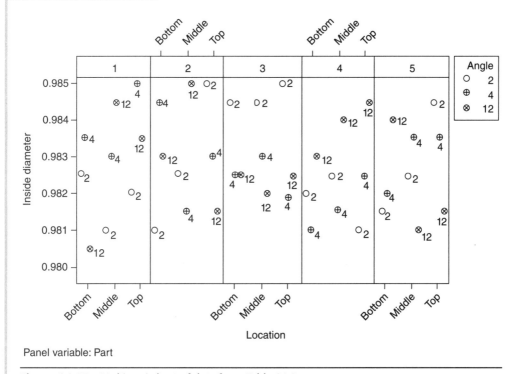

Figure 24.15   Multi-vari chart of data from Table 24.9.

So the question is, What could be causing random differences in diameters? At this point, a second shift operator mentioned the fact that after the ID is cut, a burnishing tool is passed across the surface. He said, "I don't think we get all the machining chips out before we burnish, and some of those chips may be burnished into the surface, causing small diameter differences." He suggested that the parts be removed from the chuck and pressure washed before the burnish operation. Some team members stated that this had been tried a year ago with no noticeable improvement. Others pointed out, however, that at that time the large part-to-part variation would have masked reduction in the minor variation now being seen. The team agreed that the pressure wash should be tried again. The resulting measurements are shown in Table 24.10.

Plotting this data in Figure 24.16 shows that the out-of-round variation has been noticeably reduced. One of the team members noticed a remaining pattern of variation and suggested a tooling change that reduced the variation even further.

Example 24.14 *(continued)*

Table 24.10 Casting data for Example 24.14 after pressure wash..

Angle	Part #1			Part #2			Part #3			Part #4			Part #5		
	T	M	B	T	M	B	T	M	B	T	M	B	T	M	B
12	0.9825	0.9825	0.9815	0.9830	0.9830	0.9815	0.9830	0.9820	0.9820	0.9820	0.9825	0.9820	0.9835	0.9830	0.9820
2	0.9835	0.9830	0.9825	0.9840	0.9830	0.9825	0.9835	0.9825	0.9820	0.9830	0.9825	0.9825	0.9840	0.9830	0.9825
4	0.9820	0.9820	0.9820	0.9832	0.9820	0.9820	0.9825	0.9825	0.9812	0.9820	0.9820	0.9820	0.9835	0.9830	0.9820

Example 24.14 *(continued)*

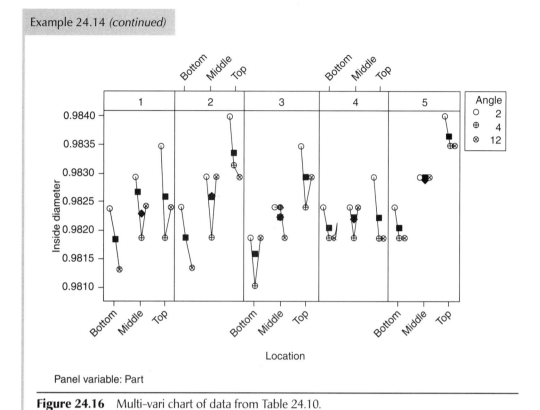

Figure 24.16   Multi-vari chart of data from Table 24.10.

Hopefully, the power of multi-vari analysis is evident from the examples. This simple graphical technique can be quickly applied and potential components of variation readily identified. However, it should be emphasized that this approach is not a substitute for performing an analytical investigation to determine actual statistical significance.

ATTRIBUTES DATA ANALYSIS

> Analyze attributes data using logit, probit, logistic regression, etc., to investigate sources of variation. (Analyze)
>
> **Body of Knowledge VI.A.5**

In sections VI.A.1 and VI.A.2, we looked at simple and multiple linear regression analysis, respectively. Though commonly used, these techniques are applicable when dealing with continuous variables. When the response variables are discrete, we must resort to the following types of tools:

- Binary logistic regression—The response variable for this type of regression has two distinct categories usually of the following type: yes/no, on/off, and so forth.

- Nominal logistic regression—The response variable for this type of regression has three or more distinct categories, but with no natural ordering. Such categories might include math/science/arts, apparel/tools/automotive, and so forth.

- Ordinal logistic regression—The response variable for this type of regression has three or more distinct categories, but with a natural ordering. Such categories might include survival level 1/level 2/level 3, first grade/second grade/third grade, and so forth.

Recall that with linear regression, an equation is derived that permits the prediction of an exact response variable value. However, logistic regression provides probabilities for each level of the response variable by finding a linear relationship between the predictor and response variables through the use of a link function.

A *link function* transforms probabilities of a response variable from the closed interval, (0,1), to a continuous scale that is unbounded. Once the transformation is complete, the relationship between the predictor and response variable can be modeled with linear regression. Three types of link functions are commonly used:

- Logit—The logit link function is of the form

$$g(p_i) = \log\left(\frac{p_i}{1 - p_i}\right)$$

- Normit or probit—The normit or probit link function is of the form

$$g(p_i) = \Phi^{-1}(p_i)$$

- Gompit—The gompit link function is of the form

$$g(p_i) = \log[-\log(1 - p_i)]$$

In these link functions, we have

$$p_i = \text{probabilities associated with each response variable}$$

$$\Phi^{-1} = \text{inverse cumulative standard normal function}$$

Link functions should be chosen to provide the best goodness-of-fit test results. Each of these tools will now be explored through the following examples.

Example 24.15

Using the resting pulse data collected in Table 24.11, perform a binary logistic regression analysis using Minitab.

Example 24.15 *(continued)*

Table 24.11 Resting pulse data for Example 24.15. Obtained from Minitab.

Resting pulse	Smokes	Weight		Resting pulse	Smokes	Weight
Low	No	140		Low	No	150
Low	No	145		High	Yes	180
Low	Yes	160		Low	No	160
Low	Yes	190		Low	No	135
Low	No	155		Low	No	160
Low	No	165		Low	Yes	130
High	No	150		Low	Yes	155
Low	No	190		Low	Yes	150
Low	No	195		Low	No	148
Low	No	138		High	No	155
High	Yes	160		Low	No	150
Low	No	155		High	Yes	140
High	Yes	153		Low	No	180
Low	No	145		Low	Yes	190
Low	No	170		High	No	145
Low	No	175		High	Yes	150
Low	Yes	175		Low	Yes	164
Low	Yes	170		Low	No	140
Low	Yes	180		Low	No	142
Low	No	135		High	No	136
Low	No	170		Low	No	123
Low	No	157		Low	No	155
Low	No	130		High	No	130
Low	Yes	185		Low	No	120
High	No	140		Low	No	130
Low	No	120		High	Yes	131
Low	Yes	130		Low	No	120
High	No	138		Low	No	118
High	Yes	121		Low	No	125

Continued

Example 24.15 *(continued)*

Table 24.11 Resting pulse data for Example 24.15. Obtained from Minitab. *Continued*

Resting pulse	Smokes	Weight		Resting pulse	Smokes	Weight
Low	No	125		High	Yes	135
High	No	116		Low	No	125
Low	No	145		High	No	118
High	Yes	150		Low	No	122
Low	Yes	112		Low	No	115
Low	No	125		Low	No	102
Low	No	190		Low	No	115
Low	No	155		Low	No	150
Low	Yes	170		Low	No	110
Low	No	155		High	No	116
Low	No	215		Low	Yes	108
Low	Yes	150		High	No	95
Low	Yes	145		High	Yes	125
Low	No	155		Low	No	133
Low	No	155		Low	No	110
Low	No	150		High	No	150
Low	Yes	155		Low	No	108

Setup:

Choose *Stat > Regression > Binary Logistic Regression*. Select "Resting Pulse" for *Response*. Select "Smokes" and "Weight" for *Model*. Select "Delta chi-square vs. probability" and "Delta chi-square vs. leverage" in the *Graphs* dialog box. Select "In addition, list of factor level values, tests for terms with more than 1 degree of freedom, and 2 additional goodness-of-fit tests" in the *Results* dialog box. The resulting analysis is depicted in Figures 24.17–24.19.

Example 24.15 *(continued)*

```
Binary Logistic Regression: RestingPulse versus Smokes, Weight

Link Function: Logit


Response Information

Variable        Value    Count
RestingPulse    Low        70     (Event)
                High       22
                Total      92



Factor Information

Factor    Levels    Values
Smokes      2       No, Yes



Logistic Regression Table

                                                        Odds        95% CI
Predictor          Coef      SE Coef       Z       P    Ratio    Lower   Upper
Constant        -1.98717    1.67930     -1.18   0.237
Smokes
  Yes           -1.19297    0.552980    -2.16   0.031   0.30     0.10    0.90
Weight          0.0250226   0.0122551    2.04   0.041   1.03     1.00    1.05


Log-Likelihood = -46.820
Test that all slopes are zero: G = 7.574, DF = 2, P-Value = 0.023



Goodness-of-Fit Tests

Method                   Chi-Square    DF       P
Pearson                    40.8477     47    0.724
Deviance                   51.2008     47    0.312
Hosmer-Lemeshow             4.7451      8    0.784
Brown:
General Alternative         0.9051      2    0.636
Symmetric Alternative       0.4627      1    0.496
```

Figure 24.17   Minitab session window output for the binary logistic regression based on data given in Table 24.9.

Continued

Example 24.15 *(continued)*

```
Table of Observed and Expected Frequencies:
(See Hosmer-Lemeshow Test for the Pearson Chi-Square Statistic)

                              Group
Value     1     2     3     4     5     6     7     8     9    10   Total
Low
  Obs     4     6     6     8     8     6     8    12    10     2      70
  Exp   4.4   6.4   6.3   6.6   6.9   7.2   8.3  12.9   9.1   1.9
High
  Obs     5     4     3     1     1     3     2     3     0     0      22
  Exp   4.6   3.6   2.7   2.4   2.1   1.8   1.7   2.1   0.9   0.1
Total     9    10     9     9     9     9    10    15    10     2      92


Measures of Association:
(Between the Response Variable and Predicted Probabilities)

Pairs         Number   Percent   Summary Measures
Concordant     1045     67.9     Somers' D                0.38
Discordant      461     29.9     Goodman-Kruskal Gamma    0.39
Ties             34      2.2     Kendall's Tau-a          0.14
Total          1540    100.0
```

Figure 24.17 Minitab session window output for the binary logistic regression based on data given in Table 24.9. *Continued*

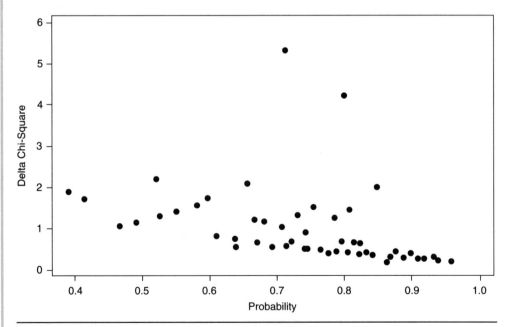

Figure 24.18 Delta chi-square versus probability analysis for Example 24.15.

Example 24.15 *(continued)*

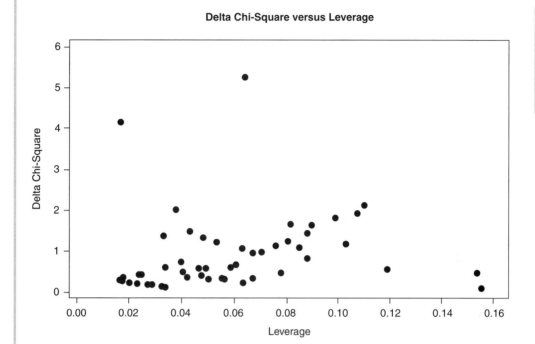

Figure 24.19   Delta chi–square versus leverage analysis for Example 24.15.

Analysis:

From Figure 24.17, we see that 70 individuals had a low resting pulse, while 22 were high. The logistic regression table indicates that the regression coefficients are not 0, due to the low p-values. However, the odds ratio for weight is close to 1, indicating that a 1-pound increase in weight has little practical effect on the resting pulse. The coefficient of -1.19297, along with an odds ratio of 0.3, indicates that individuals who smoke tend to have a higher resting pulse than individuals who don't smoke. Alternately, the odds ratio can be interpreted as the odds of smokers having 30% of the odds of nonsmokers having a low pulse for the same weight. The log-likelihood test indicates that there is sufficient evidence to conclude that at least one coefficient is not zero. Note the p-value is 0.023. All of the goodness-of-fit tests have p-values much greater than $\alpha = 0.05$, indicating that we should accept the null hypothesis that the model fits the data adequately. This is confirmed by observing the similarities of the observed and expected frequencies. The values for the summary measures range between 0 and 1. The higher the value, the better the predictability of the model. The highest summary measure value is 0.39, indicating that despite the adequacy of the model fit, it offers a low level of predictability.

Taken together, Figures 24.18 and 24.19 indicate that the model does not fit two observations very well. These two observations are evident by their high delta chi-square values.

Example 24.16

Using the subject and teaching method data collected in Table 24.12, perform a nominal logistic regression analysis using Minitab.

Table 24.12 Favorite subject data for Example 24.16. Obtained from Minitab.

Subject	Teaching method	Age
math	discuss	10
science	discuss	10
science	discuss	10
math	lecture	10
math	discuss	10
science	lecture	10
math	discuss	10
math	lecture	11
arts	lecture	11
science	discuss	11
arts	lecture	11
math	discuss	11
science	lecture	11
science	discuss	11
arts	lecture	11
science	lecture	12
science	lecture	12
science	discuss	12
arts	lecture	12
math	discuss	12
math	discuss	12
arts	lecture	12
arts	discuss	13
math	discuss	13
arts	lecture	13
arts	lecture	13
math	discuss	13
science	discuss	13
math	lecture	13
arts	lecture	13

Example 24.16 *(continued)*

Setup:

Choose *Stat* > *Regression* > *Nominal Logistic Regression.* Select "Subject" for *Response.* Select "Teaching Method" and "Age" for *Model.* Select "Teaching Method" for *Factors (optional).* Select "In addition, list of factor level values, tests for terms with more than 1 degree of freedom" in the *Results* dialog box. The resulting analysis is depicted in Figure 24.20.

```
Nominal Logistic Regression: Subject versus TeachingMethod, Age

Response Information

Variable    Value     Count
Subject     science     10    (Reference Event)
            math        11
            arts         9
            Total       30


Factor Information

Factor              Levels   Values
TeachingMethod           2   discuss, lecture


Logistic Regression Table

                                                               95%
                                                      Odds      CI
Predictor                Coef    SE Coef     Z      P  Ratio  Lower
Logit 1: (math/science)
Constant             -1.12266    4.56425  -0.25  0.806
TeachingMethod
 lecture             -0.563115   0.937591 -0.60  0.548  0.57   0.09
Age                   0.124674   0.401079  0.31  0.756  1.13   0.52
Logit 2: (arts/science)
Constant             -13.8485    7.24256  -1.91  0.056
TeachingMethod
 lecture              2.76992    1.37209   2.02  0.044 15.96   1.08
Age                   1.01354    0.584494  1.73  0.083  2.76   0.88
```

Figure 24.20 Minitab session window output for the nominal logistic regression based on data given in Table 24.9.

Continued

Example 24.16 *(continued)*

```
Predictor                    Upper
Logit 1: (math/science)
Constant
TeachingMethod
  lecture                     3.58
Age                          2.49
Logit 2: (arts/science)
Constant
TeachingMethod
  lecture                   234.91
Age                          8.66


Log-Likelihood = -26.446
Test that all slopes are zero: G = 12.825, DF = 4, P-Value = 0.012


Goodness-of-Fit Tests

Method      Chi-Square    DF       P
Pearson       6.95295     10    0.730
Deviance      7.88622     10    0.640
```

Figure 24.20   Minitab session window output for the nominal logistic regression based on data given in Table 24.9. *Continued*

Analysis:

Since the reference event is "science," Minitab produced logit functions for math and science and for language arts and science, as seen in Figure 24.20. The high *p*-values for the first logit function indicate that there is sufficient evidence to conclude that a change in the teaching method or age affected the choice of math as a favorite subject compared to science. However, due to the low *p*-values, the second logit function suggests that the teaching method or age affected the choice of language arts as a favorite subject compared to science. The large odds ratio of 15.96 indicates that the odds of choosing language arts over science are almost 16 times greater when the teaching method changes to a lecture. The log-likelihood test indicates that there is sufficient evidence to conclude that at least one coefficient is not zero. Both goodness-of-fit tests have *p*-values much greater than $\alpha = 0.05$, indicating that we should accept the null hypothesis that the model fits the data adequately.

Example 24.17

Using the toxicity data collected in Table 24.13, perform an ordinal logistic regression analysis using Minitab.

Example 24.17 *(continued)*

Table 24.13   Toxicity data for Example 24.17 Obtained from Minitab.

Survival	Region	Toxic level	Survival	Region	Toxic level
1	1	62.00	2	1	40.50
1	2	46.00	2	2	60.00
2	1	48.50	3	1	57.50
3	2	32.00	2	1	48.75
2	1	63.50	2	1	44.50
1	1	41.25	1	1	49.50
2	2	40.00	2	2	33.75
3	1	34.25	2	1	43.50
2	1	34.75	2	2	48.00
1	2	46.25	3	1	34.00
2	1	43.50	1	1	50.00
2	2	46.00	3	2	35.00
2	1	42.50	1	1	49.00
1	2	53.00	2	2	43.50
1	2	43.50	3	2	37.25
1	1	56.00	3	2	39.00
2	1	40.00	3	1	34.50
1	2	48.00	2	1	47.50
2	1	46.50	1	2	42.00
2	2	72.00	2	2	45.50
2	2	31.00	2	2	38.50
1	1	48.00	2	1	36.50
2	2	36.50	2	2	37.50
2	2	43.75	3	1	38.50
2	1	34.25	2	2	47.00
2	1	41.25	2	2	39.75
2	2	41.75	1	1	60.00
2	2	45.25	2	2	41.00
2	1	43.50	2	1	41.00

Continued

Example 24.17 *(continued)*

Table 24.13 Toxicity data for Example 24.17 Obtained from Minitab. *Continued*

Survival	Region	Toxic level	Survival	Region	Toxic level
2	2	53.00	3	1	30.00
3	1	38.00	2	2	45.00
2	2	59.00	2	2	51.00
2	1	52.50	2	2	35.25
2	2	42.75	1	2	40.50
2	2	31.50	2	2	39.50
2	2	43.50	3	2	36.00
2	2	40.00			

Setup:

Choose *Stat > Regression > Nominal Logistic Regression*. Select "Survival" for *Response*. Select "Region" and "Toxic Level" for *Model*. Select "Region" for *Factors (optional)*. Select "In addition, list of factor level values, tests for terms with more than 1 degree of freedom" in the *Results* dialog box. The resulting analysis is depicted in Figure 24.21.

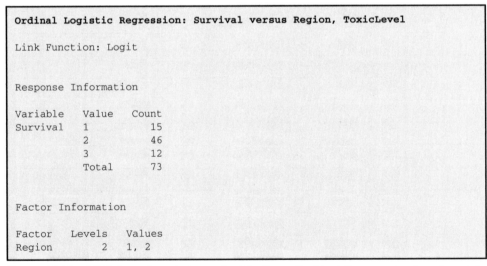

Figure 24.21 Minitab session window output for the ordinal logistic regression based on data given in Table 24.9.

Example 24.17 *(continued)*

```
Logistic Regression Table

                                                    Odds      95% CI
Predictor          Coef     SE Coef       Z      P  Ratio  Lower  Upper
Const(1)        -7.04343    1.68017   -4.19  0.000
Const(2)        -3.52273    1.47108   -2.39  0.017
Region
  2              0.201456   0.496153    0.41  0.685   1.22   0.46   3.23
ToxicLevel       0.121289   0.0340510   3.56  0.000   1.13   1.06   1.21


Log-Likelihood = -59.290
Test that all slopes are zero: G = 14.713, DF = 2, P-Value = 0.001


Goodness-of-Fit Tests

Method     Chi-Square     DF       P
Pearson      122.799     122   0.463
Deviance     100.898     122   0.918


Measures of Association:
(Between the Response Variable and Predicted Probabilities)

Pairs          Number   Percent   Summary Measures
Concordant       1127      79.3   Somers' D              0.59
Discordant        288      20.3   Goodman-Kruskal Gamma  0.59
Ties                7       0.5   Kendall's Tau-a        0.32
Total            1422     100.0
```

Figure 24.21   Minitab session window output for the ordinal logistic regression based on data given in Table 24.9. *Continued*

Analysis:

From Figure 24.21, we see that due to the high *p*-value of 0.685, we cannot conclude that region has a significant effect on survival time. In contrast, the low *p*-value for "toxic level" indicates that toxic level affects survival time. The log-likelihood test indicates that there is sufficient evidence to conclude that at least one coefficient is not zero. Both goodness-of-fit tests have *p*-values much greater than $\alpha = 0.05$, indicating that we should accept the null hypothesis that the model fits the data adequately. The values for the summary measures range between 0 and 1. The higher the value, the better the predictability of the model. In this example, the summary measure values range from 0.032 to 0.59, indicating the model fit offers a low-to-moderate level of predictability.

Although more complicated to perform and interpret, logistic regressions permit us to develop models that fit categorical regressor and response variables, thus overcoming the limitation inherent to simple and multiple regression analyses.

Chapter 25

Hypothesis Testing

TERMINOLOGY

> Define and interpret the significance level,
> power, type I, and type II errors of statistical tests.
> (Evaluate)
>
> **Body of Knowledge VI.B.1**

Every hypothesis test uses samples to infer properties of a population on the basis of an analysis of a sample. Therefore, there is some chance that although the analysis is flawless, the conclusion may be incorrect. These sampling errors are not errors in the usual sense, because they can't be corrected (without using 100% sampling with no measurement errors).

Two types of errors can be made when testing hypotheses:

- Type I error—This error occurs when the null hypothesis is rejected when it is true. We refer to the P(Type I error) = P(rejecting H_0 when H_0 is true) = α. A Type I error is also known as an α error and error of the first kind. The P(Type I error) is also known as α-value, producer's risk, level of significance, and significance level (see the note accompanying the definition of p-value).

- Type II error—This error occurs when the alternative hypothesis is accepted when it is false. We refer to the P(Type II error) = P(not rejecting H_0 when H_0 is false) = β. A Type II error is also known as a β error and error of the second kind. The P(Type II error) is also known as β-value or consumer's risk.

Figure 25.1 illustrates the relationship between Type I and Type II errors.

Concepts related to Type I and Type II errors include p-value and power. These terms are defined as:

- p-value—This is the *smallest* level of significance leading to the rejection of the null hypothesis. (Note: In Minitab, we look for a p-value less than our stated α-value in order to reject the null hypothesis. Some authors have used a level of significance and/or significance level synonymous with p-value.)

- Power—This is the probability of rejecting the null hypothesis when the alternative is true. We write this as P(rejecting $H_0 | H_0$ is not true) = $1 - \beta$.

		Nature (true condition)	
		H_0 is true	H_0 is false
Conclusion	H_0 is rejected	Type I error P (Type I) $= \alpha$	**Correct decision**
	H_0 is not rejected	**Correct decision**	Type II error P (Type II) $= \beta$

Figure 25.1   Four outcomes associated with statistical hypotheses.

The stronger the power of a hypothesis test, the more sensitive it is to detecting small differences.

STATISTICAL VS. PRACTICAL SIGNIFICANCE

Define, compare, and interpret statistical and practical significance. (Evaluate)

Body of Knowledge VI.B.2

In some situations it may be possible to detect a statistically significant difference between two populations when the difference has no practical importance. For example, suppose that a test is devised to determine whether there is a statistically significant difference in the surface finish when a lathe is operated at 400 rpm and at 700 rpm. If large sample sizes are used, it may be possible to determine that the 400 rpm population has a tiny, but statistically significant improved surface. However, if both speeds produce surface finishes capable of meeting the specifications, it may be better to go with the faster speed because of its associated increase in throughput. Thus, we must ask ourselves, What does it take to translate a statistical significant difference into a practical significant difference? How much time, effort, cost, and energy are required? Is it worth it? For example, Can we just change the setting on the machine to achieve 700 rpm or is it necessary to purchase another costly machine?

SAMPLE SIZE

Calculate sample size for common hypothesis tests (e.g., equality of means, equality of proportions, etc.). (Apply)

Body of Knowledge VI.B.3

In order to make a statistically significant decision, it is important that a hypothesis test and confidence intervals use the proper sample size.

Table 25.1 incorporates some of the most commonly used sample size formulas for the following:

Table 25.1 Sample size formulas. Always round n up to the next highest integer.

Parameter	Sample size formula	Purpose
μ	$$n = \left(\frac{z_{\alpha/2}\sigma}{E}\right)^2$$	Estimating the mean μ of a normal distribution with known variance σ^2. Replace $z_{\alpha/2}$ with z_α for a one-sided alternative hypothesis.
p	$$n = \left(\frac{z_{\alpha/2}}{E}\right)^2 \hat{p}(1-\hat{p})$$	Estimating the proportion p with an initial estimate $\hat{p}$. Replace $z_{\alpha/2}$ with z_α for a one-sided alternative hypothesis.
μ	$$n = \frac{\left(z_{\alpha/2}+z_\beta\right)^2 \sigma^2}{E^2} ; E = \mu - \mu_0$$	Detecting a difference of size E from the mean μ from a normal distribution with known variance σ^2. Replace $z_{\alpha/2}$ with z_α for a one-sided alternative hypothesis.
p	$$n = \frac{z_{\alpha/2}\sqrt{p_0(1-p_0)}+z_\beta\sqrt{p(1-p)}}{p-p_0}$$	Detecting a difference in the true population proportion μ.
$\mu_1 - \mu_2$	$$n = n_1 = n_2 = \frac{\left(z_{\alpha/2}+z_\beta\right)^2 \left(\sigma_1^2+\sigma_2^2\right)}{E^2}$$	Detecting a true difference of size E between population means from normal distributions. Replace $z_{\alpha/2}$ with z_α for a one-sided alternative hypothesis.
$\mu_1 - \mu_2$	$$n = n_1 = n_2 = \frac{\left(z_{\alpha/2}\right)^2 \left(\sigma_1^2+\sigma_2^2\right)}{E^2}$$	Detecting a difference of size E between population means from normal distributions and known variances σ_1^2 and σ_2^2 when estimating $\mu_1 - \mu_2$ by $\bar{X}_1 - \bar{X}_2$. Replace $z_{\alpha/2}$ with z_α for a one-sided alternative hypothesis.
$p_1 - p_2$	$$n = n_1 = n_2 = \frac{\left[z_{\alpha/2}\sqrt{(p_1+p_2)\dfrac{(q_1+q_2)}{2}}+z_\beta\sqrt{p_1 q_1+p_2 q_2}\right]^2}{\left(p_1-p_2\right)^2}$$ $$q = 1-p$$	Detecting a difference between two proportions. Replace $z_{\alpha/2}$ with z_α for a one-sided alternative hypothesis.

- Means

- Difference between means

- Proportions

- Difference between proportions

All of the sample size formulas given in Table 25.1 reflect a two-sided alternative hypothesis. However, it is easy to obtain the one-sided alternative hypothesis formula by simply substituting $z_{\alpha/2}$ with z_{α}. Note that z_{β} is *not* changed.

Also note that the formulas given in Table 25.1 will most likely generate non-integer sample sizes. When this occurs, always round up to the next whole number to ensure statistically valid conclusions based on the stated α and β values.

Example 25.1

A Six Sigma professional wants to determine with 95% confidence whether the mean diameter of a fiber optic cable differs by 0.5 mm. From past experience it is known that $\sigma = 2$ mm.

From Appendix 12, we know that $z_{\alpha/2} = 1.96$. Also, we have

$$\alpha = 0.05$$

$$\sigma = 2$$

$$E = 0.5$$

We will use the following formula from Table 25.1 for our problem:

$$n = \left(\frac{z_{\alpha/2}\sigma}{E} \right)^2$$

Filling in the numbers, we obtain

$$n = \left(\frac{z_{\alpha/2}\sigma}{E} \right)^2 = \left[\frac{(1.96)(2)}{0.5} \right]^2 = 61.47 \Rightarrow 62$$

Thus, a sample size of 62 is required.

Example 25.2

A Six Sigma professional wants to determine with 95% confidence whether the true proportion defective in a lot of fiber optic cable is no larger than 0.05. From past experience, we estimate p using $\hat{p} = 0.15$.

From Appendix 12, we know that $z_{\alpha/2} = 1.96$. Also, we have

$$\alpha = 0.05$$

$$E = 0.05$$

Example 25.2 *(continued)*

We will use the following formula from Table 25.1 for our problem:

$$n = \left(\frac{z_{\alpha/2}}{E}\right)^2 \hat{p}(1-\hat{p})$$

Filling in the numbers, we obtain

$$n = \left(\frac{z_{\alpha/2}}{E}\right)^2 \hat{p}(1-\hat{p}) = \left(\frac{1.96}{0.05}\right)^2 (0.15)(1-0.15) = 196.92 \Rightarrow 197$$

Thus, a sample size of 197 is required. However, it might be more practical to sample an even 200 units of fiber optic cable.

POINT AND INTERVAL ESTIMATES

Define and distinguish between confidence and prediction intervals. Define and interpret the efficiency and bias of estimators. Calculate tolerance and confidence intervals. (Evaluate)

Body of Knowledge VI.B.4

Unbiased Estimators

An *unbiased estimator* is a point estimate of a parameter such that the expected value of the estimate equals the parameter. Mathematically, we write this as $E(\hat{\theta}) = \theta$.

Example 25.3

The sample variance is written as

$$s^2 = \frac{\sum_{i=1}^{n}(X_i - \bar{X})^2}{n-1}$$

Maybe you have wondered why it isn't written as

$$s^2 = \frac{\sum_{i=1}^{n}(X_i - \bar{X})^2}{n}$$

Example 25.3 *(continued)*

The reason is that

$$E(s^2) = E\left[\frac{\sum_{i-1}^{n}\left(X_i - \bar{X}\right)^2}{n-1}\right] = \sigma^2$$

The

$$E(s^2) = E\left[\frac{\sum_{i=1}^{n}\left(X_i - \bar{X}\right)^2}{n}\right] \neq \sigma^2$$

Readers who are interested in the specific mathematics of why this is true are encouraged to read a more advanced book on statistics.

Efficient Estimators

Efficiency is one measure of an estimator. If we have an unbiased estimator, T, the efficiency of the estimator is given by $e(T) = \dfrac{1/\Psi(\theta)}{\text{var}(T)}$ such that $e(T) \leq 1$ and where $\Psi(\theta)$ is known as the Fisher transformation. When $e(T) = 1$ for all values of the parameter θ, the estimator is said to be efficient.

Prediction Intervals

A *prediction interval* is similar to a confidence interval, but it is based on the predicted value that is likely to contain the values of future observations. It will be wider than the confidence interval because it contains bounds on individual observations rather than a bound on the mean of a group of observations. The $100(1 - \alpha)\%$ prediction interval for a single future observation from a normal distribution is given by

$$\bar{X} - t_{\alpha/2}s\sqrt{1+\frac{1}{n}} \leq X_{n+1} \leq \bar{X} + t_{\alpha/2}s\sqrt{1+\frac{1}{n}}$$

Example 25.4

A Six Sigma professional wants to determine the 95% prediction interval on the 26th observation of a piece of fiber optic cable. The 25 observations yielded $\bar{X} = 15$; $s = 2$.

Example 25.4 *(continued)*

From Appendix 14, we know that $t_{\alpha/2} = 2.064$. Also, we have

$$\alpha = 0.05$$

$$n = 25$$

$$\bar{X} = 15$$

$$s = 2$$

Filling in the numbers, we obtain

$$15 - (2.064)(2)\sqrt{1 + \frac{1}{25}} \leq X_{26} \leq 15 + (2.064)(2)\sqrt{1 + \frac{1}{25}}$$

$$10.7902 \leq X_{26} \leq 19.2093$$

Tolerance Intervals

A *tolerance interval* (also known as a statistical tolerance interval) is an interval estimator determined from a random sample so as to provide a level of confidence that the interval covers at least a specified proportion of the sampled population. The lower tolerance limit (*LTL*) and the upper tolerance limit (*UTL*) are given by

$$LTL : \bar{X} - Ks$$

$$UTL : \bar{X} + Ks$$

where

$\bar{X}$ = sample mean

s = sample standard deviation

K = a factor found in Appendices 26 and 27

Like confidence intervals, tolerance intervals may be one sided or two sided.

Example 25.5

A 15-piece sample from a process has a mean of $\bar{X} = 10.821$ and a standard deviation of $s = 0.027$. Find the tolerance interval so that there is 95% confidence that it will contain 99% of the population.

From Appendix 27, we know that $K = 3.867$. Also, we have

$$\alpha = 0.05$$

$$n = 15$$

$$\bar{X} = 10.821$$

$$s = 0.027$$

Filling in the numbers, we obtain

$$LTL = \bar{X} - Ks = 10.821 - (3.867)(0.027) = 10.7166$$
$$UTL = \bar{X} + Ks = 10.821 + (3.867)(0.027) = 10.9254$$

Point Estimates and Confidence Intervals

A *point estimate* is a statistic used to estimate a parameter of a population. Examples include the sample mean and sample proportion defective. However, point estimates provide no information regarding how close the estimate is to the actual population parameter. In other words, how well does $\bar{X}$, the sample mean, estimate μ, the population mean?

To address this question, we turn our attention to one type of interval estimate known as a confidence interval. A *confidence interval* is defined mathematically as

$$P(\text{lower limit} \leq parameter \leq \text{upper limit}) = 1 - \alpha$$

Both the lower and upper limits are determined by the parameter and the sample data and are referred to as confidence limits. $(1 - \alpha)$ is known as the confidence level. Confidence intervals may be one sided (for example, lower or upper) or two sided.

In simpler terms, a confidence interval represents the degree of certainty to which the interval contains the true population parameter.

Confidence Intervals for Means

Table 25.2 provides seven commonly used confidence intervals for means.

Table 25.2 Confidence intervals for means.

Test name	Assumption	$100(1 - \alpha)\%$ confidence interval
z test for a population mean	Variance known, normal	$\bar{X} - z_{\alpha/2}\dfrac{\sigma}{\sqrt{n}} \leq \mu \leq \bar{X} + z_{\alpha/2}\dfrac{\sigma}{\sqrt{n}}$
z test for two population means	Variances known and equal, normal	$(\bar{X}_1 - \bar{X}_2) - z_{\alpha/2}\sigma\sqrt{\dfrac{1}{n_1} + \dfrac{1}{n_2}} \leq (\mu_1 - \mu_2) \leq (\bar{X}_1 - \bar{X}_2) + z_{\alpha/2}\sigma\sqrt{\dfrac{1}{n_1} + \dfrac{1}{n_2}}$
z test for two population means	Variances known and unequal, normal	$(\bar{X}_1 - \bar{X}_2) - z_{\alpha/2}\sqrt{\dfrac{\sigma_1^2}{n_1} + \dfrac{\sigma_2^2}{n_2}} \leq (\mu_1 - \mu_2) \leq (\bar{X}_1 - \bar{X}_2) + z_{\alpha/2}\sqrt{\dfrac{\sigma_1^2}{n_1} + \dfrac{\sigma_2^2}{n_2}}$
t test for a population mean	Variance unknown, normal	$\bar{X} - t_{\alpha/2,n-1}\dfrac{s}{\sqrt{n}} \leq \mu \leq \bar{X} + t_{\alpha/2,n-1}\dfrac{s}{\sqrt{n}}$ $s = \sqrt{\dfrac{\left(X_i - \bar{X}\right)^2}{n-1}}$
t test for two population means	Variances unknown and equal, normal	$(\bar{X}_1 - \bar{X}_2) - t_{\alpha/2,n_1+n_2-2}s_p\sqrt{\dfrac{1}{n_1} + \dfrac{1}{n_2}} \leq (\mu_1 - \mu_2) \leq (\bar{X}_1 - \bar{X}_2) + t_{\alpha/2,n_1+n_2-2}s_p\sqrt{\dfrac{1}{n_1} + \dfrac{1}{n_2}}$ $s_p = \dfrac{(n_1-1)s_1^2 + (n_2-1)s_2^2}{n_1 + n_2 - 2}$

Table 25.2   Confidence intervals for means. *Continued*

Test name	Assumption	$100(1 - \alpha)\%$ confidence interval
t test for population means	Variances unknown and unequal, normal	$(\bar{X}_1 - \bar{X}_2) - t_{\alpha/2,\nu}\sqrt{\dfrac{s_1^2}{n_1} + \dfrac{s_2^2}{n_2}} \leq (\mu_1 - \mu_2) \leq (\bar{X}_1 - \bar{X}_2) + t_{\alpha/2,\nu}\sqrt{\dfrac{s_1^2}{n_1} + \dfrac{s_2^2}{n_2}}$ $$\nu = \frac{\left(\dfrac{s_1^2}{n_1} + \dfrac{s_2^2}{n_2}\right)^2}{\dfrac{\left(s_1^2/n_1\right)^2}{n_1 - 1} + \dfrac{\left(s_2^2/n_2\right)^2}{n_2 - 1}}$$ Round ν down to the next whole number
t test for population means (paired *t* test)	Each data element in one population is paired with one data element in the other population, normal	$\bar{D} - t_{\alpha/2,n-1}\,s_D/\sqrt{n} \leq \mu_D \leq \bar{D} + t_{\alpha/2,n-1}\,s_D/\sqrt{n}$ $$s_D = \sqrt{\frac{\sum_{i=1}^{n}\left(D_i - \bar{D}\right)^2}{n-1}}$$ $\bar{D}$ = average of the n differences $D_1, D_2, \ldots, D_n$

Example 25.6

Suppose an estimate is needed for the average coating thickness for a population of 1000 circuit boards received from a supplier. Rather than measure the coating thickness on all 1000 boards, one might randomly select a sample of 36 for measurement. Suppose that the average coating thickness on these 36 boards is 0.003, and the standard deviation of the 36 coating measurements is 0.0005. The standard deviation is assumed known from past experience. Determine the 95% confidence interval for the true mean.

From Appendix 12, we know that $z_{\alpha/2} = 1.96$. Also, we have

$$\alpha = 0.05$$

$$\bar{X} = 0.003$$

$$\sigma = 0.0005$$

$$n = 36$$

We will use the following formula from Table 25.2 for our problem:

$$\bar{X} - z_{\alpha/2} \frac{\sigma}{\sqrt{n}} \le \mu \le \bar{X} + z_{\alpha/2} \frac{\sigma}{\sqrt{n}}$$

Filling in the numbers, we obtain

$$0.003 - (1.96)\frac{0.0005}{\sqrt{36}} \le \mu \le 0.003 + (1.96)\frac{0.0005}{\sqrt{36}}$$

$$0.00284 \le \mu \le 0.00316$$

Thus, the 95% confidence interval for the mean is (0.00284, 0.00316).

Confidence Intervals for Variances

Table 25.3 provides three commonly used confidence intervals for variances or ratios of variances.

Table 25.3 Confidence intervals for variances.

Test name	Assumption	$100(1 - \alpha)\%$ confidence interval
χ^2 test between a sample variance and an assumed population variance σ_0^2	Sample is drawn from a normal population	$\dfrac{(n-1)s^2}{\chi^2_{\alpha/2,n-1}} \le \sigma^2 \le \dfrac{(n-1)s^2}{\chi^2_{1-\alpha/2,n-1}}$
F test for two population variances	Both samples are taken from a normal distribution	$\dfrac{s_1^2}{s_2^2} f_{1-\alpha/2,v_2,v_1} \le \dfrac{\sigma_1^2}{\sigma_2^2} \le \dfrac{s_1^2}{s_2^2} f_{\alpha/2,v_2,v_1}$
χ^2 test between a population variance and an assumed variance σ_0^2	Sample is taken from a normal distribution	$\dfrac{(n-1)s^2}{\chi^2_{\alpha/2,n-1}} \le \sigma^2 \le \dfrac{(n-1)s^2}{\chi^2_{1-\alpha/2,n-1}}$

Example 25.7

Let's assume the same data given in Example 25.6 with the exception that the variance is not known and our sampling process yields $s = 0.1$. Determine the 95% confidence interval for the true variance.

From Appendix 15, we know that $\chi^2_{\alpha/2,n-1} = 53.203$; $\chi^2_{1-\alpha/2,n-1} = 53.203$. Also, we have

$$\alpha = 0.05$$

$$\bar{X} = 0.003$$

$$s = 0.1$$

$$n = 36$$

We will use the following formula from Table 25.3 for our problem:

$$\frac{(n-1)s^2}{\chi^2_{\alpha/2,n-1}} \le \sigma^2 \le \frac{(n-1)s^2}{\chi^2_{1-\alpha/2,n-1}}$$

Filling in the numbers, we obtain

$$\frac{(35)(0.1)^2}{53.203} \le \sigma^2 \le \frac{(35)(0.1)^2}{20.569}$$

$$0.00658 \le \sigma^2 \le 0.01702$$

Thus, the 95% confidence interval for the variance is (0.00658, 0.01702).

Confidence Intervals for Proportions

Table 25.4 provides two commonly used confidence intervals for proportions.

Table 25.4 Confidence intervals for proportions.

Test name	Assumption	$100(1-\alpha)\%$ confidence interval
z test for a given proportion p_0	Same size, $n \geq 30$	$\hat{p} - z_{\alpha/2}\sqrt{\dfrac{\hat{p}(1-\hat{p})}{n}} \leq p \leq \hat{p} + z_{\alpha/2}\sqrt{\dfrac{\hat{p}(1-\hat{p})}{n}}$ $\hat{p} = \dfrac{X}{n}$; X is the number of observations of interest in the respective sample
z test of the equality of two proportions	Same size, $n \geq 30$	$(\hat{p}_1 - \hat{p}_2) - z_{\alpha/2}\sqrt{\dfrac{\hat{p}_1(1-\hat{p}_1)}{n_1} + \dfrac{\hat{p}_2(1-\hat{p}_2)}{n_2}} \leq (p_1 - p_2) \leq (\hat{p}_1 - \hat{p}_2) + z_{\alpha/2}\sqrt{\dfrac{\hat{p}_1(1-\hat{p}_1)}{n_1} + \dfrac{\hat{p}_2(1-\hat{p}_2)}{n_2}}$ $\hat{p}_1 = \dfrac{X_1}{n_1}$; $\hat{p}_2 = \dfrac{X_2}{n_2}$; X_1, X_2 are the numbers of observations of interest in their respective samples

Example 25.8

Let's assume the same data given in Example 25.6 with the exception that our sampling process yields four defectives. Determine the 95% confidence interval for the true proportion.

From Appendix 12, we know that $z_{\alpha/2}$ = 1.96. Also, we have

$$\alpha = 0.05$$

$$\hat{p} = \frac{4}{36} = 0.1111$$

$$n = 36$$

We will use the following formula from Table 25.4 for our problem:

$$\hat{p} - z_{\alpha/2}\sqrt{\frac{\hat{p}(1-\hat{p})}{n}} \leq p \leq \hat{p} + z_{\alpha/2}\sqrt{\frac{\hat{p}(1-\hat{p})}{n}}$$

Filling in the numbers, we obtain

$$0.1111 - (1.96)\sqrt{\frac{(0.1111)(1-0.1111)}{36}} \leq p \leq 0.1111 + (1.96)\sqrt{\frac{(0.1111)(1-0.1111)}{36}}$$

$$0.00844 \leq p \leq 0.21376$$

Thus, the 95% confidence interval for the proportion is (0.00844, 0.21376).

TESTS FOR MEANS, VARIANCES, AND PROPORTIONS

> Use and interpret the results of hypothesis tests
> for means, variances, and proportions. (Evaluate)
>
> **Body of Knowledge VI.B.5**

Hypothesis Tests

To ensure that hypothesis tests are carried out properly, it is useful to have a well-defined process for conducting them:

1. Specify the parameter to be tested

2. State the null and alternative hypotheses (H_0, H_A)

3. State the α value

4. Determine the test statistic

5. Define the rejection criteria

6. Compute the critical values

7. Compute the test statistic

8. State the conclusion of the test

Note that the null hypothesis is either rejected or not rejected. It is never accepted.

Many Six Sigma professionals like to conduct hypothesis tests using a two-sided alternative hypothesis. On the surface this may seem correct. However, one should recognize that the job of the Six Sigma professional is to improve things. This suggests a one-sided hypothesis test. Of course, the direction of the alternative hypothesis depends on which direction represents "better." This does not mean that we should abandon the two-sided alternative hypothesis; it just means that we need to think more carefully about which alternative hypothesis is more appropriate.

Hypothesis Tests for Means

Table 25.5 provides seven commonly used hypothesis tests for means.

Table 25.5   Hypothesis tests for means.

Test name	Assumption	Test statistic	Null hypothesis	Alternative hypotheses	Rejection criteria
z test for a population mean	Variance known, normal	$z_0 = \dfrac{\bar{X} - \mu_0}{\sigma/\sqrt{n}}$	$\mu = \mu_0$	$\mu \neq \mu_0$ $\mu > \mu_0$ $\mu < \mu_0$	$\lvert z_0 \rvert > z_{\alpha/2}$ $z_0 > z_\alpha$ $z_0 < -z_\alpha$
z test for two population means	Variances known and equal, normal	$z_0 = \dfrac{(\bar{X}_1 - \bar{X}_2) - (\mu_1 - \mu_2)}{\sigma\sqrt{\dfrac{1}{n_1} + \dfrac{1}{n_2}}}$ $\delta = \mu_1 - \mu_2$	$\mu_1 - \mu_2 = \delta$	$\mu_1 - \mu_2 \neq \delta$ $\mu_1 - \mu_2 > \delta$ $\mu_1 - \mu_2 < \delta$	$\lvert z_0 \rvert > z_{\alpha/2}$ $z_0 > z_\alpha$ $z_0 < -z_\alpha$
z test for two population means	Variances known and unequal, normal	$z_0 = \dfrac{(\bar{X}_1 - \bar{X}_2) - (\mu_1 - \mu_2)}{\sqrt{\dfrac{\sigma_1^2}{n_1} + \dfrac{\sigma_2^2}{n_2}}}$ $\delta = \mu_1 - \mu_2$	$\mu_1 - \mu_2 = \delta$	$\mu_1 - \mu_2 \neq \delta$ $\mu_1 - \mu_2 > \delta$ $\mu_1 - \mu_2 < \delta$	$\lvert z_0 \rvert > z_{\alpha/2}$ $z_0 > z_\alpha$ $z_0 < -z_\alpha$
t test for a population mean	Variance unknown, normal	$t_0 = \dfrac{\bar{X} - \mu_0}{s/\sqrt{n}}$ $s = \sqrt{\dfrac{\left(X_i - \bar{X}\right)^2}{n-1}}$	$\mu = \mu_0$	$\mu \neq \mu_0$ $\mu > \mu_0$ $\mu < \mu_0$	$\lvert t_0 \rvert > t_{\alpha/2, n-1}$ $t_0 > t_{\alpha, n-1}$ $t_0 < -t_{\alpha, n-1}$

Continued

Part VI.B.5

Table 25.5 Hypothesis tests for means. *Continued*

Test name	Assumption	Test statistic	Null hypothesis	Alternative hypotheses	Rejection criteria
t test for two population means	Variances unknown and equal, normal	$t_0 = \dfrac{(\bar{X}_1 - \bar{X}_2) - (\mu_1 - \mu_2)}{s_p \sqrt{\dfrac{1}{n_1} + \dfrac{1}{n_2}}}$ $\delta = \mu_1 - \mu_2$ $s_p = \dfrac{(n_1 - 1)s_1^2 + (n_2 - 1)s_2^2}{n_1 + n_2 - 2}$	$\mu_1 - \mu_2 = \delta$	$\mu_1 - \mu_2 \neq \delta$ $\mu_1 - \mu_2 > \delta$ $\mu_1 - \mu_2 < \delta$	$|t_0| > t_{\alpha/2,\, n_1+n_2-2}$ $t_0 > t_{\alpha,\, n_1+n_2-2}$ $t_0 < -t_{\alpha,\, n_1+n_2-2}$
t test for population means	Variances unknown and unequal, normal	$t_0 = \dfrac{(\bar{X}_1 - \bar{X}_2) - (\mu_1 - \mu_2)}{\sqrt{\dfrac{s_1^2}{n_1} + \dfrac{s_2^2}{n_2}}}$ $\delta = \mu_1 - \mu_2$ $v = \dfrac{\left(\dfrac{s_1^2}{n_1} + \dfrac{s_2^2}{n_2}\right)^2}{\dfrac{\left(s_1^2/n_1\right)^2}{n_1 - 1} + \dfrac{\left(s_2^2/n_2\right)^2}{n_2 - 1}}$ Round *v* down to the next whole number	$\mu_1 - \mu_2 = \delta$	$\mu_1 - \mu_2 \neq \delta$ $\mu_1 - \mu_2 > \delta$ $\mu_1 - \mu_2 < \delta$	$|t_0| > t_{\alpha/2,\, v}$ $t_0 > t_{\alpha,\, v}$ $t_0 < -t_{\alpha,\, v}$

Continued

Table 25.5 Hypothesis tests for means. *Continued*

Test name	Assumption	Test statistic	Null hypothesis	Alternative hypotheses	Rejection criteria
t test for population means (paired t test)	Each data element in one population is paired with one data element in the other population, normal	$t_0 = \dfrac{(\bar{X}_1 - \bar{X}_2) - \delta}{s_D/\sqrt{n}}$ $s_D = \sqrt{\dfrac{\sum\limits_{i=1}^{n}(D_i - \bar{D})^2}{n-1}}$ $\bar{D}$ = average of the n differences D_1, D_2, ..., D_n	$\mu_D = \delta$	$\mu_D \neq \delta$ $\mu_D > \delta$ $\mu_D < \delta$	$\lvert t_0 \rvert > t_{\alpha/2, n-1}$ $t_0 > t_{\alpha}, n-1$ $t_0 < -t_{\alpha}, n-1$

Example 25.9

We have just received a lot of 1000 circuit boards. The supplier is expected to coat the boards to a thickness of 0.0025 with a standard deviation of 0.0005. The standard deviation is assumed known from past experience. After randomly sampling 36 boards, we compute a mean thickness of 0.003. Has there been a change in the mean thickness?

1. The parameter to be tested is μ

2. $H_0 : \mu = \mu_0; H_A : \mu > \mu_0$

3. $\alpha = 0.05$

4. $z_0 = \dfrac{\bar{X} - \mu_0}{\sigma/\sqrt{n}}$

5. Reject H_0 if $z_0 > z_\alpha$

6. From Appendix 12, $z_{0.05} = 1.645$

7. $z_0 = \dfrac{0.003 - 0.0025}{0.0005/\sqrt{36}} = 6$

8. Since the test statistic falls in the reject region, we reject the null hypothesis and conclude that there has been a change in the mean thickness of the coating on the circuit boards

Hypothesis Tests for Variances

Table 25.6 provides three commonly used confidence intervals for variances or ratios of variances.

Table 25.6 Hypothesis tests for variances or ratios of variances.

Test name	Assumption	Test statistic	Null hypothesis	Alternative hypotheses	Rejection criteria
χ^2 test between a sample variance and an assumed population variance σ_0^2	Sample is drawn from a normal population	$\chi_0^2 = \dfrac{(n-1)s^2}{\sigma_0^2}$	$\sigma^2 = \sigma_0^2$	$\sigma^2 \neq \sigma_0^2$ $\sigma^2 > \sigma_0^2$ $\sigma^2 < \sigma_0^2$	$\chi_0^2 > \chi_{\alpha/2,n-1}^2$ or $\chi_0^2 < \chi_{1-\alpha/2,n-1}^2$ $\chi_0^2 > \chi_{\alpha,n-1}^2$ $\chi_0^2 < \chi_{1-\alpha,n-1}^2$
F test for two population variances	Both samples are taken from a normal distribution	$F_0 = \dfrac{s_1^2}{s_2^2}$ $f_{1-\alpha,v_1,v_2} = \dfrac{1}{f_{\alpha,v_2,v_1}}$	$\sigma_1^2 = \sigma_2^2$	$\sigma_1^2 \neq \sigma_2^2$ $\sigma_1^2 > \sigma_2^2$ $\sigma_1^2 < \sigma_2^2$	$F_0 > f_{\alpha/2,n_1-1,n_2-1}$ or $F_0 < f_{1-\alpha/2,n_1-1,n_2-1}$ $F_0 > f_{\alpha,n_1-1,n_2}$ $F_0 < f_{1-\alpha,n_1-1,n_2-1}$
χ^2 test between a population variance and an assumed variance σ_0^2	Sample is taken from a normal distribution	$\chi_0^2 = \dfrac{(n-1)s^2}{\sigma_0^2}$	$\sigma^2 = \sigma_0^2$	$\sigma^2 \neq \sigma_0^2$ $\sigma^2 > \sigma_0^2$ $\sigma^2 < \sigma_0^2$	$\chi_0^2 > \chi_{\alpha/2,n-1}^2$ or $\chi_0^2 < \chi_{1-\alpha/2,n-1}^2$ $\chi_0^2 > \chi_{\alpha,n-1}^2$ $\chi_0^2 < \chi_{1-\alpha,n-1}^2$

Example 25.10

Recently, a Six Sigma Black Belt project was undertaken to reduce the variance of the coating on circuit boards from 0.0005. We have just received a lot of 1000 circuit boards. After randomly sampling 36 boards, we compute a mean thickness of 0.003 and a variance of 0.00025. Has the variance been reduced?

1. The parameter to be tested is σ^2

2. $H_0 : \sigma^2 = \sigma_0^2; H_A : \sigma^2 < \sigma_0^2$

3. $\alpha = 0.05$

4. $\chi_0^2 = \dfrac{(n-1)s^2}{\sigma_0^2}$

5. Reject H_0 if $\chi_0^2 < \chi_{1-\alpha,n-1}^2$

6. From Appendix 15, $\chi_{0.95,35}^2 = 22.465$

7. $\chi_0^2 = \dfrac{(35)(0.00025)}{0.0005} = 17.5$

8. Since the test statistic falls in the reject region, we reject the null hypothesis and conclude that there has been a reduction in the variance of the coating thickness.

Hypothesis Tests for Proportions

Table 25.7 provides two commonly used confidence intervals for proportions.

Table 25.7 Hypothesis tests for proportions.

Test name	Assumption	Test statistic	Null hypothesis	Alternative hypotheses	Rejection criteria
z test for a given proportion p_0	Same size, $n \geq 30$	$z_0 = \dfrac{p - p_0}{\sqrt{\dfrac{p_0(1-p_0)}{n}}}$	$p = p_0$	$p \neq p_0$ $p > p_0$ $p < p_0$	$\lvert z_0 \rvert > z_{\alpha/2}$ $z_0 > z_\alpha$ $z_0 < -z_\alpha$
z test of the equality of two proportions	Same size, $n \geq 30$	$z_0 = \dfrac{p_1 - p_2}{\sqrt{P(1-P)\left(\dfrac{1}{n_1} + \dfrac{1}{n_2}\right)}}$ $P = \dfrac{n_1 p_1 + n_2 p_2}{n_1 + n_2}$	$p_1 = p_2$	$p_1 \neq p_2$ $p_1 > p_2$ $p_1 < p_2$	$\lvert z_0 \rvert > z_{\alpha/2}$ $z_0 > z_\alpha$ $z_0 < -z_\alpha$

Example 25.11

Let's assume the same data given in Example 25.9 with the exception that our sampling process yields two defectives. We want to determine whether our recent improvement efforts have been successful in reducing the proportion defective from 0.10. Has the proportion defective been reduced?

1. The parameter to be tested is p

2. $H_0 : p = p_0; H_A : p < p_0$

3. $\alpha = 0.05$

4. $z_0 = \dfrac{p - p_0}{\sqrt{\dfrac{p_0(1 - p_0)}{n}}}$

5. Reject H_0 if $z_0 < -z_\alpha$

6. From Appendix 12, $-z_{0.05} = -1.645$

7. $z_0 = \dfrac{0.0556 - 0.10}{\sqrt{\dfrac{(0.10)(1 - 0.10)}{36}}} = -0.888$

8. Since the test statistic does not fall in the reject region, we do not reject the null hypothesis and conclude there has been no change in the proportion defective.

Figures 25.2–25.4 provide a flowchart to help determine which hypothesis test to use.

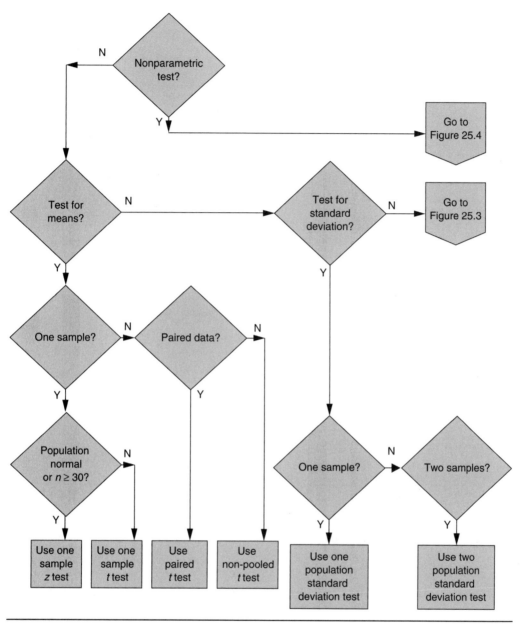

Figure 25.2 Hypothesis test flowchart (part 1).

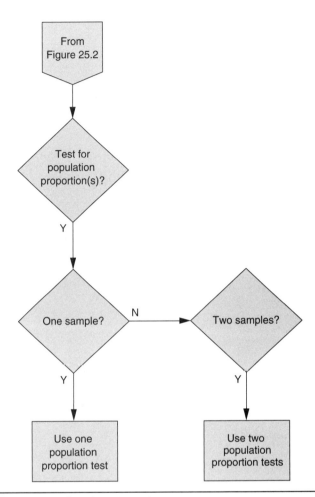

Figure 25.3 Hypothesis test flowchart (part 2).

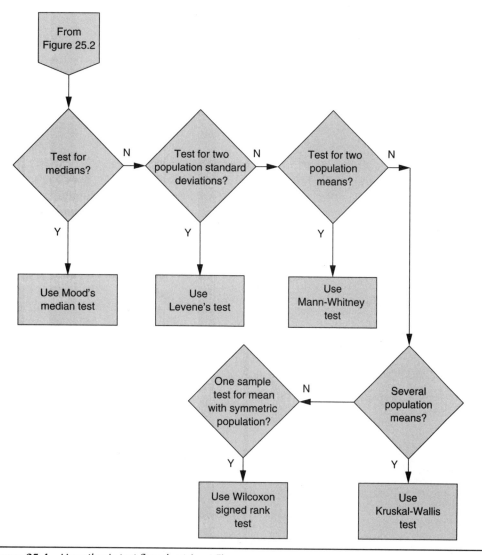

Figure 25.4 Hypothesis test flowchart (part 3).

ANALYSIS OF VARIANCE (ANOVA)

Select, calculate, and interpret the results of
ANOVAs. (Evaluate)

Body of Knowledge VI.B.6

The ANOVA procedures extend the hypothesis tests for means that were discussed
in the previous section to the means of more than two populations.

One-Way ANOVA

The one-way ANOVA procedure is used to determine whether the data from three or more populations formed by the treatment options from a single factor designed experiment indicate that the population means are different. A treatment is a specific factor level. The hypotheses being tested are

$$H_0 : \mu_1 = \mu_2 = \ldots = \mu_k$$

H_A : Not all means are equal

From these hypotheses, we know that there are k factor levels.

Essentially, the idea behind ANOVA is to determine whether the variation due to the treatments is sufficiently large compared with the experimental error (that is, within treatment variation). Although the null hypothesis is stated in terms of means, this determination is made through the use of the F test, described previously.

To ensure that the ANOVA is carried out properly, it is useful to have a well-defined process for conducting it:

1. State the null and alternative hypotheses (H_0, H_A)

2. State the α value

3. Determine the test statistic

4. Define the rejection criteria

5. Compute the critical values

6. Construct the source table

7. Compute the test statistics

8. State the conclusion of the test using the ANOVA source table

Table 25.8 illustrates an ANOVA source table where

$$k = \text{number of treatments}$$

$$n = \text{number of readings per treatment}$$

$$N = kn = \text{total number of readings}$$

$$\sum_{i=1}^{k} \sum_{j=1}^{n} y_{ij} = \text{total of all responses}$$

$$SS_T = \sum_{i=1}^{k} \sum_{j=1}^{n} y_{ij}^2 - \frac{y_{..}^2}{N}$$

$$SS_{\text{treatments}} = \sum_{i=1}^{k} \frac{y_i^2}{n} - \frac{y_{..}^2}{N}$$

$$SS_E = SS_T - SS_{\text{treatments}}$$

$$y_{ij} = i^{th} \text{ treatment, } j^{th} \text{ measurement}$$

The underlying assumptions of ANOVA are that the data are independent, are normally distributed, and are of equal variance.

Table 25.8   Example of a one-way ANOVA source table.

Source of variation	Sum of squares	Degrees of freedom	Mean squares	F statistic
Between treatments	SS_B	$k-1$	$MS_B = \dfrac{SS_B}{k-1}$	$F_0 = \dfrac{MS_B}{MS_E}$
Within treatments (error)	SS_E	$N-k$	$MS_E = \dfrac{SS_E}{N-k}$	
Total	SS_T	$N-1$		

Example 25.12

A process can be run at any of three temperatures: 180°F, 200°F, and 220°F. Using the data in Table 25.9 and assuming $\alpha = 0.05$, determine whether temperature significantly affects the moisture content.

Table 25.9   Moisture content data for Example 25.12.

Level	Temperature (°F)		
	180	200	220
1	10.8	11.4	14.3
2	10.4	11.9	12.6
3	11.2	11.6	13.0
4	9.9	12.0	14.2

From the problem statement, we can determine

$$\alpha = 0.05$$

$$k = 3$$

$$n = 4$$

$$N = kn = 12$$

$$\sum_{i=1}^{k}\sum_{j=1}^{n} y_{ij} = 143.3$$

$$SS_T = \sum_{i=1}^{k}\sum_{j=1}^{n} y_{ij}^2 - \frac{y_{..}^2}{N} = 1732.3 - \frac{(143.3)^2}{12} = 1732.27 - 1711.24 = 21.03$$

$$SS_{\text{treatments}} = \sum_{i=1}^{k} \frac{y_i^2}{n} - \frac{y_{..}^2}{N} = 1728.93 - 1711.24 = 17.69$$

$$SS_E = SS_T - SS_{\text{treatments}} = 21.03 - 17.69 = 3.34$$

Example 25.12 *(continued)*

Let's complete the ANOVA steps:

1. $H_0 = \mu_1 = \mu_2 = \ldots = \mu_k$; H_A = Not all means are equal

2. $\alpha = 0.05$

3. F statistic given in Table 25.8

4. Reject H_0 if $F_0 > F_{\alpha,k-1,N-k}$

5. From Appendix 21, the critical value is $F_{0.05,2,9} = 4.26$

6. See Table 25.10 for the completed ANOVA source table

7. From Table 25.10, the test statistic is 23.92

8. Since the test statistic, 23.92, exceeds the critical value, 4.26, we reject the null hypothesis and conclude that temperature affects the moisture content

Table 25.10 Completed one-way ANOVA source table for the data given in Table 25.9.

Source of variation	Sum of squares	Degrees of freedom	Mean squares	F statistic
Between treatments	17.69	2	8.85	23.92
Within treatments (error)	3.34	9	0.37	
Total	21.03	11		

Two-Way ANOVA

The two-way ANOVA test can be used in the analysis of two-factor experiments. It differs from the one-way ANOVA procedure only in the details of the ANOVA table, so this discussion will focus on construction of the table.

In two-factor experiments, the effects to be analyzed are the main effects of factor A, the main effects of factor B, and the interaction between them (as will be discussed in Chapter 28). The two-way ANOVA source table is given in Table 25.11.

The structure of the table is similar to that of the one-way ANOVA table. The F statistics in the last column are compared with the critical values in an F table to determine if there is a statistically significant effect due to factor A, factor B, or the interaction between them. Formulas for the sum of squares values are similar to those for one-way ANOVA. The equations for the two-way ANOVA are not provided. Though they are similar to the equations for the one-way ANOVA, they are tedious to apply. As a result, most two-way ANOVAs are computed using readily available statistical software.

As with the one-way ANOVA, the F statistic measures the ratio between the effect and the experimental error. If the variation due to the effect is sufficiently large relative to the experimental error, the effect is considered statistically significant at a specified α value.

Table 25.11   Example of a two–way ANOVA source table.

Source of variation	Sum of squares	Degrees of freedom	Mean squares	F statistic
Factor A	SS_A	$a - 1$	$MS_A = \dfrac{SS_A}{a - 1}$	$F_0 = \dfrac{MS_A}{MS_E}$
Factor B	SS_B	$b - 1$	$MS_B = \dfrac{SS_B}{b - 1}$	$F_0 = \dfrac{MS_B}{MS_E}$
Interaction of factors A and B	SS_{AB}	$(a - 1)(b - 1)$	$MS_{AB} = \dfrac{SS_{AB}}{(a - 1)(b - 1)}$	$F_0 = \dfrac{MS_{AB}}{MS_E}$
Error	SS_E	$(N - ab)$	$MS_E = \dfrac{SS_E}{N - ab}$	
Total	SS_T	$N - 1$		

GOODNESS-OF-FIT (CHI SQUARE) TESTS

Define, select, and interpret the results of these tests. (Evaluate)

Body of Knowledge VI.B.7

χ^2 Goodness-of-Fit Test

The purpose of the χ^2 goodness-of-fit test is to test the hypotheses

H_0 = The data follow a specified distribution

H_A = The data do not follow a specified distribution

To conduct the χ^2 goodness-of-fit test:

1. State the null and alternative hypotheses (H_0, H_A).

2. Arrange a random sample of size n into a frequency histogram of k class intervals.

3. Determine O_i = observed frequency in the ith class interval.

4. Determine E_i = expected frequency in the ith class interval using the hypothesis distribution. Note: It is generally accepted that the expected frequencies should be no less than five. If they are less, adjacent class intervals should be combined until the recommended minimum of five is obtained.

5. State the α value.

6. Compute the test statistic $\chi_0^2 = \sum_{i=1}^{k} \frac{(O_i - E_i)^2}{E_i}$

7. Compute the critical value. Reject H_0 if $\chi_0^2 > \chi_{\alpha,k-p-1}^2$. The value of p is the number of parameters estimated.

8. State the conclusion of the test.

Example 25.13

Table 25.12 provides historical data of defect types for a consumer product. Each defective product has been categorized into one of four defect types. Percentages of each defect type have been computed from the historical data. Additionally, current data have been randomly selected and are also depicted in Table 25.12. Is the distribution that produced the current defect data the same as the distribution that produced the historical data?

Table 25.12 Historical data of defect types along with current data from a randomly selected week for Example 25.13.

Defect type	Percent of defectives	Current data
Paint run	16	27
Paint blistered	28	60
Decal crooked	42	100
Door cracked	14	21
Total	100	208

1. H_0 = the data follow a specified distribution; H_A = the data do not follow a specified distribution. Alternatively, we would state H_0 = the distribution has not changed; H_A = the distribution has changed.

2. See the arrangement of data in Table 25.13.

3. See column D in Table 25.13.

4. See column E in Table 25.13. This column is calculated by multiplying each probability in column C by the total of column D.

5. $\alpha = 0.05$.

6. $\chi_0^2 = \sum_{i=1}^{k} \frac{(O_i - E_i)^2}{E_i} = 5.33$. This is given in the total of column G.

7. From Appendix 15, we have $\chi_{\alpha,k-p-1}^2 = \chi_{\alpha,4-0-1}^2 = \chi_{0.05,3}^2 = 7.815$. Since $\chi_0^2 <$ 7.815, do not reject the null hypothesis. The value of p is zero since no parameters were estimated.

8. Since we failed to reject the null hypothesis, we conclude that the distribution producing the current data has not changed.

Example 25.13 *(continued)*

Table 25.13   Goodness-of-fit table for Example 25.13.

A	B	C	D	E	F	G
Defect type	Percent of defectives	Probability of defective	Observed frequency	Expected frequency	(O)bserved – (E)xpected	$\dfrac{(O-E)^2}{E}$
Paint run	16	0.16	27	33.28	–6.28	1.19
Paint blistered	28	0.28	60	58.24	1.76	0.05
Decal crooked	42	0.42	100	87.36	12.64	1.83
Door cracked	14	0.14	21	29.12	–8.12	2.26
Total	**100**	**1.00**	**208**	**208**		**5.33**

CONTINGENCY TABLES

> Select, develop, and use contingency tables to determine statistical significance. (Evaluate)
>
> **Body of Knowledge VI.B.8**

Contingency tables provide us with the ability to determine whether items classified into two or more categories act independent of one another.

A contingency table analysis allows us to test the hypotheses

H_0 = The classifications are independent

H_A = The classifications are dependent

To conduct a two-way contingency table analysis:

1. Determine your variables of classification.

2. State the null and alternative hypotheses (H_0, H_A).

3. Arrange the data according to the general form given in Table 25.14. This provides the observed frequencies O_{ij}.

4. Determine the expected frequencies E_{ij} as follows:

$$E_{ij} = \frac{r_i c_j}{N}$$

Table 25.14 The general form of a two-way contingency table.

Rows (r)	Classification 1	Columns (c)		
		Classification 2		
		O_{11} O_{12} $\cdots$ O_{1c}		
		O_{21} O_{22} $\cdots$ O_{2c}		
		$\vdots$ $\vdots$ $\vdots$ $\vdots$		
		O_{r1} O_{r2} $\cdots$ O_{rc}		

where

$$r_i = \sum_{j=1}^{c} O_{ij}$$

$$c_j = \sum_{i=1}^{r} O_{ij}$$

$$N = \sum_{i=1}^{r}\sum_{j=1}^{c} O_{ij}$$

5. State the α value.

6. Compute the test statistic $\chi_0^2 = \sum_{i=1}^{r}\sum_{j=1}^{c}\dfrac{\left(O_{ij} - E_{ij}\right)^2}{E_{ij}}$.

7. Compute the critical value. Reject H_0 if $\chi_0^2 > \chi_{\alpha,(r-1)(c-1)}^2$.

8. State the conclusion of the test.

Example 25.14

Suppose there are three product families called red, blue, and yellow, and the four defect types shown in Table 25.15. Determine whether the classifications of product type and defect type are statistically independent.

Table 25.15 Observed frequencies of defectives for Example 25.14.

Defect type	Observed frequencies		
	Red	Blue	Yellow
Paint run	20	54	34
Paint blistered	35	71	50
Decal crooked	48	88	66
Door cracked	10	23	17

Example 25.14 *(continued)*

1. Product classification and defect type.

2. H_0 = The classifications are independent; H_A = The classifications are not independent.

3. See Table 25.15 for the arrangement of the data and the associated observed frequencies.

4. The expected frequencies E_{ij} are given in Table 25.16.

5. $\alpha = 0.05$.

6. Compute the test statistic:

$$\chi_0^2 = \sum_{i=1}^{r}\sum_{j=1}^{c}\frac{\left(O_{ij}-E_{ij}\right)^2}{E_{ij}} = \frac{(20-23.65)^2}{23.65} + \frac{(54-59.40)^2}{59.40} + \ldots + \frac{(17-16.18)^2}{16.18} = 377.5$$

7. Reject H_0 if $\chi_0^2 > \chi_{\alpha,(r-1)(c-1)}^2 = \chi_{0.05,6}^2 = 12.592$.

8. Since $\chi_0^2 < 12.592$, we do not reject the null hypothesis and conclude the two classifications are independent.

Table 25.16 Computation of the expected frequencies for Example 25.14.

Defect type	Observed frequencies			
	Red	Blue	Yellow	Total
Paint run	20	54	34	108
Paint blistered	35	71	50	156
Decal crooked	48	88	66	202
Door cracked	10	23	17	50
Total	113	236	167	516

Defect type	Expected frequencies			
	Red	Blue	Yellow	Total
Paint run	23.65	49.40	34.95	108
Paint blistered	34.16	71.35	50.49	156
Decal crooked	44.24	92.39	65.38	202
Door cracked	10.95	22.87	16.18	50
Total	113	236	167	516

NON-PARAMETRIC TESTS

> Select, develop, and use various non-parametric tests, including Mood's Median, Levene's test, Kruskal-Wallis, Mann-Whitney, etc. (Evaluate)
>
> **Body of Knowledge VI.B.9**

When the underlying distribution of the data is not known, we must turn to non-parametric statistics to conduct hypothesis testing. Non-parametric tests tend to be less powerful than their corresponding parametric tests. Table 25.17 compares common parametric tests with their analogous non-parametric tests. Table 25.18 provides the details around each test depicted in Table 25.17. Let's examine each of the four tests in Table 25.18.

Mood's Median Test

Mood's Median test is used to determine whether there is sufficient evidence to conclude k medians from samples of size n_j are equal. This test permits the use of unequal sample sizes. The hypotheses tested are

$$H_0 : \tilde{\mu}_1 = \tilde{\mu}_2 = ..., \tilde{\mu}_k$$

$$H_A : \tilde{\mu}_i \neq \tilde{\mu}_j \text{ for at least one pair } (i,j)$$

The procedure for using Mood's Median test is as follows:

1. State the null and alternative hypotheses (H_0, H_A).

2. Collect a random sample of size n_i for each of the k populations.

3. Compute the overall median from the total sample size N, where

$$N = \sum_{i=1}^{k} n_i.$$

Table 25.17 Comparison of parametric and non-parametric hypothesis tests.

Parametric	Non-parametric
2-sample t test	Mann-Whitney test
One-way ANOVA	Kruskal-Wallis test
One-way ANOVA	Mood's Median test
Bartlett test	Levene's test

Table 25.18   Common non-parametric hypothesis tests.

Test name	Assumption	Test statistic	Null hypothesis	Alternative hypotheses	Rejection criteria
Mood's Median test		$$M = \sum_{i=1}^{k} \frac{(o_{AMi} - e_{AMi})^2}{e_{AMi}} + \sum_{i=1}^{k} \frac{(o_{BMi} - e_{BMi})^2}{e_{BMi}}$$ AM = number above median BM = number below median	$\tilde{\mu}_1 = \tilde{\mu}_2 =, \dots, \tilde{\mu}_K$	$\tilde{\mu}_i \neq \tilde{\mu}_j$ for at least one pair (i,j)	$H > \chi^2_{a,k-1}$
Levene's test		$$L = \frac{(N-k)\sum_{j=1}^{k} n_j \left(\bar{Y}_{.j} - \bar{Y}_{..}\right)^2}{(k-1)\sum_{j=1}^{k}\sum_{i=1}^{n_j}\left(Y_{ij} - \bar{Y}_{i.}\right)^2}$$ k = number of subgroups n_j = sample size of the jth subgroup $$N = \sum_{j=1}^{k} n_j$$	$\sigma_1 = \sigma_2 =, \dots, \sigma_k$	$\sigma_i \neq \sigma_j$ for at least one pair (i,j)	$L > F_{a,k-1,N-k}$

Continued

Part VI.B.9

Table 25.18 Common non-parametric hypothesis tests. *Continued*

Test name	Assumption	Test statistic	Null hypothesis	Alternative hypotheses	Rejection criteria
Kruskal-Wallis rank sum test of k populations	Each sample size should be at least 5	$H = \left[\dfrac{12}{N(N+1)} \sum_{j=1}^{k} \dfrac{R_j^2}{n_j} \right] - 3(N+1)$ k = number of subgroups n_j = sample size of the jth subgroup $N = \sum_{j=1}^{k} n_j$ R_j = sum of the ranks for the jth subgroup	$\mu_1 = \mu_2 = , \dots , \mu_K$	$\mu_i \neq \mu_j$ for at least one pair (i,j)	$H > \chi^2_{\alpha, k-1}$
Mann-Whitney test (aka Wilcoxon rank-sum test)	Distributions have the same shape and variance	$W_2 = \dfrac{(n_1 + n_2)(n_1 + n_2 + 1)}{2} - W_1$	$\mu_1 = \mu_2$	$\mu_1 \neq \mu_2$ $\mu_1 > \mu_2$ $\mu_1 < \mu_2$	W_1 or $W_2 \neq W_{\alpha, n_1, n_2}$ $W_2 \leq W_{\alpha, n_1, n_2}$ $W_1 \leq W_{\alpha, n_1, n_2}$

4. Construct a table with one column showing the number of readings above the overall median and another showing the number of readings below the overall median for each category. Construct this table using the observed values. There are k categories, one for each population. Half the readings that are equal to the median (that is, ties) should be counted in the "above" column and half in the "below" column. Special note: A review of the literature indicates that authors handle ties in different ways. You may try to replicate this example using Minitab, only to find the results differ. Generally, this difference would be attributed to the way ties are handled.

5. Construct a table with one column showing the number of readings above the sample median and another showing the number of readings below the sample median for each category. This table will provide the expected values.

6. Compute the test statistic $\chi_0^2 = \sum_{i=1}^{k} \frac{(O_{iA} - E_{iA})^2}{E_{iA}} + \sum_{i=1}^{k} \frac{(O_{iB} - E_{iB})^2}{E_{iB}}$, where the subscripts A and B denote above and below the median, respectively.

7. State the α value.

8. Compute the critical value. Reject H_0 if $\chi_0^2 > \chi_{\alpha,k-1}^2$.

9. State the conclusion of the test.

Example 25.15

Three machines produce plastic parts with a critical location dimension. A sample size of at least 10 is collected from each machine. The dimension is measured on each part. Does Mood's Median test permit rejection at the 95% significance level of the hypothesis that the median dimensions of the three machines are the same? The data are given in Table 25.19.

1. $H_0 : \tilde{\mu}_1 = \tilde{\mu}_2 = ..., \tilde{\mu}_K; H_A : \tilde{\mu}_i \neq \tilde{\mu}_j$ for at least one pair (i,j).

2. See the data given in Table 25.19.

3. Overall median is 6.46.

4. See the top half of Table 25.20.

5. See the bottom half of Table 25.20.

6. $\chi_0^2 = \sum_{i=1}^{k} \frac{(O_{iA} - E_{iA})^2}{E_{iA}} + \sum_{i=1}^{k} \frac{(O_{iB} - E_{iB})^2}{E_{iB}} = 1.964$

7. $\alpha = 0.05$.

8. Using Appendix 15, compute the critical value. Reject H_0 if $\chi_0^2 > \chi_{\alpha,k-1}^2 = \chi_{0.05,2}^2 = 5.991$.

9. Since $\chi_0^2 = 1.964 < \chi_{0.05,2}^2 = 5.991$, do not reject the null hypothesis. Thus, we conclude the medians are drawn from the same population.

Example 25.15 *(continued)*

Table 25.19   Data for Mood's Median test in Example 25.15.

Machine 1	Machine 2	Machine 3
6.48	6.42	6.46
6.42	6.46	6.48
6.47	6.41	6.45
6.48	6.47	6.41
6.49	6.45	6.47
6.47	6.46	6.44
6.48	6.42	6.47
6.46	6.46	6.42
6.45	6.46	6.43
6.46	6.48	6.47
	6.47	6.41
	6.43	
	6.48	
	6.47	
$n_1 = 10$	$n_2 = 14$	$n_3 = 11$

Table 25.20   Computation of the expected frequencies for Example 25.15.

Machine	Observed frequencies	
	Number above median	Number below median
1	7	3
2	7	7
3	4.5	6.5

Machine	Expected frequencies	
	Number above median	Number below median
1	5	5
2	7	7
3	5.5	5.5

Levene's Test

Levene's test is used to determine whether there is sufficient evidence to conclude k variances from samples of size n_j are equal. This test permits the use of unequal sample sizes. It is an alternative to Bartlett's test when the underlying data are non-normal. The hypotheses tested are

$H_0 : \sigma_1 = \sigma_2 = \ldots = \sigma_k$

$H_A : \sigma_i \neq \sigma_j$ for at least one pair (i, j)

Levene's original work used the mean in the test statistic as follows:

- $Y_{ij} = |X_{ij} - \bar{X}_{i.}|$, where $\bar{X}_{i.}$ is the mean of the ith subgroup and is best when the underlying data follow a symmetrical distribution.

The test statistic was later modified to include both the median and the trimmed mean:

- $Y_{ij} = |X_{ij} - \tilde{X}_{i.}|$, where $\tilde{X}_{i.}$ is the median of the ith subgroup and is best when the underlying data are skewed

- $Y_{ij} = |X_{ij} - \bar{X}'_{i.}|$, where $\bar{X}'_{i.}$ is the 10% trimmed mean of the ith subgroup and is best when the underlying data follow a heavy-tailed distribution such as the Cauchy

The procedure for using Levene's test is as follows:

1. State the null and alternative hypotheses (H_0, H_A).

2. Collect a random sample of size n_j for each of the k populations.

3. Compute the median for each sample.

4. Compute $Y_{ij} = |X_{ij} - \tilde{X}_{i.}|$.

5. Compute the test statistic:

$$L = \frac{(N-k) \sum_{j=1}^{k} n_j \left(\bar{Y}_{.j} - \bar{Y}_{..} \right)^2}{(k-1) \sum_{j=1}^{k} \sum_{i=1}^{n_j} \left(Y_{ij} - \bar{Y}_{i.} \right)^2}$$

6. State the α value.

7. Compute the critical value. Reject H_0 if $L > F_{\alpha, k-1, N-k}$.

8. State the conclusion of the test.

Example 25.16

Using the data given in Table 25.21, determine whether the variances are equal.

1. $H_0 : \sigma_1 = \sigma_2 = \ldots \sigma_k$; $H_A : \sigma_i \neq \sigma_j$ for at least one pair (i, j).

2. See the data given in Table 25.21.

3. See the median computed at the bottom of Table 25.22.

4. Compute $Y_{ij} = |X_{ij} - \tilde{X}_{i.}|$. See Table 25.22.

5. Using Tables 25.22–25.25, compute the test statistic:

$$L = \frac{(N-k)\sum\limits_{j=1}^{k} n_j \left(\bar{Y}_{.j} - \bar{Y}_{..}\right)^2}{(k-1)\sum\limits_{j=1}^{k}\sum\limits_{i=1}^{n_j} \left(Y_{ij} - \bar{Y}_{i.}\right)^2} = 4.26$$

6. $\alpha = 0.05$.

7. Using Appendix 21, compute the critical value. Reject H_0 if $L > F_{\alpha,k-1,N-k} = F_{0.05,2,27} = 3.35$.

8. Since $L > F_{0.05,2,27}$, we reject the null hypothesis and conclude the variances are different.

Table 25.21 Data for Levene's test for Example 25.16.

Sample 1	Sample 2	Sample 3
27	19	10
26	23	12
22	20	15
20	27	18
15	21	14
8	23	16
7	17	8
24	18	18
27	26	15
12	25	9

Example 25.16 (continued)

Table 25.22   Levene's test for Example 25.16.

X_{i1}	X_{i2}	X_{i3}	$\tilde{X}_1$	$\tilde{X}_2$	$\tilde{X}_3$	Y_{i1}	Y_{i2}	Y_{i3}
27	19	10	21	22	14.5	6	3	4.5
26	23	12	21	22	14.5	5	1	2.5
22	20	15	21	22	14.5	1	2	0.5
20	27	18	21	22	14.5	1	5	3.5
15	21	14	21	22	14.5	6	1	0.5
8	23	16	21	22	14.5	13	1	1.5
7	17	8	21	22	14.5	14	5	6.5
24	18	18	21	22	14.5	3	4	3.5
27	26	15	21	22	14.5	6	4	0.5
12	25	8	21	22	14.5	9	3	6.5

$\sum_{i=1}^{n_j} X_{ij}$ 188   219   134

$\tilde{X}_{i.}$ 21   22   14.5

Table 25.23   Levene's test for Example 25.16 (continued).

Y_{i1}	Y_{i2}	Y_{i3}	$\bar{Y}_{i1}$	$\bar{Y}_{i2}$	$\bar{Y}_{i3}$	$Y_{i1} - \bar{Y}_{i1}$	$Y_{i2} - \bar{Y}_{i2}$	$Y_{i3} - \bar{Y}_{i3}$
6	3	4.5	6.4	2.9	3.0	−0.4	0.1	1.5
5	1	2.5	6.4	2.9	3.0	−1.4	−1.9	−0.5
1	2	0.5	6.4	2.9	3.0	−5.4	−0.9	−2.5
1	5	3.5	6.4	2.9	3.0	−5.4	2.1	0.5
6	1	0.5	6.4	2.9	3.0	−0.4	−1.9	−2.5
13	1	1.5	6.4	2.9	3.0	6.6	−1.9	−1.5
14	5	6.5	6.4	2.9	3.0	7.6	2.1	3.5
3	4	3.5	6.4	2.9	3.0	−3.4	1.1	0.5
6	4	0.5	6.4	2.9	3.0	−0.4	1.1	−2.5
9	3	6.5	6.4	2.9	3.0	2.6	0.1	3.5

$\sum_{i=1}^{n_j} X_{ij}$ 64   29   30

$\bar{Y}_{i.}$ 6.4   2.9   3.0

$\bar{Y}_{..} = \dfrac{\sum_{j=1}^{k} \sum_{i=1}^{n_j} Y_{ij}}{N}$ 4.1

Example 25.16 *(continued)*

Table 25.24 Levene's test for Example 25.16 (continued).

$Y_{i1} - \bar{Y}_{i1}$	$Y_{i2} - \bar{Y}_{i2}$	$Y_{i3} - \bar{Y}_{i3}$	$(Y_{i1} - \bar{Y}_{i1})^2$	$(Y_{i2} - \bar{Y}_{i2})^2$	$(Y_{i3} - \bar{Y}_{i3})^2$
−0.4	0.1	1.5	0.16	0.01	2.25
−1.4	−1.9	−0.5	1.96	3.61	0.25
−5.4	−0.9	−2.5	29.16	0.81	6.25
−5.4	2.1	0.5	29.16	4.41	0.25
−0.4	−1.9	−2.5	0.16	3.61	6.25
6.6	−1.9	−1.5	43.56	3.61	2.25
7.6	2.1	3.5	57.76	4.41	12.25
−3.4	1.1	0.5	11.56	1.21	0.25
−0.4	1.1	−2.5	0.16	1.21	6.25
2.6	0.1	3.5	6.76	0.01	12.25

$\sum\limits_{i=1}^{n_j}(Y_{ij} - \bar{Y}_i)^2$ 180.40   22.90   48.50

$\sum\limits_{j=1}^{k}\sum\limits_{i=1}^{n_j}(Y_{ij} - \bar{Y}_i)^2$ 251.80

Table 25.25 Levene's test for Example 25.16 (continued).

$\bar{Y}_{\cdot j}$	$\bar{Y}_{\cdot\cdot}$	$\bar{Y}_{\cdot j} - \bar{Y}_{\cdot\cdot}$	$(\bar{Y}_{\cdot j} - \bar{Y}_{\cdot\cdot})^2$	n_j	$n_j(\bar{Y}_{\cdot j} - \bar{Y}_{\cdot\cdot})^2$
6.4	4.1	2.3	5.29	10	52.9
2.9	4.1	−1.2	1.44	10	14.4
3.0	4.1	−1.1	1.21	10	12.1

$\sum\limits_{j=1}^{k}n_j(\bar{Y}_{\cdot j} - \bar{Y}_{\cdot\cdot})^2$ 79.4

Kruskal-Wallis Test

The Kruskal-Wallis test is used to determine whether there is sufficient evidence to conclude k means from samples of size n_j are equal. This test permits the use of unequal sample sizes. The hypotheses tested are

$H_0 : \mu_1 = \mu_2 =, \ldots, \mu_k$

$H_A : \mu_i \neq \mu_j$ for at least one pair (i, j)

The procedure for using the Kruskal-Wallis test is as follows:

1. State the null and alternative hypotheses (H_0, H_A).

2. Collect a random sample of size n_j for each of the k populations.

3. Compute the ranks and average ranks where ties exist using the format shown in Table 25.27 for combined samples.

4. Compute the test statistic $H = \left[\dfrac{12}{N(N+1)} \sum_{j=1}^{k} \dfrac{R_j^2}{n_j} \right] - 3(N+1)$.

5. State the α value.

6. Compute the critical value. Reject H_0 if $H > \chi^2_{\alpha,k-1}$.

7. State the conclusion of the test.

Example 25.17

Random samples of a population of fourth graders from three school districts were given a math test. The scores are listed in Table 25.26. Assuming the populations have the same shape, determine whether all means are equal.

1. $H_0 : \mu_1 = \mu_2 =, \ldots, \mu_k$; $H_A : \mu_i \neq \mu_j$ for at least one pair (i, j).

2. See the data given in Table 25.26.

3. See Table 25.27 for the ranks and average ranks.

4. Using Table 25.28 to assist in the calculations, compute the test statistic:

$$H = \left[\frac{12}{N(N+1)} \sum_{j=1}^{k} \frac{R_j^2}{n_j} \right] - 3(N+1) = 10.36$$

5. $\alpha = 0.05$.

Table 25.26 Data for Kruskal-Wallis test for Example 25.17.

District 1	District 2	District 3
104	100	103
106	106	111
111	103	108
108	102	113
110	101	112
104	102	109
107	106	107

Example 25.17 *(continued)*

Table 25.27 Determining ranks for Example 25.17.

Combined samples	Rank	Average rank
100	1	1
101	2	2
102	3, 4	3.5
103	5, 6	5.5
104	7, 8	7.5
106	9, 10, 11	10
107	12, 13	12.5
108	14, 15	14.5
109	16	16
110	17	17
111	18, 19	18.5
112	20	20
113	21	21

6. Using Appendix 15, compute the critical value. Reject H_0 if $H > \chi^2_{\alpha,k-1} = \chi^2_{0.05,2} = 5.991$.

7. Since $H > \chi^2_{\alpha,k-1} = \chi^2_{0.05,2} = 5.991$, we reject the null hypothesis and conclude the means are different.

Example 25.17 (continued)

Table 25.28 Kruskal-Wallis test for Example 25.17.

District 1	District 1 rank	District 2	District 2 rank	District 3	District 3 rank
104	7.5	100	1	103	5.5
106	10	106	10	111	18.5
111	18.5	103	5.5	108	14.5
108	14.5	102	3.5	113	21
110	17	101	2	112	20
104	7.5	102	3.5	109	16
107	12.5	106	10	107	12.5
Total rank	87.5		35.5		108.0
Ranks squared	7656.3		1260.3		11,664.0
n_j	7		7		7
$\dfrac{R_j^2}{n_j}$	1094		180		1666
$\displaystyle\sum_{j=1}^{k} \dfrac{R_j^2}{n_j}$					2940

Mann-Whitney Test

The Mann-Whitney test is used to determine whether there is sufficient evidence to conclude two means from samples of size n_j are equal. This test permits the use of unequal sample sizes. The hypotheses tested are

$$H_0 : \mu_1 = \mu_2$$

$$H_A : \mu_1 \neq \mu_2 \text{ or } \mu_1 > \mu_2 \text{ or } \mu_1 < \mu_2$$

The procedure for using the Mann-Whitney test is as follows:

1. State the null and alternative hypotheses (H_0, H_A).

2. Collect a random sample of size n_j for each of the two populations.

3. Compute the ranks and average ranks where ties exist using the format shown in Table 25.30 for combined samples.

4. Let W_1 be the sum of the ranks in the smaller sample.

5. Compute the test statistic $W_2 = \dfrac{(n_1 + n_2)(n_1 + n_2 + 1)}{2} - W_1$, if W_2 is necessary for the test.

6. State the α value.

7. Compute the critical value. Reject H_0 if

$$W_1 \text{ or } W_2 \neq W_{\alpha, n_1, n_2}$$

$$W_2 \leq W_{\alpha, n_1, n_2}$$

$$W_1 \leq W_{\alpha, n_1, n_2}$$

8. State the conclusion of the test.

Example 25.18

Steel parts are painted by two shifts. A sample from each shift is inspected, and the number of paint bubbles is recorded for each part. The data are given in Table 25.29. Assuming the two populations have the same shape, determine whether the first shift produces more bubbles than the second shift.

1. $H_0 : \mu_1 = \mu_2 ; H_A : \mu_1 < \mu_2$.

2. See the data given in Table 25.29.

3. Compute the ranks and average ranks where ties exist using the format shown in Table 25.30.

4. Let W_1 be the sum of the ranks in the smaller sample.

5. Using Table 25.31, we obtain $W_1 = 88.0$.

6. $= 0.05$.

Table 25.29   Data for Mann–Whitney test for Example 25.18.

Shift 1	Shift 2
12	8
11	7
13	9
12	8
9	7
10	8
9	8
	9
	9

Example 25.18 *(continued)*

Table 25.30 Determining ranks for Example 25.18.

Combined samples	Rank	Average rank
7	1, 2	1.5
8	3, 4, 5, 6	4.5
9	7, 8, 9, 10, 11	9
10	12	12
11	13	13
12	14, 15	14.5
13	16	16

Table 25.31 Mann–Whitney test for Example 25.18.

Shift 1	Rank for shift 1	Shift 2
12	14.5	8
11	13	7
13	16	9
12	14.5	8
9	9	7
10	12	8
9	9	8
		9
		9
Total ranks	**88.0**	

7. Using Appendix 29, compute the critical value. Reject H_0 if $W_1 \leq W_{\alpha,n_1,n_2} = W_{0.05,7,9} = 37$.

8. Since W_1 is greater than the critical value, we do not reject the null hypothesis and conclude that both shifts produce the same number of bubbles.

Chapter 26

Failure Mode and Effects Analysis (FMEA)

FAILURE MODE AND EFFECTS ANALYSIS (FMEA)

> Describe the purpose and elements of FMEA, including risk priority number (RPN), and evaluate FMEA results for processes, products, and services. Distinguish between design FMEA (DFMEA) and process FMEA (PFMEA), and interpret results from each. (Evaluate)
>
> **Body of Knowledge VI.C**

A failure mode and effects analysis (FMEA) is a prevention-based tool that focuses the user or team on systematically:

- Identifying and anticipating potential failures
- Identifying potential causes for the failures
- Prioritizing failures
- Taking action to reduce, mitigate, or eliminate failures

There are two primary types of FMEAs:

- Process FMEA (PFMEA)—focuses on processes
- Design FMEA (DFMEA)—focuses on product or component parts

Figure 26.1 provides a partial example of a PFMEA, and Figure 26.2 provides a partial example of a DFMEA. Other than the first column, the forms are similar. In the PFMEA, the first column identifies the process step; in the DFMEA, the first column identifies a product or component part.

Most of the columns in the examples are self-explanatory, but the ones with numerical entries merit further discussion. There are four numerical columns:

- Severity (SEV)—The entry in this column serves to quantify the severity of the impact of the failure mode. The scale for severity ranges from "no effect" on the low end to "safety hazard (up to and including loss of life) with no warning" on the high end.

Process step/input	Potential failure mode	Potential failure effects	S E V	Potential causes	O C C	Current controls	D E T	R P N	Actions recommended	Responsible person	Actions taken	S E V	O C C	D E T	R P N
What is the process step/ input under investigation?	In what ways does the key input go wrong?	What is the impact on the key output variables (customer requirements) or internal requirements?	How severe is the effect on the customer?	What causes the key input to go wrong?	How often does the cause or failure mode occur?	What are the existing controls and procedures (inspection and test) that prevent either the cause or the failure mode? **Should include an SOP number.**	How well can you detect cause or failure mode?		What are the actions for reducing the occurrence of the cause or improving detection? **Should have actions only on high RPN's or easy fixes.**	Who is responsible for the recommended action?	What are the completed actions taken with the recalculated RPN? **Be sure to include completion month/year.**				
Install part A	Part not installed	Device does not work	1	Process step skipped	5	SOP 123: process routing sheet	10	50	Modify program to halt production	M. Jones 04-08-08	Guides added				0
Install part A	Wrong part installed	Device overheats	9	Parts comingled in bin	7	None	7	441	Place different parts in different bins	M. Jones 04-08-08	Guides added	9	1	7	63
								0							0
								0							0
								0							0

Figure 26.1 Example of a PFMEA form.

Product/ Component	Potential failure mode	Potential failure effects	S E V	Potential causes	O C C	Current controls	D E T	R P N	Actions recommended	Responsible person	Actions taken	S E V	O C C	D E T	R P N
What is the product or component under investigation?	In what ways can the product or component fail?	What is the impact on the internal customer, external customer, or end user if the product or component fails?	How severe is the effect on the customer?	What causes the product or component to fail?	How often does cause or failure mode occur?	What are the existing controls and procedures (inspection and test) that prevent either the cause or the failure mode?	How well can you detect cause or failure mode?		What are the actions for reducing the occurrence of the cause or improving detection? **Should have actions only on high RPN's or easy fixes.**	Who is responsible for the recommended action?	What are the completed actions taken with the recalculated RPN? **Be sure to include completion month/year.**				
V-1298 tank overflow value	Valve stem sticks	Tank overflows	7	Packing ID undersize	3	Test valve after assembly	5	105	Install alignment guides	M. Jones 04-08-08	Guides added	7	3	3	63
V-1298 tank overflow value	Valve stem sticks	Tank overflows	7	Stem OD oversize	7	Test valve after assembly	9	441	Install alignment guides	M. Jones 04-08-08	Guides added	5	5	9	225
								0							0
								0							0
								0							0

Figure 26.2 Example of a DFMEA form.

- Occurrence (OCC)—The entry in this column serves to quantify the frequency of occurrence of the failure mode. The scale for occurrence ranges from "very unlikely" on the low end to "highly likely" on the high end. Some users, teams, and organizations will go to great lengths to provide absolute definitions for frequency of occurrences. For example, the Automotive Industry Action Group (AIAG; 1995) has gone as far as stating that an occurrence entry value of 1 designates a possible failure rate ≤ 0.01 per thousand vehicles/items, and an entry value of 10 designates a possible failure rate ≥ 100 per thousand vehicles/items.

- Detection (DET)—The entry in this column serves to quantify the ability to detect the failure at a specific process step (that is, not at a previous or subsequent step, but at the step under consideration) or at the product or component part level. The scale for detection ranges from "almost certain" on the low end to "not possible" on the high end.

- Risk priority number (RPN)—The entry in this column represents the multiplicative effect (that is, RPN = severity value × occurrence value × detection value) of values assigned to each of the previous three columns. Although teams generally work the highest RPNs first, they may set additional prioritization criteria, such as working any line item on the FMEA where the detection value or the severity value is at the highest level.

Note that on each of the FMEA forms, there is a second set of columns for severity, occurrence, detection, and RPN. The team will fill in these values after it has acted on the high-priority line items. The purpose is to determine whether such actions had the desired effect. For example, notice the second line item in Figure 26.1. The action the team decided on was to "place different parts in different bins." The purpose of this action was to reduce one or more of the RPN components. In this case, the effect was to reduce the occurrence value from 7 to 1. This had the overall effect on the FMEA of reducing the RPN value from 441 to 63.

For FMEAs to be successful, a team must give considerable thought to the scales it will use to assign values to each component of the RPN. Some authors advocate the use of a 10-point scale. If severity was being considered, a severity value of 1 would mean that the failure has no effect, whereas a severity value of 10 would mean that a failure results in a safety hazard (up to and including loss of life) without warning. One issue with a 10-point scale is that it tends to promote debate over whether to assign an item a 2 versus a 3, a 5 versus a 6, and so forth. In such instances, the overall influence on the RPN value may be minimal, yet the team wastes significant time and energy debating values that are so close together. In contrast, other authors advocate the use of scales that are skewed and sparse in terms of assignable values. For example, instead of selecting a 1–10 scale, some teams will choose 1, 3, 7, and 10 scales or something similar. The benefit of this type of scale is that it minimizes meaningless debate over close numbers and forces the team to discuss how to assign values. Regardless of the scales used, they should be well defined, consistent, and clearly understood by each team member.

FMEAs should be considered living documents and updated on an ongoing basis. FMEAs require intensive work up front on the part of the team, but their value is almost immeasurable in terms of providing a positive impact on quality and a delightful experience for the customer.

Reference

Automotive Industry Action Group. 1995. *(QS-9000) Measurement Systems Analysis (MSA) Reference Manual.* 2nd ed. Southfield, MI: Chrysler, Ford, and GM.

Chapter 27
Additional Analysis Methods

GAP ANALYSIS

> Use various tools and techniques (gap analysis, scenario planning, etc.) to compare the current and future state in terms of pre-defined metrics. (Analyze)
>
> **Body of Knowledge VI.D.1**

A *gap analysis* is a tool used to identify a performance difference between a current state and a desired or future state. The desired or future state may be set by recognizing potential performance determined through activities such as benchmarking. Gap analyses are performed at multiple levels:

- Business level—A business may compare its performance directly with that of competitors or the general average industry performance. Gaps at this level are usually financial in nature.

- Process level—The current performance of a process might be compared with the cost, cycle time, and quality characteristics of other processes or at performance levels required to remain competitive.

- Product level—Gaps at this level are usually identified through differences in features and capabilities, cost, quality, or generally by critical-to-X perspectives.

If the gap between the current state and the future state is sufficiently large, a series of intermediate steps or milestones may be required, with more achievable gaps between each one. However, it is important to recognize that gaps are usually never stationary. Therefore, it may be necessary to account for an increasing gap over time, particularly when future states are set relative to competitor performance.

ROOT CAUSE ANALYSIS

> Define and describe the purpose of root cause analysis, recognize the issues involved in identifying a root cause, and use various tools (e.g., the 5 whys, Pareto charts, fault tree analysis, cause and effect diagrams, etc.) for resolving chronic problems. (Evaluate)
>
> **Body of Knowledge VI.D.2**

Solving a process problem means identifying the root cause and eliminating it. The ultimate test of whether the root cause has been eliminated is the ability to toggle the problem on and off by removing and reintroducing the root cause.

A number of tools for identifying root causes are discussed in the following paragraphs.

5 Whys

The *5 whys* is a technique used to drill down through the layers of cause and effect to the root cause. It consists of looking at an undesired result and asking, Why did this occur? When the question is answered, the next question is, And why did that occur? and so on. The number five is, of course, arbitrary.

Example 27.1

Undesired result: A customer is not satisfied.

"Why is the customer not satisfied?"
Because the order arrived late.

"Why did the order arrive late?"
Because it was shipped late.

"Why was it shipped late?"
Because final assembly wasn't completed on time.

"Why wasn't final assembly completed on time?"
Because a part was received from the paint line late.

"Why was the part from the paint line late?"
Because it arrived late from the fabrication department.

"Why was it late from the fabrication department?"
Because the fabrication machine was running another part for the same order.

Example 27.1 *(continued)*

"Why was the fabrication machine running another part for the same order?"
Because that machine always runs these two parts.

"Could they be on separate machines simultaneously when a delivery date is imminent?"
Um, yes.

Cause-and-Effect Diagram

A *cause-and-effect diagram* (also called the Ishikawa or fishbone diagram) traditionally divides causes into several generic categories. In use, a large empty diagram is often drawn on a whiteboard or flip chart, as shown in Figure 27.1.

An undesirable end effect is specified, and a brainstorming session is usually held to identify potential causes, subcauses, and so on. The participants in the session should include people with a working knowledge of the process as well as subject matter experts. For example, suppose a circuit board plating operation is producing defects. After a few steps of brainstorming, the diagram might look like Figure 27.2. Notice that the main branches of the diagram are the 7Ms, which were discussed in Chapter 20.

Pareto Chart

An excellent tool for seeking out and prioritizing potential root causes is the *Pareto chart* or diagram. An example of a Pareto chart for defect types is illustrated in Figure 27.3. Let's take a moment to analyze this chart. Notice that a list of mutually exclusive categories is given along the *x* axis. Each defect type is graphed, and the

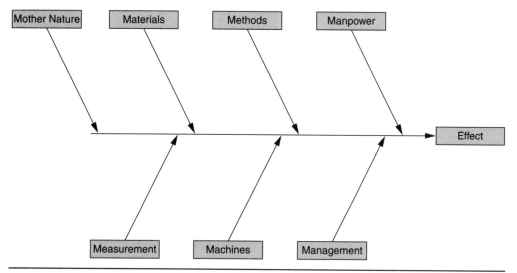

Figure 27.1   Example of a blank cause-and-effect diagram.

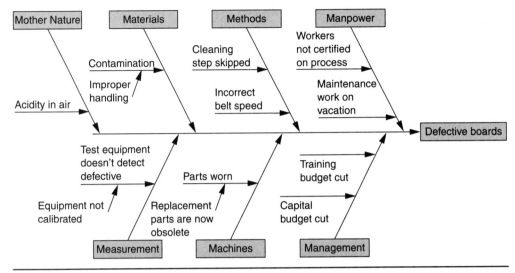

Figure 27.2 Example of a cause-and-effect diagram after a few brainstorming steps.

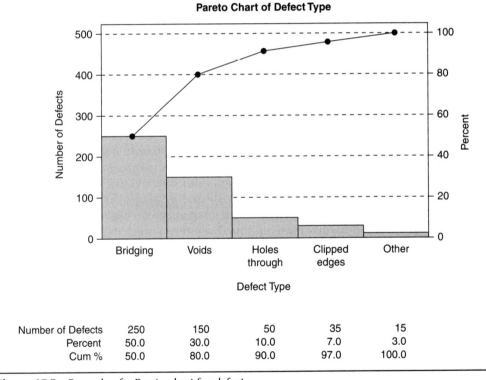

Number of Defects	250	150	50	35	15
Percent	50.0	30.0	10.0	7.0	3.0
Cum %	50.0	80.0	90.0	97.0	100.0

Figure 27.3 Example of a Pareto chart for defects.

Part VI.D.2

height of each bar is proportional to the number of defects. The graph contains two *y* axes. The left *y* axis identifies the number of defects and is associated with the bar heights. The right *y* axis represents the percentage of defects. The cumulative percentage of each defect type is graphed above the bars. The purpose of the Pareto chart is to identify the "vital few" from the "trivial many." This is often reflected in what is called the 80/20 rule. Figure 27.3 illustrates that the first two bars (that is, bridging and voids) represent 80% of the defects. The remaining 20% is spread across the three subsequent bars. Notice that the last bar is identified as "other." Because there are many types of minor defects that are few in quantity, they are collected in this category. There is no real need to identify them by specific type since they make up the trivial many and will not be investigated.

Pareto charts can and are often decomposed into lower level charts. For example, an investigation into the "bridging" bar in Figure 27.3 may determine that bridging can be further subdivided into additional meaningful categories.

One drawback of Figure 27.3 is that it assumes all defects have an equal impact. However, if we quantify the cost of correcting each defect, we can weight each quantity of defect type by the cost of correction. This weight could very well yield a Pareto chart completely different from Figure 27.3.

Example 27.2

Let's consider the data given in Table 27.1. Applying the cost data in this table to Figure 27.3 yields the revised Pareto chart depicted in Figure 27.4, which illustrates a completely different picture and dictates a different course of investigation and action than Figure 27.3.

Table 27.1   Cost to correct each defect type.

Defect type	Cost to correct ($)
Bridging	1.00
Voids	5.00
Holes through	25.00
Clipped edges	100.00
Other	10.00

Example 27.2 *(continued)*

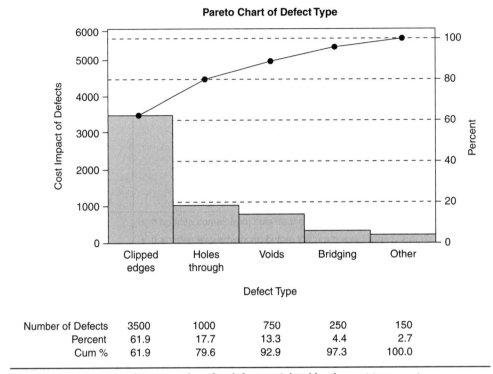

Pareto Chart of Defect Type

	Clipped edges	Holes through	Voids	Bridging	Other
Number of Defects	3500	1000	750	250	150
Percent	61.9	17.7	13.3	4.4	2.7
Cum %	61.9	79.6	92.9	97.3	100.0

Figure 27.4 Example of a Pareto chart for defects weighted by the cost to correct.

Fault Tree Analysis

Once a failure has been identified as requiring additional study, a *fault tree analysis* (FTA) can be performed. Basic symbols used in FTA are borrowed from the electronics and logic fields. The fundamental symbols are the AND gate and the OR gate. Each of these has at least two inputs and a single output. Another key gate is the voting OR gate. In this gate, the output occurs if and only if k or more of the input events occur, where k is specified, usually on the gate symbol. Common FTA gate symbols are depicted in Figure 27.5.

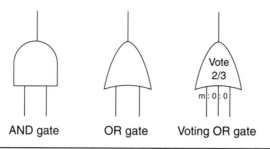

Figure 27.5   Basic FTA symbols.

The output for the AND gate occurs if and only if all inputs occur. The output for the OR gate occurs if and only if at least one input occurs. Rectangles are typically used for labeling inputs and outputs. The failure mode being studied is sometimes referred to as the "top" or "head" event. An FTA helps the user consider underlying causes for a failure mode and study relationships between various failures.

Example 27.3

The failure being studied is the stoppage of agitation in a tank before mixing is complete. This becomes the top event. Further team study indicates this will happen if any of the following occurs:

- Power loss due to both the external power source and the backup generator failing.

- Timer shuts off too soon because it is set incorrectly or has a mechanical failure.

- Agitator motor fails because it is overheated, or a fuse or capacitor fails.

- Agitator power train fails because both belts A and B break or the clutch fails or the transmission fails.

This test is symbolized by the FTA diagram shown in Figure 27.6.

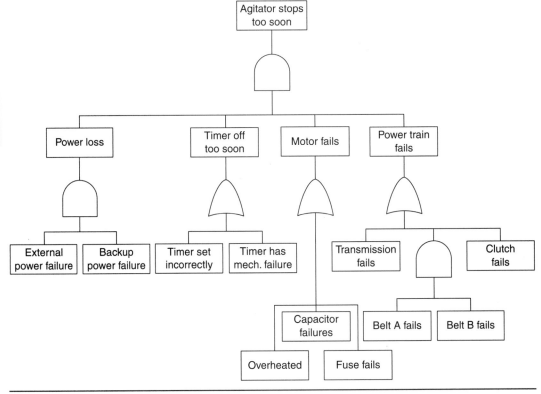

Figure 27.6 Example of stoppage of agitation in a tank.

WASTE ANALYSIS

> Identify and interpret the 7 classic wastes (over-production, inventory, defects, over-processing, waiting, motion, and transportation) and other forms of waste such as resource under-utilization, etc. (Analyze)
>
> **Body of Knowledge VI.D.3**

The National Institute for Standards and Technology (NIST) identifies eight sources of waste:

- **Overproduction:** Producing sooner or faster or in greater quantity than is needed by the next operation.

- **Inventory:** Excessive supply of parts or materials. Some accounting systems consider inventory an asset, but in light of the need to store, protect, locate, handle, and retrieve, it may be considered a liability by lean professionals.

- **Defects:** When defects occur, additional material, labor, and machine time may be required in addition to a possible increase in warranty costs and the potential for product recalls.

- **Processing:** This represents effort that does not add value. For example, a company found that parts waiting to be painted were rusting. An oil dip tank was installed to prevent rust. Of course, a de-oiling dip tank was also needed because oily parts don't paint well. The oil/degrease steps were processing waste.

- **Waiting:** Most workers can identify with this issue. Waiting for equipment, instructions, materials, and so forth, does not add value to a product or service.

- **Motion:** Movement by persons or equipment that does not add value.

- **Transportation:** Movement of parts and materials around the plant or facility usually due to poor facility layout.

- **People:** Failing to make use of all an employee has to offer in terms of ideas and creativity in making continuous improvement. This is often considered the eighth waste.

Part VII

Improve

Part VII

Chapter 28
Design of Experiments (DOE)

TERMINOLOGY

Define basic DOE terms, including independent
and dependent variables, factors and levels,
response, treatment, error, etc. (Understand)

Body of Knowledge VII.A.1

Design of experiments (DOE) is a statistical approach to designing and conducting experiments such that the experiment provides the most efficient and economical methods of determining the effect of a set of independent variables on a response variable. Knowledge of this relationship permits the experimenter to optimize a process and predict a response variable by setting the factors at specific levels. In other words, the objective of a designed experiment is to generate knowledge about a product or process and establish the mathematical relationship $y = f(x)$, where x is a list of independent variables and y is the dependent variable.

To better understand the concept of DOE, we will first provide a few fundamental definitions:

- An *effect* is the relationship between a factor and a response variable. Note that there can be many factors and response variables. Specific types include main effect, dispersion effect, and interaction effect. We will deal specifically with main and interaction effects.

- The *response variable* is the output variable that shows the observed results or value of an experimental treatment. It is sometimes known as the dependent variable or y variable. There may be multiple response variables in an experimental design.

- The *observed value* is a particular value of a response variable determined as a result of a test or measurement.

- A *factor* is an independent variable or assignable cause that may affect the responses and of which different levels are included in the experiment. Factors are also known as explanatory variables, predictor variables, or input variables.

- *Noise factor* is an independent variable that is difficult or too expensive to control as part of standard experimental conditions. In general, it is not desirable to make inferences on noise factors, but they are included in an experiment to broaden the conclusions regarding control factors.

- A *level* is the setting or assignment of a factor at a specific value.

- The *design space* is the multidimensional region of possible treatment combinations formed by the selected factors and their levels.

- Variation that occurs in the response variable beyond that accounted for by the factors, blocks, or other assignable source in an experiment is known as *experimental error*. Usually it is truncated to just "error."

- An *experimental unit* is the smallest entity receiving a particular treatment that yields a value of the response variable.

- A *treatment* is the specific setting or combination of factor levels for an experimental unit.

- An *experimental run* is a single performance of the experiment for a specific set of treatment combinations.

- n represents the number of experimental runs that will be conducted in a given experiment and is computed as

$$n = L^F$$

where

n = number of runs

L = number of levels

F = number of factors

These concepts are best illustrated by an example.

Example 28.1

Suppose a machine operator can adjust the feed, speed, and coolant temperature of a process. Further, he wishes to find the settings that will produce the best surface finish. The feed, speed, and coolant temperature are called the factors or independent variables. The surface finish is called the response or dependent variable because its value depends on the values of the independent variables through the mathematical relationship that will be determined by the experiment. There may be additional independent variables, such as the hardness of the material or humidity of the room, that have an effect on the dependent variable. In this example, hardness and humidity will be considered noise factors since they are difficult or expensive to control with regard to this experiment. The experimenter has decided that three factors will be tested at two levels each:

- Feed (*F*):   0.01 and 0.04 inches/revolution

- Speed (*S*):   1300 and 1800 revolutions/minute

- Coolant temperature (*T*):   100°F and 140°F

Example 28.1 *(continued)*

The experimenter has decided to conduct a full factorial experiment in order to generate the maximum amount of process knowledge. A full factorial experiment (discussed later in this section) tests all possible combinations of levels and factors, using one run for each combination. The number of runs in this experiment will be $n = 2^3 = 8$ since there are three factors at two levels each.

To ease the data collection process, the experiment has developed a sheet listing those eight runs with room for recording five readings of the response variable for each run, as shown in Table 28.1.

Table 28.1 A 2^3 full factorial data collection sheet for Example 28.1.

Run	Feed	Speed	Temperature	1	2	3	4	5
1	0.01	1300	100					
2	0.01	1300	140					
3	0.01	1800	100					
4	0.01	1800	140					
5	0.04	1300	100					
6	0.04	1300	140					
7	0.04	1800	100					
8	0.04	1800	140					

The factor-level combinations are also called treatments, and the additional runs of each experiment are called replication. Each run of the experiment is conducted, and the results are recorded in column 1 in Table 28.2. The experiment is conducted again, and the results are recorded in column 2. The experimenter continues in this manner until all five columns contain data.

Table 28.2 A 2^3 full factorial data collection sheet with data entered for Example 28.1.

Run	Feed	Speed	Temperature	1	2	3	4	5
1	0.01	1300	100	10.1	10.0	10.2	9.8	9.9
2	0.01	1300	140	3.0	4.0	3.0	5.0	5.0
3	0.01	1800	100	6.5	7.0	5.3	5.0	6.2
4	0.01	1800	140	1.0	3.0	3.0	1.0	2.0
5	0.04	1300	100	5.0	7.0	9.0	8.0	6.0
6	0.04	1300	140	4.0	7.0	5.0	6.0	8.0
7	0.04	1800	100	5.8	6.0	6.1	6.2	5.9
8	0.04	1800	140	3.1	2.9	3.0	2.9	3.1

Example 28.1 *(continued)*

As we might expect, the five values for a particular run are not all the same. This may be due to drift in the factor levels, variation in the measurement system, or the existence of other noise factors. The variation observed in the readings for a particular run is referred to as experimental error. If the number of replications is decreased, the calculation of experimental error is less accurate, although the experiment has a lower total cost. Therefore, the accurate determination of experimental error and cost are competing design properties.

DESIGN PRINCIPLES

> Define and apply DOE principles, including power and sample size, balance, repetition, replication, order, efficiency, randomization, blocking, interaction, confounding, resolution, etc. (Apply)
>
> **Body of Knowledge VII.A.2**

DOE is an effective tool for determining causal relationships between independent and response variables. However, considerable attention must be given to planning and conducting an experiment. Therefore, it is important to identify and define critical concepts underlying experimental designs:

- Power and sample size
- Replication
- Repeated measure (repetition)
- Confounding
- Order
- Randomization
- Blocking
- Main effects
- Interaction effects
- Balanced design
- Resolution

Each of these concepts will be discussed in detail in the following subsections.

Power and Sample Size

The concepts of power and sample size were discussed in Chapter 25. Recall that the more power a test has, the greater the sensitivity of that test to detect small differences. Power increases as the sample size increases and can be determined before actually conducting an experiment. Also, as the power of the test increases, the probability of a Type II error, β, decreases.

Replication

Replication occurs when the entire experiment is performed more than once for a given set of independent variables. Each repetition of the experiment is called a replicate. Replication differs from repeated measures in that it is a repeat of the entire experiment for a given set of independent variables, not just a repeat of measurements for the same run. Replication increases the precision of the estimates of the effects in an experiment. It is more effective when all elements contributing to the experimental error are included. In some cases, replication may be limited to repeated measures under essentially the same conditions.

Repeated Measures (Repetition)

A *repeated measure*, also known as *repetition*, is the measurement of a response variable more than once under similar conditions. Repeated measures allow one to determine the inherent variability in the measurement system. Repetition occurs when each run is conducted n times in a row. This is in contrast to replication, whereby the entire experiment is repeated n times in a row.

Confounding

Confounding, or aliasing, occurs when factors or interactions are not distinguishable from one another. Confounding occurs when using fractional factorial designs, because such designs do not include every possible combination of factors. However, higher-order interactions are generally assumed not statistically significant. (Note: In some processes, such as chemical processes, higher-order interactions must be considered.) Fortunately, we can choose which factors or interactions are confounded in order to permit the estimation of these lower-order terms.

Order

Order refers to the sequence in which the runs of an experiment will be conducted. Generally, we talk about two types of order:

- *Standard order* shows what the order of the runs in an experiment would be if the experiment was done in Yates's order. To understand Yates's order, look at the second, third, and fourth columns of Table 28.4. Notice the pattern of the lows and highs. The pattern is "cut in half" as we move from right to left.

- *Run order* shows what the order of the runs in an experiment would be if the experiment was run in random order. Random order works to spread the effects of noise variables.

Randomization

Randomization is used to assign treatments to experimental units so that each unit has an equal chance of being assigned a particular treatment, thus minimizing the effect of variation from uncontrolled noise factors. A *completely randomized design* is one in which the treatments are assigned at random to the full set of experimental units. No blocks are involved in a completely randomized design.

Example 28.2

Table 28.2 depicts eight treatments with five replications per treatment, producing 40 tests. The tests should be performed in random order, and they may be randomized in several ways. Here are two possibilities:

1. Number the tests from 1 to 40 and randomize these numbers to obtain the order in which the tests will be performed. This is referred to as a completely randomized design.

2. Randomize the run order, but once a run is set up, make all five replicates for that run.

Although it usually requires more time and effort, method 1 is better. To see that this is true, suppose that time of day is a noise factor and that products made before noon are different from those made after noon. With the completely randomized design, each run will likely have parts from both morning and afternoon.

Blocking

A *block* is a collection of experimental units more homogeneous than the full set of experimental units. Blocks are usually selected to allow for special causes, in addition to those introduced as factors to be studied. These special causes may be avoidable within blocks, thus providing a more homogeneous experimental subspace. *Blocking* refers to the method of including blocks in an experiment in order to broaden the applicability of the conclusions or minimize the impact of selected assignable causes. Randomization of the experiment is restricted and occurs within blocks. The *block effect* is the resulting effect from a block in an experimental design. Existence of a block effect generally means that the method of blocking was appropriate and that an assignable cause has been found.

An experimental design consisting of *b* blocks with *t* treatments assigned via randomization to the experimental units within each block is known as a *randomized block design* and is used to control the variability of experimental units. For completely randomized designs, no stratification of the experimental units is made. In the randomized block design, the treatments are randomly allotted within each block; that is, the randomization is restricted. Similar to the randomized block design, a *randomized block factorial design* is a design run in a randomized block design where each block includes a complete set of factorial combinations.

Example 28.3

If it is not possible to run all 40 tests under the same conditions, the experimenter may decide to use blocking. For example, if the 40 tests must be spread over two shifts, the experimenter would be concerned about the impact the shift difference could have on the results. In this experiment, the coolant temperature is probably the most difficult to adjust, so the experimenter may be tempted to perform all the 100°F runs during the first shift and the 140°F runs in the second shift. The obvious problem here is that what appears to be the impact of the change in coolant temperature may in part reflect the impact of the change in shift. A better approach would be to randomly select the runs to be performed during each shift. This is called a randomized block design. For example, the random selection might put runs 1, 4, 5, and 8 in the first shift and runs 2, 3, 6, and 7 in the second shift.

Once the data are collected, as shown in Table 28.2, the next step is to find the average of the five replication responses for each run. These averages are shown in Table 28.3.

Table 28.3 A 2^3 full factorial data collection sheet with run averages.

Run	Feed	Speed	Temperature	Average surface finish reading
1	0.01	1300	100	10
2	0.01	1300	140	4
3	0.01	1800	100	6
4	0.01	1800	140	2
5	0.04	1300	100	7
6	0.04	1300	140	6
7	0.04	1800	100	6
8	0.04	1800	140	3

Main Effects

A *main effect* is the impact or influence of a single factor on the mean of the response variable. A *main effects plot* is a graphical depiction that gives the average responses at the various levels of individual factors.

Example 28.4

Refer to the data given in Table 28.3. The first step in calculating the main effects, sometimes called the average main effects, is to average the results for each level of each factor. This is accomplished by averaging the results of the four runs for that level. For example, $F_{0.01}$ (feed at the 0.01 inches/minute level) is calculated by averaging the results of the four runs in which feed was set at the 0.01 level. These were runs 1, 2, 3, and 4, so

$$F_{0.01} = \frac{10+4+6+2}{4} = 5.5$$

Similarly, $F_{0.04}$ is obtained from runs 5, 6, 7, and 8:

$$F_{0.04} = \frac{7+6+6+3}{4} = 5.5$$

The other main effects can be determined in a similar manner:

$$S_{1300} = \frac{10+4+7+6}{4} = 6.75$$

$$S_{1800} = \frac{6+2+6+3}{4} = 4.25$$

$$T_{100} = \frac{10+6+7+6}{4} = 7.25$$

$$T_{140} = \frac{4+2+6+3}{4} = 3.75$$

Figure 28.1 graphically depicts the main effects.

A better surface finish is the one with the lowest response. Therefore, the experimenter would choose the level of each factor that produces the lowest result. The lowest response for speed is when the factor is set at 1800 revolutions/minute. Similarly, the lowest response occurs with a coolant temperature of 140°F. What feed rate should be recommended? Since both $F_{0.01}$ and $F_{0.04}$ are 5.5, the feed rate doesn't impact surface finish in this range. A feed rate of 0.04 would be appropriate since it will result in a faster operation.

Example 28.4 *(continued)*

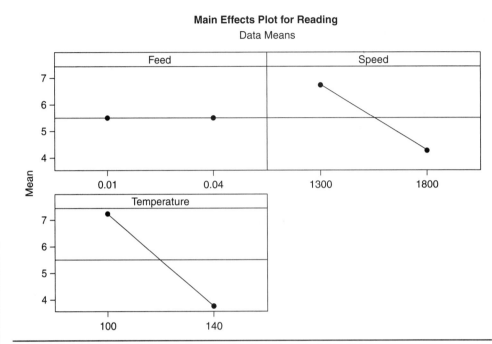

Figure 28.1 Graph of the main effects for the data given in Table 28.3.

Factors with the greatest difference between the "high" and "low" results have the greatest impact on the quality characteristic of interest (surface finish in this case). The impact of the main effect is determined by subtracting the "low level" result from the "high level" result for the factor.

Example 28.5

A quick review of the results from Example 28.4 reveals the impact of the main effects:

$$F_{0.04} - F_{0.01} = 5.5 - 5.5 = 0$$

$$S_{1800} - S_{1300} = 4.25 - 6.75 = -2.50$$

$$T_{140} - T_{100} = 3.75 - 7.25 = -3.50$$

The larger the absolute value of the main effect, the more influence that factor has on the quality characteristic. It is possible that the perceived difference between "high" and "low" results is not statistically significant. This would occur if the experimental error is so large that it would be impossible to determine whether the difference between the high and low values is due to a real difference in the dependent variable or due to experimental error. This may be determined by using ANOVA procedures, as discussed in Chapter 25.

For analysis of data from an experiment, the null hypothesis is that changing the factor level does not make a statistically significant difference in the dependent variable. The α risk is the probability that the analysis will show that there is a significant difference when there is no difference. The β risk is the probability that the analysis will show that there is no significant difference when one exists. The power of the experiment is defined as $1-\beta$, so the higher the power of the experiment, the lower the β risk. In general, a higher number of replications or a larger sample size provides a more precise estimate of experimental error, which in turn reduces the β risk.

Interaction Effects

An *interaction effect* occurs when the influence of one factor on the response variable depends on one or more other factors. Existence of an interaction effect means that the factors cannot be changed independently of one another. An *interaction plot* is a graphical depiction that gives the average responses at the combinations of levels of two distinct factors.

Interaction effects may be determined by replacing each high level with "+" and each low level with "–," as shown in Table 28.4.

Table 28.4   A 2^3 full factorial design using the + and – format.

Run	F	S	T	$F \times S$	$F \times T$	$S \times T$	$F \times S \times T$
1	–	–	–				
2	–	–	+				
3	–	+	–				
4	–	+	+				
5	+	–	–				
6	+	–	+				
7	+	+	–				
8	+	+	+				

Example 28.6

To find an entry in the $F \times S$ column, multiply the entries in the F and S columns, using the multiplication rule: If the signs are the same, the result is positive; otherwise, the result is negative. Complete the other interaction columns the same way. To complete the $F \times S \times T$ column, multiply the $F \times S$ column by the T column. The completed interaction table is shown in Table 28.5.

Example 28.6 *(continued)*

Table 28.5 A 2^3 full factorial design showing interaction columns.

Run	F	S	T	F × S	F × T	S × T	F × S × T	Response
1	–	–	–	+	+	+	–	10
2	–	–	+	+	–	–	+	4
3	–	+	–	–	+	–	+	6
4	–	+	+	–	–	+	–	2
5	+	–	–	–	–	+	+	7
6	+	–	+	–	+	–	–	6
7	+	+	–	+	–	–	–	6
8	+	+	+	+	+	+	+	3

Two-factor interaction effects for $F \times S$ are calculated as follows:

$$F^- \times T^- = \frac{10+6}{2} = 8$$

$$F^- \times T^+ = \frac{4+2}{2} = 3$$

$$F^+ \times T^- = \frac{7+6}{2} = 6.5$$

$$F^+ \times T^+ = \frac{6+3}{2} = 4.5$$

Other two-factor interactions can be computed in a similar manner.

The impact of the $F \times T$ interaction is determined by computing the difference of the averages between the interaction term at the high end and the low end. Thus, we have:

$$(F \times T)^+ = \frac{10+6+6+3}{4} = 6.25$$

$$(F \times T)^- = \frac{4+2+7+6}{4} = 4.75$$

Therefore, the impact of the interaction term is 6.25 – 4.75 = 1.50.

All of the two-factor interaction plots are shown in Figure 28.2. The presence of interactions indicates that the main effects aren't additive.

Example 28.6 *(continued)*

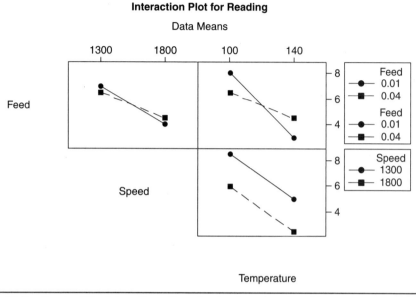

Figure 28.2 Graph of the interaction effects for the data given in Table 28.3.

Now suppose the experiment from Example 28.5 is considered too expensive to run. The experimenter can either reduce the number of replications for each run or reduce the number of runs by using a fractional factorial. However, reducing the number of replications reduces the precision of the estimate of experimental error. The experimenter decides to use a fractional factorial and chooses the one illustrated in Table 28.6. This design uses only four of the eight possible runs; therefore, the experiment itself will consume only half the resources of the design shown in Table 28.5. It still has three factors at two levels each. This design is called a 2^{3-1} design because it has two levels and three factors but only $2^{3-1} = 2^2 = 4$ runs. It is also called a half fraction of the full factorial because it has half the number of runs as the 2^3 full factorial design.

Table 28.6 Half fraction of 2^3 (also called a 2^{3-1} design).

Run	A	B	C
1	−	−	+
2	−	+	−
3	+	−	−
4	+	+	+

Balanced Design

In a *balanced design*, all treatment combinations have the same number of observations. If replication in a design exists, it would be balanced only if the replication was consistent across all the treatment combinations. In other words, the number of replicates of each treatment combination is the same.

Let's examine Table 28.6 for a moment. Notice that when factor A is at its low level in runs 1 and 2, factor B is tested once at its low level and once at its high level, and factor C is also tested once at each level. Furthermore, when factor A is at its high level in runs 3 and 4, factor B is tested once at its low level and once at its high level, and factor C is also tested once at each level. Likewise, when factor B is at its low level in runs 1 and 3, factor A is tested once at its low level and once at its high level, and factor C is also tested once at each level. And when factor C is at its low level in runs 2 and 3, factor A is tested once at its low level and once at its high level, and factor B is also tested once at each level. From this discussion, we can conclude that the fractional factorial design in Table 28.6 is balanced.

The logical next question is, "Why use a full factorial design rather than a fractional design?" To see the answer, add a column to the design for the $A \times B$ interaction, as shown in Table 28.7, and fill it, using the multiplication rule.

Note that the $A \times B$ interaction column has the same configuration as the C column. This means that when the C main effect is calculated, it is not clear whether the effect is due to factor C or the interaction between A and B or, more likely, a combination of these two causes. Statisticians say that the main effect C is confounded with the interaction effect $A \times B$. This confounding is the principal price the experimenter pays for the reduction in resource requirements of a fractional factorial. It is interesting to calculate the $A \times C$ and $B \times C$ interactions as well. We quickly determine that $A \times C$ is confounded with the B main effect, while the $B \times C$ interaction is confounded with the A main effect. So when is it safe to use fractional factorial designs? Suppose the experimenter has completed a number of full factorial designs and determined that factors A, B, and C do not interact significantly in the ranges involved. Since confounding is not an issue, the fractional factorial would be an appropriate design.

Table 28.7   Half fraction of 2^3 with completed interaction columns.

Run	A	B	C	$A \times B$	$A \times C$	$B \times C$	$A \times B \times C$
1	−	−	+	+	−	−	+
2	−	+	−	−	+	−	+
3	+	−	−	−	−	+	+
4	+	+	+	+	+	+	+

Resolution

In the context of experimental design, *resolution* refers to the level of confounding in a fractional factorial design. Resolutions are numbered with roman numerals. Common resolution designs follow:

- Resolution III
  - No main effects are confounded with another main effect
  - Main effects are confounded with two-factor interactions
- Resolution IV
  - No main effects are confounded with another main effect
  - No main effects are confounded with two-factor interactions
  - Main effects are confounded with three-factor interactions
  - Two-factor interactions may be confounded with other two-factor interactions
- Resolution V
  - No main effects are confounded with another main effect
  - No main effects are confounded with two-factor interactions
  - Main effects are confounded with four-factor interactions
  - No two-factor interactions are confounded with other two-factor interactions
  - Two-factor interactions may be confounded with three-factor interactions

Higher levels of resolution can also be achieved depending on the specific fractional factorial design.

Part VII.A.2

Example 28.7

Table 28.8 shows a full factorial 2^4 (two levels for four factors) design. Of course, the number of runs is $n = 2^4 = 16$. Table 28.9 illustrates a half fraction of the 2^4 full factorial design with interaction columns added. This half fraction was carefully selected to avoid confounding of main effects with two-factor interactions. Note that there are six two-factor interactions, four three-factor interactions, and one four-factor interaction. Also note that factor A is confounded with the BCD interaction because they have the same ($\pm$) pattern (although the A column has ($-$) where the BCD interaction has ($+$) signs and vice versa).

Similarly, factor B is confounded with the ACD interaction, factor C with the ABD interaction, and factor D with the ABC interaction. The big advantage of this particular fractional factorial is that, although there is confounding, main effects are confounded with three-factor interactions only. Since three-factor interactions are often small, the confounding of main effects is usually minor. Of course, if a three-factor interaction is significant, as it often is in chemical reactions, it will be missed with

Example 28.7 *(continued)*

Table 28.8 A 2^4 full factorial design.

Run	A	B	C	D
1	–	–	–	–
2	–	–	–	+
3	–	–	+	–
4	–	–	+	+
5	–	+	–	–
6	–	+	–	+
7	–	+	+	–
8	–	+	+	+
9	+	–	–	–
10	+	–	–	+
11	+	–	+	–
12	+	–	+	+
13	+	+	–	–
14	+	+	–	+
15	+	+	+	–
16	+	+	+	+

this design. Another downside of this design is that two-factor interactions are confounded with each other (for example, *AB* with *CD*). This means that an accurate picture of two-factor interactions is not possible.

Table 28.9 represents a resolution IV design.

Table 28.9 A 2^{4-1} fractional factorial design with interactions.

Run	A	B	C	D	AB	AC	AD	BC	BD	CD	ABC	BCD	ACD	ABD	ABCD
1	+	–	–	–	–	–	–	+	+	+	+	–	+	+	–
2	+	+	+	–	+	+	–	+	–	–	+	–	–	–	–
3	–	+	–	–	–	+	+	–	–	+	+	+	–	+	–
4	–	–	+	–	+	–	+	–	+	–	+	+	+	–	–
5	–	–	–	+	+	+	–	+	–	–	–	+	+	+	–
6	–	+	+	+	–	–	–	+	+	+	–	+	–	–	–
7	+	–	+	+	–	+	+	–	–	+	–	–	+	–	–
8	+	+	–	+	+	–	+	–	+	–	–	–	–	+	–

PLANNING EXPERIMENTS

Plan, organize, and evaluate experiments by determining the objective, selecting factors, responses, and measurement methods; choosing the appropriate design, etc. (Evaluate)

Body of Knowledge VII.A.3

When preparing to conduct an experiment, the first consideration is, "What question are we seeking to answer?" In Example 28.1, the objective was to find the combination of process settings that minimizes the surface finish reading. Examples of other experimental objectives follow:

- Find the inspection procedure that provides optimum precision

- Find the combination of mail and media ads that produces the most sales

- Find the cake recipe that produces the most consistent taste in the presence of oven temperature variation

- Find the combination of valve dimensions that produces the most linear output

Sometimes the objective derives from a question. For example, "What's causing the excess variation in hardness at the rolling mill?" could generate the objective "Identify the factors responsible for the hardness variation and find the settings that minimize it." The objective must be related to the enterprise's goals and objectives. It must also be measurable, so the next step is to establish an appropriate measurement system. If there is a tolerance on the objective quantity, the rule of 10 measurement principle says that the finest resolution of the measurement system must be less than or equal to $\frac{1}{10}$ of the tolerance. The measurement system must be reasonably simple and easy to operate.

In simpler terms, the primary objective of an experimental design is to:

- Identify which independent variables explain the most variation in the response variable

- Determine what levels of the independent variables minimize or maximize the response variable

Once the objective and a measurement system have been determined, the factors and levels are selected. People with the most experience and knowledge about the product or process should be consulted to determine what factors and what levels of each factor are important to achieve the objective. The list of factors and the levels for each factor should flow from their input.

The next step is to choose the appropriate design. The selection of the design may be constrained by such things as affordability and time available. At this stage, some experimenters establish a budget of time and other resources that may be used to reach the objective. If production equipment and personnel must be used, how much time is available? How much product and other consumables are available? Typically 20 to 40% of the available budget should be allocated to the first experiment because it seldom meets the objective and, in fact, often raises as many questions as it answers. Typical new questions are:

- What if an additional level had been used for factor *A*?

- What if an additional factor had been included instead of factor *B*?

Therefore, rather than designing a massive experiment involving many variables and levels, it is usually best to begin with more modest screening designs. A *screening design* is an experiment intended to identify a subset of the collection of factors for subsequent study. An example of a screening design is a *Plackett-Burman* design, which is used when there are many factors to study. These designs study only the main effects and are primarily used as a screening design before applying other types of designs. In general, Plackett-Burman designs are two-level, but three-, five-, and seven-level designs are available. They allow for efficient estimation of the main effects but assume that interacting terms can be initially ignored.

The activities outlined in the earlier discussion should not be left to happenstance. Instead, they should result from the development of an experimental plan. An *experimental plan* is the assignment of treatments to each experimental unit and the time order in which the treatments are to be applied. Planning an experiment requires several design considerations:

- *Noise factors* (discussed in the previous section)

- *Confounding* (discussed in the previous section)

- *Blocking*, *randomization*, and *resolution* (all of which were discussed in the previous section)

- The cost to run the experiment

- Time considerations—Limited time might be available to conduct the experiment

Montgomery (2005) offers guidelines for conducting experiments:

1. Recognition and statement of the problem—As discussed earlier, this step might start with a question, but it must eventually be translated into a statistical problem.

2. Selection of the response variable—People most familiar with the process should be consulted.

3. Choice of factors, levels, and range—As with guideline 2, the subject matter experts who are familiar with the process should be consulted.

4. Choice of experimental design—Choosing an experimental design requires consideration of an experimental plan (discussed previously).

5. Performing the experiment—It is critical that the experimenter understand the conditions under which the experiment was conducted. Ideally, these conditions should match those conditions under which the process is routinely performed.

6. Statistical analysis of the data—The data must be carefully analyzed to ensure statistical validity.

7. Conclusions and recommendations—Statistical conclusions and recommendations must be translated into terms that management and operations people can understand, particularly if they are expected to support and/or fund process changes.

The next few sections discuss various designs.

ONE-FACTOR EXPERIMENTS

> Design and conduct completely randomized, randomized block, and Latin square designs, and evaluate their results. (Evaluate)
>
> **Body of Knowledge VII.A.4**

This section addresses the following designs:

- One-way ANOVA completely randomized

- Randomized complete block design (RCBD)

- Latin square design

For the reader's convenience, the statistical models, sources tables, and definitions for the sums of squares have been summarized in three tables. This allows the reader to more readily compare and contrast each model.

Completely Randomized

A *one-factor* (that is, one-way) is a single factor analysis of variance experiment. This is the one-way ANOVA design discussed in Chapter 25.

The top portions of Tables 28.10–28.12 provide the statistical model, the source table, and the definition of the sums of squares for the one-way ANOVA. See Example 25.12.

Randomized Complete Block Design

In a *randomized complete block design* (RCBD), each block contains all treatments, and randomization is restricted within blocks.

The middle portions of Tables 28.10–28.12 provide the statistical model, the source table, and the definition of the sums of squares for the RCBD.

Part VII.A.4

Table 28.10 Statistical models for common experimental designs.

Name	Model	Hypotheses	Assumption
One-way ANOVA (completely randomized design with fixed effects)	$y_{ij} = \mu + \tau_i + \varepsilon_{ij} \begin{cases} i = 1, 2, ..., a \\ j = 1, 2, ..., n \end{cases}$ $y_{ij} = j^{th}$ observation of the ith treatment μ = overall mean τ_i = effect of the ith treatment ε_{ij} = error term	$H_0 : \mu_1 = \mu_2 = ... = \mu_k$ $H_A : \mu_i \neq \mu_j$ for at least one pair (i, j) or $H_0 : \tau_1 = \tau_2 = ... = \tau_a = 0$ $H_A : \tau_i \neq 0$ for at least one i	$\varepsilon_{ij} \sim NID(0, \sigma^2)$ and the variance σ^2 of each factor is constant for all levels
RCBD	$y_{ij} = \mu + \tau_i + \beta_j + \varepsilon_{ij} \begin{cases} i = 1, 2, ..., a \\ j = 1, 2, ..., b \end{cases}$ y_{ij} = observation in the ith treatment, j^{th} block μ = overall mean τ_i = effect of the ith treatment β_j = effect of the jth block ε_{ij} = error term	$H_0 : \mu_1 = \mu_2 = ... = \mu_p$ $H_A : \mu_i \neq \mu_j$ for at least one pair (i, j) or $H_0 : \tau_1 = \tau_2 = ... = \tau_p = 0$ $H_A : \tau_i \neq 0$ for at least one i	$\varepsilon_{ij} \sim NID(0, \sigma^2)$

Continued

Table 28.10 Statistical models for common experimental designs. *Continued*

Name	Model	Hypotheses	Assumption
Latin square design $(p \times p)$	$y_{ijk} = \mu + \alpha_i + \tau_i + \beta_k + \varepsilon_{ijk} \begin{cases} i = 1,2,...,p \\ j = 1,2,...,p \\ k = 1,2,...,p \end{cases}$ y_{ijk} = observation in the ith row, k^{th} column for the jth treatment μ = overall mean α_i = effect of the ith row τ_j = effect of the jth treatment β_k = effect of the kth column ε_{ij} = error term	$H_0 : \mu_1 = \mu_2 = ... = \mu_p$ $H_A : \mu_i \neq \mu_j$ for at least one pair (i, j) or $H_0 : \tau_1 = \tau_2 = ... = \tau_p = 0$ $H_A : \tau_i \neq 0$ for at least one i	$\varepsilon_{ij} \sim NID(0, \sigma^2)$

Note: $NID(0, \sigma^2)$ means normal and independently distributed with mean 0 and variance σ^2.

Table 28.11 Examples of source tables for the models given in Table 28.10.

Source of variation	Sum of squares	Degrees of freedom	Mean squares	F statistic
Between treatments	SS_B	$a-1$	$MS_B = \dfrac{SS_B}{a-1}$	$F_0 = \dfrac{MS_B}{MS_E}$
Error (within treatments)	SS_E	$N-a$	$MS_E = \dfrac{SS_E}{N-a}$	
Total	SS_T	$N-1$		

One-way ANOVA source table

Source of variation	Sum of squares	Degrees of freedom	Mean squares	F statistic
Treatments	$SS_{\text{treatments}}$	$a-1$	$MS_{\text{treatments}} = \dfrac{SS_{\text{treatments}}}{a-1}$	$F_0 = \dfrac{MS_{\text{treatments}}}{MS_E}$
Blocks	SS_{blocks}	$b-1$	$MS_{\text{blocks}} = \dfrac{SS_{\text{blocks}}}{b-1}$	
Error	SS_E	$(a-1)(b-1)$	$MS_E = \dfrac{SS_E}{(a-1)(b-1)}$	
Total	SS_T	$N-1$		

RCBD source table

Source of variation	Sum of squares	Degrees of freedom	Mean squares	F statistic
Treatments	$SS_{\text{treatments}}$	$p-1$	$MS_{\text{treatments}} = \dfrac{SS_{\text{treatments}}}{p-1}$	$F_0 = \dfrac{MS_{\text{treatments}}}{MS_E}$
Rows	SS_{rows}	$p-1$	$MS_{\text{rows}} = \dfrac{SS_{\text{rows}}}{p-1}$	
Columns	SS_{columns}	$p-1$	$MS_{\text{columns}} = \dfrac{SS_{\text{columns}}}{p-1}$	
Error	SS_E	$(p-2)(p-1)$	$MS_E = \dfrac{SS_E}{(p-2)(p-1)}$	
Total	SS_T	(p^2-1)		

Latin square design source table

Table 28.12 Sums of squares for the models given in Table 28.10.

Statistical model	Sums of squares (SS)
One-way ANOVA (completely randomized design with fixed effects)	$$SS_T = \sum_{i=1}^{a}\sum_{j=1}^{n} y_{ij}^2 - \frac{y_{..}^2}{N}$$ $$SS_{\text{treatments}} = \sum_{i=1}^{a} \frac{y_{.i.}^2}{n} - \frac{y_{..}^2}{N}$$ $$SS_E = SS_T - SS_{\text{treatments}}$$
RCBD	$$SS_T = \sum_{i=1}^{a}\sum_{j=1}^{b} y_{ij}^2 - \frac{y_{..}^2}{N}$$ $$SS_{\text{treatments}} = \sum_{i=1}^{a} \frac{y_{i.}^2}{b} - \frac{y_{..}^2}{N}$$ $$SS_{\text{blocks}} = \sum_{j=1}^{b} \frac{y_{.j}^2}{a} - \frac{y_{..}^2}{N}$$ $$SS_E = SS_T - SS_{\text{treatments}} - SS_{\text{blocks}}$$
Latin square design ($p \times p$)	$$SS_T = \sum_{i=1}^{p}\sum_{j=1}^{p}\sum_{k=1}^{p} y_{ijk}^2 - \frac{y_{...}^2}{N}$$ $$SS_{\text{treatments}} = \sum_{j=1}^{p} \frac{y_{.j.}^2}{p} - \frac{y_{...}^2}{N}$$ $$SS_{\text{rows}} = \sum_{i=1}^{p} \frac{y_{i..}^2}{p} - \frac{y_{...}^2}{N}$$ $$SS_{\text{columns}} = \sum_{k=1}^{p} \frac{y_{..k}^2}{p} - \frac{y_{...}^2}{N}$$ $$SS_E = SS_T - SS_{\text{treatments}} - SS_{\text{blocks}}$$

Latin Square

A *Latin square* design is generally used to eliminate two block effects by balancing out their contributions. Notice that each letter occurs exactly once in each row and column in Table 28.13. This design places restrictions on randomization as a result. A basic assumption of a Latin square design is that these block factors do not interact with the factor of interest or with each other. The design is particularly useful, when the assumptions are valid, for minimizing the amount of experimentation.

Table 28.13 Examples of Latin squares from each main class up to order 5.

Latin square size ($n \times n$)	Example 1	Example 2
2×2	$\begin{bmatrix} A & B \\ B & A \end{bmatrix}$	$\begin{bmatrix} B & A \\ A & B \end{bmatrix}$
3×3	$\begin{bmatrix} A & B & C \\ B & C & A \\ C & A & B \end{bmatrix}$	$\begin{bmatrix} A & C & B \\ B & A & C \\ C & B & A \end{bmatrix}$
4×4	$\begin{bmatrix} A & B & C & D \\ B & A & D & C \\ C & D & A & B \\ D & C & B & A \end{bmatrix}$	$\begin{bmatrix} A & B & C & D \\ B & D & A & C \\ C & A & D & B \\ D & C & B & A \end{bmatrix}$
5×5	$\begin{bmatrix} A & B & C & D & E \\ B & C & E & A & D \\ C & E & D & B & A \\ D & A & B & E & C \\ E & D & A & C & B \end{bmatrix}$	$\begin{bmatrix} A & B & C & D & E \\ B & D & A & E & C \\ C & E & D & B & A \\ D & A & E & C & B \\ E & C & B & A & D \end{bmatrix}$

The bottom portions of Tables 28.10–28.12 provide the statistical model, the source table, and the definition of the sums of squares for a $p \times p$ Latin square design.

Examples of common Latin square arrangements are shown in Table 28.13.

Example 28.8

A process can be run at 180°F, 200°F, or 220°F. What might an experimenter do to determine whether temperature significantly affects the moisture content?

Table 28.14 shows the entire Latin square analysis through a series of six tables:

- The first table provides the Latin letter assignments

- The second table links the moisture content responses to the letter assignment given in the first table

- The third table computes $\dfrac{y_{...}^2}{N}$ since this factor is used in every calculation

- The fourth table computes SS_{rows}

- The fifth table computes $SS_{columns}$

- The sixth table computes SS_T

Example 28.8 *(continued)*

Table 28.14 Latin square analysis for Example 28.8.

Day	Machine 1	Machine 2	Machine 3
1	A	B	C
2	B	C	A
3	C	A	B

Day	Machine 1	Machine 2	Machine 3
1	10.8	11.4	14.3
2	10.4	11.9	12.6
3	11.2	11.6	13.0

Latin letter	Machine 1	Machine 2	Machine 3	Total	Total squared
A	10.8	11.6	12.6	35.0	1225.00
B	10.4	11.4	13.0	34.8	1211.04
C	11.2	11.9	14.3	37.4	1398.76

Average	**1278.267**
$\dfrac{y_{...}^2}{N}$	**1276.871**
$SS_{treatment}$	**1.396**

Day	Machine 1	Machine 2	Machine 3	Total	Average	Total squared
1	10.8	11.4	14.3	36.5	12.2	1332.25
2	10.4	11.9	12.6	34.9	11.6	1218.01
3	11.2	11.6	13.0	35.8	11.9	1281.64

Total	**3831.900**
Average	**1277.300**
$\dfrac{y_{...}^2}{N}$	**1276.871**
SS_{rows}	**0.429**

Continued

Example 28.8 *(continued)*

Table 28.14 Latin square analysis for Example 28.8. *Continued*

Day	Machine 1	2	3
1	10.8	11.4	14.3
2	10.4	11.9	12.6
3	11.2	11.6	13.0
Total	32.4	34.9	39.9
Average	10.8	11.6	13.3
Total squared	1049.76	1218.01	1592.01

Total	**3859.8**
Average	**1286.593**
$\dfrac{y_{...}^2}{N}$	**1276.871**
SS_{columns}	**9.722**

Day	Machine 1	2	3
1	116.640	129.960	204.490
2	108.160	141.610	158.760
3	125.440	134.560	169.000

$\displaystyle\sum_{i=1}^{p}\sum_{j=1}^{p}\sum_{k=1}^{p} y_{ijk}^2$	**1288.620**
$\dfrac{y_{...}^2}{N}$	**1276.871**
SS_T	**11.749**

Now we must compute SS_E by subtraction:

$$SS_E = SS_T - SS_{\text{treatments}} - SS_{\text{rows}} - SS_{\text{columns}}$$

$$= 11.749 - 1.396 - 0.429 - 9.722$$

$$= 0.202$$

We will reject the null hypothesis if $F_0 > F_{0.05,(p-1)(p-2)(p-1)} = F_{0.05,3,2} = 19.16$. Since F_0 does not exceed the critical value, we do not reject the null hypothesis and conclude there is no difference in the moisture content.

Example 28.8 *(continued)*

Table 28.15 illustrates the completed source table.

Table 28.15   Completed Latin square source table for Example 28.8.

Source of variation	Sum of squares	Degrees of freedom	Mean squares	F statistic
Treatments (moisture)	1.396	2	0.6980	6.911
Rows (day)	0.429	2	0.2145	
Columns (machine)	9.722	2	0.4861	
Error	0.202	2	0.101	
Total	**11.749**	**8**		

TWO-LEVEL FRACTIONAL FACTORIAL EXPERIMENTS

Design, analyze, and interpret these types of experiments, and describe how confounding affects their use. (Evaluate)

Body of Knowledge VII.A.5

A *factorial design* is an experimental design consisting of all possible treatments formed from two or more factors, with each factor being studied at two or more levels. When all combinations are run, the interaction effects as well as the main effects can be estimated. By contrast, a *fractional factorial design* is an experimental design consisting of a subset (fraction) of the factorial design. Typically, the fraction is a simple proportion of the full set of possible treatment combinations. For example, half-fractions, quarter-fractions, and so forth are common. While fractional factorial designs require fewer runs, some degree of confounding occurs.

Full factorial experiments (described in the next section) require a large number of runs, especially if several factors or several levels are involved. Recall that the formula for number of runs in a full factorial experiment is

$$n = L^F$$

where

n = number of runs

L = number of levels

F = number of factors

For example, an experiment with eight two-level factors has $2^8 = 256$ runs, and an experiment with five three-level factors has $3^5 = 243$ runs. If runs are replicated, the numbers of tests will be multiples of these values. As you can see, full factorial experiments require significant numbers of runs, which can be very costly and time consuming.

Furthermore, if the experiment is testing the effect of various factors on product quality in a manufacturing process, the tests typically must be run sequentially rather than simultaneously. A full factorial experiment with several factors and/ or levels may require a piece of production equipment be taken out of production for a considerable amount of time. Because of the extensive resource requirements of full factorial experiments, fractional factorial experimental designs were developed.

An example of a fractional factorial experiment was given in the "Balanced Design" subsection and illustrated in Table 28.7. Recall that confounding occurs with fractional factorial designs since all treatment possible combinations are not included.

Example 28.9

Consider the 2^{4-1} fractional factorial design and data given in Table 28.16. This is a resolution IV design. Analyze this design to determine which factors are significant.

Table 28.16 A 2^{4-1} fractional factorial for Example 28.9.

StdOrder	RunOrder	CenterPt	Blocks	A	B	C	D	Response
2	1	1	1	1	−1	−1	1	83
4	2	1	1	1	1	−1	−1	75
6	3	1	1	1	−1	1	−1	67
1	4	1	1	−1	−1	−1	−1	10
7	5	1	1	−1	1	1	−1	25
3	6	1	1	−1	1	−1	1	5
5	7	1	1	−1	−1	1	1	20
8	8	1	1	1	1	1	1	87

The following illustrates the analysis of this design:

- The session window for this analysis is depicted in Table 28.17. Initially, the three-factor interaction term *ABC* was assumed to be not significant and used for the error term.

- The first analysis indicates that factor *A* is the only one that is significant.

Example 28.9 *(continued)*

- The analysis is run again with only factor *A*. All other terms were used for the error term. From the session window, we see that the main effects are significant for $\alpha = 0.05$.

- The main effects are plotted and confirm that factor *A* is the only significant factor. The main effects are plotted in Table 28.18.

- The interaction effects are plotted and confirm that no interactions are significant. The interaction effects are plotted in Table 28.19.

- Finally, the residuals are plotted and shown in Table 28.20. The normal probability plot appears to be somewhat acceptable though the histogram does not suggest normality. Remember, only eight points are plotted. The "residuals versus fitted values," though polarized, indicates that the residuals remain fixed while the fitted values increase, suggesting a constant variance. The "residuals versus observation order" does not indicate the presence of a pattern given only eight points.

Table 28.17 Session window from Minitab for the data given in Table 28.16.

```
Results for: Worksheet 1

Fractional Factorial Design

Factors:   4   Base Design:        4, 8   Resolution:   IV
Runs:      8   Replicates:            1   Fraction:    1/2
Blocks:    1   Center pts (total):    0

Design Generators: D = ABC

Alias Structure

I + ABCD

A + BCD
B + ACD
C + ABD
D + ABC
AB + CD
AC + BD
AD + BC
```

Continued

Example 28.9 *(continued)*

Table 28.17   Session window from Minitab for the data given in Table 28.16. *Continued*

```
Factorial Fit: Response versus A, B, C

Estimated Effects and Coefficients for Response (coded units)

Term       Effect    Coef   SE Coef      T       P
Constant            46.500   2.250   20.67   0.031
A          63.000  31.500    2.250   14.00   0.045
B           3.000   1.500    2.250    0.67   0.626
C           6.500   3.250    2.250    1.44   0.386
A*B         3.000   1.500    2.250    0.67   0.626
A*C        -8.500  -4.250    2.250   -1.89   0.310
B*C         9.500   4.750    2.250    2.11   0.282


S = 6.36396      PRESS = 2592
R-Sq = 99.52%   R-Sq(pred) = 69.23%   R-Sq(adj) = 96.63%


Analysis of Variance for Response (coded units)

Source             DF    Seq SS    Adj SS    Adj MS      F      P
Main Effects        3   8040.50   8040.50   2680.17  66.18  0.090
2-Way Interactions  3    343.00    343.00    114.33   2.82  0.406
Residual Error      1     40.50     40.50     40.50
Total               7   8424.00


Alias Structure
I
A
B
C
A*B
A*C
B*C


Factorial Fit: Response versus A

Estimated Effects and Coefficients for Response (coded units)

Term       Effect    Coef   SE Coef      T       P
Constant            46.50    3.182   14.61   0.000
A          63.00   31.50     3.182    9.90   0.000


S = 9            PRESS = 864
R-Sq = 94.23%   R-Sq(pred) = 89.74%   R-Sq(adj) = 93.27%
```

Continued

Example 28.9 *(continued)*

Table 28.17 Session window from Minitab for the data given in Table 28.16. *Continued*

```
Analysis of Variance for Response (coded units)

Source          DF  Seq SS  Adj SS   Adj MS      F      P
Main Effects     1  7938.0  7938.0  7938.00  98.00  0.000
Residual Error   6   486.0   486.0    81.00
  Pure Error     6   486.0   486.0    81.00
Total            7  8424.0

Alias Structure
I
A
```

Residual Plots for Response

Table 28.18 Minitab main effects plot for the analysis given in Table 28.17.

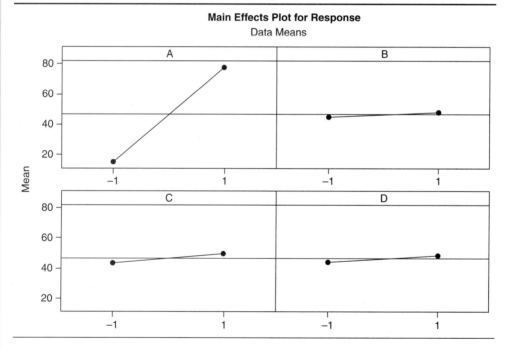

Example 28.9 *(continued)*

Table 28.19 Minitab interaction effects plot for the analysis given in Table 28.17.

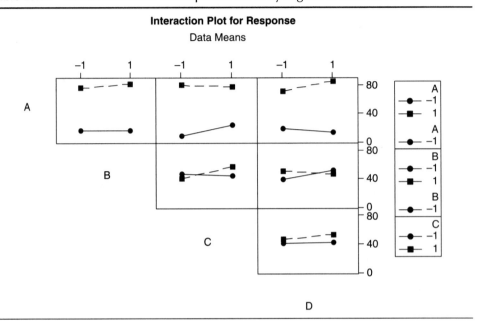

Example 28.9 *(continued)*

Table 28.20   Minitab analysis of residuals for the data given in Table 28.16.

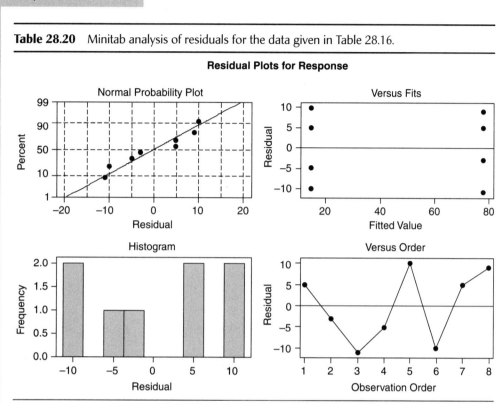

FULL FACTORIAL EXPERIMENTS

Design, conduct, and analyze full factorial
experiments. (Evaluate)

Body of Knowledge VII.A.6

Table 28.21 provides the statistical model, source table, and the definition of the
sums of squares for a full factorial design.

Table 28.21 Relevant tables for two–way full factorial design.

Name	Model	Hypotheses	Assumption
Two-way ANOVA (completely randomized design with fixed effects)	$y_{ijk} = \mu + \tau_i + (\tau\beta)_{ij} + \varepsilon_{ijk}$ $\begin{cases} i = 1, 2, ..., a \\ j = 1, 2, ..., b \\ k = 1, 2, ..., n \end{cases}$ y_{ijk} = observation in the ith row, j^{th} column for the kth replicate μ = overall mean τ_i = effect of the ith level of row factor A β_j = effect of the jth level of column factor B ε_{ijk} = error term	$H_0 : \tau_1 = \tau_2 = ... = \tau_a = 0$ $H_A : \tau_i \neq 0$ for at least one i $H_0 : \beta_1 = \beta_2 = ... = \beta_b = 0$ $H_A : \beta_j \neq 0$ for at least one j $H_0 : (\tau\beta)_{ij} = 0$ for all i, j $H_A : (\tau\beta)_{ij} \neq 0$ for at least one i, j	$\varepsilon_{ijk} \sim NID(0, \sigma^2)$ and the variance σ^2 of each factor is constant for all levels

Statistical model for the two-way ANOVA

Continued

Table 28.21   Relevant tables for two-way full factorial design. *Continued*

Source of variation	Sum of squares	Degrees of freedom	Mean squares	F statistic
Factor A	SS_A	$a-1$	$MS_A = \dfrac{SS_A}{a-1}$	$F_0 = \dfrac{MS_A}{MS_E}$
Factor B	SS_B	$b-1$	$MS_B = \dfrac{SS_B}{b-1}$	$F_0 = \dfrac{MS_B}{MS_E}$
Interaction AB	SS_{AB}	$(a-1)(b-1)$	$MS_{AB} = \dfrac{SS_{AB}}{(a-1)(b-1)}$	$F_0 = \dfrac{MS_{AB}}{MS_E}$
Error	SS_E	$ab(n-1)$	$MS_E = \dfrac{SS_E}{ab(n-1)}$	
Total	SS_T	$N-1$		

Two-way ANOVA source table

Continued

Part VII.A.6

Table 28.21 Relevant tables for two-way full factorial design. *Continued*

Statistical model	Sums of squares (SS)
Two-way ANOVA (completely randomized design with fixed effects)	$SS_T = \sum_{i=1}^{a} \sum_{j=1}^{b} \sum_{k=1}^{n} y_{ijk}^2 - \dfrac{y_{...}^2}{abn}$ $SS_A = \sum_{i=1}^{a} \dfrac{y_{i..}^2}{bn} - \dfrac{y_{...}^2}{abn}$ $SS_B = \sum_{j=1}^{b} \dfrac{y_{.j.}^2}{an} - \dfrac{y_{...}^2}{abn}$ $SS_{AB} = \sum_{i=1}^{a} \sum_{j=1}^{b} \dfrac{y_{ij.}^2}{n} - \dfrac{y_{...}^2}{abn} - SS_A - SS_B$ $SS_E = SS_T - SS_A - SS_B - SS_{AB}$

Sums of squares for the two-way ANOVA

Example 28.10

Determine the effect that acidity and bromine have on nitrogen oxide (NOx) emissions.

A 2^2 full factorial experiment (that is, two levels of acidity and two levels of bromine) with three replications has been established. The three replications will provide us with an estimate of experimental error. The order of the 12 tests has been randomized. The completed data table is shown in Table 28.22.

The following illustrates the analysis of this design:

Table 28.22   Data for a 2^2 full factorial experiment with three replicates.

StdOrder	RunOrder	CenterPt	Blocks	(A)cidity	(B)romine	Response
7	1	1	1	−1	1	20.8
6	2	1	1	1	−1	20.6
8	3	1	1	1	1	28.7
11	4	1	1	−1	1	50.0
9	5	1	1	−1	−1	41.3
10	6	1	1	1	−1	46.5
12	7	1	1	1	1	23.6
5	8	1	1	−1	−1	14.6
1	9	1	1	−1	−1	18.9
4	10	1	1	1	1	40.2
2	11	1	1	1	−1	31.2
3	12	1	1	−1	1	27.6

- The session window for this analysis is depicted in Table 28.23. A review of the table indicates that both factors are significant, but the interaction is not significant at $\alpha = 0.05$.

Table 28.23   Session window results for the data given in Table 28.22.

```
Two-way ANOVA: Response versus A, B

Source        DF        SS        MS       F       P
A              1     223.60    223.60    8.69   0.018
B              1    1001.01   1001.01   38.92   0.000
Interaction    1      55.47     55.47    2.16   0.180
Error          8     205.78     25.72
Total         11    1485.87

S = 5.072    R-Sq = 86.15%    R-Sq(adj) = 80.96%
```

Example 28.10 *(continued)*

- The main effects are plotted and confirm that factors *A* and *B* are both significant. The main effects are plotted in Table 28.24.

- The interaction effect is plotted and confirms that the interaction is not significant. The interaction effect is plotted in Table 28.25.

Table 28.24   Main effects plot for the data given in Table 28.22.

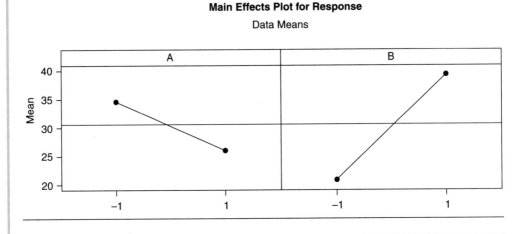

Table 28.25   Interaction plot for the data given in Table 28.22.

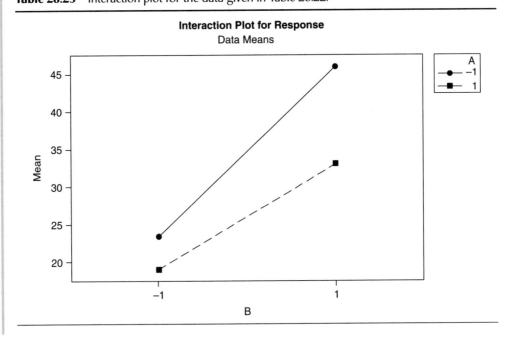

Example 28.10 *(continued)*

- Finally, the residuals are plotted and shown in Table 28.26. The normal probability plot indicates some concern regarding normality, as does the histogram. Remember, only 12 points are plotted. The "residuals versus fitted values" indicates that the variances of the residuals may not be constant. The "residuals versus observation order" does not indicate the presence of a pattern, given only 12 points.

Table 28.26 Residual plots for the data given in Table 28.22.

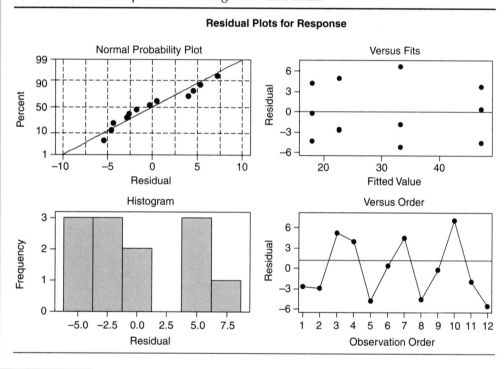

Reference

Montgomery, Douglas C. 2005. *Design and Analysis of Experiments*. 6th ed. Hoboken, NJ: John Wiley.

Chapter 29
Waste Elimination

WASTE ELIMINATION

> Select and apply tools and techniques for eliminating or preventing waste, including pull systems, kanban, 5S, standard work, poka-yoke, etc. (Analyze)
>
> **Body of Knowledge VII.B**

Over the years a great deal of effort has gone into improving value-added activities—those activities that impact the form or function of the product. Lean thinking focuses on non-value-added activities—those activities that occur in every enterprise but do not add value for the customer. Some of these activities can be eliminated, and some can be simplified, improved, combined, and so forth. Tools for identifying and eliminating or reducing waste of all kinds is the topic of this chapter.

Kanban

A *kanban* is a system that signals the need to replenish stock or materials or to produce more of an item. Kanban is also known as a "pull" approach. Kanban systems need not be elaborate, sophisticated, or even computerized to be effective. Toyota's Taiichi Ohno developed the concept of a kanban system after visiting a U.S. supermarket.

A system is best controlled when material and information flow into and out of the process in a smooth and rational manner. If process inputs arrive before they are needed, unnecessary confusion, inventory, and costs generally occur. If process outputs are not synchronized with downstream processes, the result is often delays, disappointed customers, and associated costs. A kanban system may be used to simplify and improve resupply procedures.

Example 29.1

In a typical two-bin kanban arrangement, as the first bin is emptied, the user signals resupply personnel. The signal is usually visual and may involve displaying a card that came with the bin, turning on a light, or just showing the empty bin. The resupply employee gathers the information on supplies needed and replenishes the bins.

Sometimes the bins are resupplied from a stockroom, although often it is from a closer supply point, sometimes referred to as a supermarket. In some cases, bins are replenished directly by an outside vendor. The entire string of events occurs routinely, often with no paperwork. The result is a smoother flow requiring less inventory. A properly administered kanban system improves system control by ensuring timely movement of products and information.

Pull Systems

In a *pull system*, the customer order process withdraws the needed items from a supermarket, and the supplying process produces to replenish what was withdrawn. Also known as a kanban system, a pull system is the opposite of the traditional push system.

From the definition of the pull system, it can be seen that many manufacturing enterprises traditionally operate in a push system. This refers to the fact that raw materials and subassemblies are pushed through the production process with the anticipation that they will be needed by customers.

Example 29.2

An appliance manufacturer receives an order for 50 model XYZs. The warehouse ships the appliances to the customer, which leaves a blank space "open kanban" in the warehouse. This signals the assembly department to assemble 50 appliances to replenish those that have been sold. As the assembly department draws down the inventory of various subassemblies and purchased parts, the empty kanbans signal primary operations and purchasing agents to replenish those items.

The main question is how large should the kanbans be? When the kanbans are too small, purchase orders are placed more often and stockouts occur with greater frequency. When the kanbans are too large, work-in-process inventory (one of the waste categories) builds up and incurs carrying costs that may include a tax burden as well.

5Ss

5Ss, or Five Ss, derives its name from the five Japanese terms beginning with "s" utilized to create a workplace suited for visual control and lean production. Collectively, the 5Ss are about how to create a workplace that is visibly organized, free of clutter, neatly arranged, and sparkling clean. Each "S" of the 5Ss is defined as follows:

- **Seiri (sort or sifting)**—to separate needed tools, parts, and instructions from unneeded materials and to remove the latter

- **Seiton (set in order)**—to neatly arrange and identify parts and tools for ease of use

- **Seiso (shine; also, sanitize or scrub)**—to conduct a cleanup campaign

- **Seiketsu (standardize)**—to conduct seiri, seiton, and seiso at frequent, indeed daily, intervals to maintain a workplace in perfect condition

- **Shitsuke (sustain or self-discipline)**—to form the habit of always following the first four Ss

A process is impacted by its environment, as is the ability of personnel to respond to process change. Improvements in the general state of the work area, including access to hand tools, aid in process control. Especially critical is the cleanliness, lighting, and general housekeeping status for any area where measurements are conducted, since process control data are filtered through the measurement system.

The 5S system is often a starting place for implementing lean operations, so it is important that it be done properly and periodically. Remember shitsuke, the fifth "S," which essentially calls for performing the first four Ss on an ongoing basis.

Standard Work

Standard work is a concept whereby each work activity is organized around human motion to minimize waste. Each work activity is precisely described, including specifying cycle time, takt time, task sequence, and the minimum inventory of parts on hand required to conduct the activity. Standard work is also known as standardized work.

Finding better ways of producing an ever more consistent product (or delivering an ever more consistent service) is the essence of process control. Standard work contributes to this effort by ensuring that product or service flowing into a process has minimal variation and that there is a reduction in the variation caused by the process. In addition, work is performed the same way every time.

Example 29.3

An assembly line worker installs a wiring harness that is connected to various components in subsequent stations. Through conversations with fellow assemblers, it was discovered that if the wiring harness was always placed in a certain configuration, downstream work was simplified. Subsequently, a change was made to the product routing sheets to incorporate the wiring harness change to ensure that all assembly line workers install wiring harnesses in the same configuration. This change to the product routing sheets was supplemented with training.

Some organizations have found that rotating jobs helps everyone become acquainted with additional standard work opportunities.

Poka-Yoke

Poka-yoke is a term that means to mistake proof a process by building safeguards into the system that avoid or immediately find errors. A poka-yoke device is one that prevents incorrect parts from being made or assembled or easily identifies a flaw or error. The term comes from the Japanese terms *poka*, which means "error," and *yokeru*, which means "to avoid." Poka-yoke is also known as error proofing, foolproofing, and mistake proofing.

Poka-yoke activities enable process control by automatically eliminating a source of variation.

Example 29.4

Several people place documents in four separate trays, depending on the document type. A kaizen team discovered that a person sorts the trays at the end of the day because about 5% of the documents are in the wrong tray, even though signs clearly state the document type. The team recommended printing the documents on different colored paper and also printing the signs on the corresponding paper color. This reduced the number of documents placed in the wrong tray to 0.7% and made the sorting job much easier. Note that the poka-yoke activity did not completely prevent errors, but the color-coding scheme did permit ready and immediate identification of an error.

Poka-yoke methods are also helpful in reducing the occurrence of rare events.

Example 29.5

A manufacturer finds that about 1 in 2000 of its assemblies shipped is missing one of its 165 components. A poka-yoke technique was used to eliminate this defect. The manufacturer now uses a bar code on each component and scans the serial number and bar code on each component as it is added to the assembly. The software is written so that the printer at the shipping department will not print a shipping label if any component is missing or otherwise incorrect.

Example 29.6

Another poka-yoke solution involves the selection of the correct part from a rack of bins with similar contents. As the product reaches the workstation, its bar code is read. Light beams crisscross the front of the bins. If the operator reaches into the wrong bin, the conveyor stops until appropriate corrections have been made.

With the increase in flexible work assignments and cross-trained personnel, poka-yoke becomes even more important.

Part VII.B

Example 29.7

A newly assigned press operator placed finished parts on a pallet in the incorrect orientation. The next operator didn't notice the error; thus, several hundred products were spoiled. A fixture for the pallet now makes it impossible to stack the parts in an incorrect orientation.

Kaizen

Kaizen is a term that means gradual unending improvement by doing little things better and setting and achieving increasingly higher standards. The kaizen approach is usually implemented as a small, intensive event or project over a relatively short duration, such as a week. It is advantageous to use the kaizen approach in the following situations:

- The responsibility for implementation of change as a result of the kaizen activity lies mostly within the team and the risk of failure is small

- Projects are time bounded and results must be demonstrated quickly

- Projects are clearly defined

- Improvement opportunities are readily identifiable, such as excess waste

Process control can be enhanced through kaizen events that reduce non-value-added activities. The resulting work is more productive and permits a closer process focus by all involved. Kaizen events are discussed in more detail in Chapter 31.

Example 29.8

A kaizen team observed that fan blades were retrieved from a large box that the operator was required to move around to accommodate model changes. A kaizen team designed a "Christmas tree" with arms holding the appropriate fan blade, which the assemblers could easily reach from their workstation.

Chapter 30
Cycle-Time Reduction

CYCLE-TIME REDUCTION

> Use various tools and techniques for reducing cycle time, including continuous flow, single-minute exchange of die (SMED), etc. (Analyze)
>
> **Body of Knowledge VII.C**

Cycle time is the time required to complete one cycle of an operation. It is useful to find ways to reduce cycle time and cycle time variation. Reducing variation in cycle time makes a system more predictable. Sometimes the cycle time variation can be analyzed by studying the cycle times of subactivities instead. For example, suppose the activity consists of using a word processor to modify a standard bid form. Subactivities might include inserting client information, listing the proposed budget, detailing alternatives, and so on. The total time to prepare the bid might vary a great deal, while the time required to accomplish each subactivity should show less variation. The activities performed should be continually studied in an effort to eliminate non-value-added components and find better and faster ways to complete the value-added components. One successful technique for accomplishing these goals goes by many names: kaizen methods, kaizen blitz, rapid continuous improvement (RCI), and similar titles. The usual procedure is to form a small team that is given a process to improve and a limited time frame, often only a few days. The team should include the people who perform the targeted activity, outsiders who can provide a fresh perspective, and people authorized to approve changes. The team observes the process and raises questions about its various parts, including:

- Why is that stored there? Is there a better place to put it?
- Why do things in that order?
- Would a different table height work better?
- Could your supplier (internal or external) provide a better service?
- Does your supplier know what you need?

- Are you providing your customer (internal or external) with the best possible service?

- Do you know what your customer needs?

- Should parts of this activity be performed by the customer or the supplier?

- Are there steps that can be eliminated?

- Is there enough light, fresh air, and so on, to do the job efficiently?

- Would another tool, software package, and so on, be more helpful?

- Are tools conveniently and consistently stored?

- Can the distance the person and/or product moves be reduced?

- Should this activity be moved closer to the supplier or customer?

- How many of these items should be kept on hand?

- Would it help to do this activity in less space?

In other words, the team questions everything about the process and its environment. Kaizen activity usually results in making several small improvements. In many situations the team actually implements a change and studies the result before making a recommendation.

Another useful time-based measure is *takt time*, which is sometimes confused with cycle time. However, the discussion immediately following should alleviate any confusion.

Takt time is determined by customer demand. It is defined as

$$\text{Takt time} = \frac{\text{Time available}}{\text{Units required}}$$

Example 30.1

If 285 units are to be produced in a shift consisting of 27,000 seconds,

$$\text{Takt time} = \frac{27,000 \text{ seconds}}{285 \text{ units}} = 94.7 \text{ seconds/unit}$$

The system must average one unit approximately every 95 seconds. To meet this demand rate, the cycle time for each process must be less than 95 seconds. So, to meet demand, the basic relationship between cycle time and takt time is

$$\text{Cycle time} \leq \text{Takt time}$$

Takt time is recalculated whenever the production schedule changes.

Example 30.2

If the number of units scheduled is increased to 312 from 285, the takt time is reduced to 86.5 from 94.7 seconds. Adjustments to cycle times, due to adding people or equipment, may be necessary.

It is important to note that if cycle time for every operation in a complete process can be reduced to equal the takt time, products can be made in single-piece flow or simply a batch size of one. Achieving a batch size of one serves as the basis for continuous flow manufacturing, discussed in the next section.

Continuous Flow Manufacturing

Continuous flow manufacturing, commonly referred to as CFM, is a method in which items are produced and moved from one processing step to the next, one piece at a time. Each process makes only the one piece that the next process needs, and the transfer batch size is one. CFM is sometimes known as one-piece flow or single-piece flow.

However, the traditional manufacturing wisdom has been to study the marketplace to obtain a forecast of sales of various products. This forecast is used as a basis for orders that are issued to suppliers and to departments responsible for fabrication and assembly. This is referred to as a "push" system. One major problem with this strategy is that if the forecast is imperfect, products are produced that customers don't want and/or products that customers want are not available. A second major problem with the forecast-based strategy is the increasing expectation by customers for exactly the product they want, exactly when they want it. These two problems have led to a response by the manufacturing community that is sometimes called mass customization. As illustrated by the automotive industry, a customer order of a vehicle with a choice among dozens of options with perhaps hundreds of possible combinations cannot be accurately forecast. Instead, the customer order initiates the authorization to build the product. This is referred to as a "pull" system, because the pull of the customer instead of the push of the forecast activates the system.

Rather than producing batches of identical products, a pull-oriented organization produces a mix of products with the mix of features that customers order. In the ideal pull system, the receipt of the customer order initiates orders for the component parts to be delivered to the assembly line at scheduled times. The mixture of features on the components as they continuously flow to and through the line results in exactly the product the customer needs. Making this happen in a reasonable amount of time would have been unthinkable only a few years ago.

If a system were to achieve the state of perfection, each activity would move a component through the value stream so that it arrives at the next activity at the time it is needed. Achieving and maintaining this state may require a great deal of flexibility in allocating resources to various activities. Cross-training of personnel is essential. The resulting flexibility and system nimbleness would permit reduction of work-in-process. Excessive cycle times are a barrier to CFM.

Reducing Changeover Time

Lean thinking is built on timely satisfaction of customer demand. This means there must be a system for quickly responding to changes in customer requirements. In metal-forming industries, for example, it was common practice to produce hundreds or even thousands of a particular part before changing the machine's dies and then producing hundreds of another part. This often led to vast inventories of work-in-process and the associated waste. These procedures were "justified" because changeover time of dies took several hours. *Changeover time* is the time between the last good piece off the current run and the first good piece off the next run. This includes the time required to modify a system or workstation, which involves both teardown time for the existing condition and setup time for the new condition.

A system used to reduce changeover time and improve timely response to demand is based on a method known as *single-minute exchange of dies* (SMED). SMED is a series of techniques pioneered by Shigeo Shingo for changeovers of production machinery in less than 10 minutes. The long-term objective is always zero setup, in which changeovers are instantaneous and do not interfere in any way with continuous flow. Setup in a single minute is not required but used as a reference. SMED is also known as *rapid exchange of tooling and dies* (RETAD).

The initial application of SMED often requires considerable resources in special staging tables, die storage areas, and so on. SMED is based on the concept that activities done while the machine is down are referred to as *internal activities*, whereas *external activities* are performed in preparation or follow-up to the die change. Shingo's method is to move as many activities from internal to external as possible. A useful technique is to make a video recording of a typical changeover and have the user identify internal activities that can be converted to external activities. Positioning correct tooling, equipment, and manpower should all be done in external time.

The Shingo methodology can be summarized as follows:

- Identify and classify internal and external activities

- Make a video of the changeover process

- Separate internal and external activities

- Convert internal to external activities

- Apply engineering changes to convert any remaining internal activities to external activities as appropriate

- Minimize external activity time

Example 30.3

A procedure for changing cameras requires several steps:

1. Shoot last good picture with camera A

2. Remove camera A and its power supply and place in storage cupboard

Example 30.3 *(continued)*

3. Remove type A tripod

4. Remove type A lighting and reflectors

5. Install type B lighting and reflectors

6. Install type B tripod. Measure distance to subject with tape measure

7. Locate camera B in cupboard and install it and its power supply

8. Shoot first good picture with camera B

A team working to reduce changeover time designed a fitting so both cameras could use the same tripod. By purchasing extra cables, the team was able to avoid moving power supplies. More flexible lighting reflectors were designed so that one set will work for both cameras. Tape was placed on the floor to mark the location of the tripod feet, thus avoiding the use of a tape measure.

Of course, another alternative would be to obtain a more versatile camera that would not need to be changed. However, such an approach may be cost prohibitive.

Part VII.C

Chapter 31
Kaizen and Kaizen Blitz

KAIZEN AND KAIZEN BLITZ

> Define and distinguish between these two
> methods and apply them in various situations.
> (Apply)
>
> **Body of Knowledge VII.D**

Kaizen is a Japanese term made famous by Masaaki Imai in his book *Kaizen: The Key to Japan's Competitive Success* (1986). It refers to a mind-set in which all employees are responsible for making continuous incremental improvements to the functions they perform. The aggregate effect of this approach is the cost-effective and practical improvements that have instant buy-in by those who use them.

Example 31.1

An overhead chain assembly line is populated by 35 workers. Each person can stop the line when he or she sees an opportunity for improvement. A clock that is visible to all is set at 12:00 at the start of each shift and runs only when the line is stopped for these improvements. Management policy is that the clock should have about 30–40 minutes each shift because, "Only when the clock is running are we solving problems and making things better. . . . We need around 30–40 minutes of improvements each shift."

Kaizen, then, is really an approach to process and enterprise management that recognizes the importance of each employee's creative ability and interest in continuous improvement. This approach may be difficult to instill in organizations with a history of top-down management. Barriers include an adversarial attitude and the feeling that "It's not my job to make my job better." In some situations this may be overcome by demonstrating successful kaizen blitz events.

A *kaizen blitz* is performed by a team in a short amount of time, usually a few days. The team focuses on a specific work area with the intent of making low-cost improvements that are easy to implement and are often installed during the blitz. The team should consist of people from the work area, others from similar work areas, technical support, supervisory personnel with decision-making responsi-bilities, and outsiders who can see with "fresh eyes." The blitz begins with some training and team-building activities and quickly proceeds to the work area, where each function is observed and explained in detail. Teams may split into subteams assigned to specific tasks. At some point the entire team hears reports and recommendations from the subteams and reaches a consensus on changes to be implemented. In some cases these changes can be carried out immediately, and in others a schedule of future implementation efforts is prepared. This schedule should include deadlines and persons responsible. The team sometimes makes a report to the next higher level of management, which provides recognition. Some organizations have found these reports and the time spent to prepare for them to be unnecessary as blitz events become routine and a part of the standard way of operating. A side benefit of blitz events is that employees begin to see that their input is valuable and valued, which may lead to more support for the incremental kaizen mind-set.

Example 31.2

A team is assigned to perform a blitz event on an assembly line for an appliance manufacturer. The team consists of the departmental foreman, a group leader, three line workers (including one from a similar line elsewhere in the plant), one engineer with assembly line responsibilities, a technician, and a guest from a nearby factory. After introductory training, communication of the ground rules and expectations, and a discussion of previous kaizen events, the team proceeds to the observation phase, which takes about three hours. Special attention is given to material handling and resupply, availability of tools, and motion by individual workers. The team then splits into subteams. Two of the subteams will work on specific resupply problems, one will work with workplace organization and clutter, and a fourth will examine the need for better flow of subassemblies to the line.

The results of this blitz event included better designs and positioning of material racks, with the stockroom responsible for making sure that the next item on the rack is the next item needed on the line. (Note: This is especially important when the sched-ule calls for a model change.) New routes for the resupply personnel were defined. Designated areas for subassemblies were signed and painted. Standard work issues were resolved and documented so that some assemblers now have slightly modified jobs that will make downstream functions more efficient. Material storage racks were redesigned.

In summary, the term "kaizen" is used to describe the gradual but continuous improvement process that extends over time. It has been found to improve pro-cesses, products, and morale. "Kaizen blitz" describes a short-term event designed to make quick and easy improvements and set the stage for the mind-set required for the long-term kaizen approach.

Part VII.D

Chapter 32

Theory of Constraints (TOC)

THEORY OF CONSTRAINTS (TOC)

> Define and describe this concept and its uses.
> (Understand)
>
> **Body of Knowledge VII.E**

The *theory of constraints* (TOC) is a problem-solving methodology that focuses on the weakest link in a chain of processes. Usually the constraint is the slowest process. Flow rate through the system cannot increase unless the rate at the constraint increases. The TOC lists five steps to system improvement:

1. Identify—Find the process that limits the effectiveness of the system. If throughput is the concern, the constraint will often have work-in-process (WIP) awaiting action.

2. Exploit—Use kaizen or other methods to improve the rate of the constraining process.

3. Subordinate—Adjust (or subordinate) the rates of other processes in the chain to match that of the constraining process.

4. Elevate—If the system rate needs further improvement, the constraining process may require extensive revision (or elevation). This could mean investment in additional equipment or new technology.

5. Repeat—If these steps have improved the process to the point where it is no longer the constraint, the system rate can be further improved by repeating these steps with a new constraint.

The strength of the TOC is that it employs a systems approach, emphasizing that improvements to individual processes will not improve the rate of the system unless they improve the performance of the constraining process.

Figure 32.1 The Drum–Buffer–Rope subordinate step analogy—no rope.

Drum-Buffer-Rope

The "subordinate" step requires further explanation. To illustrate how to manage operations, Goldratt (1997) uses a squad of soldiers walking in single file as an analogy for a string of production processes (see Figure 32.1). As the first soldier moves forward, that soldier receives unprocessed material, the fresh ground. Each succeeding soldier performs another process by walking on that same ground. As the last soldier passes over the ground, it becomes finished goods. Thus, the individual processes are moving over fixed material rather than the other way around. *Lead time* is the time it takes for the squad to pass a certain point. If each soldier moves as fast as possible, the lead time tends to lengthen, with the slower soldiers falling behind and holding up those behind them, since passing is not permitted.

The system constraint is the slowest soldier. The ground can't be processed faster than this soldier can move. This soldier sets the drum beat for the entire system. To avoid lengthening the lead time, a rope connects the lead soldier to the slowest soldier (see Figure 32.2).

The length of the rope is the size of the *buffer*. When the lead soldier, marching faster than the constraint, gets far enough ahead, the rope becomes taut and signals the soldier to stop. In this way, maximum lead time and WIP are fixed.

If a soldier behind the slowest soldier happens to drop his rifle, he'll fall behind a little but will be able to catch up since he is not the slowest soldier. This is analogous to a minor process problem at one station. If a soldier in front of the slowest soldier drops her rifle, the squad will not have to stop unless the slowest soldier catches up with the one in front of him. So if the squad has a high tendency to drop rifles, the rope must be longer. The length of the rope is the size of the buffer. In summary, to avoid long lead times and excess WIP, all system processes should be slowed down (via the rope) to the speed of the slowest process (the drum), and the amount of WIP (or buffer) is determined by the dependability of the individual processes.

Figure 32.2 The Drum–Buffer–Rope subordinate step analogy—with rope.

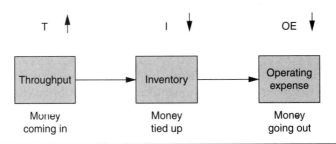

Figure 32.3 The interdependence of throughput, inventory, and operating expense measures.

The TOC as described by Goldratt has significant impact on three key interdependent operating measures of a business. Briefly these are as described by Dettmer (2007):

- Throughput (designated as T)—the rate at which the entire system generates money through sales

- Inventory (designated as I)—the money the system invests in things it intends to sell

- Operating expense (designated as OE)—the money the system spends turning inventory into throughput

Figure 32.3 illustrates the relationship among these operating measures. Notice that as throughput increases, the other two measures decrease. This makes sense, because as constraints are removed, throughput increases. Increased throughput means less inventory tied up in the system. Less inventory, along with a higher throughput, means that less money (that is, operating expense) is required to turn inventory into throughput (or output as the case may be).

References

Dettmer, H. William. 2007. *The Logical Thinking Process: A Systems Approach to Complex Problem Solving*. New edition to *Goldratt's Theory of Constraints*. Milwaukee, WI: ASQ Quality Press.

Goldratt, Eliyahu M. 1997. *Critical Chain*. Great Barrington, MA: The North River Press.

Chapter 33
Implementation

IMPLEMENTATION

> Develop plans for implementing the improved
> process (i.e., conduct pilot tests, simulations,
> etc.) and evaluate results to select the optimum
> solution. (Evaluate)
>
> **Body of Knowledge VII.F**

Once the root causes have been identified, the next step should be to identify
a potential set of solutions. These should be considered tentative until they are
evaluated. When evaluating a set of solutions, it is important that specific criteria
be established. Examples of such criteria include cost of implementation, ease of
implementation, maintainability, reliability, organizational acceptance, customer
impact, impact to the bottom line, and so forth. Whatever criteria are chosen, they
should be relevant, well defined, and a result of team consensus.

Figure 33.1 depicts a matrix of potential solutions and the associated evaluation criteria. Also depicted are weights associated with each criterion. For each
potential solution, a rank can be assigned to each cell, with the best being the
highest number and the worst being the lowest number. Decimal values indicate

	Weight value	Potential solution				
		A	B	C	D	E
Percent process improvement	0.25	5	1	2.5	2.5	4
Cost of implementation	0.20	2	3	5	4	1
Reliability	0.15	5	3.5	2	1	3.5
Maintainability	0.10	4	5	1.5	1.5	3
Installation resources required	0.10	2	5	4	1	3
Adverse impact	0.20	3	2	4	5	1
		3.60	2.78	3.28	2.83	2.53

Figure 33.1 Example of a ranking matrix with criteria weights shown.

ties between two rank values. For instance, if multiple criteria are tied for a specific rank, each would be assigned the average rank value. Once each cell has been assigned a value, the corresponding weight value is multiplied by each of the assigned values and totaled. The potential solution with the highest weighted value becomes the solution of focus for implementation.

However, one big question remains, How are the various cell values determined? These values may be obtained in various ways. Following is a list of common and very useful approaches that yield highly actionable insight:

- **Pilot run**—a short, limited production run usually terminated by elapsed time or quantity produced. A pilot run provides the team with valuable information regarding how an improved process will run, since the pilot represents actual production. It also provides significant insight into issues or problems that were overlooked. Hence, an additional opportunity is available to correct outstanding problems prior to full-scale implementation.

- **Simulation**—usually performed with computer software and can be either deterministic or probabilistic in design. A deterministic simulation provides little information other than to ensure that process flows are correct and that the general design of the simulation matches the operational environment. A probabilistic or stochastic simulation provides insight into the statistical and operational measures associated with the process being simulated. However, careful attention must be given to interpreting the statistical output to ensure parameters are being estimated properly. Overall, simulation provides the ability to "implement" solutions off-line but draw conclusions regarding how the process improvement will operate online. When conducting simulations, caution is warranted. Simulations must be both verified and validated before use.

- **Model**—a smaller physical representation developed on a specified scale. Unlike simulations, models simply provide a three-dimensional miniature version of whatever is being modeled and are a very effective means of communicating an improvement alternative since they play to the visual sense.

- **Prototype**—a representation of the actual product in terms of form, fit, and functionality with perhaps some limitations on functions and/or features. Prototypes provide the team with the ability to experiment with a product by adjusting a wide range of both product and process parameters at usually a lower cost.

Once the team settles on a particular solution, it must then establish an implementation strategy. A first step in this approach might be the development of a force field analysis. Recall that a force field analysis is useful for identifying those forces that both support and oppose the process implementation. These forces can be integrated into the implementation strategy to ensure that those forces that support the implementation are retained or strengthened, and those that oppose are eliminated or mitigated.

Although many authors purport various improvement implementation strategies and methodologies, they are all usually offered in a one-size-fits-all approach. Implementation of any initiative or process improvement must be performed with care and due consideration of the organization's culture. With respect to this idea, consider the following framework, which can be tailored to a specific organization's needs during an improvement implementation:

- Infrastructure—This includes everything necessary to ensure a successful implementation. Examples include changes to hardware or software, training, acquisition of talent, organizational changes, facilities, and so forth.

- Communication plan—A communication plan should be specific with regard to:

  - Who communicates it—It is important that communication start at the top; however, the message needs to cascade down through all levels of management until it reaches those who need to know. This cascading level of communication cannot be emphasized enough, as it creates and reinforces a sense of urgency. Furthermore, it reinforces the message that management believes it is important to implement the process improvement.

  - What is communicated—What should be communicated is the "Who," "What," "When," "Where," and "Why." If each of these questions is addressed, then a clear and concise message will be delivered. No communication should raise more questions than it answers. And it should not assume an existing knowledge of the improvement implementation on the part of the recipient of the communication. What is to be communicated must remain consistent throughout. Thus, the development of "canned" presentations, a script, and so forth, are beneficial in maintaining that consistency.

  - When it is communicated—The timeliness of a communication is, at best, tricky, and often more than one communication is required. Communications may be timed for release just prior to the phases of the implementation schedule. Occasionally it is prudent to issue an overarching, up-front communication and support it with phased communications throughout the implementation. Regardless of the approach chosen, there are three important considerations:

    1. Multiple communications may be necessary

    2. Communications should reinforce and progress logically

    3. Timely communications should occur before a phase is executed, not after

  - Where it is communicated—This speaks to the geographic, demographic, and organizational areas of the communication. For example, the communication may be intended for the engineering function located in North Carolina.

– How it is communicated—All communication media are not created equal. An effective communication plan should recognize that most organizations have a variety of communication media available to them. Choosing the right medium for the right audience is essential. Examples of media include newsletters, e-mail, video, staff meetings, town halls, net meetings, telephone broadcasts, and so forth. It is important to keep in mind that for any given audience, multiple delivery media may be appropriate.

– To whom it is communicated—Without a doubt, it is critical to communicate to all who might be impacted by the improvement implementation. This includes not only those responsible for carrying out the process, but also upstream suppliers and downstream customers.

• Competition for time, energy, and resources—As with most organizations, the team's improvement initiative is not the only critical activity in the organization that demands resources. Therefore, it is essential to outline the requirements for implementation in advance and to secure approval by management. An actual document requiring "sign-off" is helpful in this regard.

• Management commitment—By now, "management commitment" has become cliché. In terms of the framework, this item is pivotal. Nothing will be accomplished without it. Management must be visible, active, and engaged to ensure a successful implementation. Lip service won't cut it. If there is no management commitment, the only assurance the team has is that it will fail.

Chapter 34
Risk Analysis and Mitigation

RISK ANALYSIS AND MITIGATION

> Use tools such as feasibility studies, SWOT analysis (strengths, weaknesses, opportunities, and threats), PEST analysis (political, environmental, social, and technological), and consequential metrics to analyze and mitigate risk. (Apply)
>
> **Body of Knowledge VII.G**

Feasibility Study

A *feasibility study* is a preliminary investigation to determine the viability of a project, business venture, or the like. Such a study may look at the feasibility from the perspective of cost, technology, culture, legal, and so forth. At the conclusion of a feasibility study, management usually determines whether to proceed with the project or business venture.

Risk Analysis

When analyzing risk, we often deal with the concept of expected profit. Expected profit is defined as follows:

$$\text{Expected profit} = \sum_{i=1}^{n} (\text{Profit}_i \times \text{Probability}_i)$$

where

n = total number of outcomes

Example 34.1

A gambler is considering whether to bet $1.00 on red at a roulette table. If the ball falls into a red cell, the gambler will receive a $1.00 profit. Otherwise the gambler will lose the $1.00 bet. The wheel has 38 cells, and 18 are red.

Example 34.1 *(continued)*

Assuming a fair wheel, the probability of winning is 18/38 = 0.474, and the probability of losing is 20/38 = 0.526. This risk analysis is best represented in a table similar to Table 34.1.

Table 34.1 Data for Example 34.1.

Outcome	Profit	Probability	Profit × probability ($M)
Win	$1.00	0.474	$0.474
Lose	($1.00)	0.526	($0.526)
		Expected profit =	($0.052)

In this case, the gambler can expect to lose an average of about a nickel (–$0.052) for each $1.00 bet.

Risk analysis for real-life problems tends to be less precise primarily because the probabilities are usually not known and must be estimated. However, the overall concept is similar.

Example 34.2

A proposed Six Sigma project is aimed at improving quality enough to attract one or two new customers. The project will cost $3 million (M). Previous experience indicates that the probability of getting customer A is between 60% and 70%, and the probability of getting customer B is between 10% and 20%. The probability of getting both A and B is between 5% and 10%. One way to analyze this problem is to make two tables, one for the worst case and the other for the best case, as indicated in Table 34.2.

Table 34.2 Data for Example 34.2.

	Worst case			Best case		
Outcome	Profit ($M)	Probability	Profit × probability ($M)	Profit ($M)	Probability	Profit × probability ($M)
A only	2.00	0.60	1.20	2.00	0.70	1.40
B only	2.00	0.10	0.20	2.00	0.20	0.40
A and B	7.00	0.05	0.35	7.00	0.10	0.70
None	(3.00)	0.25	(0.75)	(3.00)	0.00	0.00
		Expected profit =	1.00		Expected profit =	2.50

Assuming that the data are correct, the project will improve profit of the enterprise by between $1M and $2.5M.

SWOT

A *SWOT* (strengths, weaknesses, opportunities, and threats) is an effective strategic planning tool applicable to a business or project objective.

Strengths and weaknesses are identified with respect to the internal capabilities of an organization. They provide an introspective view. Strengths and weaknesses should not be considered opposites. This can be readily seen in Figure 34.1.

On the other hand, opportunities and threats look outside the organization. Quite simply, we are trying to identify opportunities for the organization and threats to the organization.

When analyzing a SWOT, the question to ask is, "How can the organization leverage its strengths or improve its weaknesses to take advantage of the opportunities while mitigating or eliminating the threats?"

Example 34.3

A private higher-education institution has experienced declining enrollment for four consecutive years, particularly from the two major cities in the state where it is located. This declining enrollment has impacted profitability. The president is feeling pressure from the board of directors, which wants answers as to why the enrollment levels are declining. The industrial engineering department has proposed a Six Sigma project aimed at improving the enrollment rate for students from these two major cities. As the department prepares to make probability estimates, it produces the SWOT analysis shown in Figure 34.1.

	Strengths	Weaknesses
Internal	• High academic entrance requirements • Strong general education program • High percentage of full-time faculty • New endowments for faculty chairs • Fundraising goals are being met each year • Well-designed internship and study abroad opportunities	• Print communications for prospective students are bland and generic • Recruitment staff is too passive in contacting prospective students • Uneven implementation of assessment and program review methods • Student-centered customer focus is not recognized throughout the institution
	Opportunities	**Threats**
External	• Metropolitan area location has population advantages • Area corporations offer tuition reimbursements • Reputable business program with a global studies focus is not marketed as well as it could be	• The number of traditional-age prospective students is expected to decline • With the cost of education escalating, community colleges have recently become viable competitors • Public universities have undertaken significant marketing efforts to position themselves as comparable in experience to private colleges

Figure 34.1   SWOT analysis for Example 34.3.

PEST

A similar analysis to SWOT is the *PEST analysis,* which brings together four environmental scanning perspectives that serve as useful input into an organization's strategic planning process:

- Political—This perspective looks at political stability, threats of wars, regulatory issues, tax considerations, labor problems, laws, and so forth

- Economic—This perspective looks at exchange rates, market conditions, unemployment rates, inflation factors, interest rates, and so forth

- Social—This perspective looks at education considerations, demographics, health factors, cultural implications, and so forth

- Technological—This perspective looks at new technology developments, rate of technological change, cost impact of technology, and so forth

Example 34.4

A nonprofit organization seeks to improve quality of life for citizens in a neighborhood by upgrading storm sewers. Its PEST analysis would look similar to Figure 34.2.

Political	Economic
• The proposal will be competing with other projects for public money • The neighborhood must have adequate representation on the governing bodies • Other neighborhoods will be improved as a result of the proposal, so they should support it • The current situation allows storm water to infiltrate the sanitary sewer system, which impacts all users	• An increase in real estate taxes for two years will be necessary to cover the costs of the upgrade • Environmental costs will be associated with increased stream and river pollution that occurs from ponded storm water
Social	Technological
• People in the affected neighborhood tend to feel disenfranchised and mistreated by the government decision makers, which may impact attitudes toward others • Lack of an adequate storm sewer system has lead to an increasing trend of gastrointestinal illnesses as the population increases and more demand is placed on the existing sewer system	• A study should be commissioned to determine which approach will best solve the storm water problem • New pipe-TV techniques are now available

Figure 34.2   PEST analysis for Example 34.4.

Unintended Consequences

A system may be thought of as the set of processes that make up an enterprise. When improvements are proposed, it is important to take a systems approach. This means that consideration should be given to the effect the proposed changes will have on other processes within the system and therefore on the enterprise as a whole. Operating a system at less than its best mode is called suboptimization. Changes in a system may optimize individual processes but suboptimize the system as a whole. It is important to put measurement systems in place that reflect unintended consequences of proposed actions.

Example 34.5

The resources invested in improving process A might be more profitably invested in process B.

Example 34.6

The improvement of the throughput rate for process A exceeds the ability of process B, thus creating a bottleneck at process B. As result, the work-in-process increases dramatically.

Example 34.7

A distribution center loads its trucks in a manner that minimizes its work. However, this method requires the receiving organization to expend more time, energy, resources, and dollars to unload the trucks. A different loading arrangement may be more expensive to the distribution center, but it would significantly reduce costs for the entire system.

Part VIII
Control

Part VIII

Chapter 35

Statistical Process Control (SPC)

OBJECTIVES

> Define and describe the objectives of SPC, including monitoring and controlling process performance, tracking trends, runs, etc., and reducing variation in a process. (Understand)
>
> **Body of Knowledge VIII.A.1**

The goal of any quality activity is to meet the needs of the customer. Statistical process control (SPC) consists of a set of tools and activities that contribute to this goal through the following objectives:

- Quantifying and reducing variation
- Improving understanding of products and processes
- Improving product and process design
- Monitoring processes in real time
- Making statistically valid decisions
- Centering the process
- Determining when and when not to take action on the process
- Determining the type of action to take (for example, actions to eliminate special causes, actions to improve the overall process)

The SPC tools achieve these objectives by collecting and analyzing data. Figure 35.1 depicts SPC as a machine that uses data as input and has information as its output. The SPC tools squeeze the information out of the raw data.

When setting out to improve a process, the first step is to form a data collection plan. The general rule is to collect as much data as possible, because data collection costs money. In some cases, historical data may be available, but they should be used with caution unless information is available on the conditions under which they were collected. Once data have been collected, they are often placed on a histogram and the mean and the standard deviation calculated. The histogram provides a visual picture of the variation and center of the process, and the mean

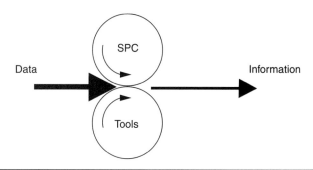

Figure 35.1 Function of SPC tools.

and the standard deviation provide numerical values for comparison. Other charts often used include scatter diagrams, run charts, and control charts. In addition, machine capability and gage repeatability and reproducibility (GR&R) can be calculated by using the techniques discussed in Chapter 20.

The statistical inference techniques discussed in Chapter 25 can be used when more sophisticated analysis is required.

These and other SPC tools are available in various SPC software packages and in some spreadsheets, such as Microsoft Excel.

Special versus Common Causes

Every process has variation. The sources of process variation can be divided into two categories: special and common. *Common causes* are those that are inherent to the process and generally are not controllable by process operators. Examples of common causes include variation in raw materials, variation in ambient temperature and humidity, variation in electrical or pneumatic sources, and variation within equipment, such as worn bearings. In the case of service processes, common causes typically include variation in the input data, variations in customer load, and variation in computer operations. Some authors refer to common cause variation as natural variation.

Special causes of variation include unusual events that the operator, when properly alerted, can usually remove or adjust. Examples include tool wear, large changes in raw materials, and broken equipment. Special causes are sometimes called assignable causes.

A principal problem in process management is the separation of special and common causes. If the process operator tries to adjust a process in response to common cause variation, the result is usually more variation rather than less. This is sometimes called overadjustment or overcontrol. If a process operator fails to respond to the presence of a special cause of variation, this cause is likely to produce additional process variation. This is referred to as underadjustment or undercontrol.

The principal purpose of control charts is to help the process operator recognize the presence of special causes so that appropriate action can be taken in a timely manner. Control charts are discussed in detail in the following paragraphs.

Part VIII.A.1

SELECTION OF VARIABLES

> Identify and select critical characteristics for
> control chart monitoring. (Apply)
>
> **Body of Knowledge VIII.A.2**

When a control chart is to be used, a variable must be selected for monitoring. Sometimes that variable is the most critical dimension on the product. In some cases, the variable of choice is a "leading indicator" of special causes—one that detects special causes before others do. Contractual requirements with a customer sometimes specify the variable(s) to be monitored via control chart. If the root cause of the special variation is known, an input variable may be monitored. Often, the variable to be monitored is the one that is the most difficult to hold, as determined by capability analyses. It is possible to monitor several variables on separate control charts, especially if computerized charting is employed. Ultimately, the selection of the variable to be charted depends on experience and judgment.

RATIONAL SUBGROUPING

> Define and apply the principle of rational
> subgrouping. (Apply)
>
> **Body of Knowledge VIII.A.3**

The method used to select samples for a control chart must be logical, or "rational." In the case of the $\bar{X} - R$ chart, it is desirable that any process shift be detected by the $\bar{X}$ chart, while the R chart should capture only common cause variation. That means there should be a high probability of variation between successive samples while the variation within the sample is kept low. Therefore, to minimize the within-sample variation, samples frequently consist of parts that are produced successively by the same process. The next sample is chosen somewhat later so that any process shifts that have occurred will be displayed on the chart as between-sample variation. Choosing the rational subgroup requires care to make sure the same process is producing each item. For example, suppose a candy-making process uses 40 pistons to deposit 40 gobs of chocolate on a moving sheet of waxed paper in a 5×8 array, as shown in Figure 35.2. How should rational subgroups of size five be selected? Choosing the first five chocolates in each row, as indicated in Figure 35.2, would have the five elements of the sample being produced by five different processes (the five different pistons). A better choice would be to select the upper left-hand chocolate in five consecutive arrays, as shown in Figure 35.3, because they are all formed by the same piston. This rational subgrouping scheme minimizes the within-subgroup variation, thus allowing subgroup-to-subgroup variation to become more prominent.

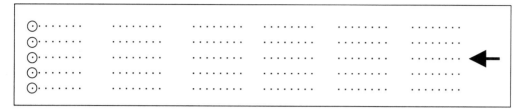

Figure 35.2 Conveyor belt in chocolate-making process.

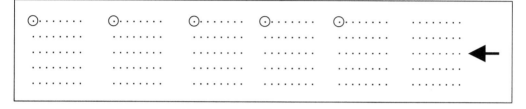

Figure 35.3 Conveyor belt in chocolate-making process with rational subgroup choice.

The choice of sample size depends to some extent on the resources available to do the measuring. However, the larger the sample size, the more sensitive the chart.

CONTROL CHART SELECTION

> Select and use the following control charts in various situations: $\bar{X} - R$, $\bar{X} - s$ individual and moving range (ImR), p, np, c, u, short-run SPC and moving average. (Apply)
>
> **Body of Knowledge VIII.A.4**

Variables Charts

The $\bar{X} - R$ chart is the flagship of the control charts. It is called a variables chart because the data to be plotted result from measurement on a variable or continuous scale. This type of measurement occurs when, for each pair of values, there are an infinite number of possible values between them. On an inch scale, for instance, there are an infinite number of values between 1.250 and 1.251—values such as 1.2503, 1.2508, and so on.

The $\bar{X} - s$ chart is another variables control chart. With this chart, the sample standard deviation s is used to indicate dispersion instead of the range. The standard deviation is a better measure of spread, particularly when the sample size is large.

The individual and moving range chart is useful when data are expensive to obtain or occur at a rate too slow to form rational subgroups.

Appendix 3 provides useful combinations of variables control charts, and all necessary control chart constants are identified in Appendixes 4 and 5.

Control Limits

Control limits are calculated from the process data and, therefore, represent the voice of the process (VOP). They are set at $\pm 3\sigma$. The upper control limit is designated as *UCL*, and the lower control limit is designated as *LCL*. Formulas for control limits and examples of each are given in this section. Several constants are needed in the formulas. The values of these constants are given in Appendix 4. When calculating control limits, it is prudent to collect as much data as practical. Many authors suggest at least 25 subgroups. The examples in the following sections use fewer samples for simplicity. Subgroup sizes are generally held constant with variable control charts. However, subgroup sizes may vary with specific attribute control charts.

When the lower control limit computes to a negative value on the dispersion chart, it is artificially set to zero since it is not possible to have negative ranges or standard deviations.

$\bar{X} - R$ Chart

The $\bar{X} - R$ chart is typically used when the sample size of each subgroup is approximately < 10 since the range is a better estimate of dispersion for smaller sample sizes.

Control limits for an $\bar{X} - R$ chart are given by the following formulas:

k = number of subgroups

n = sample size of each subgroup

$$\bar{X}_i = \frac{\sum_{j=1}^{n} x_{ij}}{n} = \text{average of the } i^{th} \text{ subgroup; plot points}$$

$$\bar{\bar{X}} = \frac{\sum_{i=1}^{k} \bar{X}_i}{k} = \text{center line of the } \bar{X} \text{ chart}$$

R_i = range of the ith subgroup

$$\bar{R} = \frac{\sum_{i=1}^{k} R_i}{k} = \text{center line of the } R \text{ chart}$$

$$LCL_{\bar{X}} = \bar{\bar{X}} - A_2\bar{R} \qquad UCL_{\bar{X}} = \bar{\bar{X}} + A_2\bar{R}$$

$$LCL_{\bar{R}} = D_3\bar{R} \qquad UCL_R = D_4\bar{R}$$

Example 35.1

Data are collected in a face-and-plunge operation done on a lathe. The dimension being measured is the groove inside diameter (ID), which has a tolerance of 7.125 ± 0.010. Four parts are measured every hour. These values have been entered in Table 35.1.

Table 35.1   Data for Examples 35.1 and 35.2—$\bar{X} - R$ and $\bar{X} - s$ charts, respectively.

Sample	7:00 a.m.	8:00 a.m.	9:00 a.m.	10:00 a.m.	11:00 a.m.	12:00 p.m.	1:00 p.m.	2:00 p.m.	3:00 p.m.	4:00 p.m.
1	7.127	7.125	7.123	7.127	7.128	7.125	7.126	7.126	7.127	7.128
2	7.123	7.126	7.129	7.127	7.125	7.125	7.123	7.126	7.129	7.123
3	7.123	7.121	7.129	7.124	7.126	7.127	7.123	7.127	7.128	7.122
4	7.126	7.122	7.124	7.125	7.127	7.128	7.125	7.128	7.129	7.124

Filling in the numbers from the earlier formulas, we have

$$\bar{\bar{X}} = 7.12565$$

$$\bar{R} = 0.00401$$

$$LCL_{\bar{X}} = 7.12565 - (0.729)(0.00401) = 7.122727$$

$$UCL_{\bar{X}} = 7.12575 + (0.729)(0.00401) = 7.128573$$

$$LCL_{\bar{R}} = D_3\bar{R} = (0)(0.00401) = 0$$

$$UCL_R = D_4\bar{R} = (2.282)(0.00401) = 0.00915$$

The values of A_2, D_3, and D_4 are found in Appendix 4 for $n = 4$. The completed $\bar{X} - R$ chart is given in Figure 35.4.

Part VIII.A.4

Example 35.1 *(continued)*

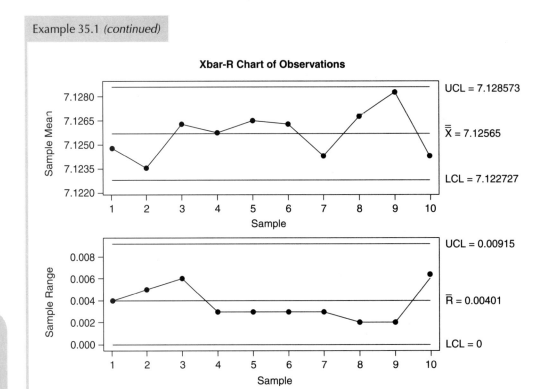

Figure 35.4 $\bar{X} - R$ chart for data given in Table 35.1.

$\bar{X} - s$ Chart

The $\bar{X} - s$ chart is typically used when the sample size of each subgroup is approximately ≥ 10 since the standard deviation is a better estimate of dispersion for larger sample sizes.

Control limits for an $\bar{X} - s$ chart are given by the following formulas:

k = number of subgroups

n = sample size of each subgroup

$$\bar{X}_i = \frac{\sum_{j=1}^{n} x_{ij}}{n} = \text{ average if the } i^{th} \text{ subgroup; plot points}$$

$$\bar{\bar{X}} = \frac{\sum_{i=1}^{k} \bar{X}_i}{k} = \text{ center line of the } \bar{X} \text{ chart}$$

s_i = range of the ith subgroup

$$\bar{s} = \frac{\sum_{i=1}^{k} s_i}{k} = \text{ center line of the } s \text{ chart}$$

$$LCL_{\bar{X}} = \bar{\bar{X}} - A_3\bar{s} \qquad UCL_{\bar{X}} = \bar{\bar{X}} + A_3\bar{s}$$

$$LCL_s = B_3\bar{s} \qquad UCL_s = B_4\bar{s}$$

Example 35.2

Using the same data provided in Table 35.1, construct an $\bar{X} - s$ chart. Filling in the numbers from the earlier formulas, we have

$$\bar{\bar{X}} = 7.12565$$

$$\bar{s} = 0.001795$$

$$LCL_{\bar{X}} = 7.12565 - (1.627)(0.001795) = 7.122727$$

$$UCL_{\bar{X}} = 7.12575 + (1.628)(0.001795) = 7.128573$$

$$LCL_s = B_3\bar{s} = (0)(0.001795) = 0$$

$$UCL_s = B_4\bar{s} = (2.266)(0.001795) = 0.004068$$

The values of A_3, B_3, and B_4 are found in Appendix 4 for $n = 4$. The completed $\bar{X} - s$ chart is given in Figure 35.5.

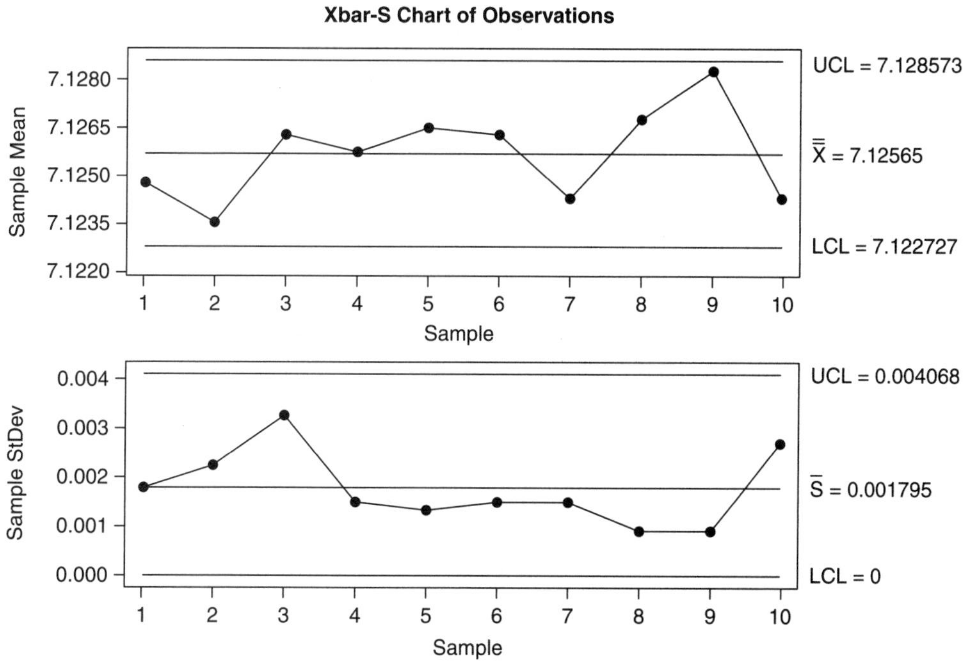

Part VIII.A.4

Figure 35.5 $\bar{X} - s$ chart for data given in Table 35.1.

Individual and Moving Range Chart

Recall that larger sample sizes produce more sensitive charts. In some situations, however, a sample size of one must be used. Examples include very slow processes or processes in which the measurement is very expensive to obtain, such as with destructive tests. If the sample size is one, an individual and moving range (also known as *ImR* or *XmR*) chart is appropriate. The moving range is calculated by taking the absolute value of the difference between each measurement and the previous one. For this reason, the moving range chart has one less point plotted than the corresponding individual chart.

Control limits for the individual and moving range chart are given by the following formulas:

$$n = \text{number of individual data measurements}$$

$$x_i = \text{individual data measurements; plot points}$$

$$\bar{X} = \frac{\sum_{i=1}^{n} x_i}{n} \quad \text{center line of the } X \text{ chart}$$

$$mR_i = |x_i - x_{i-1}| \quad \text{for } i = 2, 3, ..., n$$

$$m\bar{R} = \frac{\sum_{i=1}^{n-1} MR_i}{n-1} = \text{center line for the } mR \text{ chart (moving range)}$$

$$LCL_X = \bar{X} - E_2 m\bar{R} \qquad UCL_X = \bar{X} + E_2 m\bar{R}$$

$$LCL_{mR} = D_3 m\bar{R} \qquad UCL_{mR} = D_4 m\bar{R}$$

Example 35.3

Using the data provided in Table 35.2, construct an individual and moving range chart.

Filling in the numbers from the earlier formulas, we have

$$\bar{X} = 288.3$$

$$m\bar{R} = 2.89$$

$$LCL_X = 288.3 - (2.660)(2.89) = 280.62$$

$$UCL_X = 288.3 + (2.660)(2.89) = 295.98$$

$$LCL_{mR} = (0)(2.89) = 0$$

$$UCL_{mR} = (3.267)(2.89) = 9.44$$

The values of E_2, D_3, and D_4 are found in Appendix 4 for $n = 2$.

Example 35.3 *(continued)*

Table 35.2   Data for Example 35.3—individual and moving range chart.

Reading	Individual data element
1	290
2	288
3	285
4	290
5	291
6	287
7	284
8	290
9	290
10	288

The completed individual and moving range chart is given in Figure 35.6.

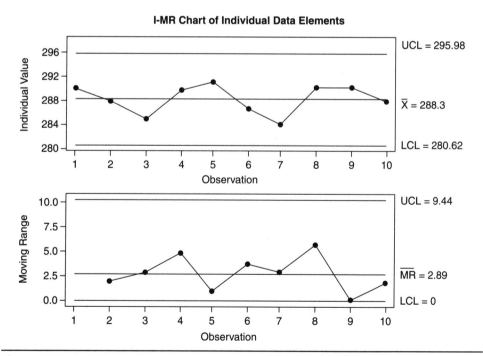

Figure 35.6   Individual and moving range chart for data given in Table 35.2.

Part VIII.A.4

Attribute Charts

Attribute charts are used for count data where each data element is classified in one of two categories, such as good or bad. *p* charts and *np* charts are used to plot percentage or proportion defective, and *c* charts and *u* charts are used to plot counts of defects. A "defective" is also known as a "nonconformance." Similarly, a "defect" is also known as a "nonconformity." The *np* chart and the *c* chart require constant sample sizes. However, the *p* chart and the *u* chart permit variable sample sizes.

When a lower control limit computes to a negative value, it is artificially set to zero since it is not possible to have a negative percentage defective or negative defect counts.

p Chart

Recall that the *p* chart is used when the sample size varies. We use this chart to plot the proportion or percentage of defectives. Note: The control limits on the chart appear ragged because they reflect each subgroup's individual sample size.

The formulas for the center line and the upper and lower control limits for the *p* chart are

$$D_i = \text{number of defective (nonconforming) units in the } i^{th} \text{ subgroup}$$

$$k = \text{number of subgroups}$$

$$n_i = \text{sample size of the } i^{th} \text{ subgroup}$$

$$p_i = \frac{D_i}{n_i} = \text{ plot points}$$

$$\bar{p} = \frac{\sum\limits_{i=1}^{k} D_i}{\sum\limits_{i=1}^{k} n_i} = \text{ center line for the } p \text{ chart}$$

$$LCL_p = \bar{p} - 3\sqrt{\frac{\bar{p}(1-\bar{p})}{n_i}} \qquad UCL_p = \bar{p} + 3\sqrt{\frac{\bar{p}(1-\bar{p})}{n_i}}$$

Example 35.4

A test was conducted to determine the presence of the Rh factor in 13 samples of donated blood. The results of the test are given in Table 35.3.

Filling in the numbers from the earlier formulas, we have

$$\bar{p} = \frac{189}{1614} = 0.1171$$

Example 35.4 *(continued)*

Table 35.3 Data for Example 35.4—*p* chart.

Date	Number of defectives	Sample size
8-Sep	12	115
9-Sep	14	125
10-Sep	18	111
11-Sep	13	133
12-Sep	17	120
13-Sep	15	118
14-Sep	15	137
15-Sep	16	108
16-Sep	11	110
17-Sep	14	124
18-Sep	13	128
19-Sep	14	144
20-Sep	17	141

The enthusiastic reader will want to attempt to calculate the control limits for each value of n_i:

$$LCL_p = \bar{p} - 3\sqrt{\frac{\bar{p}(1-\bar{p})}{n_i}}$$

$$UCL_p = \bar{p} + 3\sqrt{\frac{\bar{p}(1-\bar{p})}{n_i}}$$

The completed *p* chart is given in Figure 35.7.

Part VIII.A.4

Example 35.4 *(continued)*

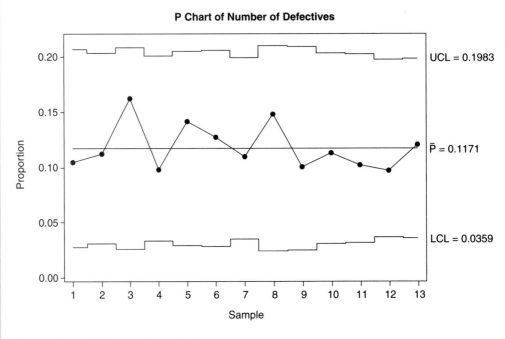

Tests performed with unequal sample sizes

Figure 35.7   *p* chart for data given in Table 35.3.

np Chart

Recall that the *np* chart is used when the sample size is constant. We use this chart to plot the number of defectives.

The formulas for the center line and the upper and lower control limits for the *np* chart are

D_i = number of defective (nonconforming) units in the ith subgroup; plot points

k = number of subgroups

n_i = sample size of each subgroup

$$n\bar{p} = n\dfrac{\sum\limits_{i=1}^{k} D_i}{\sum\limits_{i=1}^{k} n_i} = \text{ center line for the } np \text{ chart}$$

$$LCL_{np} = n\bar{p} - 3\sqrt{n\bar{p}\left(1 - \bar{p}\right)} \qquad\qquad UCL_{np} = n\bar{p} + 3\sqrt{n\bar{p}\left(1 - \bar{p}\right)}$$

Example 35.5

Packages containing 1000 lightbulbs are randomly selected, and all 1000 bulbs are light-tested. The results of the tests are given in Table 35.4.

Table 35.4   Data for Example 35.5—*np* chart.

Date	Number of defectives	Sample size
8-Sep	9	1000
9-Sep	12	1000
10-Sep	13	1000
11-Sep	12	1000
12-Sep	11	1000
13-Sep	9	1000
14-Sep	7	1000
15-Sep	0	1000
16-Sep	12	1000
17-Sep	8	1000
18-Sep	9	1000
19-Sep	7	1000
20-Sep	11	1000

Filling in the numbers from the earlier formulas, we have

$$\bar{p} = \frac{120}{13000} = 0.00923$$

$$n\bar{p} = (1000)\left(\frac{120}{13000}\right) = 9.23$$

$$LCL_{np} = 9.23 - 3\sqrt{(1000)(0.00923)(1 - 0.00923)} = 0.16$$

$$UCL_{np} = 9.23 + 3\sqrt{(1000)(0.00923)(1 - 0.00923)} = 18.30$$

The completed *np* chart is given in Figure 35.8.

Example 35.5 *(continued)*

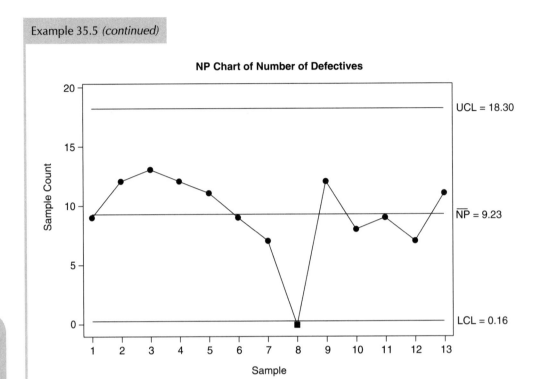

Figure 35.8 *np* chart for data given in Table 35.4.

c Chart

Recall that the *c* chart is used when the sample size is constant. We use this chart to plot the number of defects.

The formulas for the center line and the upper and lower control limits for the *c* chart are

c_i = number of defective (nonconformities) in the ith subgroup; plot points

k = number of subgroups

n = sample size of each subgroup

$$\bar{c} = \frac{\sum_{i=1}^{k} c_i}{k}$$

$$LCL_c = \bar{c} - 3\sqrt{\bar{c}} \qquad\qquad UCL_c = \bar{c} + 3\sqrt{\bar{c}}$$

Example 35.6

Panes of glass are inspected for defects such as bubbles, scratches, chips, inclusions, waves, and dips. The results of the inspection are given in Table 35.5.

Table 35.5   Data for Example 35.6—c chart.

Date	Number of defects	Sample size
15-May	19	150
16-May	12	150
17-May	13	150
18-May	12	150
19-May	18	150
20-May	19	150
21-May	17	150
22-May	20	150
23-May	22	150
24-May	18	150
25-May	19	150
26-May	17	150
27-May	11	150

Filling in the numbers from the earlier formulas, we have

$$\bar{c} = \frac{217}{13} = 16.69$$

$$LCL_c = 16.69 - 3\sqrt{16.69} = 4.44$$

$$UCL_c = 16.69 + 3\sqrt{16.69} = 28.95$$

The completed c chart is given in Figure 35.9.

Example 35.6 *(continued)*

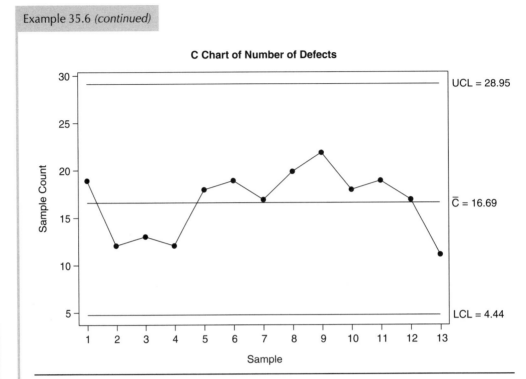

Figure 35.9 *c* chart for data given in Table 35.5.

u Chart

Recall that the *u* chart is used when the sample size varies. We use this chart to plot the number of defects per unit. Note: The control limits on the chart appear ragged because they reflect each subgroup's individual sample size.

The formulas for the center line and the upper and lower control limits for the *u* chart are

$$c_i = \text{number of defects (nonconformities) units in the } i^{th} \text{ subgroup}$$

$$k = \text{number of subgroups}$$

$$n_i = \text{sample size of the } i^{th} \text{ subgroup}$$

$$u_i = \frac{c_i}{n_i} = \text{number of defects per unit in the } i^{th} \text{ subgroup; plot points}$$

$$\bar{u} = \frac{\sum_{i=1}^{k} D_i}{\sum_{i=1}^{k} n_i} = \text{center line for the } u \text{ chart}$$

$$LCL_u = \bar{u} - 3\sqrt{\frac{\bar{u}}{n_i}}$$

$$UCL_u = \bar{u} + 3\sqrt{\frac{\bar{u}}{n_i}}$$

Example 35.7

Panes of glass are inspected for defects such as bubbles, scratches, chips, inclusions, waves, and dips. The results of the inspection are given in Table 35.6.

Table 35.6   Data for Example 35.7—u chart.

Date	Number of defects	Sample size
4-Jul	4	125
5-Jul	8	111
6-Jul	3	133
7-Jul	7	120
8-Jul	5	118
9-Jul	5	137
10-Jul	6	108
11-Jul	10	110
12-Jul	4	124
13-Jul	3	128
14-Jul	4	144
15-Jul	7	138
16-Jul	11	150

Filling in the numbers from the earlier formulas, we have

$$\bar{u} = \frac{77}{1646} = 0.0468$$

The enthusiastic reader will want to attempt to calculate the control limits for each value of n_i:

$$LCL_u = \bar{u} - 3\sqrt{\frac{\bar{u}}{n_i}}$$

$$UCL_u = \bar{u} + 3\sqrt{\frac{\bar{u}}{n_i}}$$

Example 35.7 *(continued)*

The completed *u* chart is given in Figure 35.10.

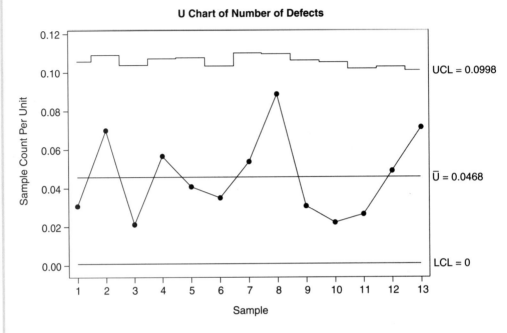

U Chart of Number of Defects

UCL = 0.0998

$\bar{U}$ = 0.0468

LCL = 0

Tests performed with unequal sample sizes

Figure 35.10   *u* chart for data given in Table 35.6.

Short-Run Control Charts

Short-run control charts should be considered when data are collected infrequently or aperiodically. They may be used with historical target or target values, attribute or variable data, and individual or subgrouped averages.

While the subject of short-run control charts is not overly difficult, it can be particularly confusing due to the use of various nomenclatures and terminologies used by authors. For this reason, the following tables and figures have been prepared:

- Figure 35.11: This flowchart will aid the reader in determining what type of chart is most appropriate and will link to a comprehensive set of examples.

- Table 35.7: This table contains all the formulas needed to construct the short-run charts discussed in this subsection. Furthermore, an attempt has been made to provide the reader with alternate names of charts so that recognition is possible among the various sources and references.

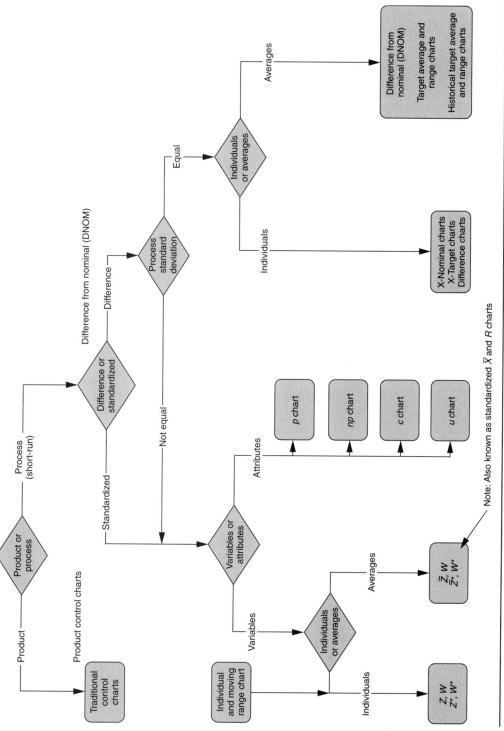

Figure 35.11   Short-run SPC decision flowchart.

Part VIII.A.4

Part VIII.A.4

Table 35.7 Summary of formulas for short-run SPC charts.

Chart type	Paired charts		Individuals — Paired charts		Paired charts	
	Difference (X-nominal, X-target)	mR	Z	W	Z*	W*
Plot points	$X - Nom$	$mR_{X\text{-}nominal}$	$Z = \dfrac{X - Nom}{Sigma(X)}$	mR_Z	$Z^{*} = \dfrac{X - Nom}{\overline{R}}$	$mR_{Z'}$
CL	0.0	$\overline{mR}$	0.0	d_2	0.0	1.0
UCL	$+A_3\overline{mR}$	$D_4\overline{mR}$	+3.0	$d_2 + 3d_3$	$+A_3$	D_4
LCL	$-A_3\overline{mR}$	$D_3\overline{mR}$	–3.0	0	$-A_3$	D_3

Where Nom = *Nominal* or *Target* and $Sigma(X) = \dfrac{\overline{R}}{d_2}$ and $n = 2$

Continued

Table 35.7 Summary of formulas for short-run SPC charts. *Continued*

	Averages					
	Paired charts		**Paired charts**		**Paired charts**	
Chart type	Difference	R	$\bar{Z}$ (standardized average)	W (standardized range)	$\bar{Z}^*$ (standardized average)	W^* (standardized range)
Plot points	$\bar{X} - Nom$	R	$Z = \dfrac{\bar{X} - Nom}{Sigma(\bar{X})}$	$\dfrac{R}{Sigma(X)}$	$Z^* = \dfrac{\bar{X} - Nom}{\bar{R}}$	$\dfrac{R}{\bar{R}}$
CL	0.0	$\bar{R}$	0.0	d_2	0.0	1.0
UCL	$+A_2\bar{R}$	$D_4\bar{R}$	+3.0	$d_2 + 3d_3$	$+A_2$	D_4
LCL	$-A_2\bar{R}$	$D_3\bar{R}$	−3.0	$d_2 - 3d_3$	$-A_2$	D_3

Where Nom = *Nominal or Target* and $Sigma(\bar{X}) = \dfrac{\bar{R}}{d_2\sqrt{n}}$ and $n > 2$

	Attributes			
Chart type	Standardized p	Standardized np	c	u
Plot points	$Z_i = \dfrac{p_i - \bar{p}}{\sqrt{\bar{p}(1-\bar{p})/n}}$	$Z_i = \dfrac{np_i - n\bar{p}}{\sqrt{n\bar{p}(1-\bar{p})}/n}$	$Z_i = \dfrac{c_i - \bar{c}}{\sqrt{\bar{c}}}$	$Z_i = \dfrac{u_i - \bar{u}}{\sqrt{\bar{u}/n}}$
CL	0.0	0.0	0.0	0.0
UCL	+3.0	+3.0	+3.0	+3.0
LCL	−3.0	−3.0	−3.0	−3.0

Part VIII.A.4

The focus of this subsection will be on selecting the appropriate chart or pair of charts and computing the corresponding statistics to be plotted. Since formulas are provided and the construction of most tables and charts is fundamentally similar, an example table will be developed for plotting the $\bar{Z}$, W and $\bar{Z}^*$, and W^* charts only. Little attention will be given to the actual plotting of the data.

Key Considerations When Using a Short-Run Chart

Griffith (1996) recommends the following rules when dealing with short-run control charts:

- Focus on the process, not the parts. Traditional (or product) control charts should be used to monitor parts.

- Be sure the process stream is the same. For example, parts may vary in size, shape, and material, but the process remains the same.

- Look for generic families of product made by the process.

- Use coded data. This permits different parts, dimensions, tolerances, and so on, to be used together.

- Use the 20 subgroups minimum rule. The immediately preceding bullets all work to help meet this requirement.

- Variation between different parts aggregated on a chart must be the same. Statistically, we call this homogeneity of variance. Various tests are available to determine homogeneity of variance.

When homogeneity of variance is not present in the data, the reader will note from Figure 35.11 that standardized charts must be used.

Also, it is important to point out that the measurement system should be sufficiently granular to detect variation. This is a particularly important consideration when dealing with parts of varying size, shape, and other measured characteristics.

A special word of caution is in order when interpreting short-run charts. Remember, these types of charts reflect multiple part numbers. Subsequently, the short-run chart may be in control but not the specific part numbers that compose it. Undoubtedly, the reader will notice we are frequently working with coded data (that is, differences from target or historical target for averages and ranges). Therefore, it is critical that the data for each part be coded with their own target or historical target. This point cannot be emphasized enough.

Constructing a Short-Run Chart

1. Determine the historical average and historical range for each product

2. Collect a set of data—$X_1, X_2, \ldots, X_n$—for a number of different products that follow the same process

3. Compute the average and range for each subgroup

4. Compute Sigma (X) or Sigma ($\bar{X}$), depending on the set of charts to be developed

5. Compute $\bar{Z}$, W and $\bar{Z}^*$, W^*, depending on the set of charts to be developed

6. Compute the *LCL* and the *UCL* for the moving range chart, using the appropriate formulas given in the "Averages" section of Table 35.7

7. Compute the center line for the moving average chart, using the appropriate formulas given in the "Averages" section of Table 35.7

8. Compute the *LCL* and the *UCL* for the moving average chart, using the appropriate formulas given in the "Averages" section of Table 35.7

9. Plot the data, center line, *LCL*, and *UCL* for both of the chosen pairs of charts

10. Interpret results and take action accordingly

Example 35.8

The data shown in Table 35.8 are taken from Wheeler (1991).

1. The product, historical average, and historical range are given in columns B–D, respectively.

2. The data collected by product in time order by subgroup are given in columns E–I, respectively. A subgroup size of five has been used.

3. The average and range for each subgroup have been computed and are given in columns J and K, respectively.

4. For $n = 5$, $d_2 = 2.326$, Sigma (X) is given in column L, and Sigma ($\bar{X}$) is given in column M. Note: The average range given in column D is used to compute the values for each product.

5. Using the formulas given in Table 35.7, the values for $\bar{Z}$, W and $\bar{Z}^*$, and W^* are computed as reflected in columns N–Q, respectively.

Steps 6–10 are common to most control charts and will be left to the enjoyment of the reader.

Example 35.8 *(continued)*

Table 35.8 Short-run chart data for Example 35.8.

Column A	Column B	Column C	Column D	Column E	Column F	Column G	Column H	Column I	Column J	Column K	Column L	Column M	Column N	Column O	Column P	Column Q
Date	Product	Target/ Nominal value	Average range	X_1	X_1	X_1	X_1	X_1	$\bar{X}$	R	$Sigma(X)$	$Sigma(\bar{X})$	$\bar{Z}$	W	$\bar{Z}'$	W'
11-Jul	1407	9.5	10.50	16	11	13	7	10	11.4	9	4.51	2.02	0.94	2.0	0.18	0.9
12-Jul	1407	9.5	10.50	14	15	15	10	16	14.0	6	4.51	2.02	2.23	1.3	0.43	0.6
15-Jul	1404	4.5	4.10	4	0	6	4	4	3.6	6	1.76	0.79	-1.14	3.4	-0.22	1.5
16-Jul	1404	4.5	4.10	2	4	5	8	5	4.8	6	1.76	0.79	0.38	3.4	0.07	1.5
17-Jul	1404	4.5	4.10	5	8	3	5	3	4.8	5	1.76	0.79	0.38	2.8	0.07	1.2
18-Jul	1404	4.5	4.10	6	6	5	3	5	5.0	3	1.76	0.79	0.63	1.7	0.12	0.7
19-Jul	1404	4.5	4.10	4	5	4	2	8	4.6	6	1.76	0.79	0.13	3.4	0.02	1.5
22-Jul	1407	9.5	10.50	5	7	7	8	15	8.4	10	4.51	2.02	-0.54	2.2	-0.10	1.0
23-Jul	1408	8.5	7.90	0	9	9	7	0	5.0	9	3.40	1.52	-2.30	2.6	-0.44	1.1
24-Jul	1408	8.5	7.90	5	7	7	12	8	7.8	7	3.40	1.52	-0.46	2.1	-0.09	0.9
25-Jul	1404	4.5	4.10	4	2	7	2	2	3.4	5	1.76	0.79	-1.40	2.8	-0.27	1.2
26-Jul	1404	4.5	4.10	3	6	4	2	6	4.2	4	1.76	0.79	-0.38	2.3	-0.07	1.0
29-Jul	1407	9.5	10.50	3	10	16	6	10	9.0	13	4.51	2.02	-0.25	2.9	-0.05	1.2
30-Jul	1408	8.5	7.90	9	7	8	8	13	9.0	6	3.40	1.52	0.33	1.8	0.06	0.8
31-Jul	1407	9.5	10.50	5	15	9	5	10	8.8	10	4.51	2.02	-0.35	2.2	-0.07	1.0
1-Aug	1408	8.5	7.90	8	8	8	10	10	8.8	2	3.40	1.52	0.20	0.6	0.04	0.3
2-Aug	1407	9.5	10.50	11	15	12	8	14	12.0	7	4.51	2.02	1.24	1.6	0.24	0.7
5-Aug	1404	4.5	4.10	3	2	5	4	4	3.6	3	1.76	0.79	-1.14	1.7	-0.22	0.7
6-Aug	1404	4.5	4.10	4	5	5	4	8	5.2	4	1.76	0.79	0.89	2.3	0.17	1.0
7-Aug	1404	4.5	4.10	2	3	1	4	1	2.2	3	1.76	0.79	-2.92	1.7	-0.56	0.7

Part VIII.A.4

Moving Average and Moving Range Control Charts

The moving average and moving range (MAMR) chart may be suitable in the following situations:

- When data are collected periodically or when it takes time to produce a single item

- When it may be desirable to dampen the effects of overcontrol

- When it may be necessary to detect smaller shifts in the process than with a comparable Shewhart chart

Key Considerations When Using an MAMR Chart

The user of an MAMR chart must address the following:

- Selection of a moving average length: The overall sensitivity of the chart to detect process shifts is affected by the selection of the moving average length. Generally, the longer the length, the less sensitive the chart is to detecting shifts. However, specific selection of the length should be made with consideration to the out-of-control detection rules being used. Wheeler (1995) presents and compares a series of power function curves (that is, probability of detecting a shift in the process average) for n – point moving averages to various "Chart for Individuals" detection rules. When the moving average length becomes a practical consideration, the reader is encouraged to consult a more rigorous source on this topic. Note: Minitab allows the user to set the size of the moving average length.

- Selection of a method for estimating σ: Wheeler (1995) suggests two methods:

  - Average moving range: An example using this method is given in a later section. The average moving range will be designated $\bar{R}_{MR}$ to distinguish it from the standard moving range $m\bar{R}$.

  - Median moving range: When using this method for estimating α, the following formulas apply:

    1. Moving average chart: Center line $\pm A_4\tilde{R}$, where $\tilde{R}$ is the median moving range and A_4 is a constant found in Appendix 4.

    2. Moving range chart: $LCL = D_5\tilde{R}$ and $UCL = D_6\tilde{R}$, where D_5 and D_6 are constants found in Appendix 4.

Although the use of the average moving range is more popular, variability present in the data may suggest the use of the dispersion statistics. However, Wheeler (1995) computes control limits by using a variety of dispersion statistics (for example, range, median moving range, standard deviation) and concludes that "there is no practical difference between any of the sets of limits."

The following two considerations are particularly important when using moving average charts:

- Rational subgrouping: As with any control chart, consideration to rational subgrouping remains paramount. Example 35.9 assumes a rational subgroup of one with a moving average length of three. If statistical and technical considerations were appropriate for a rational subgroup of five, the average of each subgroup would constitute a point in the moving average of length five. Note: Minitab allows the user to set the subgroup size.

- Interpretation of the charts: By nature of their construction, points on moving average charts and moving range charts do not represent independent subgroups. Hence, these points are correlated. While single points exceeding the control limits may still be used as out of control, other tests such as zone run tests may lead to false conclusions. Some software packages such as Minitab recognize this and limit the out-of-control tests on the moving range charts to the following:

  - One point more than three sigma from the center line

  - Nine points in a row on the same side of the center line

  - Six points in a row, all increasing or all decreasing

  - Fourteen points in a row, alternating up and down

Constructing an MAMR Chart

Use the following steps when constructing an MAMR chart:

1. Collect a set of data: $X_1, X_2, \ldots, X_n$

2. Specify the length of the moving average (for example, 2, 3, . . .)

3. Calculate the moving averages

4. Calculate the moving ranges

5. Calculate the center line of the moving average chart

6. Calculate the center line of the moving range chart

7. Compute the *LCL* and the *UCL* for the moving range chart, using $LCL = D_3\bar{R}_{MR}$ and $UCL = D_4\bar{R}_{MR}$, where D_3 and D_4 are constants found in Appendix 4

8. Compute the *LCL* and the *UCL* for the moving average chart, using $\bar{X}_{MA} \pm A_2\bar{R}_{MR}$, where A_2 is a constant found in Appendix 4

9. Plot the data, center line, *LCL*, and *UCL* for both the moving average and moving range charts

10. Interpret results and take action accordingly

Example 35.9

The data shown in Table 35.9 are taken from Griffith (1996).

1. The data are given in column B, Table 35.9.

2. The moving average length will be set at three.

3. The moving averages are given in column C.

4. The moving ranges are given in column D.

5. The center line of the moving average chart is $\bar{X}_{MA} = 10.6$, given at the bottom of column C.

6. The center line of the moving range chart is $\bar{R}_{MR} = 1.99$, given at the bottom of column D.

7. Steps 7–10 are common to most control charts and will be left to the enjoyment of the reader. The plots are given in Figures 35.12 and 35.13.

Note: Computational differences and/or rounding differences occur between Microsoft Excel and Minitab, and account for slight numerical discrepancies in center line and control limit values.

Part VIII.A.4

Example 35.9 *(continued)*

Table 35.9 MAMR data for Example 35.9.

Column A	Column B	Column C	Column D	Column E	Column F	Column G	Column H	Column I	Column J	Column K	Column L	Column M
No.	X_i	Moving average	Moving range	A_2	D_3	D_4	Average moving average	Average moving range	LCL_{MA}	UCL_{MA}	LCL_{MR}	UCL_{MR}
1	8.0											
2	8.5											
3	7.4	8.0	1.1	1.023	0.000	2.574	10.6	1.99	8.61	12.68	0.00	5.12
4	10.5	8.8	3.1	1.023	0.000	2.574	10.6	1.99	8.61	12.68	0.00	5.12
5	9.3	9.1	3.1	1.023	0.000	2.574	10.6	1.99	8.61	12.68	0.00	5.12
6	11.1	10.3	1.8	1.023	0.000	2.574	10.6	1.99	8.61	12.68	0.00	5.12
7	10.4	10.3	1.8	1.023	0.000	2.574	10.6	1.99	8.61	12.68	0.00	5.12
8	10.4	10.6	0.7	1.023	0.000	2.574	10.6	1.99	8.61	12.68	0.00	5.12
9	9.0	9.9	1.4	1.023	0.000	2.574	10.6	1.99	8.61	12.68	0.00	5.12
10	10.0	9.8	1.4	1.023	0.000	2.574	10.6	1.99	8.61	12.68	0.00	5.12
11	11.7	10.2	2.7	1.023	0.000	2.574	10.6	1.99	8.61	12.68	0.00	5.12
12	10.3	10.7	1.7	1.023	0.000	2.574	10.6	1.99	8.61	12.68	0.00	5.12
13	16.2	12.7	5.9	1.023	0.000	2.574	10.6	1.99	8.61	12.68	0.00	5.12
14	11.6	12.7	5.9	1.023	0.000	2.574	10.6	1.99	8.61	12.68	0.00	5.12
15	11.5	13.1	4.7	1.023	0.000	2.574	10.6	1.99	8.61	12.68	0.00	5.12
16	11.0	11.4	0.6	1.023	0.000	2.574	10.6	1.99	8.61	12.68	0.00	5.12
17	12.0	11.5	1.0	1.023	0.000	2.574	10.6	1.99	8.61	12.68	0.00	5.12
18	11.0	11.3	1.0	1.023	0.000	2.574	10.6	1.99	8.61	12.68	0.00	5.12

Continued

Part VIII.A.4

Example 35.9 *(continued)*

Table 35.9 MAMR data for Example 35.9. *Continued*

Column A	Column B	Column C	Column D	Column E	Column F	Column G	Column H	Column I	Column J	Column K	Column L	Column M
No.	X_i	Moving average	Moving range	A_2	D_3	D_4	Average moving average	Average moving range	LCL_{MA}	UCL_{MA}	LCL_{MR}	UCL_{MR}
19	10.2	11.1	1.8	1.023	0.000	2.574	10.6	1.99	8.61	12.68	0.00	5.12
20	10.1	10.4	0.9	1.023	0.000	2.574	10.6	1.99	8.61	12.68	0.00	5.12
21	10.5	10.3	0.4	1.023	0.000	2.574	10.6	1.99	8.61	12.68	0.00	5.12
22	10.3	10.3	0.4	1.023	0.000	2.574	10.6	1.99	8.61	12.68	0.00	5.12
23	11.5	10.8	1.2	1.023	0.000	2.574	10.6	1.99	8.61	12.68	0.00	5.12
24	11.1	11.0	1.2	1.023	0.000	2.574	10.6	1.99	8.61	12.68	0.00	5.12
Average		10.6	1.99									

Part VIII.A.4

Example 35.9 *(continued)*

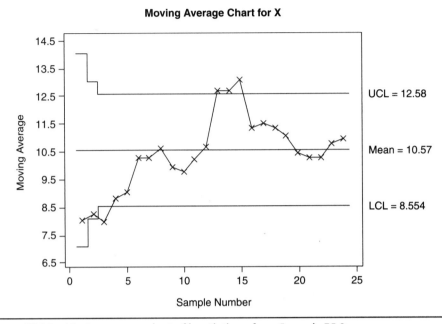

Figure 35.12 Moving average chart of length three from Example 35.9.

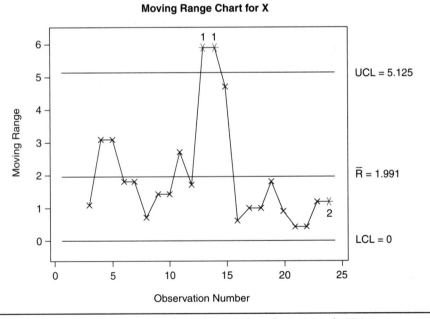

Figure 35.13 Moving average range chart of length three from Example 35.9.

See the interpretation and analysis of charts later in the chapter.

CONTROL CHART ANALYSIS

> Interpret control charts and distinguish between common and special causes using rules for determining statistical control. (Analyze)
>
> **Body of Knowledge VIII.A.5**

Recall that control limit formulas represent the VOP and are set at $\pm 3\sigma$. These limits are said to constitute an economic trade-off between looking for special cause variation when it does not exist and not looking for it when it does exist. Also, $\pm 3\sigma$ limits covers approximately 99.73% of the data. Points falling within the control limits are due to common cause variation. Points falling outside the limits or that meet any of the out-of-control rules outlined later in this section are said to be attributed to special or assignable cause variation. Such points, regardless of whether they constitute "good" or "bad" occurrences, should be investigated immediately, while the cause-and-effect relationships are fresh. The motto "Time is of the essence" is most appropriate. Ideally, "good" out-of-control conditions are incorporated into the process, while "bad" out-of-control conditions are removed. However, a word of caution is in order. Adjusting a process when it is not warranted by out-of-control conditions constitutes process tampering. This usually results in destabilizing a process, causing it to go out of control.

The probability of out-of-control points occurring is relatively small. With the exception of points exceeding the control limits, most out-of-control conditions are subtle and would likely go unnoticed without the aid of a control chart. The control chart permits us to detect small changes in a process, thus allowing us to take systematic action to discover the root cause of the variation or permit adjustment or other actions on the process before serious damage occurs.

Analyzing Control Chart Behavior

A critical tool useful in analyzing control charts, particularly when special cause variation is present, is the *process log*. The process log may be a separate document, or it may be maintained as part of the control chart itself. Entries in the log should be identified by date and time and include all changes to the process and the process environment. Such changes might include occurrences of preventive or corrective maintenance, raw material from different suppliers, machine adjustments, tool replacement, incorporation or replacement of new part fixtures, and so forth. Also, some Six Sigma professionals have found it useful to construct a list of things to check when certain out-of-control conditions occur. Such a list may be developed from discussions with experienced subject matter experts as well as from data from the process log.

When variables charts are being used, the chart used to measure process variation (for example, $\bar{R}$, $\bar{s}$, and $\overline{MR}$) should be reviewed first. Out-of-control conditions on this chart constitute changes of within-subgroup variation. Remember from rational subgrouping that we would like the variation of subgroups on this chart to be as small as possible since this measure of dispersion is used to compute the control limits on the corresponding process average chart (for example, $\bar{X}$ and X). The tighter the control limits on the process average chart, the easier it is to detect subgroup-to-subgroup variation.

Commonly used rules or tests have been devised to detect out-of-control conditions. The software package Minitab uses eight rules:

1. One point more than 3σ from the center line (either side)

2. Nine points in a row on the same side of the center line

3. Six points in a row, all increasing or all decreasing

4. Fourteen points in a row, alternating up and down

5. Two out of three points more than 2σ from the center line (same side)

6. Four out of five points more than 1σ from the center line (same side)

7. Fifteen points in a row within 1σ of the center line (either side)

8. Eight points in a row more than 1σ from the center line (either side)

Table 35.10 provides a list of possible reasons for these out-of-control conditions. Minitab's eight rules are depicted in Figures 35.14–35.21. Any points that violate a rule are circled.

The Automotive Industry Action Group (AIAG) identifies six rules in its SPC manual:

1. Points beyond the control limits

2. Seven points in a row on one side of the average

3. Seven points in a row that are consistently increasing (equal or greater than the preceding points) or consistently decreasing

4. Over 90% of the plotted points are in the middle third of the control limit region (for 25 or more subgroups)

5. Less than 40% of the plotted points are in the middle third of the control limit region (for 25 or more subgroups)

6. Obvious nonrandom patterns such as cycles

Table 35.10 Interpreting control chart out-of-control conditions used by Minitab.

Out-of-control condition	Possible reasons	Chart type						
		Variables			Attributes			
		$\bar{X},R$	$\bar{X},s$	XmR	p	np	c	u
One point more than 3σ from the center line (either side)	*Freaks*: error in plotting, calculation error, breakdown of facilities, extraneous causes	X	X	X	X	X	X	X
Nine points in a row on the same side of the center line (Note: References to 6–9 points in a row on the same side of the center line appear in the literature.)	A shift in the process mean has likely occurred	X	X	X	X	X	X	X
Six points in a row, all increasing or all decreasing	*Trend*: tool wear, skill improvement, deteriorating maintenance	X	X	X	X	X	X	X
Fourteen points in a row, alternating up and down	Alternating cause systems are present, such as two suppliers, etc. Unlike stratification, the subgroups are homogeneous	X	X	X	X	X	X	X
Two out of three points more than 2σ from the center line (same side)	Early warning of a potential process shift	X	X	X				
Four out of five points more than 1σ from the center line (same side)	Early warning of a potential process shift	X	X	X				
Fifteen points in a row within 1σ of the center line (either side)	*Stratification*: two or more cause systems are present in every subgroup	X	X	X				
Eight points in a row more than 1σ from the center line (either side)	*Mixture*: two operators being used, two machines, etc.	X	X	X				

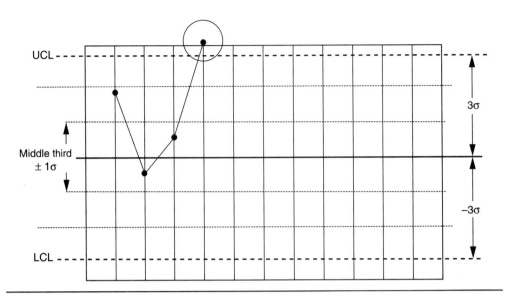

Figure 35.14   Example of out-of-control condition #1 from Minitab.

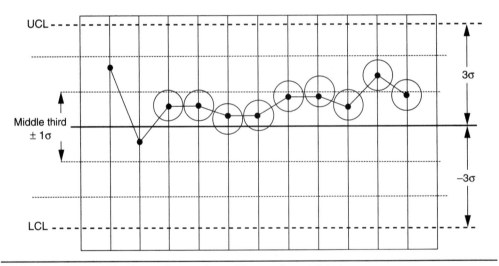

Figure 35.15   Example of out-of-control condition #2 from Minitab.

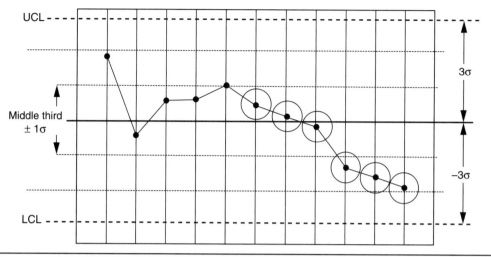

Figure 35.16   Example of out-of-control condition #3 from Minitab.

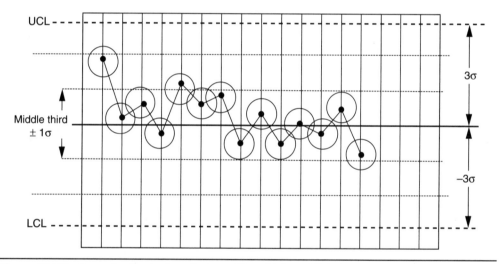

Figure 35.17   Example of out-of-control condition #4 from Minitab.

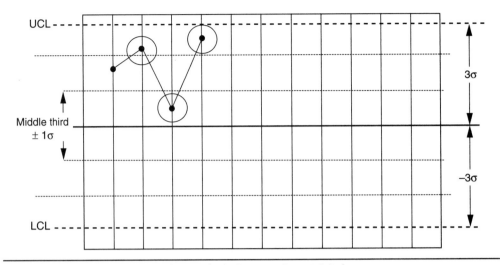

Figure 35.18 Example of out-of-control condition #5 from Minitab.

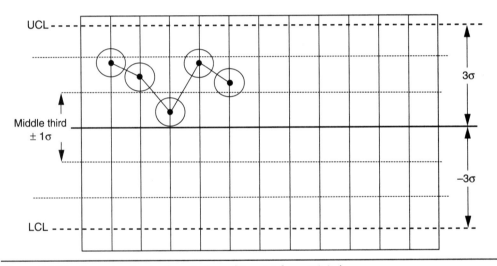

Figure 35.19 Example of out-of-control condition #6 from Minitab.

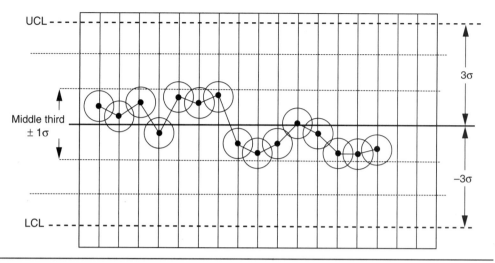

Figure 35.20   Example of out-of-control condition #7 from Minitab.

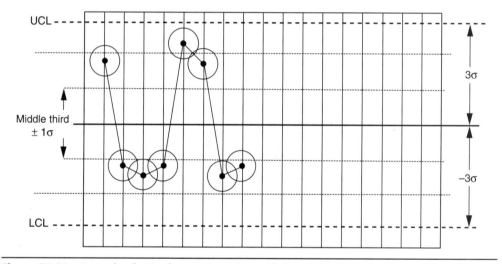

Figure 35.21   Example of out-of-control condition #8 from Minitab.

Part VIII.A.5

AIAG's rules are depicted in Figures 35.22–35.27. Any points that violate a rule are circled.

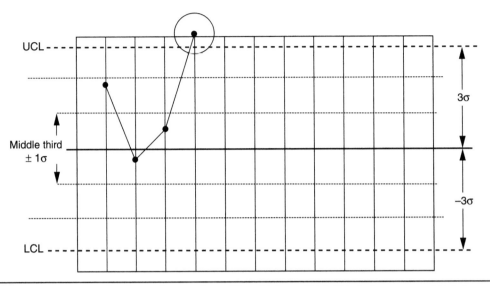

Figure 35.22 Example of out-of-control condition #1 from AIAG. This is the same as Minitab out-of-control condition #1.

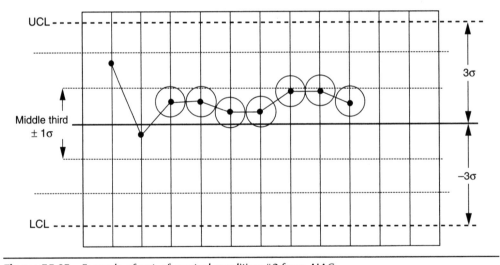

Figure 35.23 Example of out-of-control condition #2 from AIAG.

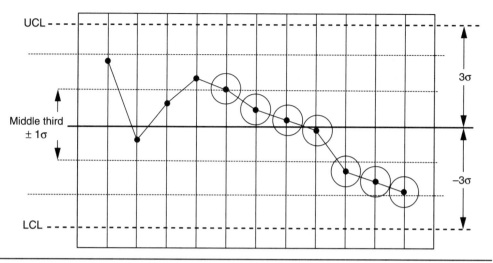

Figure 35.24   Example of out-of-control condition #3 from AIAG.

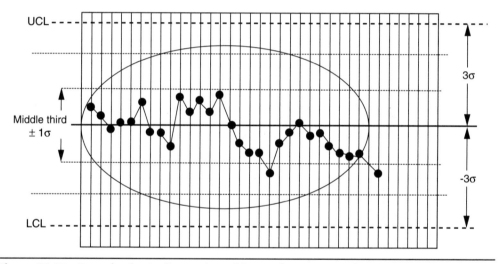

Figure 35.25   Example of out-of-control condition #4 from AIAG.

Part VIII.A.5

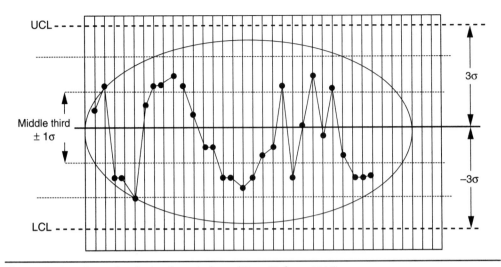

Figure 35.26 Example of out-of-control condition #5 from AIAG.

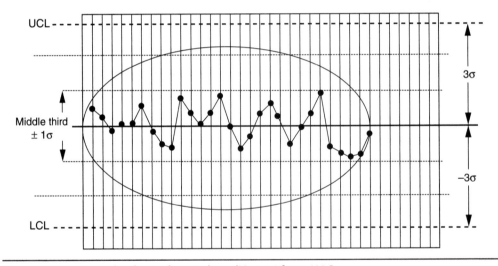

Figure 35.27 Example of out-of-control condition #6 from AIAG.

These examples should motivate the reader to look for more out-of-control conditions than simply points exceeding the control limits.

The Six Sigma professional may find it useful to make up additional tests for particular situations. For instance, if an increase of values represents a safety hazard, it is not necessary to wait for the specified number of successively increasing points to take action.

Finally, note that a control chart is really a graphical hypothesis test. The null hypothesis is that the process hasn't changed. The alternative hypothesis is that it has changed. As each point is plotted, the chart is examined to determine whether there is sufficient evidence to reject the null hypothesis and conclude that the process has changed.

References

Griffith, Gary K. 1996. *Statistical Process Control Methods for Long and Short Runs.* 2nd ed. Milwaukee, WI: ASQC Quality Press.

Wheeler, Donald J. 1991. *Short Run SPC.* Knoxville, TN: SPC Press.

————. 1995. *Advanced Topics in Statistical Process Control: The Power of Shewhart's Charts.* Knoxville, TN: SPC Press.

Chapter 36

Other Control Tools

Part VIII.B.1

Once a process has been improved, the next, and sometimes most difficult, challenge is to hold the gain. One reason this is so difficult is that it often requires people to change the way they do things. Two tools for holding the gain are total productive maintenance and the visual factory.

TOTAL PRODUCTIVE MAINTENANCE (TPM)

Define the elements of TPM and describe how it can be used to control the improved process. (Understand)

Body of Knowledge VIII.B.1

Total productive maintenance (TPM) is a methodology pioneered by Nippondenso (a member of the Toyota group) that works to ensure that every machine in a production process is always able to perform its required tasks so that production is never interrupted. TPM maximizes equipment effectiveness by using a preventive maintenance program throughout the life of the equipment.

In any situation where mechanical devices are used, the working state of those devices has an impact on the control of the process. If equipment deteriorates even subtly, the process output may be affected, often in unsuspected ways. For lean systems to work, all equipment must be ready to quickly respond to customer needs. This requires a system that foresees maintenance needs and takes appropriate action. A TPM system uses historical data, manufacturer's recommendations, reports by alert operators, diagnostic tests, and other techniques to schedule maintenance activity so machine downtime can be minimized. TPM goes beyond keeping everything running. An effective TPM system includes continuous improvement initiatives as it seeks more effective and efficient ways to predict and diagnose maintenance-related problems.

Example 36.1

A punch press operation experienced a stoppage to repair damage caused by the breakage of a die spring. The repair entailed reworking the die, a process that sometimes takes two weeks. When the die was disassembled, it was determined that there were actually two broken die springs. It was speculated that a single spring broke and the machine continued to operate normally until the extra stress put on the other springs caused a second spring to break. The operators who were monitoring a particular dimension with an SPC chart noticed a slight jump in the range chart for that dimension an hour or so before the second die spring broke. The next time that shift occurred they called maintenance and said, "We think we have a broken die spring." The maintenance person said, "No you don't; the die would have crashed." After some discussion, the maintenance person agreed to disassemble the die. A single broken spring was found inside. It was replaced, and the machine was back online in less than an hour.

Example 36.2

The resolver on a pick-and-place robot was malfunctioning, causing sporadic part defects due to incorrect positioning of parts in a machine. A TPM team investigated the problem and determined the malfunction was due to a buildup of contaminant located in and around the machine. As a result of this key learning, the team modified the robot maintenance schedule without creating any additional downtime.

In addition to using TPM to minimize equipment downtime, it can also be used to maintain process control by recognizing it as one component of total process variation. When we discuss measurement systems analysis, we look at total process variation as

$$\sigma^2_{\text{measurement}} + \sigma^2_{\text{process}} = \sigma^2_{\text{total}}$$

However, we can further decompose $\sigma^2_{\text{process}}$ as follows:

$$\sigma^2_{\text{TPM}} + \sigma^2_{\text{part}} + \sigma^2_{\text{operator}} + \ldots = \sigma^2_{\text{process}}$$

Having isolated the variation component due to TPM, it can now be monitored and improved using a variety of tools and techniques discussed in other chapters.

VISUAL FACTORY

Define the elements of a visual factory and describe how they can help control the improved process. (Understand)

Body of Knowledge VIII.B.2

Part VIII.B.2

Visual controls, sometimes known as the *visual factory,* are approaches and techniques that permit one to visually determine the status of a system, factory, or process at a glance and prevent or minimize process variation. To some degree, it can be viewed as a minor form of mistake proofing. Some examples of visual controls include:

- Signage
- Product line identification
- Color-coded items such as parts, bins, racks, documentation, walkways, and so forth
- Schedule boards
- Conspicuous posting of performance indicators

Visual controls work to provide a constant focus and attention on the process. This level of attention can help stabilize variation at the improved level of a process.

Chapter 37
Maintain Controls

MEASUREMENT SYSTEM RE-ANALYSIS

> Review and evaluate measurement system capability as process capability improves, and ensure that measurement capability is sufficient for its intended use. (Evaluate)
>
> **Body of Knowledge VIII.C.1**

There are many reasons why a re-analysis of the measurement system is required; examples include change in process, change in customer specifications, new measuring devices, equipment calibration issues, and so on. Of course, most of these reasons are fairly obvious. One reason that is not so obvious is the impact that continuous process improvement has on the measurement system.

The total observed variation in a process is made up of two components: process variation and measurement variation. We usually write this as

$$\sigma^2_{\text{total observed}} = \sigma^2_{\text{process}} + \sigma^2_{\text{measurement system}}$$

Hopefully, process improvement efforts result in reduced process variation. This, in turn, results in reduced total observed variation. However, the measurement system variation remains unchanged. As a result, measurement system variation increases as a percentage of total observed variation. Depending on the percentage value, the current measurement system could become unacceptably large.

Measurement variation can be calculated by performing a gage repeatability and reproducibility (GR&R) analysis, as described in Chapter 20. The following guidelines are typically used to determine the acceptability of a measurement system:

- < 10% error—The measurement system is considered acceptable.

- 10% to 30% error—The measurement system may be considered acceptable on the basis of importance of application, cost of gage, cost of repairs, and so on. This is a gray area and depends on the situation at hand.

- 30% error—The measurement system is considered unacceptable, and improvement is necessary.

Figure 37.1 depicts an acceptable measurement system using the above percentage guidelines, whereas Figure 37.2 depicts one that is unacceptable.

Other rules or standards exist for determining the acceptability of measurement system variation:

- 10:1 ratio rule—This rule states that the increments of the measurement instrument should be no greater than the smaller of the process variation or the specification tolerance

- 4:1 ratio (25%) rule—This rule states that measurement uncertainty should be no greater than 25% of the specification tolerance

Note that these two rules are based on the specification tolerance, whereas the GR&R calculation is based on the process control limits.

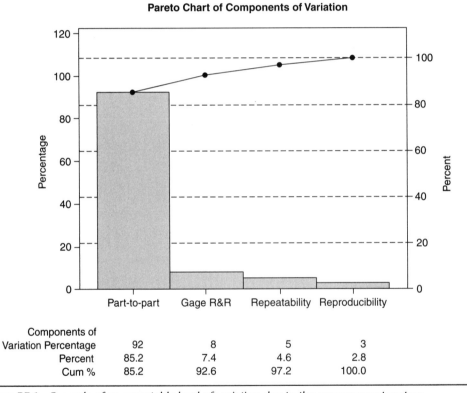

Pareto Chart of Components of Variation

	Part-to-part	Gage R&R	Repeatability	Reproducibility
Components of Variation Percentage	92	8	5	3
Percent	85.2	7.4	4.6	2.8
Cum %	85.2	92.6	97.2	100.0

Figure 37.1 Example of an acceptable level of variation due to the measurement system.

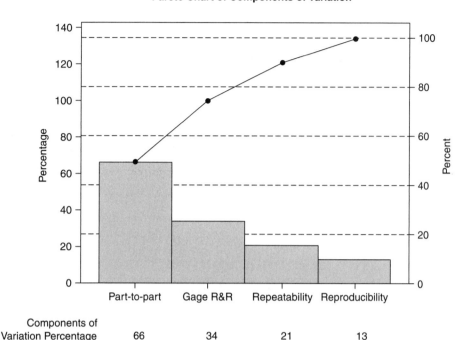

Pareto Chart of Components of Variation

Components of Variation Percentage	66	34	21	13
Percent	49.3	25.4	15.7	9.7
Cum %	49.3	74.6	90.3	100.0

Figure 37.2   Example of an unacceptable level of variation due to the measurement system.

Part VIII.C.1

Example 37.1

An initial GR&R study determined the measurement system percentage to be 12%. In addition, the 10:1 ratio rule was met. Thus the measurement system was judged acceptable. However, after a series of improvement projects, the part-to-part process variation was reduced by 75%. A re-analysis of the measurement system now showed that the GR&R increased to 35% and that the 10:1 ratio rule was still satisfied since the measuring devices and specification limits did not change. As a result, the organization must determine whether the measurement system is acceptable or needs improvement on the basis of intended use, customer specification, and cost of implementation.

In the previous example, any future projects aimed at reducing process variation will most likely fail to produce the desired results. This is due to the large amount of measurement variation. The measurement system does not have adequate resolution within the process control limits and will not be able to detect the changes in the process variation. Future activities in this area will need to address the adequacy of the measurement system before any project to further reduce process variation is undertaken.

CONTROL PLAN

> Develop a control plan for ensuring the ongoing
> success of the improved process including the
> transfer of responsibility from the project team to
> the process owner. (Apply)
>
> **Body of Knowledge VIII.C.2**

A *control plan* is a living document that identifies critical input or output variables and associated activities that must be performed to maintain control of the variation of processes, products, and services in order to minimize deviation from their preferred values.

Control plans are formulated during the control phase of DMAIC and are intended to ensure that process improvement gains are not lost over time. Examples of different formats for control plans are illustrated in Figure 37.3.

Control plan for process XYZ					
Activity/ Step	**Input**	**Specification characteristic to be controlled**	**Control method**	**Control description**	**Responsibility**
1	Copper cable	Cross-section diameter	Measure per SOP 481-4.7	$\bar{X}$, R control chart Out-of-control condition: Do not complete operation, notify production engineer immediately	Operator
2	Resistor	Resistance	Measure per SOP 596-2.4	$\bar{X}$, R control chart Out-of-control condition: Pull lot from production, notify supplier, draw new lot	Production engineer

Control plan for process XYZ					
Control factor	**Specification or tolerance**	**Measurement technique**	**Sample size**	**Sampling method/ Frequency**	**Reaction plan**	**Responsibility**
Cable diameter	0.5 mm ± 0.05 mm	Caliper, measure per SOP	7	$\bar{X}$, R control chart, random sampling with a probability of 0.25	Out-of-control condition: Do not complete operation, notify production engineer immediately	Operator
Cable length	12.0 mm ± 0.10 mm	GKRD-45 optical reader, measure per SOP	5	$\bar{X}$, R control chart, random sampling with a probability of 0.10	Out-of-control condition: Pull lot from production, notify supplier, draw new lot	Production engineer

Figure 37.3 Example of two different formats for control plans.

Notice that both plans identify the individual responsible for taking the actions defined in the control plan. The control uses the basic premise that things get done when accountability is assigned.

Further, a control plan is defined as a living document. It is designed to be maintained. Common triggers for updating control charts include:

- Process changes

- Specification changes

- Measurement technology changes

- Organizational changes

- Personnel turnover

- Defined period reviews

To reiterate, control plans hold the gains achieved from process improvement activities. A weak or inadequate control plan is a key failure mode for DMAIC projects. To this point, organizations with existing process or quality audit functions may want to consider adding control plans to their list of audit items.

Part VIII.C.2

Chapter 38
Sustain Improvements

LESSONS LEARNED

> Document the lessons learned from all phases of a project and identify how improvements can be replicated and applied to other processes in the organization. (Apply)
>
> **Body of Knowledge VIII.D.1**

Organizational Memory

Many organizations find that they solve the same problems more than once. This is often because of poor documentation, poor communication, internal employee churn, or external attrition. Moreover, the organization's memory may exist only in the minds of employees. When a problem recurs or occurs in a slightly different form, it is often solved again, particularly if the people who worked on it before are not involved. This problem is only exacerbated by organizational downsizing, whereby the bottom line may receive some short-term benefit, but the organization has been crippled due to a significant loss of its intellectual capital and memory.

The recognition of the need to maintain an organization's memory has given rise to the concept of knowledge management. While the definition of knowledge management remains vague, it can be characterized by its requirements to identify an organization's knowledge base and intellectual capital; maintain this information; and distribute it, make it accessible, or otherwise communicate it to those in the organization who have the need to use it.

Current technologies allow organizations to maintain and distribute information rather easily. The difficulty lies in capturing it.

With respect to Six Sigma, the opportunity to capture project information and related lessons learned can easily be embedded into the control phase of the methodology. Organizations can readily establish requirements such that no project can be closed out without first capturing relevant project information and lessons learned in some permanent repository. Once captured, project information can be searched and compared against future project opportunities such that decisions can be made to charter a project, replicate a past success, or even kick-start new or innovative thinking on an existing project.

TRAINING PLAN DEPLOYMENT

> Develop and implement training plans to ensure continued support of the improved process. (Apply)
>
> **Body of Knowledge VIII.D.2**

A critical element for ensuring the gains of an improved process are maintained is the training of the personnel responsible for executing the process. Training is often overlooked or viewed as an unnecessary cost or imposition on the time of already overworked employees.

Training comes in two main forms:

- Initial—This type is used for existing employees who have been responsible for executing the old process and will continue to be responsible for executing the new process. It also addresses the needs of employees who are new to the process. Furthermore, it may be conducted off the job or on the job or both. The correct combination depends on the skill levels required, process complexity, and experience levels, among other factors. Initial training serves to calibrate employees and minimize variation in how the process is performed.

- Recurring—This type is used to minimize deterioration in the process performance over time. Deterioration usually occurs as employees become comfortable with the new process and fail to recognize minor changes or tweaks to the process either through carelessness, poor documentation, or perhaps even a system that permits obsolete documentation to remain in the process stream. In addition, on-the-job training is another factor that often adversely impacts process performance. In a manner similar to the children's game of "telephone" that permits the description, interpretation, and understanding of an initial whispered message to transform itself into something entirely different after it has passed through a series of children trying to communicate the original message, so too does on-the-job training. Specific facts, details, and nuances are frequently left out as they pass from worker to worker. Recurring training restores the process execution to its original design. The frequency of recurring training should be determined on the basis of process metrics and employee performance. Such training may be offered at specified intervals or conducted as required to serve the needs of underperforming employees.

When developing process-related training plans, important considerations include:

- Providing employees with the minimum skills and information needed to perform the functions required by the position. This goes beyond "how to turn on the screw gun." It includes how to read and interpret documentation and safety precautions, how to supply required data, and other skills as needed.

- Providing employees with additional skills and information that will ensure a broader view of what the position accomplishes for the enterprise. If the position entails installing 200 bimetallic oven controls each day, the employee should know how a bimetallic control works, which metals can be used, and perhaps a little history regarding earlier models.

- Providing employees with cross training for additional functions. This often involves training employees on the processes immediately before and after the process for which they are responsible.

Other, larger training plan considerations beyond the immediate process include:

- Providing employees with opportunities for further education outside the enterprise on topics not directly related to the current organization needs. This is done under the assumption that exposure to ideas outside the box is valuable.

- Providing incentives and requirements that motivate employees to continue to seek education and training opportunities.

- Providing employees with experiences that demonstrate the need the organization has for their ideas for continuous improvement.

- Providing employees with the opportunity to help formulate a customized annual training plan. Such a plan should be routinely maintained, supported by readily accessible records, and monitor progress toward plan completion.

These considerations should help employees make positive contributions toward the ability of the organization to sustain process improvements over the long term.

DOCUMENTATION

> Develop or modify documents including standard operating procedures (SOPs), work instructions, etc., to ensure that the improvements are sustained over time. (Apply)
>
> **Body of Knowledge VIII.D.3**

Part VIII.D.3

Many organizations have found that documented standard operating procedures (SOPs) and work instructions (known in the lean manufacturing literature as "standard work") help reduce process variation. The purpose of these documents is to make certain that the activity is performed the same way over time. This is especially important when multiskilled, cross-trained personnel move into a variety of positions.

The development and updating of these documents must involve the people who perform the work. The documentation process is begun by listing the major steps. Succeeding iterations examine the steps from the previous one and break them into smaller substeps. This process can continue until further deconstruction is not useful.

Two main considerations include:

- Documents must be kept current. In an era of continuous improvement, processes may be continuously changing. As a result, it is possible that different documentation releases for the same documentation may be in use simultaneously. Therefore, it is vital that employees always have access to the appropriate documentation based on effectivity of the change. It is easy to see how the complexity of managing such a documentation system can grow exponentially. With today's Web-based and other technologies, documentation configuration management systems can be designed and developed to ensure that the proper documentation is available for the right process on the right part at the right time.

- Multiple documentation formats exist. The right choice depends on how the documentation is to be used, by whom, and at what skill level. However, documentation best practices suggest developing documents that are color-coded; rely heavily on graphics, illustrations, and photographs; and are light on words. Photographs of acceptable and unacceptable product and procedures have been found to be very useful. Some organizations have had success with the use of videotapes for depicting complex operations. As always, the level of detail provided in any set of documentation should reflect the skills and education levels of the personnel doing the actual work and the degree to which variation must be controlled. Remember, robust processes usually require less detailed documentation than nonrobust processes.

ONGOING EVALUATION

Identify and apply tools for ongoing evaluation of the improved process, including monitoring for new constraints, additional opportunities for improvement, etc. (Apply)

Body of Knowledge VIII.D.4

Part VIII.D.4

Once a process has been improved, it must be monitored to ensure the gains are maintained and to determine when additional improvements are required. Several tools and methods are available to assist in this regard:

- Control charts—These are used to monitor the stability of the process, determine when special cause is present, and when to take appropriate action. The choice of a particular control chart depends on the nature of the process. When out-of-control conditions occur, action is required to restore stability. Control charts represent the voice of the process.

- Process capability studies—These studies provide us with the opportunity to understand how the voice of the process (that is, control limits) compares with the voice of the customer (that is, specifications) and helps us determine whether the process average must be shifted or recentered or the variation reduced.

- Process metrics—This includes a wide variety of in-process and end-of-process metrics that measure the overall efficiency and effectivness of the process. Examples include cycle times, takt time, take rate, work-in-process, backlog, defect rates, rework rates, and scrap rates.

Taken collectively, these tools and methods help us gauge the overall health of a process and provide triggers for reevaluating a process for further improvement.

Part IX

Design for Six Sigma (DFSS) Frameworks and Methodologies

Part IX

Chapter 39

Common DFSS Methodologies

While DMAIC may be traditionally viewed as the foundation for Six Sigma, its application is primarily limited to improving existing processes; it does little to address the design of new product or processes. Fortunately, several additional structured methodologies exist. These include DMADV and DMADOV.

DMADV (DEFINE, MEASURE, ANALYZE, DESIGN, AND VALIDATE)

> Identify and describe this methodology.
> (Understand)
>
> **Body of Knowledge IX.A.1**

DMADV is a well-recognized Design for Six Sigma (DFSS) methodology and an acronym for define, measure, analyze, design, and verify. Note the ASQ Body of Knowledge replaces "verify" with "validate." The difference is likely because, although different, "verify" and "validate" are often used synonymously. In this chapter, however, "V" will stand for "verify."

The DMA portion of DMADV has been covered elsewhere in this book, so we'll concentrate on the remaining DV portion:

- Design—Quite simply, this means carrying out the process of designing a product or process. Many organizations have well-established policies and procedures for their respective design processes. One valuable Six Sigma technique that supports the design process is quality function deployment (QFD), the details of which were discussed in Chapter 15. Additional tools useful in this phase include pilot runs, simulations, prototypes, and models (addressed in Chapter 33).

- Verify—This phase is directed at ensuring that the design output meets the design requirements and specifications and is performed on the final product or process. Basically, verification speaks to the design meeting customer requirements and ensures that the design yields the correct product or process. By contrast, validation speaks to the effectiveness of the design process itself and is intended to ensure that it is capable of meeting the requirements of the final product or process.

Both verification and validation are necessary functions in any design process. As such, this suggests that DMADV might be more appropriately named DMADVV.

DMADOV (DEFINE, MEASURE, ANALYZE, DESIGN, OPTIMIZE, AND VALIDATE)

> Identify and describe this methodology. (Understand)
>
> **Body of Knowledge IX.A.2**

The basic difference between DMADV and DMADOV is that "O" for "optimize" has been added. This sounds like a trivial observation, but many organizations' design processes do not include this refinement action. They are intended solely to produce a minimally workable product or process. DMADOV forces attention on the need to optimize the design. Additional tools useful in this phase include design of experiments, response surface methodology (RSM), and evolutionary operations (EVOP). These methods help the design team establish and refine design parameters.

Part IX.A.2

Chapter 40

Design for X (DFX)

DESIGN FOR X (DFX)

> Describe design constraints, including
> design for cost, design for manufacturability
> and producibility, design for test, design for
> maintainability, etc. (Understand)
>
> **Body of Knowledge IX.B**

Traditionally, the design process was conducted almost in isolation, without regard to the downstream functions that might be impacted by that design. Once the design was complete, it was handed off to manufacturing, production, or the assembly function, whose job was to translate the design from concept to reality. Unfortunately, many design functions failed to address the capability of these downstream organizations. This frequently resulted in escalating production costs and numerous engineering change orders that created a significant divergence between the "as designed" and the "as built" configurations.

This scenario led to the development of the design-by-team approach known as concurrent or simultaneous engineering. For the first time, stakeholders in the design function had a voice in how a product or process was designed. With fully cross-functional design teams in place, organizations could begin improving the efficiency and effectiveness of designs to benefit both the organization and the customer.

The concept behind Design for X (DFX), where X is a variable such as cost, manufacturability, producibility, testability, maintainability, and so forth, is simply that "X" becomes the focus of or constraint to the design process. Let's look at some of the more familiar "Xs":

- **Design-for-Cost (better known as Design-to-Cost [DTC])**—The need for DTC usually arises when an organization establishes a fixed design budget in an effort to become more fiscally responsible, or perhaps a major customer has dictated what it is willing to spend. As a result, the design focus is shifted from "what works" to "what works within budget." The disciplines of value engineering and value analysis are keystones under a DTC scenario.

- **Design for Manufacturing/Design for Producibility/Design for Assembly**—Although some degree of difference exists among the three terms, they are grouped together because the underlying DFX issues remain the same. Under these scenarios, the design team must recognize that limitations might exist with respect to manufacturing, producing, or assembling a product. Common examples include designs calling for:

  - Equipment not currently available.

  - Methods unfamiliar to the manufacturing or assembly workforce. An example might be requiring an automated method of soldering when the assembly workforce is skilled only in manual soldering.

  - Expensive fixtures.

  - Specialized tooling.

  - Workplace redesign.

  - Operators/assembly worker to use asymmetrical motions.

  - Limited accessibility.

  - Obsolete or hard-to-find parts.

  - Use of exotic material when unnecessary.

  - Special manufacturing, operator, or assembly worker skills.

  - Tolerances beyond that which can be achieved given the available equipment or processes.

- **Design for Test (also known as Design for Testability)**—Testing may be an integral part of ensuring quality, or it may be demanded by the customer. In such cases, designs must accommodate an assemble-test-assemble type of production assembly process rather than rely entirely on functional tests of the finished product. Such considerations are common with complex electromechanical equipment including avionics and mass market consumer electronic products.

- **Design for Maintainability**—Customer loyalty depends on long-term satisfaction. For many products, this means that the ability to perform routine maintenance must be considered during the design process. Cars that require a floor jack to remove spark plugs or a contortionist to replace a shock absorber do not inspire customer confidence in other aspects of the product. Industrial products that require long downtimes for repair can be of paramount interest particularly when the customer is concerned with managing a product's or process's overall life-cycle costs.

- **Design for Robustness**—In this scenario, designs must accommodate increased variation in the inputs while still producing the required output within defined specifications. For example, the impedance of a supplier's resistors is known to follow a normal distribution with a rather large variance. The design should be capable of accepting parts with such variation and still produce a tight output distribution.

Chapter 41

Robust Design and Process

ROBUST DESIGN AND PROCESS

> Describe the elements of robust product design, tolerance design, and statistical tolerancing.
> (Apply)
>
> **Body of Knowledge IX.C**

Functional Requirements

The concepts of functional requirements are perhaps best understood with an example. A producer of black rubber provides door and window seals for the automotive industry. For many years the automobile designers have specified the hardness, toughness, and elasticity of the material; the geometry of the cross section; and other specifications. As might be expected, the rubber company has struggled to meet the specifications of its customers.

More recently, the designers have been specifying such things as "will not leak under a 20 mph wind and 2 inches of rain per hour for two hours." Such a statement is known as a *functional requirement*. It defines how the product is to perform and under what conditions.

Many companies have decided that their suppliers probably know more about the products they supply than they do and are probably in a better position to design a product that can be manufactured efficiently.

The use of functional requirements is sometimes referred to as "black box" engineering because the customer says, in essence, "I am not going to specify the design details; here's how I want it to function." Of course, the customer typically puts some constraints on the design, perhaps providing the space available, the relationship to other components, and so on. When specifications include functional and nonfunctional requirements, it is referred to as a "gray box" design.

Noise Strategies

Noise factors were introduced in Chapter 28. Figure 41.1 illustrates a response curve with three acceptable values for the input variable P. Regardless of the value of P chosen, a certain amount of variation or noise can be expected. This noise in

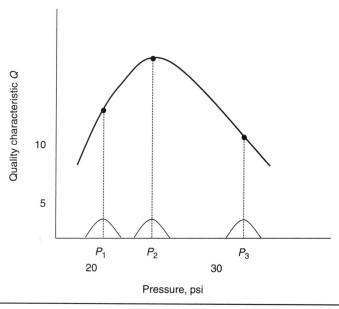

Figure 41.1   Nonlinear response curve with input noise.

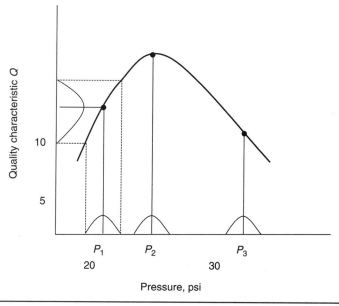

Figure 41.2   Nonlinear response curve showing the impact on Q of input noise at P_1.

the input variable is represented by the normal curves sketched on the horizontal axis. Figure 41.2 illustrates the impact on the output variable Q when $P = P_1$. Figure 41.3 shows the impact of noise at each of the three values of P. It is clear that the amount of variation in Q depends on the location of P. In fact, the location of P that minimizes "transmitted noise" is the area where the response curve is flattest—P_2 in this example.

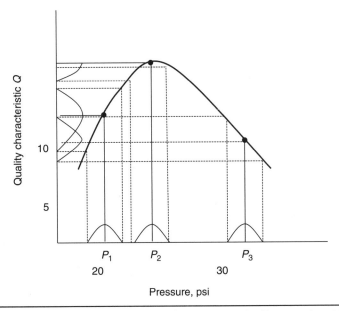

Figure 41.3 Nonlinear response curve showing the impact on Q of input noise at P_1, P_2, and P_3.

The noise strategy, then, is to conduct a designed experiment or set of experiments, as shown in Chapter 28, and when nonlinear response curves are found, locate the flattest part of the curve, as there will be a point along this section that will minimize transmitted noise.

Tolerance Design

Tolerance design uses the concept of transmitted noise to help determine product tolerance. For example, suppose a fabricator who uses steel to produce parts finds that the hardness of the steel impacts a quality characteristic of a formed part. As a result, a hardness tolerance is applied to the steel. What should the tolerance be? The amount of acceptable variation in the quality characteristic due to hardness is reflected back through the response curve to determine the amount of acceptable variation in hardness (see Figure 41.4). If a designed experiment determines that it is possible to operate at a relatively flat spot on the response curve relating hardness to the quality characteristic, the hardness tolerance can be looser than it would otherwise have to be. Therefore, tolerance design is considered a cost-saving technique since loosening tolerances on a specification generally reduces costs.

Statistical Tolerancing

In this section, we will address two methods for determining tolerance:

- Conventional tolerances
- Statistical tolerances

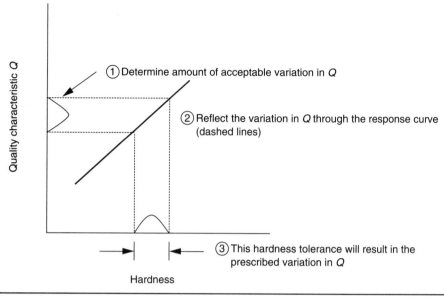

Figure 41.4 Using a response curve to determine tolerance.

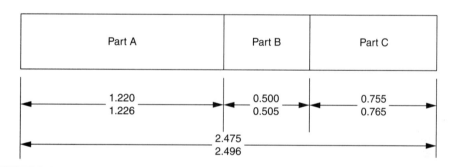

Figure 41.5 Conventional stack tolerance dimensioning.

Conventional Tolerances

The conventional or traditional way to determine tolerance involves a situation in which several parts are stacked together, as shown in Figure 41.5.

Example 41.1

The method to compute the overall tolerance on the length is as follows:

1. Use the sum of the minimum lengths of the three components as the lower tolerance limit:

$$\text{Lower tolerance limit} = 1.220 + 0.500 + 0.755 = 2.475$$

Example 41.1 *(continued)*

2. Use the sum of the maximum lengths of the three components as the upper tolerance limit:

Upper tolerance limit = 1.226 + 0.505 + 0.765 = 2.496

Therefore, the tolerance on the overall length is the sum of the tolerances on the individual parts:

Tolerance on the length = 0.006 + 0.005 + 0.010 = 0.021 = ±0.0105

Statistical Tolerances

If the processes producing the lengths of parts A, B, and C are capable and generate normal distributions, the tolerances on these parts are directly related to the standard deviations. But, unlike tolerances, standard deviations are not additive. Therefore, we must add the variances as follows:

$$\sigma^2_{stack} = \sigma^2_A + \sigma^2_B + \sigma^2_C$$

$$\sigma_{stack} = \sqrt{\sigma^2_A + \sigma^2_B + \sigma^2_C}$$

If we recognize that the worst-case scenario that occurs with the tolerance is exactly 6 standard deviations in width (that is, ±3 deviations), we can now write

$$\text{Nominal}_{total} = \text{Nominal}_A + \text{Nominal}_B + \text{Nominal}_C$$

and

$$\frac{T}{3} = \sqrt{\frac{T_A}{3} + \frac{T_B}{3} + \frac{T_C}{3}} \text{ or}$$

$$T_{stack} = \sqrt{T^2_A + T^2_B + T^2_C}$$

Applying the appropriate numerical values, we have

$$\text{Nominal}_{total} = 1.223 + 0.5025 + 0.76 = 2.4855$$

and

$$T_{stack} = \sqrt{(0.003)^2 + (0.0025)^2 + (0.005)^2} = \sqrt{0.00004025} = \pm0.0063$$

Given this, we might want to inquire how the statistical tolerances might change in the previous equation such that we still achieve the tolerance of the stack obtained using the conventional approach. If we assume, for the moment, that each of the statistical tolerances is equal, we obtain the equation

$$T_{stack} = \sqrt{3T^2_{part}}$$

Solving for T_{part}, we compute

$$T_{part} = \frac{T_{stack}}{\sqrt{3}}$$

Applying the numbers, we get

$$T_{part} = \frac{0.0105}{\sqrt{3}} = 0.0061$$

Note that the tolerance of the part ($T_{part} = 0.0061$) is greater than any of the part tolerances (that is, 0.003, 0.0025, and 0.005) using the conventional approach.

Thus, by using a statistical tolerance approach, the tolerance of the individual parts can be increased, giving the designer greater latitude.

Tolerance and Process Capability

If a process capability study has been completed, the process mean and standard deviation can be used to calculate tolerances. The formula used depends on the number of standard deviations to be included in the tolerance interval. The traditional number is 6 (that is, ±3).

Example 41.2

A painting process produces coatings with a thickness of 0.0005 and a standard deviation of 0.00002. What should the tolerance limits be for this process?

$$0.0005 \pm 3 \times 0.00002$$

$$0.0005 \pm 0.00006$$

$$(0.00044, 0.00056)$$

Tolerance Intervals

See Chapter 25, section VI.B.4.

Chapter 42

Special Design Tools

Planning may be subdivided into three categories: strategic, tactical, and operational (that is, day-to-day) activities. This chapter deals with strategic and tactical planning. Strategic planning typically looks at a three-to-five-year horizon, while tactical planning covers one to three years.

STRATEGIC

> Describe how Porter's five forces analysis, portfolio architecting, and other tools can be used in strategic design and planning. (Understand)
>
> **Body of Knowledge IX.D.1**

In general, a strategic planning process must do three things:

- Study the current state (that is, the business environment in which we operate)

- Envision the ideal future state (that is, where we'd like to be in three to five years)

- Plan the path (that is, how we'll get from here to there)

Strategic planning must be a priority of top management. For strategic planning to be successful, senior management must be actively engaged in the process. It is not something that can be delegated. Further, successful strategic planning must create a line of sight from strategic to tactical to operational activities. This does not mean that individuals executing activities at the lowest level of the organization must understand the details of the strategic plan. However, it does mean that their actions are traceable back to the strategic plan itself.

Various strategic planning models have been proposed, as described in the following subsections.

Porter's Five Forces

In 1979, Michael Porter listed five forces that affect the success of an enterprise:

- The bargaining power of customers—This force represents the ability and buying power of your customers to drive prices down

- The bargaining power of suppliers—This force represents the ability and power of your suppliers to drive up prices of their products

- The threat of new entrants—This force represents the ease by which new competitors can enter the market and drive prices down

- The threat of substitute products—This force represents the extent to which different products or services can be substituted for your own

- The intensity of competitive rivalry—This force represents strength of the competition in your industry

An organization should analyze each of these forces as it forms its strategic plan. It should also continually monitor each force because such forces can be highly dynamic, and changes in any one of these forces can require a change in strategy.

Portfolio Architecting

Portfolio architecting is the process of determining which products to produce. As a strategic planning tool it can be used to add to a current product line or to develop an entirely new family of products. The strategic advantage of this approach is that the product family will have common modules that will make manufacturing and inventory more efficient and permit "mass customization." The steps in portfolio architecting are as follows:

1. Study basic physical/chemical/biological principles involved (for example, How does powder coating work at the molecular level?)

2. Use the basic principles studied in step 1 to outline a family of products (for example, power coating spray guns, curing systems, turnkey systems)

3. List the modules required for each product

4. Form a matrix with products composing the rows and function modules composing the columns (see Figure 42.1)

5. Study the matrix to determine which products to build

Steps 3–5 are repeated in an iterative fashion, adjusting modules, adding or deleting products, and redesigning modules until a final combination is determined.

Hoshin Planning

Hoshin planning is a very tightly controlled planning and execution protocol that requires goal setting beginning at the highest level. Each lower level of the organization is required to form objectives and goals that support those of the next higher level.

Part IX.D.1

Product	Module						
	A	B	C	D	E	F	G
Systems for custom auto shops	Y	Y		Y		Y	Y
Systems for education and training	Y	Y		Y			
Home systems	Y	Y		Y		Y	
Commercial turnkey systems	Y	Y	Y	Y	Y	Y	
Systems for coating wood	Y		Y	Y	Y	Y	Y
Systems for using thermosets	Y	Y	Y		Y		Y
Systems for curing other finishes		Y		Y	Y	Y	
Stand-alone spray guns		Y		Y			

Figure 42.1   Example of a product family matrix.

Following are the basic steps in the hoshin planning process at each level of the hierarchy:

- Statement of the organization's goals (occasionally referred to as objectives)

- Strategies that support achievement of the goals

- Time-based tactics that support achievement of each strategy

- Development of metrics that measure the progress toward achieving each strategy

- Assignment of accountability for strategies and tactics

- Regular reviews to assess actual performance of plan

- Establishment of recovery plans or the adjustment of strategies and tactics as necessary

A key advantage of an effectively implemented hoshin planning process is that strategies are deployed and aligned both horizontally and vertically throughout an organization.

TACTICAL

> Describe and use the theory of inventive problem-solving (TRIZ), systematic design, critical parameter management, and Pugh analysis in designing products or processes. (Apply)
>
> **Body of Knowledge IX.D.2**

Tactical plans are designed to support strategic plans. This section describes some tools for executing tactical plans.

TRIZ

TRIZ is an acronym for the Russian words *Teorija Rezbenija Izobretaltelshih Zadach*, meaning "theory of inventive problem solving." TRIZ provides another approach for solving difficult design problems. According to Rantanen and Domb (2002), the following are core concepts of this theory:

- Contradiction—Many problems have an inherent contradiction. For example, How many stages should an air conditioner have? The more stages, the more efficiently it can respond to varying demand. However, additional stages are more expensive. The contradiction is that additional stages are both good and bad. Solving the problem consists of resolving the contradiction—preferably by removing it. Can a single-stage compressor become more efficient so that additional stages aren't needed? Can a multistage compressor be designed that is less expensive to build?

- Resources—TRIZ procedures require the analysis of items, information, energy, or material properties to determine which of them can be useful in resolving the contradiction.

- Ideality—In the beginning stages of problem solving, the ideal solution should be defined. In the case of the air conditioner, an ideal solution might be a single infinitely variable stage.

- Patterns of evolution—Studies have shown that innovation tends to follow certain patterns. One such pattern is the move toward a more macro perspective, integrating a device or idea with others to form a new device or idea. An example would be the integration of the hand lawnmower with the small gasoline engine to form the power mower.

- Inventive principles—40 inventive principles extracted from a worldwide review of patents resulted in engineering hints aimed at creating inventive and patentable designs to specific problems.

A Russian engineer, Genrich Altshuller, developed eight engineering system laws. According to Breyfogle (2003), Altshuller's laws are:

- Law of completeness of the system—Systems are derived from synthesis of separate parts into a functional system.

- Law of energy transfer in the system—Shaft, gears, magnetic fields, and charged particles are the heart of many inventive problems.

- Law of increasing ideality—Function is created with minimum complexity, which can be considered a ratio of system usefulness to its harmful effects. The ideal system has the desired outputs with no harmful effects, that is, no machine, just the function(s).

- Law of harmonization—Transferring energy more efficiently.

- Law of uneven development of parts—Not all parts evolve at the same pace. The least will limit the overall system.

- Law of transition to a super system—The solution system becomes the subsystem of a larger system.

- Law of transition from macro to micro—The use of physically smaller solutions (for example, electronic tubes to chips).

- Law of increasing substance-field involvement—Viewing and modeling systems as composed of two substances interacting through a field.

Axiomatic Design

Axiomatic design, yet another aid to the designer, divides the universe of the designer into four domains:

- Customer domain—lists the features the customer wants

- Functional domain—lists the various ways the product must work to meet the items in the customer domain

- Physical domain—lists the parameters in the design that satisfy the items in the functional domain

- Process domain—lists the processes that produce the product with the parameters listed in the physical domain

These domains are used sequentially in the design process:

- Concept design uses the customer domain to form the functional domain

- Product design uses the functional domain to form the physical domain

- Process design uses the physical domain to form the process domain

There are two fundamental axioms of good design:

- A good design can be partitioned into sections so that changes in one section have minimal effect on the other sections

- A good design requires a minimal amount of information to describe it

Systematic Design

Systematic design refers to the current trend toward applying design principles to the design function itself. Some organizations are constructing a value stream map for the processes involved, finding waste, excess waiting, unneeded processing, and so forth. The result is a design process that is more efficient and better able to respond to changes in the marketplace. Improving the design process has a positive impact on the ability to produce and execute tactical plans.

Critical Parameter Management

In a manufacturing process, critical dimensions are carefully monitored by the use of SPC charts or other data collection and analysis techniques. Tactical planning must determine which information is critical to the success of the plan and establish a process for data collection and analysis. The tactical plan must also detail appropriate responses to changes in these critical parameters. This process is called *critical parameter management.*

Pugh Analysis

Pugh analysis, also called a decision matrix or Pugh matrix, is appropriate to use when a single option must be selected from several and when multiple criteria are to be used. Thus, it can have frequent applications in the design of products and processes. The matrix is formed by listing the criteria in the first column and identifying the options across the top of the remaining columns, as shown in Figure 42.2.

Next, the team assigns each criterion a weight, as shown in Figure 42.3. The more important the criterion, the higher the number assigned.

A baseline option is established, and for each criterion, all other options are ranked with regard to how they compare to the baseline. The value –1 is used for worse than the baseline, 0 is used when the criterion-option combination is the same as the baseline, and +1 is used for better than the baseline (see Figure 42.4). Of course, finer scales may be used. For example, –2, –1, 0, 1, and 2 may be more appropriate.

The final step is to multiply criteria weights by each cell value and calculate column totals. See Figure 42.5.

	Option					
Criteria	**A**	**B**	**C**	**D**	**E**	**F**
Profitable						
No new equipment required						
No new training required						
Doesn't require (work unknown)						
Doesn't require more floor space						

Figure 42.2   First step in forming a Pugh matrix.

		Option					
Criteria	**Weight**	**A**	**B**	**C**	**D**	**E**	**F**
Profitable	5						
No new equipment required	3						
No new training required	2						
Doesn't require (work unknown)	4						
Doesn't require more floor space	1						

Figure 42.3   Second step in forming a Pugh matrix.

Part IX.D.2

Criteria	Weight	Option					
		A	B	C	D	E	F
Profitable	5	1	0	B	1	−1	1
No new equipment required	3	−1	0	B	1	0	1
No new training required	2	−1	1	B	1	−1	−1
Doesn't require (work unknown)	4	0	1	B	1	1	1
Doesn't require more floor space	1	−1	−1	B	−1	−1	0
	Total						

Figure 42.4 Third step in forming a Pugh matrix.

Criteria	Weight	Option					
		A	B	C	D	E	F
Profitable	5	1	0	B	1	−1	1
No new equipment required	3	−1	0	B	1	0	1
No new training required	2	−1	1	B	1	−1	−1
Doesn't require (work unknown)	4	0	1	B	1	1	1
Doesn't require more floor space	1	−1	−1	B	−1	−1	0
	Total	−1	5		13	−4	10

Figure 42.5 Final step in forming a Pugh matrix.

From Figure 42.5, we see that option D results in the highest positive score against the baseline. Although option D may not be the option ultimately selected, it is the relative score of each criterion that will generate discussion and debate regarding which option is most appropriate.

References

Breyfogle, Forrest W. III. 2003. *Implementing Six Sigma: Smarter Solutions Using Statistical Methods*. 2nd ed. Hoboken, NJ: John Wiley.

Porter, Michael. 1979. "How Competitive Forces Shape Strategy." *Harvard Business Review*, March/April.

Rantanen, K., and E. Domb. 2002. *Simplified TRIZ: New Problem-Solving Applications for Engineers and Manufacturing Professionals*. Boca Raton, FL: St. Lucie Press.

Part X
Appendices

Part X

Appendix 1
ASQ Code of Ethics (May 2005)

FUNDAMENTAL PRINCIPLES

ASQ requires its members and certification holders to conduct themselves ethically by:

    I. Being honest and impartial in serving the public, their employers, customers, and clients.

    II. Striving to increase the competence and prestige of the quality profession, and

    III. Using their knowledge and skill for the enhancement of human welfare.

Members and certification holders are required to observe the tenets set forth below:

Relations with the Public

Article 1—Hold paramount the safety, health, and welfare of the public in the performance of their professional duties.

Relations with Employers and Clients

Article 2—Perform services only in their areas of competence.

Article 3—Continue their professional development throughout their careers and provide opportunities for the professional and ethical development of others.

Article 4—Act in a professional manner in dealings with ASQ staff and each employer, customer, or client.

Article 5—Act as faithful agents or trustees and avoid conflict of interest and the appearance of conflicts of interest.

Relations with Peers

Article 6—Build their professional reputation on the merit of their services and not compete unfairly with others.

Article 7—Assure that credit for the work of others is given to those to whom it is due.

Appendix 2A

ASQ Six Sigma Black Belt Certification Body of Knowledge (2007)

The topics in this Body of Knowledge include additional detail in the form of subtext explanations and the cognitive level at which the questions will be written. This information will provide useful guidance for both the Examination Development Committee and the candidates preparing to take the exam. The subtext is not intended to limit the subject matter or be all-inclusive of what might be covered in an exam. It is meant to clarify the type of content to be included in the exam. The descriptor in parentheses at the end of each entry refers to the maximum cognitive level at which the topic will be tested. A more complete description of cognitive levels is provided at the end of this document.

I. Enterprise-Wide Deployment [9 Questions]

A. Enterprise-wide view

1. **History of continuous improvement**

   Describe the origins of continuous improvement and its impact on other improvement models. (Remember)

2. **Value and foundations of Six Sigma**

   Describe the value of Six Sigma, its philosophy, history, and goals. (Understand)

3. **Value and foundations of Lean**

   Describe the value of Lean, its philosophy, history, and goals. (Understand)

4. **Integration of Lean and Six Sigma**

   Describe the relationship between Lean and Six Sigma. (Understand)

5. **Business processes and systems**

   Describe the relationship among various business processes (design, production, purchasing, accounting, sales, etc.) and the impact these relationships can have on business systems. (Understand)

6. **Six Sigma and Lean applications**

   Describe how these tools are applied to processes in all types of enterprises: manufacturing, service, transactional, product and process design, innovation, etc. (Understand)

B. **Leadership**

1. **Enterprise leadership responsibilities**

    Describe the responsibilities of executive leaders and how they affect the deployment of Six Sigma in terms of providing resources, managing change, communicating ideas, etc. (Understand)

2. **Organizational roadblocks**

    Describe the impact an organization's culture and inherent structure can have on the success of Six Sigma, and how deployment failure can result from the lack of resources, management support, etc.; identify and apply various techniques to overcome these barriers. (Apply)

3. **Change management**

    Describe and use various techniques for facilitating and managing organizational change. (Apply)

4. **Six Sigma projects and kaizen events**

    Describe how projects and kaizen events are selected, when to use Six Sigma instead of other problem-solving approaches, and the importance of aligning their objectives with organizational goals. (Apply)

5. **Six Sigma roles and responsibilities**

    Describe the roles and responsibilities of Six Sigma participants: Black Belt, Master Black Belt, Green Belt, Champion, process owners, and project sponsors. (Understand)

II. **Organizational Process Management and Measures [9 Questions]**

A. **Impact on stakeholders**

    Describe the impact Six Sigma projects can have on customers, suppliers, and other stakeholders. (Understand)

B. **Critical to x (CTx) requirements**

    Define and describe various CTx requirements (critical to quality (CTQ), cost (CTC), process (CTP), safety (CTS), delivery (CTD), etc.) and the importance of aligning projects with those requirements. (Apply)

C. **Benchmarking**

    Define and distinguish between various types of benchmarking, including best practices, competitive, collaborative, etc. (Apply)

D. **Business performance measures**

    Define and describe various business performance measures, including balanced scorecard, key performance indicators (KPIs), the financial impact of customer loyalty, etc. (Understand)

E. **Financial measures**

    Define and use financial measures, including revenue growth, market share, margin, cost of quality (COQ), net present value (NPV), return on investment (ROI), cost-benefit analysis, etc. (Apply)

III. Team Management [16 Questions]

A. Team formation

1. Team types and constraints

Define and describe various types of teams (e.g., formal, informal, virtual, cross-functional, self-directed, etc.), and determine what team model will work best for a given situation. Identify constraining factors including geography, technology, schedules, etc. (Apply)

2. Team roles

Define and describe various team roles and responsibilities, including leader, facilitator, coach, individual member, etc. (Understand)

3. Team member selection

Define and describe various factors that influence the selection of team members, including required skills sets, subject matter expertise, availability, etc. (Apply)

4. Launching teams

Identify and describe the elements required for launching a team, including having management support; establishing clear goals, ground rules, and timelines; and how these elements can affect the team's success. (Apply)

B. Team facilitation

1. Team motivation

Describe and apply techniques that motivate team members and support and sustain their participation and commitment. (Apply)

2. Team stages

Facilitate the team through the classic stages of development: forming, storming, norming, performing, and adjourning. (Apply)

3. Team communication

Identify and use appropriate communication methods (both within the team and from the team to various stakeholders) to report progress, conduct milestone reviews, and support the overall success of the project. (Apply)

C. Team dynamics

Identify and use various techniques (e.g., coaching, mentoring, intervention, etc.) to overcome various group dynamic challenges, including overbearing/dominant or reluctant participants, feuding and other forms of unproductive disagreement, unquestioned acceptance of opinions as facts, groupthink, floundering, rushing to accomplish or finish, digressions, tangents, etc. (Evaluate)

D. **Time management for teams**

Select and use various time management techniques including publishing agendas with time limits on each entry, adhering to the agenda, requiring pre-work by attendees, ensuring that the right people and resources are available, etc. (Apply)

E. **Team decision-making tools**

Define, select, and use tools such as brainstorming, nominal group technique, multi-voting, etc. (Apply)

F. **Management and planning tools**

Define, select, and apply the following tools: affinity diagrams, tree diagrams, process decision program charts (PDPC), matrix diagrams, interrelationship digraphs, prioritization matrices, and activity network diagrams. (Apply)

G. **Team performance evaluation and reward**

Measure team progress in relation to goals, objectives, and other metrics that support team success, and reward and recognize the team for its accomplishments. (Analyze)

IV. **Define [15 Questions]**

A. **Voice of the customer**

1. **Customer identification**

   Segment customers for each project and show how the project will impact both internal and external customers. (Apply)

2. **Customer feedback**

   Identify and select the appropriate data collection method (surveys, focus groups, interviews, observation, etc.) to gather customer feedback to better understand customer needs, expectations, and requirements. Ensure that the instruments used are reviewed for validity and reliability to avoid introducing bias or ambiguity in the responses. (Apply)

3. **Customer requirements**

   Define, select, and use appropriate tools to determine customer requirements, such as CTQ flow-down, quality function deployment (QFD), and the Kano model. (Apply)

B. **Project charter**

1. **Problem statement**

   Develop and evaluate the problem statement in relation to the project's baseline performance and improvement goals. (Create)

2. **Project scope**

   Develop and review project boundaries to ensure that the project has value to the customer. (Analyze)

Appendix 2A

3. **Goals and objectives**

   Develop the goals and objectives for the project on the basis of the problem statement and scope. (Apply)

4. **Project performance measures**

   Identify and evaluate performance measurements (e.g., cost, revenue, schedule, etc.) that connect critical elements of the process to key outputs. (Analyze)

C. **Project tracking**

   Identify, develop, and use project management tools, such as schedules, Gantt charts, toll-gate reviews, etc., to track project progress. (Create)

V. **Measure [26 Questions]**

   A. **Process characteristics**

      1. **Input and output variables**

         Identify these process variables and evaluate their relationships using SIPOC and other tools. (Evaluate)

      2. **Process flow metrics**

         Evaluate process flow and utilization to identify waste and constraints by analyzing work in progress (WIP), work in queue (WIQ), touch time, takt time, cycle time, throughput, etc. (Evaluate)

      3. **Process analysis tools**

         Analyze processes by developing and using value stream maps, process maps, flowcharts, procedures, work instructions, spaghetti diagrams, circle diagrams, etc. (Analyze)

   B. **Data collection**

      1. **Types of data**

         Define, classify, and evaluate qualitative and quantitative data, continuous (variables) and discrete (attributes) data, and convert attributes data to variables measures when appropriate. (Evaluate)

      2. **Measurement scales**

         Define and apply nominal, ordinal, interval, and ratio measurement scales. (Apply)

      3. **Sampling methods**

         Define and apply the concepts related to sampling (e.g., representative selection, homogeneity, bias, etc.). Select and use appropriate sampling methods (e.g., random sampling, stratified sampling, systematic sampling, etc.) that ensure the integrity of data. (Evaluate)

      4. **Collecting data**

         Develop data collection plans, including consideration of how the data will be collected (e.g., check sheets, data coding techniques, automated data collection, etc.) and how it will be used. (Apply)

C. Measurement systems

1. Measurement methods

Define and describe measurement methods for both continuous and discrete data. (Understand)

2. Measurement systems analysis

Use various analytical methods (e.g., repeatability and reproducibility (R&R), correlation, bias, linearity, precision to tolerance, percent agreement, etc.) to analyze and interpret measurement system capability for variables and attributes measurement systems. (Evaluate)

3. Measurement systems in the enterprise

Identify how measurement systems can be applied in marketing, sales, engineering, research and development (R&D), supply chain management, customer satisfaction, and other functional areas. (Understand)

4. Metrology

Define and describe elements of metrology, including calibration systems, traceability to reference standards, the control and integrity of standards and measurement devices, etc. (Understand)

D. Basic statistics

1. Basic terms

Define and distinguish between population parameters and sample statistics (e.g., proportion, mean, standard deviation, etc.) (Apply)

2. Central limit theorem

Describe and use this theorem and apply the sampling distribution of the mean to inferential statistics for confidence intervals, control charts, etc. (Apply)

3. Descriptive statistics

Calculate and interpret measures of dispersion and central tendency, and construct and interpret frequency distributions and cumulative frequency distributions. (Evaluate)

4. Graphical methods

Construct and interpret diagrams and charts, including box-and-whisker plots, run charts, scatter diagrams, histograms, normal probability plots, etc. (Evaluate)

5. Valid statistical conclusions

Define and distinguish between enumerative (descriptive) and analytic (inferential) statistical studies, and evaluate their results to draw valid conclusions. (Evaluate)

E. Probability

1. Basic concepts

Describe and apply probability concepts such as independence, mutually exclusive events, multiplication rules, complementary probability, joint occurrence of events, etc. (Apply)

2. Commonly used distributions

Describe, apply, and interpret the following distributions: normal, Poisson, binomial, chi square, Student's *t*, and *F* distributions. (Evaluate)

3. Other distributions

Describe when and how to use the following distributions: hypergeometric, bivariate, exponential, lognormal, and Weibull. (Apply)

F. Process capability

1. Process capability indices

Define, select, and calculate C_p and C_{pk} to assess process capability. (Evaluate)

2. Process performance indices

Define, select, and calculate P_p, P_{pk}, and C_{pm} to assess process performance. (Evaluate)

3. Short-term and long-term capability

Describe and use appropriate assumptions and conventions when only short-term data or attributes data are available and when long-term data are available. Interpret the relationship between long-term and short-term capability. (Evaluate)

4. Process capability for non-normal data

Identify non-normal data and determine when it is appropriate to use Box-Cox or other transformation techniques. (Apply)

5. Process capability for attributes data

Calculate the process capability and process sigma level for attributes data. (Apply)

6. Process capability studies

Describe and apply elements of designing and conducting process capability studies, including identifying characteristics and specifications, developing sampling plans, and verifying stability and normality. (Evaluate)

7. Process performance vs. specification

Distinguish between natural process limits and specification limits, and calculate process performance metrics such as percent defective, parts per million (PPM), defects per million opportunities (DPMO), defects per unit (DPU), process sigma, rolled throughput yield (RTY), etc. (Evaluate)

VI. Analyze [24 Questions]

A. Measuring and modeling relationships between variables

1. Correlation coefficient

Calculate and interpret the correlation coefficient and its confidence interval, and describe the difference between correlation and causation. (Analyze)

NOTE: Serial correlation will not be tested.

2. Regression

Calculate and interpret regression analysis, and apply and interpret hypothesis tests for regression statistics. Use the regression model for estimation and prediction, analyze the uncertainty in the estimate, and perform a residuals analysis to validate the model. (Evaluate)

NOTE: Models that have non-linear parameters will not be tested.

3. Multivariate tools

Use and interpret multivariate tools such as principal components, factor analysis, discriminant analysis, multiple analysis of variance (MANOVA), etc., to investigate sources of variation. (Analyze)

4. Multi-vari studies

Use and interpret charts of these studies and determine the difference between positional, cyclical, and temporal variation. (Analyze)

5. Attributes data analysis

Analyze attributes data using logit, probit, logistic regression, etc., to investigate sources of variation. (Analyze)

B. Hypothesis testing

1. Terminology

Define and interpret the significance level, power, type I, and type II errors of statistical tests. (Evaluate)

2. Statistical vs. practical significance

Define, compare, and interpret statistical and practical significance. (Evaluate)

3. Sample size

Calculate sample size for common hypothesis tests (e.g., equality of means, equality of proportions, etc.). (Apply)

4. Point and interval estimates

Define and distinguish between confidence and prediction intervals. Define and interpret the efficiency and bias of estimators. Calculate tolerance and confidence intervals. (Evaluate)

5. Tests for means, variances, and proportions

Use and interpret the results of hypothesis tests for means, variances, and proportions. (Evaluate)

6. **Analysis of variance (ANOVA)**

   Select, calculate, and interpret the results of ANOVAs. (Evaluate)

7. **Goodness-of-fit (chi square) tests**

   Define, select, and interpret the results of these tests. (Evaluate)

8. **Contingency tables**

   Select, develop, and use contingency tables to determine statistical significance. (Evaluate)

9. **Non-parametric tests**

   Select, develop, and use various non-parametric tests, including Mood's Median, Levene's test, Kruskal-Wallis, Mann-Whitney, etc. (Evaluate)

C. **Failure mode and effects analysis (FMEA)**

   Describe the purpose and elements of FMEA, including risk priority number (RPN), and evaluate FMEA results for processes, products, and services. Distinguish between design FMEA (DFMEA) and process FMEA (PFMEA), and interpret results from each. (Evaluate)

D. **Additional analysis methods**

   1. **Gap analysis**

      Use various tools and techniques (gap analysis, scenario planning, etc.) to compare the current and future state in terms of pre-defined metrics. (Analyze)

   2. **Root cause analysis**

      Define and describe the purpose of root cause analysis, recognize the issues involved in identifying a root cause, and use various tools (e.g., the 5 whys, Pareto charts, fault tree analysis, cause and effect diagrams, etc.) for resolving chronic problems. (Evaluate)

   3. **Waste analysis**

      Identify and interpret the 7 classic wastes (overproduction, inventory, defects, over-processing, waiting, motion, and transportation) and other forms of waste such as resource under-utilization, etc. (Analyze)

VII. **Improve [23 Questions]**

   A. **Design of experiments (DOE)**

      1. **Terminology**

         Define basic DOE terms, including independent and dependent variables, factors and levels, response, treatment, error, etc. (Understand)

      2. **Design principles**

         Define and apply DOE principles, including power and sample size, balance, repetition, replication, order, efficiency, randomization, blocking, interaction, confounding, resolution, etc. (Apply)

3. **Planning experiments**

   Plan, organize, and evaluate experiments by determining the objective, selecting factors, responses, and measurement methods; choosing the appropriate design, etc. (Evaluate)

4. **One-factor experiments**

   Design and conduct completely randomized, randomized block, and Latin square designs, and evaluate their results. (Evaluate)

5. **Two-level fractional factorial experiments**

   Design, analyze, and interpret these types of experiments, and describe how confounding affects their use. (Evaluate)

6. **Full factorial experiments**

   Design, conduct, and analyze full factorial experiments. (Evaluate)

B. **Waste elimination**

   Select and apply tools and techniques for eliminating or preventing waste, including pull systems, kanban, 5S, standard work, poka-yoke, etc. (Analyze)

C. **Cycle-time reduction**

   Use various tools and techniques for reducing cycle time, including continuous flow, single-minute exchange of die (SMED), etc. (Analyze)

D. **Kaizen and kaizen blitz**

   Define and distinguish between these two methods and apply them in various situations. (Apply)

E. **Theory of constraints (TOC)**

   Define and describe this concept and its uses. (Understand)

F. **Implementation**

   Develop plans for implementing the improved process (i.e., conduct pilot tests, simulations, etc.), and evaluate results to select the optimum solution. (Evaluate)

G. **Risk analysis and mitigation**

   Use tools such as feasibility studies, SWOT analysis (strengths, weaknesses, opportunities, and threats), PEST analysis (political, environmental, social, and technological), and consequential metrics to analyze and mitigate risk. (Apply)

VIII. **Control [21 Questions]**

A. **Statistical process control (SPC)**

   1. **Objectives**

      Define and describe the objectives of SPC, including monitoring and controlling process performance, tracking trends, runs, etc., and reducing variation in a process. (Understand)

2. **Selection of variables**

   Identify and select critical characteristics for control chart monitoring. (Apply)

3. **Rational subgrouping**

   Define and apply the principle of rational subgrouping. (Apply)

4. **Control chart selection**

   Select and use the following control charts in various situations: $\bar{X} - R, \bar{X} - s$, individual and moving range (ImR), p, np, c, u, short-run SPC, and moving average. (Apply)

5. **Control chart analysis**

   Interpret control charts and distinguish between common and special causes using rules for determining statistical control. (Analyze)

B. **Other control tools**

   1. **Total productive maintenance (TPM)**

      Define the elements of TPM and describe how it can be used to control the improved process. (Understand)

   2. **Visual factory**

      Define the elements of a visual factory and describe how they can help control the improved process. (Understand)

C. **Maintain controls**

   1. **Measurement system re-analysis**

      Review and evaluate measurement system capability as process capability improves, and ensure that measurement capability is sufficient for its intended use. (Evaluate)

   2. **Control plan**

      Develop a control plan for ensuring the ongoing success of the improved process including the transfer of responsibility from the project team to the process owner. (Apply)

D. **Sustain improvements**

   1. **Lessons learned**

      Document the lessons learned from all phases of a project and identify how improvements can be replicated and applied to other processes in the organization. (Apply)

   2. **Training plan deployment**

      Develop and implement training plans to ensure continued support of the improved process. (Apply)

   3. **Documentation**

      Develop or modify documents including standard operating procedures (SOPs), work instructions, etc., to ensure that the improvements are sustained over time. (Apply)

4. **Ongoing evaluation**

    Identify and apply tools for ongoing evaluation of the improved process, including monitoring for new constraints, additional opportunities for improvement, etc. (Apply)

IX. **Design for Six Sigma (DFSS) Frameworks and Methodologies [7 Questions]**

   A. **Common DFSS methodologies**

       Identify and describe these methodologies. (Understand)

       1. DMADV (define, measure, analyze, design, and validate)

       2. DMADOV (define, measure, analyze, design, optimize, and validate)

   B. **Design for X (DFX)**

       Describe design constraints, including design for cost, design for manufacturability and producibility, design for test, design for maintainability, etc. (Understand)

   C. **Robust design and process**

       Describe the elements of robust product design, tolerance design, and statistical tolerancing. (Apply)

   D. **Special design tools**

       1. **Strategic**

          Describe how Porter's five forces analysis, portfolio architecting, and other tools can be used in strategic design and planning. (Understand)

       2. **Tactical**

          Describe and use the theory of inventive problem-solving (TRIZ), systematic design, critical parameter management, and Pugh analysis in designing products or processes. (Apply)

SIX LEVELS OF COGNITION BASED ON BLOOM'S TAXONOMY—REVISED (2001)

In addition to *content* specifics, the subtext for each topic in this BOK also indicates the intended *complexity level* of the test questions for that topic. These levels are based on "Levels of Cognition" (from Bloom's Taxonomy—Revised, 2001) and are presented below in rank order, from least complex to most complex.

Remember

Recall or recognize terms, definitions, facts, ideas, materials, patterns, sequences, methods, principles, etc.

Understand

Read and understand descriptions, communications, reports, tables, diagrams, directions, regulations, etc.

Apply

Know when and how to use ideas, procedures, methods, formulas, principles, theories, etc.

Analyze

Break down information into its constituent parts and recognize their relationship to one another and how they are organized; identify sublevel factors or salient data from a complex scenario.

Evaluate

Make judgments about the value of proposed ideas, solutions, etc., by comparing the proposal to specific criteria or standards.

Create

Put parts or elements together in such a way as to reveal a pattern or structure not clearly there before; identify which data or information from a complex set is appropriate to examine further or from which supported conclusions can be drawn.

Appendix 2B

ASQ Six Sigma Black Belt Certification Body of Knowledge (2001)

The topics in this Body of Knowledge include additional detail in the form of sub-text explanations and the cognitive level at which the questions will be written. This information will provide useful guidance for both the Examination Development Committee and the candidates preparing to take the exam. The subtext is not intended to limit the subject matter or be all-inclusive of what might be covered in an exam. It is meant to clarify the type of content to be included in the exam. The descriptor in parentheses at the end of each entry refers to the maximum cognitive level at which the topic will be tested. A more complete description of cognitive levels is provided at the end of this document.

I. Enterprise-Wide Deployment (9 Questions)

A. Enterprise view

1. **Value of Six Sigma**

   Understand the organizational value of Six Sigma, its philosophy, goals, and definition. (Comprehension)

2. **Business systems and processes**

   Understand and distinguish interrelationships between business systems and processes. (Comprehension)

3. **Process inputs, outputs, and feedback**

   Describe how process inputs, outputs, and feedback of the system impact the enterprise system as a whole. (Comprehension)

B. Leadership

1. **Enterprise leadership**

   Understand leadership roles in the deployment of Six Sigma (e.g., resources, organizational structure). (Comprehension)

2. **Six Sigma roles and responsibilities**

   Understand the roles/responsibilities of Black Belt, Master Black Belt, Green Belt, Champion, executive, process owners. (Comprehension)

C. Organizational goals and objectives

Understanding key drivers for business; understand key metrics/ scorecards

447

1. **Linking projects to organizational goals**

   Describe the project selection process including knowing when to use Six Sigma improvement methodology (DMAIC) as opposed to other problem-solving tools, and confirm link back to organizational goals. (Comprehension)

2. **Risk analysis**

   Describe the purpose and benefit of strategic risk analysis (e.g., strengths, weaknesses, opportunities, threats (SWOT), scenario planning), including the risk of optimizing elements in a project or process resulting in suboptimizing the whole. (Comprehension)

3. **Closed-loop assessment/knowledge management**

   Document the objectives achieved and manage the lessons learned to identify additional opportunities. (Comprehension)

D. **History of organizational improvement/foundations of Six Sigma**

   Understand origin of continuous improvement tools used in Six Sigma (e.g., Deming, Juran, Shewhart, Ishikawa, Taguchi). (Comprehension)

II. **Business Process Management (9 Questions)**

A. **Process vs. functional view**

1. **Process elements**

   Understand process components and boundaries. (Analysis)

2. **Owners and stakeholders**

   Identify process owners, internal and external customers, and other stakeholders. (Analysis)

3. **Project management and benefits**

   Understand the difference between managing projects and maximizing their benefits to the business. (Analysis)

4. **Project measures**

   Establish key performance metrics and appropriate project documentation. (Analysis)

B. **Voice of the customer**

1. **Identify customer**

   Segment customers as applicable to a particular project; list specific customers impacted by project within each segment; show how a project impacts internal and external customers; recognize the financial impact of customer loyalty. (Analysis)

2. **Collect customer data**

   Use various methods to collect customer feedback (surveys, focus groups, interviews, observation, etc.) and understand the strengths and weaknesses of each approach; recognize the key elements that make surveys, interviews, and other feedback tools effective; review questions for integrity (bias, vagueness, etc.). (Application)

3. Analyze customer data

Use graphical, statistical, and qualitative tools to understand customer feedback. (Analysis)

4. Determine critical customer requirements

Translate customer feedback into strategic project focus areas using QFD or similar tools, and establish key project metrics that relate to the voice of the customer and yield process insights. (Analysis)

[NOTE: The analysis of QFD matrices is covered in section X.A.]

C. Business results

1. Process performance metrics

Calculate DPU, RTY, and DPMO sigma levels; understand how metrics propagate upward and allocate downward; compare and contrast capability, complexity, and control; manage the use of sigma performance measures (e.g., PPM, DPMO, DPU, RTY, COPQ) to drive enterprise decisions. (Analysis)

2. Benchmarking

Understand the importance of benchmarking. (Knowledge)

3. Financial benefits

Understand and present financial measures and other benefits (soft and hard) of a project; understand and use basic financial models (e.g., NPV, ROI); describe, apply, evaluate, and interpret cost of quality concepts, including quality cost categories, data collection, reporting, etc. (Application)

III. Project Management (15 Questions)

A. Project charter and plan

1. Charter/plan elements

Compare, select, and explain elements of a project's charter and plan. (Analysis)

2. Planning tools

Plan the project using tools such as Gantt chart, PERT chart, planning trees, etc. (Application)

3. Project documentation

Create data-driven and fact-driven project documentation using spreadsheets, storyboards, phased reviews, management reviews, presentations to the executive team, etc. (Synthesis)

4. Charter negotiation

Create and negotiate the charter, including objectives, scope, boundaries, resources, project transition, and project closure. (Analysis)

B. Team leadership

1. Initiating teams

Know the elements of launching a team and why they are important: clear purpose, goals, commitment, ground rules, roles and responsibilities of team members, schedules, support from management, and team empowerment. (Application)

2. Selecting team members

Select team members who have appropriate skills sets (e.g., self-facilitation, technical/subject-matter expertise), and create teams with appropriate numbers of members and representation. (Application)

3. Team stages

Facilitate the stages of team evolution, including forming, storming, norming, performing, adjourning, and recognition. (Application)

C. Team dynamics and performance

1. Team-building techniques

Recognize and apply the basic steps in team building: goals, roles and responsibilities, introductions, and both stated and hidden agendas. (Synthesis)

2. Team facilitation techniques

Apply coaching, mentoring, and facilitation techniques to guide a team and overcome problems such as overbearing, dominant, or reluctant participants; the unquestioned acceptance of opinions as facts; group-think; feuding; floundering; the rush to accomplishment; attribution; discounts and plops; digressions and tangents; etc. (Application)

3. Team performance evaluation

Measure team progress in relation to goals, objectives, and metrics that support team success. (Analysis)

4. Team tools

Define, select, and apply team tools such as nominal group technique, force field analysis, multivoting, conversion/diversion. (Application)

D. Change agent

1. Managing change

Understand and apply techniques for facilitating or managing organizational change through change agent methodologies. (Application)

2. Organizational roadblocks

Understand the inherent structures of an organization (e.g., its cultures and constructs) that present basic barriers to improvement; select and apply techniques to overcome them. (Application)

3. **Negotiation and conflict resolution techniques**

   Define, select, and apply tools such as consensus techniques, brainstorming, effort/impact, multivoting, interest-based bargaining to help conflicting parties (e.g., departments, groups, leaders, staff) recognize common goals and how to work together to achieve them. (Application)

4. **Motivation techniques**

   Define, select, and apply techniques that support and sustain team member participation and commitment. (Application)

5. **Communication**

   Use effective and appropriate communication techniques for different situations to overcome organizational barriers to success. (Application)

E. **Management and Planning Tools**

   Define, select, and use 1) affinity diagrams, 2) interrelationship digraphs, 3) tree diagrams, 4) prioritization matrices, 5) matrix diagrams, 6) process decision program charts (PDPC), and 7) activity network diagrams. (Application)

IV. **Six Sigma Improvement Methodology and Tools—***Define* **(9 Questions)**

A. **Project scope**

   Determine project definition/scope using Pareto charts, top-level process (macro) maps, etc. (Synthesis)

B. **Metrics**

   Establish primary and consequential metrics (quality, cycle time, cost). (Analysis)

C. **Problem statement**

   Develop problem statement, including baseline and improvement goals. (Synthesis)

V. **Six Sigma Improvement Methodology and Tools—***Measure* **(30 Questions)**

A. **Process analysis and documentation**

   1. **Tools**

      Develop and review process maps, written procedures, work instructions, flowcharts, etc. (Analysis)

   2. **Process inputs and outputs**

      Identify process input variables and process output variables, and document their relationships through cause and effect diagrams, relational matrices, etc. (Evaluation)

B. **Probability and statistics**

   1. **Drawing valid statistical conclusions**

      Distinguish between enumerative (descriptive) and analytical (inferential) studies, and distinguish between a population parameter and a sample statistic. (Evaluation)

2. **Central limit theorem and sampling distribution of the mean**

Define the central limit theorem and understand its significance in the application of inferential statistics for confidence intervals, control charts, etc. (Application)

3. **Basic probability concepts**

Describe and apply concepts such as independence, mutually exclusive, multiplication rules, complementary probability, joint occurrence of events, etc. (Application)

C. **Collecting and summarizing data**

1. **Types of data**

Identify, define, classify and compare continuous (variables) and discrete (attributes) data, and recognize opportunities to convert attributes data to variables measures. (Evaluation)

2. **Measurement scales**

Define and apply nominal, ordinal, interval, and ratio measurement scales. (Application)

3. **Methods for collecting data**

Define and apply methods for collecting data such as check sheets, coding data, automatic gaging, etc. (Evaluation)

4. **Techniques for assuring data accuracy and integrity**

Define and apply techniques for assuring data accuracy and integrity such as random sampling, stratified sampling, sample homogeneity, etc. (Evaluation)

5. **Descriptive statistics**

Define, compute, and interpret measures of dispersion and central tendency, and construct and interpret frequency distributions and cumulative frequency distributions. (Evaluation)

[NOTE: Measures of the geometric and harmonic mean will not be tested.]

6. **Graphical methods**

Depict *relationships* by constructing, applying and interpreting diagrams and charts such as stem-and-leaf plots, box-and-whisker plots, run charts, scatter diagrams, etc., and depict *distributions* by constructing, applying and interpreting diagrams such as histograms, normal probability plots, Weibull plots, etc. (Evaluation)

D. **Properties and applications of probability distributions**

1. **Distributions commonly used by Black Belts**

Describe and apply binomial, Poisson, normal, chi-square, Student's *t*, and *F* distributions. (Evaluation)

2. **Other distributions**

Recognize when to use hypergeometric, bivariate, exponential, lognormal, and Weibull distributions. (Application)

E. Measurement systems

1. Measurement methods

Describe and review measurement methods such as attribute screens, gauge blocks, calipers, micrometers, optical comparators, tensile strength, titration, etc. (Comprehension)

2. Measurement system analysis

Calculate, analyze, and interpret measurement system capability using repeatability and reproducibility, measurement correlation, bias, linearity, percent agreement, precision/tolerance (P/T), precision/total variation (P/TV), and use both ANOVA and control chart methods for non-destructive, destructive, and attribute systems. (Evaluation)

3. Metrology

Understand traceability to calibration standards, measurement error, calibration systems, control and integrity of standards and measurement devices. (Comprehension)

F. Analyzing process capability

1. Designing and conducting process capability studies

Identify, describe, and apply the elements of designing and conducting process capability studies, including identifying characteristics, identifying specifications/tolerances, developing sampling plans, and verifying stability and normality. (Evaluation)

2. Calculating process performance vs. specification

Distinguish between natural process limits and specification limits, and calculate process performance metrics such as percent defective. (Evaluation)

3. Process capability indices

Define, select, and calculate C_p, C_{pk}, and assess process capability. (Evaluation)

4. Process performance indices

Define, select, and calculate P_p, P_{pk}, C_{pm}, and assess process performance. (Evaluation)

5. Short-term vs. long-term capability

Understand the assumptions and conventions appropriate when only short-term data are collected and when only attributes data are available; understand the changes in relationships that occur when long-term data are used; interpret relationships between long-term and short-term capability as it relates to technology and/or control problems. (Evaluation)

6. Non-normal data transformations (process capability for non-normal data)

Understand the cause of non-normal data and determine when it is appropriate to transform. (Application)

7. **Process capability for attributes data**

Compute sigma level and understand its relationship to P_{pk}. (Application)

VI. **Six Sigma Improvement Methodology and Tools—*Analyze* (23 Questions)**

A. **Exploratory data analysis**

1. **Multi-vari studies**

Use multi-vari studies to interpret the difference between positional, cyclical, and temporal variation; design sampling plans to investigate the largest sources of variation; create and interpret multi-vari charts. (Application)

2. **Measuring and modeling relationships between variables**

a. **Simple and multiple least-squares linear regression**

Calculate the regression equation; apply and interpret hypothesis tests for regression statistics; use the regression model for estimation and prediction, and analyze the uncertainty in the estimate. (Models that have non-linear parameters will not be tested.) (Evaluation)

b. **Simple linear correlation**

Calculate and interpret the correlation coefficient and its confidence interval; apply and interpret a hypothesis test for the correlation coefficient; understand the difference between correlation and causation. (Serial correlation will not be tested.) (Evaluation)

c. **Diagnostics**

Analyze residuals of the model. (Analysis)

B. **Hypothesis testing**

1. **Fundamental concepts of hypothesis testing**

a. **Statistical vs. practical significance**

Define, compare, and contrast statistical and practical significance. (Evaluation)

b. **Significance level, power, type I and type II errors**

Apply and interpret the significance level, power, type I and type II errors of statistical tests. (Evaluation)

c. **Sample Size**

Understand how to calculate sample size for any given hypothesis test. (Application)

2. **Point and interval estimation**

Define and interpret the efficiency and bias of estimators; compute, interpret and draw conclusions from statistics such as standard error, tolerance intervals, and confidence intervals; understand the distinction between confidence intervals and prediction intervals. (Analysis)

3. **Tests for means, variances, and proportions**

   Apply hypothesis tests for means, variances, and proportions, and interpret the results. (Evaluation)

4. **Paired-comparison tests**

   Define, determine applicability, and apply paired-comparison parametric hypothesis tests, and interpret the results. (Evaluation)

5. **Goodness-of-fit tests**

   Define, determine applicability, and apply chi-square tests and interpret the results. (Evaluation)

6. **Analysis of variance (ANOVA)**

   Define, determine applicability, and apply ANOVAs and interpret the results. (Evaluation)

7. **Contingency tables**

   Define, determine applicability, and construct a contingency table and use it to determine statistical significance. (Evaluation)

8. **Non-parametric tests**

   Define, determine applicability, and construct various non-parametric tests including Mood's Median, Levene's test, Kruskal-Wallis, Mann-Whitney, etc. (Analysis)

VII. **Six Sigma Improvement Methodology and Tools—***Improve* **(22 Questions)**

   A. **Design of experiments (DOE)**

   1. **Terminology**

      Define independent and dependent variables, factors and levels, response, treatment, error, and replication. (Comprehension)

   2. **Planning and organizing experiments**

      Describe and apply the basic elements of experiment planning and organizing, including determining the experiment objective, selecting factors, responses, and measurement methods, choosing the appropriate design, etc. (Evaluation)

   3. **Design principles**

      Define and apply the principles of power and sample size, balance, replication, order, efficiency, randomization and blocking, interaction, and confounding. (Application)

   4. **Design and analysis of one-factor experiments**

      Construct these experiments such as completely randomized, randomized block and Latin square designs, and apply computational and graphical methods to analyze and evaluate the significance of results. (Evaluation)

5. **Design and analysis of full-factorial experiments**

   Construct these experiments and apply computational and graphical methods to analyze and evaluate the significance of results. (Evaluation)

6. **Design and analysis of two-level fractional factorial experiments**

   Construct experiments (including Taguchi designs) and apply computational and graphical methods to analyze and evaluate the significance of results; understand limitations of fractional factorials due to confounding. (Evaluation)

7. **Taguchi robustness concepts**

   Apply Taguchi robustness concepts and techniques such as signal-to-noise ratio, controllable and noise factors, and robustness to external sources of variability. (Analysis)

8. **Mixture experiments**

   Construct these experiments and apply computational and graphical methods to analyze and evaluate the significance of results. (Analysis)

B. **Response surface methodology**

   1. **Steepest ascent/descent experiments**

      Construct these experiments and apply computational and graphical methods to analyze the significance of results. (Analysis)

   2. **Higher-order experiments**

      Construct experiments such as CCD, Box-Behnken, etc., and apply computational and graphical methods to analyze the significance of results. (Analysis)

C. **Evolutionary operations (EVOP)**

   Understand the application and strategy of EVOP. (Comprehension)

VIII. **Six Sigma Improvement Methodology and Tools—*Control* (15 Questions)**

A. **Statistical process control**

   1. **Objectives and benefits**

      Understand objectives and benefits of SPC (e.g., controlling process performance, distinguishing special from common causes). (Comprehension)

   2. **Selection of variable**

      Select critical characteristics for monitoring by control chart. (Application)

   3. **Rational subgrouping**

      Define and apply the principle of rational subgrouping. (Application)

4. **Selection and application of control charts**

   Identify, select, construct and apply the following types of control charts: $\bar{X} - R$, $\bar{X} - s$, individual and moving range (ImR/XmR), median, p, np, c, and u. (Application)

5. **Analysis of control charts**

   Interpret control charts and distinguish between common and special causes using rules for determining statistical control. (Analysis)

6. **PRE-control**

   Define and explain PRE-control and perform PRE-control calculations and analysis. (Analysis)

B. **Advanced statistical process control**

   Understand appropriate uses of short-run SPC, EWMA, CuSum, and moving average. (Comprehension)

C. **Lean tools for control**

   Apply appropriate lean tools (e.g., 5S, visual factory, kaizen, kanban, poka-yoke, total productive maintenance, standard work) as they relate to the control phase of DMAIC. (Application)

   [NOTE: The use of lean tools in other areas of DMAIC is covered in section IX.C.]

D. **Measurement system re-analysis**

   Understand the need to improve measurement system capability as process capability improves; evaluate the use of control measurement systems (e.g., attributes, variables, destructive), and ensure that measurement capability is sufficient for its intended use. (Evaluation)

IX. **Lean Enterprise (9 Questions)**

A. **Lean concepts**

1. **Theory of constraints**

   Describe the theory of constraints. (Comprehension)

2. **Lean thinking**

   Describe concepts such as value, value chain, flow, pull, perfection, etc. (Comprehension)

3. **Continuous flow manufacturing (CFM)**

   Describe the concept CFM. (Comprehension)

4. **Non-value-added activities**

   Identify these activities in terms inventory, space, test inspection, rework, transportation, storage, etc. (Application)

5. **Cycle-time reduction**

   Describe how cycle-time reduction can be used to identify defects and non-value-added activities using kaizen-type methods to reduce waste of space, inventory, labor, and distance. (Comprehension)

B. **Lean tools**

Define, select, and apply tools such as visual factory, kanban, poka-yoke, standard work, SMED, etc., in areas outside of DMAIC-Control. (Application)

[NOTE: The use of lean tools in DMAIC-Control is covered in section VIII.C.]

C. **Total productive maintenance (TPM)**

Understand the concept of TPM. (Comprehension)

X. **Design for Six Sigma (DFSS) (9 Questions)**

A. **Quality function deployment (QFD)**

Analyze a completed QFD matrix. (Analysis)

B. **Robust design and process**

1. **Functional requirements**

Understand functional requirements of a design. (Comprehension)

2. **Noise strategies**

Develop a robust design using noise strategies. (Application)

3. **Tolerance design**

Understand the concepts of tolerance design and statistical tolerancing. (Analysis)

4. **Tolerance and process capability**

Calculate tolerances using process capability data. (Analysis)

C. **Failure mode and effects analysis (FMEA)**

Understand the terminology, purpose, and use of scale criteria (RPN) and be able to apply it to a process, product, or service; understand the distinction between and interpret data associated with DFMEA and PFMEA. (Analysis)

D. **Design for X (DFX)**

Understand design constraints such as design for cost, design for manufacturability and producibility, design for test, design for maintainability, etc. (Comprehension)

E. **Special design tools**

Understand the concept of special design tools such as the theory of inventive problem-solving (TRIZ), axiomatic design (conceptual structure robustness), etc. (Knowledge)

SIX LEVELS OF COGNITION BASED ON BLOOM'S TAXONOMY (1956)

In addition to *content* specifics, the subtext detail also indicates the intended *complexity level* of the test questions for that topic. These levels are based on "Levels of Cognition" (from Bloom's Taxonomy, 1956) and are presented below in rank order, from least complex to most complex.

Knowledge Level

(Also commonly referred to as recognition, recall, or rote knowledge.) Being able to remember or recognize terminology, definitions, facts, ideas, materials, patterns, sequences, methodologies, principles, etc.

Comprehension Level

Being able to read and understand descriptions, communications, reports, tables, diagrams, directions, regulations, etc.

Application Level

Being able to apply ideas, procedures, methods, formulas, principles, theories, etc., in job-related situations.

Analysis

Being able to break down information into its constituent parts and recognize the parts' relationship to one another and how they are organized; identify sublevel factors or salient data from a complex scenario.

Synthesis

Being able to put parts or elements together in such a way as to show a pattern or structure not clearly there before; identify which data or information from a complex set is appropriate to examine further or from which supported conclusions can be drawn.

Evaluation

Being able to make judgments regarding the value of proposed ideas, solutions, methodologies, etc., by using appropriate criteria or standards to estimate accuracy, effectiveness, economic benefits, etc.

Appendix 3

Control Chart Combinations for Measurement Data

Averages				Natural Process Limits			
Chart	Center line	LCL	UCL	Chart	Center line	UNPL	LNPL
$\bar{X}$	$\bar{\bar{X}}$	$\bar{\bar{X}} - A_2\bar{R}$	$\bar{\bar{X}} + A_2\bar{R}$	I	$\bar{\bar{X}}$	$\bar{\bar{X}} - E_2\bar{R}$	$\bar{\bar{X}} + E_2\bar{R}$
R	$\bar{R}$	$D_3\bar{R}$	$D_4\bar{R}$	R	$\bar{R}$	$D_3\bar{R}$	$D_4\bar{R}$
$\bar{X}$	$\bar{\bar{X}}$	$\bar{\bar{X}} - A_4\tilde{R}$	$\bar{\bar{X}} + A_4\tilde{R}$	I	$\bar{\bar{X}}$	$\bar{\bar{X}} - E_5\tilde{R}$	$\bar{\bar{X}} + E_5\tilde{R}$
R	$\tilde{R}$	$D_5\tilde{R}$	$D_6\tilde{R}$	R	$\tilde{R}$	$D_5\tilde{R}$	$D_6\tilde{R}$
$\bar{X}$	$\bar{\bar{X}}$	$\bar{\bar{X}} - A_1\bar{\sigma}_{RMS}$	$\bar{\bar{X}} + A_1\bar{\sigma}_{RMS}$	I	$\bar{\bar{X}}$	$\bar{\bar{X}} - E_1\bar{\sigma}_{RMS}$	$\bar{\bar{X}} + E_1\bar{\sigma}_{RMS}$
σ_{RMS}	$\bar{\sigma}_{RMS}$	$B_3\bar{\sigma}_{RMS}$	$B_4\bar{\sigma}_{RMS}$	σ_{RMS}	$\bar{\sigma}_{RMS}$	$B_3\bar{\sigma}_{RMS}$	$B_4\bar{\sigma}_{RMS}$
$\bar{X}$	$\bar{\bar{X}}$	$\bar{\bar{X}} - A_5\tilde{\sigma}_{RMS}$	$\bar{\bar{X}} + A_5\tilde{\sigma}_{RMS}$	I	$\bar{\bar{X}}$	$\bar{\bar{X}} - E_4\tilde{\sigma}_{RMS}$	$\bar{\bar{X}} + E_4\tilde{\sigma}_{RMS}$
σ_{RMS}	$\tilde{\sigma}_{RMS}$	$B_9\tilde{\sigma}_{RMS}$	$B_{10}\tilde{\sigma}_{RMS}$	σ_{RMS}	$\tilde{\sigma}_{RMS}$	$B_9\tilde{\sigma}_{RMS}$	$B_{10}\tilde{\sigma}_{RMS}$
$\bar{X}$	$\bar{\bar{X}}$	$\bar{\bar{X}} - A_3\bar{s}$	$\bar{\bar{X}} + A_3\bar{s}$	I	$\bar{\bar{X}}$	$\bar{\bar{X}} - E_3\bar{s}$	$\bar{\bar{X}} + E_3\bar{s}$
s	$\bar{s}$	$B_3\bar{s}$	$B_4\bar{s}$	s	$\bar{s}$	$B_3\bar{s}$	$B_4\bar{s}$
$\bar{X}$	$\bar{\bar{X}}$	$\bar{\bar{X}} - A_{10}\tilde{s}$	$\bar{\bar{X}} + A_{10}\tilde{s}$	I	$\bar{\bar{X}}$	$\bar{\bar{X}} - E_6\tilde{s}$	$\bar{\bar{X}} + E_6\tilde{s}$
s	$\tilde{s}$	$B_9\tilde{s}$	$B_{10}\tilde{s}$	s	$\tilde{s}$	$B_9\tilde{s}$	$B_{10}\tilde{s}$
$\bar{X}$	$\bar{\bar{X}}$	$\bar{\bar{X}} - A_7\sqrt{\bar{s}^2}$ $\approx \bar{\bar{X}} - A\sqrt{\bar{s}^2}$	$\bar{\bar{X}} + A_7\sqrt{\bar{s}^2}$ $\approx \bar{\bar{X}} + A\sqrt{\bar{s}^2}$	—	—	—	—
s	$\sqrt{\bar{s}^2}$	$B_7\sqrt{\bar{s}^2}$ $\approx B_5\sqrt{\bar{s}^2}$	$B_8\sqrt{\bar{s}^2}$ $\approx B_6\sqrt{\bar{s}^2}$	—	—	—	—
$\bar{X}$	$\bar{\bar{X}}$	$\bar{\bar{X}} - A_7\sqrt{\bar{s}^2}$ $\approx \bar{\bar{X}} - A\sqrt{\bar{s}^2}$	$\bar{\bar{X}} + A_7\sqrt{\bar{s}^2}$ $\approx \bar{\bar{X}} + A\sqrt{\bar{s}^2}$	—	—	—	—
s^2	$\bar{s}^2$	$B_{11}\bar{s}^2$	$B_{12}\bar{s}^2$	—	—	—	—
$\tilde{X}$	$\bar{\tilde{X}}$	$\bar{\tilde{X}} - A_6\bar{R}$	$\bar{\tilde{X}} + A_6\bar{R}$	I	$\bar{\tilde{X}}$	$\bar{\tilde{X}} - E_2\bar{R}$	$\bar{\tilde{X}} + E_2\bar{R}$
R	$\bar{R}$	$D_3\bar{R}$	$D_4\bar{R}$	R	$\bar{R}$	$D_3\bar{R}$	$D_4\bar{R}$
$\tilde{X}$	$\bar{\tilde{X}}$	$\bar{\tilde{X}} - A_9\tilde{R}$	$\bar{\tilde{X}} + A_9\tilde{R}$	I	$\bar{\tilde{X}}$	$\bar{\tilde{X}} - E_5\tilde{R}$	$\bar{\tilde{X}} + E_5\tilde{R}$
R	$\tilde{R}$	$D_5\tilde{R}$	$D_6\tilde{R}$	R	$\tilde{R}$	$D_5\tilde{R}$	$D_6\tilde{R}$

	Averages				Natural Process Limits		
Chart	Center line	LCL	UCL	Chart	Center line	UNPL	LNPL
$\bar{X}$	Nominal	Nominal $- A\sigma_x$	Nominal $+ A\sigma_x$	I	Nominal	Nominal $- 3\sigma_x$	Nominal $+ 3\sigma_x$
R	$d_2\sigma_x$	$D_1\sigma_x$	$D_2\sigma_x$	R	$d_2\sigma_x$	$D_1\sigma_x$	$D_2\sigma_x$
$\bar{X}$	Nominal	Nominal $- A\sigma_x$	Nominal $+ A\sigma_x$	I	Nominal	Nominal $- 3\sigma_x$	Nominal $+ 3\sigma_x$
σ_{RMS}	$c_2\sigma_x$	$B_1\sigma_x$	$B_2\sigma_x$	σ_{RMS}	$c_2\sigma_x$	$B_1\sigma_x$	$B_2\sigma_x$
$\bar{X}$	Nominal	Nominal $- A\sigma_x$	Nominal $+ A\sigma_x$	I	Nominal	Nominal $- 3\sigma_x$	Nominal $+ 3\sigma_x$
s	$c_4\sigma_x$	$B_5\sigma_x$	$B_6\sigma_x$	s	$c_4\sigma_x$	$B_5\sigma_x$	$B_6\sigma_x$
$\tilde{X}$	Nominal	Nominal $- A_8\sigma_x$	Nominal $+ A_8\sigma_x$	I	Nominal	Nominal $- 3\sigma_x$	Nominal $+ 3\sigma_x$
R	$d_2\sigma_x$	$D_1\sigma_x$	$D_2\sigma_x$	R	$d_2\sigma_x$	$D_1\sigma_x$	$D_2\sigma_x$
—	—	—	—	I	$\bar{X}$	$\bar{X} - E_2 m\bar{R}$	$\bar{X} + E_2 m\bar{R}$
—	—	—	—	R	$m\bar{R}$	$D_3 m\bar{R}$	$D_4 m\bar{R}$
—	—	—	—	I	$\bar{X}$	$\bar{X} - E_5 m\tilde{R}$	$\bar{X} + E_5 m\tilde{R}$
—	—	—	—	R	$m\tilde{R}$	$D_5 m\tilde{R}$	$D_6 m\tilde{R}$

Notes:

When subgroups are involved, assume k subgroups of size n.

$\bar{R}$ is the average range of k subgroups of size n.

$\tilde{R}$ is the median range.

$m\bar{R}$ is the average moving range.

$m\tilde{R}$ is the median range of all the subgroup ranges.

σ_{RMS} is the average root mean squared deviation and computed as $\sqrt{\dfrac{\sum_{i=1}^{n}(X_i - \bar{X})^2}{n}}$.

"Nominal" may be construed as given, known, target, and historical or past values.

See Appendix 6 for various ways of computing σ_x.

Appendix 4
Control Chart Constants

n	A	A_1	A_2	A_3	A_4	A_5	A_6	A_8	A_9	A_{10}	B_1	B_2	B_3	B_4	B_5	B_6	n
2	2.121	3.760	1.881	2.659	2.224	4.447				3.143	0.000	1.843	0.000	3.266	0.000	2.606	2
3	1.732	2.394	1.023	1.954	1.091	2.547	1.187	2.010	1.265	2.082	0.000	1.858	0.000	2.568	0.000	2.276	3
4	1.500	1.880	0.729	1.628	0.758	1.951				1.689	0.000	1.808	0.000	2.266	0.000	2.088	4
5	1.342	1.596	0.577	1.427	0.594	1.638	0.691	1.607	0.712	1.465	0.000	1.757	0.000	2.089	0.000	1.964	5
6	1.225	1.410	0.483	1.287	0.495	1.438				1.313	0.026	1.711	0.030	1.970	0.029	1.874	6
7	1.134	1.277	0.419	1.182	0.429	1.297	0.509	1.377	0.520	1.201	0.104	1.672	0.118	1.882	0.113	1.806	7
8	1.061	1.175	0.373	1.099	0.380	1.190				1.114	0.167	1.638	0.185	1.815	0.178	1.752	8
9	1.000	1.094	0.337	1.032	0.343	1.107	0.412	1.223	0.419	1.044	0.219	1.609	0.239	1.761	0.232	1.707	9
10	0.949	1.028	0.308	0.975	0.314	1.039				0.985	0.261	1.584	0.284	1.716	0.277	1.669	10
11	0.905	0.973	0.285	0.927	0.290	0.982	0.350	1.110	0.356	0.936	0.299	1.561	0.322	1.678	0.314	1.637	11
12	0.866	0.925	0.266	0.886	0.270	0.933				0.893	0.330	1.542	0.354	1.646	0.346	1.609	12
13	0.832	0.884	0.249	0.850	0.253	0.891	0.308	1.026	0.312	0.856	0.359	1.523	0.381	1.619	0.374	1.585	13
14	0.802	0.848	0.235	0.817	0.239	0.854				0.823	0.384	1.506	0.407	1.593	0.399	1.563	14
15	0.775	0.816	0.223	0.789	0.226	0.821	0.276	0.958	0.280	0.794	0.406	1.492	0.428	1.572	0.420	1.544	15
16	0.750	0.788	0.212	0.763	0.215						0.427	1.477	0.448	1.552	0.441	1.526	16
17	0.728	0.762	0.203	0.739	0.206						0.445	1.466	0.466	1.534	0.458	1.511	17
18	0.707	0.738	0.194	0.718	0.197						0.461	1.455	0.482	1.518	0.475	1.496	18
19	0.688	0.717	0.187	0.698	0.189						0.477	1.443	0.496	1.504	0.490	1.483	19
20	0.671	0.697	0.180	0.680	0.182						0.490	1.434	0.510	1.490	0.503	1.471	20
21	0.655	0.679	0.173	0.663	0.176						0.504	1.423	0.523	1.477	0.517	1.459	21
22	0.640	0.662	0.167	0.647	0.170						0.517	1.414	0.535	1.465	0.529	1.448	22
23	0.626	0.647	0.162	0.633	0.164						0.528	1.406	0.545	1.455	0.539	1.438	23
24	0.612	0.632	0.157	0.619	0.159						0.539	1.398	0.555	1.445	0.549	1.429	24
25	0.600	0.619	0.153	0.606	0.155						0.544	1.395	0.564	1.436	0.558	1.421	25

Notes: Only odd values of n are given for A_6, A_8, and A_9. Otherwise, the median for an even n is simply the average of the two middle values of the subgroup.

See Appendix 5 for values of A_7, B_7, and B_8.

Appendix 4

Appendix 4

n	E_6	E_5	E_4	E_3	E_2	E_1	D_6	D_5	D_4	D_3	D_2	D_1	B_{12}	B_{11}	B_{10}	B_9	n
2	4.444	3.145	6.289	3.760	2.660	5.317	3.863	0.000	3.267	0.000	3.686	0.000	5.243	0.000	3.864		2
3	3.606	1.889	4.412	3.385	1.772	4.146	2.744	0.000	2.574	0.000	4.358	0.000	4.000	0.000	2.733		3
4	3.378	1.517	4.115	3.256	1.457	3.760	2.375	0.000	2.282	0.000	4.698	0.000	3.449	0.000	2.351		4
5	3.275	1.329	3.663	3.191	1.290	3.568	2.179	0.000	2.114	0.000	4.918	0.000	3.121	0.000	2.145		5
6	3.215	1.214	3.521	3.153	1.184	3.454	2.054	0.000	2.004	0.000	5.078	0.000	2.897	0.000	2.008	0.031	6
7	3.178	1.134	3.432	3.127	1.109	3.378	1.967	0.077	1.924	0.076	5.204	0.204	2.732	0.000	1.913	0.120	7
8	3.151	1.075	3.367	3.109	1.054	3.323	1.901	0.139	1.864	0.136	5.306	0.388	2.604	0.000	1.839	0.188	8
9	3.132	1.029	3.322	3.095	1.010	3.283	1.850	0.188	1.816	0.184	5.393	0.547	2.500	0.000	1.782	0.242	9
10	3.115	0.992	3.286	3.084	0.975	3.251	1.809	0.227	1.777	0.223	5.469	0.687	2.414	0.000	1.735	0.287	10
11	3.106	0.961	3.257	3.076	0.945	3.226	1.773	0.260	1.744	0.256	5.535	0.811	2.342	0.000	1.695	0.324	11
12	3.093	0.935	3.233	3.069	0.921	3.205	1.744	0.288	1.717	0.283	5.594	0.923	2.279	0.000	1.661	0.357	12
13	3.086	0.913	3.212	3.063	0.899	3.188	1.719	0.312	1.693	0.307	5.647	1.025	2.225	0.000	1.631	0.384	13
14	3.080	0.894	3.195	3.058	0.881	3.174	1.697	0.333	1.672	0.328	5.696	1.118	2.177	0.000	1.604	0.409	14
15	3.074	0.877	3.181	3.054	0.864	3.161	1.678	0.352	1.653	0.347	5.741	1.203	2.134	0.000	1.582	0.431	15
16		0.862		3.050	0.849	3.150	1.660	0.368	1.637	0.363	5.782	1.282	2.095	0.000			16
17		0.848		3.047	0.836	3.141	1.645	0.383	1.622	0.378	5.820	1.356	2.061	0.000			17
18		0.835		3.044	0.824	3.133	1.631	0.397	1.609	0.391	5.856	1.424	2.029	0.000			18
19		0.824		3.042	0.813	3.125	1.618	0.409	1.597	0.403	5.890	1.489	2.000	0.000			19
20		0.814		3.040	0.803	3.119	1.606	0.420	1.585	0.415	5.921	1.549	1.973	0.027			20
21		0.804		3.038	0.794	3.113	1.598	0.428	1.577	0.423	5.960	1.596	1.949	0.051			21
22		0.796		3.036	0.786	3.107	1.585	0.440	1.566	0.434	5.979	1.659	1.926	0.074			22
23		0.787		3.034	0.778	3.102	1.576	0.449	1.557	0.443	6.006	1.710	1.905	0.095			23
24		0.780		3.033	0.770	3.098	1.568	0.457	1.548	0.452	6.031	1.759	1.885	0.115			24
25		0.773		3.032	0.763	3.094	1.560	0.465	1.541	0.459	6.056	1.806	1.866	0.134			25

Notes: Only odd values of n are given for A_6, A_8, and A_9. Otherwise, the median for an even n is simply the average of the two middle values of the subgroup.
See Appendix 5 for values of A_7, B_7, and B_8.

Appendix 5

Constants for A_7, B_7, and B_8

n	k	A_7	B_7	B_8		n	k	A_7	B_7	B_8
2	2	2.3937	0.0000	2.9409		3	6	1.7685	0.0000	2.3238
2	3	2.3025	0.0000	2.8289		3	7	1.7632	0.0000	2.3170
2	4	2.2568	0.0000	2.7727		3	8	1.7593	0.0000	2.3118
2	5	2.2294	0.0000	2.7391		3	9	1.7563	0.0000	2.3078
2	6	2.2112	0.0000	2.7167		3	10	1.7538	0.0000	2.3046
2	7	2.1982	0.0000	2.7008		3	11	1.7518	0.0000	2.3020
2	8	2.1885	0.0000	2.6888		3	12	1.7502	0.0000	2.2998
2	9	2.1809	0.0000	2.6796		3	13	1.7488	0.0000	2.2980
2	10	2.1749	0.0000	2.6722		3	14	1.7476	0.0000	2.2964
2	11	2.1700	0.0000	2.6661		3	15	1.7465	0.0000	2.2950
2	12	2.1659	0.0000	2.6611		3	16	1.7456	0.0000	2.2938
2	13	2.1625	0.0000	2.6569		3	17	1.7448	0.0000	2.2928
2	14	2.1595	0.0000	2.6532		3	18	1.7441	0.0000	2.2918
2	15	2.1569	0.0000	2.6501		3	19	1.7435	0.0000	2.2910
2	16	2.1547	0.0000	2.6473		3	20	1.7429	0.0000	2.2902
2	17	2.1527	0.0000	2.6449		3	21	1.7424	0.0000	2.2896
2	18	2.1510	0.0000	2.6427		3	22	1.7419	0.0000	2.2889
2	19	2.1494	0.0000	2.6408		3	23	1.7415	0.0000	2.2884
2	20	2.1480	0.0000	2.6391		3	24	1.7411	0.0000	2.2879
2	21	2.1467	0.0000	2.6375		3	25	1.7407	0.0000	2.2874
2	22	2.1456	0.0000	2.6361		4	2	1.5635	0.0000	2.1762
2	23	2.1445	0.0000	2.6348		4	3	1.5422	0.0000	2.1464
2	24	2.1435	0.0000	2.6336		4	4	1.5315	0.0000	2.1316
2	25	2.1426	0.0000	2.6325		4	5	1.5252	0.0000	2.1228
3	2	1.8426	0.0000	2.4213		4	6	1.5210	0.0000	2.1169
3	3	1.8054	0.0000	2.3724		4	7	1.5180	0.0000	2.1127
3	4	1.7869	0.0000	2.3480		4	8	1.5157	0.0000	2.1096
3	5	1.7758	0.0000	2.3335		4	9	1.5140	0.0000	2.1072

Note: Values are based on k subgroups of size n.

n	k	A_7	B_7	B_8
4	10	1.5125	0.0000	2.1052
4	11	1.5114	0.0000	2.1036
4	12	1.5105	0.0000	2.1023
4	13	1.5096	0.0000	2.1012
4	14	1.5090	0.0000	2.1002
4	15	1.5084	0.0000	2.0994
4	16	1.5078	0.0000	2.0987
4	17	1.5074	0.0000	2.0980
4	18	1.5070	0.0000	2.0974
4	19	1.5066	0.0000	2.0969
4	20	1.5063	0.0000	2.0965
4	21	1.5060	0.0000	2.0961
4	22	1.5057	0.0000	2.0957
4	23	1.5054	0.0000	2.0953
4	24	1.5052	0.0000	2.0950
4	25	1.4955	0.0000	2.0815
5	2	1.3841	0.0000	2.0258
5	3	1.3699	0.0000	2.0049
5	4	1.3628	0.0000	1.9945
5	5	1.3585	0.0000	1.9883
5	6	1.3557	0.0000	1.9842
5	7	1.3537	0.0000	1.9812
5	8	1.3522	0.0000	1.9790
5	9	1.3510	0.0000	1.9773
5	10	1.3501	0.0000	1.9759
5	11	1.3493	0.0000	1.9748
5	12	1.3486	0.0000	1.9739
5	13	1.3481	0.0000	1.9731
5	14	1.3476	0.0000	1.9724
5	15	1.3472	0.0000	1.9718
5	16	1.3469	0.0000	1.9713
5	17	1.3466	0.0000	1.9709
5	18	1.3463	0.0000	1.9705
5	19	1.3461	0.0000	1.9701
5	20	1.3458	0.0000	1.9698
5	21	1.3456	0.0000	1.9695
5	22	1.3455	0.0000	1.9692
5	23	1.3453	0.0000	1.9690
5	24	1.3451	0.0000	1.9687

n	k	A_7	B_7	B_8
5	25	1.3450	0.0000	1.9685
6	2	1.2557	0.0296	1.9215
6	3	1.2453	0.0294	1.9056
6	4	1.2401	0.0293	1.8977
6	5	1.2371	0.0292	1.8930
6	6	1.2350	0.0291	1.8899
6	7	1.2335	0.0291	1.8876
6	8	1.2324	0.0291	1.8859
6	9	1.2316	0.0291	1.8846
6	10	1.2309	0.0290	1.8836
6	11	1.2303	0.0290	1.8827
6	12	1.2299	0.0290	1.8820
6	13	1.2295	0.0290	1.8814
6	14	1.2291	0.0290	1.8809
6	15	1.2288	0.0290	1.8804
6	16	1.2286	0.0290	1.8800
6	17	1.2284	0.0290	1.8797
6	18	1.2282	0.0290	1.8794
6	19	1.2280	0.0290	1.8791
6	20	1.2278	0.0290	1.8789
6	21	1.2277	0.0290	1.8786
6	22	1.2275	0.0290	1.8784
6	23	1.2274	0.0290	1.8783
6	24	1.2273	0.0290	1.8781
6	25	1.2272	0.0289	1.8779
7	2	1.1577	0.1153	1.8438
7	3	1.1497	0.1145	1.8311
7	4	1.1458	0.1141	1.8247
7	5	1.1434	0.1138	1.8209
7	6	1.1418	0.1137	1.8184
7	7	1.1407	0.1136	1.8166
7	8	1.1398	0.1135	1.8153
7	9	1.1392	0.1134	1.8142
7	10	1.1386	0.1134	1.8134
7	11	1.1382	0.1133	1.8127
7	12	1.1378	0.1133	1.8121
7	13	1.1375	0.1133	1.8116
7	14	1.1373	0.1132	1.8112
7	15	1.1370	0.1132	1.8109

Note: Values are based on *k* subgroups of size *n*.

n	k	A_7	B_7	B_8
7	16	1.1369	0.1132	1.8105
7	17	1.1367	0.1132	1.8103
7	18	1.1365	0.1132	1.8100
7	19	1.1364	0.1132	1.8098
7	20	1.1363	0.1131	1.8096
7	21	1.1361	0.1131	1.8094
7	22	1.1360	0.1131	1.8093
7	23	1.1359	0.1131	1.8091
7	24	1.1359	0.1131	1.8090
7	25	1.1358	0.1131	1.8088
8	2	1.0798	0.1818	1.7830
8	3	1.0734	0.1808	1.7724
8	4	1.0702	0.1802	1.7671
8	5	1.0683	0.1799	1.7640
8	6	1.0670	0.1797	1.7619
8	7	1.0661	0.1795	1.7604
8	8	1.0654	0.1794	1.7593
8	9	1.0649	0.1793	1.7584
8	10	1.0645	0.1793	1.7577
8	11	1.0641	0.1792	1.7571
8	12	1.0638	0.1791	1.7567
8	13	1.0636	0.1791	1.7563
8	14	1.0634	0.1791	1.7559
8	15	1.0632	0.1790	1.7556
8	16	1.0630	0.1790	1.7554
8	17	1.0629	0.1790	1.7551
8	18	1.0628	0.1790	1.7549
8	19	1.0627	0.1790	1.7547
8	20	1.0626	0.1789	1.7546
8	21	1.0625	0.1789	1.7544
8	22	1.0624	0.1789	1.7543
8	23	1.0623	0.1789	1.7542
8	24	1.0622	0.1789	1.7541
8	25	1.0622	0.1789	1.7539
9	2	1.0157	0.2354	1.7337
9	3	1.0105	0.2342	1.7247
9	4	1.0078	0.2336	1.7202
9	5	1.0063	0.2332	1.7175
9	6	1.0052	0.2330	1.7157

n	k	A_7	B_7	B_8
9	7	1.0045	0.2328	1.7145
9	8	1.0039	0.2327	1.7135
9	9	1.0035	0.2326	1.7128
9	10	1.0031	0.2325	1.7122
9	11	1.0028	0.2325	1.7117
9	12	1.0026	0.2324	1.7113
9	13	1.0024	0.2324	1.7109
9	14	1.0022	0.2323	1.7106
9	15	1.0021	0.2323	1.7104
9	16	1.0020	0.2322	1.7102
9	17	1.0018	0.2322	1.7100
9	18	1.0017	0.2322	1.7098
9	19	1.0016	0.2322	1.7096
9	20	1.0016	0.2322	1.7095
9	21	1.0015	0.2321	1.7094
9	22	1.0014	0.2321	1.7093
9	23	1.0014	0.2321	1.7091
9	24	1.0013	0.2321	1.7091
9	25	1.0013	0.2321	1.7090
10	2	0.9619	0.2798	1.6927
10	3	0.9575	0.2785	1.6849
10	4	0.9553	0.2779	1.6810
10	5	0.9540	0.2775	1.6787
10	6	0.9531	0.2772	1.6771
10	7	0.9525	0.2770	1.6760
10	8	0.9520	0.2769	1.6752
10	9	0.9516	0.2768	1.6745
10	10	0.9513	0.2767	1.6740
10	11	0.9511	0.2766	1.6736
10	12	0.9509	0.2766	1.6732
10	13	0.9507	0.2765	1.6729
10	14	0.9506	0.2765	1.6727
10	15	0.9504	0.2765	1.6725
10	16	0.9503	0.2764	1.6723
10	17	0.9502	0.2764	1.6721
10	18	0.9501	0.2764	1.6719
10	19	0.9501	0.2764	1.6718
10	20	0.9500	0.2763	1.6717
10	21	0.9499	0.2763	1.6716

Note: Values are based on k subgroups of size n.

n	k	A_7	B_7	B_8		n	k	A_7	B_7	B_8
10	22	0.9499	0.2763	1.6715		12	13	0.8675	0.3462	1.6124
10	23	0.9498	0.2763	1.6714		12	14	0.8674	0.3461	1.6122
10	24	0.9498	0.2763	1.6713		12	15	0.8673	0.3461	1.6120
10	25	0.9497	0.2763	1.6712		12	16	0.8673	0.3461	1.6118
11	2	0.9159	0.3173	1.6579		12	17	0.8672	0.3460	1.6117
11	3	0.9121	0.3160	1.6510		12	18	0.8671	0.3460	1.6116
11	4	0.9102	0.3153	1.6476		12	19	0.8671	0.3460	1.6115
11	5	0.9091	0.3149	1.6455		12	20	0.8670	0.3460	1.6114
11	6	0.9083	0.3147	1.6442		12	21	0.8670	0.3460	1.6113
11	7	0.9078	0.3145	1.6432		12	22	0.8669	0.3459	1.6112
11	8	0.9074	0.3143	1.6425		12	23	0.8669	0.3459	1.6111
11	9	0.9071	0.3142	1.6419		12	24	0.8668	0.3459	1.6111
11	10	0.9068	0.3141	1.6414		12	25	0.8668	0.3459	1.6110
11	11	0.9066	0.3141	1.6411		13	2	0.8408	0.3776	1.6017
11	12	0.9064	0.3140	1.6408		13	3	0.8378	0.3763	1.5962
11	13	0.9063	0.3140	1.6405		13	4	0.8364	0.3756	1.5934
11	14	0.9062	0.3139	1.6403		13	5	0.8355	0.3753	1.5917
11	15	0.9060	0.3139	1.6401		13	6	0.8349	0.3750	1.5906
11	16	0.9059	0.3139	1.6399		13	7	0.8345	0.3748	1.5898
11	17	0.9059	0.3138	1.6397		13	8	0.8342	0.3747	1.5892
11	18	0.9058	0.3138	1.6396		13	9	0.8340	0.3746	1.5888
11	19	0.9057	0.3138	1.6395		13	10	0.8338	0.3745	1.5884
11	20	0.9057	0.3138	1.6394		13	11	0.8336	0.3744	1.5881
11	21	0.9056	0.3137	1.6393		13	12	0.8335	0.3743	1.5879
11	22	0.9056	0.3137	1.6392		13	13	0.8334	0.3743	1.5877
11	23	0.9055	0.3137	1.6391		13	14	0.8333	0.3743	1.5875
11	24	0.9055	0.3137	1.6390		13	15	0.8332	0.3742	1.5873
11	25	0.9054	0.3137	1.6390		13	16	0.8331	0.3742	1.5872
12	2	0.8759	0.3495	1.6279		13	17	0.8331	0.3742	1.5871
12	3	0.8726	0.3482	1.6218		13	18	0.8330	0.3741	1.5869
12	4	0.8710	0.3475	1.6187		13	19	0.8330	0.3741	1.5869
12	5	0.8700	0.3472	1.6169		13	20	0.8329	0.3741	1.5868
12	6	0.8693	0.3469	1.6156		13	21	0.8329	0.3741	1.5867
12	7	0.8688	0.3467	1.6148		13	22	0.8328	0.3741	1.5866
12	8	0.8685	0.3466	1.6141		13	23	0.8328	0.3740	1.5865
12	9	0.8682	0.3465	1.6136		13	24	0.8328	0.3740	1.5865
12	10	0.8680	0.3464	1.6132		13	25	0.8327	0.3740	1.5864
12	11	0.8678	0.3463	1.6129		14	2	0.8095	0.4024	1.5785
12	12	0.8677	0.3462	1.6126		14	3	0.8069	0.4011	1.5735

Note: Values are based on *k* subgroups of size *n*.

n	k	A_7	B_7	B_8
14	4	0.8056	0.4004	1.5710
14	5	0.8049	0.4001	1.5695
14	6	0.8044	0.3998	1.5684
14	7	0.8040	0.3996	1.5677
14	8	0.8037	0.3995	1.5672
14	9	0.8035	0.3994	1.5668
14	10	0.8033	0.3993	1.5664
14	11	0.8032	0.3992	1.5662
14	12	0.8031	0.3992	1.5659
14	13	0.8030	0.3991	1.5657
14	14	0.8029	0.3991	1.5656
14	15	0.8028	0.3990	1.5654
14	16	0.8027	0.3990	1.5653
14	17	0.8027	0.3990	1.5652
14	18	0.8026	0.3989	1.5651
14	19	0.8026	0.3989	1.5650
14	20	0.8026	0.3989	1.5649
14	21	0.8025	0.3989	1.5649
14	22	0.8025	0.3989	1.5648
14	23	0.8025	0.3988	1.5647
14	24	0.8024	0.3988	1.5647
14	25	0.8024	0.3988	1.5646
15	2	0.7815	0.4244	1.5578

n	k	A_7	B_7	B_8
15	3	0.7792	0.4231	1.5532
15	4	0.7781	0.4225	1.5509
15	5	0.7774	0.4221	1.5495
15	6	0.7769	0.4219	1.5486
15	7	0.7766	0.4217	1.5479
15	8	0.7763	0.4216	1.5475
15	9	0.7761	0.4215	1.5471
15	10	0.7760	0.4214	1.5468
15	11	0.7759	0.4213	1.5465
15	12	0.7758	0.4213	1.5463
15	13	0.7757	0.4212	1.5461
15	14	0.7756	0.4212	1.5460
15	15	0.7755	0.4211	1.5458
15	16	0.7755	0.4211	1.5457
15	17	0.7754	0.4211	1.5456
15	18	0.7754	0.4210	1.5455
15	19	0.7753	0.4210	1.5455
15	20	0.7753	0.4210	1.5454
15	21	0.7753	0.4210	1.5453
15	22	0.7752	0.4210	1.5453
15	23	0.7752	0.4210	1.5452
15	24	0.7752	0.4209	1.5452
15	25	0.7752	0.4209	1.5452

Note: Values are based on k subgroups of size n.

Appendix 6

Factors for Estimating σ_X

n	c_2	c_4	d_2	d_3	d_4	n
2	0.5642	0.7979	1.128	0.8525	0.954	2
3	0.7236	0.8862	1.693	0.8884	1.588	3
4	0.7979	0.9213	2.059	0.8798	1.978	4
5	0.8407	0.9400	2.326	0.8641	2.257	5
6	0.8686	0.9515	2.534	0.8480	2.472	6
7	0.8882	0.9594	2.704	0.8332	2.645	7
8	0.9027	0.9650	2.847	0.8198	2.791	8
9	0.9139	0.9693	2.970	0.8078	2.915	9
10	0.9227	0.9727	3.078	0.7971	3.024	10
11	0.9300	0.9754	3.173	0.7873	3.121	11
12	0.9359	0.9776	3.258	0.7785	3.207	12
13	0.9410	0.9794	3.336	0.7704	3.285	13
14	0.9453	0.9810	3.407	0.7630	3.356	14
15	0.9490	0.9823	3.472	0.7562	3.422	15
16	0.9523	0.9835	3.532	0.7499	3.482	16
17	0.9551	0.9845	3.588	0.7441	3.538	17
18	0.9576	0.9854	3.640	0.7386	3.591	18
19	0.9599	0.9862	3.689	0.7335	3.640	19
20	0.9619	0.9869	3.735	0.7287	3.686	20
21	0.9638	0.9876	3.778	0.7272	3.730	21
22	0.9655	0.9882	3.819	0.7199	3.771	22
23	0.9670	0.9887	3.858	0.7159	3.811	23
24	0.9684	0.9892	3.895	0.7121	3.847	24
25	0.9695	0.9896	3.931	0.7084	3.883	25

Note: σ_x may be estimated from k subgroups of size n:

$$\frac{\bar{\sigma}_{RMS}}{c_2} \qquad \frac{\bar{s}}{c_4}$$

$$\frac{\bar{R}}{d_2} \qquad \frac{\overline{mR}}{d_2}$$

$$\frac{\tilde{R}}{d_4}$$

Appendix 7

Control Charts Count Data

Chart	Center line	LCL	UCL	Plot point
p	$\bar{p} = \dfrac{\sum_{i=1}^{k} D_i}{\sum_{i=1}^{k} n_i}$	$LCL_p = \bar{p} - 3\sqrt{\dfrac{\bar{p}(1-\bar{p})}{n_i}}$	$UCL_p = \bar{p} + 3\sqrt{\dfrac{\bar{p}(1-\bar{p})}{n_i}}$	$p_i = \dfrac{D_i}{n_i}$
D_i = number of defective (nonconforming) units in the ith subgroup				
np	$n\bar{p} = n\dfrac{\sum_{i=1}^{k} D_i}{\sum_{i=1}^{k} n_i}$	$LCL_{np} = n\bar{p} - 3\sqrt{n\bar{p}(1-\bar{p})}$	$UCL_{np} = n\bar{p} + 3\sqrt{n\bar{p}(1-\bar{p})}$	D_i
c	$\bar{c} = \dfrac{\sum_{i=1}^{k} c_i}{k}$	$LCL_c = \bar{c} - 3\sqrt{\bar{c}}$	$UCL = \bar{c} + 3\sqrt{\bar{c}}$	c_i
c_i = number of defects (nonconformities) in the ith subgroup				
u	$\bar{u} = \dfrac{\sum_{i=1}^{k} D_i}{\sum_{i=1}^{k} n_i}$	$LCL_u = \bar{u} - 3\sqrt{\dfrac{\bar{u}}{n_i}}$	$UCL_u = \bar{u} + 3\sqrt{\dfrac{\bar{u}}{n_i}}$	$u_i = \dfrac{c_i}{n_i}$

Appendix 8
Binomial Distribution Table

$$Pr(X=x) = f(n;x,p) = \binom{n}{k} p^k (1-p)^{n-k}$$

Probability of x occurrences in a sample of size n

n	x	0.05	0.10	0.15	0.20	0.25	0.30	0.35	0.40	0.45	0.50	0.55	0.60	0.65	0.70	0.75	0.80	0.85	0.90	0.95	x	n
1	0	0.9500	0.9000	0.8500	0.8000	0.7500	0.7000	0.6500	0.6000	0.5500	0.5000	0.4500	0.4000	0.3500	0.3000	0.2500	0.2000	0.1500	0.1000	0.0500	0	1
	1	0.0500	0.1000	0.1500	0.2000	0.2500	0.3000	0.3500	0.4000	0.4500	0.5000	0.5500	0.6000	0.6500	0.7000	0.7500	0.8000	0.8500	0.9000	0.9500	1	
2	0	0.9025	0.8100	0.7225	0.6400	0.5625	0.4900	0.4225	0.3600	0.3025	0.2500	0.2025	0.1600	0.1225	0.0900	0.0625	0.0400	0.0225	0.0100	0.0025	0	2
	1	0.0950	0.1800	0.2550	0.3200	0.3750	0.4200	0.4550	0.4800	0.4950	0.5000	0.4950	0.4800	0.4550	0.4200	0.3750	0.3200	0.2550	0.1800	0.0950	1	
	2	0.0025	0.0100	0.0225	0.0400	0.0625	0.0900	0.1225	0.1600	0.2025	0.2500	0.3025	0.3600	0.4225	0.4900	0.5625	0.6400	0.7225	0.8100	0.9025	2	
3	0	0.8574	0.7290	0.6141	0.5120	0.4219	0.3430	0.2746	0.2160	0.1664	0.1250	0.0911	0.0640	0.0429	0.0270	0.0156	0.0080	0.0034	0.0010	0.0001	0	3
	1	0.1354	0.2430	0.3251	0.3840	0.4219	0.4410	0.4436	0.4320	0.4084	0.3750	0.3341	0.2880	0.2389	0.1890	0.1406	0.0960	0.0574	0.0270	0.0071	1	
	2	0.0071	0.0270	0.0574	0.0960	0.1406	0.1890	0.2389	0.2880	0.3341	0.3750	0.4084	0.4320	0.4436	0.4410	0.4219	0.3840	0.3251	0.2430	0.1354	2	
	3	0.0001	0.0010	0.0034	0.0080	0.0156	0.0270	0.0429	0.0640	0.0911	0.1250	0.1664	0.2160	0.2746	0.3430	0.4219	0.5120	0.6141	0.7290	0.8574	3	
4	0	0.8145	0.6561	0.5220	0.4096	0.3164	0.2401	0.1785	0.1296	0.0915	0.0625	0.0410	0.0256	0.0150	0.0081	0.0039	0.0016	0.0005	0.0001	0.0000	0	4
	1	0.1715	0.2916	0.3685	0.4096	0.4219	0.4116	0.3845	0.3456	0.2995	0.2500	0.2005	0.1536	0.1115	0.0756	0.0469	0.0256	0.0115	0.0036	0.0005	1	
	2	0.0135	0.0486	0.0975	0.1536	0.2109	0.2646	0.3105	0.3456	0.3675	0.3750	0.3675	0.3456	0.3105	0.2646	0.2109	0.1536	0.0975	0.0486	0.0135	2	
	3	0.0005	0.0036	0.0115	0.0256	0.0469	0.0756	0.1115	0.1536	0.2005	0.2500	0.2995	0.3456	0.3845	0.4116	0.4219	0.4096	0.3685	0.2916	0.1715	3	
	4	0.0000	0.0001	0.0005	0.0016	0.0039	0.0081	0.0150	0.0256	0.0410	0.0625	0.0915	0.1296	0.1785	0.2401	0.3164	0.4096	0.5220	0.6561	0.8145	4	
5	0	0.7738	0.5905	0.4437	0.3277	0.2373	0.1681	0.1160	0.0778	0.0503	0.0313	0.0185	0.0102	0.0053	0.0024	0.0010	0.0003	0.0001	0.0000	0.0000	0	5
	1	0.2036	0.3281	0.3915	0.4096	0.3955	0.3602	0.3124	0.2592	0.2059	0.1563	0.1128	0.0768	0.0488	0.0284	0.0146	0.0064	0.0022	0.0005	0.0000	1	
	2	0.0214	0.0729	0.1382	0.2048	0.2637	0.3087	0.3364	0.3456	0.3369	0.3125	0.2757	0.2304	0.1811	0.1323	0.0879	0.0512	0.0244	0.0081	0.0011	2	
	3	0.0011	0.0081	0.0244	0.0512	0.0879	0.1323	0.1811	0.2304	0.2757	0.3125	0.3369	0.3456	0.3364	0.3087	0.2637	0.2048	0.1382	0.0729	0.0214	3	
	4	0.0000	0.0005	0.0022	0.0064	0.0146	0.0284	0.0488	0.0768	0.1128	0.1563	0.2059	0.2592	0.3124	0.3602	0.3955	0.4096	0.3915	0.3281	0.2036	4	
	5	0.0000	0.0000	0.0001	0.0003	0.0010	0.0024	0.0053	0.0102	0.0185	0.0313	0.0503	0.0778	0.1160	0.1681	0.2373	0.3277	0.4437	0.5905	0.7738	5	

Appendix 8

Appendix 8

$$Pr(X = x) = f(n; x, p) = \binom{n}{k} p^k (1-p)^{n-k}$$

Probability of x occurrences in a sample of size n

n	x	0.05	0.10	0.15	0.20	0.25	0.30	0.35	0.40	0.45	0.50	0.55	0.60	0.65	0.70	0.75	0.80	0.85	0.90	0.95	n	x
6	0	0.7351	0.5314	0.3771	0.2621	0.1780	0.1176	0.0754	0.0467	0.0277	0.0156	0.0083	0.0041	0.0018	0.0007	0.0002	0.0001	0.0000	0.0000	0.0000	6	0
	1	0.2321	0.3543	0.3993	0.3932	0.3560	0.3025	0.2437	0.1866	0.1359	0.0938	0.0609	0.0369	0.0205	0.0102	0.0044	0.0015	0.0004	0.0001	0.0000		1
	2	0.0305	0.0984	0.1762	0.2458	0.2966	0.3241	0.3280	0.3110	0.2780	0.2344	0.1861	0.1382	0.0951	0.0595	0.0330	0.0154	0.0055	0.0012	0.0001		2
	3	0.0021	0.0146	0.0415	0.0819	0.1318	0.1852	0.2355	0.2765	0.3032	0.3125	0.3032	0.2765	0.2355	0.1852	0.1318	0.0819	0.0415	0.0146	0.0021		3
	4	0.0001	0.0012	0.0055	0.0154	0.0330	0.0595	0.0951	0.1382	0.1861	0.2344	0.2780	0.3110	0.3280	0.3241	0.2966	0.2458	0.1762	0.0984	0.0305		4
	5	0.0000	0.0001	0.0004	0.0015	0.0044	0.0102	0.0205	0.0369	0.0609	0.0938	0.1359	0.1866	0.2437	0.3025	0.3560	0.3932	0.3993	0.3543	0.2321		5
	6	0.0000	0.0000	0.0000	0.0001	0.0002	0.0007	0.0018	0.0041	0.0083	0.0156	0.0277	0.0467	0.0754	0.1176	0.1780	0.2621	0.3771	0.5314	0.7351		6
7	0	0.6983	0.4783	0.3206	0.2097	0.1335	0.0824	0.0490	0.0280	0.0152	0.0078	0.0037	0.0016	0.0006	0.0002	0.0001	0.0000	0.0000	0.0000	0.0000	7	0
	1	0.2573	0.3720	0.3960	0.3670	0.3115	0.2471	0.1848	0.1306	0.0872	0.0547	0.0320	0.0172	0.0084	0.0036	0.0013	0.0004	0.0001	0.0000	0.0000		1
	2	0.0406	0.1240	0.2097	0.2753	0.3115	0.3177	0.2985	0.2613	0.2140	0.1641	0.1172	0.0774	0.0466	0.0250	0.0115	0.0043	0.0012	0.0002	0.0000		2
	3	0.0036	0.0230	0.0617	0.1147	0.1730	0.2269	0.2679	0.2903	0.2918	0.2734	0.2388	0.1935	0.1442	0.0972	0.0577	0.0287	0.0109	0.0026	0.0002		3
	4	0.0002	0.0026	0.0109	0.0287	0.0577	0.0972	0.1442	0.1935	0.2388	0.2734	0.2918	0.2903	0.2679	0.2269	0.1730	0.1147	0.0617	0.0230	0.0036		4
	5	0.0000	0.0002	0.0012	0.0043	0.0115	0.0250	0.0466	0.0774	0.1172	0.1641	0.2140	0.2613	0.2985	0.3177	0.3115	0.2753	0.2097	0.1240	0.0406		5
	6	0.0000	0.0000	0.0001	0.0004	0.0013	0.0036	0.0084	0.0172	0.0320	0.0547	0.0872	0.1306	0.1848	0.2471	0.3115	0.3670	0.3960	0.3720	0.2573		6
	7	0.0000	0.0000	0.0000	0.0000	0.0001	0.0002	0.0006	0.0016	0.0037	0.0078	0.0152	0.0280	0.0490	0.0824	0.1335	0.2097	0.3206	0.4783	0.6983		7
8	0	0.6634	0.4305	0.2725	0.1678	0.1001	0.0576	0.0319	0.0168	0.0084	0.0039	0.0017	0.0007	0.0002	0.0001	0.0000	0.0000	0.0000	0.0000	0.0000	8	0
	1	0.2793	0.3826	0.3847	0.3355	0.2670	0.1977	0.1373	0.0896	0.0548	0.0313	0.0164	0.0079	0.0033	0.0012	0.0004	0.0001	0.0000	0.0000	0.0000		1
	2	0.0515	0.1488	0.2376	0.2936	0.3115	0.2965	0.2587	0.2090	0.1569	0.1094	0.0703	0.0413	0.0217	0.0100	0.0038	0.0011	0.0002	0.0000	0.0000		2
	3	0.0054	0.0331	0.0839	0.1468	0.2076	0.2541	0.2786	0.2787	0.2568	0.2188	0.1719	0.1239	0.0808	0.0467	0.0231	0.0092	0.0026	0.0004	0.0000		3
	4	0.0004	0.0046	0.0185	0.0459	0.0865	0.1361	0.1875	0.2322	0.2627	0.2734	0.2627	0.2322	0.1875	0.1361	0.0865	0.0459	0.0185	0.0046	0.0004		4
	5	0.0000	0.0004	0.0026	0.0092	0.0231	0.0467	0.0808	0.1239	0.1719	0.2188	0.2568	0.2787	0.2786	0.2541	0.2076	0.1468	0.0839	0.0331	0.0054		5
	6	0.0000	0.0000	0.0002	0.0011	0.0038	0.0100	0.0217	0.0413	0.0703	0.1094	0.1569	0.2090	0.2587	0.2965	0.3115	0.2936	0.2376	0.1488	0.0515		6
	7	0.0000	0.0000	0.0000	0.0001	0.0004	0.0012	0.0033	0.0079	0.0164	0.0313	0.0548	0.0896	0.1373	0.1977	0.2670	0.3355	0.3847	0.3826	0.2793		7
	8	0.0000	0.0000	0.0000	0.0000	0.0000	0.0001	0.0002	0.0007	0.0017	0.0039	0.0084	0.0168	0.0319	0.0576	0.1001	0.1678	0.2725	0.4305	0.6634		8

$$\Pr(X = x) = f(n; x, p) = \binom{n}{k} p^k (1-p)^{n-k}$$

Probability of x occurrences in a sample of size n

n	x	0.05	0.10	0.15	0.20	0.25	0.30	0.35	0.40	0.45	0.50	0.55	0.60	0.65	0.70	0.75	0.80	0.85	0.90	0.95
9	0	0.6302	0.3874	0.2316	0.1342	0.0751	0.0404	0.0207	0.0101	0.0046	0.0020	0.0008	0.0003	0.0001	0.0000	0.0000	0.0000	0.0000	0.0000	0.0000
	1	0.2985	0.3874	0.3679	0.3020	0.2253	0.1556	0.1004	0.0605	0.0339	0.0176	0.0083	0.0035	0.0013	0.0004	0.0001	0.0000	0.0000	0.0000	0.0000
	2	0.0629	0.1722	0.2597	0.3020	0.3003	0.2668	0.2162	0.1612	0.1110	0.0703	0.0407	0.0212	0.0098	0.0039	0.0012	0.0003	0.0000	0.0000	0.0000
	3	0.0077	0.0446	0.1069	0.1762	0.2336	0.2668	0.2716	0.2508	0.2119	0.1641	0.1160	0.0743	0.0424	0.0210	0.0087	0.0028	0.0006	0.0001	0.0000
	4	0.0006	0.0074	0.0283	0.0661	0.1168	0.1715	0.2194	0.2508	0.2600	0.2461	0.2128	0.1672	0.1181	0.0735	0.0389	0.0165	0.0050	0.0008	0.0000
	5	0.0000	0.0008	0.0050	0.0165	0.0389	0.0735	0.1181	0.1672	0.2128	0.2461	0.2600	0.2508	0.2194	0.1715	0.1168	0.0661	0.0283	0.0074	0.0006
	6	0.0000	0.0001	0.0006	0.0028	0.0087	0.0210	0.0424	0.0743	0.1160	0.1641	0.2119	0.2508	0.2716	0.2668	0.2336	0.1762	0.1069	0.0446	0.0077
	7	0.0000	0.0000	0.0000	0.0003	0.0012	0.0039	0.0098	0.0212	0.0407	0.0703	0.1110	0.1612	0.2162	0.2668	0.3003	0.3020	0.2597	0.1722	0.0629
	8	0.0000	0.0000	0.0000	0.0000	0.0001	0.0004	0.0013	0.0035	0.0083	0.0176	0.0339	0.0605	0.1004	0.1556	0.2253	0.3020	0.3679	0.3874	0.2985
	9	0.0000	0.0000	0.0000	0.0000	0.0000	0.0000	0.0001	0.0003	0.0008	0.0020	0.0046	0.0101	0.0207	0.0404	0.0751	0.1342	0.2316	0.3874	0.6302
10	0	0.5987	0.3487	0.1969	0.1074	0.0563	0.0282	0.0135	0.0060	0.0025	0.0010	0.0003	0.0001	0.0000	0.0000	0.0000	0.0000	0.0000	0.0000	0.0000
	1	0.3151	0.3874	0.3474	0.2684	0.1877	0.1211	0.0725	0.0403	0.0207	0.0098	0.0042	0.0016	0.0005	0.0001	0.0000	0.0000	0.0000	0.0000	0.0000
	2	0.0746	0.1937	0.2759	0.3020	0.2816	0.2335	0.1757	0.1209	0.0763	0.0439	0.0229	0.0106	0.0043	0.0014	0.0004	0.0001	0.0000	0.0000	0.0000
	3	0.0105	0.0574	0.1298	0.2013	0.2503	0.2668	0.2522	0.2150	0.1665	0.1172	0.0746	0.0425	0.0212	0.0090	0.0031	0.0008	0.0001	0.0000	0.0000
	4	0.0010	0.0112	0.0401	0.0881	0.1460	0.2001	0.2377	0.2508	0.2384	0.2051	0.1596	0.1115	0.0689	0.0368	0.0162	0.0055	0.0012	0.0001	0.0000
	5	0.0001	0.0015	0.0085	0.0264	0.0584	0.1029	0.1536	0.2007	0.2340	0.2461	0.2340	0.2007	0.1536	0.1029	0.0584	0.0264	0.0085	0.0015	0.0001
	6	0.0000	0.0001	0.0012	0.0055	0.0162	0.0368	0.0689	0.1115	0.1596	0.2051	0.2384	0.2508	0.2377	0.2001	0.1460	0.0881	0.0401	0.0112	0.0010
	7	0.0000	0.0000	0.0001	0.0008	0.0031	0.0090	0.0212	0.0425	0.0746	0.1172	0.1665	0.2150	0.2522	0.2668	0.2503	0.2013	0.1298	0.0574	0.0105
	8	0.0000	0.0000	0.0000	0.0001	0.0004	0.0014	0.0043	0.0106	0.0229	0.0439	0.0763	0.1209	0.1757	0.2335	0.2816	0.3020	0.2759	0.1937	0.0746
	9	0.0000	0.0000	0.0000	0.0000	0.0000	0.0001	0.0005	0.0016	0.0042	0.0098	0.0207	0.0403	0.0725	0.1211	0.1877	0.2684	0.3474	0.3874	0.3151
	10	0.0000	0.0000	0.0000	0.0000	0.0000	0.0000	0.0000	0.0001	0.0003	0.0010	0.0025	0.0060	0.0135	0.0282	0.0563	0.1074	0.1969	0.3487	0.5987

Appendix 8

Appendix 9

Cumulative Binomial Distribution Table

$$Pr(X \le x) = F(n; x, p) = \sum_{k=0}^{x} \binom{n}{x} p^k (1-p)^{n-k}$$

Probability of ≤ x occurrences in a sample of size n

n	x	0.05	0.10	0.15	0.20	0.25	0.30	0.35	0.40	0.45	0.50	0.55	0.60	0.65	0.70	0.75	0.80	0.85	0.90	0.95
1	0	0.9500	0.9000	0.8500	0.8000	0.7500	0.7000	0.6500	0.6000	0.5500	0.5000	0.4500	0.4000	0.3500	0.3000	0.2500	0.2000	0.1500	0.1000	0.0500
	1	1.0000	1.0000	1.0000	1.0000	1.0000	1.0000	1.0000	1.0000	1.0000	1.0000	1.0000	1.0000	1.0000	1.0000	1.0000	1.0000	1.0000	1.0000	1.0000
2	0	0.9025	0.8100	0.7225	0.6400	0.5625	0.4900	0.4225	0.3600	0.3025	0.2500	0.2025	0.1600	0.1225	0.0900	0.0625	0.0400	0.0225	0.0100	0.0025
	1	0.9975	0.9900	0.9775	0.9600	0.9375	0.9100	0.8775	0.8400	0.7975	0.7500	0.6975	0.6400	0.5775	0.5100	0.4375	0.3600	0.2775	0.1900	0.0975
	2	1.0000	1.0000	1.0000	1.0000	1.0000	1.0000	1.0000	1.0000	1.0000	1.0000	1.0000	1.0000	1.0000	1.0000	1.0000	1.0000	1.0000	1.0000	1.0000
3	0	0.8574	0.7290	0.6141	0.5120	0.4219	0.3430	0.2746	0.2160	0.1664	0.1250	0.0911	0.0640	0.0429	0.0270	0.0156	0.0080	0.0034	0.0010	0.0001
	1	0.9928	0.9720	0.9393	0.8960	0.8438	0.7840	0.7183	0.6480	0.5748	0.5000	0.4253	0.3520	0.2818	0.2160	0.1563	0.1040	0.0608	0.0280	0.0073
	2	0.9999	0.9990	0.9966	0.9920	0.9844	0.9730	0.9571	0.9360	0.9089	0.8750	0.8336	0.7840	0.7254	0.6570	0.5781	0.4880	0.3859	0.2710	0.1426
	3	1.0000	1.0000	1.0000	1.0000	1.0000	1.0000	1.0000	1.0000	1.0000	1.0000	1.0000	1.0000	1.0000	1.0000	1.0000	1.0000	1.0000	1.0000	1.0000
4	0	0.8145	0.6561	0.5220	0.4096	0.3164	0.2401	0.1785	0.1296	0.0915	0.0625	0.0410	0.0256	0.0150	0.0081	0.0039	0.0016	0.0005	0.0001	0.0000
	1	0.9860	0.9477	0.8905	0.8192	0.7383	0.6517	0.5630	0.4752	0.3910	0.3125	0.2415	0.1792	0.1265	0.0837	0.0508	0.0272	0.0120	0.0037	0.0005
	2	0.9995	0.9963	0.9880	0.9728	0.9492	0.9163	0.8735	0.8208	0.7585	0.6875	0.6090	0.5248	0.4370	0.3483	0.2617	0.1808	0.1095	0.0523	0.0140
	3	1.0000	0.9999	0.9995	0.9984	0.9961	0.9919	0.9850	0.9744	0.9590	0.9375	0.9085	0.8704	0.8215	0.7599	0.6836	0.5904	0.4780	0.3439	0.1855
	4	1.0000	1.0000	1.0000	1.0000	1.0000	1.0000	1.0000	1.0000	1.0000	1.0000	1.0000	1.0000	1.0000	1.0000	1.0000	1.0000	1.0000	1.0000	1.0000
5	0	0.7738	0.5905	0.4437	0.3277	0.2373	0.1681	0.1160	0.0778	0.0503	0.0313	0.0185	0.0102	0.0053	0.0024	0.0010	0.0003	0.0001	0.0000	0.0000
	1	0.9774	0.9185	0.8352	0.7373	0.6328	0.5282	0.4284	0.3370	0.2562	0.1875	0.1312	0.0870	0.0540	0.0308	0.0156	0.0067	0.0022	0.0005	0.0000
	2	0.9988	0.9914	0.9734	0.9421	0.8965	0.8369	0.7648	0.6826	0.5931	0.5000	0.4069	0.3174	0.2352	0.1631	0.1035	0.0579	0.0266	0.0086	0.0012
	3	1.0000	0.9995	0.9978	0.9933	0.9844	0.9692	0.9460	0.9130	0.8688	0.8125	0.7438	0.6630	0.5716	0.4718	0.3672	0.2627	0.1648	0.0815	0.0226
	4	1.0000	1.0000	0.9999	0.9997	0.9990	0.9976	0.9947	0.9898	0.9815	0.9688	0.9497	0.9222	0.8840	0.8319	0.7627	0.6723	0.5563	0.4095	0.2262
	5	1.0000	1.0000	1.0000	1.0000	1.0000	1.0000	1.0000	1.0000	1.0000	1.0000	1.0000	1.0000	1.0000	1.0000	1.0000	1.0000	1.0000	1.0000	1.0000

Appendix 9

Appendix 9

$$Pr(X \leq x) = F(n;x,p) = \sum_{k=0}^{x} \binom{n}{x} p^k (1-p)^{n-k}$$

Probability of $\leq x$ occurrences in a sample of size n

n	x	0.05	0.10	0.15	0.20	0.25	0.30	0.35	0.40	0.45	0.50	0.55	0.60	0.65	0.70	0.75	0.80	0.85	0.90	0.95	x	n
6	0	0.7351	0.5314	0.3771	0.2621	0.1780	0.1176	0.0754	0.0467	0.0277	0.0156	0.0083	0.0041	0.0018	0.0007	0.0002	0.0001	0.0000	0.0000	0.0000	0	6
	1	0.9672	0.8857	0.7765	0.6554	0.5339	0.4202	0.3191	0.2333	0.1636	0.1094	0.0692	0.0410	0.0223	0.0109	0.0046	0.0016	0.0004	0.0001	0.0000	1	
	2	0.9978	0.9842	0.9527	0.9011	0.8306	0.7443	0.6471	0.5443	0.4415	0.3438	0.2553	0.1792	0.1174	0.0705	0.0376	0.0170	0.0059	0.0013	0.0001	2	
	3	0.9999	0.9987	0.9941	0.9830	0.9624	0.9295	0.8826	0.8208	0.7447	0.6563	0.5585	0.4557	0.3529	0.2557	0.1694	0.0989	0.0473	0.0159	0.0022	3	
	4	1.0000	0.9999	0.9996	0.9984	0.9954	0.9891	0.9777	0.9590	0.9308	0.8906	0.8364	0.7667	0.6809	0.5798	0.4661	0.3446	0.2235	0.1143	0.0328	4	
	5	1.0000	1.0000	1.0000	0.9999	0.9998	0.9993	0.9982	0.9959	0.9917	0.9844	0.9723	0.9533	0.9246	0.8824	0.8220	0.7379	0.6229	0.4686	0.2649	5	
	6	1.0000	1.0000	1.0000	1.0000	1.0000	1.0000	1.0000	1.0000	1.0000	1.0000	1.0000	1.0000	1.0000	1.0000	1.0000	1.0000	1.0000	1.0000	1.0000	6	
7	0	0.6983	0.4783	0.3206	0.2097	0.1335	0.0824	0.0490	0.0280	0.0152	0.0078	0.0037	0.0016	0.0006	0.0002	0.0001	0.0000	0.0000	0.0000	0.0000	0	7
	1	0.9556	0.8503	0.7166	0.5767	0.4449	0.3294	0.2338	0.1586	0.1024	0.0625	0.0357	0.0188	0.0090	0.0038	0.0013	0.0004	0.0001	0.0000	0.0000	1	
	2	0.9962	0.9743	0.9262	0.8520	0.7564	0.6471	0.5323	0.4199	0.3164	0.2266	0.1529	0.0963	0.0556	0.0288	0.0129	0.0047	0.0012	0.0002	0.0000	2	
	3	0.9998	0.9973	0.9879	0.9667	0.9294	0.8740	0.8002	0.7102	0.6083	0.5000	0.3917	0.2898	0.1998	0.1260	0.0706	0.0333	0.0121	0.0027	0.0002	3	
	4	1.0000	0.9998	0.9988	0.9953	0.9871	0.9712	0.9444	0.9037	0.8471	0.7734	0.6836	0.5801	0.4677	0.3529	0.2436	0.1480	0.0738	0.0257	0.0038	4	
	5	1.0000	1.0000	0.9999	0.9996	0.9987	0.9962	0.9910	0.9812	0.9643	0.9375	0.8976	0.8414	0.7662	0.6706	0.5551	0.4233	0.2834	0.1497	0.0444	5	
	6	1.0000	1.0000	1.0000	1.0000	0.9999	0.9998	0.9994	0.9984	0.9963	0.9922	0.9848	0.9720	0.9510	0.9176	0.8665	0.7903	0.6794	0.5217	0.3017	6	
	7	1.0000	1.0000	1.0000	1.0000	1.0000	1.0000	1.0000	1.0000	1.0000	1.0000	1.0000	1.0000	1.0000	1.0000	1.0000	1.0000	1.0000	1.0000	1.0000	7	
8	0	0.6634	0.4305	0.2725	0.1678	0.1001	0.0576	0.0319	0.0168	0.0084	0.0039	0.0017	0.0007	0.0002	0.0001	0.0000	0.0000	0.0000	0.0000	0.0000	0	8
	1	0.9428	0.8131	0.6572	0.5033	0.3671	0.2553	0.1691	0.1064	0.0632	0.0352	0.0181	0.0085	0.0036	0.0013	0.0004	0.0001	0.0000	0.0000	0.0000	1	
	2	0.9942	0.9619	0.8948	0.7969	0.6785	0.5518	0.4278	0.3154	0.2201	0.1445	0.0885	0.0498	0.0253	0.0113	0.0042	0.0012	0.0002	0.0000	0.0000	2	
	3	0.9996	0.9950	0.9786	0.9437	0.8862	0.8059	0.7064	0.5941	0.4770	0.3633	0.2604	0.1737	0.1061	0.0580	0.0273	0.0104	0.0029	0.0004	0.0000	3	
	4	1.0000	0.9996	0.9971	0.9896	0.9727	0.9420	0.8939	0.8263	0.7396	0.6367	0.5230	0.4059	0.2936	0.1941	0.1138	0.0563	0.0214	0.0050	0.0004	4	
	5	1.0000	1.0000	0.9998	0.9988	0.9958	0.9887	0.9747	0.9502	0.9115	0.8555	0.7799	0.6846	0.5722	0.4482	0.3215	0.2031	0.1052	0.0381	0.0058	5	
	6	1.0000	1.0000	1.0000	0.9999	0.9996	0.9987	0.9964	0.9915	0.9819	0.9648	0.9368	0.8936	0.8309	0.7447	0.6329	0.4967	0.3428	0.1869	0.0572	6	
	7	1.0000	1.0000	1.0000	1.0000	1.0000	0.9999	0.9998	0.9993	0.9983	0.9961	0.9916	0.9832	0.9681	0.9424	0.8999	0.8322	0.7275	0.5695	0.3366	7	
	8	1.0000	1.0000	1.0000	1.0000	1.0000	1.0000	1.0000	1.0000	1.0000	1.0000	1.0000	1.0000	1.0000	1.0000	1.0000	1.0000	1.0000	1.0000	1.0000	8	

$$Pr(X \le x) = F(n;x,p) = \sum_{k=0}^{x} \binom{n}{x} p^k (1-p)^{n-k}$$

Probability of ≤ x occurrences in a sample of size n

n	x	0.05	0.10	0.15	0.20	0.25	0.30	0.35	0.40	0.45	0.50	0.55	0.60	0.65	0.70	0.75	0.80	0.85	0.90	0.95
9	0	0.6302	0.3874	0.2316	0.1342	0.0751	0.0404	0.0207	0.0101	0.0046	0.0020	0.0008	0.0003	0.0001	0.0000	0.0000	0.0000	0.0000	0.0000	0.0000
	1	0.9288	0.7748	0.5995	0.4362	0.3003	0.1960	0.1211	0.0705	0.0385	0.0195	0.0091	0.0038	0.0014	0.0004	0.0001	0.0000	0.0000	0.0000	0.0000
	2	0.9916	0.9470	0.8591	0.7382	0.6007	0.4628	0.3373	0.2318	0.1495	0.0898	0.0498	0.0250	0.0112	0.0043	0.0013	0.0003	0.0000	0.0000	0.0000
	3	0.9994	0.9917	0.9661	0.9144	0.8343	0.7297	0.6089	0.4826	0.3614	0.2539	0.1658	0.0994	0.0536	0.0253	0.0100	0.0031	0.0006	0.0001	0.0000
	4	1.0000	0.9991	0.9944	0.9804	0.9511	0.9012	0.8283	0.7334	0.6214	0.5000	0.3786	0.2666	0.1717	0.0988	0.0489	0.0196	0.0056	0.0009	0.0000
	5	1.0000	0.9999	0.9994	0.9969	0.9900	0.9747	0.9464	0.9006	0.8342	0.7461	0.6386	0.5174	0.3911	0.2703	0.1657	0.0856	0.0339	0.0083	0.0006
	6	1.0000	1.0000	1.0000	0.9997	0.9987	0.9957	0.9888	0.9750	0.9502	0.9102	0.8505	0.7682	0.6627	0.5372	0.3993	0.2618	0.1409	0.0530	0.0084
	7	1.0000	1.0000	1.0000	1.0000	0.9999	0.9996	0.9986	0.9962	0.9909	0.9805	0.9615	0.9295	0.8789	0.8040	0.6997	0.5638	0.4005	0.2252	0.0712
	8	1.0000	1.0000	1.0000	1.0000	1.0000	1.0000	0.9999	0.9997	0.9992	0.9980	0.9954	0.9899	0.9793	0.9596	0.9249	0.8658	0.7684	0.6126	0.3698
	9	1.0000	1.0000	1.0000	1.0000	1.0000	1.0000	1.0000	1.0000	1.0000	1.0000	1.0000	1.0000	1.0000	1.0000	1.0000	1.0000	1.0000	1.0000	1.0000
10	0	0.5987	0.3487	0.1969	0.1074	0.0563	0.0282	0.0135	0.0060	0.0025	0.0010	0.0003	0.0001	0.0000	0.0000	0.0000	0.0000	0.0000	0.0000	0.0000
	1	0.9139	0.7361	0.5443	0.3758	0.2440	0.1493	0.0860	0.0464	0.0233	0.0107	0.0045	0.0017	0.0005	0.0001	0.0000	0.0000	0.0000	0.0000	0.0000
	2	0.9885	0.9298	0.8202	0.6778	0.5256	0.3828	0.2616	0.1673	0.0996	0.0547	0.0274	0.0123	0.0048	0.0016	0.0004	0.0001	0.0000	0.0000	0.0000
	3	0.9990	0.9872	0.9500	0.8791	0.7759	0.6496	0.5138	0.3823	0.2660	0.1719	0.1020	0.0548	0.0260	0.0106	0.0035	0.0009	0.0001	0.0000	0.0000
	4	0.9999	0.9984	0.9901	0.9672	0.9219	0.8497	0.7515	0.6331	0.5044	0.3770	0.2616	0.1662	0.0949	0.0473	0.0197	0.0064	0.0014	0.0001	0.0000
	5	1.0000	0.9999	0.9986	0.9936	0.9803	0.9527	0.9051	0.8338	0.7384	0.6230	0.4956	0.3669	0.2485	0.1503	0.0781	0.0328	0.0099	0.0016	0.0001
	6	1.0000	1.0000	0.9999	0.9991	0.9965	0.9894	0.9740	0.9452	0.8980	0.8281	0.7340	0.6177	0.4862	0.3504	0.2241	0.1209	0.0500	0.0128	0.0010
	7	1.0000	1.0000	1.0000	0.9999	0.9996	0.9984	0.9952	0.9877	0.9726	0.9453	0.9004	0.8327	0.7384	0.6172	0.4744	0.3222	0.1798	0.0702	0.0115
	8	1.0000	1.0000	1.0000	1.0000	1.0000	0.9999	0.9995	0.9983	0.9955	0.9893	0.9767	0.9536	0.9140	0.8507	0.7560	0.6242	0.4557	0.2639	0.0861
	9	1.0000	1.0000	1.0000	1.0000	1.0000	1.0000	1.0000	0.9999	0.9997	0.9990	0.9975	0.9940	0.9865	0.9718	0.9437	0.8926	0.8031	0.6513	0.4013
	10	1.0000	1.0000	1.0000	1.0000	1.0000	1.0000	1.0000	1.0000	1.0000	1.0000	1.0000	1.0000	1.0000	1.0000	1.0000	1.0000	1.0000	1.0000	1.0000

Appendix 9

Appendix 10
Poisson Distribution Table

$$\Pr(X = x) = f(x; \lambda) = \frac{\lambda^x}{x!} e^{-\lambda}$$

	Probability of *x* occurrences												
λ	0	1	2	3	4	5	6	7	8	9	10	11	12	13
0.05	0.9512	0.0476	0.0012	0.0000	0.0000	0.0000	0.0000	0.0000	0.0000	0.0000	0.0000	0.0000	0.0000	0.0000
0.10	0.9048	0.0905	0.0045	0.0002	0.0000	0.0000	0.0000	0.0000	0.0000	0.0000	0.0000	0.0000	0.0000	0.0000
0.15	0.8607	0.1291	0.0097	0.0005	0.0000	0.0000	0.0000	0.0000	0.0000	0.0000	0.0000	0.0000	0.0000	0.0000
0.20	0.8187	0.1637	0.0164	0.0011	0.0001	0.0000	0.0000	0.0000	0.0000	0.0000	0.0000	0.0000	0.0000	0.0000
0.25	0.7788	0.1947	0.0243	0.0020	0.0001	0.0000	0.0000	0.0000	0.0000	0.0000	0.0000	0.0000	0.0000	0.0000
0.30	0.7408	0.2222	0.0333	0.0033	0.0003	0.0000	0.0000	0.0000	0.0000	0.0000	0.0000	0.0000	0.0000	0.0000
0.35	0.7047	0.2466	0.0432	0.0050	0.0004	0.0000	0.0000	0.0000	0.0000	0.0000	0.0000	0.0000	0.0000	0.0000
0.40	0.6703	0.2681	0.0536	0.0072	0.0007	0.0001	0.0000	0.0000	0.0000	0.0000	0.0000	0.0000	0.0000	0.0000
0.45	0.6376	0.2869	0.0646	0.0097	0.0011	0.0001	0.0000	0.0000	0.0000	0.0000	0.0000	0.0000	0.0000	0.0000
0.50	0.6065	0.3033	0.0758	0.0126	0.0016	0.0002	0.0000	0.0000	0.0000	0.0000	0.0000	0.0000	0.0000	0.0000
0.55	0.5769	0.3173	0.0873	0.0160	0.0022	0.0002	0.0000	0.0000	0.0000	0.0000	0.0000	0.0000	0.0000	0.0000
0.60	0.5488	0.3293	0.0988	0.0198	0.0030	0.0004	0.0000	0.0000	0.0000	0.0000	0.0000	0.0000	0.0000	0.0000
0.65	0.5220	0.3393	0.1103	0.0239	0.0039	0.0005	0.0001	0.0000	0.0000	0.0000	0.0000	0.0000	0.0000	0.0000
0.70	0.4966	0.3476	0.1217	0.0284	0.0050	0.0007	0.0001	0.0000	0.0000	0.0000	0.0000	0.0000	0.0000	0.0000
0.75	0.4724	0.3543	0.1329	0.0332	0.0062	0.0009	0.0001	0.0000	0.0000	0.0000	0.0000	0.0000	0.0000	0.0000
0.80	0.4493	0.3595	0.1438	0.0383	0.0077	0.0012	0.0002	0.0000	0.0000	0.0000	0.0000	0.0000	0.0000	0.0000
0.85	0.4274	0.3633	0.1544	0.0437	0.0093	0.0016	0.0002	0.0000	0.0000	0.0000	0.0000	0.0000	0.0000	0.0000
0.90	0.4066	0.3659	0.1647	0.0494	0.0111	0.0020	0.0003	0.0000	0.0000	0.0000	0.0000	0.0000	0.0000	0.0000
0.95	0.3867	0.3674	0.1745	0.0553	0.0131	0.0025	0.0004	0.0001	0.0000	0.0000	0.0000	0.0000	0.0000	0.0000
1.00	0.3679	0.3679	0.1839	0.0613	0.0153	0.0031	0.0005	0.0001	0.0000	0.0000	0.0000	0.0000	0.0000	0.0000
1.10	0.3329	0.3662	0.2014	0.0738	0.0203	0.0045	0.0008	0.0001	0.0000	0.0000	0.0000	0.0000	0.0000	0.0000
1.20	0.3012	0.3614	0.2169	0.0867	0.0260	0.0062	0.0012	0.0002	0.0000	0.0000	0.0000	0.0000	0.0000	0.0000
1.30	0.2725	0.3543	0.2303	0.0998	0.0324	0.0084	0.0018	0.0003	0.0001	0.0000	0.0000	0.0000	0.0000	0.0000
1.40	0.2466	0.3452	0.2417	0.1128	0.0395	0.0111	0.0026	0.0005	0.0001	0.0000	0.0000	0.0000	0.0000	0.0000
1.50	0.2231	0.3347	0.2510	0.1255	0.0471	0.0141	0.0035	0.0008	0.0001	0.0000	0.0000	0.0000	0.0000	0.0000
1.60	0.2019	0.3230	0.2584	0.1378	0.0551	0.0176	0.0047	0.0011	0.0002	0.0000	0.0000	0.0000	0.0000	0.0000
1.70	0.1827	0.3106	0.2640	0.1496	0.0636	0.0216	0.0061	0.0015	0.0003	0.0001	0.0000	0.0000	0.0000	0.0000
1.80	0.1653	0.2975	0.2678	0.1607	0.0723	0.0260	0.0078	0.0020	0.0005	0.0001	0.0000	0.0000	0.0000	0.0000
1.90	0.1496	0.2842	0.2700	0.1710	0.0812	0.0309	0.0098	0.0027	0.0006	0.0001	0.0000	0.0000	0.0000	0.0000
2.00	0.1353	0.2707	0.2707	0.1804	0.0902	0.0361	0.0120	0.0034	0.0009	0.0002	0.0000	0.0000	0.0000	0.0000
2.10	0.1225	0.2572	0.2700	0.1890	0.0992	0.0417	0.0146	0.0044	0.0011	0.0003	0.0001	0.0000	0.0000	0.0000
2.20	0.1108	0.2438	0.2681	0.1966	0.1082	0.0476	0.0174	0.0055	0.0015	0.0004	0.0001	0.0000	0.0000	0.0000
2.30	0.1003	0.2306	0.2652	0.2033	0.1169	0.0538	0.0206	0.0068	0.0019	0.0005	0.0001	0.0000	0.0000	0.0000
2.40	0.0907	0.2177	0.2613	0.2090	0.1254	0.0602	0.0241	0.0083	0.0025	0.0007	0.0002	0.0000	0.0000	0.0000
2.50	0.0821	0.2052	0.2565	0.2138	0.1336	0.0668	0.0278	0.0099	0.0031	0.0009	0.0002	0.0000	0.0000	0.0000
2.60	0.0743	0.1931	0.2510	0.2176	0.1414	0.0735	0.0319	0.0118	0.0038	0.0011	0.0003	0.0001	0.0000	0.0000
2.70	0.0672	0.1815	0.2450	0.2205	0.1488	0.0804	0.0362	0.0139	0.0047	0.0014	0.0004	0.0001	0.0000	0.0000

$$\Pr(X = x) = f(x; \lambda) = \frac{\lambda^x}{x!} e^{-\lambda}$$

λ	14	15	16	17	18	19	20	21	22	23	24	25	λ
0.05	0.0000	0.0000	0.0000	0.0000	0.0000	0.0000	0.0000	0.0000	0.0000	0.0000	0.0000	0.0000	0.05
0.10	0.0000	0.0000	0.0000	0.0000	0.0000	0.0000	0.0000	0.0000	0.0000	0.0000	0.0000	0.0000	0.10
0.15	0.0000	0.0000	0.0000	0.0000	0.0000	0.0000	0.0000	0.0000	0.0000	0.0000	0.0000	0.0000	0.15
0.20	0.0000	0.0000	0.0000	0.0000	0.0000	0.0000	0.0000	0.0000	0.0000	0.0000	0.0000	0.0000	0.20
0.25	0.0000	0.0000	0.0000	0.0000	0.0000	0.0000	0.0000	0.0000	0.0000	0.0000	0.0000	0.0000	0.25
0.30	0.0000	0.0000	0.0000	0.0000	0.0000	0.0000	0.0000	0.0000	0.0000	0.0000	0.0000	0.0000	0.30
0.35	0.0000	0.0000	0.0000	0.0000	0.0000	0.0000	0.0000	0.0000	0.0000	0.0000	0.0000	0.0000	0.35
0.40	0.0000	0.0000	0.0000	0.0000	0.0000	0.0000	0.0000	0.0000	0.0000	0.0000	0.0000	0.0000	0.40
0.45	0.0000	0.0000	0.0000	0.0000	0.0000	0.0000	0.0000	0.0000	0.0000	0.0000	0.0000	0.0000	0.45
0.50	0.0000	0.0000	0.0000	0.0000	0.0000	0.0000	0.0000	0.0000	0.0000	0.0000	0.0000	0.0000	0.50
0.55	0.0000	0.0000	0.0000	0.0000	0.0000	0.0000	0.0000	0.0000	0.0000	0.0000	0.0000	0.0000	0.55
0.60	0.0000	0.0000	0.0000	0.0000	0.0000	0.0000	0.0000	0.0000	0.0000	0.0000	0.0000	0.0000	0.60
0.65	0.0000	0.0000	0.0000	0.0000	0.0000	0.0000	0.0000	0.0000	0.0000	0.0000	0.0000	0.0000	0.65
0.70	0.0000	0.0000	0.0000	0.0000	0.0000	0.0000	0.0000	0.0000	0.0000	0.0000	0.0000	0.0000	0.70
0.75	0.0000	0.0000	0.0000	0.0000	0.0000	0.0000	0.0000	0.0000	0.0000	0.0000	0.0000	0.0000	0.75
0.80	0.0000	0.0000	0.0000	0.0000	0.0000	0.0000	0.0000	0.0000	0.0000	0.0000	0.0000	0.0000	0.80
0.85	0.0000	0.0000	0.0000	0.0000	0.0000	0.0000	0.0000	0.0000	0.0000	0.0000	0.0000	0.0000	0.85
0.90	0.0000	0.0000	0.0000	0.0000	0.0000	0.0000	0.0000	0.0000	0.0000	0.0000	0.0000	0.0000	0.90
0.95	0.0000	0.0000	0.0000	0.0000	0.0000	0.0000	0.0000	0.0000	0.0000	0.0000	0.0000	0.0000	0.95
1.00	0.0000	0.0000	0.0000	0.0000	0.0000	0.0000	0.0000	0.0000	0.0000	0.0000	0.0000	0.0000	1.00
1.10	0.0000	0.0000	0.0000	0.0000	0.0000	0.0000	0.0000	0.0000	0.0000	0.0000	0.0000	0.0000	1.10
1.20	0.0000	0.0000	0.0000	0.0000	0.0000	0.0000	0.0000	0.0000	0.0000	0.0000	0.0000	0.0000	1.20
1.30	0.0000	0.0000	0.0000	0.0000	0.0000	0.0000	0.0000	0.0000	0.0000	0.0000	0.0000	0.0000	1.30
1.40	0.0000	0.0000	0.0000	0.0000	0.0000	0.0000	0.0000	0.0000	0.0000	0.0000	0.0000	0.0000	1.40
1.50	0.0000	0.0000	0.0000	0.0000	0.0000	0.0000	0.0000	0.0000	0.0000	0.0000	0.0000	0.0000	1.50
1.60	0.0000	0.0000	0.0000	0.0000	0.0000	0.0000	0.0000	0.0000	0.0000	0.0000	0.0000	0.0000	1.60
1.70	0.0000	0.0000	0.0000	0.0000	0.0000	0.0000	0.0000	0.0000	0.0000	0.0000	0.0000	0.0000	1.70
1.80	0.0000	0.0000	0.0000	0.0000	0.0000	0.0000	0.0000	0.0000	0.0000	0.0000	0.0000	0.0000	1.80
1.90	0.0000	0.0000	0.0000	0.0000	0.0000	0.0000	0.0000	0.0000	0.0000	0.0000	0.0000	0.0000	1.90
2.00	0.0000	0.0000	0.0000	0.0000	0.0000	0.0000	0.0000	0.0000	0.0000	0.0000	0.0000	0.0000	2.00
2.10	0.0000	0.0000	0.0000	0.0000	0.0000	0.0000	0.0000	0.0000	0.0000	0.0000	0.0000	0.0000	2.10
2.20	0.0000	0.0000	0.0000	0.0000	0.0000	0.0000	0.0000	0.0000	0.0000	0.0000	0.0000	0.0000	2.20
2.30	0.0000	0.0000	0.0000	0.0000	0.0000	0.0000	0.0000	0.0000	0.0000	0.0000	0.0000	0.0000	2.30
2.40	0.0000	0.0000	0.0000	0.0000	0.0000	0.0000	0.0000	0.0000	0.0000	0.0000	0.0000	0.0000	2.40
2.50	0.0000	0.0000	0.0000	0.0000	0.0000	0.0000	0.0000	0.0000	0.0000	0.0000	0.0000	0.0000	2.50
2.60	0.0000	0.0000	0.0000	0.0000	0.0000	0.0000	0.0000	0.0000	0.0000	0.0000	0.0000	0.0000	2.60
2.70	0.0000	0.0000	0.0000	0.0000	0.0000	0.0000	0.0000	0.0000	0.0000	0.0000	0.0000	0.0000	2.70

Probability of x occurrences

Appendix 10

$$\Pr(X = x) = f(x;\lambda) = \frac{\lambda^x}{x!}e^{-\lambda}$$

λ	0	1	2	3	4	5	6	7	8	9	10	11	12	13
							Probability of x occurrences							
2.80	0.0608	0.1703	0.2384	0.2225	0.1557	0.0872	0.0407	0.0163	0.0057	0.0018	0.0005	0.0001	0.0000	0.0000
2.90	0.0550	0.1596	0.2314	0.2237	0.1622	0.0940	0.0455	0.0188	0.0068	0.0022	0.0006	0.0002	0.0000	0.0000
3.00	0.0498	0.1494	0.2240	0.2240	0.1680	0.1008	0.0504	0.0216	0.0081	0.0027	0.0008	0.0002	0.0001	0.0000
3.10	0.0450	0.1397	0.2165	0.2237	0.1733	0.1075	0.0555	0.0246	0.0095	0.0033	0.0010	0.0003	0.0001	0.0000
3.20	0.0408	0.1304	0.2087	0.2226	0.1781	0.1140	0.0608	0.0278	0.0111	0.0040	0.0013	0.0004	0.0001	0.0000
3.30	0.0369	0.1217	0.2008	0.2209	0.1823	0.1203	0.0662	0.0312	0.0129	0.0047	0.0016	0.0005	0.0001	0.0000
3.40	0.0334	0.1135	0.1929	0.2186	0.1858	0.1264	0.0716	0.0348	0.0148	0.0056	0.0019	0.0006	0.0002	0.0000
3.50	0.0302	0.1057	0.1850	0.2158	0.1888	0.1322	0.0771	0.0385	0.0169	0.0066	0.0023	0.0007	0.0002	0.0001
3.60	0.0273	0.0984	0.1771	0.2125	0.1912	0.1377	0.0826	0.0425	0.0191	0.0076	0.0028	0.0009	0.0003	0.0001
3.70	0.0247	0.0915	0.1692	0.2087	0.1931	0.1429	0.0881	0.0466	0.0215	0.0089	0.0033	0.0011	0.0003	0.0001
3.80	0.0224	0.0850	0.1615	0.2046	0.1944	0.1477	0.0936	0.0508	0.0241	0.0102	0.0039	0.0013	0.0004	0.0001
3.90	0.0202	0.0789	0.1539	0.2001	0.1951	0.1522	0.0989	0.0551	0.0269	0.0116	0.0045	0.0016	0.0005	0.0002
4.00	0.0183	0.0733	0.1465	0.1954	0.1954	0.1563	0.1042	0.0595	0.0298	0.0132	0.0053	0.0019	0.0006	0.0002
4.10	0.0166	0.0679	0.1393	0.1904	0.1951	0.1600	0.1093	0.0640	0.0328	0.0150	0.0061	0.0023	0.0008	0.0002
4.20	0.0150	0.0630	0.1323	0.1852	0.1944	0.1633	0.1143	0.0686	0.0360	0.0168	0.0071	0.0027	0.0009	0.0003
4.30	0.0136	0.0583	0.1254	0.1798	0.1933	0.1662	0.1191	0.0732	0.0393	0.0188	0.0081	0.0032	0.0011	0.0004
4.40	0.0123	0.0540	0.1188	0.1743	0.1917	0.1687	0.1237	0.0778	0.0428	0.0209	0.0092	0.0037	0.0013	0.0005
4.50	0.0111	0.0500	0.1125	0.1687	0.1898	0.1708	0.1281	0.0824	0.0463	0.0232	0.0104	0.0043	0.0016	0.0006
4.60	0.0101	0.0462	0.1063	0.1631	0.1875	0.1725	0.1323	0.0869	0.0500	0.0255	0.0118	0.0049	0.0019	0.0007
4.70	0.0091	0.0427	0.1005	0.1574	0.1849	0.1738	0.1362	0.0914	0.0537	0.0281	0.0132	0.0056	0.0022	0.0008
4.80	0.0082	0.0395	0.0948	0.1517	0.1820	0.1747	0.1398	0.0959	0.0575	0.0307	0.0147	0.0064	0.0026	0.0009
4.90	0.0074	0.0365	0.0894	0.1460	0.1789	0.1753	0.1432	0.1002	0.0614	0.0334	0.0164	0.0073	0.0030	0.0011
5.00	0.0067	0.0337	0.0842	0.1404	0.1755	0.1755	0.1462	0.1044	0.0653	0.0363	0.0181	0.0082	0.0034	0.0013
5.10	0.0061	0.0311	0.0793	0.1348	0.1719	0.1753	0.1490	0.1086	0.0692	0.0392	0.0200	0.0093	0.0039	0.0015
5.20	0.0055	0.0287	0.0746	0.1293	0.1681	0.1748	0.1515	0.1125	0.0731	0.0423	0.0220	0.0104	0.0045	0.0018
5.30	0.0050	0.0265	0.0701	0.1239	0.1641	0.1740	0.1537	0.1163	0.0771	0.0454	0.0241	0.0116	0.0051	0.0021
5.40	0.0045	0.0244	0.0659	0.1185	0.1600	0.1728	0.1555	0.1200	0.0810	0.0486	0.0262	0.0129	0.0058	0.0024
5.50	0.0041	0.0225	0.0618	0.1133	0.1558	0.1714	0.1571	0.1234	0.0849	0.0519	0.0285	0.0143	0.0065	0.0028
5.60	0.0037	0.0207	0.0580	0.1082	0.1515	0.1697	0.1584	0.1267	0.0887	0.0552	0.0309	0.0157	0.0073	0.0032
5.70	0.0033	0.0191	0.0544	0.1033	0.1472	0.1678	0.1594	0.1298	0.0925	0.0586	0.0334	0.0173	0.0082	0.0036
5.80	0.0030	0.0176	0.0509	0.0985	0.1428	0.1656	0.1601	0.1326	0.0962	0.0620	0.0359	0.0190	0.0092	0.0041
5.90	0.0027	0.0162	0.0477	0.0938	0.1383	0.1632	0.1605	0.1353	0.0998	0.0654	0.0386	0.0207	0.0102	0.0046
6.00	0.0025	0.0149	0.0446	0.0892	0.1339	0.1606	0.1606	0.1377	0.1033	0.0688	0.0413	0.0225	0.0113	0.0052
6.10	0.0022	0.0137	0.0417	0.0848	0.1294	0.1579	0.1605	0.1399	0.1066	0.0723	0.0441	0.0244	0.0124	0.0058
6.20	0.0020	0.0126	0.0390	0.0806	0.1249	0.1549	0.1601	0.1418	0.1099	0.0757	0.0469	0.0265	0.0137	0.0065
6.30	0.0018	0.0116	0.0364	0.0765	0.1205	0.1519	0.1595	0.1435	0.1130	0.0791	0.0498	0.0285	0.0150	0.0073
6.40	0.0017	0.0106	0.0340	0.0726	0.1162	0.1487	0.1586	0.1450	0.1160	0.0825	0.0528	0.0307	0.0164	0.0081

$$Pr(X = x) = f(x;\lambda) = \frac{\lambda^x}{x!}e^{-\lambda}$$

λ	14	15	16	17	18	19	20	21	22	23	24	25	λ
					Probability of x occurrences								
2.80	0.0000	0.0000	0.0000	0.0000	0.0000	0.0000	0.0000	0.0000	0.0000	0.0000	0.0000	0.0000	2.80
2.90	0.0000	0.0000	0.0000	0.0000	0.0000	0.0000	0.0000	0.0000	0.0000	0.0000	0.0000	0.0000	2.90
3.00	0.0000	0.0000	0.0000	0.0000	0.0000	0.0000	0.0000	0.0000	0.0000	0.0000	0.0000	0.0000	3.00
3.10	0.0000	0.0000	0.0000	0.0000	0.0000	0.0000	0.0000	0.0000	0.0000	0.0000	0.0000	0.0000	3.10
3.20	0.0000	0.0000	0.0000	0.0000	0.0000	0.0000	0.0000	0.0000	0.0000	0.0000	0.0000	0.0000	3.20
3.30	0.0000	0.0000	0.0000	0.0000	0.0000	0.0000	0.0000	0.0000	0.0000	0.0000	0.0000	0.0000	3.30
3.40	0.0000	0.0000	0.0000	0.0000	0.0000	0.0000	0.0000	0.0000	0.0000	0.0000	0.0000	0.0000	3.40
3.50	0.0000	0.0000	0.0000	0.0000	0.0000	0.0000	0.0000	0.0000	0.0000	0.0000	0.0000	0.0000	3.50
3.60	0.0000	0.0000	0.0000	0.0000	0.0000	0.0000	0.0000	0.0000	0.0000	0.0000	0.0000	0.0000	3.60
3.70	0.0000	0.0000	0.0000	0.0000	0.0000	0.0000	0.0000	0.0000	0.0000	0.0000	0.0000	0.0000	3.70
3.80	0.0000	0.0000	0.0000	0.0000	0.0000	0.0000	0.0000	0.0000	0.0000	0.0000	0.0000	0.0000	3.80
3.90	0.0000	0.0000	0.0000	0.0000	0.0000	0.0000	0.0000	0.0000	0.0000	0.0000	0.0000	0.0000	3.90
4.00	0.0001	0.0000	0.0000	0.0000	0.0000	0.0000	0.0000	0.0000	0.0000	0.0000	0.0000	0.0000	4.00
4.10	0.0001	0.0000	0.0000	0.0000	0.0000	0.0000	0.0000	0.0000	0.0000	0.0000	0.0000	0.0000	4.10
4.20	0.0001	0.0000	0.0000	0.0000	0.0000	0.0000	0.0000	0.0000	0.0000	0.0000	0.0000	0.0000	4.20
4.30	0.0001	0.0000	0.0000	0.0000	0.0000	0.0000	0.0000	0.0000	0.0000	0.0000	0.0000	0.0000	4.30
4.40	0.0001	0.0000	0.0000	0.0000	0.0000	0.0000	0.0000	0.0000	0.0000	0.0000	0.0000	0.0000	4.40
4.50	0.0002	0.0001	0.0000	0.0000	0.0000	0.0000	0.0000	0.0000	0.0000	0.0000	0.0000	0.0000	4.50
4.60	0.0002	0.0001	0.0000	0.0000	0.0000	0.0000	0.0000	0.0000	0.0000	0.0000	0.0000	0.0000	4.60
4.70	0.0003	0.0001	0.0000	0.0000	0.0000	0.0000	0.0000	0.0000	0.0000	0.0000	0.0000	0.0000	4.70
4.80	0.0003	0.0001	0.0000	0.0000	0.0000	0.0000	0.0000	0.0000	0.0000	0.0000	0.0000	0.0000	4.80
4.90	0.0004	0.0001	0.0000	0.0000	0.0000	0.0000	0.0000	0.0000	0.0000	0.0000	0.0000	0.0000	4.90
5.00	0.0005	0.0002	0.0000	0.0000	0.0000	0.0000	0.0000	0.0000	0.0000	0.0000	0.0000	0.0000	5.00
5.10	0.0006	0.0002	0.0001	0.0000	0.0000	0.0000	0.0000	0.0000	0.0000	0.0000	0.0000	0.0000	5.10
5.20	0.0007	0.0002	0.0001	0.0000	0.0000	0.0000	0.0000	0.0000	0.0000	0.0000	0.0000	0.0000	5.20
5.30	0.0008	0.0003	0.0001	0.0000	0.0000	0.0000	0.0000	0.0000	0.0000	0.0000	0.0000	0.0000	5.30
5.40	0.0009	0.0003	0.0001	0.0000	0.0000	0.0000	0.0000	0.0000	0.0000	0.0000	0.0000	0.0000	5.40
5.50	0.0011	0.0004	0.0001	0.0000	0.0000	0.0000	0.0000	0.0000	0.0000	0.0000	0.0000	0.0000	5.50
5.60	0.0013	0.0005	0.0002	0.0001	0.0000	0.0000	0.0000	0.0000	0.0000	0.0000	0.0000	0.0000	5.60
5.70	0.0015	0.0006	0.0002	0.0001	0.0000	0.0000	0.0000	0.0000	0.0000	0.0000	0.0000	0.0000	5.70
5.80	0.0017	0.0007	0.0002	0.0001	0.0000	0.0000	0.0000	0.0000	0.0000	0.0000	0.0000	0.0000	5.80
5.90	0.0019	0.0008	0.0003	0.0001	0.0000	0.0000	0.0000	0.0000	0.0000	0.0000	0.0000	0.0000	5.90
6.00	0.0022	0.0009	0.0003	0.0001	0.0000	0.0000	0.0000	0.0000	0.0000	0.0000	0.0000	0.0000	6.00
6.10	0.0025	0.0010	0.0004	0.0001	0.0000	0.0000	0.0000	0.0000	0.0000	0.0000	0.0000	0.0000	6.10
6.20	0.0029	0.0012	0.0005	0.0002	0.0001	0.0000	0.0000	0.0000	0.0000	0.0000	0.0000	0.0000	6.20
6.30	0.0033	0.0014	0.0005	0.0002	0.0001	0.0000	0.0000	0.0000	0.0000	0.0000	0.0000	0.0000	6.30
6.40	0.0037	0.0016	0.0006	0.0002	0.0001	0.0000	0.0000	0.0000	0.0000	0.0000	0.0000	0.0000	6.40

$$Pr(X = x) = f(x;\lambda) = \frac{\lambda^x}{x!}e^{-\lambda}$$

	Probability of *x* occurrences													
λ	0	1	2	3	4	5	6	7	8	9	10	11	12	13
6.50	0.0015	0.0098	0.0318	0.0688	0.1118	0.1454	0.1575	0.1462	0.1188	0.0858	0.0558	0.0330	0.0179	0.0089
6.60	0.0014	0.0090	0.0296	0.0652	0.1076	0.1420	0.1562	0.1472	0.1215	0.0891	0.0588	0.0353	0.0194	0.0099
6.70	0.0012	0.0082	0.0276	0.0617	0.1034	0.1385	0.1546	0.1480	0.1240	0.0923	0.0618	0.0377	0.0210	0.0108
6.80	0.0011	0.0076	0.0258	0.0584	0.0992	0.1349	0.1529	0.1486	0.1263	0.0954	0.0649	0.0401	0.0227	0.0119
6.90	0.0010	0.0070	0.0240	0.0552	0.0952	0.1314	0.1511	0.1489	0.1284	0.0985	0.0679	0.0426	0.0245	0.0130
7.00	0.0009	0.0064	0.0223	0.0521	0.0912	0.1277	0.1490	0.1490	0.1304	0.1014	0.0710	0.0452	0.0263	0.0142
7.10	0.0008	0.0059	0.0208	0.0492	0.0874	0.1241	0.1468	0.1489	0.1321	0.1042	0.0740	0.0478	0.0283	0.0154
7.20	0.0007	0.0054	0.0194	0.0464	0.0836	0.1204	0.1445	0.1486	0.1337	0.1070	0.0770	0.0504	0.0303	0.0168
7.30	0.0007	0.0049	0.0180	0.0438	0.0799	0.1167	0.1420	0.1481	0.1351	0.1096	0.0800	0.0531	0.0323	0.0181
7.40	0.0006	0.0045	0.0167	0.0413	0.0764	0.1130	0.1394	0.1474	0.1363	0.1121	0.0829	0.0558	0.0344	0.0196
7.50	0.0006	0.0041	0.0156	0.0389	0.0729	0.1094	0.1367	0.1465	0.1373	0.1144	0.0858	0.0585	0.0366	0.0211
7.60	0.0005	0.0038	0.0145	0.0366	0.0696	0.1057	0.1339	0.1454	0.1381	0.1167	0.0887	0.0613	0.0388	0.0227
7.70	0.0005	0.0035	0.0134	0.0345	0.0663	0.1021	0.1311	0.1442	0.1388	0.1187	0.0914	0.0640	0.0411	0.0243
7.80	0.0004	0.0032	0.0125	0.0324	0.0632	0.0986	0.1282	0.1428	0.1392	0.1207	0.0941	0.0667	0.0434	0.0260
7.90	0.0004	0.0029	0.0116	0.0305	0.0602	0.0951	0.1252	0.1413	0.1395	0.1224	0.0967	0.0695	0.0457	0.0278
8.00	0.0003	0.0027	0.0107	0.0286	0.0573	0.0916	0.1221	0.1396	0.1396	0.1241	0.0993	0.0722	0.0481	0.0296
8.10	0.0003	0.0025	0.0100	0.0269	0.0544	0.0882	0.1191	0.1378	0.1395	0.1256	0.1017	0.0749	0.0505	0.0315
8.20	0.0003	0.0023	0.0092	0.0252	0.0517	0.0849	0.1160	0.1358	0.1392	0.1269	0.1040	0.0776	0.0530	0.0334
8.30	0.0002	0.0021	0.0086	0.0237	0.0491	0.0816	0.1128	0.1338	0.1388	0.1280	0.1063	0.0802	0.0555	0.0354
8.40	0.0002	0.0019	0.0079	0.0222	0.0466	0.0784	0.1097	0.1317	0.1382	0.1290	0.1084	0.0828	0.0579	0.0374
8.50	0.0002	0.0017	0.0074	0.0208	0.0443	0.0752	0.1066	0.1294	0.1375	0.1299	0.1104	0.0853	0.0604	0.0395
8.60	0.0002	0.0016	0.0068	0.0195	0.0420	0.0722	0.1034	0.1271	0.1366	0.1306	0.1123	0.0878	0.0629	0.0416
8.70	0.0002	0.0014	0.0063	0.0183	0.0398	0.0692	0.1003	0.1247	0.1356	0.1311	0.1140	0.0902	0.0654	0.0438
8.80	0.0002	0.0013	0.0058	0.0171	0.0377	0.0663	0.0972	0.1222	0.1344	0.1315	0.1157	0.0925	0.0679	0.0459
8.90	0.0001	0.0012	0.0054	0.0160	0.0357	0.0635	0.0941	0.1197	0.1332	0.1317	0.1172	0.0948	0.0703	0.0481
9.00	0.0001	0.0011	0.0050	0.0150	0.0337	0.0607	0.0911	0.1171	0.1318	0.1318	0.1186	0.0970	0.0728	0.0504
9.10	0.0001	0.0010	0.0046	0.0140	0.0319	0.0581	0.0881	0.1145	0.1302	0.1317	0.1198	0.0991	0.0752	0.0526
9.20	0.0001	0.0009	0.0043	0.0131	0.0302	0.0555	0.0851	0.1118	0.1286	0.1315	0.1210	0.1012	0.0776	0.0549
9.30	0.0001	0.0009	0.0040	0.0123	0.0285	0.0530	0.0822	0.1091	0.1269	0.1311	0.1219	0.1031	0.0799	0.0572
9.40	0.0001	0.0008	0.0037	0.0115	0.0269	0.0506	0.0793	0.1064	0.1251	0.1306	0.1228	0.1049	0.0822	0.0594
9.50	0.0001	0.0007	0.0034	0.0107	0.0254	0.0483	0.0764	0.1037	0.1232	0.1300	0.1235	0.1067	0.0844	0.0617
9.60	0.0001	0.0007	0.0031	0.0100	0.0240	0.0460	0.0736	0.1010	0.1212	0.1293	0.1241	0.1083	0.0866	0.0640
9.70	0.0001	0.0006	0.0029	0.0093	0.0226	0.0439	0.0709	0.0982	0.1191	0.1284	0.1245	0.1098	0.0888	0.0662
9.80	0.0001	0.0005	0.0027	0.0087	0.0213	0.0418	0.0682	0.0955	0.1170	0.1274	0.1249	0.1112	0.0908	0.0685
9.90	0.0001	0.0005	0.0025	0.0081	0.0201	0.0398	0.0656	0.0928	0.1148	0.1263	0.1250	0.1125	0.0928	0.0707
10.00	0.0000	0.0005	0.0023	0.0076	0.0189	0.0378	0.0631	0.0901	0.1126	0.1251	0.1251	0.1137	0.0948	0.0729

$$\Pr(X = x) = f(x;\lambda) = \frac{\lambda^x}{x!}e^{-\lambda}$$

λ	\multicolumn{12}{c}{Probability of x occurrences}	λ
	14	15	16	17	18	19	20	21	22	23	24	25	
6.50	0.0041	0.0018	0.0007	0.0003	0.0001	0.0000	0.0000	0.0000	0.0000	0.0000	0.0000	0.0000	6.50
6.60	0.0046	0.0020	0.0008	0.0003	0.0001	0.0000	0.0000	0.0000	0.0000	0.0000	0.0000	0.0000	6.60
6.70	0.0052	0.0023	0.0010	0.0004	0.0001	0.0001	0.0000	0.0000	0.0000	0.0000	0.0000	0.0000	6.70
6.80	0.0058	0.0026	0.0011	0.0004	0.0002	0.0001	0.0000	0.0000	0.0000	0.0000	0.0000	0.0000	6.80
6.90	0.0064	0.0029	0.0013	0.0005	0.0002	0.0001	0.0000	0.0000	0.0000	0.0000	0.0000	0.0000	6.90
7.00	0.0071	0.0033	0.0014	0.0006	0.0002	0.0001	0.0000	0.0000	0.0000	0.0000	0.0000	0.0000	7.00
7.10	0.0078	0.0037	0.0016	0.0007	0.0003	0.0001	0.0000	0.0000	0.0000	0.0000	0.0000	0.0000	7.10
7.20	0.0086	0.0041	0.0019	0.0008	0.0003	0.0001	0.0000	0.0000	0.0000	0.0000	0.0000	0.0000	7.20
7.30	0.0095	0.0046	0.0021	0.0009	0.0004	0.0001	0.0001	0.0000	0.0000	0.0000	0.0000	0.0000	7.30
7.40	0.0104	0.0051	0.0024	0.0010	0.0004	0.0002	0.0001	0.0000	0.0000	0.0000	0.0000	0.0000	7.40
7.50	0.0113	0.0057	0.0026	0.0012	0.0005	0.0002	0.0001	0.0000	0.0000	0.0000	0.0000	0.0000	7.50
7.60	0.0123	0.0062	0.0030	0.0013	0.0006	0.0002	0.0001	0.0000	0.0000	0.0000	0.0000	0.0000	7.60
7.70	0.0134	0.0069	0.0033	0.0015	0.0006	0.0003	0.0001	0.0000	0.0000	0.0000	0.0000	0.0000	7.70
7.80	0.0145	0.0075	0.0037	0.0017	0.0007	0.0003	0.0001	0.0000	0.0000	0.0000	0.0000	0.0000	7.80
7.90	0.0157	0.0083	0.0041	0.0019	0.0008	0.0003	0.0001	0.0001	0.0000	0.0000	0.0000	0.0000	7.90
8.00	0.0169	0.0090	0.0045	0.0021	0.0009	0.0004	0.0002	0.0001	0.0000	0.0000	0.0000	0.0000	8.00
8.10	0.0182	0.0098	0.0050	0.0024	0.0011	0.0005	0.0002	0.0001	0.0000	0.0000	0.0000	0.0000	8.10
8.20	0.0196	0.0107	0.0055	0.0026	0.0012	0.0005	0.0002	0.0001	0.0000	0.0000	0.0000	0.0000	8.20
8.30	0.0210	0.0116	0.0060	0.0029	0.0014	0.0006	0.0002	0.0001	0.0000	0.0000	0.0000	0.0000	8.30
8.40	0.0225	0.0126	0.0066	0.0033	0.0015	0.0007	0.0003	0.0001	0.0000	0.0000	0.0000	0.0000	8.40
8.50	0.0240	0.0136	0.0072	0.0036	0.0017	0.0008	0.0003	0.0001	0.0001	0.0000	0.0000	0.0000	8.50
8.60	0.0256	0.0147	0.0079	0.0040	0.0019	0.0009	0.0004	0.0002	0.0001	0.0000	0.0000	0.0000	8.60
8.70	0.0272	0.0158	0.0086	0.0044	0.0021	0.0010	0.0004	0.0002	0.0001	0.0000	0.0000	0.0000	8.70
8.80	0.0289	0.0169	0.0093	0.0048	0.0024	0.0011	0.0005	0.0002	0.0001	0.0000	0.0000	0.0000	8.80
8.90	0.0306	0.0182	0.0101	0.0053	0.0026	0.0012	0.0005	0.0002	0.0001	0.0000	0.0000	0.0000	8.90
9.00	0.0324	0.0194	0.0109	0.0058	0.0029	0.0014	0.0006	0.0003	0.0001	0.0000	0.0000	0.0000	9.00
9.10	0.0342	0.0208	0.0118	0.0063	0.0032	0.0015	0.0007	0.0003	0.0001	0.0000	0.0000	0.0000	9.10
9.20	0.0361	0.0221	0.0127	0.0069	0.0035	0.0017	0.0008	0.0003	0.0001	0.0001	0.0000	0.0000	9.20
9.30	0.0380	0.0235	0.0137	0.0075	0.0039	0.0019	0.0009	0.0004	0.0002	0.0001	0.0000	0.0000	9.30
9.40	0.0399	0.0250	0.0147	0.0081	0.0042	0.0021	0.0010	0.0004	0.0002	0.0001	0.0000	0.0000	9.40
9.50	0.0419	0.0265	0.0157	0.0088	0.0046	0.0023	0.0011	0.0005	0.0002	0.0001	0.0000	0.0000	9.50
9.60	0.0439	0.0281	0.0168	0.0095	0.0051	0.0026	0.0012	0.0006	0.0002	0.0001	0.0000	0.0000	9.60
9.70	0.0459	0.0297	0.0180	0.0103	0.0055	0.0028	0.0014	0.0006	0.0003	0.0001	0.0000	0.0000	9.70
9.80	0.0479	0.0313	0.0192	0.0111	0.0060	0.0031	0.0015	0.0007	0.0003	0.0001	0.0001	0.0000	9.80
9.90	0.0500	0.0330	0.0204	0.0119	0.0065	0.0034	0.0017	0.0008	0.0004	0.0002	0.0001	0.0000	9.90
10.00	0.0521	0.0347	0.0217	0.0128	0.0071	0.0037	0.0019	0.0009	0.0004	0.0002	0.0001	0.0000	10.00

Appendix 11
Cumulative Poisson Distribution Table

$$Pr(X \le x) = F(x; \lambda) = \sum_{x=0}^{n} \frac{\lambda^x}{x!} e^{-\lambda}$$

	Probability of less than or equal to *x* occurrences													
λ	0	1	2	3	4	5	6	7	8	9	10	11	12	13
0.05	0.9512	0.9988	1.0000	1.0000	1.0000	1.0000	1.0000	1.0000	1.0000	1.0000	1.0000	1.0000	1.0000	1.0000
0.10	0.9048	0.9953	0.9998	1.0000	1.0000	1.0000	1.0000	1.0000	1.0000	1.0000	1.0000	1.0000	1.0000	1.0000
0.15	0.8607	0.9898	0.9995	1.0000	1.0000	1.0000	1.0000	1.0000	1.0000	1.0000	1.0000	1.0000	1.0000	1.0000
0.20	0.8187	0.9825	0.9989	0.9999	1.0000	1.0000	1.0000	1.0000	1.0000	1.0000	1.0000	1.0000	1.0000	1.0000
0.25	0.7788	0.9735	0.9978	0.9999	1.0000	1.0000	1.0000	1.0000	1.0000	1.0000	1.0000	1.0000	1.0000	1.0000
0.30	0.7408	0.9631	0.9964	0.9997	1.0000	1.0000	1.0000	1.0000	1.0000	1.0000	1.0000	1.0000	1.0000	1.0000
0.35	0.7047	0.9513	0.9945	0.9995	1.0000	1.0000	1.0000	1.0000	1.0000	1.0000	1.0000	1.0000	1.0000	1.0000
0.40	0.6703	0.9384	0.9921	0.9992	0.9999	1.0000	1.0000	1.0000	1.0000	1.0000	1.0000	1.0000	1.0000	1.0000
0.45	0.6376	0.9246	0.9891	0.9988	0.9999	1.0000	1.0000	1.0000	1.0000	1.0000	1.0000	1.0000	1.0000	1.0000
0.50	0.6065	0.9098	0.9856	0.9982	0.9998	1.0000	1.0000	1.0000	1.0000	1.0000	1.0000	1.0000	1.0000	1.0000
0.55	0.5769	0.8943	0.9815	0.9975	0.9997	1.0000	1.0000	1.0000	1.0000	1.0000	1.0000	1.0000	1.0000	1.0000
0.60	0.5488	0.8781	0.9769	0.9966	0.9996	1.0000	1.0000	1.0000	1.0000	1.0000	1.0000	1.0000	1.0000	1.0000
0.65	0.5220	0.8614	0.9717	0.9956	0.9994	0.9999	1.0000	1.0000	1.0000	1.0000	1.0000	1.0000	1.0000	1.0000
0.70	0.4966	0.8442	0.9659	0.9942	0.9992	0.9999	1.0000	1.0000	1.0000	1.0000	1.0000	1.0000	1.0000	1.0000
0.75	0.4724	0.8266	0.9595	0.9927	0.9989	0.9999	1.0000	1.0000	1.0000	1.0000	1.0000	1.0000	1.0000	1.0000
0.80	0.4493	0.8088	0.9526	0.9909	0.9986	0.9998	1.0000	1.0000	1.0000	1.0000	1.0000	1.0000	1.0000	1.0000
0.85	0.4274	0.7907	0.9451	0.9889	0.9982	0.9997	1.0000	1.0000	1.0000	1.0000	1.0000	1.0000	1.0000	1.0000
0.90	0.4066	0.7725	0.9371	0.9865	0.9977	0.9997	1.0000	1.0000	1.0000	1.0000	1.0000	1.0000	1.0000	1.0000
0.95	0.3867	0.7541	0.9287	0.9839	0.9971	0.9995	0.9999	1.0000	1.0000	1.0000	1.0000	1.0000	1.0000	1.0000
1.00	0.3679	0.7358	0.9197	0.9810	0.9963	0.9994	0.9999	1.0000	1.0000	1.0000	1.0000	1.0000	1.0000	1.0000
1.10	0.3329	0.6990	0.9004	0.9743	0.9946	0.9990	0.9999	1.0000	1.0000	1.0000	1.0000	1.0000	1.0000	1.0000
1.20	0.3012	0.6626	0.8795	0.9662	0.9923	0.9985	0.9997	1.0000	1.0000	1.0000	1.0000	1.0000	1.0000	1.0000
1.30	0.2725	0.6268	0.8571	0.9569	0.9893	0.9978	0.9996	0.9999	1.0000	1.0000	1.0000	1.0000	1.0000	1.0000
1.40	0.2466	0.5918	0.8335	0.9463	0.9857	0.9968	0.9994	0.9999	1.0000	1.0000	1.0000	1.0000	1.0000	1.0000
1.50	0.2231	0.5578	0.8088	0.9344	0.9814	0.9955	0.9991	0.9998	1.0000	1.0000	1.0000	1.0000	1.0000	1.0000
1.60	0.2019	0.5249	0.7834	0.9212	0.9763	0.9940	0.9987	0.9997	1.0000	1.0000	1.0000	1.0000	1.0000	1.0000
1.70	0.1827	0.4932	0.7572	0.9068	0.9704	0.9920	0.9981	0.9996	0.9999	1.0000	1.0000	1.0000	1.0000	1.0000
1.80	0.1653	0.4628	0.7306	0.8913	0.9636	0.9896	0.9974	0.9994	0.9999	1.0000	1.0000	1.0000	1.0000	1.0000
1.90	0.1496	0.4337	0.7037	0.8747	0.9559	0.9868	0.9966	0.9992	0.9998	1.0000	1.0000	1.0000	1.0000	1.0000
2.00	0.1353	0.4060	0.6767	0.8571	0.9473	0.9834	0.9955	0.9989	0.9998	1.0000	1.0000	1.0000	1.0000	1.0000
2.10	0.1225	0.3796	0.6496	0.8386	0.9379	0.9796	0.9941	0.9985	0.9997	0.9999	1.0000	1.0000	1.0000	1.0000
2.20	0.1108	0.3546	0.6227	0.8194	0.9275	0.9751	0.9925	0.9980	0.9995	0.9999	1.0000	1.0000	1.0000	1.0000
2.30	0.1003	0.3309	0.5960	0.7993	0.9162	0.9700	0.9906	0.9974	0.9994	0.9999	1.0000	1.0000	1.0000	1.0000
2.40	0.0907	0.3084	0.5697	0.7787	0.9041	0.9643	0.9884	0.9967	0.9991	0.9998	1.0000	1.0000	1.0000	1.0000
2.50	0.0821	0.2873	0.5438	0.7576	0.8912	0.9580	0.9858	0.9958	0.9989	0.9997	0.9999	1.0000	1.0000	1.0000
2.60	0.0743	0.2674	0.5184	0.7360	0.8774	0.9510	0.9828	0.9947	0.9985	0.9996	0.9999	1.0000	1.0000	1.0000
2.70	0.0672	0.2487	0.4936	0.7141	0.8629	0.9433	0.9794	0.9934	0.9981	0.9995	0.9999	1.0000	1.0000	1.0000

$$\Pr(X \le x) = F(x;\lambda) = \sum_{x=0}^{n} \frac{\lambda^{x}}{x!}e^{-\lambda}$$

	Probability of less than or equal to x occurrences												
λ	14	15	16	17	18	19	20	21	22	23	24	25	λ
0.05	1.0000	1.0000	1.0000	1.0000	1.0000	1.0000	1.0000	1.0000	1.0000	1.0000	1.0000	1.0000	0.05
0.10	1.0000	1.0000	1.0000	1.0000	1.0000	1.0000	1.0000	1.0000	1.0000	1.0000	1.0000	1.0000	0.10
0.15	1.0000	1.0000	1.0000	1.0000	1.0000	1.0000	1.0000	1.0000	1.0000	1.0000	1.0000	1.0000	0.15
0.20	1.0000	1.0000	1.0000	1.0000	1.0000	1.0000	1.0000	1.0000	1.0000	1.0000	1.0000	1.0000	0.20
0.25	1.0000	1.0000	1.0000	1.0000	1.0000	1.0000	1.0000	1.0000	1.0000	1.0000	1.0000	1.0000	0.25
0.30	1.0000	1.0000	1.0000	1.0000	1.0000	1.0000	1.0000	1.0000	1.0000	1.0000	1.0000	1.0000	0.30
0.35	1.0000	1.0000	1.0000	1.0000	1.0000	1.0000	1.0000	1.0000	1.0000	1.0000	1.0000	1.0000	0.35
0.40	1.0000	1.0000	1.0000	1.0000	1.0000	1.0000	1.0000	1.0000	1.0000	1.0000	1.0000	1.0000	0.40
0.45	1.0000	1.0000	1.0000	1.0000	1.0000	1.0000	1.0000	1.0000	1.0000	1.0000	1.0000	1.0000	0.45
0.50	1.0000	1.0000	1.0000	1.0000	1.0000	1.0000	1.0000	1.0000	1.0000	1.0000	1.0000	1.0000	0.50
0.55	1.0000	1.0000	1.0000	1.0000	1.0000	1.0000	1.0000	1.0000	1.0000	1.0000	1.0000	1.0000	0.55
0.60	1.0000	1.0000	1.0000	1.0000	1.0000	1.0000	1.0000	1.0000	1.0000	1.0000	1.0000	1.0000	0.60
0.65	1.0000	1.0000	1.0000	1.0000	1.0000	1.0000	1.0000	1.0000	1.0000	1.0000	1.0000	1.0000	0.65
0.70	1.0000	1.0000	1.0000	1.0000	1.0000	1.0000	1.0000	1.0000	1.0000	1.0000	1.0000	1.0000	0.70
0.75	1.0000	1.0000	1.0000	1.0000	1.0000	1.0000	1.0000	1.0000	1.0000	1.0000	1.0000	1.0000	0.75
0.80	1.0000	1.0000	1.0000	1.0000	1.0000	1.0000	1.0000	1.0000	1.0000	1.0000	1.0000	1.0000	0.80
0.85	1.0000	1.0000	1.0000	1.0000	1.0000	1.0000	1.0000	1.0000	1.0000	1.0000	1.0000	1.0000	0.85
0.90	1.0000	1.0000	1.0000	1.0000	1.0000	1.0000	1.0000	1.0000	1.0000	1.0000	1.0000	1.0000	0.90
0.95	1.0000	1.0000	1.0000	1.0000	1.0000	1.0000	1.0000	1.0000	1.0000	1.0000	1.0000	1.0000	0.95
1.00	1.0000	1.0000	1.0000	1.0000	1.0000	1.0000	1.0000	1.0000	1.0000	1.0000	1.0000	1.0000	1.00
1.10	1.0000	1.0000	1.0000	1.0000	1.0000	1.0000	1.0000	1.0000	1.0000	1.0000	1.0000	1.0000	1.10
1.20	1.0000	1.0000	1.0000	1.0000	1.0000	1.0000	1.0000	1.0000	1.0000	1.0000	1.0000	1.0000	1.20
1.30	1.0000	1.0000	1.0000	1.0000	1.0000	1.0000	1.0000	1.0000	1.0000	1.0000	1.0000	1.0000	1.30
1.40	1.0000	1.0000	1.0000	1.0000	1.0000	1.0000	1.0000	1.0000	1.0000	1.0000	1.0000	1.0000	1.40
1.50	1.0000	1.0000	1.0000	1.0000	1.0000	1.0000	1.0000	1.0000	1.0000	1.0000	1.0000	1.0000	1.50
1.60	1.0000	1.0000	1.0000	1.0000	1.0000	1.0000	1.0000	1.0000	1.0000	1.0000	1.0000	1.0000	1.60
1.70	1.0000	1.0000	1.0000	1.0000	1.0000	1.0000	1.0000	1.0000	1.0000	1.0000	1.0000	1.0000	1.70
1.80	1.0000	1.0000	1.0000	1.0000	1.0000	1.0000	1.0000	1.0000	1.0000	1.0000	1.0000	1.0000	1.80
1.90	1.0000	1.0000	1.0000	1.0000	1.0000	1.0000	1.0000	1.0000	1.0000	1.0000	1.0000	1.0000	1.90
2.00	1.0000	1.0000	1.0000	1.0000	1.0000	1.0000	1.0000	1.0000	1.0000	1.0000	1.0000	1.0000	2.00
2.10	1.0000	1.0000	1.0000	1.0000	1.0000	1.0000	1.0000	1.0000	1.0000	1.0000	1.0000	1.0000	2.10
2.20	1.0000	1.0000	1.0000	1.0000	1.0000	1.0000	1.0000	1.0000	1.0000	1.0000	1.0000	1.0000	2.20
2.30	1.0000	1.0000	1.0000	1.0000	1.0000	1.0000	1.0000	1.0000	1.0000	1.0000	1.0000	1.0000	2.30
2.40	1.0000	1.0000	1.0000	1.0000	1.0000	1.0000	1.0000	1.0000	1.0000	1.0000	1.0000	1.0000	2.40
2.50	1.0000	1.0000	1.0000	1.0000	1.0000	1.0000	1.0000	1.0000	1.0000	1.0000	1.0000	1.0000	2.50
2.60	1.0000	1.0000	1.0000	1.0000	1.0000	1.0000	1.0000	1.0000	1.0000	1.0000	1.0000	1.0000	2.60
2.70	1.0000	1.0000	1.0000	1.0000	1.0000	1.0000	1.0000	1.0000	1.0000	1.0000	1.0000	1.0000	2.70

Appendix 11

$$\Pr(X \le x) = F(x;\lambda) = \sum_{x=0}^{n} \frac{\lambda^x}{x!} e^{-\lambda}$$

	Probability of less than or equal to x occurrences														
λ	0	1	2	3	4	5	6	7	8	9	10	11	12	13	
2.80	0.0608	0.2311	0.4695	0.6919	0.8477	0.9349	0.9756	0.9919	0.9976	0.9993	0.9998	1.0000	1.0000	1.0000	2
2.90	0.0550	0.2146	0.4460	0.6696	0.8318	0.9258	0.9713	0.9901	0.9969	0.9991	0.9998	0.9999	1.0000	1.0000	2
3.00	0.0498	0.1991	0.4232	0.6472	0.8153	0.9161	0.9665	0.9881	0.9962	0.9989	0.9997	0.9999	1.0000	1.0000	3
3.10	0.0450	0.1847	0.4012	0.6248	0.7982	0.9057	0.9612	0.9858	0.9953	0.9986	0.9996	0.9999	1.0000	1.0000	3
3.20	0.0408	0.1712	0.3799	0.6025	0.7806	0.8946	0.9554	0.9832	0.9943	0.9982	0.9995	0.9999	1.0000	1.0000	3
3.30	0.0369	0.1586	0.3594	0.5803	0.7626	0.8829	0.9490	0.9802	0.9931	0.9978	0.9994	0.9998	1.0000	1.0000	3
3.40	0.0334	0.1468	0.3397	0.5584	0.7442	0.8705	0.9421	0.9769	0.9917	0.9973	0.9992	0.9998	0.9999	1.0000	3
3.50	0.0302	0.1359	0.3208	0.5366	0.7254	0.8576	0.9347	0.9733	0.9901	0.9967	0.9990	0.9997	0.9999	1.0000	3
3.60	0.0273	0.1257	0.3027	0.5152	0.7064	0.8441	0.9267	0.9692	0.9883	0.9960	0.9987	0.9996	0.9999	1.0000	3
3.70	0.0247	0.1162	0.2854	0.4942	0.6872	0.8301	0.9182	0.9648	0.9863	0.9952	0.9984	0.9995	0.9999	1.0000	3
3.80	0.0224	0.1074	0.2689	0.4735	0.6678	0.8156	0.9091	0.9599	0.9840	0.9942	0.9981	0.9994	0.9998	1.0000	3
3.90	0.0202	0.0992	0.2531	0.4532	0.6484	0.8006	0.8995	0.9546	0.9815	0.9931	0.9977	0.9993	0.9998	0.9999	3
4.00	0.0183	0.0916	0.2381	0.4335	0.6288	0.7851	0.8893	0.9489	0.9786	0.9919	0.9972	0.9991	0.9997	0.9999	4
4.10	0.0166	0.0845	0.2238	0.4142	0.6093	0.7693	0.8786	0.9427	0.9755	0.9905	0.9966	0.9989	0.9997	0.9999	4
4.20	0.0150	0.0780	0.2102	0.3954	0.5898	0.7531	0.8675	0.9361	0.9721	0.9889	0.9959	0.9986	0.9996	0.9999	4
4.30	0.0136	0.0719	0.1974	0.3772	0.5704	0.7367	0.8558	0.9290	0.9683	0.9871	0.9952	0.9983	0.9995	0.9998	4
4.40	0.0123	0.0663	0.1851	0.3594	0.5512	0.7199	0.8436	0.9214	0.9642	0.9851	0.9943	0.9980	0.9993	0.9998	4
4.50	0.0111	0.0611	0.1736	0.3423	0.5321	0.7029	0.8311	0.9134	0.9597	0.9829	0.9933	0.9976	0.9992	0.9997	4
4.60	0.0101	0.0563	0.1626	0.3257	0.5132	0.6858	0.8180	0.9049	0.9549	0.9805	0.9922	0.9971	0.9990	0.9997	
4.70	0.0091	0.0518	0.1523	0.3097	0.4946	0.6684	0.8046	0.8960	0.9497	0.9778	0.9910	0.9966	0.9988	0.9996	
4.80	0.0082	0.0477	0.1425	0.2942	0.4763	0.6510	0.7908	0.8867	0.9442	0.9749	0.9896	0.9960	0.9986	0.9995	
4.90	0.0074	0.0439	0.1333	0.2793	0.4582	0.6335	0.7767	0.8769	0.9382	0.9717	0.9880	0.9953	0.9983	0.9994	
5.00	0.0067	0.0404	0.1247	0.2650	0.4405	0.6160	0.7622	0.8666	0.9319	0.9682	0.9863	0.9945	0.9980	0.9993	
5.10	0.0061	0.0372	0.1165	0.2513	0.4231	0.5984	0.7474	0.8560	0.9252	0.9644	0.9844	0.9937	0.9976	0.9992	
5.20	0.0055	0.0342	0.1088	0.2381	0.4061	0.5809	0.7324	0.8449	0.9181	0.9603	0.9823	0.9927	0.9972	0.9990	
5.30	0.0050	0.0314	0.1016	0.2254	0.3895	0.5635	0.7171	0.8335	0.9106	0.9559	0.9800	0.9916	0.9967	0.9988	
5.40	0.0045	0.0289	0.0948	0.2133	0.3733	0.5461	0.7017	0.8217	0.9027	0.9512	0.9775	0.9904	0.9962	0.9986	
5.50	0.0041	0.0266	0.0884	0.2017	0.3575	0.5289	0.6860	0.8095	0.8944	0.9462	0.9747	0.9890	0.9955	0.9983	
5.60	0.0037	0.0244	0.0824	0.1906	0.3422	0.5119	0.6703	0.7970	0.8857	0.9409	0.9718	0.9875	0.9949	0.9980	
5.70	0.0033	0.0224	0.0768	0.1800	0.3272	0.4950	0.6544	0.7841	0.8766	0.9352	0.9686	0.9859	0.9941	0.9977	
5.80	0.0030	0.0206	0.0715	0.1700	0.3127	0.4783	0.6384	0.7710	0.8672	0.9292	0.9651	0.9841	0.9932	0.9973	
5.90	0.0027	0.0189	0.0666	0.1604	0.2987	0.4619	0.6224	0.7576	0.8574	0.9228	0.9614	0.9821	0.9922	0.9969	
6.00	0.0025	0.0174	0.0620	0.1512	0.2851	0.4457	0.6063	0.7440	0.8472	0.9161	0.9574	0.9799	0.9912	0.9964	
6.10	0.0022	0.0159	0.0577	0.1425	0.2719	0.4298	0.5902	0.7301	0.8367	0.9090	0.9531	0.9776	0.9900	0.9958	
6.20	0.0020	0.0146	0.0536	0.1342	0.2592	0.4141	0.5742	0.7160	0.8259	0.9016	0.9486	0.9750	0.9887	0.9952	
6.30	0.0018	0.0134	0.0498	0.1264	0.2469	0.3988	0.5582	0.7017	0.8148	0.8939	0.9437	0.9723	0.9873	0.9945	
6.40	0.0017	0.0123	0.0463	0.1189	0.2351	0.3837	0.5423	0.6873	0.8033	0.8858	0.9386	0.9693	0.9857	0.9937	
6.50	0.0015	0.0113	0.0430	0.1118	0.2237	0.3690	0.5265	0.6728	0.7916	0.8774	0.9332	0.9661	0.9840	0.9929	
6.60	0.0014	0.0103	0.0400	0.1052	0.2127	0.3547	0.5108	0.6581	0.7796	0.8686	0.9274	0.9627	0.9821	0.9920	
6.70	0.0012	0.0095	0.0371	0.0988	0.2022	0.3406	0.4953	0.6433	0.7673	0.8596	0.9214	0.9591	0.9801	0.9909	

$$Pr(X \leq x) = F(x;\lambda) = \sum_{x=0}^{n} \frac{\lambda^x}{x!} e^{-\lambda}$$

	Probability of less than or equal to x occurrences												
λ	14	15	16	17	18	19	20	21	22	23	24	25	λ
2.80	1.0000	1.0000	1.0000	1.0000	1.0000	1.0000	1.0000	1.0000	1.0000	1.0000	1.0000	1.0000	2.80
2.90	1.0000	1.0000	1.0000	1.0000	1.0000	1.0000	1.0000	1.0000	1.0000	1.0000	1.0000	1.0000	2.90
3.00	1.0000	1.0000	1.0000	1.0000	1.0000	1.0000	1.0000	1.0000	1.0000	1.0000	1.0000	1.0000	3.00
3.10	1.0000	1.0000	1.0000	1.0000	1.0000	1.0000	1.0000	1.0000	1.0000	1.0000	1.0000	1.0000	3.10
3.20	1.0000	1.0000	1.0000	1.0000	1.0000	1.0000	1.0000	1.0000	1.0000	1.0000	1.0000	1.0000	3.20
3.30	1.0000	1.0000	1.0000	1.0000	1.0000	1.0000	1.0000	1.0000	1.0000	1.0000	1.0000	1.0000	3.30
3.40	1.0000	1.0000	1.0000	1.0000	1.0000	1.0000	1.0000	1.0000	1.0000	1.0000	1.0000	1.0000	3.40
3.50	1.0000	1.0000	1.0000	1.0000	1.0000	1.0000	1.0000	1.0000	1.0000	1.0000	1.0000	1.0000	3.50
3.60	1.0000	1.0000	1.0000	1.0000	1.0000	1.0000	1.0000	1.0000	1.0000	1.0000	1.0000	1.0000	3.60
3.70	1.0000	1.0000	1.0000	1.0000	1.0000	1.0000	1.0000	1.0000	1.0000	1.0000	1.0000	1.0000	3.70
3.80	1.0000	1.0000	1.0000	1.0000	1.0000	1.0000	1.0000	1.0000	1.0000	1.0000	1.0000	1.0000	3.80
3.90	1.0000	1.0000	1.0000	1.0000	1.0000	1.0000	1.0000	1.0000	1.0000	1.0000	1.0000	1.0000	3.90
4.00	1.0000	1.0000	1.0000	1.0000	1.0000	1.0000	1.0000	1.0000	1.0000	1.0000	1.0000	1.0000	4.00
4.10	1.0000	1.0000	1.0000	1.0000	1.0000	1.0000	1.0000	1.0000	1.0000	1.0000	1.0000	1.0000	4.10
4.20	1.0000	1.0000	1.0000	1.0000	1.0000	1.0000	1.0000	1.0000	1.0000	1.0000	1.0000	1.0000	4.20
4.30	1.0000	1.0000	1.0000	1.0000	1.0000	1.0000	1.0000	1.0000	1.0000	1.0000	1.0000	1.0000	4.30
4.40	0.9999	1.0000	1.0000	1.0000	1.0000	1.0000	1.0000	1.0000	1.0000	1.0000	1.0000	1.0000	4.40
4.50	0.9999	1.0000	1.0000	1.0000	1.0000	1.0000	1.0000	1.0000	1.0000	1.0000	1.0000	1.0000	4.50
4.60	0.9999	1.0000	1.0000	1.0000	1.0000	1.0000	1.0000	1.0000	1.0000	1.0000	1.0000	1.0000	4.60
4.70	0.9999	1.0000	1.0000	1.0000	1.0000	1.0000	1.0000	1.0000	1.0000	1.0000	1.0000	1.0000	4.70
4.80	0.9999	1.0000	1.0000	1.0000	1.0000	1.0000	1.0000	1.0000	1.0000	1.0000	1.0000	1.0000	4.80
4.90	0.9998	0.9999	1.0000	1.0000	1.0000	1.0000	1.0000	1.0000	1.0000	1.0000	1.0000	1.0000	4.90
5.00	0.9998	0.9999	1.0000	1.0000	1.0000	1.0000	1.0000	1.0000	1.0000	1.0000	1.0000	1.0000	5.00
5.10	0.9997	0.9999	1.0000	1.0000	1.0000	1.0000	1.0000	1.0000	1.0000	1.0000	1.0000	1.0000	5.10
5.20	0.9997	0.9999	1.0000	1.0000	1.0000	1.0000	1.0000	1.0000	1.0000	1.0000	1.0000	1.0000	5.20
5.30	0.9996	0.9999	1.0000	1.0000	1.0000	1.0000	1.0000	1.0000	1.0000	1.0000	1.0000	1.0000	5.30
5.40	0.9995	0.9998	0.9999	1.0000	1.0000	1.0000	1.0000	1.0000	1.0000	1.0000	1.0000	1.0000	5.40
5.50	0.9994	0.9998	0.9999	1.0000	1.0000	1.0000	1.0000	1.0000	1.0000	1.0000	1.0000	1.0000	5.50
5.60	0.9993	0.9998	0.9999	1.0000	1.0000	1.0000	1.0000	1.0000	1.0000	1.0000	1.0000	1.0000	5.60
5.70	0.9991	0.9997	0.9999	1.0000	1.0000	1.0000	1.0000	1.0000	1.0000	1.0000	1.0000	1.0000	5.70
5.80	0.9990	0.9996	0.9999	1.0000	1.0000	1.0000	1.0000	1.0000	1.0000	1.0000	1.0000	1.0000	5.80
5.90	0.9988	0.9996	0.9999	1.0000	1.0000	1.0000	1.0000	1.0000	1.0000	1.0000	1.0000	1.0000	5.90
6.00	0.9986	0.9995	0.9998	0.9999	1.0000	1.0000	1.0000	1.0000	1.0000	1.0000	1.0000	1.0000	6.00
6.10	0.9984	0.9994	0.9998	0.9999	1.0000	1.0000	1.0000	1.0000	1.0000	1.0000	1.0000	1.0000	6.10
6.20	0.9981	0.9993	0.9997	0.9999	1.0000	1.0000	1.0000	1.0000	1.0000	1.0000	1.0000	1.0000	6.20
6.30	0.9978	0.9992	0.9997	0.9999	1.0000	1.0000	1.0000	1.0000	1.0000	1.0000	1.0000	1.0000	6.30
6.40	0.9974	0.9990	0.9996	0.9999	1.0000	1.0000	1.0000	1.0000	1.0000	1.0000	1.0000	1.0000	6.40
6.50	0.9970	0.9988	0.9996	0.9998	0.9999	1.0000	1.0000	1.0000	1.0000	1.0000	1.0000	1.0000	6.50
6.60	0.9966	0.9986	0.9995	0.9998	0.9999	1.0000	1.0000	1.0000	1.0000	1.0000	1.0000	1.0000	6.60
6.70	0.9961	0.9984	0.9994	0.9998	0.9999	1.0000	1.0000	1.0000	1.0000	1.0000	1.0000	1.0000	6.70

$$\Pr(X \le x) = F(x;\lambda) = \sum_{x=0}^{n} \frac{\lambda^{x}}{x!} e^{-\lambda}$$

λ	Probability of less than or equal to x occurrences													
	0	**1**	**2**	**3**	**4**	**5**	**6**	**7**	**8**	**9**	**10**	**11**	**12**	**13**
6.80	0.0011	0.0087	0.0344	0.0928	0.1920	0.3270	0.4799	0.6285	0.7548	0.8502	0.9151	0.9552	0.9779	0.9898
6.90	0.0010	0.0080	0.0320	0.0871	0.1823	0.3137	0.4647	0.6136	0.7420	0.8405	0.9084	0.9510	0.9755	0.9885
7.00	0.0009	0.0073	0.0296	0.0818	0.1730	0.3007	0.4497	0.5987	0.7291	0.8305	0.9015	0.9467	0.9730	0.9872
7.10	0.0008	0.0067	0.0275	0.0767	0.1641	0.2881	0.4349	0.5838	0.7160	0.8202	0.8942	0.9420	0.9703	0.9857
7.20	0.0007	0.0061	0.0255	0.0719	0.1555	0.2759	0.4204	0.5689	0.7027	0.8096	0.8867	0.9371	0.9673	0.9841
7.30	0.0007	0.0056	0.0236	0.0674	0.1473	0.2640	0.4060	0.5541	0.6892	0.7988	0.8788	0.9319	0.9642	0.9824
7.40	0.0006	0.0051	0.0219	0.0632	0.1395	0.2526	0.3920	0.5393	0.6757	0.7877	0.8707	0.9265	0.9609	0.9805
7.50	0.0006	0.0047	0.0203	0.0591	0.1321	0.2414	0.3782	0.5246	0.6620	0.7764	0.8622	0.9208	0.9573	0.9784
7.60	0.0005	0.0043	0.0188	0.0554	0.1249	0.2307	0.3646	0.5100	0.6482	0.7649	0.8535	0.9148	0.9536	0.9762
7.70	0.0005	0.0039	0.0174	0.0518	0.1181	0.2203	0.3514	0.4956	0.6343	0.7531	0.8445	0.9085	0.9496	0.9739
7.80	0.0004	0.0036	0.0161	0.0485	0.1117	0.2103	0.3384	0.4812	0.6204	0.7411	0.8352	0.9020	0.9454	0.9714
7.90	0.0004	0.0033	0.0149	0.0453	0.1055	0.2006	0.3257	0.4670	0.6065	0.7290	0.8257	0.8952	0.9409	0.9687
8.00	0.0003	0.0030	0.0138	0.0424	0.0996	0.1912	0.3134	0.4530	0.5925	0.7166	0.8159	0.8881	0.9362	0.9658
8.10	0.0003	0.0028	0.0127	0.0396	0.0940	0.1822	0.3013	0.4391	0.5786	0.7041	0.8058	0.8807	0.9313	0.9628
8.20	0.0003	0.0025	0.0118	0.0370	0.0887	0.1736	0.2896	0.4254	0.5647	0.6915	0.7955	0.8731	0.9261	0.9595
8.30	0.0002	0.0023	0.0109	0.0346	0.0837	0.1653	0.2781	0.4119	0.5507	0.6788	0.7850	0.8652	0.9207	0.9561
8.40	0.0002	0.0021	0.0100	0.0323	0.0789	0.1573	0.2670	0.3987	0.5369	0.6659	0.7743	0.8571	0.9150	0.9524
8.50	0.0002	0.0019	0.0093	0.0301	0.0744	0.1496	0.2562	0.3856	0.5231	0.6530	0.7634	0.8487	0.9091	0.9486
8.60	0.0002	0.0018	0.0086	0.0281	0.0701	0.1422	0.2457	0.3728	0.5094	0.6400	0.7522	0.8400	0.9029	0.9445
8.70	0.0002	0.0016	0.0079	0.0262	0.0660	0.1352	0.2355	0.3602	0.4958	0.6269	0.7409	0.8311	0.8965	0.9403
8.80	0.0002	0.0015	0.0073	0.0244	0.0621	0.1284	0.2256	0.3478	0.4823	0.6137	0.7294	0.8220	0.8898	0.9358
8.90	0.0001	0.0014	0.0068	0.0228	0.0584	0.1219	0.2160	0.3357	0.4689	0.6006	0.7178	0.8126	0.8829	0.9311
9.00	0.0001	0.0012	0.0062	0.0212	0.0550	0.1157	0.2068	0.3239	0.4557	0.5874	0.7060	0.8030	0.8758	0.9261
9.10	0.0001	0.0011	0.0058	0.0198	0.0517	0.1098	0.1978	0.3123	0.4426	0.5742	0.6941	0.7932	0.8684	0.9210
9.20	0.0001	0.0010	0.0053	0.0184	0.0486	0.1041	0.1892	0.3010	0.4296	0.5611	0.6820	0.7832	0.8607	0.9156
9.30	0.0001	0.0009	0.0049	0.0172	0.0456	0.0986	0.1808	0.2900	0.4168	0.5479	0.6699	0.7730	0.8529	0.9100
9.40	0.0001	0.0009	0.0045	0.0160	0.0429	0.0935	0.1727	0.2792	0.4042	0.5349	0.6576	0.7626	0.8448	0.9042
9.50	0.0001	0.0008	0.0042	0.0149	0.0403	0.0885	0.1649	0.2687	0.3918	0.5218	0.6453	0.7520	0.8364	0.8981
9.60	0.0001	0.0007	0.0038	0.0138	0.0378	0.0838	0.1574	0.2584	0.3796	0.5089	0.6329	0.7412	0.8279	0.8919
9.70	0.0001	0.0007	0.0035	0.0129	0.0355	0.0793	0.1502	0.2485	0.3676	0.4960	0.6205	0.7303	0.8191	0.8853
9.80	0.0001	0.0006	0.0033	0.0120	0.0333	0.0750	0.1433	0.2388	0.3558	0.4832	0.6080	0.7193	0.8101	0.8786
9.90	0.0001	0.0005	0.0030	0.0111	0.0312	0.0710	0.1366	0.2294	0.3442	0.4705	0.5955	0.7081	0.8009	0.8716
10.00	0.0000	0.0005	0.0028	0.0103	0.0293	0.0671	0.1301	0.2202	0.3328	0.4579	0.5830	0.6968	0.7916	0.8645

$$\Pr(X \le x) = F(x;\lambda) = \sum_{x=0}^{n} \frac{\lambda^x}{x!} e^{-\lambda}$$

λ	14	15	16	17	18	19	20	21	22	23	24	25	λ
	\multicolumn{12}{c}{Probability of less than or equal to x occurrences}	
6.80	0.9956	0.9982	0.9993	0.9997	0.9999	1.0000	1.0000	1.0000	1.0000	1.0000	1.0000	1.0000	6.80
6.90	0.9950	0.9979	0.9992	0.9997	0.9999	1.0000	1.0000	1.0000	1.0000	1.0000	1.0000	1.0000	6.90
7.00	0.9943	0.9976	0.9990	0.9996	0.9999	1.0000	1.0000	1.0000	1.0000	1.0000	1.0000	1.0000	7.00
7.10	0.9935	0.9972	0.9989	0.9996	0.9998	0.9999	1.0000	1.0000	1.0000	1.0000	1.0000	1.0000	7.10
7.20	0.9927	0.9969	0.9987	0.9995	0.9998	0.9999	1.0000	1.0000	1.0000	1.0000	1.0000	1.0000	7.20
7.30	0.9918	0.9964	0.9985	0.9994	0.9998	0.9999	1.0000	1.0000	1.0000	1.0000	1.0000	1.0000	7.30
7.40	0.9908	0.9959	0.9983	0.9993	0.9997	0.9999	1.0000	1.0000	1.0000	1.0000	1.0000	1.0000	7.40
7.50	0.9897	0.9954	0.9980	0.9992	0.9997	0.9999	1.0000	1.0000	1.0000	1.0000	1.0000	1.0000	7.50
7.60	0.9886	0.9948	0.9978	0.9991	0.9996	0.9999	1.0000	1.0000	1.0000	1.0000	1.0000	1.0000	7.60
7.70	0.9873	0.9941	0.9974	0.9989	0.9996	0.9998	0.9999	1.0000	1.0000	1.0000	1.0000	1.0000	7.70
7.80	0.9859	0.9934	0.9971	0.9988	0.9995	0.9998	0.9999	1.0000	1.0000	1.0000	1.0000	1.0000	7.80
7.90	0.9844	0.9926	0.9967	0.9986	0.9994	0.9998	0.9999	1.0000	1.0000	1.0000	1.0000	1.0000	7.90
8.00	0.9827	0.9918	0.9963	0.9984	0.9993	0.9997	0.9999	1.0000	1.0000	1.0000	1.0000	1.0000	8.00
8.10	0.9810	0.9908	0.9958	0.9982	0.9992	0.9997	0.9999	1.0000	1.0000	1.0000	1.0000	1.0000	8.10
8.20	0.9791	0.9898	0.9953	0.9979	0.9991	0.9997	0.9999	1.0000	1.0000	1.0000	1.0000	1.0000	8.20
8.30	0.9771	0.9887	0.9947	0.9977	0.9990	0.9996	0.9998	0.9999	1.0000	1.0000	1.0000	1.0000	8.30
8.40	0.9749	0.9875	0.9941	0.9973	0.9989	0.9995	0.9998	0.9999	1.0000	1.0000	1.0000	1.0000	8.40
8.50	0.9726	0.9862	0.9934	0.9970	0.9987	0.9995	0.9998	0.9999	1.0000	1.0000	1.0000	1.0000	8.50
8.60	0.9701	0.9848	0.9926	0.9966	0.9985	0.9994	0.9998	0.9999	1.0000	1.0000	1.0000	1.0000	8.60
8.70	0.9675	0.9832	0.9918	0.9962	0.9983	0.9993	0.9997	0.9999	1.0000	1.0000	1.0000	1.0000	8.70
8.80	0.9647	0.9816	0.9909	0.9957	0.9981	0.9992	0.9997	0.9999	1.0000	1.0000	1.0000	1.0000	8.80
8.90	0.9617	0.9798	0.9899	0.9952	0.9978	0.9991	0.9996	0.9998	0.9999	1.0000	1.0000	1.0000	8.90
9.00	0.9585	0.9780	0.9889	0.9947	0.9976	0.9989	0.9996	0.9998	0.9999	1.0000	1.0000	1.0000	9.00
9.10	0.9552	0.9760	0.9878	0.9941	0.9973	0.9988	0.9995	0.9998	0.9999	1.0000	1.0000	1.0000	9.10
9.20	0.9517	0.9738	0.9865	0.9934	0.9969	0.9986	0.9994	0.9998	0.9999	1.0000	1.0000	1.0000	9.20
9.30	0.9480	0.9715	0.9852	0.9927	0.9966	0.9985	0.9993	0.9997	0.9999	1.0000	1.0000	1.0000	9.30
9.40	0.9441	0.9691	0.9838	0.9919	0.9962	0.9983	0.9992	0.9997	0.9999	1.0000	1.0000	1.0000	9.40
9.50	0.9400	0.9665	0.9823	0.9911	0.9957	0.9980	0.9991	0.9996	0.9999	0.9999	1.0000	1.0000	9.50
9.60	0.9357	0.9638	0.9806	0.9902	0.9952	0.9978	0.9990	0.9996	0.9998	0.9999	1.0000	1.0000	9.60
9.70	0.9312	0.9609	0.9789	0.9892	0.9947	0.9975	0.9989	0.9995	0.9998	0.9999	1.0000	1.0000	9.70
9.80	0.9265	0.9579	0.9770	0.9881	0.9941	0.9972	0.9987	0.9995	0.9998	0.9999	1.0000	1.0000	9.80
9.90	0.9216	0.9546	0.9751	0.9870	0.9935	0.9969	0.9986	0.9994	0.9997	0.9999	1.0000	1.0000	9.90
10.00	0.9165	0.9513	0.9730	0.9857	0.9928	0.9965	0.9984	0.9993	0.9997	0.9999	1.0000	1.0000	10.00

Appendix 12

Standard Normal Distribution Table

$$Pr(Z \geq z) = 1 - \Phi(Z \leq z) = \int_{z}^{\infty} \frac{1}{\sqrt{2\pi}} e^{-\mu^2/2} d\mu$$

Z	0.00	0.01	0.02	0.03	0.04	0.05	0.06	0.07	0.08	0.09	Z
0.0	0.5000	0.4960	0.4920	0.4880	0.4840	0.4801	0.4761	0.4721	0.4681	0.4641	0.0
0.1	0.4602	0.4562	0.4522	0.4483	0.4443	0.4404	0.4364	0.4325	0.4286	0.4247	0.1
0.2	0.4207	0.4168	0.4129	0.4090	0.4052	0.4013	0.3974	0.3936	0.3897	0.3859	0.2
0.3	0.3821	0.3783	0.3745	0.3707	0.3669	0.3632	0.3594	0.3557	0.3520	0.3483	0.3
0.4	0.3446	0.3409	0.3372	0.3336	0.3300	0.3264	0.3228	0.3192	0.3156	0.3121	0.4
0.5	0.3085	0.3050	0.3015	0.2981	0.2946	0.2912	0.2877	0.2843	0.2810	0.2776	0.5
0.6	0.2743	0.2709	0.2676	0.2643	0.2611	0.2578	0.2546	0.2514	0.2483	0.2451	0.6
0.7	0.2420	0.2389	0.2358	0.2327	0.2296	0.2266	0.2236	0.2206	0.2177	0.2148	0.7
0.8	0.2119	0.2090	0.2061	0.2033	0.2005	0.1977	0.1949	0.1922	0.1894	0.1867	0.8
0.9	0.1841	0.1814	0.1788	0.1762	0.1736	0.1711	0.1685	0.1660	0.1635	0.1611	0.9
1.0	0.1587	0.1562	0.1539	0.1515	0.1492	0.1469	0.1446	0.1423	0.1401	0.1379	1.0
1.1	0.1357	0.1335	0.1314	0.1292	0.1271	0.1251	0.1230	0.1210	0.1190	0.1170	1.1
1.2	0.1151	0.1131	0.1112	0.1093	0.1075	0.1056	0.1038	0.1020	0.1003	0.0985	1.2
1.3	0.0968	0.0951	0.0934	0.0918	0.0901	0.0885	0.0869	0.0853	0.0838	0.0823	1.3
1.4	0.0808	0.0793	0.0778	0.0764	0.0749	0.0735	0.0721	0.0708	0.0694	0.0681	1.4
1.5	0.0668	0.0655	0.0643	0.0630	0.0618	0.0606	0.0594	0.0582	0.0571	0.0559	1.5
1.6	0.0548	0.0537	0.0526	0.0516	0.0505	0.0495	0.0485	0.0475	0.0465	0.0455	1.6
1.7	0.0446	0.0436	0.0427	0.0418	0.0409	0.0401	0.0392	0.0384	0.0375	0.0367	1.7
1.8	0.0359	0.0351	0.0344	0.0336	0.0329	0.0322	0.0314	0.0307	0.0301	0.0294	1.8
1.9	0.0287	0.0281	0.0274	0.0268	0.0262	0.0256	0.0250	0.0244	0.0239	0.0233	1.9
2.0	0.0228	0.0222	0.0217	0.0212	0.0207	0.0202	0.0197	0.0192	0.0188	0.0183	2.0
2.1	0.0179	0.0174	0.0170	0.0166	0.0162	0.0158	0.0154	0.0150	0.0146	0.0143	2.1
2.2	0.0139	0.0136	0.0132	0.0129	0.0125	0.0122	0.0119	0.0116	0.0113	0.0110	2.2

$$\Pr(Z \geq z) = 1 - \Phi(Z \leq z) = \int_z^\infty \frac{1}{\sqrt{2\pi}} e^{-\mu^2/2} d\mu$$

Z	0.00	0.01	0.02	0.03	0.04	0.05	0.06	0.07	0.08	0.09	Z
2.3	0.0107	0.0104	0.0102	0.0099	0.0096	0.0094	0.0091	0.0089	0.0087	0.0084	2.3
2.4	0.0082	0.0080	0.0078	0.0075	0.0073	0.0071	0.0069	0.0068	0.0066	0.0064	2.4
2.5	0.0062	0.0060	0.0059	0.0057	0.0055	0.0054	0.0052	0.0051	0.0049	0.0048	2.5
2.6	0.0047	0.0045	0.0044	0.0043	0.0041	0.0040	0.0039	0.0038	0.0037	0.0036	2.6
2.7	0.0035	0.0034	0.0033	0.0032	0.0031	0.0030	0.0029	0.0028	0.0027	0.0026	2.7
2.8	0.0026	0.0025	0.0024	0.0023	0.0023	0.0022	0.0021	0.0021	0.0020	0.0019	2.8
2.9	0.0019	0.0018	0.0018	0.0017	0.0016	0.0016	0.0015	0.0015	0.0014	0.0014	2.9
3.0	0.0013	0.0013	0.0013	0.0012	0.0012	0.0011	0.0011	0.0011	0.0010	0.0010	3.0
3.1	0.00097	0.00094	0.00090	0.00087	0.00084	0.00082	0.00079	0.00076	0.00074	0.00071	3.1
3.2	0.00069	0.00066	0.00064	0.00062	0.00060	0.00058	0.00056	0.00054	0.00052	0.00050	3.2
3.3	0.00048	0.00047	0.00045	0.00043	0.00042	0.00040	0.00039	0.00038	0.00036	0.00035	3.3
3.4	0.00034	0.00032	0.00031	0.00030	0.00029	0.00028	0.00027	0.00026	0.00025	0.00024	3.4
3.5	0.00023	0.00022	0.00022	0.00021	0.00020	0.00019	0.00019	0.00018	0.00017	0.00017	3.5
3.6	0.00016	0.00015	0.00015	0.00014	0.00014	0.00013	0.00013	0.00012	0.00012	0.00011	3.6
3.7	0.00011	0.00010	0.00010	0.00010	0.00009	0.00009	0.00008	0.00008	0.00008	0.00008	3.7
3.8	0.00007	0.00007	0.00007	0.00006	0.00006	0.00006	0.00006	0.00005	0.00005	0.00005	3.8
3.9	0.00005	0.00005	0.00004	0.00004	0.00004	0.00004	0.00004	0.00004	0.00003	0.00003	3.9
4.0	0.00003	0.00003	0.00003	0.00003	0.00003	0.00003	0.00002	0.00002	0.00002	0.00002	4.0
4.1	0.00002	0.00002	0.00002	0.00002	0.00002	0.00002	0.00002	0.00002	0.00001	0.00001	4.1
4.2	0.00001	0.00001	0.00001	0.00001	0.00001	0.00001	0.00001	0.00001	0.00001	0.00001	4.2
4.3	0.00001	0.00001	0.00001	0.00001	0.00001	0.00001	0.00001	0.00001	0.00001	0.00001	4.3
4.4	0.000005	0.000005	0.000005	0.000005	0.000004	0.000004	0.000004	0.000004	0.000004	0.000004	4.4
4.5	0.000003	0.000003	0.000003	0.000003	0.000003	0.000003	0.000003	0.000002	0.000002	0.000002	4.5
4.6	0.000002	0.000002	0.000002	0.000002	0.000002	0.000002	0.000002	0.000002	0.000001	0.000001	4.6
4.7	0.000001	0.000001	0.000001	0.000001	0.000001	0.000001	0.000001	0.000001	0.000001	0.000001	4.7
4.8	0.000001	0.000001	0.000001	0.000001	0.000001	0.000001	0.000001	0.000001	0.000001	0.000001	4.8
4.9	0.000000	0.000000	0.000000	0.000000	0.000000	0.000000	0.000000	0.000000	0.000000	0.000000	4.9
5.0	0.000000	0.000000	0.000000	0.000000	0.000000	0.000000	0.000000	0.000000	0.000000	0.000000	5.0
5.1	0.000000	0.000000	0.000000	0.000000	0.000000	0.000000	0.000000	0.000000	0.000000	0.000000	5.1
5.2	0.000000	0.000000	0.000000	0.000000	0.000000	0.000000	0.000000	0.000000	0.000000	0.000000	5.2
5.3	0.000000	0.000000	0.000000	0.000000	0.000000	0.000000	0.000000	0.000000	0.000000	0.000000	5.3
5.4	0.000000	0.000000	0.000000	0.000000	0.000000	0.000000	0.000000	0.000000	0.000000	0.000000	5.4
5.5	0.000000	0.000000	0.000000	0.000000	0.000000	0.000000	0.000000	0.000000	0.000000	0.000000	5.5

Appendix 12

$$\Pr(Z \ge z) = 1 - \Phi\left(Z \le z\right) = \int_{z}^{\infty} \frac{1}{\sqrt{2\pi}} e^{-\mu^2/2} d\mu$$

Z	0.00	0.01	0.02	0.03	0.04	0.05	0.06	0.07	0.08	0.09	Z
5.6	0.000000	0.000000	0.000000	0.000000	0.000000	0.000000	0.000000	0.000000	0.000000	0.000000	5.6
5.7	0.000000	0.000000	0.000000	0.000000	0.000000	0.000000	0.000000	0.000000	0.000000	0.000000	5.7
5.8	0.000000	0.000000	0.000000	0.000000	0.000000	0.000000	0.000000	0.000000	0.000000	0.000000	5.8
5.9	0.000000	0.000000	0.000000	0.000000	0.000000	0.000000	0.000000	0.000000	0.000000	0.000000	5.9
6.0	0.000000	0.000000	0.000000	0.000000	0.000000	0.000000	0.000000	0.000000	0.000000	0.000000	6.0

Appendix 12

Appendix 13

Cumulative Standard Normal Distribution Table

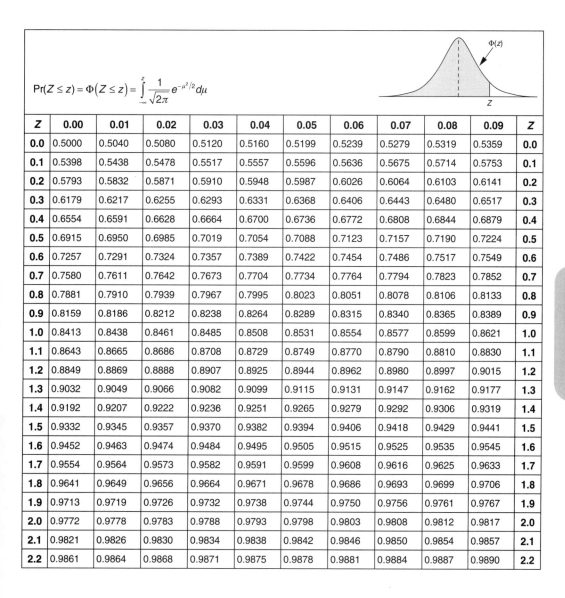

$$Pr(Z \le z) = \Phi(Z \le z) = \int_{-\infty}^{z} \frac{1}{\sqrt{2\pi}} e^{-\mu^2/2} d\mu$$

Z	0.00	0.01	0.02	0.03	0.04	0.05	0.06	0.07	0.08	0.09	Z
0.0	0.5000	0.5040	0.5080	0.5120	0.5160	0.5199	0.5239	0.5279	0.5319	0.5359	0.0
0.1	0.5398	0.5438	0.5478	0.5517	0.5557	0.5596	0.5636	0.5675	0.5714	0.5753	0.1
0.2	0.5793	0.5832	0.5871	0.5910	0.5948	0.5987	0.6026	0.6064	0.6103	0.6141	0.2
0.3	0.6179	0.6217	0.6255	0.6293	0.6331	0.6368	0.6406	0.6443	0.6480	0.6517	0.3
0.4	0.6554	0.6591	0.6628	0.6664	0.6700	0.6736	0.6772	0.6808	0.6844	0.6879	0.4
0.5	0.6915	0.6950	0.6985	0.7019	0.7054	0.7088	0.7123	0.7157	0.7190	0.7224	0.5
0.6	0.7257	0.7291	0.7324	0.7357	0.7389	0.7422	0.7454	0.7486	0.7517	0.7549	0.6
0.7	0.7580	0.7611	0.7642	0.7673	0.7704	0.7734	0.7764	0.7794	0.7823	0.7852	0.7
0.8	0.7881	0.7910	0.7939	0.7967	0.7995	0.8023	0.8051	0.8078	0.8106	0.8133	0.8
0.9	0.8159	0.8186	0.8212	0.8238	0.8264	0.8289	0.8315	0.8340	0.8365	0.8389	0.9
1.0	0.8413	0.8438	0.8461	0.8485	0.8508	0.8531	0.8554	0.8577	0.8599	0.8621	1.0
1.1	0.8643	0.8665	0.8686	0.8708	0.8729	0.8749	0.8770	0.8790	0.8810	0.8830	1.1
1.2	0.8849	0.8869	0.8888	0.8907	0.8925	0.8944	0.8962	0.8980	0.8997	0.9015	1.2
1.3	0.9032	0.9049	0.9066	0.9082	0.9099	0.9115	0.9131	0.9147	0.9162	0.9177	1.3
1.4	0.9192	0.9207	0.9222	0.9236	0.9251	0.9265	0.9279	0.9292	0.9306	0.9319	1.4
1.5	0.9332	0.9345	0.9357	0.9370	0.9382	0.9394	0.9406	0.9418	0.9429	0.9441	1.5
1.6	0.9452	0.9463	0.9474	0.9484	0.9495	0.9505	0.9515	0.9525	0.9535	0.9545	1.6
1.7	0.9554	0.9564	0.9573	0.9582	0.9591	0.9599	0.9608	0.9616	0.9625	0.9633	1.7
1.8	0.9641	0.9649	0.9656	0.9664	0.9671	0.9678	0.9686	0.9693	0.9699	0.9706	1.8
1.9	0.9713	0.9719	0.9726	0.9732	0.9738	0.9744	0.9750	0.9756	0.9761	0.9767	1.9
2.0	0.9772	0.9778	0.9783	0.9788	0.9793	0.9798	0.9803	0.9808	0.9812	0.9817	2.0
2.1	0.9821	0.9826	0.9830	0.9834	0.9838	0.9842	0.9846	0.9850	0.9854	0.9857	2.1
2.2	0.9861	0.9864	0.9868	0.9871	0.9875	0.9878	0.9881	0.9884	0.9887	0.9890	2.2

$$\Pr(Z \le z) = \Phi\left(Z \le z\right) = \int_{-\infty}^{z} \frac{1}{\sqrt{2\pi}} e^{-\mu^2/2} d\mu$$

Z	0.00	0.01	0.02	0.03	0.04	0.05	0.06	0.07	0.08	0.09	Z
2.3	0.9893	0.9896	0.9898	0.9901	0.9904	0.9906	0.9909	0.9911	0.9913	0.9916	2.3
2.4	0.9918	0.9920	0.9922	0.9925	0.9927	0.9929	0.9931	0.9932	0.9934	0.9936	2.4
2.5	0.9938	0.9940	0.9941	0.9943	0.9945	0.9946	0.9948	0.9949	0.9951	0.9952	2.5
2.6	0.9953	0.9955	0.9956	0.9957	0.9959	0.9960	0.9961	0.9962	0.9963	0.9964	2.6
2.7	0.9965	0.9966	0.9967	0.9968	0.9969	0.9970	0.9971	0.9972	0.9973	0.9974	2.7
2.8	0.9974	0.9975	0.9976	0.9977	0.9977	0.9978	0.9979	0.9979	0.9980	0.9981	2.8
2.9	0.9981	0.9982	0.9982	0.9983	0.9984	0.9984	0.9985	0.9985	0.9986	0.9986	2.9
3.0	0.9987	0.9987	0.9987	0.9988	0.9988	0.9989	0.9989	0.9989	0.9990	0.9990	3.0
3.1	0.99903	0.99906	0.99910	0.99913	0.99916	0.99918	0.99921	0.99924	0.99926	0.99929	3.1
3.2	0.99931	0.99934	0.99936	0.99938	0.99940	0.99942	0.99944	0.99946	0.99948	0.99950	3.2
3.3	0.99952	0.99953	0.99955	0.99957	0.99958	0.99960	0.99961	0.99962	0.99964	0.99965	3.3
3.4	0.99966	0.99968	0.99969	0.99970	0.99971	0.99972	0.99973	0.99974	0.99975	0.99976	3.4
3.5	0.99977	0.99978	0.99978	0.99979	0.99980	0.99981	0.99981	0.99982	0.99983	0.99983	3.5
3.6	0.99984	0.99985	0.99985	0.99986	0.99986	0.99987	0.99987	0.99988	0.99988	0.99989	3.6
3.7	0.99989	0.99990	0.99990	0.99990	0.99991	0.99991	0.99992	0.99992	0.99992	0.99992	3.7
3.8	0.99993	0.99993	0.99993	0.99994	0.99994	0.99994	0.99994	0.99995	0.99995	0.99995	3.8
3.9	0.99995	0.99995	0.99996	0.99996	0.99996	0.99996	0.99996	0.99996	0.99997	0.99997	3.9
4.0	0.99997	0.99997	0.99997	0.99997	0.99997	0.99997	0.99998	0.99998	0.99998	0.99998	4.0
4.1	0.99998	0.99998	0.99998	0.99998	0.99998	0.99998	0.99998	0.99998	0.99999	0.99999	4.1
4.2	0.99999	0.99999	0.99999	0.99999	0.99999	0.99999	0.99999	0.99999	0.99999	0.99999	4.2
4.3	0.99999	0.99999	0.99999	0.99999	0.99999	0.99999	0.99999	0.99999	0.99999	0.99999	4.3
4.4	0.999995	0.999995	0.999995	0.999995	0.999996	0.999996	0.999996	0.999996	0.999996	0.999996	4.4
4.5	0.999997	0.999997	0.999997	0.999997	0.999997	0.999997	0.999997	0.999998	0.999998	0.999998	4.5
4.6	0.999998	0.999998	0.999998	0.999998	0.999998	0.999998	0.999998	0.999998	0.999999	0.999999	4.6
4.7	0.999999	0.999999	0.999999	0.999999	0.999999	0.999999	0.999999	0.999999	0.999999	0.999999	4.7
4.8	0.999999	0.999999	0.999999	0.999999	0.999999	0.999999	0.999999	0.999999	0.999999	0.999999	4.8
4.9	1.000000	1.000000	1.000000	1.000000	1.000000	1.000000	1.000000	1.000000	1.000000	1.000000	4.9
5.0	1.000000	1.000000	1.000000	1.000000	1.000000	1.000000	1.000000	1.000000	1.000000	1.000000	5.0
5.1	1.000000	1.000000	1.000000	1.000000	1.000000	1.000000	1.000000	1.000000	1.000000	1.000000	5.1
5.2	1.000000	1.000000	1.000000	1.000000	1.000000	1.000000	1.000000	1.000000	1.000000	1.000000	5.2
5.3	1.000000	1.000000	1.000000	1.000000	1.000000	1.000000	1.000000	1.000000	1.000000	1.000000	5.3
5.4	1.000000	1.000000	1.000000	1.000000	1.000000	1.000000	1.000000	1.000000	1.000000	1.000000	5.4
5.5	1.000000	1.000000	1.000000	1.000000	1.000000	1.000000	1.000000	1.000000	1.000000	1.000000	5.5

Appendix 13

$$Pr(Z \le z) = \Phi(Z \le z) = \int_{-\infty}^{z} \frac{1}{\sqrt{2\pi}} e^{-\mu^2/2} d\mu$$

Z	0.00	0.01	0.02	0.03	0.04	0.05	0.06	0.07	0.08	0.09	Z
5.6	1.000000	1.000000	1.000000	1.000000	1.000000	1.000000	1.000000	1.000000	1.000000	1.000000	5.6
5.7	1.000000	1.000000	1.000000	1.000000	1.000000	1.000000	1.000000	1.000000	1.000000	1.000000	5.7
5.8	1.000000	1.000000	1.000000	1.000000	1.000000	1.000000	1.000000	1.000000	1.000000	1.000000	5.8
5.9	1.000000	1.000000	1.000000	1.000000	1.000000	1.000000	1.000000	1.000000	1.000000	1.000000	5.9
6.0	1.000000	1.000000	1.000000	1.000000	1.000000	1.000000	1.000000	1.000000	1.000000	1.000000	6.0

Appendix 14

t Distribution Table

	α					
ν	0.10	0.05	0.025	0.01	0.005	*ν*
1	3.078	6.314	12.706	31.821	63.657	1
2	1.886	2.920	4.303	6.965	9.925	2
3	1.638	2.353	3.182	4.541	5.841	3
4	1.533	2.132	2.776	3.747	4.604	4
5	1.476	2.015	2.571	3.365	4.032	5
6	1.440	1.943	2.447	3.143	3.707	6
7	1.415	1.895	2.365	2.998	3.499	7
8	1.397	1.860	2.306	2.896	3.355	8
9	1.383	1.833	2.262	2.821	3.250	9
10	1.372	1.812	2.228	2.764	3.169	10
11	1.363	1.796	2.201	2.718	3.106	11
12	1.356	1.782	2.179	2.681	3.055	12
13	1.350	1.771	2.160	2.650	3.012	13
14	1.345	1.761	2.145	2.624	2.977	14
15	1.341	1.753	2.131	2.602	2.947	15
16	1.337	1.746	2.120	2.583	2.921	16
17	1.333	1.740	2.110	2.567	2.898	17
18	1.330	1.734	2.101	2.552	2.878	18
19	1.328	1.729	2.093	2.539	2.861	19
20	1.325	1.725	2.086	2.528	2.845	20
21	1.323	1.721	2.080	2.518	2.831	21
22	1.321	1.717	2.074	2.508	2.819	22
23	1.319	1.714	2.069	2.500	2.807	23
24	1.318	1.711	2.064	2.492	2.797	24

	α					
ν	0.10	0.05	0.025	0.01	0.005	ν
25	1.316	1.708	2.060	2.485	2.787	25
26	1.315	1.706	2.056	2.479	2.779	26
27	1.314	1.703	2.052	2.473	2.771	27
28	1.313	1.701	2.048	2.467	2.763	28
29	1.311	1.699	2.045	2.462	2.756	29
30	1.310	1.697	2.042	2.457	2.750	30
40	1.303	1.684	2.021	2.423	2.704	40
50	1.299	1.676	2.009	2.403	2.678	50
60	1.296	1.671	2.000	2.390	2.660	60
70	1.294	1.667	1.994	2.381	2.648	70
80	1.292	1.664	1.990	2.374	2.639	80
90	1.291	1.662	1.987	2.368	2.632	90
100	1.290	1.660	1.984	2.364	2.626	100
120	1.289	1.658	1.980	2.358	2.617	120
∞	1.282	1.645	1.960	2.326	2.576	∞

Appendix 14

Appendix 15
Chi-Square Distribution Table

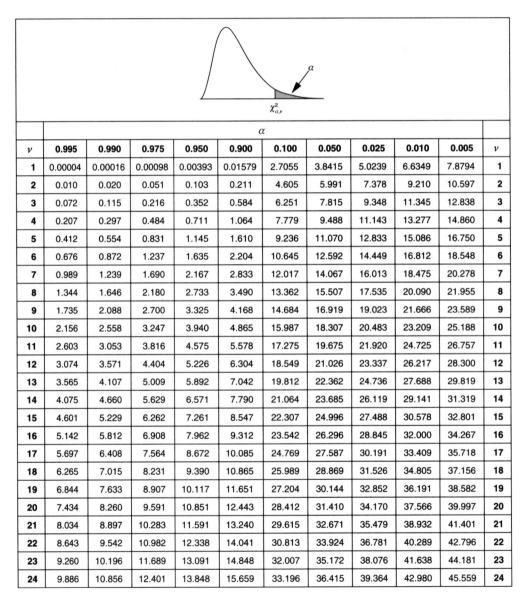

					α						
ν	0.995	0.990	0.975	0.950	0.900	0.100	0.050	0.025	0.010	0.005	ν
1	0.00004	0.00016	0.00098	0.00393	0.01579	2.7055	3.8415	5.0239	6.6349	7.8794	1
2	0.010	0.020	0.051	0.103	0.211	4.605	5.991	7.378	9.210	10.597	2
3	0.072	0.115	0.216	0.352	0.584	6.251	7.815	9.348	11.345	12.838	3
4	0.207	0.297	0.484	0.711	1.064	7.779	9.488	11.143	13.277	14.860	4
5	0.412	0.554	0.831	1.145	1.610	9.236	11.070	12.833	15.086	16.750	5
6	0.676	0.872	1.237	1.635	2.204	10.645	12.592	14.449	16.812	18.548	6
7	0.989	1.239	1.690	2.167	2.833	12.017	14.067	16.013	18.475	20.278	7
8	1.344	1.646	2.180	2.733	3.490	13.362	15.507	17.535	20.090	21.955	8
9	1.735	2.088	2.700	3.325	4.168	14.684	16.919	19.023	21.666	23.589	9
10	2.156	2.558	3.247	3.940	4.865	15.987	18.307	20.483	23.209	25.188	10
11	2.603	3.053	3.816	4.575	5.578	17.275	19.675	21.920	24.725	26.757	11
12	3.074	3.571	4.404	5.226	6.304	18.549	21.026	23.337	26.217	28.300	12
13	3.565	4.107	5.009	5.892	7.042	19.812	22.362	24.736	27.688	29.819	13
14	4.075	4.660	5.629	6.571	7.790	21.064	23.685	26.119	29.141	31.319	14
15	4.601	5.229	6.262	7.261	8.547	22.307	24.996	27.488	30.578	32.801	15
16	5.142	5.812	6.908	7.962	9.312	23.542	26.296	28.845	32.000	34.267	16
17	5.697	6.408	7.564	8.672	10.085	24.769	27.587	30.191	33.409	35.718	17
18	6.265	7.015	8.231	9.390	10.865	25.989	28.869	31.526	34.805	37.156	18
19	6.844	7.633	8.907	10.117	11.651	27.204	30.144	32.852	36.191	38.582	19
20	7.434	8.260	9.591	10.851	12.443	28.412	31.410	34.170	37.566	39.997	20
21	8.034	8.897	10.283	11.591	13.240	29.615	32.671	35.479	38.932	41.401	21
22	8.643	9.542	10.982	12.338	14.041	30.813	33.924	36.781	40.289	42.796	22
23	9.260	10.196	11.689	13.091	14.848	32.007	35.172	38.076	41.638	44.181	23
24	9.886	10.856	12.401	13.848	15.659	33.196	36.415	39.364	42.980	45.559	24

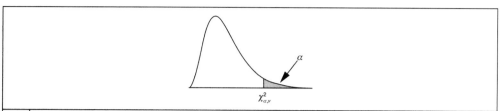

v	0.995	0.990	0.975	0.950	0.900	0.100	0.050	0.025	0.010	0.005	v
25	10.520	11.524	13.120	14.611	16.473	34.382	37.652	40.646	44.314	46.928	25
26	11.160	12.198	13.844	15.379	17.292	35.563	38.885	41.923	45.642	48.290	26
27	11.808	12.879	14.573	16.151	18.114	36.741	40.113	43.195	46.963	49.645	27
28	12.461	13.565	15.308	16.928	18.939	37.916	41.337	44.461	48.278	50.993	28
29	13.121	14.256	16.047	17.708	19.768	39.087	42.557	45.722	49.588	52.336	29
30	13.787	14.953	16.791	18.493	20.599	40.256	43.773	46.979	50.892	53.672	30
35	17.192	18.509	20.569	22.465	24.797	46.059	49.802	53.203	57.342	60.275	35
40	20.707	22.164	24.433	26.509	29.051	51.805	55.758	59.342	63.691	66.766	40
45	24.311	25.901	28.366	30.612	33.350	57.505	61.656	65.410	69.957	73.166	45
50	27.991	29.707	32.357	34.764	37.689	63.167	67.505	71.420	76.154	79.490	50
55	31.735	33.570	36.398	38.958	42.060	68.796	73.311	77.380	82.292	85.749	55
60	35.534	37.485	40.482	43.188	46.459	74.397	79.082	83.298	88.379	91.952	60
65	39.383	41.444	44.603	47.450	50.883	79.973	84.821	89.177	94.422	98.105	65
70	43.275	45.442	48.758	51.739	55.329	85.527	90.531	95.023	100.425	104.215	70
75	47.206	49.475	52.942	56.054	59.795	91.061	96.217	100.839	106.393	110.286	75
80	51.172	53.540	57.153	60.391	64.278	96.578	101.879	106.629	112.329	116.321	80
85	55.170	57.634	61.389	64.749	68.777	102.079	107.522	112.393	118.236	122.325	85
90	59.196	61.754	65.647	69.126	73.291	107.565	113.145	118.136	124.116	128.299	90
95	63.250	65.898	69.925	73.520	77.818	113.038	118.752	123.858	129.973	134.247	95
100	67.328	70.065	74.222	77.929	82.358	118.498	124.342	129.561	135.807	140.169	100

Appendix 16
F(0.99) Distribution Table

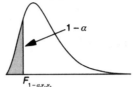

Degrees of freedom for the numerator

(v_1)

Degrees of freedom for the denominator

(v_2)	1	2	3	4	5	6	7	8	9	10	11	12	13	14	15	16	17	(v_2)
1	0.00	0.01	0.03	0.05	0.06	0.07	0.08	0.09	0.09	0.10	0.10	0.11	0.11	0.11	0.12	0.12	0.12	1
2	0.00	0.01	0.03	0.06	0.08	0.09	0.10	0.12	0.12	0.13	0.14	0.14	0.15	0.15	0.16	0.16	0.16	2
3	0.00	0.01	0.03	0.06	0.08	0.10	0.12	0.13	0.14	0.15	0.16	0.17	0.17	0.18	0.18	0.19	0.19	3
4	0.00	0.01	0.03	0.06	0.09	0.11	0.13	0.14	0.16	0.17	0.18	0.18	0.19	0.20	0.20	0.21	0.21	4
5	0.00	0.01	0.04	0.06	0.09	0.11	0.13	0.15	0.17	0.18	0.19	0.20	0.21	0.21	0.22	0.23	0.23	5
6	0.00	0.01	0.04	0.07	0.09	0.12	0.14	0.16	0.17	0.19	0.20	0.21	0.22	0.22	0.23	0.24	0.24	6
7	0.00	0.01	0.04	0.07	0.10	0.12	0.14	0.16	0.18	0.19	0.20	0.22	0.23	0.23	0.24	0.25	0.25	7
8	0.00	0.01	0.04	0.07	0.10	0.12	0.15	0.17	0.18	0.20	0.21	0.22	0.23	0.24	0.25	0.26	0.26	8
9	0.00	0.01	0.04	0.07	0.10	0.13	0.15	0.17	0.19	0.20	0.22	0.23	0.24	0.25	0.26	0.26	0.27	9
10	0.00	0.01	0.04	0.07	0.10	0.13	0.15	0.17	0.19	0.21	0.22	0.23	0.24	0.25	0.26	0.27	0.28	10
11	0.00	0.01	0.04	0.07	0.10	0.13	0.15	0.17	0.19	0.21	0.22	0.24	0.25	0.26	0.27	0.28	0.28	11
12	0.00	0.01	0.04	0.07	0.10	0.13	0.15	0.18	0.20	0.21	0.23	0.24	0.25	0.26	0.27	0.28	0.29	12
13	0.00	0.01	0.04	0.07	0.10	0.13	0.16	0.18	0.20	0.22	0.23	0.24	0.26	0.27	0.28	0.29	0.29	13
14	0.00	0.01	0.04	0.07	0.10	0.13	0.16	0.18	0.20	0.22	0.23	0.25	0.26	0.27	0.28	0.29	0.30	14
15	0.00	0.01	0.04	0.07	0.10	0.13	0.16	0.18	0.20	0.22	0.24	0.25	0.26	0.27	0.28	0.29	0.30	15
16	0.00	0.01	0.04	0.07	0.10	0.13	0.16	0.18	0.20	0.22	0.24	0.25	0.26	0.28	0.29	0.30	0.31	16
17	0.00	0.01	0.04	0.07	0.10	0.13	0.16	0.18	0.20	0.22	0.24	0.25	0.27	0.28	0.29	0.30	0.31	17
18	0.00	0.01	0.04	0.07	0.10	0.13	0.16	0.18	0.21	0.22	0.24	0.26	0.27	0.28	0.29	0.30	0.31	18
19	0.00	0.01	0.04	0.07	0.10	0.13	0.16	0.19	0.21	0.23	0.24	0.26	0.27	0.28	0.29	0.30	0.31	19
20	0.00	0.01	0.04	0.07	0.10	0.14	0.16	0.19	0.21	0.23	0.24	0.26	0.27	0.29	0.30	0.31	0.32	20
21	0.00	0.01	0.04	0.07	0.10	0.14	0.16	0.19	0.21	0.23	0.25	0.26	0.27	0.29	0.30	0.31	0.32	21
22	0.00	0.01	0.04	0.07	0.11	0.14	0.16	0.19	0.21	0.23	0.25	0.26	0.28	0.29	0.30	0.31	0.32	22
23	0.00	0.01	0.04	0.07	0.11	0.14	0.16	0.19	0.21	0.23	0.25	0.26	0.28	0.29	0.30	0.31	0.32	23
24	0.00	0.01	0.04	0.07	0.11	0.14	0.16	0.19	0.21	0.23	0.25	0.26	0.28	0.29	0.30	0.31	0.32	24
25	0.00	0.01	0.04	0.07	0.11	0.14	0.17	0.19	0.21	0.23	0.25	0.27	0.28	0.29	0.31	0.32	0.33	25
26	0.00	0.01	0.04	0.07	0.11	0.14	0.17	0.19	0.21	0.23	0.25	0.27	0.28	0.29	0.31	0.32	0.33	26
27	0.00	0.01	0.04	0.07	0.11	0.14	0.17	0.19	0.21	0.23	0.25	0.27	0.28	0.30	0.31	0.32	0.33	27
28	0.00	0.01	0.04	0.07	0.11	0.14	0.17	0.19	0.21	0.23	0.25	0.27	0.28	0.30	0.31	0.32	0.33	28
29	0.00	0.01	0.04	0.07	0.11	0.14	0.17	0.19	0.21	0.23	0.25	0.27	0.28	0.30	0.31	0.32	0.33	29
30	0.00	0.01	0.04	0.07	0.11	0.14	0.17	0.19	0.22	0.24	0.25	0.27	0.29	0.30	0.31	0.32	0.33	30
40	0.00	0.01	0.04	0.07	0.11	0.14	0.17	0.20	0.22	0.24	0.26	0.28	0.29	0.31	0.32	0.33	0.34	40
60	0.00	0.01	0.04	0.07	0.11	0.14	0.17	0.20	0.22	0.24	0.26	0.28	0.30	0.31	0.33	0.34	0.35	60
100	0.00	0.01	0.04	0.07	0.11	0.14	0.17	0.20	0.23	0.25	0.27	0.29	0.31	0.32	0.34	0.35	0.36	100
∞	0.00	0.01	0.04	0.07	0.11	0.15	0.18	0.21	0.23	0.26	0.28	0.30	0.32	0.33	0.35	0.36	0.38	∞

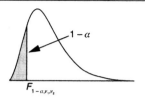

(ν_2)	18	19	20	21	22	23	24	25	26	27	28	29	30	40	60	100	∞	(ν_2)
1	0.12	0.12	0.12	0.12	0.13	0.13	0.13	0.13	0.13	0.13	0.13	0.13	0.13	0.14	0.14	0.15	0.15	1
2	0.17	0.17	0.17	0.17	0.17	0.18	0.18	0.18	0.18	0.18	0.18	0.18	0.19	0.19	0.20	0.21	0.22	2
3	0.20	0.20	0.20	0.21	0.21	0.21	0.21	0.21	0.22	0.22	0.22	0.22	0.22	0.23	0.24	0.25	0.26	3
4	0.22	0.22	0.23	0.23	0.23	0.23	0.24	0.24	0.24	0.24	0.25	0.25	0.25	0.26	0.27	0.28	0.30	4
5	0.24	0.24	0.24	0.25	0.25	0.25	0.26	0.26	0.26	0.26	0.27	0.27	0.27	0.28	0.30	0.31	0.33	5
6	0.25	0.25	0.26	0.26	0.27	0.27	0.27	0.28	0.28	0.28	0.28	0.29	0.29	0.30	0.32	0.33	0.36	6
7	0.26	0.27	0.27	0.27	0.28	0.28	0.29	0.29	0.29	0.30	0.30	0.30	0.30	0.32	0.34	0.35	0.38	7
8	0.27	0.28	0.28	0.29	0.29	0.29	0.30	0.30	0.30	0.31	0.31	0.31	0.32	0.33	0.35	0.37	0.40	8
9	0.28	0.28	0.29	0.29	0.30	0.30	0.31	0.31	0.31	0.32	0.32	0.32	0.33	0.35	0.37	0.39	0.42	9
10	0.29	0.29	0.30	0.30	0.31	0.31	0.32	0.32	0.32	0.33	0.33	0.33	0.34	0.36	0.38	0.40	0.43	10
11	0.29	0.30	0.30	0.31	0.31	0.32	0.32	0.33	0.33	0.33	0.34	0.34	0.34	0.37	0.39	0.41	0.44	11
12	0.30	0.30	0.31	0.32	0.32	0.33	0.33	0.33	0.34	0.34	0.35	0.35	0.35	0.38	0.40	0.42	0.46	12
13	0.30	0.31	0.31	0.32	0.33	0.33	0.34	0.34	0.34	0.35	0.35	0.36	0.36	0.38	0.41	0.43	0.47	13
14	0.31	0.31	0.32	0.33	0.33	0.34	0.34	0.35	0.35	0.35	0.36	0.36	0.36	0.39	0.42	0.44	0.48	14
15	0.31	0.32	0.32	0.33	0.34	0.34	0.35	0.35	0.36	0.36	0.36	0.37	0.37	0.40	0.43	0.45	0.49	15
16	0.31	0.32	0.33	0.33	0.34	0.35	0.35	0.36	0.36	0.36	0.37	0.37	0.38	0.40	0.43	0.46	0.50	16
17	0.32	0.32	0.33	0.34	0.34	0.35	0.35	0.36	0.36	0.37	0.37	0.38	0.38	0.41	0.44	0.46	0.51	17
18	0.32	0.33	0.33	0.34	0.35	0.35	0.36	0.36	0.37	0.37	0.38	0.38	0.38	0.41	0.44	0.47	0.52	18
19	0.32	0.33	0.34	0.34	0.35	0.36	0.36	0.37	0.37	0.38	0.38	0.38	0.39	0.42	0.45	0.48	0.52	19
20	0.32	0.33	0.34	0.35	0.35	0.36	0.37	0.37	0.38	0.38	0.38	0.39	0.39	0.42	0.45	0.48	0.53	20
21	0.33	0.34	0.34	0.35	0.36	0.36	0.37	0.37	0.38	0.38	0.39	0.39	0.40	0.43	0.46	0.49	0.54	21
22	0.33	0.34	0.35	0.35	0.36	0.37	0.37	0.38	0.38	0.39	0.39	0.40	0.40	0.43	0.46	0.49	0.55	22
23	0.33	0.34	0.35	0.35	0.36	0.37	0.37	0.38	0.38	0.39	0.39	0.40	0.40	0.43	0.47	0.50	0.55	23
24	0.33	0.34	0.35	0.36	0.36	0.37	0.38	0.38	0.39	0.39	0.40	0.40	0.41	0.44	0.47	0.50	0.56	24
25	0.34	0.34	0.35	0.36	0.37	0.37	0.38	0.38	0.39	0.39	0.40	0.40	0.41	0.44	0.48	0.51	0.56	25
26	0.34	0.35	0.35	0.36	0.37	0.37	0.38	0.39	0.39	0.40	0.40	0.41	0.41	0.44	0.48	0.51	0.57	26
27	0.34	0.35	0.36	0.36	0.37	0.38	0.38	0.39	0.39	0.40	0.40	0.41	0.41	0.45	0.48	0.52	0.57	27
28	0.34	0.35	0.36	0.36	0.37	0.38	0.38	0.39	0.40	0.40	0.41	0.41	0.41	0.45	0.49	0.52	0.58	28
29	0.34	0.35	0.36	0.37	0.37	0.38	0.39	0.39	0.40	0.40	0.41	0.41	0.42	0.45	0.49	0.52	0.58	29
30	0.34	0.35	0.36	0.37	0.37	0.38	0.39	0.39	0.40	0.40	0.41	0.41	0.42	0.45	0.49	0.53	0.59	30
40	0.35	0.36	0.37	0.38	0.39	0.39	0.40	0.41	0.41	0.42	0.42	0.43	0.43	0.47	0.52	0.56	0.63	40
60	0.36	0.37	0.38	0.39	0.40	0.41	0.42	0.42	0.43	0.44	0.44	0.45	0.45	0.50	0.54	0.59	0.68	60
100	0.37	0.38	0.39	0.40	0.41	0.42	0.43	0.44	0.44	0.45	0.46	0.46	0.47	0.52	0.57	0.63	0.74	100
∞	0.39	0.40	0.41	0.42	0.43	0.44	0.45	0.46	0.47	0.48	0.48	0.49	0.50	0.55	0.62	0.70	1.00	∞

Degrees of freedom for the numerator (ν_1)

Degrees of freedom for the denominator

Appendix 16

Appendix 17

F(0.975) Distribution Table

Appendix 17

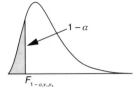

$$F_{1-\alpha, v_1, v_2}$$

	Degrees of freedom for the numerator																	
	(v_1)																	
(v_2)	1	2	3	4	5	6	7	8	9	10	11	12	13	14	15	16	17	(v_2)
1	0.00	0.03	0.06	0.08	0.10	0.11	0.12	0.13	0.14	0.14	0.15	0.15	0.16	0.16	0.16	0.16	0.17	1
2	0.00	0.03	0.06	0.09	0.12	0.14	0.15	0.17	0.17	0.18	0.19	0.20	0.20	0.21	0.21	0.21	0.22	2
3	0.00	0.03	0.06	0.10	0.13	0.15	0.17	0.18	0.20	0.21	0.22	0.22	0.23	0.24	0.24	0.25	0.25	3
4	0.00	0.03	0.07	0.10	0.14	0.16	0.18	0.20	0.21	0.22	0.23	0.24	0.25	0.26	0.26	0.27	0.27	4
5	0.00	0.03	0.07	0.11	0.14	0.17	0.19	0.21	0.22	0.24	0.25	0.26	0.27	0.27	0.28	0.29	0.29	5
6	0.00	0.03	0.07	0.11	0.14	0.17	0.20	0.21	0.23	0.25	0.26	0.27	0.28	0.29	0.29	0.30	0.31	6
7	0.00	0.03	0.07	0.11	0.15	0.18	0.20	0.22	0.24	0.25	0.27	0.28	0.29	0.30	0.30	0.31	0.32	7
8	0.00	0.03	0.07	0.11	0.15	0.18	0.20	0.23	0.24	0.26	0.27	0.28	0.30	0.30	0.31	0.32	0.33	8
9	0.00	0.03	0.07	0.11	0.15	0.18	0.21	0.23	0.25	0.26	0.28	0.29	0.30	0.31	0.32	0.33	0.34	9
10	0.00	0.03	0.07	0.11	0.15	0.18	0.21	0.23	0.25	0.27	0.28	0.30	0.31	0.32	0.33	0.33	0.34	10
11	0.00	0.03	0.07	0.11	0.15	0.18	0.21	0.24	0.26	0.27	0.29	0.30	0.31	0.32	0.33	0.34	0.35	11
12	0.00	0.03	0.07	0.11	0.15	0.19	0.21	0.24	0.26	0.28	0.29	0.31	0.32	0.33	0.34	0.35	0.35	12
13	0.00	0.03	0.07	0.11	0.15	0.19	0.22	0.24	0.26	0.28	0.29	0.31	0.32	0.33	0.34	0.35	0.36	13
14	0.00	0.03	0.07	0.12	0.15	0.19	0.22	0.24	0.26	0.28	0.30	0.31	0.32	0.34	0.35	0.35	0.36	14
15	0.00	0.03	0.07	0.12	0.16	0.19	0.22	0.24	0.27	0.28	0.30	0.31	0.33	0.34	0.35	0.36	0.37	15
16	0.00	0.03	0.07	0.12	0.16	0.19	0.22	0.25	0.27	0.29	0.30	0.32	0.33	0.34	0.35	0.36	0.37	16
17	0.00	0.03	0.07	0.12	0.16	0.19	0.22	0.25	0.27	0.29	0.30	0.32	0.33	0.34	0.36	0.37	0.37	17
18	0.00	0.03	0.07	0.12	0.16	0.19	0.22	0.25	0.27	0.29	0.31	0.32	0.34	0.35	0.36	0.37	0.38	18
19	0.00	0.03	0.07	0.12	0.16	0.19	0.22	0.25	0.27	0.29	0.31	0.32	0.34	0.35	0.36	0.37	0.38	19
20	0.00	0.03	0.07	0.12	0.16	0.19	0.22	0.25	0.27	0.29	0.31	0.33	0.34	0.35	0.36	0.37	0.38	20
21	0.00	0.03	0.07	0.12	0.16	0.19	0.22	0.25	0.27	0.29	0.31	0.33	0.34	0.35	0.36	0.38	0.38	21
22	0.00	0.03	0.07	0.12	0.16	0.19	0.23	0.25	0.27	0.30	0.31	0.33	0.34	0.36	0.37	0.38	0.39	22
23	0.00	0.03	0.07	0.12	0.16	0.19	0.23	0.25	0.28	0.30	0.31	0.33	0.34	0.36	0.37	0.38	0.39	23
24	0.00	0.03	0.07	0.12	0.16	0.20	0.23	0.25	0.28	0.30	0.32	0.33	0.35	0.36	0.37	0.38	0.39	24
25	0.00	0.03	0.07	0.12	0.16	0.20	0.23	0.25	0.28	0.30	0.32	0.33	0.35	0.36	0.37	0.38	0.39	25
26	0.00	0.03	0.07	0.12	0.16	0.20	0.23	0.25	0.28	0.30	0.32	0.33	0.35	0.36	0.37	0.38	0.39	26
27	0.00	0.03	0.07	0.12	0.16	0.20	0.23	0.26	0.28	0.30	0.32	0.33	0.35	0.36	0.37	0.39	0.40	27
28	0.00	0.03	0.07	0.12	0.16	0.20	0.23	0.26	0.28	0.30	0.32	0.34	0.35	0.36	0.38	0.39	0.40	28
29	0.00	0.03	0.07	0.12	0.16	0.20	0.23	0.26	0.28	0.30	0.32	0.34	0.35	0.36	0.38	0.39	0.40	29
30	0.00	0.03	0.07	0.12	0.16	0.20	0.23	0.26	0.28	0.30	0.32	0.34	0.35	0.37	0.38	0.39	0.40	30
40	0.00	0.03	0.07	0.12	0.16	0.20	0.23	0.26	0.29	0.31	0.33	0.34	0.36	0.37	0.39	0.40	0.41	40
60	0.00	0.03	0.07	0.12	0.16	0.20	0.24	0.26	0.29	0.31	0.33	0.35	0.37	0.38	0.40	0.41	0.42	60
100	0.00	0.03	0.07	0.12	0.16	0.20	0.24	0.27	0.29	0.32	0.34	0.36	0.37	0.39	0.40	0.42	0.43	100
∞	0.00	0.03	0.07	0.12	0.17	0.21	0.24	0.27	0.30	0.32	0.35	0.37	0.39	0.40	0.42	0.43	0.44	∞

Degrees of freedom for the denominator

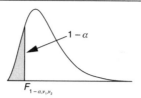

	Degrees of freedom for the numerator																	
	(ν_1)																	
(ν_2)	18	19	20	21	22	23	24	25	26	27	28	29	30	40	60	100	∞	(ν_2)
1	0.17	0.17	0.17	0.17	0.17	0.17	0.17	0.18	0.18	0.18	0.18	0.18	0.18	0.18	0.19	0.19	0.20	1
2	0.22	0.22	0.22	0.23	0.23	0.23	0.23	0.23	0.23	0.24	0.24	0.24	0.24	0.25	0.25	0.26	0.27	2
3	0.25	0.26	0.26	0.26	0.26	0.27	0.27	0.27	0.27	0.27	0.28	0.28	0.28	0.29	0.30	0.31	0.32	3
4	0.28	0.28	0.28	0.29	0.29	0.29	0.30	0.30	0.30	0.30	0.30	0.31	0.31	0.32	0.33	0.34	0.36	4
5	0.30	0.30	0.30	0.31	0.31	0.31	0.32	0.32	0.32	0.32	0.33	0.33	0.33	0.34	0.36	0.37	0.39	5
6	0.31	0.32	0.32	0.32	0.33	0.33	0.33	0.34	0.34	0.34	0.34	0.35	0.35	0.36	0.38	0.39	0.42	6
7	0.32	0.33	0.33	0.34	0.34	0.34	0.35	0.35	0.35	0.36	0.36	0.36	0.36	0.38	0.40	0.41	0.44	7
8	0.33	0.34	0.34	0.35	0.35	0.36	0.36	0.36	0.37	0.37	0.37	0.37	0.38	0.40	0.41	0.43	0.46	8
9	0.34	0.35	0.35	0.36	0.36	0.37	0.37	0.37	0.38	0.38	0.38	0.39	0.39	0.41	0.43	0.45	0.47	9
10	0.35	0.35	0.36	0.37	0.37	0.37	0.38	0.38	0.39	0.39	0.39	0.40	0.40	0.42	0.44	0.46	0.49	10
11	0.36	0.36	0.37	0.37	0.38	0.38	0.39	0.39	0.39	0.40	0.40	0.40	0.41	0.43	0.45	0.47	0.50	11
12	0.36	0.37	0.37	0.38	0.38	0.39	0.39	0.40	0.40	0.41	0.41	0.41	0.41	0.44	0.46	0.48	0.51	12
13	0.37	0.37	0.38	0.38	0.39	0.40	0.40	0.40	0.41	0.41	0.42	0.42	0.42	0.44	0.47	0.49	0.53	13
14	0.37	0.38	0.38	0.39	0.40	0.40	0.41	0.41	0.41	0.42	0.42	0.42	0.43	0.45	0.48	0.50	0.54	14
15	0.37	0.38	0.39	0.39	0.40	0.41	0.41	0.41	0.42	0.42	0.43	0.43	0.43	0.46	0.49	0.51	0.55	15
16	0.38	0.39	0.39	0.40	0.40	0.41	0.41	0.42	0.42	0.43	0.43	0.44	0.44	0.46	0.49	0.52	0.55	16
17	0.38	0.39	0.40	0.40	0.41	0.41	0.42	0.42	0.43	0.43	0.44	0.44	0.44	0.47	0.50	0.52	0.56	17
18	0.39	0.39	0.40	0.41	0.41	0.42	0.42	0.43	0.43	0.44	0.44	0.44	0.45	0.47	0.50	0.53	0.57	18
19	0.39	0.40	0.40	0.41	0.42	0.42	0.43	0.43	0.44	0.44	0.44	0.45	0.45	0.48	0.51	0.54	0.58	19
20	0.39	0.40	0.41	0.41	0.42	0.42	0.43	0.43	0.44	0.44	0.45	0.45	0.46	0.48	0.51	0.54	0.59	20
21	0.39	0.40	0.41	0.42	0.42	0.43	0.43	0.44	0.44	0.45	0.45	0.46	0.46	0.49	0.52	0.55	0.59	21
22	0.40	0.40	0.41	0.42	0.42	0.43	0.44	0.44	0.45	0.45	0.45	0.46	0.46	0.49	0.52	0.55	0.60	22
23	0.40	0.41	0.41	0.42	0.43	0.43	0.44	0.44	0.45	0.45	0.46	0.46	0.47	0.49	0.53	0.56	0.60	23
24	0.40	0.41	0.42	0.42	0.43	0.43	0.44	0.45	0.45	0.46	0.46	0.46	0.47	0.50	0.53	0.56	0.61	24
25	0.40	0.41	0.42	0.42	0.43	0.44	0.44	0.45	0.45	0.46	0.46	0.47	0.47	0.50	0.54	0.56	0.62	25
26	0.40	0.41	0.42	0.43	0.43	0.44	0.45	0.45	0.46	0.46	0.47	0.47	0.47	0.50	0.54	0.57	0.62	26
27	0.40	0.41	0.42	0.43	0.44	0.44	0.45	0.45	0.46	0.46	0.47	0.47	0.48	0.51	0.54	0.57	0.63	27
28	0.41	0.41	0.42	0.43	0.44	0.44	0.45	0.45	0.46	0.46	0.47	0.47	0.48	0.51	0.55	0.58	0.63	28
29	0.41	0.42	0.42	0.43	0.44	0.44	0.45	0.46	0.46	0.47	0.47	0.48	0.48	0.51	0.55	0.58	0.63	29
30	0.41	0.42	0.43	0.43	0.44	0.45	0.45	0.46	0.46	0.47	0.47	0.48	0.48	0.51	0.55	0.58	0.64	30
40	0.42	0.43	0.44	0.45	0.45	0.46	0.47	0.47	0.48	0.48	0.49	0.49	0.50	0.53	0.57	0.61	0.67	40
60	0.43	0.44	0.45	0.46	0.47	0.47	0.48	0.49	0.49	0.50	0.51	0.51	0.52	0.55	0.60	0.64	0.72	60
100	0.44	0.45	0.46	0.47	0.48	0.49	0.49	0.50	0.51	0.51	0.52	0.53	0.53	0.57	0.63	0.67	0.77	100
∞	0.46	0.47	0.48	0.49	0.50	0.51	0.52	0.52	0.53	0.54	0.55	0.55	0.56	0.61	0.67	0.74	1.00	∞

Degrees of freedom for the denominator

Appendix 17

Appendix 18

F(0.95) Distribution Table

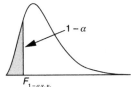

$$F_{1-\alpha,\nu_1,\nu_2}$$

		Degrees of freedom for the numerator																
		(ν_1)																
(ν_2)	1	2	3	4	5	6	7	8	9	10	11	12	13	14	15	16	17	(ν_2)
1	0.01	0.05	0.10	0.13	0.15	0.17	0.18	0.19	0.20	0.20	0.21	0.21	0.21	0.22	0.22	0.22	0.22	1
2	0.01	0.05	0.10	0.14	0.17	0.19	0.21	0.22	0.23	0.24	0.25	0.26	0.26	0.27	0.27	0.28	0.28	2
3	0.00	0.05	0.11	0.15	0.18	0.21	0.23	0.25	0.26	0.27	0.28	0.29	0.29	0.30	0.30	0.31	0.31	3
4	0.00	0.05	0.11	0.16	0.19	0.22	0.24	0.26	0.28	0.29	0.30	0.31	0.31	0.32	0.33	0.33	0.34	4
5	0.00	0.05	0.11	0.16	0.19	0.23	0.25	0.27	0.29	0.30	0.31	0.32	0.33	0.34	0.34	0.35	0.36	5
6	0.00	0.05	0.11	0.16	0.20	0.23	0.26	0.28	0.30	0.31	0.32	0.33	0.34	0.35	0.36	0.36	0.37	6
7	0.00	0.05	0.11	0.16	0.21	0.24	0.26	0.29	0.30	0.32	0.33	0.34	0.35	0.36	0.37	0.38	0.38	7
8	0.00	0.05	0.11	0.17	0.21	0.24	0.27	0.29	0.31	0.33	0.34	0.35	0.36	0.37	0.38	0.39	0.39	8
9	0.00	0.05	0.11	0.17	0.21	0.24	0.27	0.30	0.31	0.33	0.35	0.36	0.37	0.38	0.39	0.39	0.40	9
10	0.00	0.05	0.11	0.17	0.21	0.25	0.27	0.30	0.32	0.34	0.35	0.36	0.37	0.38	0.39	0.40	0.41	10
11	0.00	0.05	0.11	0.17	0.21	0.25	0.28	0.30	0.32	0.34	0.35	0.37	0.38	0.39	0.40	0.41	0.41	11
12	0.00	0.05	0.11	0.17	0.21	0.25	0.28	0.30	0.33	0.34	0.36	0.37	0.38	0.39	0.40	0.41	0.42	12
13	0.00	0.05	0.11	0.17	0.21	0.25	0.28	0.31	0.33	0.35	0.36	0.38	0.39	0.40	0.41	0.42	0.42	13
14	0.00	0.05	0.11	0.17	0.22	0.25	0.28	0.31	0.33	0.35	0.37	0.38	0.39	0.40	0.41	0.42	0.43	14
15	0.00	0.05	0.11	0.17	0.22	0.25	0.28	0.31	0.33	0.35	0.37	0.38	0.39	0.41	0.42	0.43	0.43	15
16	0.00	0.05	0.12	0.17	0.22	0.25	0.29	0.31	0.33	0.35	0.37	0.38	0.40	0.41	0.42	0.43	0.44	16
17	0.00	0.05	0.12	0.17	0.22	0.26	0.29	0.31	0.34	0.36	0.37	0.39	0.40	0.41	0.42	0.43	0.44	17
18	0.00	0.05	0.12	0.17	0.22	0.26	0.29	0.32	0.34	0.36	0.37	0.39	0.40	0.41	0.42	0.43	0.44	18
19	0.00	0.05	0.12	0.17	0.22	0.26	0.29	0.32	0.34	0.36	0.38	0.39	0.40	0.42	0.43	0.44	0.45	19
20	0.00	0.05	0.12	0.17	0.22	0.26	0.29	0.32	0.34	0.36	0.38	0.39	0.41	0.42	0.43	0.44	0.45	20
21	0.00	0.05	0.12	0.17	0.22	0.26	0.29	0.32	0.34	0.36	0.38	0.39	0.41	0.42	0.43	0.44	0.45	21
22	0.00	0.05	0.12	0.17	0.22	0.26	0.29	0.32	0.34	0.36	0.38	0.40	0.41	0.42	0.43	0.44	0.45	22
23	0.00	0.05	0.12	0.17	0.22	0.26	0.29	0.32	0.34	0.36	0.38	0.40	0.41	0.42	0.44	0.45	0.45	23
24	0.00	0.05	0.12	0.17	0.22	0.26	0.29	0.32	0.34	0.37	0.38	0.40	0.41	0.43	0.44	0.45	0.46	24
25	0.00	0.05	0.12	0.17	0.22	0.26	0.29	0.32	0.35	0.37	0.38	0.40	0.41	0.43	0.44	0.45	0.46	25
26	0.00	0.05	0.12	0.17	0.22	0.26	0.29	0.32	0.35	0.37	0.39	0.40	0.42	0.43	0.44	0.45	0.46	26
27	0.00	0.05	0.12	0.17	0.22	0.26	0.29	0.32	0.35	0.37	0.39	0.40	0.42	0.43	0.44	0.45	0.46	27
28	0.00	0.05	0.12	0.17	0.22	0.26	0.30	0.32	0.35	0.37	0.39	0.40	0.42	0.43	0.44	0.45	0.46	28
29	0.00	0.05	0.12	0.17	0.22	0.26	0.30	0.32	0.35	0.37	0.39	0.40	0.42	0.43	0.44	0.45	0.46	29
30	0.00	0.05	0.12	0.17	0.22	0.26	0.30	0.32	0.35	0.37	0.39	0.41	0.42	0.43	0.45	0.46	0.47	30
40	0.00	0.05	0.12	0.17	0.22	0.26	0.30	0.33	0.35	0.38	0.40	0.41	0.43	0.44	0.45	0.46	0.48	40
60	0.00	0.05	0.12	0.18	0.23	0.27	0.30	0.33	0.36	0.38	0.40	0.42	0.44	0.45	0.46	0.47	0.49	60
100	0.00	0.05	0.12	0.18	0.23	0.27	0.31	0.34	0.36	0.39	0.41	0.43	0.44	0.46	0.47	0.48	0.49	100
∞	0.00	0.05	0.12	0.18	0.23	0.27	0.31	0.34	0.37	0.39	0.42	0.44	0.45	0.47	0.48	0.50	0.51	∞

Degrees of freedom for the denominator

Appendix 18

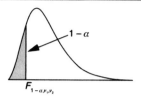

	Degrees of freedom for the numerator																	
	(v_1)																	
(v_2)	18	19	20	21	22	23	24	25	26	27	28	29	30	40	60	100	∞	(v_2)
1	0.23	0.23	0.23	0.23	0.23	0.23	0.23	0.24	0.24	0.24	0.24	0.24	0.24	0.24	0.25	0.25	0.26	1
2	0.28	0.28	0.29	0.29	0.29	0.29	0.29	0.30	0.30	0.30	0.30	0.30	0.30	0.31	0.32	0.32	0.33	2
3	0.32	0.32	0.32	0.33	0.33	0.33	0.33	0.33	0.34	0.34	0.34	0.34	0.34	0.35	0.36	0.37	0.38	3
4	0.34	0.35	0.35	0.35	0.36	0.36	0.36	0.36	0.36	0.37	0.37	0.37	0.37	0.38	0.40	0.41	0.42	4
5	0.36	0.36	0.37	0.37	0.38	0.38	0.38	0.38	0.39	0.39	0.39	0.39	0.39	0.41	0.42	0.43	0.45	5
6	0.38	0.38	0.38	0.39	0.39	0.40	0.40	0.40	0.40	0.41	0.41	0.41	0.41	0.43	0.44	0.46	0.48	6
7	0.39	0.39	0.40	0.40	0.41	0.41	0.41	0.42	0.42	0.42	0.42	0.43	0.43	0.44	0.46	0.48	0.50	7
8	0.40	0.40	0.41	0.41	0.42	0.42	0.42	0.43	0.43	0.43	0.44	0.44	0.44	0.46	0.48	0.49	0.52	8
9	0.41	0.41	0.42	0.42	0.43	0.43	0.43	0.44	0.44	0.44	0.45	0.45	0.45	0.47	0.49	0.51	0.53	9
10	0.41	0.42	0.43	0.43	0.44	0.44	0.44	0.45	0.45	0.45	0.46	0.46	0.46	0.48	0.50	0.52	0.55	10
11	0.42	0.43	0.43	0.44	0.44	0.45	0.45	0.45	0.46	0.46	0.46	0.47	0.47	0.49	0.51	0.53	0.56	11
12	0.43	0.43	0.44	0.44	0.45	0.45	0.46	0.46	0.47	0.47	0.47	0.48	0.48	0.50	0.52	0.54	0.57	12
13	0.43	0.44	0.44	0.45	0.46	0.46	0.46	0.47	0.47	0.48	0.48	0.48	0.48	0.51	0.53	0.55	0.58	13
14	0.44	0.44	0.45	0.46	0.46	0.47	0.47	0.47	0.48	0.48	0.48	0.49	0.49	0.51	0.54	0.56	0.59	14
15	0.44	0.45	0.45	0.46	0.46	0.47	0.47	0.48	0.48	0.49	0.49	0.49	0.50	0.52	0.54	0.57	0.60	15
16	0.44	0.45	0.46	0.46	0.47	0.47	0.48	0.48	0.49	0.49	0.49	0.50	0.50	0.53	0.55	0.57	0.61	16
17	0.45	0.46	0.46	0.47	0.47	0.48	0.48	0.49	0.49	0.50	0.50	0.50	0.51	0.53	0.56	0.58	0.62	17
18	0.45	0.46	0.46	0.47	0.48	0.48	0.49	0.49	0.50	0.50	0.50	0.51	0.51	0.54	0.56	0.59	0.62	18
19	0.45	0.46	0.47	0.47	0.48	0.49	0.49	0.49	0.50	0.50	0.51	0.51	0.51	0.54	0.57	0.59	0.63	19
20	0.46	0.46	0.47	0.48	0.48	0.49	0.49	0.50	0.50	0.51	0.51	0.51	0.52	0.54	0.57	0.60	0.64	20
21	0.46	0.47	0.47	0.48	0.49	0.49	0.50	0.50	0.51	0.51	0.51	0.52	0.52	0.55	0.58	0.60	0.64	21
22	0.46	0.47	0.48	0.48	0.49	0.49	0.50	0.50	0.51	0.51	0.52	0.52	0.52	0.55	0.58	0.61	0.65	22
23	0.46	0.47	0.48	0.48	0.49	0.50	0.50	0.51	0.51	0.52	0.52	0.52	0.53	0.55	0.58	0.61	0.65	23
24	0.47	0.47	0.48	0.49	0.49	0.50	0.50	0.51	0.51	0.52	0.52	0.53	0.53	0.56	0.59	0.61	0.66	24
25	0.47	0.47	0.48	0.49	0.50	0.50	0.51	0.51	0.52	0.52	0.52	0.53	0.53	0.56	0.59	0.62	0.66	25
26	0.47	0.48	0.48	0.49	0.50	0.50	0.51	0.51	0.52	0.52	0.53	0.53	0.53	0.56	0.59	0.62	0.67	26
27	0.47	0.48	0.49	0.49	0.50	0.50	0.51	0.52	0.52	0.52	0.53	0.53	0.54	0.57	0.60	0.63	0.67	27
28	0.47	0.48	0.49	0.49	0.50	0.51	0.51	0.52	0.52	0.53	0.53	0.54	0.54	0.57	0.60	0.63	0.68	28
29	0.47	0.48	0.49	0.50	0.50	0.51	0.51	0.52	0.52	0.53	0.53	0.54	0.54	0.57	0.60	0.63	0.68	29
30	0.47	0.48	0.49	0.50	0.50	0.51	0.52	0.52	0.53	0.53	0.54	0.54	0.54	0.57	0.61	0.64	0.69	30
40	0.48	0.49	0.50	0.51	0.52	0.52	0.53	0.53	0.54	0.54	0.55	0.55	0.56	0.59	0.63	0.66	0.72	40
60	0.50	0.51	0.51	0.52	0.53	0.54	0.54	0.55	0.55	0.56	0.57	0.57	0.57	0.61	0.65	0.69	0.76	60
100	0.51	0.52	0.52	0.53	0.54	0.55	0.56	0.56	0.57	0.57	0.58	0.58	0.59	0.63	0.68	0.72	0.80	100
∞	0.52	0.53	0.54	0.55	0.56	0.57	0.58	0.58	0.59	0.60	0.60	0.61	0.62	0.66	0.72	0.78	1.00	∞

Degrees of freedom for the denominator

Appendix 18

Appendix 19

F(0.90) Distribution Table

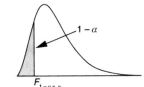

$$F_{1-\alpha, \nu_1, \nu_2}$$

	Degrees of freedom for the numerator																	
	(ν_1)																	
(ν_2)	1	2	3	4	5	6	7	8	9	10	11	12	13	14	15	16	17	(ν_2)
1	0.03	0.12	0.18	0.22	0.25	0.26	0.28	0.29	0.30	0.30	0.31	0.31	0.32	0.32	0.33	0.33	0.33	1
2	0.02	0.11	0.18	0.23	0.26	0.29	0.31	0.32	0.33	0.34	0.35	0.36	0.36	0.37	0.37	0.37	0.38	2
3	0.02	0.11	0.19	0.24	0.28	0.30	0.33	0.34	0.36	0.37	0.38	0.38	0.39	0.40	0.40	0.41	0.41	3
4	0.02	0.11	0.19	0.24	0.28	0.31	0.34	0.36	0.37	0.38	0.39	0.40	0.41	0.42	0.42	0.43	0.43	4
5	0.02	0.11	0.19	0.25	0.29	0.32	0.35	0.37	0.38	0.40	0.41	0.42	0.43	0.43	0.44	0.45	0.45	5
6	0.02	0.11	0.19	0.25	0.29	0.33	0.35	0.37	0.39	0.41	0.42	0.43	0.44	0.45	0.45	0.46	0.46	6
7	0.02	0.11	0.19	0.25	0.30	0.33	0.36	0.38	0.40	0.41	0.43	0.44	0.45	0.46	0.46	0.47	0.48	7
8	0.02	0.11	0.19	0.25	0.30	0.34	0.36	0.39	0.40	0.42	0.43	0.45	0.46	0.46	0.47	0.48	0.49	8
9	0.02	0.11	0.19	0.25	0.30	0.34	0.37	0.39	0.41	0.43	0.44	0.45	0.46	0.47	0.48	0.49	0.49	9
10	0.02	0.11	0.19	0.26	0.30	0.34	0.37	0.39	0.41	0.43	0.44	0.46	0.47	0.48	0.49	0.49	0.50	10
11	0.02	0.11	0.19	0.26	0.30	0.34	0.37	0.40	0.42	0.43	0.45	0.46	0.47	0.48	0.49	0.50	0.51	11
12	0.02	0.11	0.19	0.26	0.31	0.34	0.37	0.40	0.42	0.44	0.45	0.47	0.48	0.49	0.50	0.50	0.51	12
13	0.02	0.11	0.19	0.26	0.31	0.35	0.38	0.40	0.42	0.44	0.46	0.47	0.48	0.49	0.50	0.51	0.52	13
14	0.02	0.11	0.19	0.26	0.31	0.35	0.38	0.40	0.43	0.44	0.46	0.47	0.48	0.49	0.50	0.51	0.52	14
15	0.02	0.11	0.19	0.26	0.31	0.35	0.38	0.41	0.43	0.45	0.46	0.48	0.49	0.50	0.51	0.52	0.52	15
16	0.02	0.11	0.19	0.26	0.31	0.35	0.38	0.41	0.43	0.45	0.46	0.48	0.49	0.50	0.51	0.52	0.53	16
17	0.02	0.11	0.19	0.26	0.31	0.35	0.38	0.41	0.43	0.45	0.47	0.48	0.49	0.50	0.51	0.52	0.53	17
18	0.02	0.11	0.19	0.26	0.31	0.35	0.38	0.41	0.43	0.45	0.47	0.48	0.49	0.51	0.52	0.52	0.53	18
19	0.02	0.11	0.19	0.26	0.31	0.35	0.38	0.41	0.43	0.45	0.47	0.48	0.50	0.51	0.52	0.53	0.53	19
20	0.02	0.11	0.19	0.26	0.31	0.35	0.39	0.41	0.44	0.45	0.47	0.49	0.50	0.51	0.52	0.53	0.54	20
21	0.02	0.11	0.19	0.26	0.31	0.35	0.39	0.41	0.44	0.46	0.47	0.49	0.50	0.51	0.52	0.53	0.54	21
22	0.02	0.11	0.19	0.26	0.31	0.35	0.39	0.41	0.44	0.46	0.47	0.49	0.50	0.51	0.52	0.53	0.54	22
23	0.02	0.11	0.19	0.26	0.31	0.35	0.39	0.42	0.44	0.46	0.48	0.49	0.50	0.51	0.53	0.53	0.54	23
24	0.02	0.11	0.19	0.26	0.31	0.35	0.39	0.42	0.44	0.46	0.48	0.49	0.50	0.52	0.53	0.54	0.54	24
25	0.02	0.11	0.19	0.26	0.31	0.36	0.39	0.42	0.44	0.46	0.48	0.49	0.51	0.52	0.53	0.54	0.55	25
26	0.02	0.11	0.19	0.26	0.31	0.36	0.39	0.42	0.44	0.46	0.48	0.49	0.51	0.52	0.53	0.54	0.55	26
27	0.02	0.11	0.19	0.26	0.31	0.36	0.39	0.42	0.44	0.46	0.48	0.49	0.51	0.52	0.53	0.54	0.55	27
28	0.02	0.11	0.19	0.26	0.31	0.36	0.39	0.42	0.44	0.46	0.48	0.50	0.51	0.52	0.53	0.54	0.55	28
29	0.02	0.11	0.19	0.26	0.31	0.36	0.39	0.42	0.44	0.46	0.48	0.50	0.51	0.52	0.53	0.54	0.55	29
30	0.02	0.11	0.19	0.26	0.32	0.36	0.39	0.42	0.44	0.46	0.48	0.50	0.51	0.52	0.53	0.54	0.55	30
40	0.02	0.11	0.19	0.26	0.32	0.36	0.39	0.42	0.45	0.47	0.49	0.50	0.52	0.53	0.54	0.55	0.56	40
60	0.02	0.11	0.19	0.26	0.32	0.36	0.40	0.43	0.45	0.47	0.49	0.51	0.53	0.54	0.55	0.56	0.57	60
100	0.02	0.11	0.19	0.26	0.32	0.36	0.40	0.43	0.46	0.48	0.50	0.52	0.53	0.55	0.56	0.57	0.58	100
∞	0.02	0.11	0.19	0.27	0.32	0.37	0.40	0.44	0.46	0.49	0.51	0.53	0.54	0.56	0.57	0.58	0.59	∞

Degrees of freedom for the denominator

Appendix 19

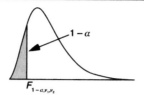

	Degrees of freedom for the numerator																	
	(ν_1)																	
(ν_2)	18	19	20	21	22	23	24	25	26	27	28	29	30	40	60	100	∞	(ν_2)
1	0.33	0.33	0.34	0.34	0.34	0.34	0.34	0.34	0.34	0.34	0.35	0.35	0.35	0.35	0.36	0.36	0.37	1
2	0.38	0.38	0.39	0.39	0.39	0.39	0.39	0.40	0.40	0.40	0.40	0.40	0.40	0.41	0.42	0.42	0.43	2
3	0.41	0.42	0.42	0.42	0.43	0.43	0.43	0.43	0.43	0.44	0.44	0.44	0.44	0.45	0.46	0.47	0.48	3
4	0.44	0.44	0.44	0.45	0.45	0.45	0.46	0.46	0.46	0.46	0.46	0.47	0.47	0.48	0.49	0.50	0.51	4
5	0.46	0.46	0.46	0.47	0.47	0.47	0.48	0.48	0.48	0.48	0.48	0.49	0.49	0.50	0.51	0.52	0.54	5
6	0.47	0.47	0.48	0.48	0.49	0.49	0.49	0.49	0.50	0.50	0.50	0.50	0.50	0.52	0.53	0.55	0.56	6
7	0.48	0.49	0.49	0.49	0.50	0.50	0.50	0.51	0.51	0.51	0.51	0.52	0.52	0.53	0.55	0.56	0.58	7
8	0.49	0.50	0.50	0.50	0.51	0.51	0.52	0.52	0.52	0.52	0.53	0.53	0.53	0.55	0.56	0.58	0.60	8
9	0.50	0.50	0.51	0.51	0.52	0.52	0.52	0.53	0.53	0.53	0.54	0.54	0.54	0.56	0.58	0.59	0.61	9
10	0.51	0.51	0.52	0.52	0.53	0.53	0.53	0.54	0.54	0.54	0.54	0.55	0.55	0.57	0.59	0.60	0.63	10
11	0.51	0.52	0.52	0.53	0.53	0.54	0.54	0.54	0.55	0.55	0.55	0.55	0.56	0.58	0.60	0.61	0.64	11
12	0.52	0.52	0.53	0.53	0.54	0.54	0.55	0.55	0.55	0.56	0.56	0.56	0.56	0.58	0.60	0.62	0.65	12
13	0.52	0.53	0.53	0.54	0.54	0.55	0.55	0.56	0.56	0.56	0.56	0.57	0.57	0.59	0.61	0.63	0.66	13
14	0.53	0.53	0.54	0.54	0.55	0.55	0.56	0.56	0.56	0.57	0.57	0.57	0.58	0.60	0.62	0.64	0.66	14
15	0.53	0.54	0.54	0.55	0.55	0.56	0.56	0.56	0.57	0.57	0.57	0.58	0.58	0.60	0.62	0.64	0.67	15
16	0.53	0.54	0.55	0.55	0.56	0.56	0.56	0.57	0.57	0.58	0.58	0.58	0.59	0.61	0.63	0.65	0.68	16
17	0.54	0.54	0.55	0.55	0.56	0.56	0.57	0.57	0.58	0.58	0.58	0.59	0.59	0.61	0.63	0.65	0.69	17
18	0.54	0.55	0.55	0.56	0.56	0.57	0.57	0.58	0.58	0.58	0.59	0.59	0.59	0.62	0.64	0.66	0.69	18
19	0.54	0.55	0.55	0.56	0.57	0.57	0.58	0.58	0.58	0.59	0.59	0.59	0.60	0.62	0.64	0.66	0.70	19
20	0.54	0.55	0.56	0.56	0.57	0.57	0.58	0.58	0.59	0.59	0.59	0.60	0.60	0.62	0.65	0.67	0.70	20
21	0.55	0.55	0.56	0.57	0.57	0.58	0.58	0.58	0.59	0.59	0.60	0.60	0.60	0.63	0.65	0.67	0.71	21
22	0.55	0.56	0.56	0.57	0.57	0.58	0.58	0.59	0.59	0.60	0.60	0.60	0.61	0.63	0.66	0.68	0.71	22
23	0.55	0.56	0.56	0.57	0.58	0.58	0.59	0.59	0.59	0.60	0.60	0.60	0.61	0.63	0.66	0.68	0.72	23
24	0.55	0.56	0.57	0.57	0.58	0.58	0.59	0.59	0.60	0.60	0.60	0.61	0.61	0.64	0.66	0.68	0.72	24
25	0.55	0.56	0.57	0.57	0.58	0.58	0.59	0.59	0.60	0.60	0.61	0.61	0.61	0.64	0.66	0.69	0.73	25
26	0.56	0.56	0.57	0.58	0.58	0.59	0.59	0.60	0.60	0.60	0.61	0.61	0.62	0.64	0.67	0.69	0.73	26
27	0.56	0.56	0.57	0.58	0.58	0.59	0.59	0.60	0.60	0.61	0.61	0.61	0.62	0.64	0.67	0.69	0.73	27
28	0.56	0.57	0.57	0.58	0.58	0.59	0.59	0.60	0.60	0.61	0.61	0.62	0.62	0.64	0.67	0.70	0.74	28
29	0.56	0.57	0.57	0.58	0.59	0.59	0.60	0.60	0.61	0.61	0.61	0.62	0.62	0.65	0.68	0.70	0.74	29
30	0.56	0.57	0.58	0.58	0.59	0.59	0.60	0.60	0.61	0.61	0.62	0.62	0.62	0.65	0.68	0.70	0.75	30
40	0.57	0.58	0.59	0.59	0.60	0.60	0.61	0.61	0.62	0.62	0.63	0.63	0.64	0.66	0.70	0.72	0.77	40
60	0.58	0.59	0.60	0.60	0.61	0.62	0.62	0.63	0.63	0.64	0.64	0.65	0.65	0.68	0.72	0.75	0.81	60
100	0.59	0.60	0.61	0.61	0.62	0.63	0.63	0.64	0.64	0.65	0.65	0.66	0.66	0.70	0.74	0.77	0.84	100
∞	0.60	0.61	0.62	0.63	0.64	0.65	0.65	0.66	0.67	0.67	0.68	0.68	0.69	0.73	0.77	0.82	1.00	∞

Degrees of freedom for the denominator

Appendix 19

Appendix 20

F(0.10) Distribution Table

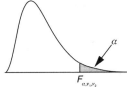

	Degrees of freedom for the numerator																	
	(v_1)																	
(v_2)	1	2	3	4	5	6	7	8	9	10	11	12	13	14	15	16	17	(v_2)
1	39.86	49.50	53.59	55.83	57.24	58.20	58.91	59.44	59.86	60.19	60.47	60.71	60.90	61.07	61.22	61.35	61.46	1
2	8.53	9.00	9.16	9.24	9.29	9.33	9.35	9.37	9.38	9.39	9.40	9.41	9.41	9.42	9.42	9.43	9.43	2
3	5.54	5.46	5.39	5.34	5.31	5.28	5.27	5.25	5.24	5.23	5.22	5.22	5.21	5.20	5.20	5.20	5.19	3
4	4.54	4.32	4.19	4.11	4.05	4.01	3.98	3.95	3.94	3.92	3.91	3.90	3.89	3.88	3.87	3.86	3.86	4
5	4.06	3.78	3.62	3.52	3.45	3.40	3.37	3.34	3.32	3.30	3.28	3.27	3.26	3.25	3.24	3.23	3.22	5
6	3.78	3.46	3.29	3.18	3.11	3.05	3.01	2.98	2.96	2.94	2.92	2.90	2.89	2.88	2.87	2.86	2.85	6
7	3.59	3.26	3.07	2.96	2.88	2.83	2.78	2.75	2.72	2.70	2.68	2.67	2.65	2.64	2.63	2.62	2.61	7
8	3.46	3.11	2.92	2.81	2.73	2.67	2.62	2.59	2.56	2.54	2.52	2.50	2.49	2.48	2.46	2.45	2.45	8
9	3.36	3.01	2.81	2.69	2.61	2.55	2.51	2.47	2.44	2.42	2.40	2.38	2.36	2.35	2.34	2.33	2.32	9
10	3.29	2.92	2.73	2.61	2.52	2.46	2.41	2.38	2.35	2.32	2.30	2.28	2.27	2.26	2.24	2.23	2.22	10
11	3.23	2.86	2.66	2.54	2.45	2.39	2.34	2.30	2.27	2.25	2.23	2.21	2.19	2.18	2.17	2.16	2.15	11
12	3.18	2.81	2.61	2.48	2.39	2.33	2.28	2.24	2.21	2.19	2.17	2.15	2.13	2.12	2.10	2.09	2.08	12
13	3.14	2.76	2.56	2.43	2.35	2.28	2.23	2.20	2.16	2.14	2.12	2.10	2.08	2.07	2.05	2.04	2.03	13
14	3.10	2.73	2.52	2.39	2.31	2.24	2.19	2.15	2.12	2.10	2.07	2.05	2.04	2.02	2.01	2.00	1.99	14
15	3.07	2.70	2.49	2.36	2.27	2.21	2.16	2.12	2.09	2.06	2.04	2.02	2.00	1.99	1.97	1.96	1.95	15
16	3.05	2.67	2.46	2.33	2.24	2.18	2.13	2.09	2.06	2.03	2.01	1.99	1.97	1.95	1.94	1.93	1.92	16
17	3.03	2.64	2.44	2.31	2.22	2.15	2.10	2.06	2.03	2.00	1.98	1.96	1.94	1.93	1.91	1.90	1.89	17
18	3.01	2.62	2.42	2.29	2.20	2.13	2.08	2.04	2.00	1.98	1.95	1.93	1.92	1.90	1.89	1.87	1.86	18
19	2.99	2.61	2.40	2.27	2.18	2.11	2.06	2.02	1.98	1.96	1.93	1.91	1.89	1.88	1.86	1.85	1.84	19
20	2.97	2.59	2.38	2.25	2.16	2.09	2.04	2.00	1.96	1.94	1.91	1.89	1.87	1.86	1.84	1.83	1.82	20
21	2.96	2.57	2.36	2.23	2.14	2.08	2.02	1.98	1.95	1.92	1.90	1.87	1.86	1.84	1.83	1.81	1.80	21
22	2.95	2.56	2.35	2.22	2.13	2.06	2.01	1.97	1.93	1.90	1.88	1.86	1.84	1.83	1.81	1.80	1.79	22
23	2.94	2.55	2.34	2.21	2.11	2.05	1.99	1.95	1.92	1.89	1.87	1.84	1.83	1.81	1.80	1.78	1.77	23
24	2.93	2.54	2.33	2.19	2.10	2.04	1.98	1.94	1.91	1.88	1.85	1.83	1.81	1.80	1.78	1.77	1.76	24
25	2.92	2.53	2.32	2.18	2.09	2.02	1.97	1.93	1.89	1.87	1.84	1.82	1.80	1.79	1.77	1.76	1.75	25
26	2.91	2.52	2.31	2.17	2.08	2.01	1.96	1.92	1.88	1.86	1.83	1.81	1.79	1.77	1.76	1.75	1.73	26
27	2.90	2.51	2.30	2.17	2.07	2.00	1.95	1.91	1.87	1.85	1.82	1.80	1.78	1.76	1.75	1.74	1.72	27
28	2.89	2.50	2.29	2.16	2.06	2.00	1.94	1.90	1.87	1.84	1.81	1.79	1.77	1.75	1.74	1.73	1.71	28
29	2.89	2.50	2.28	2.15	2.06	1.99	1.93	1.89	1.86	1.83	1.80	1.78	1.76	1.75	1.73	1.72	1.71	29
30	2.88	2.49	2.28	2.14	2.05	1.98	1.93	1.88	1.85	1.82	1.79	1.77	1.75	1.74	1.72	1.71	1.70	30
40	2.84	2.44	2.23	2.09	2.00	1.93	1.87	1.83	1.79	1.76	1.74	1.71	1.70	1.68	1.66	1.65	1.64	40
60	2.79	2.39	2.18	2.04	1.95	1.87	1.82	1.77	1.74	1.71	1.68	1.66	1.64	1.62	1.60	1.59	1.58	60
100	2.76	2.36	2.14	2.00	1.91	1.83	1.78	1.73	1.69	1.66	1.64	1.61	1.59	1.57	1.56	1.54	1.53	100
∞	2.71	2.30	2.08	1.94	1.85	1.77	1.72	1.67	1.63	1.60	1.57	1.55	1.52	1.50	1.49	1.47	1.46	∞

Degrees of freedom for the denominator

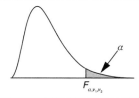

	Degrees of freedom for the numerator																
	(v_1)																
(v_2)	18	19	20	21	22	23	24	25	26	27	28	29	30	40	60	100	∞	(v_2)
1	61.57	61.66	61.74	61.81	61.88	61.95	62.00	62.05	62.10	62.15	62.19	62.23	62.26	62.53	62.79	63.01	63.33	1
2	9.44	9.44	9.44	9.44	9.45	9.45	9.45	9.45	9.45	9.45	9.46	9.46	9.46	9.47	9.47	9.48	9.49	2
3	5.19	5.19	5.18	5.18	5.18	5.18	5.18	5.17	5.17	5.17	5.17	5.17	5.17	5.16	5.15	5.14	5.13	3
4	3.85	3.85	3.84	3.84	3.84	3.83	3.83	3.83	3.83	3.82	3.82	3.82	3.82	3.80	3.79	3.78	3.76	4
5	3.22	3.21	3.21	3.20	3.20	3.19	3.19	3.19	3.18	3.18	3.18	3.18	3.17	3.16	3.14	3.13	3.10	5
6	2.85	2.84	2.84	2.83	2.83	2.82	2.82	2.81	2.81	2.81	2.81	2.80	2.80	2.78	2.76	2.75	2.72	6
7	2.61	2.60	2.59	2.59	2.58	2.58	2.58	2.57	2.57	2.56	2.56	2.56	2.56	2.54	2.51	2.50	2.47	7
8	2.44	2.43	2.42	2.42	2.41	2.41	2.40	2.40	2.40	2.39	2.39	2.39	2.38	2.36	2.34	2.32	2.29	8
9	2.31	2.30	2.30	2.29	2.29	2.28	2.28	2.27	2.27	2.26	2.26	2.26	2.25	2.23	2.21	2.19	2.16	9
10	2.22	2.21	2.20	2.19	2.19	2.18	2.18	2.17	2.17	2.17	2.16	2.16	2.16	2.13	2.11	2.09	2.06	10
11	2.14	2.13	2.12	2.12	2.11	2.11	2.10	2.10	2.09	2.09	2.08	2.08	2.08	2.05	2.03	2.01	1.97	11
12	2.08	2.07	2.06	2.05	2.05	2.04	2.04	2.03	2.03	2.02	2.02	2.01	2.01	1.99	1.96	1.94	1.90	12
13	2.02	2.01	2.01	2.00	1.99	1.99	1.98	1.98	1.97	1.97	1.96	1.96	1.96	1.93	1.90	1.88	1.85	13
14	1.98	1.97	1.96	1.96	1.95	1.94	1.94	1.93	1.93	1.92	1.92	1.92	1.91	1.89	1.86	1.83	1.80	14
15	1.94	1.93	1.92	1.92	1.91	1.90	1.90	1.89	1.89	1.88	1.88	1.88	1.87	1.85	1.82	1.79	1.76	15
16	1.91	1.90	1.89	1.88	1.88	1.87	1.87	1.86	1.86	1.85	1.85	1.84	1.84	1.81	1.78	1.76	1.72	16
17	1.88	1.87	1.86	1.86	1.85	1.84	1.84	1.83	1.83	1.82	1.82	1.81	1.81	1.78	1.75	1.73	1.69	17
18	1.85	1.84	1.84	1.83	1.82	1.82	1.81	1.80	1.80	1.80	1.79	1.79	1.78	1.75	1.72	1.70	1.66	18
19	1.83	1.82	1.81	1.81	1.80	1.79	1.79	1.78	1.78	1.77	1.77	1.76	1.76	1.73	1.70	1.67	1.63	19
20	1.81	1.80	1.79	1.79	1.78	1.77	1.77	1.76	1.76	1.75	1.75	1.74	1.74	1.71	1.68	1.65	1.61	20
21	1.79	1.78	1.78	1.77	1.76	1.75	1.75	1.74	1.74	1.73	1.73	1.72	1.72	1.69	1.66	1.63	1.59	21
22	1.78	1.77	1.76	1.75	1.74	1.74	1.73	1.73	1.72	1.72	1.71	1.71	1.70	1.67	1.64	1.61	1.57	22
23	1.76	1.75	1.74	1.74	1.73	1.72	1.72	1.71	1.70	1.70	1.69	1.69	1.69	1.66	1.62	1.59	1.55	23
24	1.75	1.74	1.73	1.72	1.71	1.71	1.70	1.70	1.69	1.69	1.68	1.68	1.67	1.64	1.61	1.58	1.53	24
25	1.74	1.73	1.72	1.71	1.70	1.70	1.69	1.68	1.68	1.67	1.67	1.66	1.66	1.63	1.59	1.56	1.52	25
26	1.72	1.71	1.71	1.70	1.69	1.68	1.68	1.67	1.67	1.66	1.66	1.65	1.65	1.61	1.58	1.55	1.50	26
27	1.71	1.70	1.70	1.69	1.68	1.67	1.67	1.66	1.65	1.65	1.64	1.64	1.64	1.60	1.57	1.54	1.49	27
28	1.70	1.69	1.69	1.68	1.67	1.66	1.66	1.65	1.64	1.64	1.63	1.63	1.63	1.59	1.56	1.53	1.48	28
29	1.69	1.68	1.68	1.67	1.66	1.65	1.65	1.64	1.63	1.63	1.62	1.62	1.62	1.58	1.55	1.52	1.47	29
30	1.69	1.68	1.67	1.66	1.65	1.64	1.64	1.63	1.63	1.62	1.62	1.61	1.61	1.57	1.54	1.51	1.46	30
40	1.62	1.61	1.61	1.60	1.59	1.58	1.57	1.57	1.56	1.56	1.55	1.55	1.54	1.51	1.47	1.43	1.38	40
60	1.56	1.55	1.54	1.53	1.53	1.52	1.51	1.50	1.50	1.49	1.49	1.48	1.48	1.44	1.40	1.36	1.29	60
100	1.52	1.50	1.49	1.48	1.48	1.47	1.46	1.45	1.45	1.44	1.43	1.43	1.42	1.38	1.34	1.29	1.21	100
∞	1.44	1.43	1.42	1.41	1.40	1.39	1.38	1.38	1.37	1.36	1.35	1.35	1.34	1.30	1.24	1.18	1.00	∞

Degrees of freedom for the denominator

Appendix 20

Appendix 21

F(0.05) Distribution Table

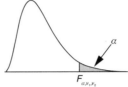

		Degrees of freedom for the numerator															
		(v_1)															
(v_2)	1	2	3	4	5	6	7	8	9	10	11	12	13	14	15	16	17
1	161.45	199.50	215.71	224.58	230.16	233.99	236.77	238.88	240.54	241.88	242.98	243.91	244.69	245.36	245.95	246.46	246.92
2	18.51	19.00	19.16	19.25	19.30	19.33	19.35	19.37	19.38	19.40	19.40	19.41	19.42	19.42	19.43	19.43	19.44
3	10.13	9.55	9.28	9.12	9.01	8.94	8.89	8.85	8.81	8.79	8.76	8.74	8.73	8.71	8.70	8.69	8.68
4	7.71	6.94	6.59	6.39	6.26	6.16	6.09	6.04	6.00	5.96	5.94	5.91	5.89	5.87	5.86	5.84	5.83
5	6.61	5.79	5.41	5.19	5.05	4.95	4.88	4.82	4.77	4.74	4.70	4.68	4.66	4.64	4.62	4.60	4.59
6	5.99	5.14	4.76	4.53	4.39	4.28	4.21	4.15	4.10	4.06	4.03	4.00	3.98	3.96	3.94	3.92	3.91
7	5.59	4.74	4.35	4.12	3.97	3.87	3.79	3.73	3.68	3.64	3.60	3.57	3.55	3.53	3.51	3.49	3.48
8	5.32	4.46	4.07	3.84	3.69	3.58	3.50	3.44	3.39	3.35	3.31	3.28	3.26	3.24	3.22	3.20	3.19
9	5.12	4.26	3.86	3.63	3.48	3.37	3.29	3.23	3.18	3.14	3.10	3.07	3.05	3.03	3.01	2.99	2.97
10	4.96	4.10	3.71	3.48	3.33	3.22	3.14	3.07	3.02	2.98	2.94	2.91	2.89	2.86	2.85	2.83	2.81
11	4.84	3.98	3.59	3.36	3.20	3.09	3.01	2.95	2.90	2.85	2.82	2.79	2.76	2.74	2.72	2.70	2.69
12	4.75	3.89	3.49	3.26	3.11	3.00	2.91	2.85	2.80	2.75	2.72	2.69	2.66	2.64	2.62	2.60	2.58
13	4.67	3.81	3.41	3.18	3.03	2.92	2.83	2.77	2.71	2.67	2.63	2.60	2.58	2.55	2.53	2.51	2.50
14	4.60	3.74	3.34	3.11	2.96	2.85	2.76	2.70	2.65	2.60	2.57	2.53	2.51	2.48	2.46	2.44	2.43
15	4.54	3.68	3.29	3.06	2.90	2.79	2.71	2.64	2.59	2.54	2.51	2.48	2.45	2.42	2.40	2.38	2.37
16	4.49	3.63	3.24	3.01	2.85	2.74	2.66	2.59	2.54	2.49	2.46	2.42	2.40	2.37	2.35	2.33	2.32
17	4.45	3.59	3.20	2.96	2.81	2.70	2.61	2.55	2.49	2.45	2.41	2.38	2.35	2.33	2.31	2.29	2.27
18	4.41	3.55	3.16	2.93	2.77	2.66	2.58	2.51	2.46	2.41	2.37	2.34	2.31	2.29	2.27	2.25	2.23
19	4.38	3.52	3.13	2.90	2.74	2.63	2.54	2.48	2.42	2.38	2.34	2.31	2.28	2.26	2.23	2.21	2.20
20	4.35	3.49	3.10	2.87	2.71	2.60	2.51	2.45	2.39	2.35	2.31	2.28	2.25	2.22	2.20	2.18	2.17
21	4.32	3.47	3.07	2.84	2.68	2.57	2.49	2.42	2.37	2.32	2.28	2.25	2.22	2.20	2.18	2.16	2.14
22	4.30	3.44	3.05	2.82	2.66	2.55	2.46	2.40	2.34	2.30	2.26	2.23	2.20	2.17	2.15	2.13	2.11
23	4.28	3.42	3.03	2.80	2.64	2.53	2.44	2.37	2.32	2.27	2.24	2.20	2.18	2.15	2.13	2.11	2.09
24	4.26	3.40	3.01	2.78	2.62	2.51	2.42	2.36	2.30	2.25	2.22	2.18	2.15	2.13	2.11	2.09	2.07
25	4.24	3.39	2.99	2.76	2.60	2.49	2.40	2.34	2.28	2.24	2.20	2.16	2.14	2.11	2.09	2.07	2.05
26	4.23	3.37	2.98	2.74	2.59	2.47	2.39	2.32	2.27	2.22	2.18	2.15	2.12	2.09	2.07	2.05	2.03
27	4.21	3.35	2.96	2.73	2.57	2.46	2.37	2.31	2.25	2.20	2.17	2.13	2.10	2.08	2.06	2.04	2.02
28	4.20	3.34	2.95	2.71	2.56	2.45	2.36	2.29	2.24	2.19	2.15	2.12	2.09	2.06	2.04	2.02	2.00
29	4.18	3.33	2.93	2.70	2.55	2.43	2.35	2.28	2.22	2.18	2.14	2.10	2.08	2.05	2.03	2.01	1.99
30	4.17	3.32	2.92	2.69	2.53	2.42	2.33	2.27	2.21	2.16	2.13	2.09	2.06	2.04	2.01	1.99	1.98
40	4.08	3.23	2.84	2.61	2.45	2.34	2.25	2.18	2.12	2.08	2.04	2.00	1.97	1.95	1.92	1.90	1.89
60	4.00	3.15	2.76	2.53	2.37	2.25	2.17	2.10	2.04	1.99	1.95	1.92	1.89	1.86	1.84	1.82	1.80
100	3.94	3.09	2.70	2.46	2.31	2.19	2.10	2.03	1.97	1.93	1.89	1.85	1.82	1.79	1.77	1.75	1.73
∞	3.84	3.00	2.60	2.37	2.21	2.10	2.01	1.94	1.88	1.83	1.79	1.75	1.72	1.69	1.67	1.64	1.62

Degrees of freedom for the denominator

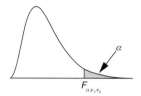

	Degrees of freedom for the numerator																		
	(v_1)																		
	18	19	20	21	22	23	24	25	26	27	28	29	30	40	60	100	∞	(v_2)
1	247.32	247.69	248.01	248.31	248.58	248.83	249.05	249.26	249.45	249.63	249.80	249.95	250.10	251.14	252.20	253.04	254.31	1
2	19.44	19.44	19.45	19.45	19.45	19.45	19.45	19.46	19.46	19.46	19.46	19.46	19.46	19.47	19.48	19.49	9.49	2
3	8.67	8.67	8.66	8.65	8.65	8.64	8.64	8.63	8.63	8.63	8.62	8.62	8.62	8.59	8.57	8.55	5.13	3
4	5.82	5.81	5.80	5.79	5.79	5.78	5.77	5.77	5.76	5.76	5.75	5.75	5.75	5.72	5.69	5.66	3.76	4
5	4.58	4.57	4.56	4.55	4.54	4.53	4.53	4.52	4.52	4.51	4.50	4.50	4.50	4.46	4.43	4.41	3.10	5
6	3.90	3.88	3.87	3.86	3.86	3.85	3.84	3.83	3.83	3.82	3.82	3.81	3.81	3.77	3.74	3.71	2.72	6
7	3.47	3.46	3.44	3.43	3.43	3.42	3.41	3.40	3.40	3.39	3.39	3.38	3.38	3.34	3.30	3.27	2.47	7
8	3.17	3.16	3.15	3.14	3.13	3.12	3.12	3.11	3.10	3.10	3.09	3.08	3.08	3.04	3.01	2.97	2.29	8
9	2.96	2.95	2.94	2.93	2.92	2.91	2.90	2.89	2.89	2.88	2.87	2.87	2.86	2.83	2.79	2.76	2.16	9
10	2.80	2.79	2.77	2.76	2.75	2.75	2.74	2.73	2.72	2.72	2.71	2.70	2.70	2.66	2.62	2.59	2.06	10
11	2.67	2.66	2.65	2.64	2.63	2.62	2.61	2.60	2.59	2.59	2.58	2.58	2.57	2.53	2.49	2.46	1.97	11
12	2.57	2.56	2.54	2.53	2.52	2.51	2.51	2.50	2.49	2.48	2.48	2.47	2.47	2.43	2.38	2.35	1.90	12
13	2.48	2.47	2.46	2.45	2.44	2.43	2.42	2.41	2.41	2.40	2.39	2.39	2.38	2.34	2.30	2.26	1.85	13
14	2.41	2.40	2.39	2.38	2.37	2.36	2.35	2.34	2.33	2.33	2.32	2.31	2.31	2.27	2.22	2.19	1.80	14
15	2.35	2.34	2.33	2.32	2.31	2.30	2.29	2.28	2.27	2.27	2.26	2.25	2.25	2.20	2.16	2.12	1.76	15
16	2.30	2.29	2.28	2.26	2.25	2.24	2.24	2.23	2.22	2.21	2.21	2.20	2.19	2.15	2.11	2.07	1.72	16
17	2.26	2.24	2.23	2.22	2.21	2.20	2.19	2.18	2.17	2.17	2.16	2.15	2.15	2.10	2.06	2.02	1.69	17
18	2.22	2.20	2.19	2.18	2.17	2.16	2.15	2.14	2.13	2.13	2.12	2.11	2.11	2.06	2.02	1.98	1.66	18
19	2.18	2.17	2.16	2.14	2.13	2.12	2.11	2.11	2.10	2.09	2.08	2.08	2.07	2.03	1.98	1.94	1.63	19
20	2.15	2.14	2.12	2.11	2.10	2.09	2.08	2.07	2.07	2.06	2.05	2.05	2.04	1.99	1.95	1.91	1.61	20
21	2.12	2.11	2.10	2.08	2.07	2.06	2.05	2.05	2.04	2.03	2.02	2.02	2.01	1.96	1.92	1.88	1.59	21
22	2.10	2.08	2.07	2.06	2.05	2.04	2.03	2.02	2.01	2.00	2.00	1.99	1.98	1.94	1.89	1.85	1.57	22
23	2.08	2.06	2.05	2.04	2.02	2.01	2.01	2.00	1.99	1.98	1.97	1.97	1.96	1.91	1.86	1.82	1.55	23
24	2.05	2.04	2.03	2.01	2.00	1.99	1.98	1.97	1.97	1.96	1.95	1.95	1.94	1.89	1.84	1.80	1.53	24
25	2.04	2.02	2.01	2.00	1.98	1.97	1.96	1.96	1.95	1.94	1.93	1.93	1.92	1.87	1.82	1.78	1.52	25
26	2.02	2.00	1.99	1.98	1.97	1.96	1.95	1.94	1.93	1.92	1.91	1.91	1.90	1.85	1.80	1.76	1.50	26
27	2.00	1.99	1.97	1.96	1.95	1.94	1.93	1.92	1.91	1.90	1.90	1.89	1.88	1.84	1.79	1.74	1.49	27
28	1.99	1.97	1.96	1.95	1.93	1.92	1.91	1.91	1.90	1.89	1.88	1.88	1.87	1.82	1.77	1.73	1.48	28
29	1.97	1.96	1.94	1.93	1.92	1.91	1.90	1.89	1.88	1.88	1.87	1.86	1.85	1.81	1.75	1.71	1.47	29
30	1.96	1.95	1.93	1.92	1.91	1.90	1.89	1.88	1.87	1.86	1.85	1.85	1.84	1.79	1.74	1.70	1.46	30
40	1.87	1.85	1.84	1.83	1.81	1.80	1.79	1.78	1.77	1.77	1.76	1.75	1.74	1.69	1.64	1.59	1.38	40
60	1.78	1.76	1.75	1.73	1.72	1.71	1.70	1.69	1.68	1.67	1.66	1.66	1.65	1.59	1.53	1.48	1.29	60
100	1.71	1.69	1.68	1.66	1.65	1.64	1.63	1.62	1.61	1.60	1.59	1.58	1.57	1.52	1.45	1.39	1.21	100
∞	1.60	1.59	1.57	1.56	1.54	1.53	1.52	1.51	1.50	1.49	1.48	1.47	1.46	1.39	1.32	1.24	1.00	∞

Degrees of freedom for the denominator

Appendix 21

Appendix 22

F(0.025) Distribution Table

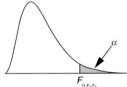

$$F_{\alpha, \nu_1, \nu_2}$$

Appendix 22

Degrees of freedom for the denominator

	Degrees of freedom for the numerator																	
	(ν_1)																	
(ν_2)	**1**	**2**	**3**	**4**	**5**	**6**	**7**	**8**	**9**	**10**	**11**	**12**	**13**	**14**	**15**	**16**	**17**	
1	647.79	799.50	864.16	899.58	921.85	937.11	948.22	956.66	963.28	968.63	973.03	976.71	979.84	982.53	984.87	986.92	988.73	
2	38.51	39.00	39.17	39.25	39.30	39.33	39.36	39.37	39.39	39.40	39.41	39.41	39.42	39.43	39.43	39.44	39.44	
3	17.44	16.04	15.44	15.10	14.88	14.73	14.62	14.54	14.47	14.42	14.37	14.34	14.30	14.28	14.25	14.23	14.21	
4	12.22	10.65	9.98	9.60	9.36	9.20	9.07	8.98	8.90	8.84	8.79	8.75	8.71	8.68	8.66	8.63	8.61	
5	10.01	8.43	7.76	7.39	7.15	6.98	6.85	6.76	6.68	6.62	6.57	6.52	6.49	6.46	6.43	6.40	6.38	
6	8.81	7.26	6.60	6.23	5.99	5.82	5.70	5.60	5.52	5.46	5.41	5.37	5.33	5.30	5.27	5.24	5.22	
7	8.07	6.54	5.89	5.52	5.29	5.12	4.99	4.90	4.82	4.76	4.71	4.67	4.63	4.60	4.57	4.54	4.52	
8	7.57	6.06	5.42	5.05	4.82	4.65	4.53	4.43	4.36	4.30	4.24	4.20	4.16	4.13	4.10	4.08	4.05	
9	7.21	5.71	5.08	4.72	4.48	4.32	4.20	4.10	4.03	3.96	3.91	3.87	3.83	3.80	3.77	3.74	3.72	
10	6.94	5.46	4.83	4.47	4.24	4.07	3.95	3.85	3.78	3.72	3.66	3.62	3.58	3.55	3.52	3.50	3.47	
11	6.72	5.26	4.63	4.28	4.04	3.88	3.76	3.66	3.59	3.53	3.47	3.43	3.39	3.36	3.33	3.30	3.28	
12	6.55	5.10	4.47	4.12	3.89	3.73	3.61	3.51	3.44	3.37	3.32	3.28	3.24	3.21	3.18	3.15	3.13	
13	6.41	4.97	4.35	4.00	3.77	3.60	3.48	3.39	3.31	3.25	3.20	3.15	3.12	3.08	3.05	3.03	3.00	
14	6.30	4.86	4.24	3.89	3.66	3.50	3.38	3.29	3.21	3.15	3.09	3.05	3.01	2.98	2.95	2.92	2.90	
15	6.20	4.77	4.15	3.80	3.58	3.41	3.29	3.20	3.12	3.06	3.01	2.96	2.92	2.89	2.86	2.84	2.81	
16	6.12	4.69	4.08	3.73	3.50	3.34	3.22	3.12	3.05	2.99	2.93	2.89	2.85	2.82	2.79	2.76	2.74	
17	6.04	4.62	4.01	3.66	3.44	3.28	3.16	3.06	2.98	2.92	2.87	2.82	2.79	2.75	2.72	2.70	2.67	
18	5.98	4.56	3.95	3.61	3.38	3.22	3.10	3.01	2.93	2.87	2.81	2.77	2.73	2.70	2.67	2.64	2.62	
19	5.92	4.51	3.90	3.56	3.33	3.17	3.05	2.96	2.88	2.82	2.76	2.72	2.68	2.65	2.62	2.59	2.57	
20	5.87	4.46	3.86	3.51	3.29	3.13	3.01	2.91	2.84	2.77	2.72	2.68	2.64	2.60	2.57	2.55	2.52	
21	5.83	4.42	3.82	3.48	3.25	3.09	2.97	2.87	2.80	2.73	2.68	2.64	2.60	2.56	2.53	2.51	2.48	
22	5.79	4.38	3.78	3.44	3.22	3.05	2.93	2.84	2.76	2.70	2.65	2.60	2.56	2.53	2.50	2.47	2.45	
23	5.75	4.35	3.75	3.41	3.18	3.02	2.90	2.81	2.73	2.67	2.62	2.57	2.53	2.50	2.47	2.44	2.42	
24	5.72	4.32	3.72	3.38	3.15	2.99	2.87	2.78	2.70	2.64	2.59	2.54	2.50	2.47	2.44	2.41	2.39	
25	5.69	4.29	3.69	3.35	3.13	2.97	2.85	2.75	2.68	2.61	2.56	2.51	2.48	2.44	2.41	2.38	2.36	
26	5.66	4.27	3.67	3.33	3.10	2.94	2.82	2.73	2.65	2.59	2.54	2.49	2.45	2.42	2.39	2.36	2.34	
27	5.63	4.24	3.65	3.31	3.08	2.92	2.80	2.71	2.63	2.57	2.51	2.47	2.43	2.39	2.36	2.34	2.31	
28	5.61	4.22	3.63	3.29	3.06	2.90	2.78	2.69	2.61	2.55	2.49	2.45	2.41	2.37	2.34	2.32	2.29	
29	5.59	4.20	3.61	3.27	3.04	2.88	2.76	2.67	2.59	2.53	2.48	2.43	2.39	2.36	2.32	2.30	2.27	
30	5.57	4.18	3.59	3.25	3.03	2.87	2.75	2.65	2.57	2.51	2.46	2.41	2.37	2.34	2.31	2.28	2.26	
40	5.42	4.05	3.46	3.13	2.90	2.74	2.62	2.53	2.45	2.39	2.33	2.29	2.25	2.21	2.18	2.15	2.13	
60	5.29	3.93	3.34	3.01	2.79	2.63	2.51	2.41	2.33	2.27	2.22	2.17	2.13	2.09	2.06	2.03	2.01	
100	5.18	3.83	3.25	2.92	2.70	2.54	2.42	2.32	2.24	2.18	2.12	2.08	2.04	2.00	1.97	1.94	1.91	
∞	5.02	3.69	3.12	2.79	2.57	2.41	2.29	2.19	2.11	2.05	1.99	1.94	1.90	1.87	1.83	1.80	1.78	

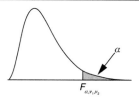

Degrees of freedom for the numerator																	
(v_1)																	
18	19	20	21	22	23	24	25	26	27	28	29	30	40	60	100	∞	(v_2)
990.35	991.80	993.10	994.29	995.36	996.35	997.25	998.08	998.85	999.56	1000.22	1000.84	1001.41	1005.60	1009.80	1013.17	1018.26	1
39.44	39.45	39.45	39.45	39.45	39.45	39.46	39.46	39.46	39.46	39.46	39.46	39.46	39.47	39.48	39.49	39.50	2
14.20	14.18	14.17	14.16	14.14	14.13	14.12	14.12	14.11	14.10	14.09	14.09	14.08	14.04	13.99	13.96	13.90	3
8.59	8.58	8.56	8.55	8.53	8.52	8.51	8.50	8.49	8.48	8.48	8.47	8.46	8.41	8.36	8.32	8.26	4
6.36	6.34	6.33	6.31	6.30	6.29	6.28	6.27	6.26	6.25	6.24	6.23	6.23	6.18	6.12	6.08	6.02	5
5.20	5.18	5.17	5.15	5.14	5.13	5.12	5.11	5.10	5.09	5.08	5.07	5.07	5.01	4.96	4.92	4.85	6
4.50	4.48	4.47	4.45	4.44	4.43	4.41	4.40	4.39	4.39	4.38	4.37	4.36	4.31	4.25	4.21	4.14	7
4.03	4.02	4.00	3.98	3.97	3.96	3.95	3.94	3.93	3.92	3.91	3.90	3.89	3.84	3.78	3.74	3.67	8
3.70	3.68	3.67	3.65	3.64	3.63	3.61	3.60	3.59	3.58	3.58	3.57	3.56	3.51	3.45	3.40	3.33	9
3.45	3.44	3.42	3.40	3.39	3.38	3.37	3.35	3.34	3.34	3.33	3.32	3.31	3.26	3.20	3.15	3.08	10
3.26	3.24	3.23	3.21	3.20	3.18	3.17	3.16	3.15	3.14	3.13	3.13	3.12	3.06	3.00	2.96	2.88	11
3.11	3.09	3.07	3.06	3.04	3.03	3.02	3.01	3.00	2.99	2.98	2.97	2.96	2.91	2.85	2.80	2.72	12
2.98	2.96	2.95	2.93	2.92	2.91	2.89	2.88	2.87	2.86	2.85	2.85	2.84	2.78	2.72	2.67	2.60	13
2.88	2.86	2.84	2.83	2.81	2.80	2.79	2.78	2.77	2.76	2.75	2.74	2.73	2.67	2.61	2.56	2.49	14
2.79	2.77	2.76	2.74	2.73	2.71	2.70	2.69	2.68	2.67	2.66	2.65	2.64	2.59	2.52	2.47	2.40	15
2.72	2.70	2.68	2.67	2.65	2.64	2.63	2.61	2.60	2.59	2.58	2.58	2.57	2.51	2.45	2.40	2.32	16
2.65	2.63	2.62	2.60	2.59	2.57	2.56	2.55	2.54	2.53	2.52	2.51	2.50	2.44	2.38	2.33	2.25	17
2.60	2.58	2.56	2.54	2.53	2.52	2.50	2.49	2.48	2.47	2.46	2.45	2.44	2.38	2.32	2.27	2.19	18
2.55	2.53	2.51	2.49	2.48	2.46	2.45	2.44	2.43	2.42	2.41	2.40	2.39	2.33	2.27	2.22	2.13	19
2.50	2.48	2.46	2.45	2.43	2.42	2.41	2.40	2.39	2.38	2.37	2.36	2.35	2.29	2.22	2.17	2.09	20
2.46	2.44	2.42	2.41	2.39	2.38	2.37	2.36	2.34	2.33	2.33	2.32	2.31	2.25	2.18	2.13	2.04	21
2.43	2.41	2.39	2.37	2.36	2.34	2.33	2.32	2.31	2.30	2.29	2.28	2.27	2.21	2.14	2.09	2.00	22
2.39	2.37	2.36	2.34	2.33	2.31	2.30	2.29	2.28	2.27	2.26	2.25	2.24	2.18	2.11	2.06	1.97	23
2.36	2.35	2.33	2.31	2.30	2.28	2.27	2.26	2.25	2.24	2.23	2.22	2.21	2.15	2.08	2.02	1.94	24
2.34	2.32	2.30	2.28	2.27	2.26	2.24	2.23	2.22	2.21	2.20	2.19	2.18	2.12	2.05	2.00	1.91	25
2.31	2.29	2.28	2.26	2.24	2.23	2.22	2.21	2.19	2.18	2.17	2.17	2.16	2.09	2.03	1.97	1.88	26
2.29	2.27	2.25	2.24	2.22	2.21	2.19	2.18	2.17	2.16	2.15	2.14	2.13	2.07	2.00	1.94	1.85	27
2.27	2.25	2.23	2.22	2.20	2.19	2.17	2.16	2.15	2.14	2.13	2.12	2.11	2.05	1.98	1.92	1.83	28
2.25	2.23	2.21	2.20	2.18	2.17	2.15	2.14	2.13	2.12	2.11	2.10	2.09	2.03	1.96	1.90	1.81	29
2.23	2.21	2.20	2.18	2.16	2.15	2.14	2.12	2.11	2.10	2.09	2.08	2.07	2.01	1.94	1.88	1.79	30
2.11	2.09	2.07	2.05	2.03	2.02	2.01	1.99	1.98	1.97	1.96	1.95	1.94	1.88	1.80	1.74	1.64	40
1.98	1.96	1.94	1.93	1.91	1.90	1.88	1.87	1.86	1.85	1.83	1.82	1.82	1.74	1.67	1.60	1.48	60
1.89	1.87	1.85	1.83	1.81	1.80	1.78	1.77	1.76	1.75	1.74	1.72	1.71	1.64	1.56	1.48	1.35	100
1.75	1.73	1.71	1.69	1.67	1.66	1.64	1.63	1.61	1.60	1.59	1.58	1.57	1.48	1.39	1.30	1.00	∞

Degrees of freedom for the denominator

Appendix 22

Appendix 23

F(0.01) Distribution Table

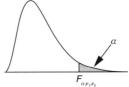

$$F_{\alpha, \nu_1, \nu_2}$$

Degrees of freedom for the numerator

(ν_1)

(ν_2)	1	2	3	4	5	6	7	8	9	10	11	12	13	14	15	16	17
1	4052.18	4999.50	5403.35	5624.58	5763.65	5858.99	5928.36	5981.07	6022.47	6055.85	6083.32	6106.32	6125.86	6142.67	6157.28	6170.10	6181.43
2	98.50	99.00	99.17	99.25	99.30	99.33	99.36	99.37	99.39	99.40	99.41	99.42	99.42	99.43	99.43	99.44	99.44
3	34.12	30.82	29.46	28.71	28.24	27.91	27.67	27.49	27.35	27.23	27.13	27.05	26.98	26.92	26.87	26.83	26.79
4	21.20	18.00	16.69	15.98	15.52	15.21	14.98	14.80	14.66	14.55	14.45	14.37	14.31	14.25	14.20	14.15	14.11
5	16.26	13.27	12.06	11.39	10.97	10.67	10.46	10.29	10.16	10.05	9.96	9.89	9.82	9.77	9.72	9.68	9.64
6	13.75	10.92	9.78	9.15	8.75	8.47	8.26	8.10	7.98	7.87	7.79	7.72	7.66	7.60	7.56	7.52	7.48
7	12.25	9.55	8.45	7.85	7.46	7.19	6.99	6.84	6.72	6.62	6.54	6.47	6.41	6.36	6.31	6.28	6.24
8	11.26	8.65	7.59	7.01	6.63	6.37	6.18	6.03	5.91	5.81	5.73	5.67	5.61	5.56	5.52	5.48	5.44
9	10.56	8.02	6.99	6.42	6.06	5.80	5.61	5.47	5.35	5.26	5.18	5.11	5.05	5.01	4.96	4.92	4.89
10	10.04	7.56	6.55	5.99	5.64	5.39	5.20	5.06	4.94	4.85	4.77	4.71	4.65	4.60	4.56	4.52	4.49
11	9.65	7.21	6.22	5.67	5.32	5.07	4.89	4.74	4.63	4.54	4.46	4.40	4.34	4.29	4.25	4.21	4.18
12	9.33	6.93	5.95	5.41	5.06	4.82	4.64	4.50	4.39	4.30	4.22	4.16	4.10	4.05	4.01	3.97	3.94
13	9.07	6.70	5.74	5.21	4.86	4.62	4.44	4.30	4.19	4.10	4.02	3.96	3.91	3.86	3.82	3.78	3.75
14	8.86	6.51	5.56	5.04	4.69	4.46	4.28	4.14	4.03	3.94	3.86	3.80	3.75	3.70	3.66	3.62	3.59
15	8.68	6.36	5.42	4.89	4.56	4.32	4.14	4.00	3.89	3.80	3.73	3.67	3.61	3.56	3.52	3.49	3.45
16	8.53	6.23	5.29	4.77	4.44	4.20	4.03	3.89	3.78	3.69	3.62	3.55	3.50	3.45	3.41	3.37	3.34
17	8.40	6.11	5.18	4.67	4.34	4.10	3.93	3.79	3.68	3.59	3.52	3.46	3.40	3.35	3.31	3.27	3.24
18	8.29	6.01	5.09	4.58	4.25	4.01	3.84	3.71	3.60	3.51	3.43	3.37	3.32	3.27	3.23	3.19	3.16
19	8.18	5.93	5.01	4.50	4.17	3.94	3.77	3.63	3.52	3.43	3.36	3.30	3.24	3.19	3.15	3.12	3.08
20	8.10	5.85	4.94	4.43	4.10	3.87	3.70	3.56	3.46	3.37	3.29	3.23	3.18	3.13	3.09	3.05	3.02
21	8.02	5.78	4.87	4.37	4.04	3.81	3.64	3.51	3.40	3.31	3.24	3.17	3.12	3.07	3.03	2.99	2.96
22	7.95	5.72	4.82	4.31	3.99	3.76	3.59	3.45	3.35	3.26	3.18	3.12	3.07	3.02	2.98	2.94	2.91
23	7.88	5.66	4.76	4.26	3.94	3.71	3.54	3.41	3.30	3.21	3.14	3.07	3.02	2.97	2.93	2.89	2.86
24	7.82	5.61	4.72	4.22	3.90	3.67	3.50	3.36	3.26	3.17	3.09	3.03	2.98	2.93	2.89	2.85	2.82
25	7.77	5.57	4.68	4.18	3.85	3.63	3.46	3.32	3.22	3.13	3.06	2.99	2.94	2.89	2.85	2.81	2.78
26	7.72	5.53	4.64	4.14	3.82	3.59	3.42	3.29	3.18	3.09	3.02	2.96	2.90	2.86	2.81	2.78	2.75
27	7.68	5.49	4.60	4.11	3.78	3.56	3.39	3.26	3.15	3.06	2.99	2.93	2.87	2.82	2.78	2.75	2.71
28	7.64	5.45	4.57	4.07	3.75	3.53	3.36	3.23	3.12	3.03	2.96	2.90	2.84	2.79	2.75	2.72	2.68
29	7.60	5.42	4.54	4.04	3.73	3.50	3.33	3.20	3.09	3.00	2.93	2.87	2.81	2.77	2.73	2.69	2.66
30	7.56	5.39	4.51	4.02	3.70	3.47	3.30	3.17	3.07	2.98	2.91	2.84	2.79	2.74	2.70	2.66	2.63
40	7.31	5.18	4.31	3.83	3.51	3.29	3.12	2.99	2.89	2.80	2.73	2.66	2.61	2.56	2.52	2.48	2.45
60	7.08	4.98	4.13	3.65	3.34	3.12	2.95	2.82	2.72	2.63	2.56	2.50	2.44	2.39	2.35	2.31	2.28
100	6.90	4.82	3.98	3.51	3.21	2.99	2.82	2.69	2.59	2.50	2.43	2.37	2.31	2.27	2.22	2.19	2.15
∞	6.63	4.61	3.78	3.32	3.02	2.80	2.64	2.51	2.41	2.32	2.25	2.18	2.13	2.08	2.04	2.00	1.97

Degrees of freedom for the denominator

Appendix 23

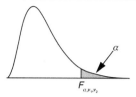

	Degrees of freedom for the numerator																	
	(v_1)																	
(v_2)	18	19	20	21	22	23	24	25	26	27	28	29	30	40	60	100	∞	(v_2)
1	6191.53	6200.58	6208.73	6216.12	6222.84	6228.99	6234.63	6239.83	6244.62	6249.07	6253.20	6257.05	6260.65	6286.78	6313.03	6334.11	6365.86	1
2	99.44	99.45	99.45	99.45	99.45	99.46	99.46	99.46	99.46	99.46	99.46	99.46	99.47	99.47	99.48	99.49	99.50	2
3	26.75	26.72	26.69	26.66	26.64	26.62	26.60	26.58	26.56	26.55	26.53	26.52	26.50	26.41	26.32	26.24	26.13	3
4	14.08	14.05	14.02	13.99	13.97	13.95	13.93	13.91	13.89	13.88	13.86	13.85	13.84	13.75	13.65	13.58	13.46	4
5	9.61	9.58	9.55	9.53	9.51	9.49	9.47	9.45	9.43	9.42	9.40	9.39	9.38	9.29	9.20	9.13	9.02	5
6	7.45	7.42	7.40	7.37	7.35	7.33	7.31	7.30	7.28	7.27	7.25	7.24	7.23	7.14	7.06	6.99	6.88	6
7	6.21	6.18	6.16	6.13	6.11	6.09	6.07	6.06	6.04	6.03	6.02	6.00	5.99	5.91	5.82	5.75	5.65	7
8	5.41	5.38	5.36	5.34	5.32	5.30	5.28	5.26	5.25	5.23	5.22	5.21	5.20	5.12	5.03	4.96	4.86	8
9	4.86	4.83	4.81	4.79	4.77	4.75	4.73	4.71	4.70	4.68	4.67	4.66	4.65	4.57	4.48	4.41	4.31	9
10	4.46	4.43	4.41	4.38	4.36	4.34	4.33	4.31	4.30	4.28	4.27	4.26	4.25	4.17	4.08	4.01	3.91	10
11	4.15	4.12	4.10	4.08	4.06	4.04	4.02	4.01	3.99	3.98	3.96	3.95	3.94	3.86	3.78	3.71	3.60	11
12	3.91	3.88	3.86	3.84	3.82	3.80	3.78	3.76	3.75	3.74	3.72	3.71	3.70	3.62	3.54	3.47	3.36	12
13	3.72	3.69	3.66	3.64	3.62	3.60	3.59	3.57	3.56	3.54	3.53	3.52	3.51	3.43	3.34	3.27	3.17	13
14	3.56	3.53	3.51	3.48	3.46	3.44	3.43	3.41	3.40	3.38	3.37	3.36	3.35	3.27	3.18	3.11	3.00	14
15	3.42	3.40	3.37	3.35	3.33	3.31	3.29	3.28	3.26	3.25	3.24	3.23	3.21	3.13	3.05	2.98	2.87	15
16	3.31	3.28	3.26	3.24	3.22	3.20	3.18	3.16	3.15	3.14	3.12	3.11	3.10	3.02	2.93	2.86	2.75	16
17	3.21	3.19	3.16	3.14	3.12	3.10	3.08	3.07	3.05	3.04	3.03	3.01	3.00	2.92	2.83	2.76	2.65	17
18	3.13	3.10	3.08	3.05	3.03	3.02	3.00	2.98	2.97	2.95	2.94	2.93	2.92	2.84	2.75	2.68	2.57	18
19	3.05	3.03	3.00	2.98	2.96	2.94	2.92	2.91	2.89	2.88	2.87	2.86	2.84	2.76	2.67	2.60	2.49	19
20	2.99	2.96	2.94	2.92	2.90	2.88	2.86	2.84	2.83	2.81	2.80	2.79	2.78	2.69	2.61	2.54	2.42	20
21	2.93	2.90	2.88	2.86	2.84	2.82	2.80	2.79	2.77	2.76	2.74	2.73	2.72	2.64	2.55	2.48	2.36	21
22	2.88	2.85	2.83	2.81	2.78	2.77	2.75	2.73	2.72	2.70	2.69	2.68	2.67	2.58	2.50	2.42	2.31	22
23	2.83	2.80	2.78	2.76	2.74	2.72	2.70	2.69	2.67	2.66	2.64	2.63	2.62	2.54	2.45	2.37	2.26	23
24	2.79	2.76	2.74	2.72	2.70	2.68	2.66	2.64	2.63	2.61	2.60	2.59	2.58	2.49	2.40	2.33	2.21	24
25	2.75	2.72	2.70	2.68	2.66	2.64	2.62	2.60	2.59	2.58	2.56	2.55	2.54	2.45	2.36	2.29	2.17	25
26	2.72	2.69	2.66	2.64	2.62	2.60	2.58	2.57	2.55	2.54	2.53	2.51	2.50	2.42	2.33	2.25	2.13	26
27	2.68	2.66	2.63	2.61	2.59	2.57	2.55	2.54	2.52	2.51	2.49	2.48	2.47	2.38	2.29	2.22	2.10	27
28	2.65	2.63	2.60	2.58	2.56	2.54	2.52	2.51	2.49	2.48	2.46	2.45	2.44	2.35	2.26	2.19	2.06	28
29	2.63	2.60	2.57	2.55	2.53	2.51	2.49	2.48	2.46	2.45	2.44	2.42	2.41	2.33	2.23	2.16	2.03	29
30	2.60	2.57	2.55	2.53	2.51	2.49	2.47	2.45	2.44	2.42	2.41	2.40	2.39	2.30	2.21	2.13	2.01	30
40	2.42	2.39	2.37	2.35	2.33	2.31	2.29	2.27	2.26	2.24	2.23	2.22	2.20	2.11	2.02	1.94	1.80	40
60	2.25	2.22	2.20	2.17	2.15	2.13	2.12	2.10	2.08	2.07	2.05	2.04	2.03	1.94	1.84	1.75	1.60	60
100	2.12	2.09	2.07	2.04	2.02	2.00	1.98	1.97	1.95	1.93	1.92	1.91	1.89	1.80	1.69	1.60	1.43	100
∞	1.93	1.90	1.88	1.85	1.83	1.81	1.79	1.77	1.76	1.74	1.72	1.71	1.70	1.59	1.47	1.36	1.00	∞

Degrees of freedom for the denominator

Appendix 23

Appendix 24
Median Ranks Table

	Sample of size n															
i	1	2	3	4	5	6	7	8	9	10	11	12	13	14	15	i
1	0.5000	0.2929	0.2063	0.1591	0.1294	0.1091	0.0943	0.0830	0.0741	0.0670	0.0611	0.0561	0.0519	0.0483	0.0452	1
2		0.7071	0.5000	0.3855	0.3136	0.2643	0.2284	0.2011	0.1797	0.1623	0.1480	0.1361	0.1259	0.1171	0.1095	2
3			0.7937	0.6145	0.5000	0.4214	0.3642	0.3207	0.2864	0.2588	0.2360	0.2169	0.2007	0.1867	0.1746	3
4				0.8409	0.6864	0.5786	0.5000	0.4402	0.3932	0.3553	0.3240	0.2978	0.2755	0.2564	0.2397	4
5					0.8706	0.7357	0.6358	0.5598	0.5000	0.4518	0.4120	0.3787	0.3504	0.3260	0.3048	5
6						0.8909	0.7716	0.6793	0.6068	0.5482	0.5000	0.4596	0.4252	0.3956	0.3698	6
7							0.9057	0.7989	0.7136	0.6447	0.5880	0.5404	0.5000	0.4652	0.4349	7
8								0.9170	0.8203	0.7412	0.6760	0.6213	0.5748	0.5348	0.5000	8
9									0.9259	0.8377	0.7640	0.7022	0.6496	0.6044	0.5651	9
10										0.9330	0.8520	0.7831	0.7245	0.6740	0.6302	10
11											0.9389	0.8639	0.7993	0.7436	0.6952	11
12												0.9439	0.8741	0.8133	0.7603	12
13													0.9481	0.8829	0.8254	13
14														0.9517	0.8905	14
15															0.9548	15
16																16
17																17
18																18
19																19
20																20
21																21
22																22
23																23
24																24
25																25
26																26
27																27
28																28
29																29
30																30

$$\text{Median rank}(i) = \begin{cases} 1 - \text{median rank}(n) & \text{for } i = 1 \\ \dfrac{i - 0.3175}{n + 0.365} & \text{for } i = 2, 3, \ldots, n-1 \\ 0.5^{1/n} & \text{for } i = n \end{cases}$$

							Sample of size n									
i	16	17	18	19	20	21	22	23	24	25	26	27	28	29	30	i
1	0.0424	0.0400	0.0378	0.0358	0.0341	0.0325	0.0310	0.0297	0.0285	0.0273	0.0263	0.0253	0.0245	0.0236	0.0228	1
2	0.1028	0.0969	0.0916	0.0869	0.0826	0.0788	0.0752	0.0720	0.0691	0.0663	0.0638	0.0615	0.0593	0.0573	0.0554	2
3	0.1639	0.1545	0.1461	0.1385	0.1317	0.1256	0.1199	0.1148	0.1101	0.1058	0.1017	0.0980	0.0946	0.0914	0.0883	3
4	0.2250	0.2121	0.2005	0.1902	0.1808	0.1724	0.1647	0.1576	0.1511	0.1452	0.1397	0.1346	0.1298	0.1254	0.1213	4
5	0.2861	0.2697	0.2550	0.2418	0.2299	0.2192	0.2094	0.2004	0.1922	0.1846	0.1776	0.1711	0.1651	0.1595	0.1542	5
6	0.3472	0.3272	0.3094	0.2934	0.2790	0.2660	0.2541	0.2432	0.2332	0.2240	0.2155	0.2077	0.2003	0.1935	0.1871	6
7	0.4083	0.3848	0.3639	0.3451	0.3281	0.3128	0.2988	0.2860	0.2743	0.2635	0.2535	0.2442	0.2356	0.2276	0.2201	7
8	0.4694	0.4424	0.4183	0.3967	0.3772	0.3596	0.3435	0.3288	0.3153	0.3029	0.2914	0.2807	0.2708	0.2616	0.2530	8
9	0.5306	0.5000	0.4728	0.4484	0.4263	0.4064	0.3882	0.3716	0.3564	0.3423	0.3293	0.3173	0.3061	0.2957	0.2859	9
10	0.5917	0.5576	0.5272	0.5000	0.4754	0.4532	0.4329	0.4144	0.3974	0.3817	0.3672	0.3538	0.3414	0.3297	0.3189	10
11	0.6528	0.6152	0.5817	0.5516	0.5246	0.5000	0.4776	0.4572	0.4384	0.4212	0.4052	0.3904	0.3766	0.3638	0.3518	11
12	0.7139	0.6728	0.6361	0.6033	0.5737	0.5468	0.5224	0.5000	0.4795	0.4606	0.4431	0.4269	0.4119	0.3978	0.3847	12
13	0.7750	0.7303	0.6906	0.6549	0.6228	0.5936	0.5671	0.5428	0.5205	0.5000	0.4810	0.4635	0.4471	0.4319	0.4177	13
14	0.8361	0.7879	0.7450	0.7066	0.6719	0.6404	0.6118	0.5856	0.5616	0.5394	0.5190	0.5000	0.4824	0.4659	0.4506	14
15	0.8972	0.8455	0.7995	0.7582	0.7210	0.6872	0.6565	0.6284	0.6026	0.5788	0.5569	0.5365	0.5176	0.5000	0.4835	15
16	0.9576	0.9031	0.8539	0.8098	0.7701	0.7340	0.7012	0.6712	0.6436	0.6183	0.5948	0.5731	0.5529	0.5341	0.5165	16
17		0.9600	0.9084	0.8615	0.8192	0.7808	0.7459	0.7140	0.6847	0.6577	0.6328	0.6096	0.5881	0.5681	0.5494	17
18			0.9622	0.9131	0.8683	0.8276	0.7906	0.7568	0.7257	0.6971	0.6707	0.6462	0.6234	0.6022	0.5823	18
19				0.9642	0.9174	0.8744	0.8353	0.7996	0.7668	0.7365	0.7086	0.6827	0.6586	0.6362	0.6153	19
20					0.9659	0.9212	0.8801	0.8424	0.8078	0.7760	0.7465	0.7193	0.6939	0.6703	0.6482	20
21						0.9675	0.9248	0.8852	0.8489	0.8154	0.7845	0.7558	0.7292	0.7043	0.6811	21
22							0.9690	0.9280	0.8899	0.8548	0.8224	0.7923	0.7644	0.7384	0.7141	22
23								0.9703	0.9309	0.8942	0.8603	0.8289	0.7997	0.7724	0.7470	23
24									0.9715	0.9337	0.8983	0.8654	0.8349	0.8065	0.7799	24
25										0.9727	0.9362	0.9020	0.8702	0.8405	0.8129	25
26											0.9737	0.9385	0.9054	0.8746	0.8458	26
27												0.9747	0.9407	0.9086	0.8787	27
28													0.9755	0.9427	0.9117	28
29														0.9764	0.9446	29
30															0.9772	30

Appendix 25
Normal Scores Table

Appendix 25

n	1	2	3	4	5	6	7	8	9	10	11	12	13	14	15	n
1	0.000	−0.545	−0.819	−0.998	−1.129	−1.231	−1.315	−1.385	−1.446	−1.499	−1.546	−1.588	−1.626	−1.662	−1.694	1
2		0.545	0.000	−0.291	−0.486	−0.630	−0.744	−0.838	−0.917	−0.985	−1.045	−1.098	−1.146	−1.189	−1.229	2
3			0.819	0.291	0.000	−0.198	−0.347	−0.466	−0.564	−0.647	−0.719	−0.783	−0.839	−0.890	−0.936	3
4				0.998	0.486	0.198	0.000	−0.150	−0.271	−0.371	−0.456	−0.531	−0.596	−0.655	−0.707	4
5					1.129	0.630	0.347	0.150	0.000	−0.121	−0.222	−0.309	−0.384	−0.451	−0.511	5
6						1.231	0.744	0.466	0.271	0.121	0.000	−0.102	−0.189	−0.265	−0.332	6
7							1.315	0.838	0.564	0.371	0.222	0.102	0.000	−0.087	−0.164	7
8								1.385	0.917	0.647	0.456	0.309	0.189	0.087	0.000	8
9									1.446	0.985	0.719	0.531	0.384	0.265	0.164	9
10										1.499	1.045	0.783	0.596	0.451	0.332	10
11											1.546	1.098	0.839	0.655	0.511	11
12												1.588	1.146	0.890	0.707	12
13													1.626	1.189	0.936	13
14														1.662	1.229	14
15															1.694	15
16																16
17																17
18																18
19																19
20																20
21																21
22																22
23																23
24																24
25																25
26																26
27																27
28																28
29																29
30																30

								n							
n	**16**	**17**	**18**	**19**	**20**	**21**	**22**	**23**	**24**	**25**	**26**	**27**	**28**	**29**	**30**	*n*
1	−1.724	−1.751	−1.777	−1.801	−1.824	−1.846	−1.866	−1.885	−1.904	−1.921	−1.938	−1.954	−1.969	−1.984	−1.998	**1**
2	−1.266	−1.299	−1.331	−1.360	−1.388	−1.414	−1.438	−1.461	−1.483	−1.504	−1.524	−1.542	−1.561	−1.578	−1.595	**2**
3	−0.978	−1.017	−1.053	−1.087	−1.118	−1.148	−1.175	−1.201	−1.226	−1.249	−1.272	−1.293	−1.313	−1.332	−1.351	**3**
4	−0.755	−0.799	−0.840	−0.877	−0.912	−0.945	−0.976	−1.004	−1.032	−1.057	−1.082	−1.105	−1.127	−1.148	−1.169	**4**
5	−0.565	−0.614	−0.659	−0.701	−0.739	−0.775	−0.809	−0.840	−0.870	−0.898	−0.925	−0.950	−0.974	−0.997	−1.019	**5**
6	−0.393	−0.448	−0.497	−0.543	−0.586	−0.625	−0.662	−0.696	−0.728	−0.759	−0.787	−0.815	−0.840	−0.865	−0.888	**6**
7	−0.232	−0.293	−0.348	−0.399	−0.445	−0.488	−0.528	−0.565	−0.600	−0.633	−0.664	−0.693	−0.721	−0.747	−0.772	**7**
8	−0.077	−0.145	−0.206	−0.262	−0.313	−0.360	−0.403	−0.443	−0.481	−0.516	−0.549	−0.581	−0.610	−0.638	−0.665	**8**
9	0.077	0.000	−0.068	−0.130	−0.186	−0.237	−0.284	−0.328	−0.368	−0.406	−0.442	−0.475	−0.507	−0.537	−0.565	**9**
10	0.232	0.145	0.068	0.000	−0.062	−0.118	−0.169	−0.216	−0.260	−0.301	−0.339	−0.375	−0.409	−0.441	−0.471	**10**
11	0.393	0.293	0.206	0.130	0.062	0.000	−0.056	−0.107	−0.155	−0.199	−0.240	−0.278	−0.314	−0.348	−0.380	**11**
12	0.565	0.448	0.348	0.262	0.186	0.118	0.056	0.000	−0.051	−0.099	−0.143	−0.184	−0.223	−0.259	−0.293	**12**
13	0.755	0.614	0.497	0.399	0.313	0.237	0.169	0.107	0.051	0.000	−0.048	−0.092	−0.133	−0.172	−0.208	**13**
14	0.978	0.799	0.659	0.543	0.445	0.360	0.284	0.216	0.155	0.099	0.048	0.000	−0.044	−0.085	−0.124	**14**
15	1.266	1.017	0.840	0.701	0.586	0.488	0.403	0.328	0.260	0.199	0.143	0.092	0.044	0.000	−0.041	**15**
16	1.724	1.299	1.053	0.877	0.739	0.625	0.528	0.443	0.368	0.301	0.240	0.184	0.133	0.085	0.041	**16**
17		1.751	1.331	1.087	0.912	0.775	0.662	0.565	0.481	0.406	0.339	0.278	0.223	0.172	0.124	**17**
18			1.777	1.360	1.118	0.945	0.809	0.696	0.600	0.516	0.442	0.375	0.314	0.259	0.208	**18**
19				1.801	1.388	1.148	0.976	0.840	0.728	0.633	0.549	0.475	0.409	0.348	0.293	**19**
20					1.824	1.414	1.175	1.004	0.870	0.759	0.664	0.581	0.507	0.441	0.380	**20**
21						1.846	1.438	1.201	1.032	0.898	0.787	0.693	0.610	0.537	0.471	**21**
22							1.866	1.461	1.226	1.057	0.925	0.815	0.721	0.638	0.565	**22**
23								1.885	1.483	1.249	1.082	0.950	0.840	0.747	0.665	**23**
24									1.904	1.504	1.272	1.105	0.974	0.865	0.772	**24**
25										1.921	1.524	1.293	1.127	0.997	0.888	**25**
26											1.938	1.542	1.313	1.148	1.019	**26**
27												1.954	1.561	1.332	1.169	**27**
28													1.969	1.578	1.351	**28**
29														1.984	1.595	**29**
30															1.998	**30**

Appendix 26

Factors for One-Sided Tolerance Limits

	Confidence level								
	0.90			0.95			0.99		
	Proportion			Proportion			Proportion		
n	0.90	0.95	0.99	0.90	0.95	0.99	0.90	0.95	0.99
4	2.955	3.668	5.040	4.255	5.293	7.291	26.036	33.146	46.579
5	2.586	3.207	4.401	3.381	4.190	5.750	7.698	9.649	13.382
6	2.378	2.950	4.048	2.962	3.667	5.025	5.281	6.572	9.055
7	2.242	2.783	3.820	2.711	3.355	4.595	4.300	5.332	7.321
8	2.145	2.663	3.659	2.541	3.145	4.307	3.759	4.652	6.373
9	2.071	2.573	3.538	2.416	2.992	4.099	3.412	4.217	5.771
10	2.012	2.503	3.442	2.321	2.875	3.940	3.168	3.913	5.352
11	1.964	2.445	3.365	2.245	2.782	3.814	2.986	3.687	5.041
12	1.924	2.397	3.301	2.182	2.706	3.712	2.844	3.511	4.800
13	1.891	2.356	3.247	2.130	2.642	3.627	2.729	3.371	4.607
14	1.861	2.321	3.201	2.085	2.589	3.554	2.635	3.255	4.449
15	1.836	2.291	3.160	2.046	2.542	3.492	2.556	3.157	4.317
16	1.813	2.264	3.125	2.013	2.501	3.438	2.488	3.074	4.204
17	1.793	2.240	3.093	1.983	2.465	3.390	2.429	3.002	4.107
18	1.775	2.218	3.065	1.956	2.433	3.347	2.377	2.939	4.022
19	1.759	2.199	3.039	1.932	2.404	3.309	2.331	2.884	3.947
20	1.744	2.181	3.016	1.910	2.378	3.274	2.290	2.834	3.880
21	1.730	2.165	2.994	1.890	2.355	3.243	2.254	2.790	3.821
22	1.717	2.150	2.975	1.872	2.333	3.214	2.220	2.749	3.766
23	1.706	2.137	2.957	1.855	2.313	3.188	2.190	2.713	3.717
24	1.695	2.124	2.940	1.840	2.295	3.164	2.162	2.679	3.673
25	1.685	2.112	2.925	1.826	2.278	3.142	2.137	2.649	3.631
26	1.676	2.101	2.911	1.812	2.262	3.121	2.113	2.620	3.594
27	1.667	2.091	2.897	1.800	2.247	3.101	2.091	2.594	3.559
28	1.659	2.081	2.885	1.788	2.234	3.083	2.071	2.569	3.526
29	1.651	2.072	2.873	1.777	2.221	3.066	2.052	2.547	3.496

	Confidence level								
	0.90			0.95			0.99		
	Proportion			Proportion			Proportion		
n	0.90	0.95	0.99	0.90	0.95	0.99	0.90	0.95	0.99
30	1.644	2.064	2.862	1.767	2.209	3.050	2.034	2.525	3.468
31	1.637	2.056	2.851	1.758	2.197	3.035	2.018	2.506	3.441
32	1.630	2.048	2.841	1.748	2.186	3.021	2.002	2.487	3.416
33	1.624	2.041	2.832	1.740	2.176	3.008	1.987	2.469	3.393
34	1.618	2.034	2.823	1.732	2.166	2.995	1.973	2.453	3.371
35	1.613	2.027	2.814	1.724	2.157	2.983	1.960	2.437	3.350
36	1.608	2.021	2.806	1.716	2.148	2.972	1.948	2.422	3.330
37	1.602	2.015	2.799	1.709	2.140	2.961	1.936	2.408	3.312
38	1.598	2.009	2.791	1.702	2.132	2.950	1.924	2.394	3.294
39	1.593	2.004	2.784	1.696	2.124	2.941	1.914	2.381	3.277
40	1.588	1.999	2.777	1.690	2.117	2.931	1.903	2.369	3.261
41	1.584	1.994	2.771	1.684	2.110	2.922	1.894	2.358	3.245
42	1.580	1.989	2.765	1.678	2.104	2.913	1.884	2.346	3.231
43	1.576	1.984	2.759	1.673	2.097	2.905	1.875	2.336	3.217
44	1.572	1.980	2.753	1.668	2.091	2.897	1.867	2.326	3.203
45	1.569	1.976	2.748	1.662	2.085	2.889	1.858	2.316	3.190
46	1.565	1.971	2.742	1.658	2.079	2.882	1.850	2.306	3.178
47	1.562	1.967	2.737	1.653	2.074	2.875	1.843	2.297	3.166
48	1.558	1.964	2.732	1.648	2.069	2.868	1.835	2.288	3.154
49	1.555	1.960	2.727	1.644	2.063	2.861	1.828	2.280	3.143
50	1.552	1.956	2.723	1.640	2.058	2.855	1.821	2.272	3.133
51	1.549	1.953	2.718	1.636	2.054	2.848	1.815	2.264	3.122
52	1.546	1.949	2.714	1.632	2.049	2.842	1.808	2.257	3.113
53	1.543	1.946	2.710	1.628	2.045	2.837	1.802	2.249	3.103
54	1.541	1.943	2.706	1.624	2.040	2.831	1.796	2.242	3.094
55	1.538	1.940	2.702	1.621	2.036	2.826	1.791	2.235	3.085
56	1.536	1.937	2.698	1.617	2.032	2.820	1.785	2.229	3.076
57	1.533	1.934	2.694	1.614	2.028	2.815	1.780	2.222	3.068
58	1.531	1.931	2.690	1.610	2.024	2.810	1.774	2.216	3.060
59	1.528	1.929	2.687	1.607	2.020	2.805	1.769	2.210	3.052
60	1.526	1.926	2.684	1.604	2.017	2.801	1.764	2.204	3.044
61	1.524	1.923	2.680	1.601	2.013	2.796	1.759	2.199	3.037
62	1.522	1.921	2.677	1.598	2.010	2.792	1.755	2.193	3.029
63	1.520	1.918	2.674	1.595	2.007	2.787	1.750	2.188	3.022
64	1.518	1.916	2.671	1.593	2.003	2.783	1.746	2.183	3.016
65	1.516	1.914	2.668	1.590	2.000	2.779	1.741	2.178	3.009
66	1.514	1.911	2.665	1.587	1.997	2.775	1.737	2.173	3.003

	Confidence level								
	0.90			**0.95**			**0.99**		
	Proportion			**Proportion**			**Proportion**		
n	**0.90**	**0.95**	**0.99**	**0.90**	**0.95**	**0.99**	**0.90**	**0.95**	**0.99**
67	1.512	1.909	2.662	1.585	1.994	2.771	1.733	2.168	2.996
68	1.510	1.907	2.659	1.582	1.991	2.767	1.729	2.163	2.990
69	1.508	1.905	2.657	1.580	1.988	2.764	1.725	2.159	2.984
70	1.506	1.903	2.654	1.577	1.985	2.760	1.721	2.154	2.978
71	1.504	1.901	2.651	1.575	1.983	2.756	1.718	2.150	2.973
72	1.503	1.899	2.649	1.573	1.980	2.753	1.714	2.145	2.967
73	1.501	1.897	2.646	1.570	1.977	2.750	1.711	2.141	2.962
74	1.499	1.895	2.644	1.568	1.975	2.746	1.707	2.137	2.957
75	1.498	1.893	2.642	1.566	1.972	2.743	1.704	2.133	2.951
76	1.496	1.891	2.639	1.564	1.970	2.740	1.701	2.129	2.946
77	1.495	1.890	2.637	1.562	1.967	2.737	1.697	2.126	2.941
78	1.493	1.888	2.635	1.560	1.965	2.734	1.694	2.122	2.937
79	1.492	1.886	2.633	1.558	1.963	2.731	1.691	2.118	2.932
80	1.490	1.885	2.630	1.556	1.961	2.728	1.688	2.115	2.927
81	1.489	1.883	2.628	1.554	1.958	2.725	1.685	2.111	2.923
82	1.488	1.881	2.626	1.552	1.956	2.722	1.682	2.108	2.918
83	1.486	1.880	2.624	1.550	1.954	2.720	1.679	2.105	2.914
84	1.485	1.878	2.622	1.549	1.952	2.717	1.677	2.101	2.910
85	1.484	1.877	2.620	1.547	1.950	2.714	1.674	2.098	2.906
86	1.482	1.875	2.618	1.545	1.948	2.712	1.671	2.095	2.902
87	1.481	1.874	2.617	1.543	1.946	2.709	1.669	2.092	2.898
88	1.480	1.872	2.615	1.542	1.944	2.707	1.666	2.089	2.894
89	1.479	1.871	2.613	1.540	1.942	2.704	1.664	2.086	2.890
90	1.477	1.870	2.611	1.539	1.940	2.702	1.661	2.083	2.886
91	1.476	1.868	2.610	1.537	1.938	2.700	1.659	2.080	2.882
92	1.475	1.867	2.608	1.535	1.937	2.697	1.656	2.077	2.879
93	1.474	1.866	2.606	1.534	1.935	2.695	1.654	2.075	2.875
94	1.473	1.864	2.605	1.532	1.933	2.693	1.652	2.072	2.872
95	1.472	1.863	2.603	1.531	1.932	2.691	1.649	2.069	2.868
96	1.471	1.862	2.601	1.530	1.930	2.688	1.647	2.067	2.865
97	1.470	1.861	2.600	1.528	1.928	2.686	1.645	2.064	2.862
98	1.469	1.859	2.598	1.527	1.927	2.684	1.643	2.062	2.858
99	1.468	1.858	2.597	1.525	1.925	2.682	1.641	2.059	2.855
100	1.467	1.857	2.595	1.524	1.923	2.680	1.639	2.057	2.852
200	1.410	1.791	2.511	1.448	1.836	2.568	1.524	1.923	2.679
300	1.385	1.763	2.476	1.416	1.799	2.521	1.476	1.868	2.609
400	1.371	1.747	2.455	1.397	1.777	2.493	1.448	1.836	2.568

	Confidence level								
	0.90			0.95			0.99		
	Proportion			Proportion			Proportion		
n	0.90	0.95	0.99	0.90	0.95	0.99	0.90	0.95	0.99
500	1.361	1.736	2.441	1.385	1.762	2.475	1.430	1.814	2.540
600	1.354	1.727	2.430	1.375	1.752	2.461	1.416	1.799	2.521
700	1.349	1.721	2.422	1.368	1.744	2.451	1.406	1.787	2.505
800	1.344	1.716	2.416	1.362	1.737	2.442	1.397	1.777	2.493
900	1.340	1.712	2.411	1.358	1.732	2.436	1.390	1.769	2.483
1000	1.337	1.708	2.406	1.354	1.727	2.430	1.385	1.762	2.475

Appendix 26

Appendix 27

Factors for Two-Sided Tolerance Limits

	Confidence level								
	0.90			**0.95**			**0.99**		
	Proportion			Proportion			Proportion		
n	0.90	0.95	0.99	0.90	0.95	0.99	0.90	0.95	0.99
4	4.166	4.930	6.420	5.368	6.353	8.274	9.397	11.121	14.483
5	3.494	4.141	5.407	4.274	5.065	6.614	6.611	7.834	10.230
6	3.131	3.713	4.856	3.712	4.402	5.757	5.336	6.328	8.277
7	2.901	3.443	4.507	3.368	3.997	5.232	4.612	5.473	7.165
8	2.742	3.255	4.265	3.135	3.722	4.876	4.147	4.922	6.449
9	2.625	3.117	4.086	2.967	3.522	4.617	3.822	4.538	5.948
10	2.535	3.010	3.948	2.838	3.371	4.420	3.582	4.254	5.578
11	2.463	2.925	3.837	2.737	3.251	4.264	3.397	4.034	5.292
12	2.404	2.856	3.747	2.655	3.153	4.137	3.249	3.860	5.064
13	2.355	2.798	3.671	2.586	3.073	4.032	3.129	3.717	4.878
14	2.313	2.748	3.607	2.529	3.005	3.943	3.029	3.599	4.723
15	2.277	2.706	3.552	2.480	2.946	3.867	2.944	3.498	4.592
16	2.246	2.669	3.503	2.437	2.895	3.801	2.871	3.412	4.479
17	2.218	2.636	3.461	2.399	2.851	3.743	2.808	3.337	4.380
18	2.194	2.607	3.423	2.366	2.812	3.691	2.752	3.271	4.294
19	2.172	2.581	3.389	2.336	2.776	3.645	2.703	3.212	4.218
20	2.152	2.558	3.358	2.310	2.745	3.604	2.659	3.160	4.149
21	2.134	2.536	3.331	2.285	2.716	3.566	2.619	3.113	4.088
22	2.118	2.517	3.305	2.264	2.690	3.532	2.584	3.071	4.032
23	2.103	2.499	3.282	2.243	2.666	3.501	2.551	3.032	3.981
24	2.089	2.483	3.261	2.225	2.644	3.473	2.521	2.996	3.935
25	2.077	2.468	3.241	2.208	2.624	3.446	2.494	2.964	3.892
26	2.065	2.454	3.223	2.192	2.606	3.422	2.469	2.934	3.853
27	2.054	2.441	3.206	2.178	2.588	3.399	2.445	2.906	3.817
28	2.044	2.429	3.190	2.164	2.572	3.378	2.424	2.881	3.783
29	2.034	2.418	3.175	2.151	2.557	3.358	2.403	2.857	3.752

	Confidence level								
	0.90			0.95			0.99		
	Proportion			Proportion			Proportion		
n	0.90	0.95	0.99	0.90	0.95	0.99	0.90	0.95	0.99
30	2.025	2.407	3.161	2.140	2.543	3.340	2.385	2.834	3.722
31	2.017	2.397	3.148	2.128	2.530	3.323	2.367	2.813	3.695
32	2.009	2.387	3.136	2.118	2.517	3.306	2.350	2.794	3.669
33	2.001	2.379	3.124	2.108	2.505	3.291	2.335	2.775	3.645
34	1.994	2.370	3.113	2.099	2.494	3.276	2.320	2.757	3.622
35	1.987	2.362	3.103	2.090	2.484	3.262	2.306	2.741	3.600
36	1.981	2.355	3.093	2.081	2.474	3.249	2.293	2.725	3.580
37	1.975	2.347	3.083	2.073	2.464	3.237	2.280	2.711	3.560
38	1.969	2.341	3.074	2.066	2.455	3.225	2.269	2.696	3.542
39	1.964	2.334	3.066	2.058	2.447	3.214	2.257	2.683	3.524
40	1.958	2.328	3.058	2.051	2.438	3.203	2.246	2.670	3.507
41	1.953	2.322	3.050	2.045	2.431	3.193	2.236	2.658	3.491
42	1.948	2.316	3.042	2.038	2.423	3.183	2.226	2.646	3.476
43	1.944	2.311	3.035	2.032	2.416	3.173	2.217	2.635	3.462
44	1.939	2.305	3.028	2.027	2.409	3.164	2.208	2.625	3.448
45	1.935	2.300	3.022	2.021	2.402	3.156	2.200	2.615	3.434
46	1.931	2.295	3.015	2.016	2.396	3.147	2.191	2.605	3.421
47	1.927	2.291	3.009	2.010	2.390	3.139	2.183	2.595	3.409
48	1.923	2.286	3.003	2.006	2.384	3.131	2.176	2.586	3.397
49	1.920	2.282	2.998	2.001	2.378	3.124	2.168	2.578	3.386
50	1.916	2.278	2.992	1.996	2.373	3.117	2.161	2.569	3.375
51	1.913	2.274	2.987	1.992	2.367	3.110	2.155	2.561	3.364
52	1.910	2.270	2.982	1.987	2.362	3.103	2.148	2.553	3.354
53	1.906	2.266	2.977	1.983	2.357	3.097	2.142	2.546	3.344
54	1.903	2.262	2.972	1.979	2.353	3.090	2.136	2.538	3.334
55	1.900	2.259	2.967	1.975	2.348	3.084	2.130	2.531	3.325
56	1.897	2.256	2.963	1.972	2.344	3.078	2.124	2.525	3.316
57	1.895	2.252	2.958	1.968	2.339	3.073	2.118	2.518	3.308
58	1.892	2.249	2.954	1.964	2.335	3.067	2.113	2.512	3.299
59	1.889	2.246	2.950	1.961	2.331	3.062	2.108	2.505	3.291
60	1.887	2.243	2.946	1.958	2.327	3.057	2.103	2.499	3.283
61	1.884	2.240	2.942	1.954	2.323	3.052	2.098	2.494	3.276
62	1.882	2.237	2.939	1.951	2.319	3.047	2.093	2.488	3.268
63	1.880	2.234	2.935	1.948	2.316	3.042	2.088	2.482	3.261
64	1.877	2.232	2.931	1.945	2.312	3.037	2.084	2.477	3.254
65	1.875	2.229	2.928	1.942	2.309	3.033	2.080	2.472	3.247
66	1.873	2.226	2.925	1.939	2.305	3.029	2.075	2.467	3.241

Appendix 27

	Confidence level								
	0.90			**0.95**			**0.99**		
	Proportion			Proportion			Proportion		
n	0.90	0.95	0.99	0.90	0.95	0.99	0.90	0.95	0.99
67	1.871	2.224	2.921	1.937	2.302	3.024	2.071	2.462	3.234
68	1.869	2.221	2.918	1.934	2.299	3.020	2.067	2.457	3.228
69	1.867	2.219	2.915	1.931	2.296	3.016	2.063	2.453	3.222
70	1.865	2.217	2.912	1.929	2.293	3.012	2.059	2.448	3.216
71	1.863	2.214	2.909	1.926	2.290	3.008	2.056	2.444	3.210
72	1.861	2.212	2.906	1.924	2.287	3.004	2.052	2.439	3.204
73	1.859	2.210	2.903	1.922	2.284	3.001	2.048	2.435	3.199
74	1.857	2.208	2.900	1.919	2.282	2.997	2.045	2.431	3.193
75	1.856	2.206	2.898	1.917	2.279	2.994	2.042	2.427	3.188
76	1.854	2.204	2.895	1.915	2.276	2.990	2.038	2.423	3.183
77	1.852	2.202	2.893	1.913	2.274	2.987	2.035	2.419	3.178
78	1.851	2.200	2.890	1.911	2.271	2.984	2.032	2.415	3.173
79	1.849	2.198	2.888	1.909	2.269	2.980	2.029	2.412	3.168
80	1.848	2.196	2.885	1.907	2.266	2.977	2.026	2.408	3.163
81	1.846	2.195	2.883	1.905	2.264	2.974	2.023	2.405	3.159
82	1.845	2.193	2.880	1.903	2.262	2.971	2.020	2.401	3.154
83	1.843	2.191	2.878	1.901	2.259	2.968	2.017	2.398	3.150
84	1.842	2.189	2.876	1.899	2.257	2.965	2.014	2.394	3.145
85	1.840	2.188	2.874	1.897	2.255	2.962	2.012	2.391	3.141
86	1.839	2.186	2.872	1.895	2.253	2.960	2.009	2.388	3.137
87	1.838	2.184	2.870	1.894	2.251	2.957	2.006	2.385	3.133
88	1.836	2.183	2.868	1.892	2.249	2.954	2.004	2.382	3.129
89	1.835	2.181	2.866	1.890	2.247	2.952	2.001	2.379	3.125
90	1.834	2.180	2.864	1.889	2.245	2.949	1.999	2.376	3.121
91	1.833	2.178	2.862	1.887	2.243	2.947	1.996	2.373	3.117
92	1.831	2.177	2.860	1.885	2.241	2.944	1.994	2.370	3.114
93	1.830	2.176	2.858	1.884	2.239	2.942	1.992	2.368	3.110
94	1.829	2.174	2.856	1.882	2.237	2.939	1.989	2.365	3.107
95	1.828	2.173	2.854	1.881	2.236	2.937	1.987	2.362	3.103
96	1.827	2.171	2.852	1.879	2.234	2.935	1.985	2.360	3.100
97	1.826	2.170	2.851	1.878	2.232	2.932	1.983	2.357	3.096
98	1.824	2.169	2.849	1.876	2.231	2.930	1.981	2.355	3.093
99	1.823	2.167	2.847	1.875	2.229	2.928	1.979	2.352	3.090
100	1.822	2.166	2.846	1.874	2.227	2.926	1.977	2.350	3.087
200	1.764	2.097	2.754	1.798	2.137	2.808	1.865	2.217	2.912
300	1.740	2.068	2.842	1.767	2.100	2.922	1.820	2.163	3.080
400	1.726	2.052	2.841	1.749	2.079	2.920	1.794	2.132	3.077

	Confidence level								
	0.90			0.95			0.99		
	Proportion			Proportion			Proportion		
n	0.90	0.95	0.99	0.90	0.95	0.99	0.90	0.95	0.99
500	1.717	2.041	2.839	1.737	2.065	2.918	1.777	2.112	3.074
600	1.710	2.033	2.838	1.728	2.055	2.916	1.764	2.097	3.071
700	1.705	2.027	2.836	1.722	2.047	2.914	1.755	2.086	3.069
800	1.701	2.022	2.835	1.717	2.041	2.912	1.747	2.077	3.066
900	1.697	2.018	2.833	1.712	2.035	2.910	1.741	2.069	3.063
1000	1.694	2.014	2.832	1.709	2.031	2.908	1.736	2.063	3.060

Appendix 27

Appendix 28

Equivalent Sigma Levels, Percent Defective, and PPM

With no sigma shift (centered)				With 1.5 sigma shift			
Sigma level	Percent in specification	Percent defective	PPM	Sigma level	Percent in specification	Percent defective	PPM
0.10	7.9656	92.0344	920344	0.10	2.5957	97.40426	974043
0.20	15.8519	84.1481	841481	0.20	5.2235	94.77650	947765
0.30	23.5823	76.4177	764177	0.30	7.9139	92.08606	920861
0.40	31.0843	68.9157	689157	0.40	10.6950	89.30505	893050
0.50	38.2925	61.7075	617075	0.50	13.5905	86.40949	864095
0.60	45.1494	54.8506	548506	0.60	16.6196	83.38043	833804
0.70	51.6073	48.3927	483927	0.70	19.7952	80.20480	802048
0.80	57.6289	42.3711	423711	0.80	23.1240	76.87605	768760
0.90	63.1880	36.8120	368120	0.90	26.6056	73.39444	733944
1.00	68.2689	31.7311	317311	1.00	30.2328	69.76721	697672
1.10	72.8668	27.1332	271332	1.10	33.9917	66.00829	660083
1.20	76.9861	23.0139	230139	1.20	37.8622	62.13784	621378
1.30	80.6399	19.3601	193601	1.30	41.8185	58.18148	581815
1.40	83.8487	16.1513	161513	1.40	45.8306	54.16937	541694
1.50	86.6386	13.3614	133614	1.50	49.8650	50.13499	501350
1.60	89.0401	10.9599	109599	1.60	53.8860	46.11398	461140
1.70	91.0869	8.9131	89131	1.70	57.8573	42.14274	421427
1.80	92.8139	7.1861	71861	1.80	61.7428	38.25720	382572
1.90	94.2567	5.7433	57433	1.90	65.5085	34.49152	344915
2.00	95.4500	4.5500	45500	2.00	69.1230	30.87702	308770
2.10	96.4271	3.5729	35729	2.10	72.5588	27.44122	274412
2.20	97.2193	2.7807	27807	2.20	75.7929	24.20715	242071
2.30	97.8552	2.1448	21448	2.30	78.8072	21.19277	211928
2.40	98.3605	1.6395	16395	2.40	81.5892	18.41082	184108
2.50	98.7581	1.2419	12419	2.50	84.1313	15.86869	158687
2.60	99.0678	0.9322	9322	2.60	86.4313	13.56867	135687
2.70	99.3066	0.6934	6934	2.70	88.4917	11.50830	115083

With no sigma shift (centered)				With 1.5 sigma shift			
Sigma level	Percent in specification	Percent defective	PPM	Sigma level	Percent in specification	Percent defective	PPM
2.80	99.4890	0.5110	5110	2.80	90.3191	9.68090	96809
2.90	99.6268	0.3732	3732	2.90	91.9238	8.07621	80762
3.00	99.7300	0.2700	2700	3.00	93.3189	6.68106	66811
3.10	99.8065	0.1935	1935	3.10	94.5199	5.48014	54801
3.20	99.8626	0.1374	1374	3.20	95.5433	4.45668	44567
3.30	99.9033	0.0967	967	3.30	96.4069	3.59311	35931
3.40	99.9326	0.0674	674	3.40	97.1283	2.87170	28717
3.50	99.9535	0.0465	465	3.50	97.7250	2.27504	22750
3.60	99.9682	0.0318	318	3.60	98.2135	1.78646	17865
3.70	99.9784	0.0216	216	3.70	98.6096	1.39035	13904
3.80	99.9855	0.0145	145	3.80	98.9276	1.07242	10724
3.90	99.9904	0.0096	96.2	3.90	99.1802	0.81976	8198
4.00	99.9937	0.0063	63.3	4.00	99.3790	0.62097	6210
4.10	99.9959	0.0041	41.3	4.10	99.5339	0.46612	4661
4.20	99.9973	0.0027	26.7	4.20	99.6533	0.34670	3467
4.30	99.9983	0.0017	17.1	4.30	99.7445	0.25551	2555
4.40	99.9989	0.0011	10.8	4.40	99.8134	0.18658	1866
4.50	**99.9993**	**0.0007**	**6.8**	4.50	99.8650	0.13499	1350
4.60	99.9996	0.0004	4.2	4.60	99.9032	0.09676	968
4.70	99.9997	0.0003	2.6	4.70	99.9313	0.06871	687
4.80	99.9998	0.0002	1.6	4.80	99.9517	0.04834	483
4.90	99.99990	0.00010	1.0	4.90	99.9663	0.03369	337
5.00	99.99994	0.00006	0.6	5.00	99.9767	0.02326	233
5.10	99.99997	0.00003	0.3	5.10	99.9841	0.01591	159
5.20	99.99998	0.00002	0.2	5.20	99.9892	0.01078	108
5.30	99.999988	0.000012	0.12	5.30	99.9928	0.00723	72.3
5.40	99.999993	0.000007	0.07	5.40	99.9952	0.00481	48.1
5.50	99.999996	0.000004	0.04	5.50	99.9968	0.00317	31.7
5.60	99.999998	0.000002	0.02	5.60	99.9979	0.00207	20.7
5.70	99.9999988	0.0000012	0.012	5.70	99.9987	0.00133	13.3
5.80	99.9999993	0.0000007	0.007	5.80	99.9991	0.00085	8.5
5.90	99.9999996	0.0000004	0.004	5.90	99.9995	0.00054	5.4
6.00	99.9999998	0.0000002	0.002	**6.00**	**99.9997**	**0.00034**	**3.4**

Appendix 28

Appendix 29

Critical Values for the Mann-Whitney Test Table (One-Tail, Alpha = 0.05)

n_2	| n_1																						
	4	5	6	7	8	9	10	11	12	13	14	15	16	17	18	19	20	21	22	23	24	25
4	12																					
5	13	19																				
6	14	20	24																			
7	15	22	25	34																		
8	16	23	26	35	45																	
9	17	25	28	37	47	59																
10	18	26	29	39	49	61	83															
11	19	27	30	40	51	63	86	101														
12	20	29	32	42	53	66	90	105	121													
13	21	30	33	44	55	68	93	109	125	143												
14	22	32	34	45	57	71	96	112	130	148	167											
15	23	33	36	47	59	73	100	116	134	152	172	192										
16	24	35	37	49	62	75	103	120	138	157	177	198	220									
17	25	36	38	50	64	78	107	124	142	162	182	203	226	249								
18	26	37	40	52	66	80	110	128	147	166	187	209	232	256	281							
19	27	39	41	54	68	83	114	132	151	171	192	215	238	262	287	314						
20	28	40	42	55	70	85	117	136	155	176	197	220	244	269	294	321	349					
21	29	42	44	57	72	88	121	140	160	181	203	226	250	275	301	328	356	386				
22	30	43	45	59	74	90	124	143	164	185	208	231	256	281	308	336	364	394	424			
23	31	45	46	61	76	93	128	147	168	190	213	237	262	288	315	343	372	402	433	465		
24	32	46	48	62	78	95	131	151	172	195	218	243	268	294	322	350	380	410	442	474	508	
25	33	47	49	64	80	97	134	155	177	200	223	248	274	301	329	358	387	418	450	483	517	552

Note: $n_2 > n_1$

Appendix 30

Critical Values for the Mann-Whitney Test Table (One-Tail, Alpha = 0.01)

n_2	4	5	6	7	8	9	10	11	12	13	14	15	16	17	18	19	20	21	22	23	24	25
4	9																					
5	10	16																				
6	11	17	24																			
7	11	18	25	34																		
8	12	19	26	35	45																	
9	12	20	28	37	47	59																
10	13	21	29	39	49	61	74															
11	14	21	30	40	51	63	76	91														
12	14	22	32	42	53	66	79	94	109													
13	15	23	33	44	55	68	82	97	113	130												
14	16	24	34	45	57	71	85	100	116	134	152											
15	16	25	36	47	59	73	88	103	120	138	156	176										
16	17	26	37	49	62	75	90	106	123	141	161	181	202									
17	18	27	38	50	64	78	93	110	127	145	165	185	207	229								
18	18	28	40	52	66	80	96	113	131	149	169	190	212	235	259							
19	19	29	41	54	68	83	99	116	134	153	174	195	217	241	265	290						
20	19	30	42	55	70	85	102	119	138	157	178	200	222	246	271	297	324					
21	20	31	44	57	72	88	104	122	141	161	182	205	228	252	277	303	330	359				
22	21	32	45	59	74	90	107	126	145	165	187	209	233	257	283	310	337	366	395			
23	21	33	46	61	76	93	110	129	149	169	191	214	238	263	289	316	344	373	403	434		
24	22	34	48	62	78	95	113	132	152	173	196	219	243	269	295	322	351	380	411	442	475	
25	23	35	49	64	80	97	116	135	156	177	200	224	248	274	301	329	358	388	418	450	483	517

(n_1 across top)

Note: $n_2 > n_1$

Appendix 31

Critical Values for the Mann-Whitney Test Table (Two-Tail, Alpha = 0.025)

n_2 \ n_1	4	5	6	7	8	9	10	11	12	13	14	15	16	17	18	19	20	21	22	23	24	25
4	11																					
5	11	18																				
6	12	19	26																			
7	13	20	28	37																		
8	14	21	29	39	49																	
9	15	22	31	40	51	63																
10	16	23	32	42	53	65	79															
11	16	25	34	44	56	68	82	96														
12	17	26	36	46	58	71	85	100	116													
13	18	27	37	48	60	74	88	103	119	137												
14	19	28	39	50	63	76	91	107	123	141	160											
15	20	30	40	52	65	79	94	110	127	145	165	185										
16	21	31	42	54	67	82	97	114	131	150	169	190	211									
17	22	32	44	56	70	85	100	117	135	154	174	195	217	240								
18	22	33	45	58	72	87	104	121	139	159	179	200	223	246	271							
19	23	34	47	60	75	90	107	124	143	163	184	205	228	252	277	303						
20	24	36	48	62	77	93	110	128	147	167	188	211	234	258	283	310	337					
21	25	37	50	64	79	96	113	132	151	172	193	216	240	264	290	317	344	373				
22	26	38	51	66	82	98	116	135	155	176	198	221	245	270	296	324	352	381	411			
23	27	39	53	68	84	101	119	139	159	180	203	226	251	276	303	330	359	389	419	451		
24	28	41	55	70	86	104	123	142	163	185	208	232	257	282	309	337	366	396	427	459	492	
25	29	42	56	72	89	107	126	146	167	189	213	237	262	289	316	344	374	404	436	468	502	536

Note: $n_2 > n_1$

Appendix 32

Critical Values for the Mann-Whitney Test Table (Two-Tail, Alpha = 0.005)

n_2	4	5	6	7	8	9	10	11	12	13	14	15	16	17	18	19	20	21	22	23	24	25
4	9																					
5	9	15																				
6	9	15	22																			
7	10	16	23	32																		
8	10	17	25	33	43																	
9	11	18	26	35	45	56																
10	11	18	27	36	47	58	70															
11	12	19	28	38	48	60	73	87														
12	12	20	29	39	50	62	75	90	105													
13	13	21	30	40	52	64	78	93	108	125												
14	13	22	31	42	54	67	81	95	111	128	146											
15	14	22	32	43	56	69	83	98	115	132	150	170										
16	14	23	34	45	57	71	86	101	118	136	155	174	195									
17	15	24	35	46	59	73	88	104	121	139	159	179	200	222								
18	15	25	36	48	61	75	91	107	125	143	163	183	205	227	251							
19	16	26	37	49	63	78	93	110	128	147	167	188	210	233	257	282						
20	16	27	38	51	65	80	96	113	131	151	171	192	215	238	262	288	314					
21	17	27	39	52	67	82	99	116	135	154	175	197	219	243	268	294	321	349				
22	17	28	40	54	69	84	101	119	138	158	179	201	224	249	274	300	327	355	385			
23	18	29	42	55	70	87	104	122	141	162	183	206	229	254	279	306	334	362	392	423		
24	18	30	43	57	72	89	106	125	145	166	187	210	234	259	285	312	340	369	399	430	463	
25	19	31	44	58	74	91	109	128	148	169	192	215	239	264	291	318	347	376	407	438	471	504

The column headers span under n_1.

Note: $n_2 > n_1$

Appendix 33

Critical Values for the Wilcoxon Signed-Rank Test

	α			
Two-tail test	**0.100**	**0.050**	**0.020**	**0.010**
One-tail test	**0.050**	**0.025**	**0.010**	**0.005**
n				
4	0			
5	1	0		
6	2	1		
7	4	2	0	
8	6	4	1	
9	8	5	2	0
10	11	8	4	2
11	14	10	6	4
12	18	14	9	6
13	21	17	12	8
14	26	21	15	11
15	31	25	19	14
16	36	30	23	18
17	41	35	27	22
18	47	40	32	26
19	54	46	37	30
20	60	52	42	35
21	68	59	48	41
22	75	66	54	47
23	83	73	61	53
24	92	81	68	59
25	101	89	76	66

Note: In most cases, the critical value is a non-integer value for a given alpha value. Therefore, the table values have been rounded down to the nearest whole number. This results in a smaller, more conservative alpha value than shown in the column headers.

Appendix 34
Glossary of Six Sigma and Related Terms

α—*see* alpha.

β—*see* beta.

C_p **(process capability index)**—an index describing process capability in relation to specified tolerance of a characteristic divided by the natural process variation for a process in a state of statistical control:

$$C_p = \frac{USL - LSL}{6\sigma}$$

where USL = upper specification limit, LSL = lower specification limit, and 6σ = the natural process variation. *See also* P_p (process performance index), a similar term, except that the process may not be in a state of statistical control; process capability index.

C_{pk} **(minimum process capability index)**—the smaller of the upper process capability index (C_{pk_U}) and the lower process capability index (C_{pk_L}). The C_{pk} considers the mean of the process with respect to the upper and lower specifications. The C_{pk} can be converted to a sigma level using sigma level = $3C_{pk}$.

C_{pk_L} **(lower process capability index; CPL)**—an index describing process capability in relation to the lower specification limit. The index is defined as

$$C_{pk_L} = \frac{\bar{x} - LSL}{3\sigma}$$

where $\bar{x}$ = process average, LSL = lower specification limit, and 3σ = half of the process capability. Note: When the process average is obtained from a control chart, $\bar{x}$ is replaced by $\bar{\bar{x}}$.

C_{pk_U} **(upper process capability index; CPU)**—an index describing process capability in relation to the upper specification limit. The index is defined as

$$C_{pk_U} = \frac{USL - \bar{x}}{3\sigma}$$

where $\bar{x}$ = process average, USL = upper specification limit, and 3σ = half of the process capability. Note: When the process average is obtained from a control chart, $\bar{x}$ is replaced by $\bar{\bar{x}}$.

C_{pm} **(process capability index of the mean)**—an index that takes into account the location of the process average relative to a target value and is defined as

$$C_{pm} = \frac{(USL - LSL)/2}{3\sqrt{\sigma^2 + (\mu - T)^2}}$$

where USL = upper specification limit, LSL = lower specification limit, σ = standard deviation, μ = expected value, and T = target value. When the process average and the target value are the same, the $C_{pm} = C_{pk}$. When the process average drifts from the target value, the $C_{pm} < C_{pk}$.

n—*see* sample size.

$1 - \alpha$—*see* confidence level.

$1 - \beta$—*see* power.

ρ—the population correlation coefficient. *See also* correlation coefficient.

p – **value**—the smallest level of significance leading to the rejection of the null hypothesis.

P_p **(process performance index)**—an index describing process performance in relation to specified tolerance:

$$P_p = \frac{USL - LSL}{6s}$$

s is used for standard deviation instead of σ since both random and special causes may be present. Note: A state of statistical control is not required. Also note the similarity to the formula for C_p.

P_{pk} **(minimum process performance index)**—the smaller of the upper process performance index (P_{pk_U}) and the lower process performance index (P_{pk_L}). The P_{pk}, similar to the C_{pk}, considers the mean of the process with respect to the upper and lower specifications. The P_{pk} is known as the potential process capability and is used in the validation stage of a new product launch. A state of statistical control is not required.

P_{pk_L} **(process performance index, lower; PPL)**—an index describing process performance in relation to the lower specification limit. The index is defined as

$$P_{pk_L} = \frac{\bar{x} - LSL}{3s}$$

where $\bar{x}$ = process average, LSL = lower specification limit, and $3s$ = half of the process capability. Note: When the process average is obtained from a control chart, $\bar{x}$ is replaced by $\bar{\bar{x}}$.

P_{pk_U} **(process performance index, upper; PPU)**—an index describing process performance in relation to the upper specification limit. The index is defined as

$$P_{pk_U} = \frac{USL - \bar{x}}{3s}$$

where $\bar{x}$ = process average, USL = upper specification limit, and $3s$ = half of the process capability. Note: When the process average is obtained from a control chart, $\bar{x}$ is replaced by $\bar{\bar{x}}$.

r—*see* correlation coefficient.

R—*see* correlation coefficient.

r^2_{adj}—*see* adjusted coefficient of determination.

R^2_{adj}—*see* adjusted coefficient of determination.

y = *f*(x)—a foundational concept of Six Sigma, this equation represents the idea that process outputs are a function of process inputs.

5Ss (Five Ss)—a term that derives its name from the five terms beginning with "s" that are used to create a workplace suited for visual control and lean production. Collectively, the 5Ss are about how to create a workplace that is visibly organized, free of clutter, neatly arranged, and sparkling clean. The 5Ss are defined as follows: **seiri (sort; also sifting)** means to separate needed tools, parts, and instructions from unneeded materials and to remove the latter; **seiton (set in order)** means to neatly arrange and identify parts and tools for ease of use; **seiso (shine; also sanitize or scrub)** means to conduct a cleanup campaign; **seiketsu (standardize)** means to conduct seiri, seiton, and seiso at frequent, indeed daily, intervals to maintain a workplace in perfect condition; and **shitsuke (sustain; also self-discipline)** means to form the habit of always following the first four Ss. *See also individual listing for each of the 5Ss.*

5 whys—a persistent questioning technique to probe deeper to reach the root cause of a problem. *See also* 5Ws & 1H.

5Ws & 1H—addressing the Who, What, Where, When, Why, and How questions is a useful technique to help develop an objective and a concise statement of a problem. *See also* 5 whys.

6Ms—typically the primary categories of the cause-and-effect diagram: machines, manpower, materials, measurements, methods, and Mother Nature. Using these categories as a structured approach provides some assurance that few causes will be overlooked. *See also* 7Ms.

7Ms—the 6Ms with the addition of management. *See also* 6Ms.

acceptance control chart—a control chart intended primarily to evaluate whether the plotted measure can be expected to satisfy specified tolerances.

acceptance quality limit (AQL)—the quality level that is the worst tolerable product average when a continuing series of lots is submitted for acceptance sampling. Note the following: (1) This concept applies only when an acceptance sampling scheme with rules for switching and discontinuation is used. (2) Although individual lots with quality as bad as the AQL can be accepted with fairly high probability, the designation of an AQL does not suggest that this is a desirable quality level. (3) Acceptance sampling schemes found in standards with their rules for switching and discontinuation of sampling inspection are designed to encourage suppliers to have process averages consistently better than the AQL. If suppliers fail to do so, there is a high probability of being switched from normal inspection to tightened inspection, where lot acceptance becomes more difficult. Once on tightened inspection, unless corrective action is taken to improve product quality, it is very likely that the rule requiring discontinuation of sampling inspection pending such improvement will be invoked unless action is taken to improve the process. (4) The use of the abbreviation AQL to mean acceptable quality level is no longer recommended since modern thinking is that no fraction defective is really acceptable. Using "acceptance quality limit" rather than "acceptable quality level" indicates a technical value where acceptance occurs.

accuracy—the closeness of agreement between a test result or measurement result and the true or reference value.

action plan—the steps taken to implement the actions needed to achieve strategic goals and objectives.

activity—an action of some type that requires a time duration for accomplishment.

activity network diagram (AND)—a tool used to illustrate a sequence of events or activities (nodes) and the interconnectivity of such nodes. It is used for scheduling and especially for determining the critical path through nodes. It is also known as an arrow diagram. The activity network diagram is one of the seven management and planning tools.

adjusted coefficient of determination (r^2_{adj})—a statistic used with multiple regression because, unlike the r^2 statistic, the adjusted coefficient of determination will increase when variables that act to decrease the mean square error are added to the model. r^2_{adj} is given by

$$r^2_{adj} = 1 - \frac{SS_E/(n-p)}{SS_T/(n-1)} = 1 - \frac{\sum_{i=1}^{n}(y_i - \hat{y}_i)^2 \Big/ (n-p)}{\sum_{i=1}^{n}(y_i - \bar{y})^2 \Big/ (n-1)}$$

where p = number of coefficients fitted in the regression equation, SS_E = sum of the squares for the error term, and SS_T = total sum of squares.

affinity diagram—a tool used to organize information and help achieve order out of the chaos that can develop in a brainstorming session. Large amounts of data, concepts, and ideas are grouped on the basis of their natural relationship to one another. It is more a creative process than a logical process. Also known as the "KJ" method, the affinity diagram is one of the seven management and planning tools.

agile approach—*see* lean approach/lean thinking.

AIAG—Automotive Industry Action Group.

alias—an effect that is completely confounded with another effect due to the nature of the designed experiment. Aliases are the result of confounding, which may or may not be deliberate.

alpha (a)—(1) The maximum probability or risk of making a Type I error when dealing with the significance level of a test. (2) The probability or risk of incorrectly deciding that a shift in the process mean has occurred when in fact the process has not changed (when referring to α in general or the p – value obtained in the test). (3) α is usually designated as producer's risk.

alpha (α) risk—*see* Type I error.

alternative hypothesis—a hypothesis formulated from new information.

analysis of means (ANOM)—a statistical procedure for troubleshooting industrial processes and analyzing the results of experimental designs with factors at fixed levels. It provides a graphical display of data. Ellis R. Ott developed the procedure in 1967 because he observed that non-statisticians had difficulty understanding analysis of variance. Analysis of means is easier for quality practitioners to use because it is an extension of the control chart. In 1973, Edward G. Schilling further extended the concept, enabling analysis of means to be used with non-normal distributions and attributes data where the normal approximation to the binomial distribution does not apply. This is referred to as analysis of means for treatment effects.

analysis of variance (ANOVA)—a basic statistical technique for analyzing experimental data. It subdivides the total variation of a data set into meaningful component parts associated with specific sources of variation in order to test a hypothesis on the parameters of the model or to estimate variance components. There are three model types: fixed, random, and mixed.

analytical thinking—breaking down a problem or situation into discrete parts to understand how each part contributes to the whole.

AND—*see* activity network diagram.

Andon board—a visual device (usually lights) displaying status alerts that can easily be seen by those who should respond.

ANOM—*see* analysis of means.

ANOVA—*see* analysis of variance.

ANSI—American National Standards Institute.

appraisal costs—the costs associated with measuring, evaluating, or auditing products or services to ensure conformance to quality standards and performance requirements. These include costs such as incoming and source inspection/test of purchased material; in-process and final inspection/test; product, process, or service audit; calibration of measuring and test equipment; and the cost of associated supplies and materials.

AQL—*see* acceptance quality limit.

arrow diagram—*see* activity network diagram.

AS-9100—a standard for the aeronautics industry embracing the ISO 9001 standard.

ASQ—American Society for Quality.

assignable cause—a specifically identified factor that contributes to variation and is detectable. Eliminating assignable causes so that the points plotted on the control chart remain within the control limits helps achieve a state of statistical control. Note: Although assignable cause is sometimes considered synonymous with special cause, a special cause is assignable only when it is specifically identified. *See also* special cause.

assumption—a condition that must be true in order for a statistical procedure to be valid.

attribute data—data that are categorized for analysis or evaluation. (Attribute data may involve measurements as long as they are used only to place given data in a category for further analysis or evaluation. Contrast with variables data.)

autonomation—*see* jidoka.

axiomatic design—a theory by Dr. Nam Pyo Suh that stresses each functional requirement be designed to achieve robustness without affecting other functional requirements.

baka-yoke—a term for a manufacturing technique for preventing mistakes by designing the manufacturing process, equipment, and tools so that an operation literally cannot be performed incorrectly. In addition to preventing incorrect operation, the technique usually provides a warning signal of some sort for incorrect performance.

balanced design—a design where all treatment combinations have the same number of observations. If replication in a design exists, it would be balanced only if the replication was consistent across all treatment combinations. In other words, the number of replicates of each treatment combination is the same.

balanced incomplete block design—incomplete block design in which each block contains the same number k of different levels from the l levels of the principal factor arranged so that every pair of levels occurs in the same number l of blocks from the b blocks. Note: This design implies that every level of the principal factor will appear the same number of times in the experiment.

balanced scorecard—translates an organization's mission and strategy into a comprehensive set of performance measures to provide a basis for strategic measurement and management, utilizing four balanced views: financial, customers, internal business processes, and learning and growth.

batch processing—running large batches of a single product through the process at one time, resulting in queues awaiting the next steps in the process.

bathtub curve—a graphic representation of the relationship of the life of a product versus the probable failure rate. The curve contains three phases: early or infant failure (break-in), a stable rate during normal use, and wear out. The bathtub curve is also known as the life-history curve.

BB—*see* Black Belt.

benchmark—an organization, a part of an organization, or a measurement that serves as a reference point or point of comparison.

benchmarking—an improvement process in which an organization measures its performance against that of best-in-class organizations (or others that are good performers), determines how those organizations achieved their performance levels, and uses the information to improve its own performance. Areas that can be benchmarked include strategies, operations, processes, and procedures.

benefit-cost analysis—a collection of the dollar value of benefits derived from an initiative divided by the associated costs incurred. A benefit-cost analysis is also known as a cost-benefit analysis.

beta (β)—(1) The maximum probability or risk of making a Type II error. (2) The probability or risk of incorrectly deciding that a shift in the process mean has not occurred when in fact the process has changed. (3) β is usually designated as consumer's risk.

beta (β) risk—*see* Type II error.

bias—a systematic difference between the mean of the test result or measurement result and a true or reference value. For example, if one measures the lengths of 10 pieces of rope that range from 1 foot to 10 feet and always concludes that the length of each piece is 2 inches shorter than the true length, then the individual is exhibiting a bias of 2 inches.

Black Belt (BB)—a Six Sigma role associated with an individual who is typically assigned full time to train and mentor Green Belts as well as lead improvement projects using specified methodologies such as define, measure, analyze, improve, and control (DMAIC); define, measure, analyze, design, and verify (DMADV); and Design for Six Sigma (DFSS).

block—a collection of experimental units more homogeneous than the full set of experimental units. Blocks are usually selected to allow for special causes, in addition to those introduced as factors to be studied. These special causes may be avoidable within blocks, thus providing a more homogeneous experimental subspace.

block diagram—a diagram that describes the operation, interrelationships, and interdependencies of components in a system. Boxes, or blocks (hence the name), represent the components; connecting lines between the blocks represent interfaces. There are two types of block diagrams: a functional block diagram, which shows a system's subsystems and lower-level products, their interrelationships, and interfaces with other systems, and a reliability block diagram, which is similar to the functional block diagram except that it is modified to emphasize those aspects influencing reliability.

block effect—an effect resulting from a block in an experimental design. Existence of a block effect generally means that the method of blocking was appropriate and that an assignable cause has been found.

blocking—including blocks in an experiment in order to broaden the applicability of the conclusions or minimize the impact of selected assignable causes. The randomization of the experiment is restricted and occurs within blocks.

brainstorming—a problem-solving tool that teams use to generate as many ideas as possible that are related to a particular subject. Team members begin by offering all their ideas; the ideas are not discussed or reviewed until after the brainstorming session.

calibration—the comparison of a measurement instrument or system of unverified accuracy to a measurement instrument or system of known accuracy to detect any variation from the true value.

capability—the performance of a process demonstrated to be in a state of statistical control. *See also* process capability; process performance.

capability index—*see* process capability index.

causal factor—a variable that when changed or manipulated in some manner serves to influence a given effect or result.

cause-and-effect analysis—the process of identifying the likely causes of any outcome. Some cause-and-effect analyses produce an output like a fishbone diagram. Others produce a cause-and-effect tree with multiple subbranches.

cause-and-effect diagram—a diagram resembling a fish skeleton that is used to illustrate the main causes and subcauses leading to an effect. One of the seven basic tools of quality, the cause-and-effect diagram is also known as the Ishikawa diagram or the fishbone diagram.

central limit theorem (CLT)—a theorem that states that irrespective of the shape of the distribution of a population, the distribution of sample means is approximately normal when the sample size is large.

central tendency—the propensity of data collected on a process to concentrate around a value situated approximately midway between the lowest and highest values. Three common measures of central tendency include (arithmetic) mean, median, and mode. *See also* mean; median; mode.

Certified Six Sigma Black Belt (CSSBB)—an ASQ certification.

Certified Six Sigma Green Belt (CSSGB)—an ASQ certification.

CFM—*see* continuous flow manufacturing.

chaku-chaku—a term meaning "load-load" in a cell layout where a part is taken from one machine and loaded into the next.

Champion—a Six Sigma role of a senior manager who ensures his or her projects are aligned with the organization's strategic goals and priorities, provides the Six Sigma team with resources, removes organizational barriers for the team, participates in project tollgate reviews, and essentially serves as the team's backer. Although many organizations define the terms "Champion" and "sponsor" differently, they are frequently used interchangeably. *See also* sponsor.

chance cause—*see* random cause.

chance variation—variation due to chance causes. *See also* random variation.

changeover time—the time interval between the last good piece off the current run and the first good piece off the next run.

characteristic—a property that helps differentiate among items of a given sample or population.

charter—a documented statement officially initiating the formation of a committee, team, project, or other effort in which a clearly stated purpose and approval are conferred.

check sheet—a simple data recording device typically used to collect the frequency of occurrences of nominal data by category. Whenever the user observes the occurrence of one of the categories, he or she places a mark next to the category. When the observation process is complete, final counts by category can then be obtained. The user custom designs the check sheet so that he or she can readily interpret the results. The check sheet is occasionally considered to be one of the seven basic tools of quality. Note: Check sheets are often confused with checklists. *See also* checklist.

checklist—a quality tool that is used for processes where there is a large human element. Examples are audit checklists and an airplane pilot's preflight checklist. Checklists serve as reminders and, depending on design, evidence that important items have been observed or appropriate actions have been taken. A well-designed checklist helps gather information to support findings and observations and serves as a guide and a place to record information. Note: Checklists are often confused with check sheets. *See also* check sheet.

circle diagram—a tool used to show linkages between various items. The circle diagram is constructed by evenly placing item descriptors around a circle. Such item descriptors might include products, services, organizations, individuals, and so forth. Arrows are drawn from each item to other items where a flow exists. Circle diagrams are highly useful in that they readily depict predecessor and successor relationships as well as potential bottlenecks. Too many inputs or outputs from any given descriptor around the circumference of the circle may indicate a limiting function. A circle diagram is also known as a hand-off map.

CLT—*see* central limit theorem.

coefficient of determination (r^2)—the square of the correlations coefficient. It represents the amount of the variation in y that is explained by the fitted simple linear equation $r^2 \leq 1$. The coefficient of determination is sometimes written as R^2.

common cause—*see* random cause.

complete block—a block that accommodates a complete set of treatment combinations.

completely randomized design—a design in which the treatments are randomly assigned to the full set of experimental units. No blocks are involved.

completely randomized factorial design—a factorial design in which all the treatments are randomly assigned to the full set of experimental units. *See also* completely randomized design.

compliance—an affirmative indication or judgment that the supplier of a product or service has met the requirements of the relevant specifications, contract, or regulation; also the state of meeting the requirements.

concurrent engineering—a way to reduce cost, improve quality, and shrink cycle time by simplifying a product's system of life-cycle tasks during the early concept stages. Concurrent engineering is a process to get all departments from engineering, purchasing, marketing, manufacturing, and finance to work on a new design at once to speed development. The emphasis is on upstream prevention versus downstream correction. Concurrent engineering is also known as simultaneous engineering.

confidence coefficient (1 – a)—*see* confidence level.

confidence interval—an estimate of the interval between two statistics that includes the true value of the parameter with some probability. This probability is called the confidence level of the estimate. Confidence levels typically used are 90%, 95%, and 99%. Either the interval contains the parameter or it does not.

confidence level (1 – a)—the probability that (1) the confidence interval described by a set of confidence limits actually includes the population parameter and (2) an interval about a sample statistic actually includes the population parameter. The confidence level is also known as the confidence coefficient.

confidence limits—the endpoints of the interval about the sample statistic that is believed, with a specified confidence level, to include the population parameter. *See also* confidence interval.

conflict resolution—a process for resolving disagreements in a manner acceptable to all parties.

Appendix 34

confounding—indistinguishably combining an effect with other effects or blocks. When done deliberately, higher-order effects are systematically aliased so as to allow estimation of lower-order effects. Sometimes, confounding results from inadvertent changes to a design during the running of an experiment or from poor planning of the design. This can diminish or even invalidate the effectiveness of the experiment.

consensus—finding a proposal acceptable enough that all team members support the decision and no member opposes it.

constraint—a bottleneck or limitation of the throughput of a process.

constraint management—pertains to identifying a constraint and working to remove or diminish it, while dealing with resistance to change.

consumer's risk (β)—the probability of acceptance when the quality level has a value stated by the acceptance sampling plan as unsatisfactory. Note: (1) such acceptance is a Type II error; (2) consumer's risk is usually designated as beta (β). Consumer's risk is also known as beta (β) risk, beta (β) error, error of the second kind, Type 2 error, and Type II error.

continuous flow manufacturing (CFM)—a method in which items are produced and moved from one processing step to the next, one piece at a time. Each process makes only the one piece that the next process needs, and the transfer batch size is one. CFM is sometimes known as one-piece flow or single-piece flow.

continuous variable—a variable whose possible values form an interval set of numbers such that between each two values in the set another member of the set occurs.

control chart—a chart that plots a statistical measure of a series of samples in a particular order to steer the process regarding that measure and to control and reduce variation. The control chart comprises the plotted points, a set of upper and lower control limits, and a center line. Specific rules are used to determine when the control chart goes out of control. Note: (1) the order is either time or sample number order based, and (2) the control chart operates most effectively when the measure is a process characteristic correlated with an ultimate product or service characteristic. The control chart is one of the seven basic tools of quality.

control chart, acceptance—*see* acceptance control chart.

control limit—a line on a control chart used for judging the stability of a process. Note: (1) control limits provide statistically determined boundaries for the deviations from the center line of the statistic plotted on a Shewhart control chart due to random causes alone; (2) control limits (with the exception of the acceptance control chart) are based on actual process data, not on specification limits; (3) other than points outside the control limits, "out-of-control" criteria can include runs, trends, cycles, periodicity, and unusual patterns within the control limits; (4) the calculation of control limits depends on the type of control chart.

control plan—a living document that identifies critical input or output variables and associated activities that must be performed to maintain control of the variation of processes, products, and services in order to minimize deviation from their preferred values.

COPQ—*see* cost of poor quality.

COQ—*see* cost of quality.

corrective action—action taken to eliminate the root cause(s) and symptom(s) of an existing deviation or nonconformity to prevent recurrence.

correlation coefficient (r)—a statistic that measures the degree of linear relationship between two sets of numbers and is computed as

$$r = \frac{S_{xy}}{\sqrt{S_{xx}S_{yy}}} = \frac{\sum_{i=1}^{n}(x_i - \bar{x})^2(y_i - \bar{y})^2}{\sqrt{\sum_{i=1}^{n}(x_i - \bar{x})^2 \sum_{i=n}^{n}(y_i - \bar{y})^2}} = \frac{\sum_{i=1}^{n}x_i y_i - \frac{\left(\sum_{i=1}^{n}x_i\right)\left(\sum_{i=1}^{n}y_i\right)}{n}}{\sqrt{\left(\sum_{i=1}^{n}x_i^2 - \frac{\left(\sum_{i=1}^{n}x_i\right)^2}{n}\right)\left(\sum_{i=1}^{n}y_i^2 - \frac{\left(\sum_{i=1}^{n}y_i\right)^2}{n}\right)}}$$

where $-1 \leq r \leq 1$. Also, r is used to estimate the population correlation coefficient ρ. Correlation values of -1 and $+1$ represent perfect linear agreement between two independent and dependent variables. An $r = 0$ means there is no linear relationship at all. If r is positive, the relationship between the variables is said to be positive. Hence, when x increases, y increases. If r is negative, the relationship is said to be negative. Hence, when x increases, y decreases. The correlation coefficient is also known as the sample correlation coefficient and is sometimes written as R.

cost of poor quality (COPQ)—the costs associated with the production of nonconforming material. These costs include both external and internal failure costs. *See also* external failure costs; internal failure costs.

cost of quality (COQ)—the costs specifically associated with the achievement or non-achievement of product or service quality, including all product or service requirements established by the organization and its contracts with customers and society. More specifically, quality costs are the total costs incurred by (1) investing in the prevention of nonconformances to requirements, (2) appraising a product or service for conformance to requirements, and (3) failing to meet requirements. These can then be categorized as prevention, appraisal, and failure. *See also* appraisal costs; failure costs; prevention costs.

cost-benefit analysis—*see* benefit-cost analysis.

CPL—*see* C_{pk_L}.

CPM—*see* critical path method.

CPU—*see* C_{pk_U}.

critical path—the sequence of tasks that takes the longest time and determines a project's completion date.

critical path method (CPM)—an activity-oriented project management technique that uses arrow-diagramming methods to demonstrate both the time and the cost required to complete a project. It provides one time estimate: normal time.

criticality—an indication of the consequences expected to result from a failure.

critical-to-quality (CTQ)—a characteristic of a product or service that is essential to ensure customer satisfaction.

Appendix 34

cross-functional team—a group consisting of members from more than one department that is organized to accomplish a project.

CSSBB—*see* Certified Six Sigma Black Belt.

CSSGB—*see* Certified Six Sigma Green Belt.

CTQ—*see* critical-to-quality.

cumulative sum (CUSUM) control chart—a control chart on which the plotted value is the cumulative sum of deviations of successive samples from a target value. The ordinate of each plotted point represents the algebraic sum of the previous ordinate and the most recent deviations from the target.

customer loyalty—a term used to describe the behavior of customers—in particular, customers who exhibit a high level of satisfaction, conduct repeat business, or provide referrals and testimonials. It is the result of an organization's processes, practices, and efforts designed to deliver its services or products in ways that drive such behavior.

CUSUM—*see* cumulative sum (CUSUM) control chart.

cycle time—the time required to complete one cycle of an operation. If cycle time for every operation in a complete process can be reduced to equal takt time, products can be made in single-piece flow. *See also* takt time.

cycle-time reduction—a method for reducing the amount of time it takes to execute a process or build a specific product. Elimination of duplicate or unnecessary tasks also reduces the time that is necessary to execute a process. Improving hand-offs, which tend to be points of substantial discontinuity, also eliminates rework or duplicate efforts.

defect—the nonfulfillment of a requirement related to an intended or specified use for a product or service. In simpler terms, a defect is anything not done correctly the first time. Note: The distinction between the concepts defect and nonconformity is important because it has legal connotations, particularly those associated with product liability issues. Consequently, the term "defect" should be used with extreme caution.

defective—a unit of product that contains one or more defects with respect to the quality characteristic(s) under consideration.

defects per million opportunities (DPMO)—a measure of capability for discrete (attribute) data found by dividing the number of defects by the opportunities for defects multiplied by a million. DPMO allows for comparison of different types of product. *See also* parts per million.

defects per unit (DPU)—a measure of capability for discrete (attribute) data found by dividing the number of defects by the number of units.

Deming cycle—*see* plan-do-study-act (PDSA) cycle.

Deming Prize—award given annually to organizations that, according to the award guidelines, have successfully applied organization-wide quality control based on statistical quality control and will keep up with it in the future. Although the award is named in honor of W. Edwards Deming, its criteria are not specifically related to Deming's teachings. There are three separate divisions for the award: the Deming Application Prize, the Deming Prize for Individuals, and the Deming Prize for

Overseas Companies. The award process is overseen by the Deming Prize Committee of the Union of Japanese Scientists and Engineers in Tokyo.

Deming wheel—*see* plan-do-study-act (PDSA) cycle.

dependability—the degree to which a product is operable and capable of performing its required function at any randomly chosen time during its specified operating time, provided that the product is available at the start of that period. (Non-operation-related influences are not included.) Dependability can be expressed by the ratio

$$\frac{\text{time available}}{\text{time available} + \text{time required}}$$

dependent events—two events, *A* and *B,* are dependent if the probability of one event occurring is higher given the occurrence of the other event.

descriptive statistics—the collection of tools and techniques for displaying and summarizing data.

design failure mode and effects analysis (DFMEA)—an analysis process used to identify and evaluate the relative risk associated with a particular design.

Design for Six Sigma (DFSS)—a structured methodology that focuses on designing new products or services with the intent of achieving Six Sigma quality levels. *See also* DMADV; DMAIC; IDOV.

Design for X (DFX)—an umbrella term whereby *X* is a variable that can assume multiple descriptions such as maintainability, manufacturability, producibility, quality, testability, or whatever component of design, logistics, production, quality, and so forth, of the product needs to be emphasized. The various components of the product are collectively referred to as the "ilities." Design for X involves the principle of designing products so that they are cost effective and achieve the objectives set forth for whatever "ilities" are of concern.

design of experiments (DOE; DOX)—the arrangement in which an experimental program is to be conducted, including the selection of factor combinations and their levels. Note: The purpose of designing an experiment is to provide the most efficient and economical methods of reaching valid and relevant conclusions from the experiment. The selection of the design is a function of many considerations, such as the type of questions to be answered, the applicability of the conclusions, the homogeneity of experimental units, the randomization scheme, and the cost to run the experiment. A properly designed experiment will permit simple interpretation of valid results.

design review—documented, comprehensive, and systematic examination of a design to evaluate its capability to fulfill the requirements for quality.

design space—the multidimensional region of possible treatment combinations formed by the selected factors and their levels.

design-for-cost (DFC)—*see* design-to-cost.

design-to-cost (DTC)—a set of tools, techniques, or methods used to set and achieve product cost goals through design trade-off analysis. Design-to-cost is also known as design-for-cost.

detection—the likelihood of finding a failure once it has occurred. Detection may be evaluated based on a 10-point scale. On the lowest end of the scale (1), it is assumed that a design control will detect a failure with certainty. On the highest end of the scale (10), it is assumed that a design control will not detect a failure when a failure occurs.

DFC—an acronym for design-for-cost. *See* design-to-cost.

DFM—an acronym for design for manufacturability. *See* Design for X.

DFMaint—an acronym for design for maintainability. *See* Design for X.

DFMEA—*see* design failure mode and effects analysis.

DFP—an acronym for design for producibility. *See* Design for X.

DFQ—an acronym for design for quality. *See* Design for X.

DFSS—*see* Design for Six Sigma.

DFT—an acronym for design for testability. *See* Design for X.

DFX—*see* Design for X.

discrete scale—a scale with only a set or sequence of distinct values. Examples include defects per unit, events in a given time period, types of defects, and number of orders on a truck.

discrete variable—a variable whose possible values form a finite or, at most, countably infinite set.

discriminant analysis—a statistical technique that is used "to classify observations into two or more groups if you have a sample with known groups. Discriminant analysis can also be used to investigate how variables contribute to group separation" (Minitab 15).

discrimination—the capability of the measurement system to detect and indicate small changes in the characteristic measured. Discrimination is also known as resolution. For example, a tape measure with gradations of one inch would be unable to distinguish between lengths of objects that fall in between the inch marks. Hence, we would say the measurement system could not properly discriminate among the objects. If an object to be measured is 2.5 inches, the measurement system (i.e., tape measure) would produce a value of 2 or 3 inches depending on how the individual decided to round. Therefore, to measure an object that is 2.5 inches, a tape measure with finer gradations would be required.

dispersion effect—the influence of a single factor on the variance of the response variable.

dissatisfiers—those features or functions that the customer or employee has come to expect, and if they are no longer present, the customer will be dissatisfied.

DMADV—a structured methodology similar to DFSS. DMADV is an acronym for define, measure, analyze, design, and verify. Variations of DMADV exist. *See also* Design for Six Sigma; DMAIC; IDOV.

DMAIC—a structured methodology that focuses on improving existing processes with the intent of achieving Six Sigma quality levels. DMAIC is an acronym for define, measure, analyze, improve, and control. *See also* Design for Six Sigma; DMADV; IDOV.

DOE—*see* design of experiments.

DOX—*see* design of experiments.

DPMO—*see* defects per million opportunities.

DPU—*see* defects per unit.

DTC—*see* design-to-cost.

effect—a relationship between factor(s) and response variable(s) based on cause. Note that there can be many factors and response variables. Specific types include main effect, dispersion effect, and interaction effect.

efficiency—an unbiased estimator is considered to be more efficient than another unbiased estimator if it has a smaller variance.

eight types of waste—the seven types of waste plus an additional waste: people. The eighth category was added by Taiichi Ohno, as he saw the underutilization of employees (e.g., brainpower, skills, experience, and talents) as a waste. *See also* seven types of waste.

eighty-twenty (80-20) rule—a term referring to the Pareto principle, which was first defined by J. M. Juran in 1950. The principle suggests most effects come from relatively few causes; that is, 80% of the effects come from 20% of the possible causes. *See also* Pareto principle.

entity—an item that can be individually described and considered.

error—(1) Error in measurement is the difference between the indicated value and the true value of a measured quantity. (2) A fault resulting from defective judgment, deficient knowledge, or carelessness. It is not to be confused with measurement error, which is the difference between a computed or measured value and the true or reference value.

error detection—a hybrid form of error proofing whereby a bad part can still be made but will be caught immediately, and corrective action will be taken to prevent another bad part from being produced. An error detection device is used to spot the error and stop the process when a bad part is made. This is used when error proofing is too expensive or not easily implemented.

error of the first kind—*see* Type I error.

error of the second kind—*see* Type II error.

error proofing—the use of process or design features to prevent the acceptance or further processing of nonconforming products. *See also* foolproofing; mistake proofing; and poka-yoke.

evolutionary operations (EVOP)—the procedure of adjusting variables in a process in small increments in search of a more optimum point on the response surface.

EVOP—*see* evolutionary operations.

expected value—the mean of a random variable.

experimental design—a formal plan that details the specifics for conducting an experiment, such as which responses, factors, levels, blocks, treatments, and tools are to be used. *See also* design of experiments.

experimental error—variation in the response variable beyond that accounted for by the factors, blocks, or other assignable sources in the conduct of the experiment.

experimental run—a single performance of the experiment for a specific set of treatment combinations.

experimental unit—the smallest entity receiving a particular treatment, subsequently yielding a value of the response variable.

explanatory variable—*see* predictor variable.

external customer—a person or organization that receives a product, service, or information but is not part of the organization supplying it. *See also* internal customer.

external failure costs—the failure costs occurring after delivery or shipment of the product, and during or after furnishing of a service, to the customer. Examples are the costs of processing customer complaints, customer returns, warranty claims, and product recalls.

facilitator—an individual responsible for creating favorable conditions that will enable a team to reach its purpose or achieve its goals by bringing together the necessary tools, information, and resources to get the job done.

factor—an independent variable or assignable cause that may affect the responses and of which different levels are included in the experiment. Factors are also known as explanatory, independent, regressor, or predictor variables.

factor analysis—a statistical technique used "to determine the underlying factors responsible for correlations in the data" (Minitab 15).

failure—the termination, due to one or more defects, of the ability of an item, product, or service to perform its required function when called upon to do so. A failure may be partial, complete, or intermittent.

failure analysis—the process of breaking down a failure to determine its cause and to put measures in place to prevent future problems.

failure costs—the costs resulting from product or services not conforming to requirements or customer/user needs. Failure costs are further divided into internal and external categories. *See also* external failure costs; internal failure costs.

failure mode—the type of defect contributing to a failure.

failure mode and effects analysis (FMEA)—a procedure in which each potential failure mode in every subitem of an item is analyzed to determine its effect on other subitems and on the required function of the item.

failure rate—the number of failures per unit time (for equal time intervals).

first-pass yield (FPY)—the percentage of units that complete a process and meet quality guidelines without being scrapped, rerun, retested, returned, or diverted into an offline repair area. FPY is calculated by dividing the units entering the process minus the defective units by the total number of units entering the process. First-pass yield is also known as the quality rate or first-time yield (FTY).

first-time yield (FTY)—*see* first-pass yield.

fishbone diagram—*see* cause-and-effect diagram.

fitness for use—a term used to indicate that a product or service fits the customer's or user's defined purpose for that product or service.

Five Ss—*see* 5Ss.

five whys—*see* 5 whys.

flowchart—a basic quality tool that uses graphical representation for the steps in a process. Effective flowcharts include decisions, inputs, and outputs as well as the sequence of process steps. The flowchart is occasionally considered to be one of the seven basic tools of quality.

FMEA—*see* failure mode and effects analysis.

foolproofing—a method of making a product or process immune to errors on the part of the user or operator. Foolproofing is synonymous with error proofing. *See also* error proofing; mistake proofing; poka-yoke.

force-field analysis—a technique for analyzing the forces that aid or hinder an organization in reaching an objective.

forming—the first stage of team growth. *See also* stages of team growth.

Fourteen (14) points—W. Edwards Deming's 14 management practices to help organizations increase their quality and productivity. They are as follows: (1) create constancy of purpose for improving products and services; (2) adopt a new philosophy; (3) cease dependence on inspection to achieve quality; (4) end the practice of awarding business on price alone; instead, minimize total cost by working with a single supplier; (5) improve constantly and forever every process for planning, production, and service; (6) institute training on the job; (7) adopt and institute leadership; (8) drive out fear; (9) break down barriers between staff areas; (10) eliminate slogans, exhortations, and targets for the workforce; (11) eliminate numerical quotas for the workforce and numerical goals for management; (12) remove barriers that rob people of pride of workmanship, and eliminate the annual rating or merit system; (13) institute a vigorous program of education and self-improvement for everyone; (14) put everybody in the company to work to accomplish the transformation.

FPY—*see* first-pass yield.

funnel experiment—an experiment that demonstrates the effects of tampering. Marbles are dropped through a funnel in an attempt to hit a mark on a flat surface target below. The experiment shows that adjusting a stable process to compensate for an undesirable result or an extraordinarily good result will produce output that is worse than if the process had been left alone.

gage repeatability and reproducibility (GR&R) study—a type of measurement system analysis done to evaluate the performance of a test method or measurement system. Such a study quantifies the capabilities and limitations of a measurement instrument, often estimating its repeatability and reproducibility. It typically involves multiple operators measuring a series of measurement items multiple times.

gantt chart—a type of bar chart used in process/project planning and control to display planned work and finished work in relation to time. Also called a milestone chart.

gap analysis—a technique that compares an organization's existing state with its desired state (typically expressed by its long-term plans) to help determine what needs to be done to remove or minimize the gap.

GB—*see* Green Belt.

GD&T—*see* geometric dimensioning and tolerancing.

Appendix 34

gemba visit—a term that means "place of work" or "the place where the truth can be found." Still others may call it "the value proposition." A gemba visit is a method of obtaining voice of customer information that requires the design team to visit and observe how the customer uses the product in his or her environment.

geometric dimensioning and tolerancing (GD&T)—a method to minimize production costs by considering the functions or relationships of part features in order to define dimensions and tolerances.

goal—a statement of general intent, aim, or desire. It is the point toward which the organization (or individual) directs its efforts; goals are often nonquantitative.

GR&R study—*see* gage repeatability and reproducibility (GR&R) study.

Green Belt (GB)—a Six Sigma role associated with an individual who retains his or her regular position within the firm but is trained in the tools, methods, and skills necessary to conduct Six Sigma improvement projects either individually or as part of larger teams.

hand-off map—*see* circle diagram.

heijunka—the act of leveling the variety or volume of items produced at a process over a period of time. Heijunka is used to avoid excessive batching of product types and volume fluctuations, especially at a pacemaker process.

histogram—a plot of a frequency distribution in the form of rectangles (cells) whose bases are equal to the class interval and whose areas are proportional to the frequencies. A histogram is a graphic summary of variation in a set of data. The graphical nature of the histogram permits easier visualization of patterns of variation that are difficult to detect in a simple table of numbers. The histogram is one of the seven basic tools of quality.

hoshin kanri—the selection of goals, projects to achieve the goals, designation of people and resources for project completion, and establishment of project metrics.

hoshin planning—a term meaning "breakthrough planning." Hoshin planning is a strategic planning process in which an organization develops up to four vision statements that indicate where the company should be in the next five years. Company goals and work plans are developed on the basis of the vision statements. Periodic audits are then conducted to monitor progress.

House of Quality—a diagram named for its house-shaped appearance that clarifies the relationship between customer needs and product features. It helps correlate market or customer requirements and analysis of competitive products with higher-level technical and product characteristics and makes it possible to bring several factors into a single figure. The House of Quality is also known as quality function deployment (QFD).

hygiene factors—a term used by Frederick Herzberg to label "dissatisfiers." *See also* dissatisfiers.

ID—*see* interrelationship digraph.

IDOV—a structured methodology as an alternative to Design for Six Sigma. IDOV is an acronym for identify, design, optimize, and validate. *See also* Design for Six Sigma.

imprecision—a measure of precision computed as a standard deviation of the test or measurement results. Less precision is reflected by a larger standard deviation.

Appendix 34

incomplete block—a block that accommodates only a subset of treatment combinations.

incomplete block design—a design in which the design space is subdivided into blocks in which there are insufficient experimental units available to run a complete replicate of the experiment.

in-control process—a condition where the existence of special causes is no longer indicated by a Shewhart control chart. This does not indicate that only random causes remain, nor does it imply that the distribution of the remaining values is normal (Gaussian). It indicates (within limits) a predictable and stable process.

independent events—two events, A and B, are called independent if the probability that they both occur is the product of the probabilities of their individual occurrences. That is, $P(A \cap B) = P(A)P(B)$.

independent variable—*see* predictor variable.

inferential statistics—techniques for reaching conclusions about a population on the basis of analysis of data from a sample.

inherent process variation—the variation in a process when the process is operating in a state of statistical control.

inspection—the process of measuring, examining, testing, gauging, or otherwise comparing the unit with the applicable requirements.

interaction effect—the effect for which the apparent influence of one factor on the response variable depends on one or more other factors. Existence of an interaction effect means that the factors cannot be changed independently of each other.

interaction plot—a plot providing the average responses at the combinations of levels of two distinct factors.

internal customer—the recipient, person, or department of another person's or department's output (product, service, or information) within an organization. *See also* external customer.

internal failure costs—the failure costs occurring prior to delivery or shipment of the product, or the furnishing of a service, to the customer. Examples are the costs of scrap, rework, re-inspection, retesting, material review, and downgrading.

internal rate of return (IRR)—a discount rate that causes net present value to equal zero.

interrelationship digraph (ID)—a tool that displays the relationship between factors in a complex situation. It identifies meaningful categories from a mass of ideas and is useful when relationships are difficult to determine. Also known as a relations diagram, the interrelationship digraph is one of the seven management and planning tools.

interval scale—a quantitative scale in which meaningful differences exist, but where multiplication and division are not allowed since there is not absolute zero. An example is temperature measured in °F, because 20°F isn't twice as warm as 10°F.

intervention—an action taken by a leader or a facilitator to support the effective functioning of a team or work group.

IRR—*see* internal rate of return.

Ishikawa diagram—*see* cause-and-effect diagram.

Appendix 34

ISO—"equal" (Greek). A prefix for a series of standards published by the International Organization for Standardization.

ISO 14000 series—a set of individual, but related, international standards and guidelines relevant to developing and sustaining an environmental management system.

ISO 9000 series—a set of individual, but related, international standards and guidelines on quality management and quality assurance developed to help organizations effectively document the quality system elements to be implemented to maintain an efficient quality system. The standards were developed by the International Organization for Standardization, a specialized international agency for standardization composed of the national standards bodies of nearly 100 countries.

jidoka—a method of autonomous control involving the adding of intelligent features to machines to start or stop operations as control parameters are reached, and to signal operators when necessary. Jidoka is also known as autonomation.

JIT manufacturing—*see* just-in-time manufacturing.

Juran trilogy—*see* quality trilogy.

just-in-time manufacturing (JIT)—a material requirement planning system for a manufacturing process in which there is little or no manufacturing material inventory on hand at the manufacturing site and little or no incoming inspection.

kaikaku—a term meaning a breakthrough improvement in eliminating waste.

kaizen—a term that means gradual unending improvement by doing little things better and setting and achieving increasingly higher standards. The kaizen approach is usually implemented as a small, intensive event or project over a relatively short duration, such as a week.

kaizen blitz/event—an intense team approach to employ the concepts and techniques of continuous improvement in a short time frame (for example, to reduce cycle time, increase throughput).

kanban—a system that signals the need to replenish stock or materials or to produce more of an item. Kanban is also known as a "pull" approach. Kanban systems need not be elaborate, sophisticated, or even computerized to be effective. Taiichi Ohno of Toyota developed the concept of a kanban system after a visit to a U.S. supermarket.

Kano model—a representation of the three levels of customer satisfaction, defined as dissatisfaction, neutrality, and delight.

KJ method—*see* affinity diagram.

lean—a comprehensive approach complemented by a collection of tools and techniques that focus on reducing cycle time, standardizing work, and reducing waste. Lean is also known as "lean approach" or "lean thinking."

lean approach—*see* lean.

lean manufacturing—applying the lean approach to improving manufacturing operations.

Lean-Six Sigma—a fact-based, data-driven philosophy of improvement that values defect prevention over defect detection. It drives customer satisfaction and bottom-line results by reducing variation, waste, and cycle time, while promoting the use of work standardization and flow, thereby creating a competitive advantage. It applies anywhere variation and waste exist, and every employee should be involved. Note: In the first edition of *The Certified Six Sigma Black Belt Handbook*, this definition was attributed to Six Sigma. However, through experience and empirical evidence, it has become clear that Lean and Six Sigma are different sides of the same coin. Both concepts are required to effectively drive sustained breakthrough improvement. Subsequently, the definition is being changed to reflect the symbiotic relationship that must exist between Lean and Six Sigma to ensure lasting and positive change.

lean thinking—*see* lean.

level—the setting or assignment of a factor at a specific value.

linearity (general sense)—the degree to which a pair of variables follows a straight-line relationship. Linearity can be measured by the correlation coefficient.

linearity (measurement system sense)—the difference in bias through the range of measurement. A measurement system that has good linearity will have a constant bias no matter the magnitude of measurement. If one views the relation between the observed measurement result on the y axis and the true value on the x axis, an ideal measurement system would have a line of slope = 1.

main effect—the influence of a single factor on the mean of the response variable.

main effects plot—the plot giving the average responses at the various levels of individual factors.

maintainability—the measure of the ability of an item to be retained or restored to a specified condition when maintenance is performed by personnel having specified skill levels, using prescribed procedures and resources, at each prescribed level of maintenance and repair.

Malcolm Baldrige National Quality Award (MBNQA)—an award established by Congress in 1987 to raise awareness of quality management and to recognize U.S. organizations that have implemented successful quality management systems. A Criteria for Performance Excellence is published each year. Three awards may be given annually in each of five categories: manufacturing businesses, service businesses, small businesses, education institutions, and health-care organizations. The award is named after the late secretary of commerce Malcolm Baldrige, a proponent of quality management. The U.S. Commerce Department's National Institute of Standards and Technology manages the award, and ASQ administers it. The major emphasis in determining success is achieving results driven by effective processes.

Master Black Belt (MBB)—a Six Sigma role associated with an individual typically assigned full time to train and mentor Black Belts as well as lead the strategy to ensure improvement projects chartered are the right strategic projects for the organization. Master Black Belts are usually the authorizing body to certify Green Belts and Black Belts within an organization.

materials review board (MRB)—a quality control committee or team usually employed in manufacturing or other materials-processing installations that has the responsibility and authority to deal with items or materials that do not conform to fitness-for-use specifications.

matrix chart—*see* matrix diagram.

matrix diagram—a tool that shows the relationships among various groups of data; it yields information about the relationships and the importance of tasks and method elements of the subjects. For each required task (listed along the left side of the diagram), the matrix diagram shows which departments were in charge, which had some involvement, and which had no involvement (listed across the top of the diagram). At each intersecting point, the relationship is either present or absent. This is frequently used to determine who or what department is responsible for the different elements of an implementation plan. The matrix diagram is one of the seven management and planning tools.

MBB—*see* Master Black Belt.

MBNQA—*see* Malcolm Baldrige National Quality Award.

mean—a measure of central tendency and the arithmetic average of all measurements in a data set.

mean-time-between-failures (MTBF)—a basic measure of reliability for repairable items. The mean number of life units during which all parts of an item perform within their specified limits, during a particular measurement interval under stated conditions.

mean-time-to-failure (MTTF)—a basic measure of system reliability for nonrepairable items. The total number of life units for an item divided by the total number of failures within that population, during a particular measurement interval under stated conditions.

mean-time-to-repair (MTTR)—a basic measure of maintainability. The sum of corrective maintenance times at any specific level of repair, divided by the total number of failures within an item repaired at that level, during a particular interval under stated conditions.

measurement error—the difference between the actual value and the measured value of a quality characteristic.

median—the middle number or center value of a set of data when all the data are arranged in increasing order.

metrology—the science and practice of measurements.

mind mapping—a technique for creating a visual representation of a multitude of issues or concerns by forming a map of the interrelated ideas.

mistake proofing—the use of process or design features to prevent manufacture of nonconforming product. It is typically engineering techniques that make the process or product sufficiently robust so as to avoid failing. *See also* error proofing; foolproofing; and poka-yoke.

mode—the value that occurs most frequently in a data set.

MRB—*see* materials review board.

MTBF—*see* mean-time-between-failures.

MTTF—*see* mean-time-to-failure.

MTTR—*see* mean-time-to-repair.

muda—an activity that consumes resources but creates no value; the seven categories are correction, processing, inventory, waiting, overproduction, internal transport, and motion. *See also* seven types of waste.

multiple analysis of variance (MANOVA)—a statistical technique that can be used to analyze both balanced and unbalanced experimental designs. MANOVA is used to perform multivariate analysis of variance for balanced designs when there is more than one dependent variable. The advantage of MANOVA over multiple one-way ANOVAs is that MANOVA controls the family error rate. By contrast, multiple one-way ANOVAs work to increase the alpha error rate.

multi-vari analysis—a graphical technique for viewing multiple sources of process variation. Different sources of variation are categorized into families of related causes and quantified to reveal the largest causes.

multivariate control chart—a variables control chart that allows plotting of more than one variable. These charts make use of the T^2 statistic to combine information from the dispersion and mean of several variables.

multi-voting—a decision-making tool that enables a group to sort through a long list of ideas to identify priorities.

natural process variation—*see* voice of the process.

natural team—a work group responsible for a particular process.

net present value—a discounted cash flow technique for finding the present value of each future year's cash flow.

next-operation-as-customer—the concept that the organization is composed of service/product providers and service/product receivers or "internal customers." *See also* internal customer.

NGT—*see* nominal group technique.

NIST—National Institute of Standards and Technology (U.S.).

noise factor—in robust parameter design, a noise factor is a predictor variable that is hard to control or is not desirable to control as part of the standard experimental conditions. In general, it is not desirable to make inference on noise factors, but they are included in an experiment to broaden the conclusions regarding control factors.

nominal group technique (NGT)—a technique similar to brainstorming that is used by teams to generate ideas on a particular subject. Team members are asked to silently come up with as many ideas as possible and write them down. Each member then shares one idea, which is recorded. After all the ideas are recorded, they are discussed and prioritized by the group.

nominal scale—a scale with unordered, labeled categories, or a scale ordered by convention. Examples include type of defect, breed of dog, and complaint category. Note: It is possible to count by category but not by order or measure.

nonconformance—*see* defective.

nonconformity—*see* defect.

non-value-added (NVA)—tasks or activities that can be eliminated with no deterioration in product or service functionality, performance, or quality in the eyes of the customer. Generally, customers are unwilling to pay for non-value-added activities.

norming—the third stage of team growth. *See also* stages of team growth.

norms—behavioral expectations, mutually agreed-upon rules of conduct, protocols to be followed, or social practices.

NPV—*see* net present value.

null hypothesis—a hypothesis that is formulated without considering any new information or formulated based on the belief that what already exists is true.

NVA—*see* non-value-added.

objective—a quantitative statement of future expectations and an indication of when the expectations should be achieved; it flows from goal(s) and clarifies what people must accomplish.

observation—the process of determining the presence or absence of attributes or measuring a variable. Also, the result of the process of determining the presence or absence of attributes or measuring a variable.

observational study—analysis of data collected from a process without imposing changes on the process.

observed value—the particular value of a response variable determined as a result of a test or measurement.

occurrence—the likelihood of a failure occurring. Occurrence is evaluated using a 10-point scale. On the lowest end of the scale (1), it is assumed the probability of a failure is unlikely. On the highest end of the scale (10), it is assumed the probability of a failure is nearly inevitable.

order—there are two types of order used by Minitab when creating experimental designs: (1) standard order (StdOrder) shows what the order of the runs in the experiment would be if the experiment was done in standard order (also called Yates' order), and (2) run order (RunOrder) shows what the order of the runs in the experiment would be if the experiment was run in random order.

ordinal scale—a scale with ordered, labeled categories. Note: (1) The borderline between ordinal and discrete scales is sometimes blurred. When subjective opinion ratings such as excellent, very good, neutral, poor, and very poor are coded (as numbers 1–5), the apparent effect is conversion from an ordinal to a discrete scale. However, such numbers should not be treated as ordinary numbers, because the distance between 1 and 2 may not be the same as that between 2 and 3, 3 and 4, and so forth. On the other hand, some categories that are ordered objectively according to magnitude—such as the Richter scale, which ranges from 0 to 8 according to the amount of energy release—could equally well be related to a discrete scale. (2) Sometimes nominal scales are ordered by convention. An example is the blood groups *A*, *B*, and *O*, which are always stated in this order. It's the same case if different categories are denoted by single letters; they are then ordered by convention, according to the alphabet.

out of control—a process is described as operating out of control when special causes are present.

parameter—a constant or coefficient that describes some characteristic of a population.

Pareto chart—a graphical tool based on the Pareto principle for ranking causes from most significant to least significant. It utilizes a vertical bar graph in which the bar height reflects the frequency or impact of causes. The graph is distinguished by the inclusion of a cumulative percentage line that identifies the vital few opportunities for improvement. It is also known as the Pareto diagram. The Pareto chart is one of the seven basic tools of quality.

Pareto diagram—*see* Pareto chart.

Pareto principle—an empirical rule named after the nineteenth-century economist Vilfredo Pareto that suggests that most effects come from relatively few causes; that is, about 80% of the effects come from about 20% of the possible causes. The Pareto principle is also known as the eighty-twenty (80-20) rule.

parts per billion (ppb)—the number of times an occurrence happens in one billion chances. In a typical quality setting it usually indicates the number of times a defective part will happen in a billion parts produced; the calculation is projected into the future on the basis of past performance. Parts per billion allows for comparison of different types of product. Two ppb corresponds to a Six Sigma level of quality assuming there is not a 1.5 shift of the mean.

parts per million (ppm)—the number of times an occurrence happens in one million chances. In a typical quality setting it usually indicates the number of times a defective part will happen in a million parts produced; the calculation is often projected into the future on the basis of past performance. Parts per million allows for comparison of different types of product. A ppm of 3.4 corresponds to a Six Sigma level of quality assuming a 1.5 shift of the mean.

payback period—the number of years it will take the results of a project or capital investment to recover the investment from net cash flows.

PDCA cycle—*see* plan-do-check-act (PDCA) cycle.

PDPC—*see* process decision program chart.

PDSA cycle—*see* plan-do-study-act (PDSA) cycle.

percent agreement—the percentage of time in an attribute GR&R study that appraisers agree with (1) themselves (i.e., repeatability), (2) other appraisers (i.e., reproducibility), or (3) a known standard (i.e., bias) when classifying or rating items using nominal or ordinal scales, respectively.

performing—the fourth stage of team growth. *See also* stages of team growth.

PERT—*see* program evaluation and review technique.

PFMEA—*see* process failure mode and effects analysis.

PIT—*see* process improvement team.

plan-do-check-act (PDCA) cycle—a four-step process for quality improvement. In the first step (plan), a plan to effect improvement is developed. In the second step (do), the plan is carried out, preferably on a small scale. In the third step (check), the effects of the plan are observed. In the last step (act), the results are studied to determine what was learned and what can be predicted. The plan-do-check-act cycle is sometimes referred to as the Shewhart cycle, after Walter A. Shewhart.

plan-do-study-act (PDSA) cycle—a variation on the plan-do-check-act (PDCA) cycle, with the variation indicating additional study is required after a change is made. The PDSA cycle is attributed to W. Edwards Deming.

Appendix 34

point estimate—the single value used to estimate a population parameter. Point estimates are commonly referred to as the points at which the interval estimates are centered; these estimates give information about how much uncertainty is associated with the estimate.

poka-yoke—a term that means to mistake proof a process by building safeguards into the system that avoid or immediately find errors. A poka-yoke device prevents incorrect parts from being made or assembled and easily identifies a flaw or error. The term comes from the Japanese terms *poka*, which means "error," and *yokeru*, which means "to avoid." *See also* baka-yoke; error proofing; foolproofing; mistake proofing.

policy—a high-level overall statement embracing the general goals and acceptable practices of a group.

PONC—*see* price of nonconformance.

population—the totality of items or units of material under consideration.

potential process capability—*see* P_{pk}.

power (1 – β)—the probability of rejecting the null hypothesis when the alternative is true. We write this as $P(\text{rejecting } H_0 \mid H_0 \text{ is not true}) = 1 - \beta$. The stronger the power of a hypothesis test, the more sensitive the test is to detecting small differences.

ppb—*see* parts per billion.

PPL—*see* P_{pk_L}.

ppm—*see* parts per million.

PPU—*see* P_{pk_U}.

precision—the closeness of agreement among randomly selected individual measurements or test results. It is that aspect of measure that addresses repeatability or consistency when an identical item is measured several times.

precision-to-tolerance ratio (PTR)—a measure of the capability of the measurement system. It can be calculated by

$$PTR = \frac{5.15\hat{\sigma}_{ms}}{USL - LSL}$$

where $\hat{\sigma}_{ms}$ is the estimated standard deviation of the total measurement system variability. In general, reducing the PTR will yield an improved measurement system.

prediction interval—similar to a confidence interval, it is based on the predicted value that is likely to contain the values of future observations. It will be wider than the confidence interval because it contains bounds on individual observations rather than a bound on the mean of a group of observations. The $100(1 - \alpha)\%$ prediction interval for a single future observation from a normal distribution is given by

$$\bar{X} - t_{\alpha/2} s \sqrt{1 + \frac{1}{n}} \le X_{n+1} \le \bar{X} + t_{\alpha/2} s \sqrt{1 + \frac{1}{n}}$$

predictor variable—a variable that can contribute to the explanation of the outcome of an experiment. A predictor variable is also known as an independent variable, explanatory variable, or regressor variable.

prevention costs—the cost of all activities specifically designed to prevent poor quality in products or services. Examples are the cost of new product review, quality planning, supplier capability surveys, process capability evaluations, quality improvement team meetings, quality improvement projects, and quality education and training.

prevention vs. detection—a phrase used to contrast two types of quality activities. Prevention refers to those activities designed to prevent nonconformances in products and services. Detection refers to those activities designed to find nonconformances already in products and services. Another phrase used to describe this distinction is "designing in quality vs. inspecting in quality."

price of nonconformance (PONC)—the cost of not doing things right the first time.

principal components—used "to form a smaller number of uncorrelated variables from a large set of data. The goal of principal components analysis is to explain the maximum amount of variance with the fewest number of principal components" (Minitab 15). Principal components have wide applicability in the social sciences and market research.

prioritization matrix—a tool used to choose among several options that have many useful benefits, but where not all of them are of equal value. The choices are prioritized according to known weighted criteria and then narrowed down to the most desirable or effective one(s) to accomplish the task or problem at hand. The prioritization matrix is one of the seven management and planning tools.

process—a series of interrelated steps consisting of resources and activities that transform inputs into outputs and work together to a common end. A process can be graphically represented using a flowchart. A process may or may not add value.

process capability—the calculated inherent variability of a characteristic of a product. It represents the best performance of the process over a period of stable operations. Process capability is expressed as $6\hat{\sigma}$, where $\hat{\sigma}$ is the sample standard deviation (short-term component of variation) of the process under a state of statistical control. Note: $\hat{\sigma}$ is often shown as σ in most process capability formulas. A process is said to be "capable" when the output of the process always conforms to the process specifications.

process capability index—a single-number assessment of ability to meet specification limits on a quality characteristic of interest. This index compares the variability of the characteristic to the specification limits. Three basic process capability indices are C_p, C_{pk}, and C_{pm}. *See also* C_p; C_{pk}; C_{pm}.

process decision program chart (PDPC)—a tool that identifies all events that can go wrong and the appropriate countermeasures for these events. It graphically represents all sequences that lead to a desirable effect. It is one of the seven management and planning tools.

process failure mode and effects analysis (PFMEA)—an analysis process used to identify and evaluate the relative risks associated with a particular process.

process improvement team (PIT)—a natural work group or cross-functional team whose responsibility is to achieve needed improvements in existing processes. The lifespan of the team is based on the completion of the team purpose and specific tasks.

process mapping—the flowcharting of a process in detail that includes the identification of inputs and outputs.

process owner—a Six Sigma role associated with an individual who coordinates the various functions and work activities at all levels of a process, has the authority or ability to make changes in the process as required, and manages the entire process cycle so as to ensure performance effectiveness.

process performance—a statistical measure of the outcome of a characteristic from a process that may not have demonstrated to be in a state of statistical control. Note: Use this measure cautiously since it may contain a component of variability from special causes of unpredictable value. It differs from process capability because a state of statistical control is not required.

process performance index—a single-number assessment of ability to meet specification limits on a quality characteristic of interest. The index compares the variability of the characteristic with the specification limits. Three basic process performance indices are P_p, P_{pk}, and P_{pm}. The P_{pm} is analogous to the C_{pm}. *See also* P_p; P_{pk}.

producer's risk (α)—the probability of nonacceptance when the quality level has a value stated by the acceptance sampling plan as acceptable. Note: (1) such nonacceptance is a Type I error; (2) producer's risk is usually designated as alpha (α); (3) quality level could relate to fraction nonconforming and acceptable to AQL; (4) interpretation of producer's risk requires knowledge of the stated quality level. Producer's risk is also known as alpha (α) risk, alpha (α) error, error of the first kind, Type 1 error, and Type I error.

product identification—a means of marking parts with a label, etching, engraving, ink, or other means so that part numbers and other key attributes can be identified.

program evaluation and review technique (PERT)—an event-oriented project management planning and measurement technique that utilizes an arrow diagram or road map to identify all major project events and demonstrates the amount of time (critical path) needed to complete a project. It provides three time estimates: optimistic, most likely, and pessimistic.

project life cycle—a typical project life cycle consists of five sequential phases in project management: concept, planning, design, implementation, and evaluation.

project management—the entire process of managing activities and events throughout a project's life cycle.

project plan—documents that contain the details of why the project is to be initiated, what the project is to accomplish, when and where it is to be implemented, who will be responsible, how implementation will be carried out, how much it will cost, what resources are required, and how the project's progress and results will be measured.

PTR—*see* precision-to-tolerance ratio.

QFD—*see* quality function deployment.

quality assurance—the planned or systematic actions necessary to provide adequate confidence that a product or service will satisfy given needs.

quality control—the operational techniques and the activities that sustain a quality of product or service that will satisfy given needs; also the use of such techniques and activities.

Appendix 34

quality council—a group within an organization that drives the quality improvement effort and usually has oversight responsibility for the implementation and maintenance of the quality management system; it operates in parallel with the normal operation of the business. A quality council is sometimes referred to as a quality steering committee.

quality function deployment (QFD)—a method used to translate voice of customer information into product requirements/CTQs and to continue deployment (e.g., cascading) of requirements to parts and process requirements. Quality function deployment is also known as the House of Quality. *See also* House of Quality.

quality improvement—the actions taken throughout an organization to increase the effectiveness and efficiency of activities and processes in order to provide added benefits to both the organization and its customers.

quality loss function—a parabolic approximation of the quality loss that occurs when a quality characteristic deviates from its target value. The quality loss function is expressed in monetary units. The cost of deviating from the target increases as a quadratic function the farther the quality characteristic moves from the target. The formula used to compute the quality loss function depends on the type of quality characteristic used. The quality loss function was first introduced in this form by Genichi Taguchi.

quality management—the totality of functions involved in organizing and leading the effort to determine and achieve quality.

quality manual—a document stating the quality policy and describing the quality system of an organization.

quality planning—the activity of establishing quality objectives and quality requirements.

quality policy—top management's formally stated intentions and direction for the organization pertaining to quality.

quality system—the organizational structure, procedures, processes, and resources needed to implement quality management.

quality trilogy—a three-pronged approach identified by J. M. Juran for managing for quality. The three legs are quality planning (developing the products and processes required to meet customer needs), quality control (meeting product and process goals), and quality improvement (achieving unprecedented levels of performance).

random cause—a source of process variation that is inherent in a process over time. Note: In a process subject only to random cause variation, the variation is predictable within statistically established limits. Random cause is also known as chance cause and common cause.

random sampling—the process of selecting units for a sample in such a manner that all combinations of units under consideration have an equal or ascertainable chance of being selected for the sample.

random variable—a variable whose value depends on chance.

random variation—variation due to random cause.

randomization—the process used to assign treatments to experimental units so that each experimental unit has an equal chance of being assigned a particular treatment.

randomized block design—an experimental design consisting of *b* blocks with *t* treatments assigned via randomization to the experimental units within each block. This is a method for controlling the variability of experimental units. For the completely randomized design, no stratification of the experimental units is made. In the randomized block design, the treatments are randomly allotted within each block; that is, the randomization is restricted.

randomized block factorial design—a factorial design run in a randomized block design where each block includes a complete set of factorial combinations.

ratio scale—a scale where meaningful differences are shown, where absolute zero exists, and where multiplication and division are permitted. One example of a ratio scale is length in inches, because zero length is defined as having no length, and 20 inches is twice as long as 10 inches.

rational subgroup—a subgroup that is expected to be as free as possible from assignable causes (usually consecutive items). In a rational subgroup, variation is presumed to be only from random cause.

red bead experiment—an experiment developed by W. Edwards Deming to illustrate that it is impossible to put employees in rank order of performance for the coming year based on their performance during the past year, because performance differences must be attributed to the system, not to the employees. Four thousand red and white beads in a jar (of which 20% are red) and six people are needed for the experiment. The participants' goal is to produce white beads, as the customer will not accept red beads. One person stirs the beads and then, blindfolded, selects a sample of 50 beads. That person hands the jar to the next person, who repeats the process, and so on. When all participants have their samples, the number of red beads for each is counted. The limits of variation between employees that can be attributed to the system are calculated. Everyone will fall within the calculated limits of variation that could arise from the system. The calculations will show that there is no evidence that one person will be a better performer than another in the future. The experiment shows that it would be a waste of management's time to try to find out why, say, John produced 4 red beads and Jane produced 15; instead, management should improve the system, making it possible for everyone to produce more white beads.

reengineering—the process of completely redesigning or restructuring a whole organization, an organizational component, or a complete process. It's a "start all over again from the beginning" approach, sometimes called a breakthrough. In terms of improvement approaches, reengineering is contrasted with incremental improvement (kaizen).

regressor variable—*see* predictor variable.

reliability—the probability that an item can perform its intended function for a specified interval under stated conditions.

repeatability—the precision under conditions where independent measurement results are obtained with the same method on identical measurement items by the same appraiser (i.e., operator) using the same equipment within a short period of time. Although misleading, repeatability is often referred to as equipment variation (*EV*). It is also referred to as within-system variation when the conditions of measurement are fixed and defined (i.e., equipment, appraiser, method and environment).

repeated measures—the measurement of a response variable more than once under similar conditions. Repeated measures allow one to determine the inherent variability in the measurement system. Repeated measures is also known as duplication or repetition.

replication—the performance of an experiment more than once for a given set of predictor variables. Each repetition of the experiment is called a replicate. Replication differs from repeated measures in that it is a repeat of the entire experiment for a given set of predictor variables, not just a repeat of measurements on the same experiment. Note: Replication increases the precision of the estimates of the effects in an experiment. It is more effective when all elements contributing to the experimental error are included.

reproducibility—the precision under conditions where independent measurement results are obtained with the same method on identical measurement items with different operators using different equipment. Although misleading, reproducibility is often referred to as appraiser variation (*AV*). The term "appraiser variation" is used because it is common practice to have different operators with identical measuring systems. Reproducibility, however, can refer to any changes in the measurement system. For example, assume the same appraiser uses the same material, equipment, and environment, but uses two different measurement methods; the reproducibility calculation will show the variation due to change in methods. It is also known as the average variation between systems or between-conditions variation of measurement.

resolution—(1) The smallest measurement increment that can be detected by the measurement system. (2) In the context of experimental design, resolution refers to the level of confounding in a fractional factorial design. For example, in a resolution III design, the main effects are confounded with the two-way interaction effects.

response variable—a variable that shows the observed results of an experimental treatment. It is sometimes known as the dependent variable or *y* variable. There may be multiple response variables in an experimental design.

RETAD—*see* single-minute exchange of dies.

return on equity (ROE)—the net profit after taxes, divided by last year's tangible stockholders' equity, and then multiplied by 100 to provide a percentage.

return on investment (ROI)—an umbrella term for a variety of ratios measuring an organization's business performance and calculated by dividing some measure of return by a measure of investment and then multiplying by 100 to provide a percentage. In its most basic form, ROI indicates what remains from all money taken in after all expenses are paid.

risk assessment/management—the process of determining what risks are present in a situation and what actions might be taken to eliminate or mediate them.

risk, consumer's (*β*)—*see* consumer's risk.

risk, producer's (*α*)—*see* producer's risk.

robust designs—products or processes that continue to perform as intended in spite of manufacturing variation and extreme environmental conditions during use.

robustness—the condition of a product or process design that remains relatively stable with a minimum of variation even though factors that influence operations or usage, such as environment and wear, are constantly changing.

ROE—*see* return on equity.

ROI—*see* return on investment.

rolled throughput yield (RTY)—the probability of a unit of product passing through an entire process defect-free. The rolled throughput yield is determined by multiplying first-pass yield from each subprocess of the total process.

root cause—a factor (i.e., original cause) that, through a chain of cause and effect, causes a defect or nonconformance to occur. Root causes should be permanently eliminated through process improvement. Note: Several root causes may be present and may work either together or independently to cause a defect.

root cause analysis—a structured approach or process of identifying root (i.e., original) causes. Many techniques and statistical tools are available for analyzing data to ultimately determine the root cause.

RTY—*see* rolled throughput yield.

run chart—a chart showing a line connecting consecutive data points collected from a process running over a period of time. The run chart is occasionally considered to be one of the seven basic tools of quality. Note: A trend is indicated when the series of collected data points head up or down.

sample—a group of units, portions of material, or observations taken from a larger collection of units, quantity of material, or observations that serves to provide information that may be used as a basis for making a decision concerning the larger quantity.

sample size (*n*)—the number of units in a sample. Note: In a multistage sample, the sample size is the total number of units at the conclusion of the final stage of sampling.

scatter diagram—a plot of two variables, one on the *y* axis and the other on the *x* axis. The resulting graph allows visual examination for patterns to determine if the variables show any relationship or if there is just random "scatter." This pattern, or lack thereof, aids in choosing the appropriate type of model for estimation. Note: Evidence of a pattern does not imply that a causal relationship exists between the variables. The scatter diagram is one of the seven tools of quality.

scatter plot—*see* scatter diagram.

scribe—the member of a team assigned to record minutes of meetings.

SDWT—*see* self-directed work team.

seiban—the name of a management practice taken from the words *sei*, which means "manufacturing," and *ban*, which means "number." A seiban number is assigned to all parts, materials, and purchase orders associated with a particular customer, job, or project. This enables a manufacturer to track everything related to a particular product, project, or customer and facilitates setting aside inventory for specific projects or priorities. Seiban is an effective practice for project and build-to-order manufacturing.

seiketsu—one of the 5Ss that means to conduct seiri, seiton, and seiso at frequent, indeed daily, intervals to maintain a workplace in perfect condition.

seiri—one of the 5Ss that means to separate needed tools, parts, and instructions from unneeded materials and to remove the latter.

seiso—one of the 5Ss that means to conduct a cleanup campaign.

seiton—one of the 5Ss that means to neatly arrange and identify parts and tools for ease of use.

self-directed work team (SDWT)—a team that requires little supervision and manages itself and the day-to-day work it does; self-directed teams are responsible for whole work processes and schedules with each individual performing multiple tasks.

seven basic tools of quality—a set of both qualitative and quantitative tools that help organizations understand and improve. Unfortunately there is no longer a unified set of seven tools that are universally agreed upon, but most authors agree that five of the seven basic tools include the cause-and-effect diagram, control charts, histogram, Pareto chart, and the scatter diagram. Additional tools suggested as part of the seven basic tools of quality include the check sheet, flowchart, graphs, run chart, trend chart, and stratification. Note: (1) graphs are sometimes included with control charts and are distinct at other times; (2) run charts are sometimes included with control charts and are distinct at other times; (3) run charts are sometimes synonymous with trend charts and are distinct at other times; (4) run charts are sometimes included with graphs and are distinct at other times. Some authors are known to have eight basic tools of quality. *See also individual entries.*

seven management and planning tools—the seven commonly recognized management and planning tools are the affinity diagram, tree diagram, process decision program chart (PDPC), matrix diagram, interrelationship diagram, prioritization matrices, and the activity network diagram. *See also individual entries.*

seven tools of quality—*see* seven basic tools of quality.

seven types of waste—Taiichi Ohno proposed value as the opposite of waste and identified seven categories: (1) defects, (2) overproduction (ahead of demand), (3) overprocessing (beyond customer requirements), (4) waiting, (5) unnecessary motions, (6) transportation, and (7) inventory (in excess of the minimum).

severity—an indicator of the degree of a failure should a failure occur. Severity can be evaluated based on a 10-point scale. On the lowest end of the scale (1), it is assumed a failure will have no noticeable effect. On the highest end of the scale (10), it is assumed a failure will impact safe operation or violate compliance with regulatory mandate.

Shewhart cycle—*see* plan-do-check-act (PDCA) cycle.

shitsuke—one of the 5Ss that means to form the habit of always following the first four Ss.

simultaneous engineering—*see* concurrent engineering.

single-minute exchange of dies (SMED)—a series of techniques pioneered by Shigeo Shingo for changeovers of production machinery in less than 10 minutes. The long-term objective is always zero setup, in which changeovers are instantaneous and do not interfere in any way with continuous flow. Setup in a single minute is not required but used as a reference. SMED is also known as rapid exchange of tooling and dies (RETAD).

SIPOC—a macro-level analysis of the suppliers, inputs, processes, outputs, and customers.

Six Sigma—can take on various definitions across a broad spectrum depending on the level of focus and implementation. (1) Philosophy—the philosophical perspective views all work as processes that can be defined, measured, analyzed, improved, and controlled (DMAIC). Processes require inputs and produce outputs. If you control the inputs, you will control the outputs. This is generally expressed as the $y = f(x)$ concept. (2) Set of tools—Six Sigma as a set of tools includes all the qualitative and quantitative techniques used by the Six Sigma practitioner to drive process improvement through defect reduction and the minimization of variation. A few such tools include statistical process control (SPC), control charts, failure mode and effects analysis, and process mapping. There is probably little agreement among Six Sigma professionals as to what constitutes the tool set. (3) Methodology—this view of Six Sigma recognizes the underlying and rigorous approach known as DMAIC. DMAIC defines the steps a Six Sigma practitioner is expected to follow, starting with identifying the problem and ending with implementing long-lasting solutions. While DMAIC is not the only Six Sigma methodology in use, it is certainly the most widely adopted and recognized. (4) Metrics—in simple terms, Six Sigma quality performance means 3.4 defects per million opportunities (accounting for a 1.5-sigma shift in the mean).

slack time—the time an activity can be delayed without delaying the entire project; it is determined by calculating the difference between the latest allowable date and the earliest expected date.

SMED—*see* single-minute exchange of dies.

SOW—*see* statement of work.

spaghetti chart—a before-improvement chart of existing steps in a process and the many back and forth interrelationships (can resemble a bowl of spaghetti); used to see the redundancies and other wasted movements of people and material.

span of control—the number of subordinates a manager can effectively and efficiently manage.

SPC—*see* statistical process control.

special cause—a source of process variation other than inherent process variation. Note: (1) sometimes special cause is considered synonymous with assignable cause, but a special cause is assignable only when it is specifically identified; (2) a special cause arises because of specific circumstances that are not always present. Therefore, in a process subject to special causes, the magnitude of the variation over time is unpredictable. *See also* assignable cause.

specification—an engineering requirement used for judging the acceptability of a particular product/service based on product characteristics such as appearance, performance, and size. In statistical analysis, specifications refer to the document that prescribes the requirements with which the product or service has to perform.

specification limits—limiting value(s) stated for a characteristic. *See also* tolerance.

sponsor—a member of management who oversees, supports, and implements the efforts of a team or initiative. Although many organizations define the terms "Champion" and "sponsor" differently, they are frequently used interchangeably. *See also* Champion.

SQC—*see* statistical quality control.

stability (of a measurement system)—the change in bias of a measurement system over time and usage when that system is used to measure a master part or standard. Thus, a stable measurement system is one in which the variation is in statistical control, which is typically demonstrated through the use of control charts.

stable process—a process that is predictable within limits; a process that is subject only to random causes. (This is also known as a state of statistical control.) Note: (1) a stable process will generally behave as though the results are simple random samples from the same population; (2) this state does not imply that the random variation is large or small, within or outside specification limits, but rather that the variation is predictable using statistical techniques; (3) the process capability of a stable process is usually improved by fundamental changes that reduce or remove some of the random causes present and/or adjusting the mean toward the target value.

stages of team growth—the four development stages through which groups typically progress: forming, storming, norming, and performing. Knowledge of the stages helps team members accept the normal problems that occur on the path from forming a group to becoming a team.

stakeholders—the people, departments, and groups that have an investment or interest in the success or actions taken by the organization.

standard—a statement, specification, or quantity of material against which measured outputs from a process may be judged as acceptable or unacceptable.

standard work—a concept whereby each work activity is organized around human motion to minimize waste. Each work activity is precisely described and includes specifying cycle time, takt time, task sequence, and the minimum inventory of parts on hand required to conduct the activity. Standard work is also known as standardized work.

statement of work (SOW)—a description of the actual work to be accomplished. It is derived from the work breakdown structure and, when combined with the project specifications, becomes the basis for the contractual agreement on the project. The statement of work is also known as scope of work.

statistic—a quantity calculated from a sample of observations, most often to form an estimate of some population parameter.

statistical control—a process is considered to be in a state of statistical control if variations among the observed sampling results from it can be attributed to a constant system of chance causes.

statistical process control (SPC)—the use of statistical techniques such as control charts to reduce variation, increase knowledge about the process, and steer the process in the desired way. Note: (1) SPC operates most efficiently by controlling variation of process or in-process characteristics that correlate with a final product characteristic; and/or by increasing the robustness of the process against this variation;

Appendix 34

(2) a supplier's final product characteristic can be a process characteristic to the next downstream supplier's process.

statistical quality control (SQC)—the application of statistical techniques to control quality. The term "statistical process control" is often used interchangeably with "statistical quality control," although statistical quality control includes acceptance sampling as well as statistical process control.

statistical tolerance interval—an interval estimator determined from a random sample so as to provide a specified level of confidence that the interval covers at least a specified proportion of the sampled population.

storming—the second stage of team growth. *See also* stages of team growth.

strategic planning—a process to set an organization's long-range goals and identify the actions needed to reach those goals.

stratification—the layering of objects or data; also, the process of classifying data into subgroups based on characteristics or categories. Stratification is occasionally considered to be one of the seven tools of quality.

subsystem—a combination of sets, groups, and so on, that performs an operational function within a system and its major subdivision of the system.

supply chain—the series of processes and/or organizations that are involved in producing and delivering a product or service to the customer or user.

SWOT analysis—an assessment of an organization's key strengths, weaknesses, opportunities, and threats. It considers factors such as the organization's industry, competitive position, functional areas, and management.

system—a composite of equipment, skills, and techniques capable of performing or supporting an operational role, or both. A complete system includes all equipment, related facilities, material, software, services, and personnel required for its operation and support to the degree that it can be considered self-sufficient in its intended operating environment.

Taguchi methods—the American Supplier Institute's trademarked term for the quality engineering methodology developed by Genichi Taguchi. In this engineering approach to quality control, Taguchi calls for off-line quality control, online quality control, and a system of experimental designs to improve quality and reduce costs.

takt time—a term derived from the German word *taktzeit*, meaning "clock cycle." Takt time is the available production time divided by the rate of customer demand. Operating under takt time sets the production pace to customer demand.

team—two or more people who are equally accountable for the accomplishment of a purpose and specific performance goals; it is also defined as a small number of people with complementary skills who are committed to a common purpose.

team building—the process of transforming a group of people into a team and developing the team to achieve its purpose.

testing—a means of determining the capability of an item to meet specified requirements by subjecting the item to a set of physical, chemical, environmental, and operating actions and conditions.

theory of constraints (TOC)—Goldratt's theory deals with techniques and tools for identifying and eliminating the constraints (bottlenecks) in a process.

theory of knowledge—a belief that management is about prediction, and people learn not only from experience but also from theory. When people study a process and develop a theory, they can compare their predictions with their observations; profound learning results.

theory X and theory Y—a theory developed by Douglas McGregor that maintains that there are two contrasting assumptions about people, each of which is based on the manager's view of human nature. Theory X managers take a negative view and assume that most employees do not like work and try to avoid it. Theory Y managers take a positive view and believe that employees want to work, will seek and accept responsibility, and can offer creative solutions to organizational problems.

theory Z—a term coined by William G. Ouchi, theory Z refers to a Japanese style of management that is characterized by long-term employment, slow promotions, considerable job rotation, consensus-style decision making, and concern for the employee as a whole.

three-sixty-degree (360°) feedback process—an evaluation method that provides feedback from the perspectives of self, peers, direct reports, superiors, customers, and suppliers.

throughput time—the total time required (processing + queue time) from concept to launch, from order received to delivery, or from raw materials received to delivery to customer.

TOC—*see* theory of constraints.

tolerance—the difference between upper and lower specification limits.

tolerance design (Taguchi)—a rational grade limit for components of a system; determines which parts and processes need to be modified and to what degree it is necessary to increase their control capacity; a method for rationally determining tolerances.

total productive maintenance (TPM)—a methodology pioneered by Nippondenso (a member of the Toyota group) that works to ensure every machine in a production process is always able to perform its required tasks such that production is never interrupted. TPM maximizes equipment effectiveness by using a preventive maintenance program throughout the life of the equipment.

TPM—*see* total productive maintenance.

treatment—the specific setting or combination of factor levels for an experimental unit.

tree diagram—a tool that depicts the hierarchy of tasks and subtasks needed to complete an objective. The finished diagram resembles a tree. The tree diagram is one of the seven management and planning tools.

trend chart—a control chart in which the deviation of the subgroup average, $\bar{X}$, from an expected trend in the process level is used to evaluate the stability of a process. The trend chart is also known as the trend control chart. The trend chart is occasionally considered to be one of the seven basic tools of quality.

Appendix 34

trend control chart—*see* trend chart.

TRIZ—a Russian acronym for "theory of inventive problem solving"; a systematic means of inventing and solving design conflicts. TRIZ involves three items to solve technical problems: (1) various tricks, (2) methods based on utilizing physical effects and phenomenon, and (3) complex methods.

Type 1 error—*see* Type I error.

Type 2 error—*see* Type II error.

Type I error—an error that occurs when the null hypothesis is rejected when it is true. We refer to the P(Type I error) = P(rejecting H_0 when H_0 is true) = α. A Type I error is also known as an alpha (α) error and error of the first kind. The P(Type I error) is also known as α – value, producer's risk, level of significance, and significance level.

Type II error—an error that occurs when the alternative hypothesis is accepted when it is false. We refer to the P(Type II error) = P(not rejecting H_0 when H_0 is false) = β. A Type II error is also known as a beta (β) error and error of the second kind. The P(Type II error) is also known as β – value and consumer's risk.

VA—*see* value-added.

validation—refers to the effectiveness of the design process itself and is intended to ensure the design process is capable of meeting the requirements of the final product or process.

value—the net difference between customer-perceived benefits and burdens; it is sometimes expressed as a ratio of benefits to burdens or a ratio of worth to cost.

value analysis—an analytical process that assumes a process, procedure, product, or service is of no value unless proved otherwise. Value analysis assigns a price to every step of a process and then computes the worth-to-cost ratio of that step. *See also* value-added.

value engineering (VE)—an engineering discipline responsible for analyzing the components and processes that create a product, with an emphasis on minimizing costs while maintaining standards required by the customer.

value stream—all activities, both value added and non value added, required to bring a product from a raw material state into the hands of the customer, a customer requirement from order to delivery, or a design from concept to launch.

value stream analysis (VSA)—an analytical process designed to enhance the benefits of a value delivery system while reducing or eliminating all non-value-adding costs associated with value delivery.

value stream mapping—a technique for following the production path for a product or service from beginning to end while drawing a visual representation of every process in the material and information flows. Subsequently, a future state map is drawn of how value should flow.

value-added (VA)—the tasks or activities that convert resources into products or services consistent with customer requirements. The customer can be internal or external to the organization. Value-added activities add worth to the product or service from the customer's perspective and typically change form, fit, or function.

variables data—data resulting from the measurement of a parameter or a variable. The resulting measurements may be recorded on a continuous scale.

VE—*see* value engineering.

verification—refers to the design meeting customer requirements and ensures the design yields the correct product or process.

virtual team—a boundaryless team functioning without a commonly shared physical structure or physical contact, using technology to link the team members. Team members are typically remotely situated and affiliated with a common organization, purpose, or project.

visual controls—the collection of approaches and techniques that permit one to visually determine the status of a system, factory, or process at a glance and to prevent or minimize process variation. To some degree, it can be viewed as a minor form of mistake proofing. Visual controls is sometimes referred to as the visual factory.

visual factory—*see* visual controls.

vital few, useful many—a phrase used by J. M. Juran to describe his use of the Pareto principle, which he first defined in 1950. (The principle was used much earlier in economics and inventory control methodologies.) The principle suggests that most effects come from relatively few causes; that is, 80% of the effects come from 20% of the possible causes. The 20% of the possible causes is referred to as the "vital few"; the remaining causes are referred to as the "useful many." When Juran first defined this principle, he was referring to the remaining causes as the "trivial many," but realizing that no problems are trivial in quality assurance, he changed it to "useful many."

VOC—*see* voice of the customer.

voice of the customer (VOC)—an organization's efforts to understand the customers' needs and expectations ("voice") and to provide products and services that truly meet them.

voice of the process (VOP)—the 6σ spread between the upper and lower control limits as determined from an in-control process. The VOP is also known as natural process variation.

VOP—*see* voice of the process.

VSA—*see* value stream analysis.

waste—any activity that consumes resources but does not add value to the product or service a customer receives. Waste is also known as muda.

work group—a group composed of people from one functional area who work together on a daily basis and share a common purpose.

Please submit suggestions, additions, corrections, or deletions to http://asqgroups.asq.org/cssbbhandbook/.

Appendix 35

Glossary of Japanese Terms

baka-yoke—a term for a manufacturing technique for preventing mistakes by designing the manufacturing process, equipment, and tools so that an operation literally cannot be performed incorrectly. In addition to preventing incorrect operation, the technique usually provides a warning signal of some sort for incorrect performance.

chaku-chaku—a term meaning "load-load" in a cell layout where a part is taken from one machine and loaded into the next.

gemba visit—a term that means "place of work" or "the place where the truth can be found." Still others may call it "the value proposition." A gemba visit is a method of obtaining voice of customer information that requires the design team to visit and observe how the customer uses the product in his or her environment.

heijunka—the act of leveling the variety or volume of items produced at a process over a period of time. Heijunka is used to avoid excessive batching of product types and volume fluctuations, especially at a pacemaker process.

hoshin kanri—the selection of goals, projects to achieve the goals, designation of people and resources for project completion, and establishment of project metrics.

hoshin planning—a term meaning "breakthrough planning." Hoshin planning is a strategic planning process in which a company develops up to four vision statements that indicate where the company should be in the next five years. Company goals and work plans are developed on the basis of the vision statements. Periodic audits are then conducted to monitor progress.

jidoka—a method of autonomous control involving the adding of intelligent features to machines to start or stop operations as control parameters are reached, and to signal operators when necessary. Jidoka is also known as autonomation.

kaikaku—a term meaning a breakthrough improvement in eliminating waste.

kaizen—a term that means gradual unending improvement by doing little things better and setting and achieving increasingly higher standards. The kaizen approach is usually implemented as a small, intensive event or project over a relatively short duration, such as a week.

kaizen blitz/event—an intense team approach to employ the concepts and techniques of continuous improvement in a short time frame (for example, to reduce cycle time, increase throughput).

kanban—a system that signals the need to replenish stock or materials or to produce more of an item. Kanban is also known as a "pull" approach. Kanban systems need not be elaborate, sophisticated, or even computerized to be effective. Taiichi Ohno of Toyota developed the concept of a kanban system after a visit to a U.S. supermarket.

muda—an activity that consumes resources but creates no value; the seven categories are correction, processing, inventory, waiting, overproduction, internal transport, and motion.

poka-yoke—a term that means to mistake proof a process by building safeguards into the system that avoid or immediately find errors. A poka-yoke device prevents incorrect parts from being made or assembled and easily identifies a flaw or error. The term comes from the Japanese terms *poka*, which means "error," and *yokeru*, which means "to avoid."

seiban—the name of a management practice taken from the words *sei*, which means "manufacturing," and *ban*, which means "number." A seiban number is assigned to all parts, materials, and purchase orders associated with a particular customer, job, or project. This enables a manufacturer to track everything related to a particular product, project, or customer and facilitates setting aside inventory for specific projects or priorities. Seiban is an effective practice for project and build-to-order manufacturing.

seiketsu—one of the 5Ss that means to conduct seiri, seiton, and seiso at frequent, indeed daily, intervals to maintain a workplace in perfect condition.

seiri—one of the 5Ss that means to separate needed tools, parts, and instructions from unneeded materials and to remove the latter.

seiso—one of the 5Ss that means to conduct a cleanup campaign.

seiton—one of the 5Ss that means to neatly arrange and identify parts and tools for ease of use.

shitsuke—one of the 5Ss that means to form the habit of always following the first four Ss.

Bibliography

Allen, Derek R., and Tanniru R. Rao. 2000. *Analysis of Customer Satisfaction Data: A Comprehensive Guide to Multivariate Statistical Analysis in Customer Satisfaction, Loyalty, and Service Quality Research.* Milwaukee, WI: ASQ Quality Press.

Alukal, George, and Anthony Manos. 2006. *Lean Kaizen: A Simplified Approach to Process Improvements.* Milwaukee, WI: ASQ Quality Press.

Andersen, Bjørn. 2007. *Business Process Improvement Toolbox,* 2nd ed. Milwaukee, WI: ASQ Quality Press.

Andersen, Bjørn, and Thomas Fagerhaug. 2006. *Root Cause Analysis: Simplified Tools and Techniques,* 2nd ed. Milwaukee, WI: ASQ Quality Press.

Andersen, Bjørn, Tom Fagerhaug, Bjørnar Henriksen, and Lars E. Onsøyen. 2008. *Mapping Work Processes,* 2nd ed. Milwaukee, WI: ASQ Quality Press.

ANSI/ASQC A1-1978 Definitions, Symbols, Formulas and Tables for Control Charts. 1978. Milwaukee, WI: ASQC Quality Press.

ANSI/ASQC B1-1985 Guide for Quality Control Charts (set of 3 standards). 1985. Milwaukee, WI: ASQC Quality Press.

ANSI/ASQC B2-1985 Control Chart Method of Analyzing Data. 1985. Milwaukee, WI: ASQC Quality Press.

ANSI/ASQC B3-1985 Control Chart Method of Controlling Quality During Production. 1985. Milwaukee, WI: ASQC Quality Press.

ASQ Statistics Division. 2000. *Improving Performance Through Statistical Thinking.* Milwaukee, WI: ASQ Quality Press.

ASQ Statistics Division. 2005. *Glossary and Tables for Statistical Quality Control,* 4th ed. Milwaukee, WI: ASQ Quality Press.

ASQC Standards Committee. 1994. *ANSI/ISO/ASQC A8402-1994 Quality Management and Quality Assurance—Vocabulary.* Milwaukee, WI: ASQC Quality Press.

ASQC Statistics Division. 1996. *Glossary and Tables for Statistical Quality Control,* 3rd ed. Milwaukee, WI: ASQC Quality Press.

AT&T Handbook Committee. 1958. *Statistical Quality Control Handbook.* Charlotte, NC: Western Electric.

Automotive Industry Action Group. 1995. *(QS-9000) Measurement Systems Analysis (MSA) Reference Manual,* 2nd ed. Southfield, MI: Chrysler, Ford, and GM.

Automotive Industry Action Group. 1995. *(QS-9000) Potential Failure Mode and Effects Analysis (FMEA) Reference Manual,* 2nd ed. Southfield, MI: Chrysler, Ford, and GM.

Automotive Industry Action Group. 1995. *(QS-9000) Statistical Process Control (SPC) Reference Manual.* Southfield, MI: Chrysler, Ford, and GM.

Barrentine, Larry B. 2003. *Concepts for R&R Studies,* 2nd ed. Milwaukee, WI: ASQ Quality Press.

Bauer, John E., Grace L. Duffy, and Russell T. Westcott. 2006. *The Quality Improvement Handbook,* 2nd ed. Milwaukee, WI: ASQ Quality Press.

Beauregard, Michael R., Raymond J. Mikulak, and Robin E. McDermott. 1997. *The Basics of Mistake-Proofing.* New York: Quality Resources.

Belair, Georgette, and John O. O'Neill. 2007. *Implementing Design for Six Sigma: A Leader's Guide.* Milwaukee, WI: ASQ Quality Press.

Benbow, Donald W., and T. M. Kubiak. 2005. *The Certified Six Sigma Black Belt Handbook.* Milwaukee, WI: ASQ Quality Press.

Bicheno, John. 2004. *The New Lean Toolbox: Towards Fast, Flexible Flow.* Buckingham, UK: PICSIE Books.

Blazey, Mark L. 2008. *Insights to Performance Excellence 2008: An Inside Look at the 2008 Baldrige Award Criteria.* Milwaukee, WI: ASQ Quality Press.

Bossert, James L. 1991. *Quality Function Deployment: A Practitioner's Approach.* Milwaukee, WI: ASQC Quality Press/Marcel Dekker.

Bothe, Davis R. 1997. *Measuring Process Capability: Techniques and Calculations for Quality and Manufacturing Engineers.* New York: McGraw-Hill.

Box, George E. P., J. Stuart Hunter, and William G. Hunter. 2005. *Statistics for Experimenters: Design, Innovation, and Discovery,* 2nd ed. Hoboken, NJ: John Wiley.

Brassard, Michael. 1989. *The Memory Jogger Plus+™.* Methuen, MA: Goal/QPC.

Brassard, Michael, Lynda Finn, Dana Ginn, and Diane Ritter. 2002. *The Six Sigma Memory Jogger II.* Salem, NH: Goal/QPC.

Breyfogle, Forrest W. III. 2003. *Implementing Six Sigma: Smarter Solutions Using Statistical Methods,* 2nd ed. Hoboken, NJ: John Wiley.

Breyfogle, Forrest W. III, James M. Cupello, and Becki Meadows. 2001. *Managing Six Sigma: A Practical Guide to Understanding, Assessing, and Implementing the Strategy That Yields Bottom-Line Success.* Hoboken, NJ: John Wiley.

Brush, Gary G. 1988. *Volume 12: How to Choose the Proper Sample Size.* Milwaukee, WI: ASQC Quality Press.

Camp, Robert C. 1995. *Business Process Benchmarking: Finding and Implementing Best Practices.* Milwaukee, WI: ASQC Quality Press.

Campanella, Jack, and ASQ Quality Costs Committee. 1999. *Principles of Quality Costs: Principles, Implementation, and Use,* 3rd ed. Milwaukee, WI: ASQ Quality Press.

Cobb, Charles G. 2005. *Enterprise Process Mapping.* Milwaukee, WI: ASQ Quality Press.

Cox, Neil D. 1986. *Volume 11: How to Perform Statistical Tolerance Analysis.* Milwaukee, WI: ASQC Quality Press.

Crossley, Mark L. 2008. *The Desk Reference of Statistical Quality Methods,* 2nd ed. Milwaukee, WI: ASQ Quality Press.

Day, Ronald G. 1993. *Quality Function Deployment: Linking a Company with Its Customers.* Milwaukee, WI: ASQC Quality Press.

DeGroot, Morris H. 1975. *Probability and Statistics.* Reading, MA: Addison-Wesley.

Deming, W. Edwards. 1982. *Quality, Productivity, and Competitive Position.* Cambridge, MA: MIT Press.

Deming, W. Edwards. 1986. *Out of the Crisis.* Cambridge, MA: MIT Press.

Dettmer, H. William. 1997. *Goldratt's Theory of Constraints: A Systems Approach to Continuous Improvement.* Milwaukee, WI: ASQ Quality Press.

Dettmer, H. William. 2007. *The Logical Thinking Process: A Systems Approach to Complex Problem Solving.* Milwaukee, WI: ASQ Quality Press.

Dixon, Wilfrid, and Frank J. Massey Jr. 1983. *Introduction to Statistical Analysis*, 4th ed. New York: McGraw-Hill.

Dodson, Bryan. 2006. *The Weibull Analysis Handbook*, 2nd ed. Milwaukee, WI: ASQ Quality Press.

Dovich, Robert A. 1990. *Reliability Statistics*. Milwaukee, WI: ASQC Quality Press.

Dovich, Robert A. 1992. *Quality Engineering Statistics*. Milwaukee, WI: ASQC Quality Press.

Duncan, Acheson J. 1974. *Quality Control and Industrial Statistics*, 4th ed. Homewood, IL: Richard D. Irwin.

Ginn, Dana, and Evelyn Varner. 2004. *The Design for Six Sigma Memory Jogger*. Salem, NH: Goal/QPC.

Goldratt, Eliyahu M. 1997. *Critical Chain*. Great Barrington, MA: The North River Press.

Grant, Eugene L., and Richard S. Leavenworth. 1988. *Statistical Quality Control*, 6th ed. New York: McGraw-Hill.

Grant, Eugene L., W. Grant Ireson, and Richard S. Leavenworth. 1976. *Principles of Engineering Economy*, 6th ed. New York: John Wiley.

Griffith, Gary K. 1996. *Statistical Process Control Methods for Long and Short Runs*, 2nd ed. Milwaukee, WI: ASQC Quality Press.

Gryna, Frank M., Richard C. H. Chua, and Joseph A. DeFeo. 2007. *Juran's Quality Planning & Analysis for Enterprise Quality*, 5th ed. New York: McGraw-Hill.

Gunst, Richard F., and Robert L. Mason. 1991. *Volume 14: How to Construct Fractional Factorial Experiments*. Milwaukee, WI: ASQC Quality Press.

Gupta, Bhisham C., and H. Fred Walker. 2005. *Applied Statistics for the Green Belt*. Milwaukee, WI: ASQ Quality Press.

Gupta, Praveen. 2005. *The Six Sigma Performance Handbook*. New York: McGraw-Hill.

Henderson, Bruce A., and Jorge Larco. 1999. *Lean Transformation: How to Change Your Business into a Lean Enterprise*. Richmond, VA: Oaklea Press.

Hogg, R. V., and E. A. Tanis. 1997. *Probability and Statistical Inference*. Upper Saddle River, NJ: Prentice-Hall.

Imai, Masaaki. 1986. *Kaizen: The Key to Japan's Competitive Success*. New York: Random House.

John, Peter W. M. 1990. *Statistical Methods in Engineering and Quality Assurance*. New York: John Wiley.

Juran, Joseph M., and A. Blanton Godfrey. 1999. *Juran's Quality Handbook*, 5th ed. New York: McGraw-Hill.

Kanji, Gopal K. 2006. *100 Statistical Tests*, 3rd ed. London: Sage Publications.

Keats, J. Bert, and Douglas C. Montgomery. 1991. *Statistical Process Control in Manufacturing*. Milwaukee, WI: ASQC Quality Press/Marcel Dekker.

Kessler, Sheila. 1996. *Measuring and Managing Customer Satisfaction: Going for the Gold*. Milwaukee, WI: ASQC Quality Press.

Krishnamoorthi, K. S. 1992. *Reliability Methods for Engineers*. Milwaukee, WI: ASQC Quality Press.

Kubiak, Thomas M. 1986. *Practical Aids*. Milwaukee, WI: ASQC Quality Press.

Lamprecht, James L. 2005. *Applied Data Analysis for Process Improvement: A Practical Guide to Six Sigma Black Belt Statistics*. Milwaukee, WI: ASQ Quality Press.

Lareau, William. 2003. *Office Kaizen: Transforming Office Operations into a Strategic Competitive Advantage*. Milwaukee, WI: ASQ Quality Press.

Levinson, William A., and Raymond A. Rerick. 2002. *Lean Enterprise: A Synergistic Approach to Minimizing Waste.* Milwaukee, WI: ASQ Quality Press.

Lipschultz, Seymour, and Marc Lipson. 2000. *Probability,* 2nd ed. New York: McGraw-Hill.

Locks, Mitchell O. 1995. *Reliability, Maintainability, and Availability Assessment,* 2nd ed. Milwaukee, WI: ASQC Quality Press.

MacInnes, Richard L. 2002. *The Lean Enterprise Memory Jogger: Create Value and Eliminate Waste throughout Your Company.* Salem, NH: Goal/QPC.

Mathews, Paul G. 2005. *Design of Experiments with Minitab.* Milwaukee, WI: ASQ Quality Press.

McDermott, Robin E., Raymond J. Mikulak, and Michael R. Beauregard. 1996. *The Basics of FMEA.* New York: Quality Resources.

McNeese, William H., and Robert A. Klein. 1991. *Statistical Methods for the Process Industries.* Milwaukee, WI: ASQC Quality Press/Marcel Dekker.

Miller, Irwin R., and John E. Freund. 1990. *Probability and Statistics for Engineers,* 4th ed. Englewood Cliffs, NJ: Prentice-Hall.

Miller, Ken. 2002. *The Change Agent's Guide to Radical Improvement.* Milwaukee, WI: ASQ Quality Press.

Moen, Ronald D., Thomas W. Nolan, and Lloyd P. Provost. 1991. *Improving Quality through Planned Experimentation.* Boston, MA: McGraw-Hill.

Montgomery, Douglas C. 2005. *Design and Analysis of Experiments,* 6th ed. Hoboken, NJ: John Wiley.

Montgomery, Douglas C. 2005. *Introduction to Statistical Quality Control,* 5th ed. Hoboken, NJ: John Wiley.

Muir, Alastair. 2006. *Lean Six Sigma Statistics: Calculating Process Efficiencies in Transactional Projects.* New York: McGraw-Hill.

Munro, Roderick A. 2002. *Six Sigma for the Shop Floor: A Pocket Guide.* Milwaukee, WI: ASQ Quality Press.

Munro, Roderick A., Matthew J. Maio, Mohamed B. Nawaz, Govindarajan Ramu, and Daniel J. Zrymiak. 2008. *The Certified Six Sigma Green Belt Handbook.* Milwaukee, WI: ASQ Quality Press.

O'Connor, Patrick D. T. 2002. *Practical Reliability Engineering,* 4th ed. Chichester, UK: John Wiley.

Ott, Ellis R., Edward G. Schilling, and Dean V. Neubauer. 2005. *Process Quality Control: Troubleshooting and Interpretation of Data,* 4th ed. Milwaukee, WI: ASQ Quality Press.

Pennella, C. Robert. 2004. *Managing the Metrology System,* 3rd ed. Milwaukee, WI: ASQ Quality Press.

Pestorius, Michael J. 2007. *Applying the Science of Six Sigma to the Art and Sales of Marketing.* Milwaukee, WI: ASQ Quality Press.

Pries, Kim H. 2006. *Six Sigma for the Next Millennium.* Milwaukee, WI: ASQ Quality Press.

Pyzdek, Thomas. 1990. *Pyzdek's Guide to SPC, Volume 1: Fundamentals.* Tucson, AZ: Quality Publishing/Milwaukee, WI: ASQC Quality Press.

Pyzdek, Thomas. 1992. *Pyzdek's Guide to SPC, Volume 2: Applications and Special Topics.* Tucson, AZ: Quality Publishing/Milwaukee, WI: ASQC Quality Press.

Pyzdek, Thomas. 1994. *Pocket Guide to Quality Tools.* Tucson, AZ: Quality Publishing, Inc.

Pyzdek, Thomas. 2003. *The Six Sigma Handbook: A Complete Guide for Green Belts, Black Belts, and Managers at All Levels: Revised and Expanded.* New York: McGraw-Hill.

Pyzdek, Thomas, and Paul A. Keller. 2003. *Quality Engineering Handbook,* 2nd ed. Boca Raton, FL: Taylor & Francis.

Rantanen, K., and E. Domb. 2002. *Simplified TRIZ: New Problem-Solving Applications for Engineers and Manufacturing Professionals.* Boca Raton, FL: St. Lucie Press.

Reidenbach, R. Eric, and Reginald W. Goeke. 2006. *Strategic Six Sigma for Champions: Key to Sustainable Competitive Advantage.* Milwaukee, WI: ASQ Quality Press.

ReVelle, Jack B. 2004. *Quality Essentials: A Reference Guide from A to Z.* Milwaukee, WI: ASQ Quality Press.

Salvendy, Gavriel. 1992. *Handbook of Industrial Engineering,* 2nd ed. New York: John Wiley & Sons.

Sarkar, Debashis. 2006. *5S for Service Organizations and Offices: A Lean Look at Improvements.* Milwaukee, WI: ASQ Quality Press.

Sarkar, Debashis. 2008. *Lean for Service Organizations and Offices: A Holistic Approach for Achieving Operational Excellence and Improvements.* Milwaukee, WI: ASQ Quality Press.

Scholtes, Peter R., Brian L. Joiner, and Barbara J. Streibel. 2003. *The Team Handbook,* 3rd ed. Madison, WI: Oriel.

Shapiro, Samuel S. 1980. *Volume 03: How to Test Normality and Other Distributional Assumptions.* Milwaukee, WI: ASQC Quality Press.

Sheridan, Bruce M. 1993. *Policy Deployment: The TQM Approach to Long-Range Planning.* Milwaukee, WI: ASQC Quality Press.

Shewhart, W. A. *Economic Control of Quality of Manufactured Product.* 1980. Milwaukee, WI: ASQC Quality Press.

Siebels, Donald L. 2004. *The Quality Improvement Glossary.* Milwaukee, WI: ASQ Quality Press.

Spiegel, Murray R., and Larry J. Stephens. 1999. *Statistics,* 3rd. ed. New York: McGraw-Hill.

Stamatis, D. H. 2003. *Failure Mode and Effect Analysis: FMEA from Theory to Execution,* 2nd ed. Milwaukee, WI: ASQ Quality Press.

Sternstein, Martin. 2005. *Statistics,* 2nd ed. Hauppauge, NY: Barron's.

Taguchi, Genichi, Subir Chowdhury, and Yuin Wu. 2005. *Taguchi's Quality Engineering Handbook.* Hoboken, NJ: John Wiley.

Tague, Nancy R. 2005. *The Quality Toolbox,* 2nd ed. Milwaukee, WI: ASQ Quality Press.

Tapping, Don, Tom Luyster, and Tom Shuker. 2002. *Value Stream Management: Eight Steps to Planning, Mapping, and Sustaining Lean Improvements.* New York: Productivity Press.

Treichler, David H., with Ronald D. Carmichael. 2004. *The Six Sigma Path to Leadership: Observations from the Trenches.* Milwaukee, WI: ASQ Quality Press.

Watson, Gregory H. 2005. *Design for Six Sigma: Innovation for Enhanced Competitiveness.* Salem, NJ: Goal/QPC.

Wedgwood, Ian D. 2007. *Lean Sigma: A Practitioner's Guide.* Upper Saddle River, NJ: Prentice-Hall.

Westcott, Russell T. 2005. *Simplified Project Management for the Quality Professional.* Milwaukee, WI: ASQ Quality Press.

Westcott, Russell T. 2006. *The Certified Manager of Quality/Organizational Excellence Handbook,* 3rd ed. Milwaukee, WI: ASQ Quality Press.

Wheeler, Donald J. 1989. *Tables of Screening Designs,* 2nd ed. Knoxville, TN: SPC Press.

Wheeler, Donald J. 1991. *Short Run.* SPC Knoxville, TN: SPC Press.

Wheeler, Donald J. 1995. *Advanced Topics in Statistical Process Control: The Power of Shewhart's Charts.* Knoxville, TN: SPC Press.

Wheeler, Donald J. 1999. *Beyond Capability Confusion: The Average Cost-of-Use.* Knoxville, TN: SPC Press.

Wheeler, Donald J. 2000. *Normality and the Process Behavior Chart.* Knoxville, TN: SPC Press.

Wheeler, Donald J. 2000. *The Process Evaluation Handbook.* Knoxville, TN: SPC Press.

Wheeler, Donald J. 2000. *Understanding Variation: The Key to Managing Chaos*, 2nd ed. Knoxville, TN: SPC Press.

Wheeler, Donald J., and David S. Chambers. 1992. *Understanding Statistical Process Control,* 2nd ed. Knoxville, TN: SPC Press.

Wheeler, Donald J., and Richard W. Lyday. 1989. *Evaluating the Measurement Process,* 2nd ed. Knoxville, TN: SPC Press.

Wilburn, Morris. 2007. *Managing the Customer Experience: A Measurement-Based Approach.* Milwaukee, WI: ASQ Quality Press.

Wilson, Paul F., Larry D. Dell, and Gaylord F. Anderson. 1993. *Root Cause Analysis: A Tool for Total Quality Management.* Milwaukee, WI: ASQC Quality Press.

Windsor, Samuel E. 2006. *Transactional Six Sigma for Green Belts.* Milwaukee, WI: ASQ Quality Press.

Womack, James P., and Daniel T. Jones. 1996. *Lean Thinking: Banish Waste and Create Wealth in Your Corporation.* New York: Simon & Schuster.

Yang, Kai, and Jayant Trewn. 2004. *Multivariate Statistical Methods in Quality Management.* New York: McGraw-Hill.

Zwillinger, Daniel, and Stephen Kokoska. 2000. *CRC Standard Probability and Statistics Tables and Formulae.* Boca Raton, FL: Chapman & Hall/CRC.

Index